JONNY TALON

WARD

BUSINESS INFORMATION PROCESSING SYSTEMS

IRWIN SERIES IN QUANTITATIVE ANALYSIS FOR BUSINESS

CONSULTING EDITOR ROBERT B. FETTER *Yale University*

Business Information Processing Systems

C. ORVILLE ELLIOTT, Ph.D., C.P.A., C.D.P.
Professor and Chairman, Department of
Accountancy and Quantitative Studies
School of Business
Western Illinois University

ROBERT S. WASLEY, Ph.D.
Professor of Accounting
School of Business
University of Colorado

Revised Edition • 1968
RICHARD D. IRWIN, INC., *Homewood, Illinois*
IRWIN-DORSEY LIMITED, *Nobleton, Ontario*

REVISED EDITION

First Printing, April, 1968

Second Printing, September, 1968

Third Printing, November, 1968

Fourth Printing, July, 1969

Library of Congress Catalog Card No. 68–14877

Printed in the United States of America

To Our Patient Wives

Helene *and* Helen

Preface

THE IDEAS and data here provided are designed to serve as a presentation of the information processing systems in use in business firms today. It is recommended that the reader should have as background either some business experience or, at least, the equivalence of a one-semester course in accounting before approaching this area of study. Some realization of the flow of data and a knowledge of business terminology are necessary prerequisites.

Our greatest desire is to provide an overall acquaintanceship with the business information processing systems in use today. To achieve this end we have provided:

Fundamentals basic to the processing of data;

The special and sometimes technical terminology used in conjunction with information processing;

Processing systems available and the equipment to implement these systems;

How the data produced by these systems may be utilized by management in performing the management function;

The control functions available and necessary to protect the assets of the firm and to assure the proper presentation of financial data, all emphasized throughout in terms of the specific information processing system being discussed; and

Particular problems which may present themselves when a change of systems is contemplated, and some approaches to be utilized in avoiding or solving these problems.

Only such an overall acquaintanceship can provide the background necessary for an understanding of the problems to be faced—and solved —in organizing, defining, implementing, and utilizing a modern information processing system. However one of the most important, and quite often least understood, factors to be considered in such a system is the human element of the firm, which must be so molded as to provide a cohesive relationship among these human factors, the work they perform, and the equipment they utilize. This is important in every system but an absolute must in the developing integrated systems involving innovation in the gathering, processing, and utilization of data in what may eventually evolve into the so-called total system.

We feel that knowledge and understanding remove fear and doubt concerning the "mysteries" of, particularly, the electronic computer. We have shown that, regardless of the information processing system considered, the same fundamentals are common to all and the logical patterns to be followed in the processing procedures are identical in each, whether it be a manual, mechanical, electromechanical, or electronic system. It is only in the equipment used, the functions performed by the given equipment units, and the speed and accuracy available through the use of equipment that these systems differ.

An attempt has been made to present the different areas covered in a manner which will permit considerable flexibility in their use. Part of this flexibility is in that some chapters—and even some areas—may be omitted without disrupting the pattern of the material presented. Such omission may be desirable where emphasis is desired on information concerning either the punched card or the computer. Each of these areas is written so that the individual, depending on his background and interest, may use the material provided as a springboard for more advanced study. An annotated bibliography is included at the end of each chapter to provide reference to other information sources.

Chapters 1 through 4 introduce the data (and their source) necessary to manage business resources and show how devices have developed, over time, to permit evolving data processing techniques to meet the demands of ever increasing volume until today we have modern information and control systems based on fundamental data processing functions.

Chapter 5 discusses the fundamental concepts of how techniques, utilizing symbols associated with flowcharting, can be used to present pictorially the flow of data and to document the related forms containing the data. These techniques used in flowcharting are most important; not only do they acquaint the reader with ideas associated with the flow of data, from its origination to finished report form, but they also assist in organizing his thinking preparatory to writing programs acceptable to given computer systems.

Chapter 6 reviews the application of manual and mechanical methods which may be utilized in the processing of data. Some of the more commonly found techniques and equipment available for these processing systems are presented.

Chapters 7 through 9 introduce and expand upon the punched card systems available to process data. The material on the punched card itself is equally as applicable to the computer system as to the punched card system, as it serves as one of the major types of computer input. In the balance of this area, stress is placed on the use of the punched card system in a business environment, the problems of its utilization, and what is to be gained by using it. Typical punched card equipment is included in this discussion as an adjunct to explaining the functions performed in these systems.

Chapters 10 through 21 are all specifically computer oriented. The first three of these chapters trace the computer from the first known such device through the development of the modern computer and its fairly recent usage in business information processing. The organization of the computer and its components stresses the relationship of the various codes used in the operation of these units. The advantages and disadvantages of the various input, output, and storage units available are discussed in conjunction with the functions they perform, their speeds, and, where applicable, their capacities.

Chapter 13 describes the concepts related to integrated information systems techniques, planning requirements, common-machine languages and associated equipment. These concepts also include those related to communication, on-line real-time, and time-sharing systems.

A discussion of the control function, and its close relationship to the audit trail and audit requirements, in Chapter 14 reemphasizes the need for adequate controls to be built into every system. The controls available in the many forms of input, processing, programmed, and output controls, are defined or discussed as to their nature and usage.

Chapters 15 through 17 provide a background in the development of software and the newly emerging techniques of multiprogramming and multiprocessing and their associated executive programs. The FORTRAN and COBOL programming languages are presented in separate chapters in a form permitting the reader to grasp some idea of the intricacies, the terminology, and techniques of the languages, as well as providing illustrative applications.

Chapter 18 illustrates, through a variety of specific applications at various levels of sophistication, management's use of the computer as it relates to the information processing system.

The remaining three chapters present most of the problems which confront management when indications develop in the firm which suggest that a systems change may be necessary to provide management with timely data. Specific and alternative approaches are provided which may be utilized in avoiding or solving the many problems which arise in any justification study or, when feasible, in converting to a new business information processing system.

Appendix A includes a pictorial and summary review of selected major computing systems and includes most of the electronic business information processing systems currently available.

Appendix B, a glossary, provides a ready reference to definitions of the many specialized terms found in the text.

It must be recognized in an undertaking of this magnitude that the authors are greatly indebted to many individuals for their suggestions, help, and encouragement. To each of them we wish to acknowledge this indebtedness and to extend our appreciation; but, especially, we thank Mrs. Ferrol L. Cramer, Daniel Grant, Konrad Kubin, and James Fischer for their aid in manuscript preparation.

Professor Robert B. Fetter, consulting editor of the Irwin Series in Quantitative Analysis for Business; Harry H. Bingham of Richard D. Irwin, Inc.; and the Irwin copy editors have all been most cooperative in suggesting organizational and writing style improvements.

Many of the changes in this revised edition were made as a result of a survey completed by a number of educators currently using this book in the classroom and for these suggestions we are most appreciative.

We are particularly indebted to all the major equipment manufacturers, and their local representatives, for their cooperation in furnishing data in general and on their equipment in particular, and for permission to use their illustrations. Each firm contacted cooperated fully to the extent asked.

April, 1968   C. ORVILLE ELLIOTT
                                                      ROBERT S. WASLEY

Table of Contents

xi

CHAPTER 1

Statistical Data for Managing Business Resources

As FAR BACK as Assyrian and Babylonian history, we have indisputable evidence of commercial transactions. A large part of commerce centered in the temples. The scribes, who were the chief accounting officers recorded all receipts and disbursements of property belonging to the local temple, the "corporate clearinghouse" of these early times. It is evident that even credit existed on an extensive scale.

The surviving facts which these early scribes recorded are meager, but they were none the less important to the people of that time. As trade and commerce expanded, the records of these business ventures also became more detailed and extensive. This dual development was brought about through the increased interest and concern in the outcome of business ventures by different groups of people; owners, as well as the taxing authorities, had a vested interest in the venture, and it was important that adequate facts surrounding the venture were made known.

WHAT ARE STATISTICAL DATA?

What are the characteristics of these facts which are of such concern to so many different organizational units and groups of people? According to Eric L. Kohler, the word "data" means "facts."[1] He goes on to say that a "statistic is any numerical measure of a physical or economic condition

---

[1] Eric L. Kohler, *A Dictionary for Accountants* (3d ed.; Englewood Cliffs, N.J.: Prentice-Hall, Inc., 1963), p. 158.

1

or activity, as a wage, a national income total, or a summation of assets."[2]

One could conclude, therefore, that statistical data are numeric facts which arise in the conduct of economic as well as physical activities. For example, the U.S. government has systems for collecting data relative to the output of the nation. It is from data supplied by these systems that the gross national product (GNP) figures are derived on an annual basis.

With the present armed conflict in Vietnam, the armed services have a tremendous data handling problem. They have had to devise systems which will make the right authorities—at the right times—aware of the manpower supply, by technical specialty, available for combat. They must also provide for adequate supplies of food, equipment, ammunition, etc., to be ready at the right place at the right time. This system must supply the right information to the Defense Department in Washington so that the necessary men and materiel are provided the battlefield commanders in Vietnam when they are needed.

All cities depend upon data, in part at least, to operate. Each year, when the budget for the city is prepared, the revenue envisioned in the budget is predicated upon anticipated tax receipts. These estimates are based on statistical facts accumulated in previous years. The planned expenditures of the city (streets, parks, police force, water, etc.) are based upon educated estimates, made in the form of numeric facts, of costs.

Statistical data are of equal importance to the managers of modern business enterprises. On this point, Walter B. McFarland of the National Association of Accountants has the following to say:

Advances in management have been one of the significant characteristics of twentieth century industrial technology.

Practically all of these advances in management are founded upon the development of information systems which enable management to act intelligently rather than blindly. Since the economy in which we live measures economic resources in terms of money, accounting is the key element in management information systems. Without reliable financial information provided by the accountant, effective operation of any but a very small business is impossible.[3]

The statistical data which management needs on a current basis are of many different types. For example:

1. Amounts owed by customers.
2. The quantity of a certain item sold last week.
3. The size of garment sold to the last customer.
4. Amount of wages paid employees the last payday.

---

[2] *Ibid.*, p. 447.

[3] Walter B. McFarland, *Concepts for Management Accounting* (New York: National Association of Accountants, August 1966), p. 1.

5. The sales tax collected and that owed to the state on the sales made last month.
6. An analysis of sales by territory, by product, for the last three years.

DEMAND FOR DATA

One of the first things to be considered in the study of data processing is *What brings about the need for data in business?* Actually, there are two broad categories of demand. These can roughly be classified as:

Those which originate *inside* the firm in connection with the daily operation of the business enterprise, and
Those which are *external* to the firm.

The internal need for data is usually that of management, which needs classified and summarized information for use in various types of analyses on a daily, weekly, or other cyclical basis. This information stems from the recording of daily transactions in a pattern which provides a historical, detailed record of the operation of the firm. From this historical record, information can be selected and accumulated as required to provide the reports used in making business decisions and in facilitating other management functions.

The external need for data normally fulfills some of the internal needs of the firm as well, but its requirements are normally not in the same form as data developed solely for internal use. Some examples of external demands for data are those for:

1. Customer invoices. Customers not only need to know the total amount they owe, they also want to know the quantity and description of what they have purchased.
2. Purchase orders and invoices. On any purchase order sent out, it is necessary to have a *precise description* of what is ordered, as well as quantity, price, size, or color information.
3. Creditors. They are usually most interested in the financial solvency of the business, indicating its ability to pay off its debts when they come due.
4. Potential investors (including stockholders). Their primary interest is in the continuing ability of the business to make an adequate return on the investment.
5. Governmental agencies. There are innumerable taxing and regulatory agencies which demand that data, prepared in a specified way, be submitted at periodic intervals.

Internal Need for Data

In the simplest form of business organizations—one person in business for himself—it might at first appear that an individual has little need for operational data because he can hold all the necessary facts in his head.

This is apt to be true as long as the size of his business and the number of his employees do not exceed the span of his personal control. As soon, however, as he feels that he must hire someone else to *assist* him in his management functions, and to whom he is planning to delegate certain responsibilities, his dependence upon statistical facts in his control function becomes paramount. At this point, also, the volume and variety of the daily transactions will have increased many times.

An important function of management is to decide upon courses of action that the business should follow. Some of these decisions must necessarily be made at frequent intervals; others need not be made as often.

SHORT-RUN DECISIONS.   Facts are of vital importance in making all types of business decisions; however, typical examples of major decisions occur under the following circumstances:

1. The cost of making our product is too high. (*At what point, and why, did the costs become excessive?*)
2. Sales have been very good for the last month, and it is important to have the merchandise needed to fill the orders. (*What types of merchandise have been sold, and what quantities remain? Do we now need to order more?*)
3. Business has been good, with even better potential. (*Are we at the point where we can afford to add another salesman?*)
4. The firm is badly in need of cash to meet current operating expenses. (*What money is owed us, and when is it likely to be collected? What course of action should the business follow to provide the needed funds?*)
5. With the growth of the business, there are many new customers, most of whom are seeking credit. (*Which customers are good credit risks and which are not?*)

A business manager also has the problem of planning activities for the business one month, three months, or six months in advance. Once more, facts concerning the past are of vital importance in making decisions as to what should be done in the immediate future. An accurate knowledge of the past can materially influence decisions affecting future actions.

LONG-RUN DECISIONS.   In the world of business we can measure the cost and the results of our activities because, for the most part, we are dealing with matters which are, or can be, expressed in terms of money. Thus a fairly precise measurement of the economic success of a business enterprise can be made. The basic economic motive behind the existence of business is the maximization of profit, or, to say it more precisely, the greatest return feasible on the capital invested in the business enterprise.

This means that a business must continuously strive in two directions: on the one hand, it must try to maximize its income through higher selling prices or larger turnover; on the other hand, it must try to minimize the unit cost of its product or service.

The basic objective of a business enterprise is not necessarily either the greatest turnover or the highest profit per unit, but that combination of turnover, profit per unit, and operating expenses which will provide the highest return on its capital.

ARRIVING AT A PLAN OF ACTION. The act of planning may be quite informal in nature in a smaller business, taking place largely in the head of the proprietor. In a larger business, on the other hand, it may be much more formal and may be largely in writing. In such a business, there may be an overall plan which consists of a number of detailed plans covering various interdependent activities. These activities include sales, production, purchasing, inventories in every phase of the business process, accounts receivable, investments in plant, equipment, etc.

A complete business plan indicates not only the physical levels of each of the various operations, such as the number of products to be manufactured, held in stock, and marketed, but also the values to be created and to be used in the business processes during a period of time. This plan is the *budget*, simply another name for a formalized program.

A formalized budget program provides a complete projection into the future of the company's probable activities, capital requirements, and profit. To enable management to be aware of deviations from the planned program, the budget should be set up with the same corresponding structure as the financial reports, which will eventually show the actual performance, so that a comparison of the budgeted and the actual figures will reveal all deviations. An analysis of these deviations should explain their causes and in many cases provide answers as how to correct them.

For example, a manufacturing firm preparing a budget for the next fiscal period would probably commence with the sales budget and would consider the following facts in its preparation:

1. Anticipated sales both in dollars and by product, determined by—
   a) past experience and/or
   b) anticipation of business prospects for the future period
      (1) possibly determined by correlating demand for products with some other measurable form of business activity.
2. Anticipated sales in dollars and by products probably will also be determined by month, by salesman and by territory.

To make a complete budget or plan, however, it is necessary that the company have detailed records on which data are recorded of past activities. It is very largely in this way that management, by referring to the trends of the past and considering expected general economic conditions, can have a reasonable idea of what the future may hold.

Need for Coordination. "Before a set of plans, each plan covering an activity, can be considered as final, they have to be coordinated to obtain a harmonious overall plan. In a growing enterprise, the number of departments, or the number of officials charged with responsibility, increases as work is divided. If coordination is lacking, there may be overlapping and delays in related and consecutive operations."[4] It becomes necessary to show the common purpose which integrates all activities and all components of the enterprise and which makes an organic whole of the enterprise, all parts of which must function and grow in balanced accord.

Coordination also involves the interpreting of company objectives, policies, and plans to all concerned. It is equally important to explain to each individual his assigned work and the relation of his work to the total work of the component and of the company.

This coordination cannot be accomplished unless there is a smooth and continuous flow of data to management personnel at all times. The demand for data in this instance is just as great, if not greater, than in any other instance previously mentioned.

Need for Control. Control, particularly in larger business organizations, is largely accomplished through having a plan of action (a budget) for each functional area of the business—and a plan that is prescribed in written form. A designated individual, in turn, is responsible for this area. The plan should describe in a quantitative manner—in pieces, items, etc., as well as in dollars—the work to be performed and the proper time to perform it.

Once a business has such a plan of action, it can compare, at frequent intervals, the results of actual actions with those which had been forecast. Since a designated person is responsible for each area of activity, there is someone who is answerable for what has occurred in each area. This is one way that control can be accomplished.

Control can also be accomplished by showing comparisons and relationships between business statistics. For example, use can be made of:

1. Ratios; i.e., like ratios can be compared for a period of time, or ratios can be compared with like ratios in the industry;
2. Percentage relationships; i.e., such percentages as those of operating expenses to net sales can be compared for a series of years, both vertically and horizontally; and percentage relationships can also be displayed graphically with good results;
3. Break-even, cost, volume, or profit analysis can be applied to divisions, territories, and products; and
4. Return on investment analysis can be applied to divisions, territories, departments, or products.

These are all typical management control devices.

---

[4] Pieter Bakker, "Long and Short Range Planning" in *The Function of Management* (Canadian Institute of Chartered Accountants, 1959), p. 28.

External Need for Data

Historically, if one were to study the business records of the English trading companies in the 17th and 18th centuries, he would find that many expeditions were joint ventures. Several people pooled their resources to outfit an expedition or trading mission. It was important to keep records of the resources which had been committed, but very little additional information was required. When the trading mission returned, all the resources of the mission would be liquidated. But it was at this point that data and records became important once again, because each member of the joint venture wanted to be certain that he received his just share of the proceeds.

In the early business history of this country, detailed business records were not maintained. The prime requisite of the records was only that they provide confidential financial statements of the company's progress to the owners at periodic intervals, and most of the companies were either single proprietorships or partnerships.

As the corporate form of business enterprise became more prevalent (in the later 1800's), the interest of the public in the activities of particular businesses began to be recognized. Ownership of these corporations became more widespread. In fact, ownership in many instances became international in character with the investment of large sums of money in the industries of this country by foreign investors. With greater public interest in the financial activities of corporations, the need for more complete data about the activities of the corporations increased. It was not long before the governments of the respective states began to legislate (in many ways) how financial affairs and the records of corporations were to be maintained, and to set up specific requirements as to how and when these corporations were to report their financial activities.

In 1913 the first federal income tax law (after the ratification of the Sixteenth Amendment) was passed, and this enactment has probably had more to do with increased public interest in business data than any other one single event. All businesses, as well as all individuals, became more conscious of business transactions, and it was now mandatory that they keep adequate record of them so that they could be reported to the federal government on an annual basis.

The revenue acts and regulations of 1918 had an important effect on improving general accounting practices. The most significant provisions of the acts related to (1) depreciation and depletion and (2) inventory valuations. Federal income tax allowance for depreciation deductions caused many companies to make more systematic record-keeping provisions than previously thought necessary.

The Securities and Exchange Act of 1934, which created the Securities and Exchange Commission, gave the Commission powers to obtain from registrants whatever detailed information it considered necessary and appropriate to protect the public interest of investors. It also required that all corporations with securities listed on a national stock exchange, or corporations desiring to offer the public an issue of securities in excess of $3 million, must file certified financial statements with the SEC.

One effect of all these government regulations was to heighten the interest and concern of most businesses in statistical data.

GOVERNMENTAL AGENCIES. Today, the regulations and demands for data by state, local, and municipal authorities are almost as great as those of the federal government. Some of the demands of governmental agencies may be summarized as follows:

1. Income taxes on employer, federal, state, and local.
2. Withholding of federal and state income taxes, and federal social security taxes, from personal income of employees.
3. Social security taxes (federal and state) on employer.
4. Sales taxes (state and local) collected from customers and paid by the seller.
5. Manufacturer's excise taxes on sales of luxury goods.

OWNERS. As business units have increased in size and complexity, the trend has been for more and more business firms to become publicly owned. This has usually been brought about by increased needs for capital. In general, the easiest method of acquiring capital in quantity has been through the sale of shares of stock which represent individual shares of ownership of the firm.

With this trend, corporate management soon recognized the obligation—as well as the public necessity—of issuing periodic financial statements supported by considerable statistical data. These financial data are of utmost importance to prospective investors as well as to financial analysts, who are concerned with the financial outlook for the business as well as the industry.

In addition to regular balance sheets and income statements, there is a growing use of statistical analyses. For example, the recently published annual report of a nationally recognized corporation contained the following analyses to aid in judging the firm's financial condition and outlook:

1. Trend of corporate sales compared with Gross National Product.
2. Trend of corporate sales compared with the sales of their largest competitors.
3. A 13-year compilation of investment in capital assets by category of asset. This was compared with depreciation charges by asset-category for the same period of time.

4. New products introduced because of research and development.
5. Earnings as a percentage of the sales dollar for a 12-year period.
6. A 10-year analysis of the average number of employees compared to the average employee compensation (including benefits) for the same period of time.
7. A 10-year graphic analysis of inventory turnover.
8. A 10-year comparison of operating statistics.

In a financial report such as the one described above, not only would the stockholders and financial analysts find information of interest, but so would creditors, labor organizations, and the public at large. Each special interest group can extract the material in which it is primarily interested for its own particular purposes.

The authors, however, would like to call the attention of the reader to the variety and quantities of business data which must be accumulated in some systematic manner in order to make such a report possible.

SOURCES OF DATA

In considering the sources of the data required in the typical business firm, it will be found that here, also, data may originate from inside or outside the firm, depending on the type of data considered.

Internal Data

The business form is usually the medium on which data are first recorded at the time a transaction occurs: for example, a sales invoice, a time ticket, a production order, or a bank check. There are many types and designs of business forms. In each instance, however, the form is designed to make the recording of data surrounding a business transaction as simple, easy, and accurate as possible. The recorded data may not have to be transcribed again throughout the entire data processing operation, depending upon the type of system used. The importance of minimizing the transcription of data, as well as the importance of keeping them in a form which can be readily processed, cannot be overemphasized.

When, however, it is necessary to transcribe data, it is important to plan the layout of the form so that it will clearly provide the data in the same order (on the page) in which it will be transcribed. The sequence in which information is transferred to a punched card versus the layout of the hard-copy business form from which the information for the punched card is taken would be a typical example.

It might also be well at this point to stop and remember that data need not always be expressed in the form of dollars to be usable by

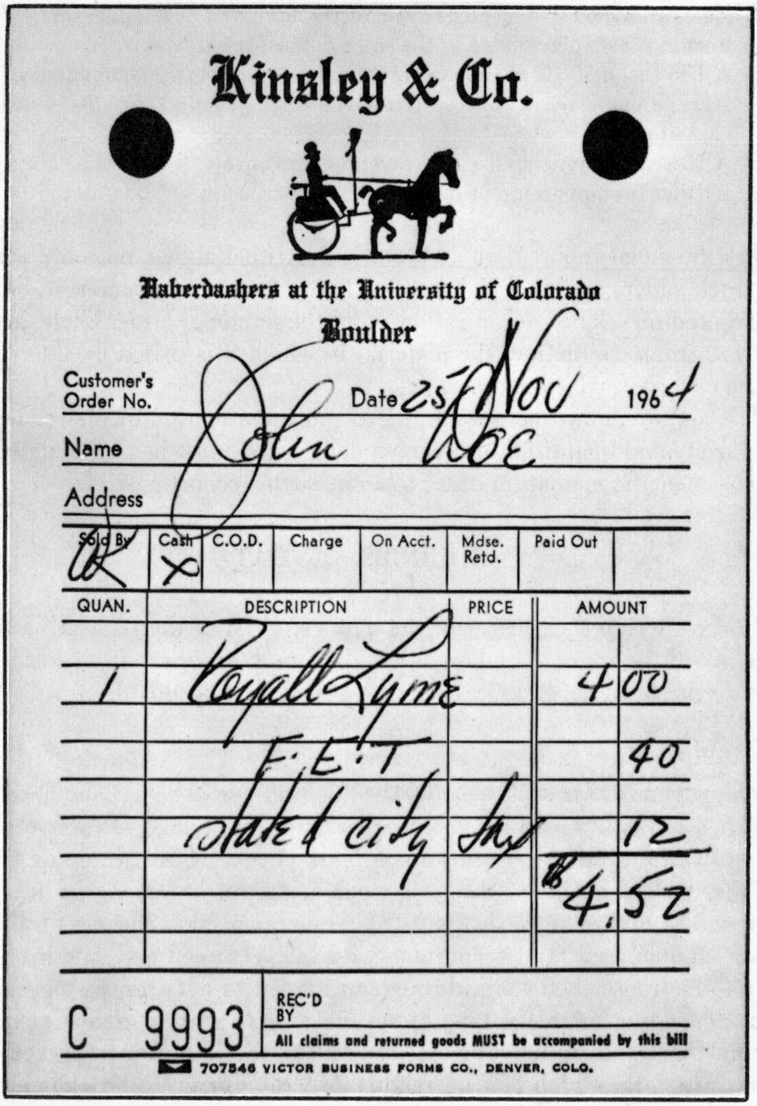

Kinsley & Co.

Haberdashers at the University of Colorado
Boulder

Customer's Order No. Date 25 Nov 1964

Name John Doe

Address

Sold By	Cash	C.O.D.	Charge	On Acct.	Mdse. Retd.	Paid Out	
	X						

QUAN.	DESCRIPTION	PRICE	AMOUNT	
1	Royall Lyme		4	00
	F.E.T			40
	State & city Tax			12
			4	52

C 9993 REC'D BY

All claims and returned goods MUST be accompanied by this bill

707546 VICTOR BUSINESS FORMS CO., DENVER, COLO.

***FIG.* 1–1. Sales Ticket.**

management; it may also include numbers and descriptions of items, man- or machine-hours, or it may be expressed in percentages, ratios, volumes, and other informational terms. For example, let us take a sales ticket (Figure 1–1) from a retail clothing store and analyze its data (Figure 1–2) with the view of recognizing the needs and uses for all the recorded data.

An employee timecard is another business form which contains much useful data, and data which is necessary to a number of different people.

Data	*Useful to Whom or for What*
Date of sale...............	Since this is a cash sale, the data on the sales ticket would facilitate the accumulation of a control figure of cash sales on April 2 with which to verify the balance of cash in the cash register.
Name and address of customer................	Identifies the customer for management.
Initials of clerk.............	Identifies clerk for possible commission purposes; also identifies clerk making sale, which is useful for control purposes.
Cash sale indicated........	Useful for purposes of sales analysis; also for control of cash received.
Description of article sold...	Useful for inventory analysis and control.
State sales tax.............	Necessary to substantiate the amounts collected and owed the state government when the next return comes due.
Federal excise tax..........	Indicates the amount owed the federal government for tax collected.
Ticket number.............	Useful to the store management to assist in controlling all of the sales tickets.

FIG. 1–2. Sales Ticket Analysis.

For example, let us examine a typical timecard and note the data it contains (Figure 1–3).

On both the sales ticket and the timecard there are a great deal of data which can be useful to management, if managers will take the time to use it. Since there are so many methods or systems whereby data can be transmitted and summarized soon after it has been recorded, the *accuracy* of the data recorded becomes paramount. In trade talk, "Garbage in, garbage out": if inaccurate data is fed into the data processing system, nothing but inaccurate data can come out of it.

Data which originates inside the firm can be controlled much more accurately as to the form used, the data to be collected, and the care exercised in the recording of the data. This control is not possible on data originating outside the firm because the firm originating the data will follow its own policies in considering any special request in this regard.

External Data

External data is usually the result of some action on the part of the firm's management. Typical of this is the invoice which is originated by a supplier after a request (usually a purchase order) by management for supplies and/or services. Another example might be a notice of taxes due that is received from some governmental agency as a result of previously prepared reports on property owned or revenues earned.

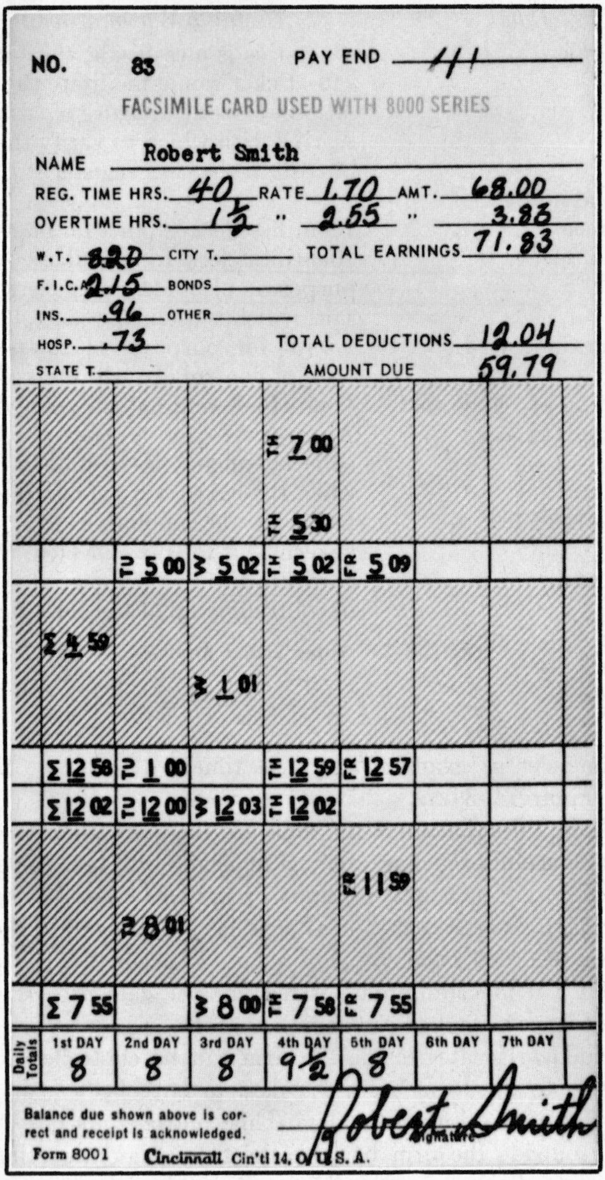

NO. 83   PAY END ___*41*___

FACSIMILE CARD USED WITH 8000 SERIES

NAME   Robert Smith

REG. TIME HRS. *40* RATE *1.70* AMT. *68.00*
OVERTIME HRS. *1½* " *2.55* " *3.83*
W.T. *8.20* CITY T.___ TOTAL EARNINGS *71.83*
F.I.C. *2.15* BONDS___
INS. *.96* OTHER___
HOSP. *.73*
STATE T.___   TOTAL DEDUCTIONS *12.04*
AMOUNT DUE *59.79*

			TH 7 00				
			TH 5 30				
	TU 5 00	3 5 02	TH 5 02	FR 5 09			
M 4 59							
		3 1 01					
M 12 58	TU 1 00		TH 12 59	FR 12 57			
M 12 02	TU 12 00	3 12 03	TH 12 02				
				FR 11 59			
	TU 8 01						
M 7 55		3 8 00	TH 7 58	FR 7 55			

Daily Totals	1st DAY	2nd DAY	3rd DAY	4th DAY	5th DAY	6th DAY	7th DAY
	8	8	8	9½	8		

Balance due shown above is correct and receipt is acknowledged.

Form 8001   Cincinnati Cin'ti 14, O./ U.S.A.   *Robert Smith* Signature

FIG. 1–3. Timecard.

Management has a real problem if it tries to dictate the information included on externally created business forms. It can specify items desired on a purchase order, and the number of invoice copies desired, and it can perhaps request that such information as purchase-order number, store number, or department number be included on the invoice, but it has no control over the arrangement of the data, the size of the document

Data	Useful to Whom or for What
Employee number..........	Systems department, payroll department, or any department responsible for controlling the number of employees being paid.
Pay period...............	Payroll department, person being paid.
Hours worked throughout the week...............	Payroll department, cost accounting department.
Tardiness................	Person responsible for control of employee attendance.
Total hours worked and rate paid...................	Payroll department, cost accounting department, person being paid.
Withholding tax, old age benefit, insurance, hospital................	Payroll department, person being paid, agencies represented by W.T., O.A.B., Insurance company, and hospital.
Amount due...............	Treasurer's department, payroll department, person being paid.
Signature of person being paid...................	Treasurer's department.

FIG. 1–4.   Time Ticket Analysis.

or its color, or the medium used in its preparation. The problem of verifying the accuracy of data is multiplied manyfold under these circumstances, yet just the possibility of these circumstances tends to slow up the entire data processing operation.

DATA FLOW

The flow of data is another important consideration. The techniques and equipment to be used in a given situation are directly dependent on the mass of data to be handled, on whether these data are produced at a constant level or in spurts, and on the urgency of timely action to record the data and produce the required output of statements and reports.

Volume

Along with the problems of assembling the needed data, accumulating it in a systematic manner on a business form, transcribing it as few times as necessary, and continually checking to verify its accuracy, there is also the problem of the quantities of data with which the business will be concerned. This problem is of particular importance in considering the method of data processing to be used. The manual methods are slower, but they are also the least costly when the volume is low. The mechanical methods would logically follow next in line, and then the electronic, in terms of relative speed and cost.

Another facet of this problem of data volume is whether the flow of data is cyclical or whether it is fairly steady and even. If the data is cyclical in nature, the questions then posed are:

1. Is it necessary that the peaks of data be processed with great rapidity?
2. Or can the data wait until other, slower methods of data processing can absorb them?

Timeliness of Data

How timely must the data output be: by seconds, minutes, hours, days, weeks, or months? Management must be able to bill its customers for their purchases as quickly as possible in order to collect these accounts when they are due. Management must also be able to plan the financial needs of the firm if it is to pay its creditors when its obligations are due. Sales volumes must be known promptly in order to plan production, or to anticipate the stock of materials that must be purchased, or to properly bill the orders that will be made by its salesmen.

Other examples of the necessity for promptness in the processing of data to furnish business information could be cited almost indefinitely. And in each of these examples, management must have timely answers to its questions to avoid such consequences as the impairment of credit, over- or underproduction, excess or insufficient purchase of goods and supplies, or other actions that could have a serious effect on the goodwill or finances of the business.

Because the method of organizing the data processing system depends upon the answers to all of the questions and problems raised above, all of these questions and problems must be correctly resolved.

ANNOTATED BIBLIOGRAPHY

AMERICAN MANAGEMENT ASSOCIATION. *Management Information Systems and the Computer.* Research Study No. 51. New York: American Management Association, 1961.

Explains the need for adequate and flexible management information systems in planning and control and gives the basic characteristics and methods of organization of a management information system.

"Business Budgets—To Each His Own," *Business Week,* May 30, 1964.

This short article explains what budgets are and what they are not supposed to be. The article explains the efforts made by the Budget Executive Institute to standardize the meaning and uses of budgets.

"How The Computer Is Changing Management Organization," *Business Management,* July, 1967.

The technology of computers is invading more and more areas of management. Some of the questions raised concern the impact of the computer on management; which department should control the computer's operation; the computer's effect on a department not in control; and how can the computer best serve management. The conclusion is that computerization should give management the option of running its business the way it should be run.

JEROME, W. T., III. *Executive Control—The Catalyst,* chap. 1. New York: John Wiley & Sons, Inc., 1961.

Chapter 1 of this book explains the need for an approach to controls broad enough to encompass the variety of needs encountered by top management. The need for more effective control data as an organization becomes larger is strongly emphasized.

RATHE, ALEX W. "Management's Need for Information," *Control Through Information: A Report on Management Information Systems.* Management Bulletin No. 24. New York: American Management Association, 1963.

QUESTIONS

1. What are data?
2. What brings about the need for data on the part of management? Explain.
3. What kinds of data can be useful to management in the making of short-run decisions? Explain.
4. How are data used by management in the making of long-run decisions?
5. How are data used in the preparation of an operating budget?
6. How is control accomplished once the budget has been prepared?
7. How also can control be accomplished other than by comparing budgeted and actual figures? Explain.
8. What are some of the external demands for data placed upon the businessman? Explain in reasonable detail.
9. Are data important to the businessman, especially when he considers the external data?
10. What are some of the usual sources of business data? Explain in reasonable detail.
11. What does the volume and the timing of data flow have to do with the problem of setting up procedures to handle the data processing in the first place?
12. What is so important about the timeliness of data?
13. What are some ways whereby data can be used by management in making long-run decisions other than in the preparation of an operating budget?
14. Enumerate five groups of people to whom data are important other than the managers of modern business enterprise. Explain why you feel the data are of importance to each group.

Historical Background

of Computing Devices

THE RECORDING of business transactions is almost as old as history itself.

Early in the development of man—who alone of all the creatures on earth has been credited with a combination of attributes that permit him to think, reason, apply logic, be inventive, and communicate through words with others of his kind—it became necessary for him to develop some technique which would permit the counting and recording of the transactions of his day.

In reviewing any related group of historical developments, it is interesting to note that at first progress is very slow, with many years or even centuries between each small change. Then, because of expanding demands and needs and the cumulative effect of inventions, the developments come faster and faster.

It is also interesting to note that at times unrelated efforts, even in widely scattered geographical locations, produce similar developments almost simultaneously.

Both of these facts, noted above, are found in the development of each of the areas of "data processing" devices and equipment to be reviewed.

EARLY MAN AND HIS RECORDS

During the Old Stone Age or Paleolithic period, man's principal concern was survival. This was the earliest and longest period since *Homo sapiens* emerged from his still more primitive ancestors. He was a nomadic hunter and food gatherer, lived in caves or rock shelters, and had only a few rudimentary stone tools. He knew about fire.

In the New Stone Age or Neolithic period, "industrial" development began with the emergence of pottery making, weaving, and carpentry.

Polished stone tools were now available. Besides the dog (tamed earlier) other domestic animals were brought into man's service, and agriculture began with the domestication of major plant crops. As the Neolithic period gave way to the Bronze Age (at least, outside the Western Hemisphere) bronze tools became available as well as such inventions as the arch and wheel, essential to further progress.

As industry and agriculture developed, a need to count also developed. The earliest attempts at counting had been through the use of the first—and basic—digital computer—the fingers or toes. The digits, or fingers, were used to count by indicating one finger, two fingers, three, four, or by closing them all into a clenched fist, "many." The use of "many" was not too satisfactory, however, and after some time they switched from fingers (or toes) to pebbles which could be arranged in stacks to keep a record of totals.

These stacks of pebbles also created problems. They could be easily knocked about or "borrowed," and the record they provided would be destroyed. This led to the use, over time of course, of such techniques as marks in wet clay which could be baked or dried to preserve the information, the use of knots tied in fibers, which were the string of the day, and notches cut into sticks. These techniques were not only utilized to record the possessions of a given individual but also the "accounts receivable" due him from those he bartered with.

At first, agricultural and pastoral pursuits were strictly tribal in nature, but eventually given individuals, or groups of individuals, became more adept at producing certain items.

This limited specialization in production brought about the need to develop some common form of value associated with the various trade items produced and a medium of exchange to equate these items. Usually, depending on the tribe, the country, etc., some item which had some permanency in form was used as such a medium. Often, this was either an item which was in great demand and could be converted to some real (actual) use in addition to serving as a medium of exchange or it was a relatively scarce item—which provided stability to the overall availability of such items. It is the latter type of exchange medium that has become money as we know it today.

EARLY DEVELOPMENTS BY CIVILIZED MAN

The ancient Egyptians discovered and perfected the use of papyrus to record their business transactions and to document their history. This reedlike plant grew along the banks of the Nile River. Its pith—when cut into strips, arranged crosswise in two or three layers, soaked in water, pressed, and dried—provided durable thin sheets which could be used as a writing surface. Our word "paper" is derived from "papyrus." The Egyptians also developed ink. They used red ink especially to indicate losses, and this practice has been carried down through the ages.

The ancient Egyptians wrote in hieroglyphics, a form of picture writing. In Mesopotamia, Babylonia, Assyria, and Persia, cuneiform writing was developed. This consisted of wedge strokes made with a stylus in soft clay or other material. Both of these forms of writing were slow and cumbersome, but they served to write the orders and historical records of the day and to provide records of the tax payments, deeds, leases, and purchase and sale of livestock, and to prepare storage receipts from granaries.

Writing, as it evolved, became a highly specialized art and was only performed by specially trained individuals, known as "scribes" and usually selected by the priests.

The Phoenicians inhabited the coast of the eastern Mediterranean and by 1250 B.C. were well established as sea traders and merchants. They

Courtesy of National Cash Register Co.

FIG. 2–1.   Evolution of the Alphabet.

extended their operations to all the seaports of the then known world. Extensive records were necessary to keep track of their business ventures, and to aid them in this, they developed the forerunner of today's alphabet (Figure 2–1). This 21-character alphabet was later extended by the Greeks to the 26 characters found in our modern alphabet.

In approximately 500 A.D., the Hindus began to develop a usable set of numbers. Previous to this the form of the numbers used was such that it was impossible to perform any of the arithmetic functions so widely used today. This new set of numbers started by using an equivalent of the digits 1 through 9 with a small dot following the number to start a second

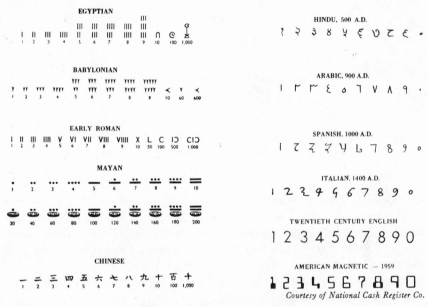

FIG. 2–2.   Evolution of Numbers.

series of numbers (1. for our 10, 2. for our 20, 1.. for our 100 etc.). This was not too usable, as the dot could be overlooked, and a small circle was later substituted. In time the small circle became the same size as the other numbers and a full-fledged digit along with the others.

The development of the Hindu set of numbers, from which later evolved the Arabic, Spanish, and finally the Italian, number system (see Figure 2–2), was a great improvement over the Roman numbers (try adding CVII to LXIV). For the first time, man had a set of numbers that could be manipulated to provide addition, subtraction, multiplication, and division as we know it today.

There appears to be considerable question as to the development of the first real computational machine or device. Various historians have dated the first use of the Chinese suan pan, or abacus, from as early as 1000 B.C. to as late as 200 B.C. (Figure 2–3). Modifications or variations of the

the *Suan Pan*
(or Chinese Abacus)

Courtesy of National Cash Register Co.

FIG. 2–3.   Abacus.

abacus have been produced in many countries and are known as the *s'choty* in Russia, the *coulba* in Turkey, the *choreb* in Armenia, and the *soroban* in Japan. These variations include the use of one button above and four below the divider bar instead of two and five respectively and the use of nine buttons without a divider bar. Considerable dexterity can be developed by users of these devices to permit the performance of surprisingly rapid arithmetic calculations.

RENAISSANCE PERIOD

Record keeping, as we know it today, was developed by the early Italians—especially the Venetians and Genoese, who were the leading merchants of the 14th and 15th centuries. In this same general period, these people formed *bancos*, which were the early counterpart of the banks of today. Credit, the use of checks, notes, etc., were all used in somewhat the same manner as today.

The twofold, dual, or double aspect of every business transaction became recognized. (As examples, every sale meant either the receipt of money or a "receivable" representing something due from others and a giving up of some trade item or the performance of a service; and the purchase of an item meant its receipt as well as its cost in terms of either the payment of money or the incurrance of a debt.) The recording and manipulation of the data resulting from business transactions utilizing this dual effect on the records became known as double-entry bookkeeping.

With the development and some general acceptance of this record-keeping technique, we have the first known written discussion of the subject. A Franciscan monk, Luca di Borgo Pacioli, wrote *Summa de arithmetica geometria proportioni et proportionalita* ("Everything about arithmetic, geometry, and proportions") in 1494. The chapter entitled *"Particularis de computis et scripturis"* clearly defined the basic techniques and principles of double-entry bookkeeping. Fra Luca Pacioli is known as "the father of accounting."

DEVELOPMENT OF CALCULATORS

Outside the development of the abacus, there was little, if any, attempt to develop mechanical devices to perform the laborious tasks of arithmetic computation until 1617. About this time John Napier (1550–1617), a Scottish mathematician, who earlier in 1614 had devised logarithm tables utilizing the base *e*, developed—just before he died—a device often called Napier's Bones, to perform multiplication problems.

This device consisted of a set of *strips of bone*, each inscribed (Figure 2–4) with one of a series of numbers representing progressive sums of that number added to itself nine times. In a given problem such as 4 × 456, we merely arrange the bone strips as shown in the illustration and list from right to left the sums of the diagonals found in the "4" row. Thus the units position would be 4, the tens position would be $2 + 0 = 2$, the hundreds position $2 + 6 = 8$, and the thousands position a 1, for an answer of 1,824.

If the problem is 10 × 456 (to which the answer 4,560 is obvious) we could use 5 × 456 two times and add the answers together (2,280 + 2,280 = 4,560), or use (3 × 456) + (3 × 456) + (4 × 456) = 1,368 + 1,368 + 1,824 = 4,560, or any other combination of multipliers to equal the multiplier 10 in our problem.

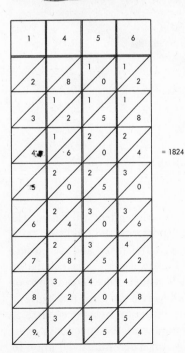

= 1824

FIG. 2–4. Napier's Bones.

Using the logarithm tables developed by Napier, William Oughtred (1574?–1660), a British mathematician, inscribed *slides of wood* or ivory with relative points—based on the values of the logarithms. These slides could be manipulated to provide very quick and fairly accurate answers to multiplication and division problems. The first such device was developed about 1622 and was circular in nature. In 1633 a rectilinear device was produced, and thus the slide rule as we know it today came into existance. This development is now credited with being the forerunner of the analog computer (see Chapter 10), which is one of the two distinct families of computers.

Blaise Pascal (1623–1662)—a noted French philosopher and scientist—developed the first true adding machine in 1642. He was then 19

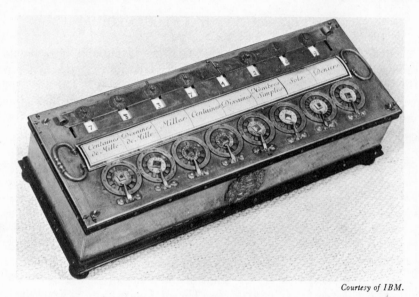

FIG. 2–5.   Pascal's Calculator.

and was working for his father, who was Superintendent of Taxes. He quickly saw the need for some device to perform the addition and subtraction calculations required in the collection of taxes and developed a *numerical wheel and rachet calculator* (Figure 2–5). This calculator registered values by the rotation of the wheels, which were in the form of cylinders, by steps from 1 through 9, with a lever to perform the "carry" from one wheel to the next when the capacity of the first was exceeded. A similar·operation is found in the mileage counter of the speedometer in today's automobile. These characteristics, though much improved upon in application, are still found in our present models of this type of equipment.

About 1666, Sir Samuel Morland of England (1625–1695) developed a more compact calculator which could multiply (by using cumulative addition) as well as add and subtract. This was a *stylus-operated* machine and is still advertised under various names today as a low-priced pocket calculator.

In 1694 Gottfried Wilhelm von Leibnitz (1646–1716), German philosopher and mathematician, completed a "stepped reckoner" which he had started in 1671. This machine had the capacity to perform all four basic arithmetical functions (addition, subtraction, multiplication, and division) as well as extract square roots. All these functions, however, were either performed by using simple addition, multiple addition, or reverse addition (subtraction) techniques.

Though several types of calculators had already been developed, these were not always reliable unless great care was spent in their use. Hahn, in Germany, developed the first really dependable calculator in 1770 to perform all four basic arithmetic functions. Its operating technique was based on Leibnitz's idea of a *stepped cylinder*, but it was considerably improved in its design.

In 1820 Charles Xavier Thomas of Colmar, France, developed a type of mechanical calculator. The major improvement over other models introduced up to this time was in the addition of a *crank* which would feed data into the machine. This machine, called an "Arithmometer," was—in 1878—the first such equipment to be manufactured in a firm established just for this purpose. The founder of this firm was Arthur Burkhardt, a German. Some models of this calculator found their way to the United States and had a strong effect in stimulating developments in this country.

D. D. Parmalee obtained a U.S. patent in 1850 for the *first key-driven* adding machine. This equipment was very limited in its operation as only a single column of data could be added at a time.

Hill, who is sometimes described as being "the father of desk calculators in the United States," developed the first *key-driven four-process* calculating device in 1857.

In the 1870's, two parallel inventions were forthcoming. Both Frank Stephen Baldwin (1838–1925) of the United States in 1872 (patented in 1875) and Willgodt Theophil Adhner of Europe in 1878 developed equipment which improved upon the design of the Leibnitz stepped-cylinder calculator. In each of the pieces of equipment, they used a thin but solid device rather than a cylinder to serve as the *wheel* to be rotated. This was accomplished by adding teeth to the edge of the wheel (much like those of a typical gear). Each tooth was assigned a given value from one through nine. This permitted the machine to be much more compact in size, and the idea has been carried forward in the design of most mechanical calculators to the present time. Baldwin's equipment is illustrated in Figure 2–6.

One of the first attempts to combine an *adding and printing device* together to produce a listing of the data was developed by E. D. Barbour in 1873. This was a very rudimentary form of listing machine and was not successful in its application.

Courtesy of Monroe Int'l Inc.

FIG. 2–6.   Baldwin's Calculator.

In 1884 William Seward Burroughs developed a powerful adding-listing machine. This equipment (Figure 2–7) was crank operated and had a *90-key keyboard* to handle a column of figures up to nine decimal digits. It was patented in 1888, and a manufacturing firm was set up to produce it in 1891.

Though not directly related to the calculators but somewhat associated in principle was the *cash register* (Figure 2–8) which was invented in 1879 by James Ritty of Dayton, Ohio. This device was developed commercially by John H. Patterson, who founded the National Cash Register Company in 1884. This firm is today one of the leading producers of cash registers, calculators, bookkeeping machines, and computers.

In 1885 a U.S. patent was granted to Dorr Eugene Felt (1862–1930) for the first successful *key-driven multiple-order* calculating-machine, which today, in improved form, is called the comptometer. A company, Felt and Tarrant, was organized to manufacture this "comptometer."

Courtesy of Burroughs Corp.

FIG. 2–7.   Burroughs Adding-Listing Machine.

Felt, later in 1889, incorporated a listing capability to his machine and produced one of the first practical devices of this nature.

Léon Bollée invented a calculator in 1887 which used a *direct method* (rather than repeated addition) to perform the function of multiplication. This was followed by an invention by Hubert Hopkins of the United States around 1900 of the first practical billing machine utilizing a direct multiplication technique. This technique was based on that developed by Bollée earlier. In 1901 Hopkins built the first adding machine to use *10-keys* instead of the "full keyboard" set of keys.

Jay R. Monroe and previously mentioned Frank Stephen Baldwin worked together to develop the first successful commercial *keyboard rotary* calculator in 1911 (See Figure 2–9). This equipment was a modification and improvement upon Baldwin's earlier equipment (1908 model of his 1872 equipment) and became known as the Monroe Calculator. This was a nonprinting calculator, but its speed of operations at performing all four basic arithmetic functions put it in a class by itself and made it a success. Together Monroe and Baldwin established the Monroe Calculating Machine Company in 1912. This firm still exists and is active in the

Courtesy of National Cash Register Co.

FIG. 2–8.   Antique Cash Register.

calculator field today under the name of Monroe International Inc., a Division of Litton Industries.

Oscar and David Sundstrand produced a successful *10-key* adding machine in 1912 and organized their own company to manufacture it. The use of only 10 keys normally increases the speed of operation considerably. This type of keyboard is very popular today.

Any number of specific brand-name calculators were put on the market from 1900 to 1930. Most of these, however, had characteristics similar to those already described and were essentially improvements in engineering design, appearance, speed, and ease of operation. Many of these were operated by electric motors, but all were mechanical in design.

Several models of punched card calculators were introduced in the late 1930's and 1940's. These will be noted and described in both the following historical data on punched card equipment and in Chapter 8. Most of these were electromechanical in design, but a few others were truly electronic calculators (Figure 2–10). In the middle and late 1950's, the

Courtesy of Monroe Int'l., Inc.

FIG. 2–9. First Monroe Keyboard Machine.

electronic calculators—which were quite expensive—were generally re-placed by smaller electronic computers which, for the same expenditure of funds, could perform many other functions besides that of calculation.

Small desk-sized electronic calculators have been introduced in the immediate past few years by most of the equipment firms. These utilize microminiature integrated circuits to perform the calculations desired in millisecond (thousandths of a second) speeds. These miniaturized components replace most of the mechanical parts previously required, and the equipment operates noiselessly. The information produced is displayed electronically and read visually on a small cathode-ray tube screen above the keyboard (Figure 2–11).

PUNCHED CARD EQUIPMENT

In the period 1725–1745, Basile Bouchon, M. Falcon, and Jacques de Vaucanson, all Frenchmen, experimented with and developed textile-weaving equipment which utilized punched holes in either paper strips or cardboard to control the weaving of cloth. These were all very rudimentary in design, but they served to stimulate thinking along this line and helped lead to future developments.

Courtesy of IBM.

FIG. 2–10. Calculator.

Joseph Marie Jacquard, another French inventor, experimented for many years with the use of punched cards to control weaving looms. In 1780 he produced equipment which used an endless belt of punched cards to automatically control the weaving of intricate designs in the production of figured patterns. The development of this equipment and other inventions resulted in his receiving a Gold Medal in 1804 from the Inspectors of Paris.

Courtesy of Victor Comptometer Corp.

FIG. 2–11.   Cathode Ray Tube Screen.

Though there was a great deal of opposition from the workers to this "automation," his equipment was widely accepted and was used throughout the Continent and in England. By 1812, 11,000 of these looms were in use in France alone. Modern models of Jacquard Looms are manufactured and used today in the production of cloth.

There is a story that the Dutch workers were so afraid of "automation"—just as their counterparts are today—that they developed a technique of "accidentally" dropping their wooden shoes (sabots) into the looms to delay production. This is said to be the origination of the word "sabotage" as it is used today.

Data Processing Equipment

In 1872 Charles Seaton, Chief Clerk of the U.S. Census Bureau, invented a mechanical tabulator which was capable of simultaneously registering both horizontal and vertical sums. This equipment could rapidly process, in sequence, large amounts of data and was used by the Bureau in statistical analysis.

Even with the development of this mechanical tabulator, it still required seven and one-half years to compile all the statistical data then deemed necessary for the 1880 census. This time span made the compiled data all but obsolete by the time the statistical work was completed. Also, with the rapid growth in population each 10 years, it was evident that, unless some new method of calculation was provided, a second census would be taken before they would be able to compile the information on the 1890 census.

Dr. Herman Hollerith, a noted statistician, had been experimenting with new techniques to compile statistical data, among which the use of punched cards was one method to show some promise. The U.S. Census Bureau heard of his experiments and engaged Dr. Hollerith as a special agent to aid it in solving its statistical data computation problems. At first, Hollerith punched data into a roll of paper using a ticket punch to punch the necessary holes. The use of paper did not prove satisfactory so he substituted a 3 × 5 inch card divided into squares approximately ¼ inch in size. These squares were punched with the data, where applicable, from a given census form, thus developing what came to be known as a "unit record" of information. The punching was still performed by hand, using the ticket punch for some time, but eventually a device was developed in which a card was inserted and a key on a keyboard depressed to punch the hole.

The hole (or holes) in the card was read at first by inserting a different colored card behind it—to make the punched holes more visible to the eye—and it was manually read. Later, the cards were inserted individually into a holder which had small electrically wired cups of mercury below each hole position in the card. A pin-press was lowered that had spring-loaded pins for each hole position, and where holes existed, electrical contact was made and recorded on counters. This contact also opened a given box lid, and the card was removed by hand and filed by given characteristics found in the card data. Thus, the punch, a manual feed reader, and a sorting box made up the original punched card installation in the Census Bureau (Figure 2–12).

An important concept was originated in the design of the punched card that was really not completely grasped until the advent of computers. This is the concept of "state" in which, in a given position in the card, there was either data (the punched hole) or no data (no punched hole) which easily adapted the punched card to the binary (two-position) number system (to be explained later). Also, for the first time, the hole in the card represented *data*—where previously the hole had merely indicated a control device (in the weaving loom)—which was electrically translatable into meaningful information.

This technique of manually punching the data into the card and individually reading each card was slow (50 to 80 cards per minute), but even with a one-fourth increase in population and an expanded statistical

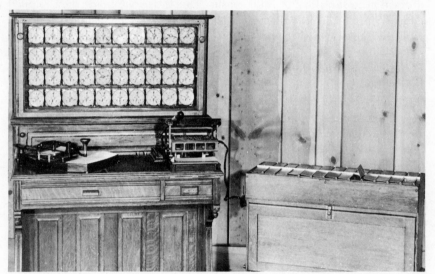

Courtesy of IBM.

FIG. 2–12.   Early Punched Card Equipment.

compilation, the 1890 census was completed in about two and one-half years time.

To promote the commercial potential of his inventions, Hollerith organized the Tabulating Machine Company in 1896. Several municipalities began using his equipment and this spurred him on to new developments. About 1900 a numerical keypunch was developed, and before his retirement in 1914, he produced other equipment, which included an automatic electric sorting machine which operated at an approximate speed of 300 cards per minute, a lever-set gang punch, and a semiautomatic accumulation tabulator.

In 1903, after some initial commercial success in marketing his equipment, Dr. Hollerith and S. N. D. North, Director of the Census Bureau, had a disagreement over patents and finances, and Hollerith left the Bureau to spend full time in the commercial field.

In 1911, the Tabulating Machine Company was merged with the International Time-Recording Company and the Dayton Scale Company to form the Computing-Tabulating-Recording Company. This company changed its name in 1924 to the International Business Machines Corporation, which is so well known today that it is most commonly referred to as IBM.

After Hollerith left the Census Bureau, Congress voted them funds to establish an equipment development laboratory. James Powers was then hired by the Bureau in 1905 to develop a new and different set of punched card equipment. As a statistical development engineer, Powers soon proved himself to be well qualified for the position. By the time the 1910 census was ready to be compiled, he had developed a set of improved equipment, all mechanical in design, to punch, sort, and automatically file punched cards. About 300 pieces of equipment were produced in the laboratory for the 1910 census.

Just as Hollerith had in the past, Powers decided that his equipment had commercial possibilities, and he left the Census Bureau in 1911 to establish his own firm. The Powers Accounting Machine Company was organized in the state of Maine in the same year he left the Bureau. This firm was merged with Remington Rand Corporation in 1927, and later became a part of the Sperry Rand Corporation.

A companion company of the Powers Accounting Machine Company, the Accounting and Tabulating Machine Company was organized to distribute Powers' equipment overseas through sales agencies.

After World War I, the British agency separated from the parent firm and continued to operate as an independent agency until 1929, when it combined with the French agency, Sociéte Anonyme des Machines à Statistics (Samas), to establish Powers-Samas Accounting Machines, Ltd., which, in turn, merged with the British Tabulating Machine Company in 1958 to establish International Computers and Tabulators, Ltd.

Improvements in punched-card equipment before 1930, made by successors to the Hollerith and Powers patents, included the mechanical verifier and electric key-punch (1917); the single-deck sorter, and the alphabetic printing tabulator (1919); an automatic control for tabulators (1921); an electric duplicating key-punch (1924); a typewriter connected to the key-punch for simultaneous punching and typing, and an 80-column card and general-purpose accounting machine (1928); and devices for remote-control accounting of merchandise inventory, customer credit and receivables, as well as for the accounting of sales clerk commissions on the basis of cards punched to indicate articles sold, customer charge plates, and sales person identification tags (about 1928). Many functional deficiencies existed in punched-card equipment in 1930; the inability to subtract, multiply, or divide through punched-card control and to punch a summary card automatically from a tabulator.

Machine developments from 1930 to 1950 included numerical interpreters; the offset-hole method of verification, and the universal printing-counting sorter (1930); the 90-column card, multiplying punch, and summary punch (1931); an alphabetic printing tabulator (1932); a test-scoring machine and alphabetic printing punch (1933); an automatic carriage for printing tabulators, and small cards (2″ × 2¾″) with 21 columns (1934); a collator to merge and separate cards (1936); a transfer posting machine, reproducing gang summary punch, and 130-column cards (two banks of 65 columns) (1938); mark sensing for cards (1939); a tape-controlled card punch and multiple-line printing from a single card (1941); cross-adding punch (1943); the calculating punch, electronic multiplier, cardtype equipment, and document originator (1946); a tape-controlled automatic carriage (1948); the non-listing high-speed punched-card adding machine, alphabetic collator, card-programmed calculator, and electronic statistical machine (1949).[1]

ELECTRONIC COMPUTERS

The basic concepts of electronic computers, as we know them today, were conceived as early as the late 1700's. Technical know-how and engineering capabilities were not developed enough in this age, however, to permit the precision construction of parts and equipment which could implement these ideas.

Even though engineering capabilities had developed over time, it was not until just before World War II that sufficient demand for the calculating capability of such equipment began to be felt. Once initial models of computers were developed, however, newer and more advanced models were quickly forthcoming. Each announcement incorporated new ideas, and the computer quickly evolved in the 1950's into a truer semblance of the *electronic brain.*

The details of this development of electronic computers will be covered in Chapter 10.

ANNOTATED BIBLIOGRAPHY

BIBBY, DAUSE L. *Your Future in the Electronic Computer Field.* New York: Richards Rosen Press, Inc., 1962.

Part I, Chapter 2 (pp. 18–27) describes the history of the computers, starting with ENIAC, the father of UNIVAC I, and mentions the inventors and developers.

BURCK, GILBERT (and the editors of *Fortune*). *The Computer Age.* New York: Harper Torchbooks, Harper & Row, Publishers, 1965.

---

[1] Robert H. Gregory and Richard L. Van Horn, *Automatic Data-Processing Systems* (Belmont, Calif.: Wadsworth Publishing Co., Inc., 1960), pp. 628–29.

This inexpensive paperback presents a great deal of basic computer background in layman's language. It gives the student an insight into the *history of the computer,* problems of the computer manufacturers, current military and civilian computer applications, and the future potential of computers.

"Computers: Yesterday and Today," *Popular Electronics,* February, 1960, p. 69.

A summarized description of the stages of the evolution of the computer from the abacus, to Pascal's calculator, to Babbage's "Difference Engine," to Hollerith and Powers, to ENIAC, UNIVAC, and later computers.

HUSKEY, HARRY D. "The Development of Computing Machines," *The Office,* January, 1962, p. 132.

A history of computing machines limited to computers. The individual equipment is noted as well as the changes which have occurred in techniques, components, and periphery devices.

SCHMIDT, RICHARD N., and MEYERS, WILLIAM E. *Electronic Business Data Processing.* New York: Holt, Rinehart & Winston, Inc., 1963.

Chapter 2 (pp. 6–17) deals with the "High Light in Computation History." Aids to computation described in this chapter range from paper-and-pencil-type aids to electronic computers.

STATLAND, N. "Information Processing; Facts, Fiction, and Future." *Data Processing Magazine,* February, 1966, pp. 18–23.

History of the computer industry. This history is divided into four periods. The late 1940's and early 1950's were characterized by laboratory developments and concentration on calculating needs. The period 1954 through 1958, where the major emphasis was placed on adapting the general-purpose computer to business applications; primarily accounting and routine report listings. The period of second generation equipment, 1958–64, was directed toward tailoring computer system configurations and information flow concepts to meet business needs. The future, 1965–68, will permit management to utilize computer systems as an extension of the decision-making process.

QUESTIONS

1. Why should people have some interest and concern in historical computing devices when we are living in the 20th century?

2. For what purposes were data manipulated and recorded in early Egypt and throughout the Middle East? Explain.

3. Would there be any correlation with your answer to question No. 2 and what you would find in our present-day environment? Explain.

4. What brought about the development of numbering systems, such as the Roman system? Explain.

5. Briefly, how does the abacus operate?

6. What was the economic environment like in Venice and Genoa in 1494 when double-entry bookkeeping was first conceived?

7. Do you feel that your answer to question No. 6 could in any way explain why the double entry system was conceived? Explain.

8. Briefly describe three of the early mechanical devices which were developed to perform arithmetic calculations.

9. Why do you suppose there were an increasing number of these inventions throughout the 17th and 18th centuries? What spurred the inventors?

10. What made the Monroe-Baldwin caculator such a success?

11. Briefly describe some of the ways whereby punched holes in paper or cardboard were used to control machines.

12. Describe the background leading to the development of punched card equipment in the United States.

13. How has the design of punched card equipment changed and improved throughout the years?

CHAPTER 3

Management Information

and Control Systems

RECORD-KEEPING SYSTEMS in the past have been almost solely concerned with telling the story of what has happened to the economic affairs of a particular business. There has been little concern for "why" the affairs were as they were, or "what" might be done about them. This is generally termed "custodial accounting," a type of accounting under which designers of record-keeping systems are oblivious to other basic needs of management, such as information for the purpose of planning and decision making and information for control by comparing actual performance with a predetermined plan. These faults, now obvious, cannot be wholly blamed on those designing these systems, as those in management were not trained in the use of such information and did not ask that it be provided.

Today, with the wide acceptance of computers for business data processing, the accounting profession, along with the business manager, is beginning to realize the potentials of this equipment as being far beyond "custodial accounting." The tremendous storage capacity provided by computers makes it possible to store vast quantities of information which can be recalled at a moment's notice to facilitate the "planning and control function" and to assist in the "decision-making function." A system utilizing these capacities is now called a *management information and control system*.

Another approach to explaining the concept of management information and control systems would be to point out that record-keeping systems have traditionally been designed to handle all of the essential clerical tasks with each task being an end in itself. Under the concept of a management information system, the problem areas associated with the management functions would first be determined. Following this, the system designer would determine the information necessary to enable management to make better and more timely decisions on problems of each of these functions.

SYSTEM DESIGN PROBLEMS

In designing a management information system, there are two major areas of consideration. The first is capturing the proper input of data to provide the basic information needed to produce all of the reports required in the operation of the firm. Such reports cover a far greater scope of information than traditional record-keeping systems. The additional information is related to personnel, production, marketing, and many other data areas.

A second area of consideration is proper control over the system itself and the business organization. This is becoming increasingly important as business firms become larger and more complex. The many aspects of control are woven throughout this and chapters to follow and will be discussed in detail in Chapter 14.

Information System

One of the systems design problems is designing the inputs to the system in such a way that all of the desired information can be accumulated and processed to provide information for the output reports and analyses required by management in its decision making and planning. Files of information, gathered from the inputs, would be stored by the computer. Such files might typically include, as part of the vast storage capability, inventory information by quantity, by class, or by location, or sales data by item, customer, department, store, etc.

A critical problem in the design of a *management information and control system* is to determine what information management might need in carrying out its duties. The systems designer needs to know as much about the problems of management as management itself, a difficult task for anyone to accomplish. This is, nevertheless, the goal of a management information system, and once the data desired have been determined and instructions prepared to ask the computer for the data, any part of these data from these files can be summarized from storage almost instantaneously so as to provide management with up-to-the-minute information.

Control System

If any system is designed to be truly both a management information and a management control system, it is essential that a clearly defined organization structure exist in which areas of authority and responsibility are clearly delineated. The chart of accounts and its codes or numeric designations then become the means of relating transactions to the persons responsible for them so that control reports can be issued upon demand to all those who have responsibility.

ORGANIZATION STRUCTURE AS IT AFFECTS THE PLANNING AND CONTROL FUNCTIONS OF MANAGEMENT

The importance of a clearly defined organization structure can be better appreciated when one considers what is involved in the planning and control functions.

Planning

Planning can be described as the exercise of creative thinking in solving business problems by relating previous knowledge and experience to current facts. Planning is accomplished by top management through determining objectives, establishing policies, formulating plans (budgets), and setting standards of performance, as well as communicating these objectives, policies, plans, and standards to all involved with their performance. *Control,* on the other hand, can be described as the act of regulating business activity in accordance with a business plan so that the objectives of a business project might be achieved.

In short, planning may be thought of as the act of expressing in numeric terms, both for the long run and the short run, a plan of action for the different segments of the enterprise. Control is implemented through the comparison of actual results with predetermined plans or goals. The judicious use of business economic data is one of the means whereby the planning and control functions can be carried out.

Management control involves setting overall objectives or measurements which will serve as yardsticks for allocating resources and for evaluating performance. If the objectives are wisely spelled out and if they are used on some rational basis, they enable managers to select the best alternative uses for a firm's resources. This process of selecting or balancing resources is what is meant by executive control.[1]

For any "plan-performance" comparison to be useful for control purposes, it is necessary first to express the plan in such terms as to enable performance to be measured and, second, to report performance on a sufficiently current basis so that corrective action is possible. Planning and control are most readily accomplished, however, where there is a formalized organization structure and where there are clear-cut lines of authority and responsibility.

Under the planning function, when top management determines objectives and policies, it does so for the entire company. However, when it comes to formulating budgets to meet company objectives and policies,

---

[1] William Travers Jerome, III, *Executive Control—The Catalyst* (New York: John Wiley & Sons, Inc., 1961), p. 23.

this can be done most successfully by calling upon all members of the management team. Their active participation is required to assure that a budget can be successfully met. This, in turn, means that each member of management, including middle and lower management, must assume certain responsibilities in the development of the budget. For this to work out satisfactorily, top management must have spelled out in advance the functions, authority, and responsibility of each. This is most frequently accomplished through an organization chart and manual. Only in this way can the individual manager appreciate the significance of the responsibility he has assumed. A relatively simple, though typical, organization chart is illustrated in Figure 3–1.

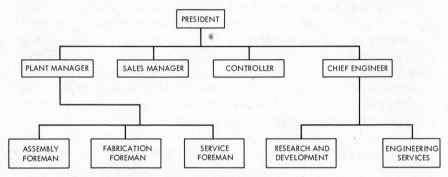

FIG. 3–1.   A Manufacturing Company Organization Chart.

Work standards are generally expressed in terms of the performance of the individual worker. Here again, the individual worker must clearly understand what is to be done, as well as how it is to be done, before he can honestly agree to endeavor to live up to specified standards of performance. This information is usually provided in a manual of procedural instructions.

Control

Control is brought about by top management through the submission, at regular intervals, of a statement to each manager of what he has accomplished compared with what he agreed to be responsible for and for which he was assigned sufficient authority. This control could never be made effective, however, if the manager had not clearly understood his duties and responsibilities beforehand.

It is of the utmost importance that the responsibility of different segments of management be spelled out in terms meaningful both to the individual manager and to members of top management concerned with certain problem areas and in the position of ultimately having to make the significant decisions.

Typical Key Items of Information

Manufacturing

Material requirements and receipt schedule
Material yield
Inventory turnover
Labor schedule
Labor productivity
Factory personnel turnover
Facility load and equipment utilization
Portion of orders shipped on time
Planned product engineering changes
Planned changes in production facilities
Quality performance
Unfilled supervisory and other positions

Marketing

Share of the market
Expected growth of industry and market
Extent of sales coverage
New business and order backlog
Sales performance and trends (by man, area, product)
Competitive activity and features of competitive products
Prices compared with competitors'
Effect of price changes upon volume
Customer complaints
Promotional plans
Market potential for new products
Market potential of styling, materials, and other changes in existing products

Finance

Return on investment and profit
Profit effect of planned actions
Break-even points
Departmental costs
Capital expenditures
Accounts receivable collection period
Working capital
Financing requirements
Cost reduction and work simplification plans
Investment analyses and plans
Potential acquisitions
EDP and other systems development plans

Source: Howard G. Johnson, "Key Item Control," *Price Waterhouse Review*, Vol. XI, No. 3 (Autumn, 1966), p. 29.

FIG. 3–2

Figure 3–2 lists reports which one author has found through experience to be significant to top management.

Chart of Accounts

A chart of accounts is a list of the ledger accounts of a business. It would not be readily possible for the information system of a business to provide the information required to complete control reports such as those illustrated, unless the chart of accounts had been devised which identified all economic data and the individuals responsible for it. One might say that the chart of accounts is the coatrack upon which the entire system of the business must hang.

It is of the greatest importance both to the planning and to the control function that the accounts used are adequate and descriptive of what management is trying to do. Some charts of accounts are not planned; they just happen. They represent an accumulation of a number of persons' contributions over years of use. Each of these contributors had his own ideas as to account classification and, as a result, added his bit of logic to that of others.

An ideal chart of accounts is one that is flexible enough to permit new accounts to be added without changing the basic accounts or hindering the accurate and rapid consolidation of accounting and financial data. If the business under discussion has several divisions or separate organizations, it is vital to use homogeneous classifications for all organizations in the corporate entity.

The accounts which are included in the chart of accounts will be determined by a variety of things:

1. The information which management desires to have in its internal and external reports.
2. The existence of a uniform system of accounts prescribed by a governmental regulatory body, or a suggested system of accounts prescribed by a trade association.
3. The type of cost accounting system in existence and whether the principle of responsibility accounting is being practiced—this point has particular relevance when, in such a system, a definite distinction is drawn between the fixed and variable costs.
4. The extent to which subsidiary ledgers and associated control accounts are to be incorporated in the system of accounts.
5. The recognition of the principle of internal control with the accompanying differentiation of accounts.

The chart of accounts adopted will dictate the arrangement of the ledger, the columnar headings of the books of original entry, and the classification of data to be collected in the auxiliary records and printed forms.

NATURAL CLASSIFICATION OF ACCOUNTS. In order to facilitate the economical and speedy preparation of financial statements, the accounts should be arranged in the sequence which will be followed in the preparation of the balance sheet, income statement, and supporting schedules.

For example:

1. Balance sheet asset accounts.
2. Balance sheet liability accounts.
3. Balance sheet owner's equity accounts.
4. Sales income accounts.
5. Manufacturing expense accounts.
6. Selling expense accounts.
7. General and administrative expense accounts.
8. Research and development expense accounts.
9. Other income accounts.
10. Other expense accounts.
11. Income tax accounts.

The caption of each account should be both brief and clearly descriptive.

Periodically the accounts which are being used should be reviewed by the controller as to their adequacy for the purposes intended. If there are accounts which are not being used, they should be deleted. On the other hand, if there are accounts which are needed and which are not presently listed in the chart, the chart should be sufficiently flexible to permit such accounts to be added with ease.

The following illustration (Figure 3–3) is a chart of accounts from a computerized accounting system for sheep ranchers in New Zealand.

EXPENSES					
4010	Wages		4050		Cash Cropping XP
	4011	Wages Manager		4051	Windrowing
	4012	Wages Permanent		4052	Heading
	4013	Wages Casual		4053	Sacks and Twine
	4014	Wages Wife		4054	Drying and Storing
	4015	Wages Meals Etc.		4055	Dressing and Certifying
	4021	Wages Sharemilker		4056	Spraying
4030	Animal Health		4057		Potato Planting
	4031	Bloat Control		4058	Potato Grading
	4032	Dips Fly Control	4060		Cultivation
	4033	Dockg Tags Gas		4061	Clearing and Bulldozing
	4034	Drenches Vaccine		4062	Initial Work
	4035	Footrot Control		4063	Final work, Sowing
	4036	Veterinary Fees	4070		Dairy Shed Expense
	4038	Health Appliances		4071	Rubber Ware
	4039	Dog Hydatid Control		4072	Brushes Brooms
4040	Breeding Expense		4073		Cleaning Materials
	4041	Artificial Breeding	4080		Electricity
	4042	Herd Testing		4081	House
	4043	Pregnancy Tests		4082	Shearing Shed
	4044	Service Fees		4083	Dairy Shed

Source: Lincoln College and University of Canterbury, Christchurch, N.Z., *Joint Project in Farm Management Accounting*, June, 1966.

FIG. 3–3

Account Coding

Definitions of the process of *account coding* vary, but most agree on the basic principles involved. Typical definitions include: "Account coding is the science of selecting and assigning account numbers to specific account lists."[2]

The National Association of Accountants in their Research Report No. 34 describe coding in this way:

The assignment of numbers, letters or other symbols according to a systematic plan for distinguishing the classification to which each item belongs and for distinguishing items within a given classification from each other.[3]

JUSTIFICATION. In any discussion of account classification, it has been traditional to include some material on different methods of numbering these accounts. The primary reason given for numbering the accounts is ease of handling the accounts, particularly when there are large numbers of them. The likelihood of error is less if the accounts can be referred to by number rather than by caption or name. The possibility of having many accounts with similar titles is always present. For each account to have a number, therefore, enables any record keeper to differentiate much more accurately between the accounts.

In recent years, the rapid advent of a host of new data processing machines, advances in punched card techniques, the increased use of punched paper tape, and the development of electronic computers, has caused a major revolution in systems and procedures techniques. Number codes form the basic language of high-speed sorters, collators, tabulators, computers, and other automated equipment. If business desires to utilize the speed, accuracy, and other capability of such equipment, it *must* convert all account titles and names into number equivalents.

The problem of developing a numbering system which will not only be adequate for existing conditions in a particular business but which will also cover all eventualities in the forseeable future is a much more difficult task than might appear.

DEVISING A CODING SYSTEM. When devising a coding system, each digit of the code should have meaning. If one is to follow this idea, the next question is, how many digits are necessary for a particular coding system? The fewer digits there are in the code, the less likelihood there is of error in recording; speed in sorting is facilitated and less storage space is required for the data on the document, in the punched card, or in the memory storage devices of electronic computers.

---

[2] Conan Doyle Whiteside, *Accounting Systems for the Small and Medium Sized Business* (Englewood Cliffs, N.J.: Prentice-Hall, Inc., 1961), p. 217.

[3] N.A.A. Research Report No. 34, *Classification and Coding Techniques to Facilitate Accounting Operations*, April 1, 1959, p. 3.

In practice, one can find business firms whose codes have a wide variety of digit combinations in them. As an example of an extreme situation, one company uses a code containing 35 digits. Reading these digits from left to right, the code would be interpreted as follows:

Digits	*Identification*
5	Commodity
6	Weight
5	Customer
2	Consignee point
1	Business
1	Shipment type
1	F. O. B.
1	Carrier type
4	Carrier
1	Shipment destination
2	State or foreign
3	County
3	City

You will note from this code that the company can have a complete analysis of every sales transaction.

TYPES OF CODES. A well-designed coding system has a number of essential ingredients: (1) the system must be simple and easily understood by any who may come in contact with it; (2) it must be capable of being easily expanded without destroying the original sequence; and (3) it must be readily adaptable to machine accounting.

A wide variety of coding systems are in use. Many of them overlap in their methods. Examples which follow are some of the more basic of the different methods used.

Block Codes. This particular type of numerical sequence code reserves a block of numbers for a definite classification of items within that block. Each number within the block identifies the item itself.

5—Fixed Assets	6—Prepaid Expenses
5–1 Land	6–1 Insurance Policy "A"
5–2 Buildings and Improvements	6–2 Insurance Policy "B"
5–3 Delivery Equipment	6–3 Rent

Group Classification Codes. This code uses one or more of its numbers to classify the items into major and minor groups. In this code, all items of any group can be identified by selecting the one number of the code which identifies the group. The larger grouping is always found on the left. Reading toward the right are found the smaller subdivisions of the group.

INCOME ACCOUNT

3111
   Revenue
      Government
         Cost reimbursable contracts
            Cost plus fixed fee subcontract

EXPENSE ACCOUNT

5461
   Expenses
      Advertising Department
         Printing media
            Brochures

In the "Expenses" classification above, those of printing brochures are classified under the Advertising Department, which has the responsibility for authorizing that expenditure. Other departments would each have their related expenditure responsibilities shown under their expense account classifications. This illustrates again the importance of having clearly defined areas of authority and responsibility.

Significant Digit Codes. Within this code all or some of the digits represent the item information (such as weight, dimension, distance and capacity). This system has most application in classifying items of inventory. It is not applicable to the classification of ledger accounts. Two examples:

31000 Files
   31040—Files 4"
   31045—Files 4½"
   31050—Files 5"

13000—Electric Light Bulbs
   13020—20 Watt
   13040—40 Watt
   13100—100 Watt
   13250—250 Watt

Decimal Codes. An example of a decimal code which has been developed with much usable data packed into a relatively small number of digits is one in which, proceeding from left to right, each column serves to emphasize the significance of the preceding column. When the entire number of columns are not needed, in analyzing an item, ciphers are inserted in the unused columns. This code consists of a one-column organizational code, a four-column general account number code, and a three-column analytical code. The three components of the code— organizational, general, and analytical—are separated by decimal points. Using zeros, the division is as follows: 0.0000.000.

With such a code arrangement, a wide range of expression is possible; flexibility is provided; and divisions, departments or products may be revised without any necessary basic changes being required in the accounts.

This classification system is ideally suited to responsibility accounting as the general account number can be subdivided organizationally to accumulate expenses by the function responsible. As an example:

Division or Plant	*Analytical Code*
1.0000.000—Division A	1.5114.200—Indirect Labor
General Account	1.5114.210—Bargaining Employees
1.5100.000—Manufacturing	1.5114.215—Inspectors
1.5110.000—Quality Control	
1.5114.000—Receiving Dept.	

Mnemonic Codes. This term is used to designate codes which have, as an integral part of their construction, some aid to the memory expressed in letters, numbers, or combinations. For example, the following is a common type of mnemonic symbol.

$$H \ 2 \ B \ W \ 12\frac{1}{2}$$

This describes a 2-pound ball peen hammer with $12\frac{1}{2}$-inch wood handle, the initial letters and dimensions being used to determine the symbol.

It is obvious that this principle cannot be employed indefinitely because of the conflict of names beginning with the same letter. Should it be desired to designate "hacksaw" for instance, in the same code, it is likely that "S" would be used, or "HK."

The sequence and position of the letters and figures constituting a symbol have a significance and, in this respect, resemble a decimal system of coding. This sequence should be arranged so that the letters of the alphabet are intermingled with the figures, as such a symbol is more easily remembered than one with all letters together and all numerals together, since the classifications are better accented.

An example of mnemonic coding may be found in the method of assigning automobile license numbers in certain states. Although these numbers are not code numbers in the strict sense, the mnemonic principle is used, inasmuch as the letters of the license are made to correspond to the initial of the county in which they are issued.

RESPONSIBILITY REPORTING—A CONTROL DEVICE

Basing the preparation of reports on responsibility assignments is not a revolutionary new idea. It merely recommends that costs be accumulated according to the various areas and levels of responsibility, as outlined and defined in the organization structure of a business firm. It also recommends that only costs which are controllable at the various levels of responsibility be reported to the responsible individuals.

In order to make such a concept workable, there are several other requirements which must be present within the organization and the accounting system.

Organization

The managerial reports with which we are concerned should tell us not only what has happened but also who is responsible for the occurrence. This means that the firm must have "a specific and precise recognition of the individual areas of responsibility specified by the firm's organization structure."[4] In turn, the organization structure has to be predicated on the objectives and policies of the firm.

CHART OF ACCOUNTS.   In order that the majority of all costs be recognized as controllable by some member of the management team, any costs which vary over the period or from period to period must be identified and related to the responsible manager. This, in turn, will require that specific ledger accounts be created so as to relate these costs to those members of management who truly have control over them.

To do this will demand not only a greatly enlarged chart of accounts but also an increased understanding on the part of the system designers of the basic nature of all of the costs incurred in the business organization.

BUDGETARY CONTROLS.   A budget tells management what it is to account for. Each supervisor should have the right to participate in the preparation of the standard by which he is to be evaluated. A complete budget for the entire business organization must be constructed from the

Radios

Month	Gross Sales Over (Under)	Gross Sales Actual Plan*	Standard Profit Contribution Amount Over (Under)	Standard Profit Contribution Amount Actual Plan*	Standard Profit Contribution Percent Sales Over (Under)	Standard Profit Contribution Percent Sales Actual Plan*	Standby Expense Spec.	Standby Expense Gen.	Pro-gram'd Exps.	Standard Product Line Earnings	Orders Received This Year	Orders Received Last Year	Order Backlog This Year	Order Backlog Last Year
Jan	(21)	2,534	(54)	937	(1.8)	37.0	35	310	44	548	2,653	2,760	92	173
Feb	(116)	2,540	(60)	968	(0.6)	38.1	35	312	56	565	2,598	2,795	113	216
Mar	79	2,901	49	1,142	0.6	30.3	36	312	42	752	3,113	2,961	301	258
Apr	33	2,922	3	1,131	-0-	38.7	35	312	39	745	3,016	3,003	275	219
May		2,889*		1,119*		38.7*	35	312	39			2,871		216
Jun		3,055		1,183*		38.7*	36	312	38			3,217		352
Jul		2,224*		862*		38.7*	35	312	39			2,219		171
Aug		3,088*		1,196*		38.7*	36	312	40			3,156		278
Sep		2,967*		1,157*		38.7*	36	312	39			2,991		207
Oct		2,822*		1,093*		38.7*	36	312	39			2,762		197
Nov		2,656*		1,028*		38.7*	35	312	36			2,461		101
Dec		2,556*		991		38.8*	35	312	48			2,333		71
Year to Date	(25)	10,897	(54)	4,178	(0.4)	38.7	141	1,246	181	2,610	11,380	11,519		
Original Plan		33,199		12,860		38.7		425	3,742	499	8,194			
Current Forecast		33,174		12,806		38.5		425	3,742	499	8,140			

SOURCE: Max F. Sporer, Partner, Touche, Ross, Bailey & Smart, "The Mechanics of Accounting under Profitable Accounting." (Company training materials.)

FIG. 3–4.   Vortex Manufacturing Company Product Line Statement of Earnings.

---

[4] William L. Ferrara, "Responsibility Accounting—A Basic Control Concept," *NAA Bulletin*, September, 1964, p. 11.

lowest echelon of management to the top and spelled out according to the responsibilities of each level of management. It is only in this way that the responsibility for the incurrence of controllable costs by any level of management will be sincerely assumed.

Timely Internal Reports

In order that control can actually take place, there must be frequent reports to all levels of management comparing, in the clearest possible manner, what had been budgeted for a particular level of management to what actually occurred. Such reports should suggest action, they should emphasize deviations from the budget plan, and they should direct thinking toward the business objectives.

Numerous ideas have been utilized as to ways whereby management can be stimulated to keep the actual controllable costs in line with the budgeted controllable costs, and these ideas must be considered when the decision is made to implement a responsibility accounting system. Figures 3–4 and 3–5 are two examples of reports which illustrate the points

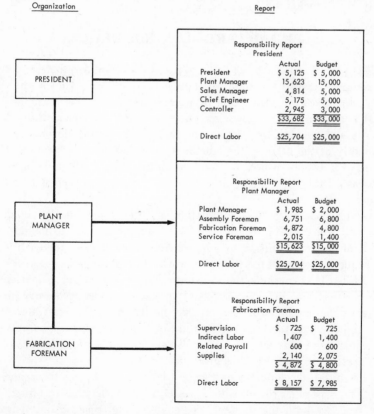

FIG. 3–5. A Manufacturing Company Responsibility Reporting— Manufacturing.

which have been made. The material contained in each of these reports is somewhat different and is worthy of careful study.

Companies which adopt a responsibility reporting system face certain problems when it comes to the preparation of the year-end financial statements because considerable data manipulation is required in order to translate data accumulated and analyzed by responsibility assignment into the typed profit and loss categories of manufacturing, selling, and administrative expense. Some companies also have the problem of reporting profits on a divisional basis, but both of these problems can be readily solved if the system is properly designed.

The use of a computer to perform the data manipulation required will, of course, expedite the preparation of the reports. In some instances, a computer will be required to provide an economically feasible method of performing all the detailed record keeping and reporting required of such a system. The cost of performing this work manually may be prohibitive.

An actual case study illustrating the implementation of a responsibility reporting system is included at the end of this chapter for additional study of this technique.

CPM AND PERT—CONTROL DEVICES

The Critical Path Method (CPM) and Program Evaluation Review Technique (PERT) had their beginnings early in 1957. They both had as their objectives the expediting of work which had to be accomplished. CPM is spoken of as following a "deterministic" approach while PERT follows a "probabilistic" approach. Each method was developed independently of the other, although the approaches are very similar. CPM deals with events which can be predicted with reasonable accuracy whereas PERT deals with situations which have not been encountered before.

As time passed, it was found that additional information could be provided using PERT techniques. These were expanded to include estimates of cost (in addition to time scheduling estimates) for each leg of the sequential steps of the PERT network and critical paths.

PERT/COST permits the consideration of various combinations of time to perform and cost involved in each activity necessary to the project. The combination chosen may be based on the least amount of time to complete, the least expenditure of funds, or some given optimum combination of time and cost depending on resource allocations available and pressure to complete by a given date.

The initial development of PERT/COST was made at the request of the Navy Special Projects Office. As early as 1962, this technique was endorsed, by both the National Aeronautics and Space Administration and the Department of Defense, as a standard tool to be used in planning and controlling schedules and costs.

Through experience the users of CPM/PERT techniques have found that they are much more appropriate in certain types of situations than in others. For example, they work best where there is a definite objective which can be achieved at a given point in time, where there is a completion date requirement, and where many identifiable and interdependent activities and events must be completed in proper sequence before the objective can be accomplished. It must also be possible for time estimates to be made for the events and activities in the network.

Planning

Planning is concerned with the sequence of work. As soon as the activities necessary to complete the task have been identified, they must be analyzed so as to see which ones must be completed before other ones may be started. In breaking down a project into its component operations, the breakdown can be made according to the nature of the work, for example, excavating, formwork, or it can be made according to who has the responsibility for the work. Another logical division of work is according to physical location.

The essence of the CPM/PERT technique is to diagram the sequence in which the activities mentioned above are to be accomplished. The diagrams are referred to as networks and they are constructed with lines with———→representing the passage of time and with circles or "Nodes" which represent the start and completion of events. Here is a simple illustration showing two sequential operations indicating that Operation

B cannot be started until Operation A is completed.

When developing a network, in order to insure its logical sequence, three questions must be asked of each operation:

1. What must precede it?
2. What must follow it?
3. What can be done concurrent with it?

All events must be numbered to facilitate identification and this should be done after the network is drawn.

Let us now consider the construction of a small concrete footpath. First the project is broken down into the following operations:

Project Approved
   Lay Out
   Excavate
   Form
   Concrete
   Cure
   Strip
   Clean up

In addition, it is necessary to:
Order timber for formwork
Prefabricate forms
Order cement and aggregate
Hire a mixer

A network or arrow diagram is drawn linking these operations together. In Figure 3–6 you will note that the lines with arrows have all

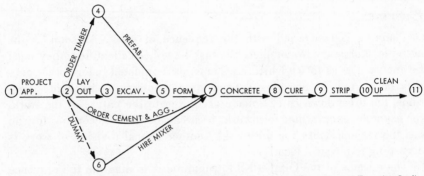

SOURCE: F.P.S. Lu, *The Critical Path Method of Construction Management* (Department of Extension Studies University of Canterbury, Christchurch, N.Z. [Christchurch, N.Z.: Carlton Press, 1964]), p. 21.

FIG. 3–6

been identified and that the nodes have all been numbered for the completion of the footpath. It is sometimes necessary to incorporate into the network dotted arrows which are called *dummy activities*. They do not represent work content but are merely used to maintain network sequence.

Scheduling

As soon as the planning has been completed, the time element must be considered. Personnel should be obtained to estimate the amount of elapsed time required to perform each individual activity, based on the following assumptions:

1. The project starts at relative time zero.
2. No job can start until all jobs upon which it depends have been completed.
3. Each job is started as early as possible.
4. Once started, each job is carried to completion.

For a task which has never before been performed, the following formula is used to determine the amount of time necessary for the completion of each job.

$$\frac{\text{Optimistic time} + 4 \times \text{Most likely time} + \text{Pessimistic time}}{6}$$

Where the task has been performed before, the estimator has something tangible to work with. As soon as the times are determined, they can be added to the network, as they have been in Figure 3–7, for the completion of the footpath.

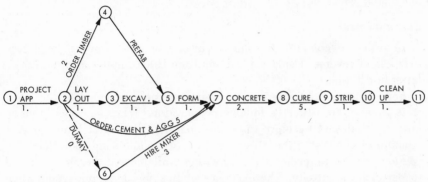

SOURCE: F.P.S. Lu, *The Critical Path Method of Construction Management* (Department of Extension Studies, University of Canterbury, Christchurch, N.Z. [Christchurch, N.Z.: Carlton Press, 1964]), p. 23.

FIG. 3–7

The Critical Path

As soon as the network or arrow diagram is drawn, one can notice that there are numerous paths which could be followed from the start to the finish of the entire project. If one were to add up the elapsed times following the different paths, one would find that they would produce differing amounts of time for the completion of the project. The path requiring the greatest amount of time is referred to as the Critical Path. Knowing the critical path should enable one to determine the completion date of the project. If the completion date is satisfactory, the project should proceed, but if it is not, it is at this time that the entire project with all of its events should be studied to see which events may be speeded up. This might be done by providing more men, money, or materials.

Note from Figure 3–7 that the path (1,2), (2,7), (7,8), (8,9), (9,10), (10,11) requires 15 days, which is the longest elapsed time of the four possible paths and therefore is the critical path. The advantage of recognizing the critical path is that resources can be shifted and specifications altered in order to improve the capacity of the system to meet the deadlines set for it before it is too late.

Earliest Times

The earliest start times of the various activities can be determined by working sequentially through the network. No activity may commence unless all previous activities have been completed. If an operation is, however, preceded by more than one operation, the earliest start time is the latest of the earliest finish times of the preceding operations. An operation can only start when all its preceding operations have been completed. The latest of these must govern.

Latest Times

In order to compute the latest times, one must work through the network in reverse. Using subtraction, one can compute each activity's latest finish time.

For each operation, the latest finish time must be equal to the latest start time of the directly following operation. When an operation is, however, followed by more than one operation, its latest finish time is equal to the earliest of the latest start time of the following operations.

Float is the difference between the time available and the time required to perform an activity. The existence of float becomes important when there is a question as to whether it will be possible to shift resources from one operation to another. If an operation doesn't have any float, it is probably on the critical path, and it is unlikely that resources can be shifted from that operation to any other.

Figure 3–8 illustrates how the earliest times and the latest times as well

Events		Description	Dura-tion (Days)	Earliest		Latest		Total Float	Critical Path
				Start	Finish	Start	Finish		
1	2	Project approved	1	0	1	0	1	0	C
2	3	Setting out	1	1	2	3	4	2	
2	4	Order timber	2	1	3	2	4	1	
3	5	Excavate	1	2	3	4	5	2	
4	5	Prefabricate	1	3	4	4	5	1	
2	6	Dummy	0	1	1	3	3	2	
2	7	Order cement and aggregate	5	1	6	1	6	0	C
5	7	Form	1	4	5	5	6	1	
6	7	Hire mixer	3	1	4	3	6	2	
7	8	Concrete	2	6	8	6	8	0	C
8	9	Cure	5	8	13	8	13	0	C
9	10	Strip	1	13	14	13	14	0	C
10	11	Clean-up	1	14	15	14	15	0	C

SOURCE: F.P.S. Lu, *The Critical Path Method of Construction Management* (Department of Extension Studies, University of Canterbury, Christchurch, N.Z. [Christchurch, N.Z.: Carlton Press, 1964]), p. 30.

FIG. 3–8.   Construction of Concrete Footpath.

as the float can be computed for the footpath illustrations in Figures 3–6 and 3–7.

Computers

The major computer manufacturers have been intensely interested in the development of CPM/PERT and have done a great deal to promote its use by developing standard computer programs for routine applications in determining the critical path.

Computers have also proven to be invaluable to management by providing timely reports pinpointing the progress of operations so that management can see, if necessary and while there is still time, where an operation stands relative to its target completion date.

Advantages of CPM/PERT

1. They involve detailed planning of a project prior to its commencement.
2. The network highlights by visual means the scope and interrelationships of a project's activities.
3. Critical activities are pinpointed.
4. Slack or float time (latest minus earliest completion time) that may exist in various activities can be quickly identified.
5. Management is provided with a scheduling method that is flexible and permits the evaluation of alternative plans.
6. If completion dates are not considered satisfactory, either of these methods highlight the activities that may require modification.
7. The manpower and equipment requirements during the project term can be forecast with greater accuracy.
8. They provide a means of controlling and evaluating the progress of a project.

In addition PERT/Cost provides benefits to managers through:

1. A continuing capability of knowing over and under expenditures at each step in the schedule through a comparison of actual costs to date with the estimate previously prepared.
2. Cost estimates for the total project may be revised and projections made of estimated average on savings to be anticipated in the completion of the project.
3. This technique has been particularly valuable in analyzing the progress of projects under incentive contracts which provide that part of any savings (or costs) may be passed on to the contractor.
4. Scarce resources of the business, such as manpower, facilities, and funds, may be allocated—and continually reviewed—to meet some given optimum usage of these resources.

CASE STUDY 3–1
RESPONSIBILITY REPORTING[5]

Background Data

Perhaps the best way to illustrate the differences between a functional and a responsibility reporting system is to describe briefly an actual case in which our firm devised and installed a complete responsibility reporting system. The case is particularly apt because it is one in which the accounting system was very satisfactory from a financial reporting viewpoint. Net income of the company was developed fairly by the system. However, the accounting reports offered little control information for management and, as was subsequently determined, some of the data were, in fact, misleading.

The company involved was basically a multi-plant, flour-milling operation. Each plant or mill had its own complete income statement. Two of the mills were separate corporations. Where centralized service functions were per-formed, the cost of such services was prorated to the individual mills on the most reasonable basis determinable. Except for intra- or inter-company elimi-nations, only a simple consolidation was necessary to present fairly the results of operations company-wide. Individual statements of operations of the mills were used to evaluate each plant. In addition, a bonus was paid to each mill manager based on his mill net income.

Corporate executives found, however, that the statements were not effective as management tools. Mill managers were always quick to enumerate reasons why the statements did not represent fairly their management efforts, and their reasons usually seemed valid. It was this situation which resulted in our assignment to review the management reporting system of the company.

Defining Responsibilities

The first step was to analyze the company's organizational structure and determine the true income and expense responsibilities throughout the com-pany. This is the first and usually most difficult step in the design of any responsibility reporting system, because very few companies have clearly defined organizational structures or responsibilities. Consequently, this step is also usually very beneficial. Until responsibilities are defined, control of expense is difficult, if not impossible, regardless of what accounting records may exist.

Sales were accounted for by actual deliveries made by each mill. They were therefore as exact as possible from a financial accounting point of view. But from a responsibility viewpoint, a different situation existed. With the excep-tion of a few local sales, almost all mill deliveries were made against bookings by the central sales department. This department established selling prices based on the daily market price of wheat. It allocated shipping orders to the

<hr>

[5] C. E. Graese, "Responsibility Reporting to Management—A Case Illustration," in *Management Controls* (New York: Peat, Marwick, Mitchell & Co., September, 1964), pp. 163–64.

various mills in a manner so as to equalize production and minimize freight cost. Typically, all export sales, which were low margin sales, were allocated to one mill because of its export shipping facilities. Thus, the mill manager had little or no control over sales volume or sales price. The existing system of management reporting disregarded this completely. Yet this was the most significant item in the determination of mill net income.

The second most significant item in the operating statement was the cost of wheat ground into flour. This area was found to be very similar to sales. Wheat costs represented the actual cost of grain shipped to each mill. However, the central grain department purchased almost all of the company's total wheat requirements in central terminal markets. Individual carloads of grain were diverted to local mills so as to minimize freight costs. It was possible, for example, for the mill filling the lowest priced sales orders to be grinding the highest cost wheat. The wheat hedging policies and transactions were also determined by the central grain department. It became apparent that the two most significant items on the income statement were almost totally beyond the control and responsibility of the mill manager.

There remained only the operating expenses. Of these, a significant portion represented allocated central office costs. It was determined that mill managers could really only control, and therefore should only be held responsible for, the actual milling costs and the conversion or grinding yield.

Designing the System

With responsibilities defined, we proceeded to design a responsibility reporting system. The concept of separate mill statements of income was discarded. Instead, only a single income statement was developed on a company-wide basis, with supporting statements for each responsibility area. For management reporting, a system was devised which would permit disregarding the separate corporate entities. In the sales area, reports were designed to establish daily the gross margin over variable wheat price on all bookings by the sales department. The wheat prices were supplied daily by the grain department. These sales reports were further broken down by salesman and proved very effective in measuring the gross margin contributed by each salesman in relation to his total volume and selling costs.

Wheat costs were accounted for by comparing actual cost of wheat purchased in total with the wheat requirements for flour orders booked by the sales department, priced at the market price in effect at time of booking. This provided a standard for measurement of the performance of the wheat department in carrying out their buying and hedging functions.

Manufacturing or mill costs and production yields were accounted for on a local mill basis. No allocations of central office costs were made.

Some Positive Results

What were the results? Perhaps it should first be mentioned that initially there was considerable reluctance on the part of both mill and central office management to eliminate complete profit-and-loss statements for each mill. But as the new concept was explained and the inequities of the old system were made known, the logic of the proposed change became obvious to all. By the time we were ready to install the system, there was considerable enthusiasm for the new approach.

One of the first positive results was that the mill managers ceased being concerned with sales prices and wheat costs of the individual orders and shipments they received. Instead, they realized that they were being evaluated on conversion cost and yield, and concentrated on this responsibility.

Another significant result occurred in the sales department. A new emphasis was placed on getting profitable business at minimum selling cost. A re-evaluation was made of certain sales efforts and lines of business.

From executive management's viewpoint, several results were noted. First, some of the low-profit mills, which were in fact being considered for shutdown, now looked quite satisfactory because they were not being penalized with low-margin orders. But most importantly, the reports received by management could be used directly to evaluate performance at each responsibility level, without fear of being challenged on the basis of arbitrary accounting allocations.

CASETTE A

Manually Operated Network Planning System Gives Many CPM Advantages to Western Utility[6]

A network planning system employing color-coded plastic strips within a frame incorporating a time scale has been used successfully by the Sierra Pacific Power Co., Reno, Nev., to devise a critical path network for a major overhaul of a 53,000-kw. turbine generator.

Cost for downtime under the simplified system ranged 20 per cent below the estimate of the generator manufacturer, and downtime itself was reduced from eight weeks to six.

The system, developed by Planalog, Inc., Philadelphia, employs color-coded, multi-faceted plastic gauges of various lengths to represent the times needed for each step of a major repair job. Various skills needed for each job are also color-coded and placed directly on each gauge, which can also carry written information showing man-hours and costs. When all steps are in place in the aluminum channels of the frame in chronological sequence, the critical path becomes readily apparent, company spokesmen say, as well as the skills required and costs and time involved for each activity.

Moreover, Sierra Pacific spokesmen say, overlapping activities are easily visible, and can be adjusted by simple realignment of the plastic strips.

The unit, somewhat similar to a Gantt chart in three-dimensional form, has the added advantage of incorporating time and cost factors, the company says, and can be used with comparatively little training by foremen to schedule their own repair activities.

---

[6] "Manually Operated Network Planning System Gives Many CPM Advantages to Western Utility," *Management Services*, March–April, 1967, p. 13.

Sierra Pacific plans to use similar units in routine preventive maintenance jobs, chemical clearing, and substation erection and maintenance and may use them in the accounting department to schedule computer operations.

CASETTE B
Expo '67 Follows Critical Path[7]

Expo '67 in Montreal, Canada, has employed the use of the critical path method (CPM) to control all phases of work on the fair, from the original feasibility studies of individual projects, through the phases of architectural and engineering design to the actual construction and, after Expo closes, their eventual demolition. In mid-1963 when work on the project began, CPM was determined to be the only way to anticipate just how long it would take to put the show together and keep track of all the projects as work progressed.

To make CPM work, a management information system was created that would coordinate the construction of some 200 buildings, access roads and bridges, a variety of underground services, a sewage treatment plant, and complete landscaping.

The result of CPM application at Expo, in addition to the fair opening on time, is the introduction of the method to many foreign countries.

ANNOTATED BIBLIOGRAPHY

American Institute of Certified Public Accountants. *Internal Control.* New York, 1949.

A report by the AICPA's Committee on Auditing Procedure stating the elements of a coordinated accounting system and its importance to management and the independent public accountant.

Beyer, Robert. "Meaningful Costs for Management Action," *Harvard Business Review,* Vol. 38, No. 5 (September–October, 1960), p. 61.

Birks, Evan G. "The Computer in a Management Information System," *Canadian Chartered Accountant,* September, 1966, pp. 172–77.

To provide an insight into the operation and potential of modern information systems, a discussion of the basic objectives of a good system and an outline of current approaches to their achievement are presented. Also considered are the components and their functions in a computer-based system, problems in the operation of a system, and trends in the future development of information systems. It is concluded that the objectives of a management information system must be realized by those businesses which want to survive and prosper.

Canadian Institute of Chartered Accountants. *The Function of Management,* Toronto, Ont., 1959.

This booklet is a guide to the many techniques and methods which

---

[7] "Expo '67 Follows 'Critical Path,'" *Business Automation,* March, 1967.

management uses to solve its problems. Four chapters concern themselves with the different types of controls used in a business, and the concluding chapter on management reports is particularly helpful in the study of accounting systems and their purposes.

COLBERT, BERTRAM A. "The Management Information System," *The Price Waterhouse Review,* Spring, 1967.

Describes in detail the importance of adequate information to enable management to carry out its functions. Divides the information which management needs into three categories: information necessary for operation and control; information required to assess future action; and information required to assess or compare performance of the company in competition or within the industry.

CUSWORTH, W. C. "The Continuing EDP Revolution: New Systems Concepts," *The Australian Accountant,* October, 1966, pp. 557–62.

It is pointed out that current concepts of data processing system or information systems are undergoing substantial change. Presented is an examination of the extent and direction of these changes. Discussed are sequential processing, centralized integrated files, multiprogramming, management information systems, integration of external system, and simulation in new models.

EVANS, W. P., and BOSWORTH, R. L. "Computerized Information System (COINS)," *Management Accounting,* October, 1966, pp. 36–44.

The total information system of one plant which has met or exceeded all of the initially set management objectives is described. Outlined and discussed are the major phases of the information system—mechanization of remaining source systems, initiation of a data control system, and mechanization of the general ledger. The relationship of these phases and their contribution to the resulting system COINS are illustrated.

FERRARA, WILLIAM, L. "Responsibility Accounting—A Basic Control Concept," *NAA Bulletin,* Vol. 46, No. 1 (September, 1964).

This article explains the uses of responsibility accounting in the control of both manufacturing and distribution activities. It also goes into the problems of dual responsibility and methods of solving this problem.

HANSEN, B. J. *Practical PERT, Including Critical Path Method.* Washington, D.C.: America House, 1965.

This book gives an excellent basic presentation of the PERT and CPM techniques.

HOROWITZ, JOSEPH. *Critical Path Scheduling—Management Control Through CPM and PERT.* New York: Ronald Press Co., 1967.

This book has been designed to provide an understandable but comprehensive introduction to CPM and its companion network method, PERT, and their applications. Basic principles are presented in simple language with numerous illustrations and examples. For the most part, the methods used require only elementary arithmetic or simple graphs.

Data Processing Techniques: Coding Methods. White Plains, N.Y., International Business Machines Corp., Form F20–8093.

Specific methods of alphabetic and numerical coding are discussed—also the way in which they may be applied. The manual lists and describes the characteristics that should be included in the construction of adequate codes.

JEROME, W. T., III. *Executive Control—The Catalyst.* New York: John Wiley & Sons, Inc., 1961.

The author tries to describe the ideas and activities that made management control an unusually effective catalyst of yet unrealized potential. This book emphasizes the businessman's overall viewpoint and avoids undue emphasis on detail or techniques.

KONVALINKA, J. W., and TRENTIN, H. G. "Management Information Systems," *Management Services,* September-October, 1965, pp. 27–39.

Timely and pertinent information is vital to good decision making. To achieve the desired level of information, sophisticated information systems are being developed. As an aid to developing sound Management Information Systems (MIS), a discussion is presented of information and decisions; development of MIS concepts; what MIS is; and how to set up MIS. Emphasis is placed on the practical rather than the theoretical aspects of MIS. Various examples are included which serve as illustrations of different information systems.

LEMKE, B. C., and EDWARDS, JAMES DON. *Administrative Control and Executive Action.* Columbus, Ohio: Charles E. Merrill Books, Inc., 1961.

This book is a collection of over 70 readings on various aspects of control. Section A groups many articles concerning the relationship of control to the management function.

MOORE, FRANCIS E., and STETTLER, HOWARD F. *Accounting Systems for Management Control.* Homewood, Ill. Richard D. Irwin, Inc., 1963.

Chapter 7 of this book gives an explanation, along with illustrations, of a chart of accounts. It also explains the function and types of symbol systems.

MORAVEC, A. F. "Basic Concepts for Designing a Fundamental Information System," *Management Services,* July–August, 1965, pp. 37–45.

Methods and techniques for designing and implementing a single information flow data processing system are explained. The basic steps are summarized as follows: determine management's needs to monitor the system as a whole; design the fundamental information flow; develop in detail the essential information that each function requires to operate efficiently; and determine each function's dependence upon the information of other functions. Administratively, the plan for conducting the systems study breaks down into three time phases, which are discussed.

NELSON, O. S., and WOODS, R. S. *Accounting Systems and Data Processing.* Cincinnati: South-Western Publishing Co., 1961.

Chapter 3 of this book gives an explanation of the use and design of a chart of accounts. Chapter 7 gives a good discussion of the necessity of an internal control system and how this should be integrated into an accounting system.

RADEMAKER, T. (ed.). *Business Systems,* Vols. I and II. Cleveland: Systems and Procedures Association, 1963.

An organized, comprehensive introduction to the entire systems field, its concepts and techniques. The two volumes assemble the contributions of a great number of members of the Systems and Procedures Association.

SCHODERBEK, PETER P. "PERT/Cost: Its Values and Limitations," *Management Services*, January–February, 1966, p. 29.

The article briefly traces the history of PERT/Cost. It provides an example of a PERT network and gives a simple explanation of the method. A natural extension to PERT/Cost is then made and explained. In addition, Schoderbek evaluates PERT/Cost's present usefulness and future potential.

SHEA, STEVENS L. *Computer-Based Management Information Systems.* American Management Association Management Bulletin, No. 30, pp. 11–13. New York, 1963.

No forward-thinking management team can afford not to consider a computer. The installation should be approached from an overall objective of profit improvement. Profit improvement is gained through more timely and more accurate decision making and utilizing the power of the computer to assimilate, digest, process, test and feed back information which is attuned to achieving short- and long-range profit objectives. The computer-based management information function will enable top management to observe the relationship of each element with a corporate function and of other corporate functions to the company's short-range and long-range profit objectives. The main advantage of this system is that it not only shows the current picture, but projects current decisions into the future and indicates the results of such decisions.

TASSO, GEORGE J. "Responsibility Accounting," *New York Certified Public Accountant*, Vol. 32 (1962). pp. 809–17.

This article defines responsibility accounting and states its purpose. It then depicts, in an organized and concise manner, the requirements for developing a successful responsibility accounting system.

WEINWURM, ERNEST H. "Satisfying Management's Data Requirement," *Journal of Data Management*, January, 1965. pp. 38–40.

Management has a pressing need for more information than that provided by existing data processing systems. An investigation of how management's demands can be satisfied is presented. An attempt is made to determine the effect the required modifications and improvements would have on the organization and design of existing data processing systems.

WENDLER, C. CLIFFORD. "An Approach to Developing a Total System," *Ideas for Management*, pp. 205–20. Cleveland, Ohio: Systems and Procedures Association, 1964.

In management's vision of an overall management information system, the electronic computer functions as the heart of the operation. This paper, based on a research study, presents in a summarized form a comprehensive approach to planning and implementing a total system utilizing a computer.

QUESTIONS

1. A prominent accounting educator recently said, "Traditional accounting has always been centered on the determination of income. The center

of thinking is now changing to that of information systems, however."
What do you think this educator had in mind when he made this statement?

2. At what point in the growth of a business does organizational structure
become important so that planning and control can be accomplished?
Explain.

3. What part do business data play in planning and control?

4. There are many successful companies which have never had or used
organization charts or manuals of procedures. How would you react if
one of these companies asked you whether it should consider using such
things? Clearly explain your answer.

5. What is responsibility accounting and how does it promote better control
in a business organization? Explain, and illustrate your answer.

6. What is the chart of accounts of a business? It is in part determined by
the existence or nonexistence of a group of elements. What are these
elements?

7. What is the relationship between the chart of accounts of a business
and its responsibility accounting system?

8. What purposes are served by assigning numbers (codes) to a chart of
accounts? Illustrate your point.

9. Are different coding systems more useful in certain situations than
others? Illustrate and explain your answer.

10. How is a coding system developed?

11. Why is a group classification code useful in a responsibility accounting
system?

12. What elements does it take in order that a responsibility accounting
system can be made workable?

13. Of what use are CPM and PERT techniques to management? In what
ways might they be useful? Explain.

14. What is the significance to management of knowing the critical path for
a project? Explain.

15. What is float, and what is its significance?

16. Discuss the relative strengths and weaknesses of PERT as a planning
and control technique.

17. Explain what each of the following terms mean relative to PERT:
    a) Activity.
    b) Nodes.
    c) Network.
    d) Critical path.
    e) Float.

CHAPTER 4

Basic Data Processing

Functions

IN EVERY procedure involving the processing of business data, there are certain basic steps to be performed. These steps must be followed regardless of the data processing system employed—handwritten, mechanical, punched card, or electronic computer. These functions, which are basic to the processing of all data, are those of originating, classifying, sorting, calculating, summarizing, recording, and communicating.

Business systems and procedures depend on business documents or forms. The system is represented by the overall techniques, or methods, used in the processing procedures to be followed. These techniques may be only those involved in a manual system where every procedure is performed by hand, a mechanical system of varying complexity, or a computer system of almost unlimited capacity. Procedures are the actual steps or operations in a system which are required in getting the job done. Practically all office and many shop procedures require the use of at least one form. Forms are the means through which, with or without the help of machines—typewriters, bookkeeping machines, and other data processing equipment—the steps or procedures are carried out. Therefore, the efficiency and economy of a procedure may hinge on the forms which make up that procedure.

Originating

Forms are basic to the data manipulation process, as they are the media on which the data are initially captured at the time a transaction occurs. It is from this point of origination, in most instances, that the act of processing data actually begins. As examples, information from a timecard (Figure 4–1) is transcribed into a punched card (Figure 4–2), so that an individual may be paid; and information from a sales invoice (Figure 4–3) is transcribed so that the customer will be billed and a claim will be set up against the customer for the amount owing. In both of

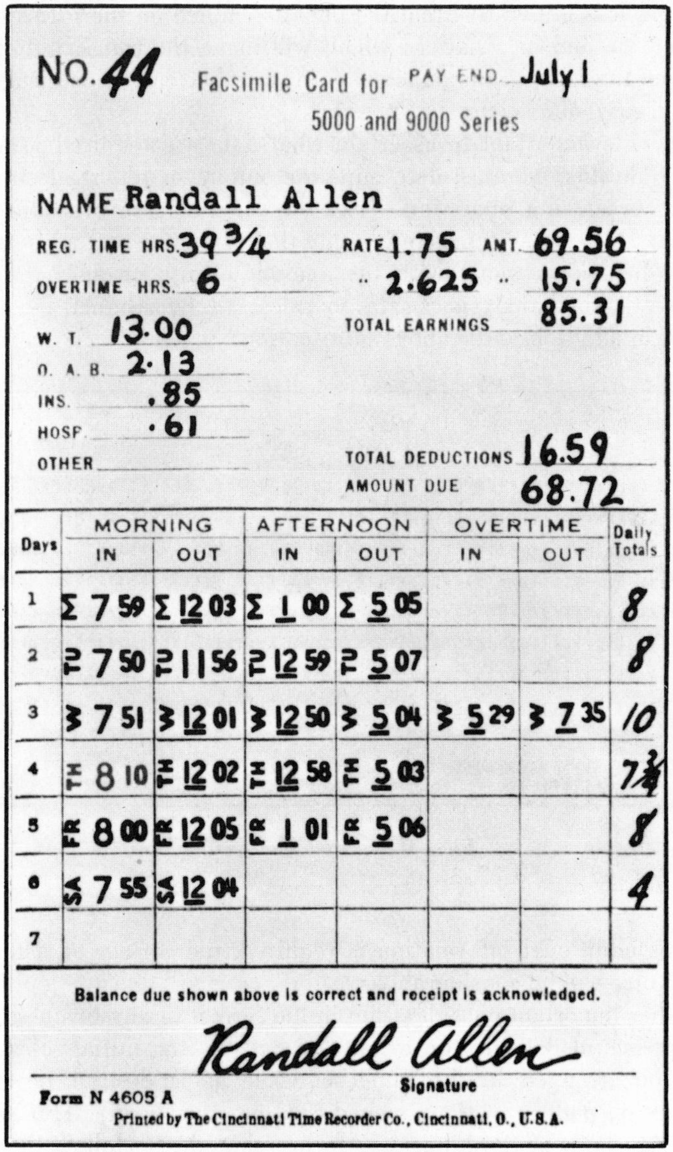

NO. **44**   Facsimile Card for   PAY END **July 1**

5000 and 9000 Series

NAME **Randall Allen**

REG. TIME HRS **39 ¾**   RATE **1.75**   AMT. **69.56**

OVERTIME HRS. **6**   " **2.625** " **15.75**

W. T. **13.00**   TOTAL EARNINGS **85.31**

O. A. B. **2.13**

INS. **.85**

HOSP. **·61**

OTHER   TOTAL DEDUCTIONS **16.59**

AMOUNT DUE **68.72**

Days	MORNING		AFTERNOON		OVERTIME		Daily Totals
	IN	OUT	IN	OUT	IN	OUT	
1	Σ 7 59	Σ 12 03	Σ 1 00	Σ 5 05			8
2	7 50	11 56	12 59	5 07			8
3	7 51	12 01	12 50	5 04	5 29	7 35	10
4	8 10	12 02	12 58	5 03			7¾
5	8 00	12 05	1 01	5 06			8
6	7 55	12 04					4
7							

Balance due shown above is correct and receipt is acknowledged.

Randall Allen

Signature

Form N 4605 A

Printed by The Cincinnati Time Recorder Co., Cincinnati, O., U.S.A.

FIG. 4–1.   Timecard.

these instances the data would be processed almost automatically after being incorporated in a punched card. But first, the data for the transaction had to be gathered and assembled on business forms which serve as originating documents—in the examples above, the timecard and sales invoice.

Since business forms become the basis of input to the data processing operation, it is imperative that the data assembled on the forms be clear and accurate and in a pattern which will make the transcription of the data from the form to the punched card, or other data processing media, as quick, easy, and accurate as possible.

First, it is important to ascertain what data are required in a procedure. To do this one must determine the output, or report, desired from the data processing operation. Take the sales invoice procedure as an example: Does the system require only that the name and address of the creditor be known along with the amount owing, or does the system require a detailed analysis of sales by salesman, by product, by size, and by color in addition to the above information?

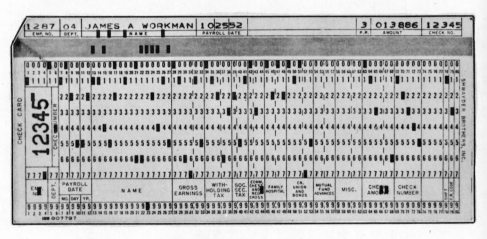

FIG. 4–2.   Punched Card.

If this additional information is required, the variety of data on the sales invoice will be considerably greater.

Another important consideration in the format of any business form is the sequence of data on the form. The data on the initial sales invoice should be arranged in the same sequence as is desired in the data transcription pattern of the punched card or other media. This sequence of data, on both of these business forms, should also follow the natural sequence required in the procedure.

The accuracy of the data on the initial business form is always of vital concern to anyone interested in the problems of data processing. Once an error is made, the accuracy of the data cannot be improved by any subsequent processing. A number of ways have been conceived as a means of alleviating this problem of being accurate in recording data in the originating document, none of which, however, completely achieve the end desired. Some of these are:

ORIGINAL INVOICE

Timary Art Supplies

15 East Huron St., Chicago, Illinois 60601

TELEPHONE
CHICAGO: INterocean 0-0000
AREA CODE 312

• SOLD TO

CUST. ORDER NO. INVOICE NO. INVOICE DATE

• SHIP TO

• SHIP VIA: TERMS: 30 DAYS NET F.O.B. SHIPPING POINT

QUANTITY	DESCRIPTION	UNIT PRICE	% DISC.	NET AMOUNT

***FIG.* 4–3. Sales Invoice.**

1. As much of the basic data surrounding the transaction as possible are preprinted on the form. If the data are not preprinted, they may be precoded on the form. In this way the accuracy of the data may be proven before use. For example, the customer number permanently impressed into the gasoline credit card (Figure 4–4) is automatically reproduced onto the sales invoice which is printed from it.

2. The forms are designed so as to be capable of being easily prepared. This is facilitated when adequate space is provided for the inser-

tion of data; when it is possible for the data to be arranged in a neat, orderly manner, and in logical groups consistent with the entire procedure; when the sequence of data flows smoothly from left to right and from top to bottom of the form and is consistent with data on related forms, and when instructions are properly located on the form and are so worded as to be easily understood.

3. A contrast is created between the preprinted data and the inserted entries. The inserted data is made to stand out plainly enough to be easily read, and the preprinted data fades into the background.

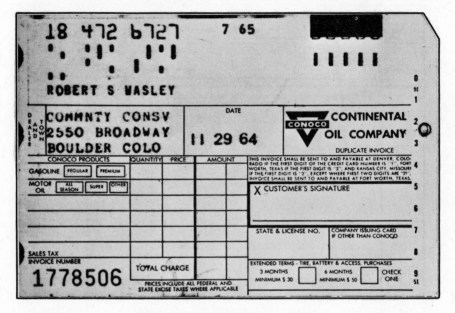

FIG. 4–4.   Gasoline Sales Invoice.

To provide the data which permits business data processing procedures, the originating data surrounding the various business transactions must first be captured. This is generally accomplished by clerks and employees at the scene of the transaction, when they fill out a business form; or the transaction may be recorded by a machine of some type, typical of which would be a cash register. Regardless of the method used in capturing this data, the importance of recording it accurately at the time of data origination cannot be overemphasized. Business forms, by their design, can do much to insure this accuracy.

Data collection and gathering systems (Chapter 13) are also utilized in the origination of data. In these systems the data are captured by the input of various types of cards, badges, and tapes on which fixed data have been prerecorded in a machine-acceptable language. Variable data related to the recording of a specific transaction are recorded by dials, knobs, or other types of manual settings. In these systems the use of prerecorded and visually observed manual input data along with available specific internal control checks (to be discussed later) provides a great deal of assurance that the data are accurate.

Classifying

Another of the functions necessary in the processing of business data is that of the classification of the data into the patterns required. Certain functions must be performed sequentially, while in other instances functions can be performed in different sequence. At times it may even be possible to perform them simultaneously.

Once business data have been originated or captured on a business document, the first step in processing them is to classify them as to what they represent. Classification has been defined as, "The identification of each item and the systematic placement of like items together according to their common features. Items grouped together under common heads are further defined according to their fundamental differences."[1] Classification is necessary in order to bring out the significance of information and is an essential step in the grouping of detailed information. It is necessary to strike a balance between the amount of detailed classification that is desirable and the cost of providing such information.

Classification of business data can in part be accomplished when the data are initially recorded on a business form. Take, for example, the sales ticket which is written out when a purchase is made in a department store on credit. The clerk, normally, will have been instructed to identify clearly certain items of data which management considers to be important, such as the name and address of the customer, a complete description of each item sold, the quantity of each item sold, the unit selling price, the total selling price, any state and/or federal taxes applicable, and the total amount of the sale to the customer. If this sales ticket form is carefully prepared, much of the data classifying function has already been accomplished.

For another example, take the student who is working one of his first accounting problems. The problem gives him some transactions, and he is asked to journalize them. When the student decides what must be debited and what must be credited, he is, in effect, classifying the data.

The manner in which data must be classified will be largely determined by the way in which management intends to use the data and by the form in which the data will be presented in the business reports which management requires from the accounting system. The format of the reports can

---

[1] NAA Research Report No. 34, *Classification and Coding Techniques to Facilitate Accounting Operations*, April 1, 1959, p. 3.

vary tremendously, depending upon the patterns of classification used in gathering and arranging the data. For example, cost data will be classified quite differently if the object of the system is that of planning and controlling cost rather than that of determining unit costs for inventory valuation purposes. In the planning and control of costs, the cost items will likely be classified, as nearly as possible, according to areas of individual responsibility. On the other hand, if the determination of unit cost is of paramount concern, the costs will probably be classified by functional groupings and then allocated to the products produced by the firm on the most equitable basis possible.

The coding activity is an intrinsic part of the classification function, also. When one codes a series of accounts he is, in effect, making it possible to classify the same basic data in several different ways—i.e., according to the plant, to the department, or to the departmental subfunction. Various methods of coding have been more fully described in Chapter 3.

Automatic coding or precoding of transactions was not discussed in Chapter 3, however. In data processing there is always the concern that

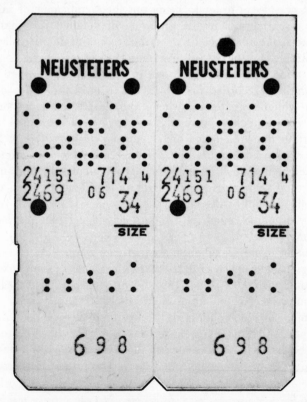

FIG. 4–5.   **Perforated Garment Ticket.**

an employee may not properly record or accurately classify or code the data when they are first originated on a business form or when they are transcribed into some other more usable form for further processing. As a result of this problem, the technique of precoding certain types of business transactions has been devised. The idea behind this is that much data are common to transactions of a certain type. Therefore, why wouldn't it be possible to identify certain transaction data before the events actually occur? In this way, the data could be verified before ever being put into process. Perforated garment tickets and charge plates are examples of ways whereby this is being done.

Perforated garment tickets (Figure 4–5) are often used in clothing stores. All pertinent data identifying the item are prepunched into the tickets and varified by the manufacturer of the garment. The tickets, in turn, are attached to each related item of clothing. When the garments are sold, one part of the ticket is retained by the salesclerk. When these tickets are accumulated and processed, a complete description of the items sold can be printed out, giving management up-to-date information on the items sold.

The charge plate (Figure 4–6) enables a store to identify accurately a

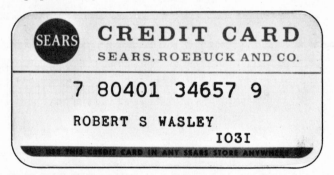

FIG. 4–6.   **Charge Plate.**

customer who has been preapproved for credit, thereby more nearly assuring the store that once the bills for the sales are sent out, they will be paid promptly.

Sorting

Sorting can be defined as the process of arranging data into some desired order according to rules dependent upon a key or field contained by each item. It may be performed manually, mechanically, electromechanically, or electronically. The complexity of the sorting task will be determined both by the number of fields by which the items being sorted are identified and by the physical volume of items to be sorted.

MANUAL SORTING. Earlier it was established that the act of determining what was to be debited and credited in a transaction was an act of classifying data. Since this is true, the act of posting these data to appropriate ledger accounts represents an illustration of the sorting process. It is as though the ledger accounts were boxes like those in a post office, with each box representing an address, and the person doing the posting was in the process of sorting mail for each address.

This same process may be carried out by using multicolumn journals (Figure 4–7). The fact that a journal has numerous columns enables one to classify data and also sort it on a simultaneous basis. Of course, the posting operation still remains, but in this case the sorting has largely been accomplished, and postings are through totals rather than individual items.

In some instances, each entry needed to represent a transaction is entered on a unit media. A job timecard would be an example of this. At the end of the day, all of the timecards would be sorted by job, totaled and posted to a Job Cost Sheet. In a manual system, the unit media would be sorted by hand.

Although the writing-board or pegboard system is a manual operation,

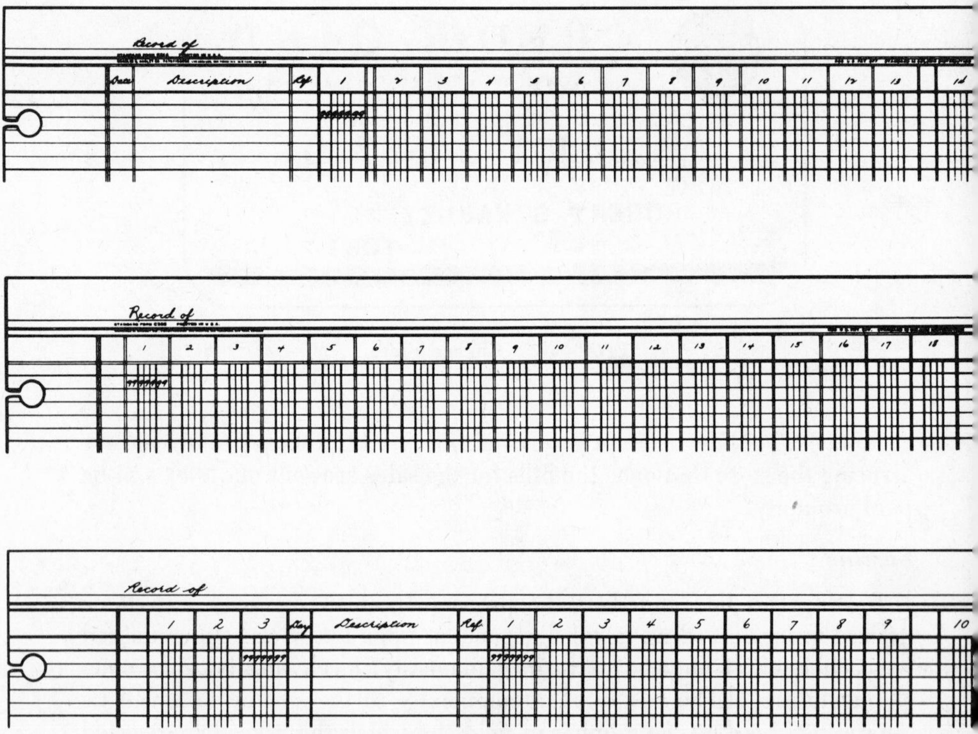

FIG. 4–7.   Multicolumn Journal Forms.

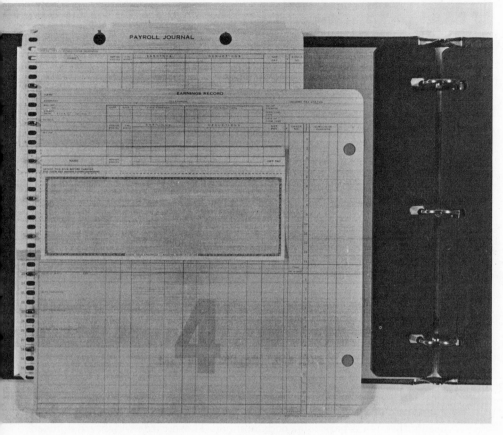

FIG. 4–8.   **Writing Board.**

it represents an endeavor to combine certain of the data processing functions and permit the overall operation to be speeded up. The physical operation of such a writing board will be described in Chapter 6. However, when one uses a writing board, the net effect is to combine the classifying, recording, summarizing, and sorting functions (see Figure 4–8). This is done through the alignment of the different forms to be prepared, and then using carbon paper to reproduce the entry simultaneously on the journals, ledgers, and other business forms. Sorting takes place when one makes entries in the various columns provided.

Edge-notched cards (Figure 4–9) are primarily a sorting device. They will also be explained more fully in Chapter 6. Briefly, however, these are cards which can be of various sizes, that contain a wide variety of information. The information on the card is coded around the edges of the card, where notches are cut out in accordance with a code. Large

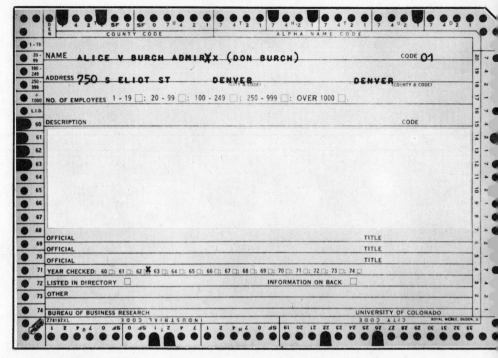

FIG. 4–9. **Edge-Notched Card.**

quantities of cards can readily be sorted by hand by running a long needle through a particular code number. Those cards which are notched at that number will fall out. In this way, information associated with a particular code can be sorted out of a mass of information rapidly.

MECHANICAL SORTING.   The method used by bookkeeping machines in keeping business records is quite similar to that used by the writing-board or pegboard systems. The forms, journals, ledgers, etc. (Figure 4–10) used are designed so that the given columns on each of them will match if they are laid on top of one another. Through the use of carbon paper, the recording of data can be completed simultaneously on these various forms through the combined use of the equivalent of both a typewriter and an adding machine. In this way, the classifying, recording, sorting, and even summarizing functions can be accomplished at the same time.

ELECTROMECHANICAL SORTING.   The sorting function can be accomplished with great rapidity when punched cards are used and a high-speed sorter (Figure 4–11) is employed to sort them in accordance with a certain code or type of information desired. Such a sorter can easily sort from 650 to 2,000 cards per minute.

ELECTRONIC SORTING.   The function of sorting, as it is performed in

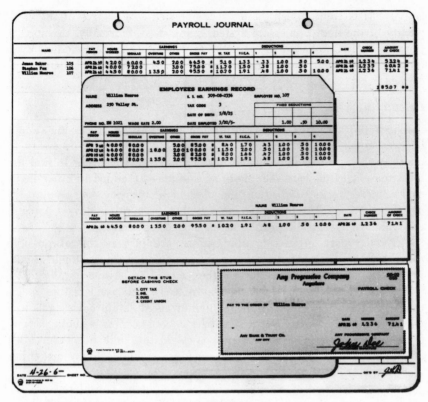

FIG. 4–10.   **Bookkeeping Machine Forms, Journals, Ledgers.**

electronic computers, involves the movement of coded electronic impulses
within the equipment. Depending on the number of digits or letters
contained in the data to be sorted and the type of equipment used,
thousands of a given type of data may be sorted in a few seconds.

In summary, sorting is an important part of the data processing

FIG. 4–11.   **IBM Punched Card Sorter.**

activity. It is continuously being accomplished irrespective of the complexity of the data processing system being used. Normally, the sorting function is accomplished in conjunction with other basic functions even though quite often it may not be specifically identified as being performed.

Calculating

The importance of the calculating function in data processing cannot be overemphasized. In a simple sales situation, it may be necessary to multiply the number of units sold by the unit price in order to find the total amount of the sale. This item of sale may be added to other items sold in order to ascertain the total amount of the sale chargeable to a certain customer. The total amount may then be multiplied by a percentage which represents either the state or local sales tax.

All other data processing applications are just as full of possible calculating applications. Therefore, since calculations must be performed, it is then only a question as to how they should be best accomplished.

Key-driven and rotary-type calculators are widely used in this operation when one is dealing with the manual forms of data processing as well as when one has a system which utilizes a bookkeeping machine. Many bookkeeping machines have rotary-type calculators built into them. Most of the calculators and bookkeeping machines available today are either electrically or electronically operated.

Two other forms of calculators which should be considered are the electronic accounting machine and the electronic data processing machine. The programming of the electronic accounting machines is performed through control-panel wiring. An example of this type of machine is the IBM 602 Calculating Punch, which is described at greater length in later chapters. The electronic data processing machines use an internally stored program to control the correct sequence of its calculating operations, and these will also be discussed more fully in later chapters.

Summarizing

The need for the summerization of data becomes more obvious when one realizes that the data discussed in this chapter have now been assembled, classified, and sorted as to classification. At periodic intervals, management needs to know where the business stands. In order to inform management on this point, the data which have been assembled by classification must be summarized.

If the accounting records are being maintained manually, the classified data have probably been posted to ledger accounts. If this is the case, it then becomes necessary to add up the sum of the debits and the credits and to find the balance in the account. Either a 10-key or a full-keyboard adding machine can be used to good advantage to facilitate this activity.

Courtesy of Burroughs Corp.

FIG. 4–12.   Bookkeeping Machine.

If the records are being maintained on a bookkeeping machine, it would be found that the bookkeeping machine (Figure 4–12) is actually a combination typewriter and adding machine. Different types of this equipment have different numbers of registers or counters in them. A register automatically accumulates figures which are recorded vertically in columns. Any information or data placed in various columns is placed there because of its classification. Therefore, if there is a register in a particular machine for each column of data recorded, the data will be automatically summarized as recorded.

In the electronic accounting machine area, the tabulator (Figure 4–13) is capable of accomplishing the same functions as the bookkeeping machine in terms of summarizing data which are recorded in columnar form. The function is accomplished automatically, however, because the machine is directed through control-panel wiring. The summation of the columns can either be printed out in report form by the tabulator or

Courtesy of IBM.

FIG. 4–13.   Tabulator.

Courtesy of IBM.

FIG. 4–14.   Reproducing Punch.

reproduced in punched cards through the use of a reproducing punch (Figure 4–14). All of this equipment will be discussed at greater length in later chapters.

Recording

The act of recording a transaction has reference to the capturing of the pertinent data surrounding an economic event at the source in reasonably permanent form.

The simplest manual method of recording a transaction is when an individual *journalizes a transaction*. The same thing could be said for entries made when recording a transaction on a *writing board* or *pegboard*. The primary difference is that when a pegboard is used, the sorting and summarizing functions would also be accomplished in addition to the recording function.

AUTOGRAPHIC REGISTER.   An *autographic register* (Figure 4–15) is a

Courtesy of Standard Register Co.

FIG. 4–15.   Autographic Register.

manual-type device for holding and feeding continuous forms and for positioning them for writing by hand. Typically, a single form may be designed for use in recording all of the following types of transactions:

Cash receipts from cash sales
Cash received on account
Paid-outs
Charge sales
Credits for returns and allowances

MARK-SENSED DATA.   In certain applications, *mark sensing* is a popular method of gathering information from outlying points. Special-type pencil marks on cards (Figure 4–16) are automatically converted to

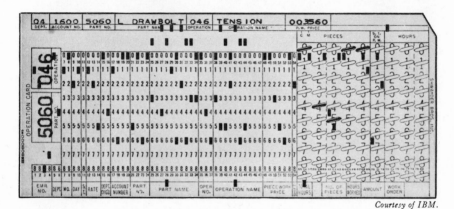

Courtesy of IBM.

FIG. 4–16.   Mark-Sensed IBM Card.

punched holes in any column of a card. Such a card becomes a source document to a punched card system, thus eliminating key punching and key verifying with a resulting savings in both machine and operator cost.

PORT-A-PUNCH.   The *Port-A-Punch* is an effective and economical answer to a great many recording problems in a wide variety of industries (Figure 4–17). The Port-A-Punch is a manual means of punching cards and is generally used at the scene of the transaction. It is frequently used in taking physical inventory and in reading utility meters. By using it, one is able to eliminate the preliminary writing or typing of a source document.

BOOKKEEPING MACHINE.   The typewriter was an early aid in the recording function because it permitted transcribing by keystroke. The *bookkeeping machine* (Figure 4–18) is an adaptation of this because it is a combination of an adding machine and a typewriter. The bookkeeping

Courtesy of IBM.

FIG. 4–17.   IBM Port-A-Punch.

machine is used in many different recording activities. At the same time it is recording, it can also classify and sort, because it is constructed to be able to journalize and post at the same time, using either carbon paper or repeat-writing techniques.

Attachments can be procured for most models of bookkeeping machines whereby punched paper tape, punched cards, or magnetic tape can be by-products of the hard-copy output of the machine operation itself. The Friden Flexowriter (Figure 4–19) may serve as an attachment for producing punched paper tape when coupled to a bookkeeping machine. With the Flexowriter, the information in the paper tape may also be used to activate the machine at a later date if so desired. This facilitates the recording operation because common information can be verified and contained on paper tape and used whenever the input of this data is necessary in the procedure performed.

SPECIAL ADDING MACHINE.   Several business machine manufacturers have devised adding machines which may be used to prepare input media for more elaborate data processing systems. Input data are prepared in

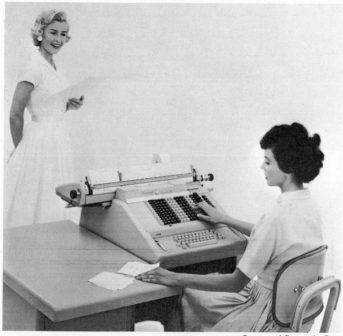

Courtesy of Burroughs Corp.

FIG. 4–18.   **Bookkeeping Machine.**

numerical code. One such machine (Figure 4–20) has a visible tape which is prepared at the same time a punched paper tape is produced. The visible tape is a means of verifying the input data, and the paper tape output may be used as input in a larger data processing system. Another make of machine has the same verification characteristics, but it may be used to produce either punched paper tape or punched cards as output. Another type of machine will produce a paper tape which is capable of being optically scanned and may, thereby, be used as input into a larger data processing machine system. All of these machines may be used to record data initially.

CASH REGISTER. A cash register is another machine which is used to record data surrounding a transaction which has just occurred. Many cash registers will distribute data into more than one classification and thus become sorting mechanisms as well as performing calculating, summarizing, and recording functions.

It is possible to have an attachment for a cash register whereby all of the information which would normally be printed on the internal tape could also be punched into a paper tape, which, in turn, could be used as input into a larger data processing system. There are also cash registers

Courtesy of Friden, Division of The Singer Co.

FIG. 4–19.   Friden 2301 FLEXOWRITER*
Automatic Writing Machine.

Courtesy of Monroe Calculating Machine Co.

FIG. 4–20.   Punched Tape Adding Machine.

which print their journal tape in a special type font which can be optically scanned and read as input into a large computer.

PUNCHED CARD EQUIPMENT.   In addition to punched cards being created as a by-product of other operations, it is universally recognized that punched cards may be created initially by an operator at a key punch (Figure 4–21) who punches the card on the basis of information concerning a transaction which was contained on an originating business form. This complete operation will be discussed at length in later chapters. The punched card, in this case, becomes a means of recording the original transaction and also performs the originating function.

---

* A trademark of Friden, Inc.

Courtesy of IBM.

FIG. 4–21.   Key Punch.

CHECK PROTECTORS.   The check protector is another important mechanical device used in the recording function (Figure 4–22). Even though this machine does not handle the complete transaction in the writing of checks, it is none the less important. A model of this machine can be purchased which is capable of performing three separate functions in this area: writing the amount of the check in a manner that protects the amount and prevents its alteration, dating the check, and signing the check in a way that the signature cannot be duplicated.

TIME CLOCK.   Time clocks (Figure 4–23) are transcribing devices which have a wide usage in manufacturing, wholesaling, and office-type situations. The clocks are built to have differing capacities, depending upon the types of jobs being performed. They are used as a means of keeping track of the elapsed time an employee has spent on the job. One type of such machine will record on a card the "In" time, the "Out" time and the "Elapsed" time of a job. You will note from the illustration (Figure 4–24) that the daily printed timecard produced by this machine is also capable of being used as input media in a punched card installation.

Another form of machine produces a timecard which is suitable for a job cost situation. In such a situation, the accounting department needs to know the time spent on each job by each employee. The card which is produced (Figure 4–25) is capable of recording the time at which an

Courtesy of Burroughs Corp.

FIG. 4–22. Check Protector.

Courtesy of the Cincinnati Time Recorder Co.

FIG. 4–23. Time Clock.

employee begins work on each job during the day as well as the time he leaves.

The time clock is a very useful piece of equipment in any transcribing process involving timing procedures.

IMPRINTERS.   The data recorder (Figure 4–26) is one example of an imprinter designed to write variable data at the same time fixed information is written from plastic plates. The variable information may be dollar-and-cent amount of a sale, number of units in a transaction, production order number, or any other information (up to five digits) that may vary with each entry.

The widest application of this method is with the sale of gasoline on

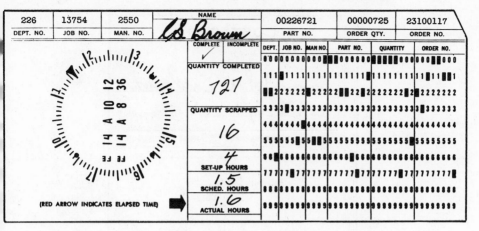

FIG. 4–24. Daily Printed Timecard.

credit. A customer is fully identified by the plastic plate he carries. The variable information is filled in by the filling station operator, indicating what has been purchased and the amount. The fixed information is quickly transferred to the sales slip by one easy motion of the printing anvil.

This method also has wide applications in hospitals, department stores, and job order shops.

Communicating

As in the case of several of the other basic data processing functions, communicating is closely related to, and predicated upon, the performance of other functions. However, the communicating function is primarily concerned with the assembly and transmission of data throughout the data processing system so that the data may be acted upon. It is also concerned with the distribution of the results, usually in the form of reports, to the users of the data. Many types of communication media are being used to accomplish this.

Several differing aspects related to the communicating function must be considered. Only a few years ago, the major emphasis in communicating was in written communication, such as we traditionally think of when we are talking about accounting work. Information was recorded in the books by hand, classified in journals and ledgers, and the results summarized and written out in the form of accounting statements for distribution. We certainly cannot belittle the preparation of written reports, as the need for written communication is as important today as in the past. In fact, it was the need for a faster, improved, and more extensive system of communicating information that resulted in the development of the techniques now used in our modern business information systems.

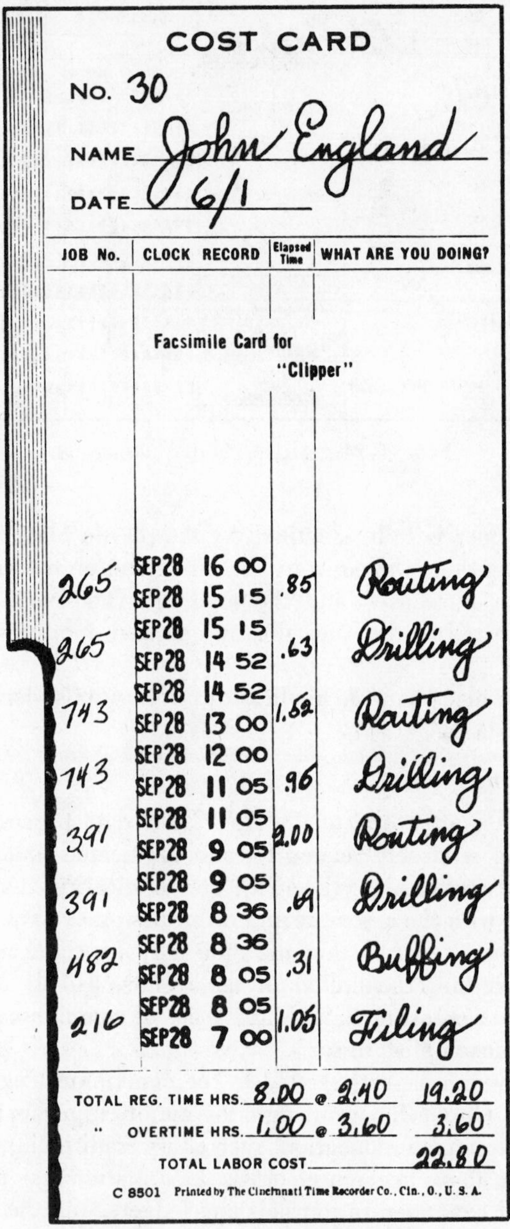

COST CARD

No. *30*

NAME *John England*

DATE *6/1*

JOB No.	CLOCK RECORD		Elapsed Time	WHAT ARE YOU DOING?

Facsimile Card for

"Clipper"

JOB No.	CLOCK RECORD		Elapsed Time	WHAT ARE YOU DOING?
265	SEP 28	16 00	.85	*Routing*
	SEP 28	15 15		
265	SEP 28	15 15	.63	*Drilling*
	SEP 28	14 52		
743	SEP 28	14 52	1.52	*Routing*
	SEP 28	13 00		
743	SEP 28	12 00	.96	*Drilling*
	SEP 28	11 05		
391	SEP 28	11 05	2.00	*Routing*
	SEP 28	9 05		
391	SEP 28	9 05	.49	*Drilling*
	SEP 28	8 36		
482	SEP 28	8 36	.31	*Buffing*
	SEP 28	8 05		
216	SEP 28	8 05	1.05	*Filing*
	SEP 28	7 00		

TOTAL REG. TIME HRS. *8.00* @ *2.40*   *19.20*

"   OVERTIME HRS. *1.00* @ *3.60*   *3.60*

TOTAL LABOR COST_____   *22.80*

C 8501   Printed by The Cincinnati Time Recorder Co., Cin., O., U. S. A.

FIG. 4–25.   Job Cost Card.

Courtesy of Addressograph-Multigraph Corp.

FIG. 4–26.   Imprinter.

Though business data may be communicated between various types of equipment systems, the ultimate end result of the communicating function will always be in some form of human-readable written communication.

As business evolved over the years, it became more complex, and better communicating systems became necessary to keep the various levels of management properly informed. As business became more widely dispersed geographically, it also became necessary that better systems of communication be developed.

In many (and in the future even more) modern computer installations, communication serves as the bridge to connect points where data originates and points where the data are to be processed and used. Computer technology has taken tremendous strides in the past few years by increasing the operational speed and storage capacity of computers while, at the same time, increasing their reliability and reducing their cost. As a direct result of these increasing capabilities, the demand for data to be processed has increased. This in turn created other problems, as a continuous flow of data must be transported to the computer at a speed sufficient to keep the equipment fully utilized if the technological development gains which have been made are to be utilized adequately.

The demand for data has resulted in many improvements and developments in both communication facilities and equipment. Communications, as a computer-associated area, is rapidly becoming a most important link in the data processing operating pattern.

Though for many years we have had what have proven to be "limited" techniques to transmit data over long distances, it is only in the relatively past few years that true communication systems have evolved.

Punched paper tape has been used in the transmission of data over teletype or telegraph systems for nearly 200 years. However, the data normally referred to as business data have only utilized teletype—in even a low-volume sense—since the 1930's. Punched cards have utilized transceivers to convert and transmit data over wires since the early 1940's, but only in the past few years has it become possible for magnetic tape to be used in the high-speed transmission of data. Even more recently, it has become possible for on-line devices to receive and transmit data directly from communication terminals to computers and for one or more computer systems to communicate directly with other computers.

Time and space are rapidly disappearing as barriers to the flow of business information. With the tools now available the question-answer-decision-reaction cycle, requiring the flow of data within and through the strata of a business organization, can be about as fast as management wants it to be, even though the organization components may be scattered throughout the world.[2]

Just as you will learn, in Chapter 11, that the width of the punched paper tape or the magnetic tape has a direct bearing on the data code used, the number of channels available, and the volume of data on a given length of tape, you will also learn, in Chapter 13, that the communication channels or circuits available in a given computer system has a direct bearing on the type, volume, and speed capabilities of the communication systems adaptable to that particular computer.

ANNOTATED BIBLIOGRAPHY

"Business Forms and Controls," *Dun's Review and Modern Industry, Special Supplement,* September, 1965, pp. 147–148.

Comments on the paperwork explosion are presented, the ways in which businesses are trying to combat and control this explosion are examined. It is suggested that the secret of paper-work control is to use the capacities of available equipment for the best information results possible, either by gathering data in a source document or by summarizing it in a report. Forms control and design are shown to require a detailed study of clerical and machine operations and of the relationship of the forms in question to the flow of other paper work.

GHERTNER, ALVIN S. "Forms Design and Control," *Encyclopedia of Accounting Forms and Records,* Vol. II, pp. 74–104. 3 vols. Englewood Cliffs, N.J.: Prentice-Hall, Inc., 1964.

The growth in size and complexity of modern business has made management aware of the ever increasing cost of paper work. Consequently, new techniques of forms control and design are being developed to meet the

---

[2] Reprinted from *Business Automation,* copyright Business Press International, Inc., March '67. Arnold E. Keller, Editor/Publisher.

problem. These techniques are detailed and explain the importance of proper design. The evaluation of real costs of possession and distribution are emphasized. The way in which one can develop and implement a forms control program is described. Other relevant topics discussed include forms specifications, value analysis of printing costs and possession of forms, the equipment and supplies, the evaluation of the results, and the maintenance of a follow-up program.

HALL, FRANK. "The Many Approaches to Sorting," *Data and Control,* Vol. 2, No. 3, March, 1964.

This article defines sorting and describes some of the more common sorting routines used. The author also corrects a few misunderstandings about the reasons for sorting.

Introduction to Data Processing. New York: Haskins and Sells, 1957.

This publication seeks to correlate the principal methods and devices of data collection with the basic operations they perform. The uses and limitations of various processing methods are discussed.

JOHNSON, ELDRED A. *Accounting Systems in Modern Business.* New York: McGraw-Hill Book Co., 1959.

Chapter 4 of this book states the important source documents used in manual accounting systems. It shows the source documents which are used in the basic operations of any industrial organization.

McMASTER, J. J., and PUNCH, J. A. "Some Consideration on Data Preparation," *Data Processing and Management Services, 36th Chartered Accountant in Australia,* January, 1966. pp. 511–19.

A review of the characteristics of established and recently introduced systems for data preparation, recording and transmission. It is felt that one of the main objectives of a well-designed data processing system involves the recording of transaction data, or information related to an event, accurately, economically, and sometimes very speedily, in a form suitable for automatic processing in terms of accounting and reporting.

MOORE, FRANCIS E., and STETTLER, HOWARD F. *Accounting Systems for Management Control.* Homewood, Ill.: Richard D. Irwin, Inc., 1963.

Chapter 8 describes the functions and design of business forms used today.

WEISS, ALLEN. "The Use of Colors to Improve Operating Efficiency," *New York Certified Public Accountant,* October, 1965. pp. 739–43.

The use of color in forms, on files, and in other respects is a suggested means of improving operating efficiency. Various illustrations of areas where color can be used in a business operation are discussed and include office forms, invoices and purchase orders, files, bound documents, and ADP records. Advantages in the use of color coding techniques are listed.

QUESTIONS

1. Discuss the usefulness of business forms in data origination.
2. A businessman was heard to say that anyone could use the preprinted

business forms which can be bought in a stationery store in a data processing system. Do you agree?

3. Why is it so important that all the data asked for on a form be properly filled in? Illustrate the need for typical data found on a typical business form.

4. What are some of the means used to insure the accuracy of data captured in the business form?

5. The classification activity is an unimportant part of the data processing function. Discuss thoroughly, indicating whether you agree or disagree.

6. Classifying and sorting both serve to give data a pattern. How do these functions differ?

7. Discuss three different methods of sorting data, making certain to note the strengths and weaknesses of each method.

8. Why do we have so many different types of equipment which will perform the calculating function? Since the computer can do nearly all the calculating needed by business firms, why not just use it?

9. Must all of the data processing functions be accomplished in sequence? Discuss your answer thoroughly.

10. Which of the data processing functions discussed in this chapter is most important? Carefully support your answer.

11. Why are there so many means of recording data? Explain.

12. Is each method of recording data reserved for a separate accounting system, or can many methods be used within any one accounting system? Explain.

13. Of what importance are all of the other data processing functions if adequate communications to transmit the data to those who are interested in them do not exist? Discuss fully.

14. Describe in as many ways as you can how the communication function is involved in the field of data processing.

CHAPTER 5

Systems Analysis

and Flowcharting

THE ACCOUNTING or data processing system of any business organization is made up of forms, procedures, records, and reports. Presumably the system will have been planned in such a way that it will assist the management of the business to meet more adequately the objectives of the business, which, among others, would certainly include: (1) the making of a satisfactory return on the investment, and (2) the conservation of the business assets.

A complete system, such as is presumed in the above statement, will probably not have been developed until the business entity has grown to considerable size and until its organization is no longer simple but represents a complex distribution of authority and responsibility. It is also quite likely that the management will not have thought through and spelled out its objectives until the business has become reasonably large, has plants in numerous locations, deals with large sums of money, and has reponsibilities delegated to a number of levels of executives.

In short, it is typical that as a business organization increases in size and becomes more involved in its operations, the data processing system must, as a necessity, be better formulated as well as more complex. However, it is also typical that the growth of the data processing system will lag behind the corresponding growth of the organization. An analysis of an existing data processing system will rarely be recognized as needed or proceed until serious problems arise which force a *felt need* on the part of management.

Before a need is apparent that a system appraisal is desirable, the present system must usually have some obvious weakness such as a lack of internal control or processing bottlenecks, or management must be dissatisfied with the information it is presently receiving. This dissatisfaction could be due to inadequate information, reports not timely enough, or a combination of these conditions.

Once management recognizes a need for systems reorganization, it must then decide whether to use company personnel to analyze the problem and to recommend a solution or to seek the assistance of outside consultants who may be representatives of either a certified public accounting or management consulting firm. Either alternative will require an analysis, in detail, of the existing system and will result in specific recommendations to correct the problems found.

The situation described in the preceeding paragraphs may very likely lead to the decision as to whether the firm ought to introduce electronic data processing equipment. This is a momentous decision for any company because it may lead to the expenditure of a great deal of time and money. Not only is the electronic equipment expensive, but any attempt to maximize its usefulness also necessitates a complete remodeling of the present system for processing data. All too often, new users of EDP equipment have tried to speed up existing procedures without giving much thought to the possibility of utilizating the tremendous capacities of the equipment in solving a broader range of problems. The net result has been that these users are soon disillusioned by the high cost of data processing. In contrast, one of the national public accounting firms urges its clients, at the time their accounting systems are being reviewed, to plan their new systems to meet tomorrow's competition rather than to try to take care solely of today's clerical problems and bottlenecks.

ANALYZING THE PRESENT SYSTEM

The task, therefore, which confronts the group which analyzes a system is to decide whether they should review all of the present system with the idea of utilizing the full capabilities of the EDP equipment or whether they should regard this as too drastic a change and limit the present review to an attempt to eliminate the current problems and bottlenecks in the system. Many people have found that the most effective compromise is for the systems review group to obtain permission to review, analyze, and design a total system, but to implement it on a building-block basis—piece by piece—over a period of time. The financial outlay to install anything close to a total system is extensive, and this is one of the reasons why many prefer to introduce the system in stages.

Once the extent of the system review has been determined, the first objective of the reviewer must be to gain an overall understanding of the business, its organization, what it is trying to do, and how it operates. This information can be gotten by talking to the operating personnel at all levels in the business as well as to the management.

When the reviewer feels that he understands the problems of the business and what the business is trying to do, he should attempt to identify the vital functions of the business. Typically, these are functions which are critical to the operation of the business and include such areas as cash control, inventories, receivables, labor cost, etc.

A system is designed by first determining what specific information is desired from the system, for what purpose it is needed, and on what time basis it must be furnished. It is only after the needs of the system have been ascertained that the inputs to the system, the procedures, records, and method of data processing, should be examined. At this point, the importance of the people who will be involved in making the proposed system work must be emphasized. All people involved with the system must be trained and educated so that they will understand and know how to deal with the proposed system when it is introduced.

Lastly, internal controls, which must be a part of all computerized systems, must be carefully thought out and included in the system.

Reports—Outputs

Broadly speaking, there are three types of financial reports with which any business is going to be concerned. First, the external financial reports, which include the income statement and the balance sheet. These are fundamental to any business organization. They are necessary to meet the requirements of stockholders, the public, labor unions, the Securities and Exchange Commission, and the various stock exchanges. Second, the internal financial reports which are prepared to meet the requirements of management at various levels within the business. Third, the reports required by governmental agencies, local, state, and national. The number, variety, and complexity of the reports required in a given business firm will, in addition to the needs of its management, also be determined by the type of business and the amount of supervision it receives from various agencies of government.

In many ways, the requirements and needs of the people or agencies which use these reports will dictate the data to be accumulated and the manner in which the data are to be summarized.

The firm's existing reports should be analyzed from the point of view of how adequately they are meeting the needs of the three groups of users of these reports. Normally, the area in which the most work will probably need to be done, due to the fact that it is often the least developed of all, is the area of internal control reports.

Factors to consider in deciding what reports are needed are:

1. Who needs information?
    a) Each person responsible for a function, an operation, a property, or for supervising a group of persons.

    b) The information needed will depend on how each individual personally carries out his responsibilities; how he personally manages and controls.

2. What information is needed?

    a) No details should be included unless necessary for control. Supporting details should be available upon request.

3. When and how frequently is the information needed?

    a) Information may be needed in case of specific operations daily, weekly or monthly, according to the several strata of management.[1]

All internal reports should have the following characteristics in common:

1. Usefulness
2. Simplicity, accuracy, and adequacy
3. Timeliness
4. Economy of preparation
5. Conciseness

Inputs—Business Forms and Records

It was pointed out early in Chapter 4 that "forms are basic to the data manipulation process." They are "the media on which the data are initially captured at the time when a transaction occurs." The analyst must certainly make himself aware of all of the sources of business information and of the forms and records on which it will be captured.

Typical detailed original records are:

Cash receipts and disbursements	Salesmen's and distributors' reports
Sales invoices and records of customers	Personnel records
Purchase orders and records of vendors	Plant and equipment records
Shipping reports	Financial transactions
Receiving reports	Credit information
Vendors invoices	Cost estimates
Production orders and reports	Standards
Time tickets or reports	Corporate records
Store requisitions	Correspondence
Stock records	Insurance and tax records[2]

In order for the analyst to understand the function of each of these forms and records, and since each of them is a part of the total data processing system, he will need to know the following about each item:

1. The nature of the form and its contents.
2. Where the form is prepared.

----

[1] C. Oliver Wellington, "Developing of Accounting Systems" in *CPA Handbook* (American Institute of Accountants, 1953), Vol. II, chap. xxii, p. 14.

[2] *Ibid.*, p. 16.

3. How it is prepared.
4. By whom it is prepared.
5. When it is prepared.
6. The number or volume of such forms prepared.
7. The frequency of reference made to any one record.
8. The reports and other records which are affected by these original forms and records.

The object of the analyst in securing the above information is to learn how these forms and records fit into the total data processing system.

Procedures

A procedures survey is a critical review of the methods by which a job is done, the tools used, and the physical location of operations. The objectives of such a review are to eliminate unessential activities, to coordinate the methods of conducting essential activities, to improve the physical location of work, and to determine staff requirements.

A management analyst uses many tools in such a procedures survey. He may interview employees and supervisors, prepare flowcharts of work, and analyze the design and use of forms and reports.

He will probably turn to the "Manual of Procedures," first of all, if one has been written. In it he should find a description of all of the procedures currently in use. However, he may not find the manual reliable because (1) conditions may have changed without the manual being rewritten, or (2) existing practices may have gotten out of line with prescribed procedures without management being aware of it.

If a computer system is being reviewed, the "Manual of Procedures" takes on added importance because in addition to the information normally included in such a manual it should include information describing how the inputs are to be prepared and how to interpret the outputs. These facts would be indispensable to anyone reviewing the existing system.

The best way to learn what is going on is to go out and talk directly with the people who are doing the work.

The analyst should begin in a clerical department by obtaining an introduction to a supervisor by the superior, thereby demonstrating management's endorsement of the project. The tone of the meeting should be friendly and informal. The supervisor should be asked to outline briefly the functions of his work and how these are related to the functions of the other departments or units of the firm. He should be questioned about the major flow steps of the paper work. This information should be obtained in broad outline form at this point, and the supervisor should be assured that all findings and questions will be discussed with him first before any changes are recommended or made.

As soon as the analyst has learned the activities of the supervisors, attention should be turned to departmental employees and their work. It is not until this has been done that a procedure survey can be considered to be complete.

Methods of Processing Data

The existing methods of processing data must be carefully studied in the light of the problems which gave rise to the systems survey in the first place. The ultimate objective to be sought is to find that method which both now and in the foreseeable future can process the data in a way and at a speed most useful to management and at a cost which management is willing to pay.

Unforeseen Benefits

When the analyst (1) has come to feel that he understands the problems of the business and what it is trying to do and (2) has studied the inputs, procedures, methods of processing data, and the outputs of the system, he is then in a position to have a good overall view of the role the data processing system should be performing in a particular business. Having gained this overall knowledge, he is often in a position to make positive recommendations for improvement. Such recommendations may include:

1. Reduction in the number of steps in a procedure.
2. Elimination of unnecessary functions.
3. Elimination of duplication.
4. Combination of operations to reduce paper handling and get acquainted time, and thereby speed up the flow of work.
5. Elimination of unnecessary reports.
6. Improvements in methods.
7. Improvements in layout.
8. Revisions and redesign of forms.

It is quite possible that many such improvements, as enumerated above, could be accomplished with relative ease and little additional cost. When one has a broad, overall view of a problem, solutions which were not recognized previously often became obvious.

FLOWCHARTING

Flowcharting, as a technique, is universally used as a means of better understanding existing or proposed procedures in business and the flow of work through a factory, or in expressing any sequence of events. A flowchart is a diagramatic representation of the flow of events.

In certain types of operations, standardized symbols have been developed to represent the flow of information or steps to be performed in given procedures. The use of these standards is not always enforced in a given plant, business, or industry and, consequently, will be found to vary somewhat in usage, depending on the individual performing the work.

A word of caution is necessary at this point. Wherever standards exist for a given type of operation, they should be adhered to as closely as possible. With the demand for skilled individuals—and those doing flow-charting would certainly fall into this classification—in today's labor market, there is a tendency for these employees to have high mobility in moving from one firm to another. This means that those preparing the flowcharts today may not necessarily be those interpreting them in the future. If nonstandard symbols are utilized, at least some level—from partial to near complete—confusion will probably arise.

In general, the flowchart illustrations to follow will use standardized symbols. Any additional symbols used in actual business illustrations will be noted so that their usage will be brought to attention.

Flowcharts are constructed to conform to our natural tendency to read

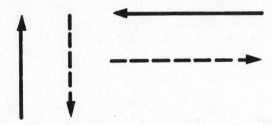

FIG. 5–1.   Direction of Flow.

from left to right and top to bottom. Variations are, however, sometimes desirable in order to achieve symmetry and to emphasize certain points. Within this framework, flow lines can be drawn horizontally, vertically, and diagonally. The primary considerations are neatness, uniformity, and clarity. Explanatory footnotes are encouraged and are frequently used.

Some symbols are used almost universally in identifying particular events in the flow of data. The flow of data itself is usually indicated by a line, and the direction of flow by an arrowhead. (Figure 5–1).

In flowcharting, solid lines are normally used to indicate the direction of flow, but occasionally it is desirable to differentiate between the physical movement of work and the mere transfer of information. This can be done by using solid lines in the first case and dotted lines in the second. For example, dotted lines are often used to illustrate accounting control functions.

Also, in order for one symbol to have a meaningful relationship to other symbols in a chart, it is necessary that it be connected to one or more other symbols in such a way as to indicate the sequence in which the operation occurs.

There are a variety of ways which can be used to flowchart an existing or proposed system so that it can be more clearly understood. Each method has a particular area of applicability. These major areas of applicability include (1) flowcharting for an informal series of steps and logical decisions; (2) flowcharting to represent symbolically the flow of documents through an organization; (3) flowcharting to show the development of the procedural steps to be followed in manually performed procedures; and (4) the technique of representing the flow of data through a punched card or electronic data processing system.

As a Series of Steps and Logical Decisions

This approach might be used where the objective is to understand the various activities, decisions, and alternatives required to achieve some

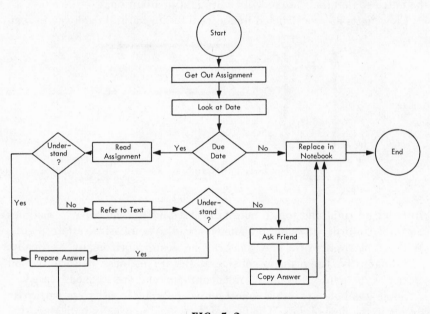

FIG. 5–2

required objective. The flowchart in Figure 5–2 illustrates the decisions a student must make when preparing his homework assignment.

In this type of flowcharting, the symbols may either be standard or nonstandard. In the illustration in Figure 5–2, there is not to be a formal implementation of the steps noted, and some of the symbols utilized are not standard. If desired, this flowchart could, however, have utilized standard symbols applicable to machine flowcharting (to be described later).

Document Flow

The flowchart technique applicable to document flow demonstrates the way various forms or other documents move from person to person, or from department to department, and is useful in representing symbolically the flow of paper work for a particular transaction or department. No special symbols are necessary, but it is useful to list the people or departments who are concerned across the top of the sheet. An illustration of flowcharting document flow is shown in Figure 5–3.

Manual Procedure

The symbols representing procedural operations which are performed manually are utilized to illustrate typical clerical operations as well as other manual procedures.

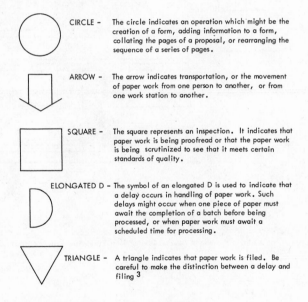

CIRCLE – The circle indicates an operation which might be the creation of a form, adding information to a form, collating the pages of a proposal, or rearranging the sequence of a series of pages.

ARROW – The arrow indicates transportation, or the movement of paper work from one person to another, or from one work station to another.

SQUARE – The square represents an inspection. It indicates that paper work is being proofread or that the paper work is being scrutinized to see that it meets certain standards of quality.

ELONGATED D – The symbol of an elongated D is used to indicate that a delay occurs in handling of paper work. Such delays might occur when one piece of paper must await the completion of a batch before being processed, or when paper work must await a scheduled time for processing.

TRIANGLE – A triangle indicates that paper work is filed. Be careful to make the distinction between a delay and filing [3]

In such illustrations each step of the operation is carefully analyzed and notes of the action involved, as well as the symbols representing the action, are placed on a procedural analysis work sheet similar to that shown in Figure 5–4.

In this illustration the component parts are: (1) described in sequential

---

[3] Systems Education Monograph #1 (Detroit: Systems and Procedures Association, 1962), p. 17.

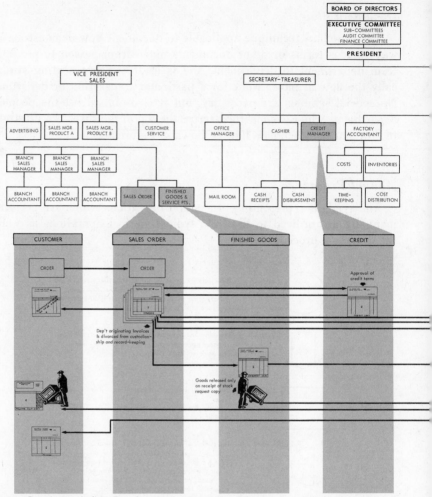

SOURCE: Committee on Auditing Procedure, *Internal Control* (New York: American Institute of Certified Public Accountants, 1949), Chart 5.

FIG. 5–3

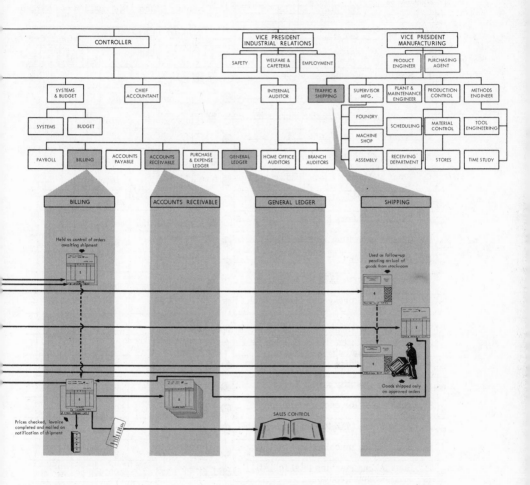

Before   Exhibit 2   (Page 1)

SUMMARY	PRESENT		PROPOSED		SAVINGS	
	NO.	HRS.	NO.	HRS.	NO.	HRS.
○ OPERATIONS	21	.57396				
⇨ TRANSPORTATIONS	8	.19128				
□ INSPECTIONS	3	.167				
D DELAYS	1	.167				
▽ STORAGES	2	–				
DISTANCE TRAVELED	741 ft.					

PROCEDURE CHARTED **Withdrawing Stationery from Central Plant Supplies**
CHART BEGINS **In Ordering Office**   CHART ENDS **Distribution of Charges**
CHARTED BY _____ DATE _____

☒ PRESENT   ☐ PROPOSED

LINE NO.	STEPS IN PROCEDURE	OPER.	TRANSP.	INSPECT.	DELAY	STORE	DISTANCE IN FEET	TIME	ELIMINATE	COMBINE	SEQUENCE	PLACE	PERSON	IMPROVE
1	A. Section Clerk inspects stock	○	⇨	■	D	▽	5	.167						
2	A. Writes one copy of Form 1772	●	⇨	□	D	▽		.083						
3	A. Carries Form 1772 to Supervisor	○	⇨	□	D	▽	40	.0167						
4	B. Supervisor signs Form 1772	●	⇨	□	D	▽		.033						
5	A. Section Clerk takes Form 1772 to Stationery Stores	○	⇨	□	D	▽	225	.083						
6	C. Plant Stationery Clerk fills requisition	●	⇨	□	D	▽		.167						
7	A. Section Clerk waits for Stationery	○	⇨	□	●	▽		.167						
8	A. Takes Stationery back to section	○	⇨	□	D	▽	225	.083						
9	C. Checks each item as it is filled	●	⇨	□	D	▽		.0167						
10	C. Initials Form 1772	●	⇨	□	D	▽		.0042						
11	C. Delivers Form 1772 to Stationery Storekeeper	○	⇨	□	D	▽	75	.0083						
12	D. Stationery Storekeeper checks each item against Kardex file	●	⇨	□	D	▽								
13	D. Determines if Stationery was originally charged to M&R or Engr. from Kardex	○	⇨	■	D	▽		.167						
14	D. Prices each item if credit must be developed and change made	●	⇨	□	D	▽								
15	D. Places red check opposite each item to be credited to Engineering	●	⇨	□	D	▽								
16	D. Extends Quantity x Unit Price	●	⇨	□	D	▽		.083						
17	D. Totals cost for each requisition	●	⇨	□	D	▽		.0167						
18	D. Sorts Form 1772 to Requisition Dept.	●	⇨	□	D	▽		.00056						
19	D. Runs adding machine total by Dept.	●	⇨	□	D	▽		.00028						
20	D. Runs adding machine total for All Engineering Credits	●	⇨	□	D	▽		.0014						
21	D. Runs adding machine total of Dept. totals	●	⇨	□	D	▽		–						
22	D. Writes out distribution of charges and credits	●	⇨	□	D	▽		.00056						
23	D. Types letter – three copies – to Accounting Dept. to make entry	●	⇨	□	D	▽		.00056						
24	D. Attaches bundle of requisitions to letter	●	⇨	□	D	▽		–						

APPROVED BY _____   DATE _____

| | TOTALS | 17 | 4 | 2 | 1 | | 570 | 1.09896 | | | | | |

PAGE 1 OF 2 PAGES

SOURCE: From *Systems Education Monograph #1* (Detroit: Systems and Procedures Association, 1962), p. 19.

FIG. 5–4.   Procedure Analysis Work Sheet.

order, (2) charted in symbolic form, (3) measured in the distance to be traveled in performing the operation, and (4) timed in terms of the elapsed time required to perform each operation.

Flowcharting for Punched Card and Electronic Systems

It would be difficult to exaggerate the crucial importance of the system's study phase in the development of a punched card or electronic data processing installation. It is at this point that the real challenge of data processing is first met. A systems study provides an opportunity for a comprehensive examination of an organization's information-handling procedures. The objective is to make the organization run more efficiently. In this connection it is well to keep in mind that the uses of data processing systems have only begun to be explored. The processing ability of today's giant computers has thus far exceeded man's ability to use them in their most sophisticated manner. At the present time the only real limit to the information-handling work that they can perform is the limit which may exist in man's ability to investigate a problem, reduce it to its basic elements, and reassemble these elements in a pattern which such a system can handle.

The significant feature of all business data processing problems is the fact that each seemingly complex problem can be broken down into combinations of elementary operations. This is the reason that such problems are readily handled by computing systems. Each of the present-day computing systems has the ability to do high-speed elementary operations such as simple addition, multiplication, and comparison. Utilizing the computer to attack a complex processing problem requires that the complex problem first be reduced to a series of logical elementary operations.

Since most data processing problems are complex, it is desirable to create a pictorial representation showing the logical elementary steps in the solution of an overall complex situation. Such a pictorial chart is also called a "flowchart."

In this chart, data provided by a source or originating document is converted to final or reporting documents.[4] A flowchart, then, provides a precise picture of the sequence in which operations are to be executed. Such a picture gives primary emphasis to the documents involved as well as to the work stations through which they pass.

Some of the functions which a flowchart fill are as follows:

1. The flowchart helps to systematize and classify intricate operations. A flowchart, with its systematic portrayal of operations, will point out logical omissions, errors and redundant operations.

---

[4] It should be noted here that in its broadest meaning a document is "any instrument conveying information." Such a definition is used in this discussion in order to include punched card, magnetic tape and paper tape in the same category as printed forms.

2. A flowchart is a valuable means of communication between persons associated with a data processing problem. This includes groups from management and systems analysis to computer operators. The flowchart, as a document, allows work plans to be reviewed, since it creates a permanent history.

3. The flowchart provides the medium or interim tool to bridge the gap between the data processing problem and the coded problem which directs the computer in solving the data processing problem.[5]

Until about 1965, the symbols utilized previously for punched card machine applications were generally used in conjunction with computer applications. These symbols varied somewhat with given equipment manufacturers but were basically those suggested by IBM, the largest such manufacturer. With the rise of specific needs for standardized symbols for computer systems and programs, it was generally felt that such standards should be developed.

In 1965 the X3.6 Subcommittee of the American Standards Association's X3 Sectional Committee on Computers and Information Processing Standards recommended and defined a standard set of flowcharting symbols for information processing problem description.

This set of symbols has been almost universally adopted, but minor variations in usage still exist among different equipment manufacturers.

In general, there are two types or levels of flowcharts used in punched card and electronic data processing. The first type is called *system flowcharts* while the second is called *program flowcharts* or *block diagrams*. The symbols used for each type have specific usage. However, as some functions represented are common to both types of flowcharting, the same symbols will be used in both cases. Also, in both types of flowcharting, flowchart work sheets similar to that of Figure 5–5 will usually be used to facilitate the placement and arrangement of the symbols.

SYSTEM FLOWCHARTS.   Flowcharts that are designed to show the sequence of major operations and that normally summarize a complete operation are known as *system flowcharts*. These are usually prepared as aids to management and systems analysts to permit them to understand some specific operation and to get an overall viewpoint of the operation.

The first step in system flowcharting is to define the data processing problem itself. In doing this, answers must be found to the following questions:

1. What information is required from the system in the form of reports?
2. What is required from this portion of the system to integrate it into the overall data processing system?

---

[5] The American University, School of Government and Public Administration, *Introduction to Flowcharting* (Center for Technology and Administration, Bulletin No. 1), November, 1961, p. 1.

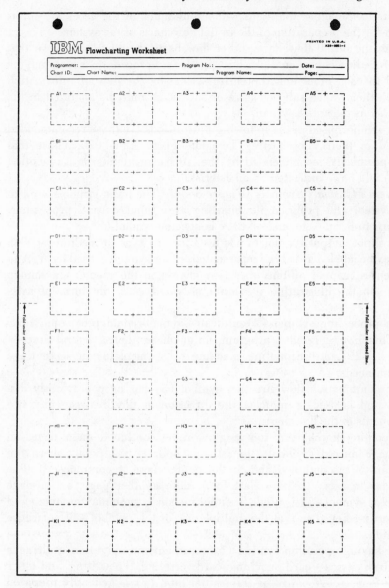

FIG. 5–5. Flowchart Work Sheet.

3. Where does the input information arise?
4. What exceptions can arise and under what circumstances?
5. How many transactions and how many exceptions of each type are involved?
6. How should each transaction and each exception be handled?
7. What files are involved and what information is involved in them?
8. Are results required on schedule or on demand?

Answers to the above questions will supply much of the necessary information for the preparation of the initial flowcharts of the system.

From the initial flowcharts, other flowcharts should be drawn so that each procedure is broken down into simpler subprocedures which may be related to each other and the entire system by the flow of information between them. Each subprocedure or subsystem must be analyzed in the same way as the entire system.

The symbols used in the following illustrations are those recommended by IBM in their Flowcharting Template Form X20–8020. Those that were specifically recommended by the American Standards Association (ASA) will be so indicated by an asterisk.

System Flowchart Symbols (Figure 5–6). The basic symbols used in both system and program flowcharting are: input/output, processing, flow-direction, on-page, and off-page connector symbols.

The input/output symbol (1) is used for any type of medium or data and may be labeled as to type represented. (This symbol is used by ASA to represent a manual off-line operation geared to the speed of a human being.) In the illustration the input provided is in the form of sales tickets.

The processing symbol (2) indicates a major data processing function. This may represent a program run or phase (2a), a central processing unit (2b), an accounting machine or a calculator to serve these different needs.

The combination flow-direction symbol (3) has been previously discussed and is used to indicate the direction of flow between any two components of the flowchart.

When the flowchart is too lengthy to be continued on a page, an on-page connector symbol (4) is used both at the point where the flowchart is discontinued and at the point where it continues. If it is necessary to carry the flowchart forward to another page, an off-page connector symbol (5) is used. In either instance, these may be numbered or otherwise keyed so that the multiple use of this symbol will not cause confusion.

The keying operation symbol (6) represents an operation utilizing a key-driven device—card punching, card verifying, typewriting, and other similar devices. A control or transmittal tape (7) is generally prepared on an adding machine and represents a batch total to accompany a batch of business documents.

Whenever a punched card is to be either keypunched or used, the punched card symbol (8) is utilized. It will also represent stub cards. The auxiliary operation symbol (9), represents a machine operation supplementing the main processing function. An example of this would be the interpreting of keypunched cards. When there is a manual off-line operation to be performed which does not require mechanical aid, the

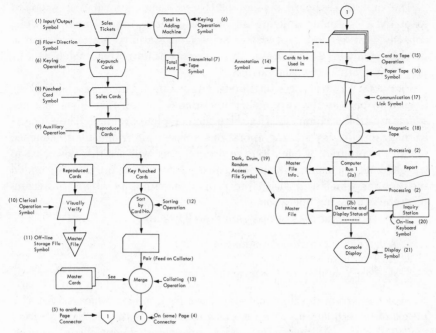

FIG. 5–6.   Illustration of Systems Symbol Usage.

symbol for a clerical operation (10) is used. Visually verifying a group of reproduced cards is an example of this.

The off-line storage file symbol (11) represents off-line storage of either paper, cards, magnetic or perforated tape, disk packs or any other medium. In Figure 5–6 the reproduced cards which have been visually verified are being put into off-line storage. Also in the illustration the keypunched cards are being *sorted* by card number. Symbols (12) and (13) represent any operation performed on sorting or collating equipment.

The processing annotation symbol (14) represents a major data processing function. When using only the basic symbols in a flowchart, this symbol represents any processing function. In Figure 5–6 symbol (15) represents a card-to-tape operation. Symbol (16) represents perforated tape, whether paper or plastic, being used as input or output on a systems flowchart. The communication link symbol (17) represents the transmission of information from one location to another via communication lines.

A circle with a line extending horizontally to the right from the bottom of the circle is the symbol used to represent data recorded on magnetic tape (18). The disk, drum, or random access file symbol (19) is used in a system flowchart to indicate the manner in which data are stored.

The on-line keyboard symbol (20) represents information supplied to or by a computer utilizing an on-line device—for example, console, console card reader, typewriter, printer, or inquiry station. When a display symbol (21) is used, it represents information which is displayed by plotters or visual devices.

PROGRAM FLOWCHARTS OR BLOCK DIAGRAMS.   This type of flowchart is used to portray the various arithmetic and logical operations or steps which must be accomplished to solve the complete problem. These charts or diagrams display specific operations and decisions and their sequence within the program. Generally, the programmer will use this flowchart to translate the elementary steps of a procedure into a program of coded instructions which will direct the proper machine operations to accomplish the processing operation.

Three important uses of program flowcharts are:

1. As an aid to program development.
2. As a guide in coding.
3. As documentation of a program.

In the program development stage, the program flowchart serves as a means of experimenting with various approaches to the mechanization of the application. At this' point, logical program segments have been established, at least tentatively, through flowcharting. Starting with blocks representing the major functions of the proposed program, the programmer develops the overall or general logical pattern by adding blocks to depict input and output functions with steps for the identification and selection of records, and decision functions.

After the overall logic of the program is tentatively established, the large segments are extracted from the general block diagram and analyzed in the same fashion. In this way, the block diagram becomes more detailed.

Once the procedure is established, and proved sound, the program flowchart becomes a guide to program coding. Unless the person who developed the flowchart is an experienced programmer for the data processing system to be used, it is almost certain that the pecularities of the machine logic will necessitate changes in the program logic. Thus, the diagram may need to be redrawn and reverified at this stage.

Final documentation of a program should include both general and detailed program flowcharts. The general block diagram helps in understanding the more detailed ones and also provides an easily understood picture of the procedure for those who might be interested in the concept only.

Program Flowchart Symbols.   There are only four additional symbols whose use is strictly limited to program flowcharting. To illustrate how the program flowchart differs from the systems flowchart, refer first to

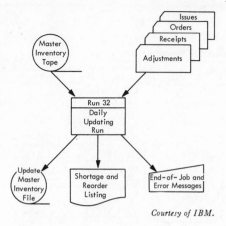

Courtesy of IBM.

FIG. 5–7.   A Systems Flowchart.

Figure 5–7, a computer system flowchart, and then to Figure 5–8, a program flowchart. The latter illustration expands the operations shown in the first into the individual steps of the program which will be coded into a machine-acceptable language to instruct the computer in processing the data to be supplied.

In Figure 5–7 the input to the computer, in this run to update the inventory status, is shown to be any current issues, orders, receipts, and adjustments along with the current inventory status file. The outputs will be a new updated current inventory status file, a notice of any shortages that would not permit sales orders to be filled and any purchase orders that need to be placed for stock items which are deleted or near deletion, and notices to be printed on the on-line keyboard of any error conditions found in the input data.

In Figure 5–8 the detail program flowchart steps are illustrated. Two of the four new symbols are introduced in this illustration. These are the decision function symbol ◇ which is used to document points in the program where a branch to alternative paths is required because of variable conditions. This symbol is used for tests to determine if one amount is higher than, equal to, or lower than, another; to check indicator settings for "on" or "off" condition; to answer a "yes" or "no" question in regard to a given condition or decision based on specific circumstances at this point in the program; and to test for the presence of specific digits which would indicate a need for alternative courses of action.

The second new symbol is the terminal symbol ⬭ which indicates the beginning, end, or a point of interruption in a program.

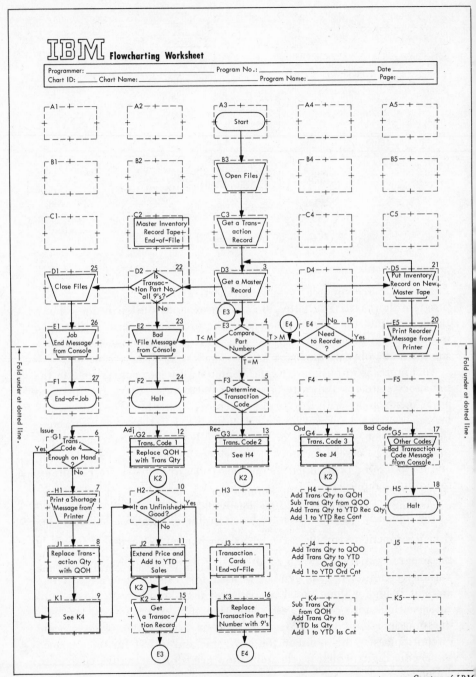

***FIG.* 5–8.   A Program Flowchart.**

Program flowchart symbols not shown in this illustration includes the program modification symbol [⟩ which indicates that an instruction or group of instructions makes some change in the program itself. The text to be written inside or coded to the symbol would explain the purpose of the modification performed.

The predefined process symbol ⟨   ⟩ represents a group of operations not detailed on the particular flowchart being used. This could indicate the insertion of some fixed and previously prepared program, such as one written to perform some mathematical function, of which a square root computation would be an example.

CASE STUDY 5–1

One large manufacturer of candies and cookies solved its problems of converting its recordkeeping system from punched cards to a computerized system in the following manner.

The company was managed by a board of managers made up of the heads of the four principal operating divisions: manufacturing, distribution, finance, and administration. These men were personally convinced that a computer was what the company needed and were ultimately responsible for installing what has proven to be a highly successful computerized system.

The organization structure was clearly defined, and all echelons of management had a clear understanding of their authority and responsibility. The board of managers asked each member of the management team to enumerate all the information he would like to have, assuming that it would be obtainable, in order that he might more adequately discharge his responsibilities. When all of the managers' requests for information were compiled, it quickly became obvious that if all this information were to be provided, the members of management would be doing nothing but reading reports. A compromise was therefore worked out to provide only the most essential data.

The proposed complete computerized data processing system was then written up in booklet form describing: (1) the various inputs to the system, how they would be prepared, and what they would contain; (2) all of the procedures which would be followed in connection with the recording and the processing of the data; and (3) exact copies of the proposed output reports. Sufficient copies of these booklets were prepared so that all members of management could have them to study. The proposed system was then discussed, criticized, and modified, where necessary, but every member of management was given to feel that he had a part to play in the development of the system. This involved two years of work prior to the actual installation of the computer.

From the point of view of the board of managers, the computer installation has been an unqualified success, and they feel that much of the success is due to the planning which went into the installation.

CASE STUDY 5–2

The illustration which follows is a flowchart representing a combination of document flow and manual procedures. It was taken from the working papers of a systems analyst who was studying the clerical operations of a large

STOCK BOOKING　　　　　　　　　　　　　　　　　　　　　　　PAREORA WORKS

FLOW CHART OF OPERATIONS

Ref.	1 Timaru Office	2 Agents Drafters	3 Transport Operators & Drivers	4 Shepherds	5 Head Shepherds	6 Booking Clerk	Time Table	Particulars of Work
				Pareora Works			To day of killing	
35							Night before kill	Receives 2 copies of killing list
36				*			Early a.m. day of kill	Write particulars from killing list in note books
37							Do	Tally stock to be killed into killing pens
38							Do	Advise head shepherd if any error in original tally
39							8 a.m. day of kill	Drive stock up ramps to sticking pens
40							Do	Hands copies of killing list to departments
41						†	During a.m. day of kill	Advises booking clerk—— stock received overnight, & any errors in tally
42							Do	Amends killing list and other stock records as advised by head shepherd
43							am–pm 11:30– 1:00 day of kill	Advises departments additions and amendments to killing list
44							During day of kill	Advises Timaru office—— particulars of stock received for killing
45							Do	Write particulars in killing book
46							Do	Advise booking clerk—— numbers drafted by each drafter
47							Do	Writes numbers drafted in book as advised

* Written record symbol
† Telephone symbol

slaughtering and meat-packing house in New Zealand preparatory to the installation of a computer.

CASE STUDY 5–3
ILLUSTRATIVE FLOWCHARTING PROBLEM[6]

The Novelty Greeting Card Co. is one of the largest producers of greeting cards and decorated wrapping paper in the country. The decorated paper product line includes, in addition to the familiar Christmas wrapping, a complete line of paper for other special occasions (birthdays, weddings, etc.)

The marketing for these products is accomplished through 73 branch field sales offices. These branches stock a complete line of products and control distribution throughout the United States. There are two separate and distinct marketing groups. The first group (which accounts for the larger sales volume) deals primarily with large accounts such as department stores, chain stores and major stationery stores. The second group works with thousands of small outlets (drug stores, general stores, variety stores, part-time agents, etc.) so that it can reach every small community and hamlet in the nation. Stocks of cards and paper are delivered to these smaller locations by a special group of field salesmen who work from the 73 branch sales offices.

There are approximately 9,000 of these "salesmen" (actually, they should be more properly called "Agents" since they are not employed by Novelty Greeting Card Co.). The "salesmen" are paid a commission monthly by the New York City home office based upon sales which they report to field offices during the prior month.

The data processing involved in this operation is depicted and explained in the accompanying flowchart and narrative entitled "Salesmen's Commission Payments."

GENERAL SYSTEM CHART NARRATIVE

(1) Salesmen remit sales tickets and cash receipts to field sales office (daily).
(2) Cashier balances cash against sales tickets, sends cash to bank (daily).
(3) Clerk determines commission due each salesman, files tickets by salesman and posts total to control sheet (daily).
(4) Clerk (monthly) completes pre-addressographed Salesmen's Commission Report received from home office by performing the following duties:
    1. Entering commissions due each salesman
    2. Entering name and address of each new salesman
    3. "Striking out" (deleting) salesmen who have been terminated
    4. "Striking out" changed addresses and entering new addresses manually
(5) Clerk adds lists of amounts shown on report, compares total to control sheet and enters totals at bottom of last sheet of report.
(6) Addressograph room (at home office) prepares plates for new salesmen,

---

[6] Lybrand, Ross Brothers, and Montgomery, Management Consulting Services, Training Program *EDP For Auditors*, (Madison, N.J.: Drew University, July 22–26, 1963).

removes from files plates of terminated salesmen, and changes addresses as required.

(7) Updated addressograph plates are used to print names and addresses on checks, names only on check register, and to create the new sales commission report for the following month. The report lists only names, addresses and salesman numbers in alpha (numeric) sequence. The report form is sent to field sales offices. Checks and check register are sent to bookkeeping machines.

(8) Bookkeeping machines "write" checks and check register. Completed checks are first sent to the controller for signature and then to the mailroom. The check register is filed.

CASE STUDY 5–4
Savings and Loan Association
Flowcharting Procedural Development

Given:

A smaller savings and loan association, chartered by the federal government. Presently using mechanical posting equipment to develop internal accounting data and maintain customer passbooks and account ledgers. This association has approximately $26 million in assets and 12,000 active savings accounts. The transaction volume is as follows:

New accounts per month......................... 250
Average monthly savings transactions..............5,500
Maximum daily savings transactions................ 800
Average daily savings transactions................. 250

The present processing method requires that upon presentation of the passbook at the window, or through the mail, the account ledger is selected and the transaction is simultaneously posted to the passbook and the ledger. Dividends are calculated on a desk calculator semiannually and posted to the customer passbook when it is presented at the window. The posting equipment develops daily totals which are used to prove cash after the windows close.

The problems being encountered are generated primarily by rapidly increasing growth both in new account activity and in transaction volume.

The association is planning on using punched card equipment for processing all transactions. It is their immediate concern to design a procedure to handle the establishment and the processing of new savings accounts using this new equipment.

In setting up the system, it will first be necessary to produce account ledger cards. It will be important to have the name, address, the amount of the deposit, and the account number on these cards. Upon further investigation it is found that it is necessary to maintain two files of these cards, one to be maintained in account number sequence and the other in alphabetical sequence.

It is also desired that a daily report be prepared of new account acquisitions, which will possibly necessitate the making of a third card.

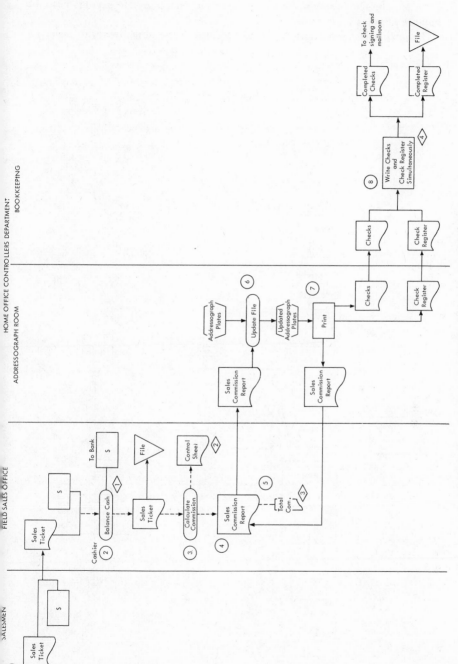

Novelty Greeting Card Co.—General System Flow Chart

In addition, it will be necessary to compute the dividends on these accounts on a semiannual basis as well as to maintain an up-to-date savings account balance file on a daily basis.

Following is a flowchart drawn to accomplish the objectives stated above.

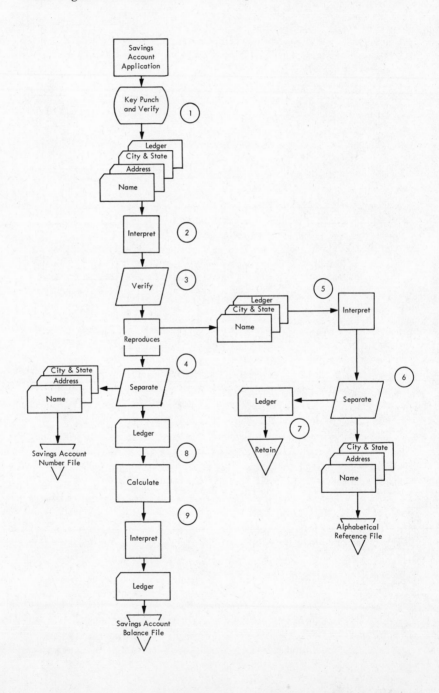

SAVINGS ACCOUNTING—ESTABLISHING NEW ACCOUNTS

1. After the accounting processes have been completed for a new savings account and the depositor issued the passbook, the application is sent to the IBM department where name and address, and the account ledger cards are keypunched and verified.
2. The cards are interpreted to provide complete visual reference.
3. The printed cards are checked against the source documents to insure the accuracy of keypunching.
4. The reproducing punch automatically produces a duplicate set of account cards and simultaneously verifies their accuracy. Original name and address cards are filed in savings account number sequence.
5. The duplicate cards are interpreted.
6. Name and address cards are filed in the cross-reference file in alphabetical sequence.
7. The duplicate account ledger is retained for use in preparing daily and monthly new account reports.
8. The savings ledger is processed through the 602 calculator to compute and automatically punch the anticipated dividend.
9. The ledger is interpreted so that anticipated dividend and dividend plus account balance are printed on the card, and then filed in the savings account balance file in account number sequence.

ANNOTATED BIBLIOGRAPHY

AMERICAN MANAGEMENT ASSOCIATION. *Advances in Management Information Systems Techniques.* Management Bulletin No. 16. New York, 1962.

The first article in this bulletin outlines some of the more important information processing techniques that are in use. The final article makes some criticisms of many management information systems in use today.

————. *Control Through Information: A Report on Management Information Systems.* Management Bulletin No. 24. New York, 1963.

This article explains the financial information needs of many of our country's industries. After the need for an integrated financial information system is explained, the areas of finance where computer-assisted action could be taken are explored.

————. *Management Information Systems and the Computer.* Research Study No. 51. New York, 1961.

Chapter 3 explains what systems work is, and it also gives some of the basic requirements in the selection of the best system for an organization.

DIEBOLD, JOHN. "Four Problems You Cannot Shirk," *Administrative Management,* Vol. 23 (July, 1962), pp. 24–25, 68–69.

This article, which is by a recognized authority on automation and systems analysis, pinpoints four problem areas caused by the innovation of computers. He elaborates on the lack of discipline in the development of information systems and the need for training and education of people to develop this discipline. He then discusses the problem of organizational change and the need for a change in business attitudes to cope with problems caused by computers.

GREENFIELD, M. S.; WEIMER, S. W.; and RANDALL, C. B.   *Systems and Procedures for Automated Accounting,* chap. xxvi. Cincinnati: South-Western Publishing Co., 1962.

Chapter 26 explains the use of flowcharting in simplifying the steps to be followed in an accounting procedure. The types of flowcharts explained are broken down into two categories: (1) data flowcharts and (2) operational flowcharts.

INTERNATIONAL BUSINESS MACHINES CORPORATION.   *Flowcharting Techniques,* #C20–8152.

Current ideas on flowcharting are both described and illustrated.

MOORE, FRANCIS E., and STETTLER, HOWARD F.   *Accounting Systems for Management Control,* chap. xxvii. Homewood, Ill.: Richard D. Irwin, Inc., 1963.

Chapter 27 explains the use of flowcharts in describing accounting procedures, and particularly punched card and EDP procedures. It also explains the use of work distribution, forms distribution, and layout charts.

SYSTEMS AND PROCEDURE ASSOCIATION.   *Business Systems,* Vol. I, chap. v. Cleveland, 1963.

A summary of the various charting symbols, the use of procedural charts (manual and mechanized), and forms and other business charts.

ZLATKOVICH, CHARLES T.   "Some Principles of Accounting Systems Design," *Accounting Review,* Vol. 33 (July, 1958), pp. 419–22.

The author in this article explains five factors which must be considered in any systems design. The system must provide needed information at the lowest cost, with adequate consideration for internal control. The system should be uniform and be capable of accommodating to change.

QUESTIONS

1. What are the ingredients of the accounting or data processing system of a business? Discuss the significance of each ingredient to the successful management of the business.

2. Why is it that small businesses are less likely to have formalized data processing systems than large?

3. In what size firm is systems analysis more apt to take place?

4. Discuss the questions which any analyst must seek answers for if he is going to endeavor to improve an existing system.

5. Should a systems analyst be concerned with organization structure? Discuss.

6. What impact does a clear definition of organization structure usually have on the internal control system of the firm?

7. What part do business forms play in a data processing system? Discuss.

8. What types of information should the system analyst seek from each

of the forms and records which are currently in use by the business being reviewed? Carefully explain your reasons for including each item on your list.

9. What is a procedures survey and what are its objectives?

10. How should the analyst approach the problem of learning about procedures in a firm?

11. What are the types of output which a business manager has a right to expect out of a data processing system? Discuss their significance and relative nature.

12. Describe flowcharting. Of what use is it to a systems analyst?

13. What is the significance of flowcharting when one is considering electronic data processing?

14. Distinguish between a program flowchart and a block diagram.

15. Using the input/output, flow direction, and processing symbols as illustrated in Figure 5–6, as well as the decision symbol which is made in the shape of a diamond, flowchart everything you did this morning from the time you left home until you reached school. (Note the decisions which you would have made and be certain that you follow each alternative decision to a proper conclusion.)

CHAPTER 6

Manual and Mechanical

Methods of Data Processing

THE MAJOR techniques used in the processing of business information may be roughly classified as manual, mechanical, electromechanical, and electronic data processing techniques. Before reviewing these techniques, however, it might be interesting to trace quickly the development of the demand for data and the impact of this demand on the origination and improvement of the equipment used in these processing techniques.

Growth in the Demand for Data

The use of modern digital computers in the processing of business data will be discussed at length in later chapters. However, we may mention here that it has been suggested that the first data compilation in the history of man was achieved through the use of "digital computers"—the digital bones of the fingers. No doubt, man did first count on his fingers and then progressed to knotted strings or fibers, marks on or grooves in stone, and finally to the use of paper (in the form of papyrus scrolls).

With the growth of "international" trade in the 13th and 14th centuries, true business records began to be required. Also, with the development and acceptance of the Arabic number system, the record keeper of the day could finally add, subtract, multiply, and even divide figures directly—which had been an impossible task using the Roman numerical system.

Business became more complex in the 16th and 17th centuries, through the use of joint ventures and partnerships, which were formed to meet the financial requirements of larger business ventures, and which brought about an ever expanding need for adequate business records to report on the results of these larger ventures. This need, in turn, began to foster the development of mechanical techniques to aid in the recording, summarizing, and other functions basic to record keeping.

The need for better business records was further intensified by the beginning in the 17th century of the corporate form of business in such colonial ventures as the East India Company, the Virginia Company, the Hudson's Bay Company, and many others. The many owners of such corporate ventures required "in-depth" reporting of the investments, expenses, and financial rewards forthcoming, and accounting, as it is known today, began to achieve professional status.

Once the corporate form of business became a legal entity,[1] this multiple-ownership form of business, with limited liability on the part of the owners, became the financial stimulus so greatly needed for the growth of our country. The rapid development of the corporation and the laws and regulations which resulted pertaining to the corporation and their stocks listed on the stock exchanges brought about a tremendous growth in the demand for data as applied to these corporations.

Another, and perhaps second most important demand for data came about through the implementation of our income tax laws, effective after the 16th Amendment to our Constitution in February, 1913, which required individuals as well as all forms of business to keep detailed records of their financial operations and to report on their tax liabilities.

Choice of Methods of Data Processing

In Chapter 5 the point was made that most businesses do not concern themselves with their accounting systems until top management becomes aware of some specific need. Such needs may, for example, include an improvement in the speed of handling certain clerical operations due to production bottlenecks or the need for more timely or more detailed data for decision-making purposes. To meet such needs requires a complete appraisal and evaluation of the existing system. A decision must be made as to the method to be employed for the manipulation of data. This decision will be influenced by the volume of data to be processed, the repetitive nature or lack of repetitive nature of the data, and the time available in which to process it. The alternative approaches available to analyze the existing system must also be a consideration.

As soon as management has decided what it wants out of the system, the problem of cost must be faced, and the factors of "cost" and "value received" must be equated.

Manual methods are less costly than mechanical methods of processing data, but they also have less speed and a more restricted ability to manipulate numerical facts. Many of the manual methods, however, have means whereby they can be connected into more elaborate systems, thereby increasing their versatility. Each of the methods of processing

---

[1] In 1888 the U.S. Supreme Court handed down the historic decision that the protection of the "due process" clause of the Constitution should be extended to the corporation as a person or entity.

data mentioned in this chapter has a unique function and purpose which must be recognized.

As soon as the systems analyst has made himself acquainted with all of the sources of business information and of the forms and records on which it will be captured, he must then determine the proper format for the forms and records in light of the demands placed upon the system by management. Do these forms and records capture the information desired by management? Is the design of the forms most appropriate for the method of data processing to be selected? Is the format for each form and record the simplest that can be conceived commensurate with the requirements of the system?

The systems analyst will be able to determine whether the existing forms are adequate or whether new ones need to be designed after he finds the answers to these questions. If new ones need to be designed or old ones modified, this will be a part of the work of this individual analyst or group, as the case may be.

MANUAL METHODS

Writing Board

In any discussion of data processing, the accuracy of input data is always stressed as being of paramount importance. One means of insuring greater accuracy in the origination of this input data is to have it transcribed as few times as possible. The writing board (Figure 6–1) is a step in this direction. This is a device which aligns and holds in place the basic documents and records involved in recording a transaction so that all are completed, by a single handwriting operation, with the original copy serving as the originating document and the carbon copies serving to record the data into the journals and ledgers.

The board itself is relatively inexpensive. The only other necessary expenditure is for the purchase of the forms which have been designed to fit on the particular board purchased. These forms, journals, and ledgers must be especially designed for each accounting procedure. This system is adaptable to such typical accounting procedures as accounts payable, accounts receivable, and payroll.

As an example, the purchase invoices may be recorded daily as they are received and processed. In addition, a voucher check and an invoice register may be prepared simultaneously. Unit purchase and expense distribution tickets may be provided as a by-product. For accounts receivable the customer's statement, the accounts receivable ledger account, and the sales journal can be prepared simultaneously. The distribution to departments or other sales classifications can be made at the same time, and all posting can be proved or cross-checked daily to assure accuracy in recording. In payroll accounting, the payroll journal, the individual earn-

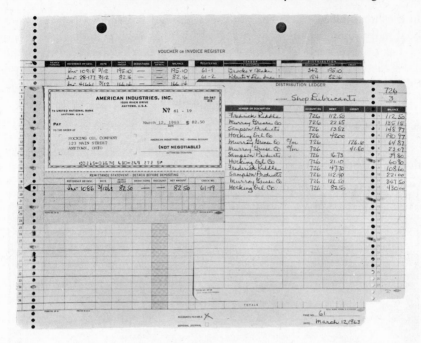

FIG. 6–1. Writing Board.

ings record, the employee's check, and the stub to explain all of the withholdings and deductions taken from the gross pay amount can all be prepared with one writing by using the writing board.

This system is extremely versatile and inexpensive to operate and should definitely be considered when planning a relatively small data processing operation.

Peg-Strip Accounting

Peg-strip accounting utilizes a device which is quite similar to the writing board in appearance. It is composed of a summary board with pegs located across the top on which standard preprinted strips of forms, with holes evenly placed across the top of them, may be "pegged" on the board.

Peg-strip accounting assumes the use of manual accounting methods. The advantage of the system is that it, like the writing board, eliminates much data transcription. The preprinted strips constitute the basic document on which data surrounding a group of transactions is assembled. Take, for example, the daily reports from salesmen in the field. The report form used may be a preprinted strip. Each day the salesman fills out these slips, itemizing his sales. These daily reports are then assembled in the home office, where they are pegged and crossadded to produce a final daily summary on another sheet which has been included at the end of the pegged reports by the personnel responsible for analyzing the assembled data. The figures on the summary strips are then added down to provide the total daily sales. At the end of the week, the daily summaries are repegged to secure a weekly summary.

Keysort Cards

Keysort cards (Figure 6–2) were primarily developed as an inexpensive device to facilitate the sorting operation. These cards are useful whenever

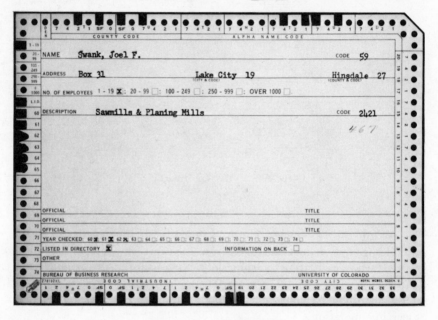

FIG. 6–2.   Keysort Card.

a business has a mass of statistical data which needs to be summarized in various ways from time to time.

The cards can be made almost any convenient size. They are then designed so that the statistical information can be conveniently recorded on the face of the card. There are many uses for such cards. For example:

1. Labor cost distribution
2. Employee records
3. Inventory control systems
4. Fixed asset records
5. Manufacturing control systems
6. Order and sales analyses
7. Research and survey work

All information recorded manually on the card which is considered relevant is then encoded around the edge of the cards. In order for this to be done, the data must be reduced to a numeric code. This code is developed by utilizing holes around the edge of the card. A particular code is indicated by notching away that portion of the card between the hole and the edge. These notches allow the notched coded cards to be separated from unnotched cards when a sorting needle is inserted in one of the holes of a group of cards. Since the notched cards have nothing to support them on the needle, they will fall away from the group, while the unnotched cards remain. Following is a description of how the numeric code around a card can be created:

Each digit of a number is indicated in a set of four holes numbered 7, 4, 2, and 1. This is called a field. The figures 0 to 9 are notched in a 7, 4, 2, 1 field as follows:

0—	0 0 0 0 7 4 2 1		5—	0 ⊔ 0 ⊔ 7 4 2 1
1—	0 0 0 ⊔ 7 4 2 1		6—	0 ⊔ ⊔ 0 7 4 2 1
2—	0 0 ⊔ 0 7 4 2 1		7—	⊔ 0 0 0 7 4 2 1
3—	0 0 ⊔ ⊔ 7 4 2 1		8—	⊔ 0 0 ⊔ 7 4 2 1
4—	0 ⊔ 0 0 7 4 2 1		9—	⊔ 0 ⊔ 0 7 4 2 1

To save handling and filing time, numbers 0 to 99 are indicated in a "group" field. The holes in this field represent groups, 0 to 24, 25 to 49, 50 to 74, and 75 to 99. Within these four groups the cards need not be in numerical order, as any card can be found very quickly. Thus we can notch cards from 0 to 99,999 (100,000 cards) in four fields.

The number 25,347 looks like this:

The notches can be read as easily as the figures on the card. The first three fields indicate that the card is in the 25,300 series.

Number 47 lies within the group 25 to 49 and therefore the second hole from the right is notched in the group field.

After the cards have been sorted into hundreds it is only necessary to drop out each group of 25.

This process was originally conceived as a manual sorting device. It still is, and should be in many instances, as it provides a useful, inexpensive process for sorting quantities of data. The only basic equipment necessary to use such a manual system are a hand punch and a sorting needle.

After the cards have been used for the purpose intended they must be refiled into the larger group of cards from which they were originally sorted. The best way to do this is manually.

The summarizing process can be automated by the use of a tab punch/reader which accepts groups of keysort cards which have been sorted by the sorting needle and automatically reads the coded values, tabulates them, and prints out summaries by classification. In addition, the machine automatically code-punches summary cards which can be used to update existing records or generate summary reports,

Keysort cards can also be used to prepare the input for an EDP system. This can be done by the use of a card converter which reads the keysort notched data and converts it into punched tape or punched cards for computer input. The card converter can expedite data handling procedures for companies with decentralized operations, organizations with a number of date-originating locations, such as hospitals, and small businesses with limited processing facilities that do not have the capacity to justify a computer in several locations. This permits their limited data to utilize keysort cards locally and to convert them to a computer input form centrally and bring the speed and processing capacity of computers to these organizations.

Document Control Register

Where it is desired to control, at the source, business forms evidencing different types of transactions, the document control register may be used (Figure 6–3). A register of this type is a metal box housing a supply of up to eight copies of a set of continuous forms with interleaved carbon. These forms are all locked in the register. There is either a hand-driven or an electrically driven feed bringing the forms to a writing surface as they

FIG. 6–3.   Document Control Register.

are needed so that all copies of a given transaction are completed by hand at the same time.

Many smaller retail establishments regard this register almost as an accounting system in itself. This is due to the many uses to which the form in the register can be put. The secret of the system is not so much in the register but in the design of the form used in the register.

At the end of the day the register is unlocked, by someone other than the person using it during the day, and the audit copies of the forms removed and summarized for posting purposes.

Thus, the document control register is still another device which enables the business firm to simplify the task of data accumulation and to control the data at its source as adequately as possible. Invariably, this device (where applicable) improves the quality of the data placed in the associated data processing system.

Source Record Punch

The source record punch is a desk-top electric data collecting machine (Figure 6–4) that records information in both human-readable language (printed) and machine-readable code (keypunched) on the same document at the same time and place in one writing. The document employed is called a ZIPCARD set (Figure 6–5), which is a carbon-interleaved set of papers which includes a standard punched card. The design of this set and the fixed information to be printed on the pages must be determined

Courtesy of Standard Register Co.

FIG. 6–4.   Source Record Punch Model 1601.

well in advance as an essential element of this system. By so doing, the recorded information is immediately ready for human use as well as for tabulator or computer processing.

The source record punch is designed to merge three different types of information: (1) constant information which is either prepunched from a master card or imprinted from an embossed plate onto a ZIPCARD set; (2) semivariable information, such as the date or department number, which is recorded by setting a mechanism in the machine which punches and prints this data on the same ZIPCARD set; and (3) variable information, such as identification codes, charges, quantities, etc., which is recorded through the use of a keyboard on the front of the machine by

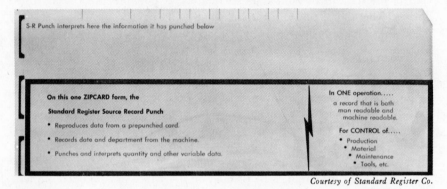

S-R Punch interprets here the information it has punched below

On this one ZIPCARD form, the

Standard Register Source Record Punch

• Reproduces data from a prepunched card.

• Records date and department from the machine.

• Punches and interprets quantity and other variable data.

In ONE operation.....
a record that is both man readable and machine readable.

For CONTROL of.....
• Production
• Material
• Maintenance
• Tools, etc.

Courtesy of Standard Register Co.

FIG. 6–5.   Zipcard Set.

simultaneously punching the data into and printing it on the ZIPCARD set.

This machine can do the entire job in one recording. It answers the need for a way to gather information at the point of origin, and through a simple operation, capture input for data processing. At the same time, this operation provides additional copies of the record for use in readable form. In this way, data to be further processed in the EDP system are gathered as hard-copy documents are provided for immediate action.

Mark-Sensing Equipment

One of the most critical problems in the whole area of data processing is how to more nearly assure the accuracy of input data. One way to achieve this accuracy is to make the original recording function as simple and as easy as possible. The mark-sensing technique was developed to provide a method of originating data that is easy to learn and simple to perform. At the same time that the data are recorded, they are incorporated in a document that is machine processable, and this eliminates any further necessity for retranscription; the data are ready to be processed in either a punched card or an electronic computer system.

Mark sensing is a manual technique which is extremely portable as all that is required in recording data is a special type of lead pencil and a stack of especially designed cards. The person recording the data merely places a pencil mark on the card in a preprinted designation. These preprinted designations are in the form of small horizontal or diagonal oblong ovals printed on the card in every position acceptable to marked data (Figure 6–6).

Care is, of course, required in marking the card, as an improperly placed, a short, or an extended mark may be interpreted by the machine equipment as a value other than that intended.

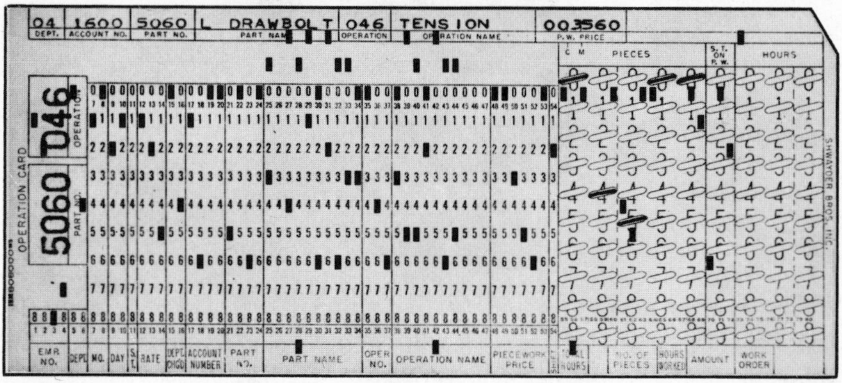

Courtesy of IBM.

FIG. 6–6.   Marked-Sensed IBM Card.

The special lead pencils required to produce the electrically conductive mark on the card contain conductive material not present in ordinary lead pencils. A mark will be effective only if the pencil, either wood or mechanical, contains the proper amount of graphite in conjunction with a reduced content of clay and wax. The position of the mark placed on the card, in relation to both the top and edge of the card, denotes the numerical value of the information recorded.

The marked cards are then assembled and passed through a piece of equipment known as a mark-sensing reproducer. Each pencil mark position on the card is read by three electrical contacts or "brushes." When a mark is encountered by these brushes, an electrical impulse flows down to the mark through the two outer brushes, then through the mark toward its center, and back out through the middle brush.

Through a series of timed electrical impulses in combination with a series of mechanical devices, the electrical impulse flowing through the mark and out the middle brush is converted into a punched hole, in a predeterminable position on either the marked or another card, whose position represents the same numerical value that was represented by the original penciled mark.

As an extension and elaboration of the mark-sensing principle, the 1231 and 1232 Optical Mark Page Readers have been developed (Figure 6–7). These provide for the entry of information, marked with *ordinary*

Courtesy of IBM.

FIG. 6–7.　Optical Mark Page Reader.

lead pencil on sheets of paper, directly into a computer or into cards for subsequent processing by punched card machines or electronic data processing systems. Both of these equipment units can read as many as 1,000 marked positions on one 8½ × 11-inch data sheet.

With the 1231 the information which is read is transferred directly to a computer at the end of each document reading cycle. The 1232 reads and transmits marked information to a cable-connected 534 card punch where either one or a number of cards may be punched for each data sheet.

The reading of the marks on the data sheets is controlled by a program which also consists of a series of pencil marks on a sheet of paper. The programmed information is entered into the equipment by means of a program control sheet. The operational controls marked on the program sheet are actually instructional directions to the equipment which is to be used in the processing of the marked data on the data sheets. This program of instructional information is loaded (read) into the machine just before the processing is started on the data sheets and remains in the equipment until a new program is entered.

Addressograph Data Recorders

Source data is written by a Data Recorder (Figure 6–8) on an 80-column-size tab card form (Figure 6–9). Plastic cards stored in the Data

Courtesy of Addressograph Multigraph Corp.

FIG. 6–8. Data Recorder.

Recorder can record fixed data on the tab card forms, while the key levers on the front of the machine control the recording of variable data, which may be visually checked in registers on the front of the machine before the data is imprinted in bar code on the tab card forms. The card forms created in this way serve as machine-readable documents for data conversion to computer input languages. The conversion of bar code data format to computer input language is done by means of the Optical Code Reader (Figure 6–10). The numeric values in bar code are electronically

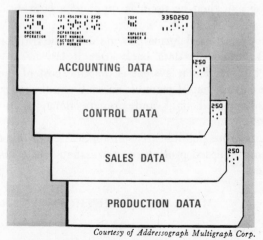

Courtesy of Addressograph Multigraph Corp.

FIG. 6–9. Eighty-Column Tab Card.

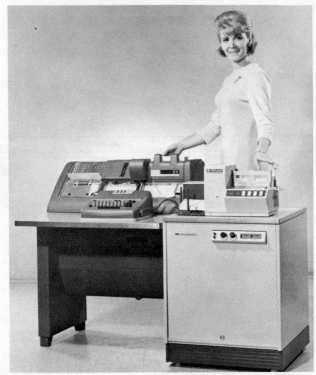

Courtesy of Addressograph Multigraph Corp.

***FIG.* 6–10.   Optical Code Reader.**

converted into an eight-channel code which is punched into paper tape. The paper tape can then be used as input to a conventional computer system.

The hard-copy tab card forms provide an audit trail or track if it is ever needed to trace the data back after it has been recorded. The advantage of this particular system is that the cost of the optical code reader is far less than that of scanners currently on the market which both scan and read printed data and prepare data input in computer-acceptable form.

There are numerous possible areas of application of this type of system in hospitals, job timecard procedures, the issuance of tools or materials, and many others.

MECHANICAL METHODS

Adding Machines

A listing-type adding machine is probably the most basic piece of mechanical equipment used in the business office today. There are two

Courtesy of National Cash Register Co.

FIG. 6–11.   Full Keyboard Adding Machine.

general types of this equipment—a full keyboard machine and a 10-key machine. The main distinguishing feature of the full keyboard (Figure 6–11) is that it has one vertical row of nine keys (number 1 to 9) which provides the place positions required for each digit of the largest amount desired. On a 10-key machine (Figure 6–12), only 10 numbered keys are provided, and the operator strikes the keys one after the other in the order in which they would be written.

On most adding machines, subtraction can be performed automatically.

Courtesy of National Cash Register Co.

FIG. 6–12.   Ten-Key Adding Machine.

Any record keeper finds one of these pieces of equipment almost indispensable in assisting in the summarizing function. The paper tape provided by a listing device gives the operator a record of the data entered into the equipment, which may be useful as either a permanent record or in checking the data entered back against the information from which the data originated.

TAPE PUNCH ADDING MACHINE.   Some adding machines also provide a punched paper tape which is machine processable in future use of the data. The basic idea of tape punch adding machines (Figure 6–13) is

Courtesy of Friden, Division of The Singer Co.

***FIG.* 6–13.   Add-Punch* Adding Machine.**

that the operator lists and encodes data from original media. At the same time as the data is being listed visually, it is being punched into paper tape. It is assumed that this operation will be taking place at the local organizational level. The paper tape, in turn, can be sent to a centralized computer location or to a data processing center to be converted into whatever type of reports or analyses management may desire.

Any basic data can be used and can be handled randomly without presorting. The operator assigns distribution codes to the data. The printed audit control tape provides a visual check of punched data. The original data remains in the control of local management. At the processing center the data can be assembled and reassembled to provide a wide variety of reports with relative ease and at low cost. Alphabetic description and up-to-date totals can be provided on any report. Processing charges are normally based on the number of items processed.

---

* A trademark of Friden, Inc.

This particular type of equipment has found wide application in the offices of accountants who perform bookkeeping and analytical services for their clients.

Calculators

Calculating machines are closely related to adding machines. However, besides having the capability to add and subtract, they can also be used to multiply and divide. These latter two functions involve either repeated addition or subtraction performed automatically.

These machines are of four types: the rotary, the key-driven, the printing, and the electronic. The rotary type (Figure 6–14) has been

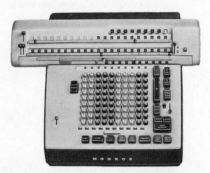

Courtesy of Monroe Calculating Machine Co.

FIG. 6–14. Rotary-Type Calculator.

most frequently used in business offices because it takes little training to operate it, but with the advent of the electronic calculator (page 135), which has greatly increased speed and provided noiseless operation with only a moderate increase in cost, the use of the rotary-type calculator in the business office is beginning to decline.

To realize the highest efficiency in the use of the key-driven calculator, formal training in its operation is highly desirable, as tremendous speed can thereby be attained. Machines of this type are commonly called "comptometers" (Figure 6–15). Their principal advantage derives from the fact that depression of a key causes a figure to be registered immediately with no time being lost by moving the hand to a motor bar or waiting for the machine to cycle. These machines are regularly used where repetitive numerical work can be made a full-time assignment.

The printing calculator (Figure 6–16) has had the numeric keys reduced to 12. The arithmetic functions can all be performed by the machine merely by the depression of a key with a record of the figures involved being printed on the tape.

Courtesy of Victor Comptometer Corp.

FIG. 6–15.   Comptometer.

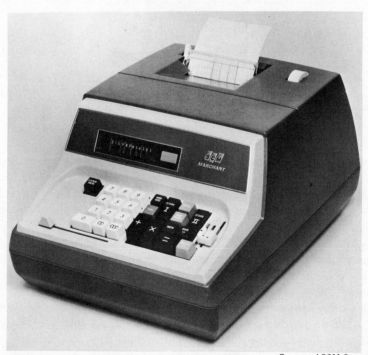

Courtesy of SCM Corp.

FIG. 6–16.   Printing Calculator.

Courtesy of Friden, Division of The Singer Co.

FIG. 6–17. 132 Electronic Calculator.

Recently a new electronic calculator (Figure 6–17) has become available. All computations are performed by solid-state electronic components. Entries and answers appear on a cathode-ray tube, very much like a small television screen. Operating speeds of this equipment are measured in milliseconds.

Cash Registers

The importance of accuracy of input data into a data processing system has already been stressed. One means of attempting to insure greater accuracy is to make certain that every transaction is recorded as quickly as possible. The cash register (Figure 6–18), if properly used, is a device for recording cash and credit transactions easily, quickly, and accurately. It is designed to be of greatest assistance in a retail situation where large volumes of transactions need to be recorded at the time payment is made. This type of transaction, as it occurs in such a store, is often most difficult to control.

The cash register is not only an excellent device for recording initial transactions, but the output of the machine, whether in the form of punched paper tape or optical journal tape, can be used as input in a completely automated data processing system.

The cash register is a manually or electrically operated accounting device of such fundamental character that it is used by almost every retail business regardless of size or kind. It serves to speed up the accounting

Courtesy of National Cash Register Co.

FIG. 6–18.   Cash Register with Locked-in Audit Tape.

data processing operations; it affords the owners or managers substantial control over cash, accounting data, and personnel; and finally, it aids materially in recording transactions and in accumulating and storing management information. The cash register was one of the first accounting machines to be developed and has served as a prototype for some of the more elaborate accounting machines in use today.

These machines are built in a wide variety of sizes and capabilities. They are most widely employed because of the various controls which they provide over the receipt of cash. Not to consider such controls when discussing cash transactions, as they affect the input of a data processing system, is to overlook some of the most important controls which ought to be recognized and understood.

Many of these controls involve the procedure which is to be followed by employees who are handling the receipt of cash. In the first place, the procedure should require that cash receipts be recorded on the cash register immediately after the sale is made. As soon as the transaction is "rung up," the amount recorded is imprinted on the audit tape locked in the machine. This audit tape is visible in some makes of equipment, while in others it is not. The purpose of the audit tape is to provide a printed record of the transaction. At the end of the day, the register totals are available to be printed on the audit tape. Once these totals are added to the tape, it will then be removed from the machine by someone other than the person handling the cash. The total of cash received according to the tape must agree with the cash amount present in the drawer after taking into consideration the amount of change money placed in the drawer at the beginning of the day.

On this same audit tape, the clerk who made the sale, the department in which the sale was made, and the item of merchandise sold may be identified by code number. This coded information can be of tremendous assistance not only in the control of cash but also in the control and handling of merchandise. This control can be accomplished by making an analysis of the sales in accordance with the coded information recorded on the tape. This permits management to determine the volume of sales each day and the items or types of inventory which are selling most rapidly.

Courtesy of National Cash Register Co.

FIG. 6–19.   Cash Register Printed Receipt.

Certain models of cash registers print receipts (Figure 6–19) for the customer, thereby involving the customer as an auditor of the transaction which has just been completed. The amount for each item sold is clearly indicated on the receipt along with the total due. This same information is visually recorded for both the clerk and the customer to see in a window at the top of the machine as the items of sale are recorded. In this way, another audit of the recorded data is accomplished.

Individual cash drawers can be provided for each clerk using the machine. Each time a sale is made, it must be charged to a particular cash drawer. This information is recorded on the audit tape by drawer or clerk number, and each individual drawer can be checked against the balance of cash which should be in the drawer at the end of the day.

Certain models of cash registers contain multiple counters which enable them to sum up individually the amounts recorded each day on different keys of the machine (Figure 6–20). Note keys marked "meat," "produce," "dairy," etc. These amounts may represent total sales, total number of transactions, sales by department, sales by salesperson, or possibly sales by merchandise class. The counters enable statistical analyses to be accomplished much more quickly, as well as permitting financial responsibility to be pinpointed more accurately.

Courtesy of National Cash Register Co.

FIG. 6–20.   Cash Register with Multiple Counters.

A model of cash register can also be procured which can perform some of the functions of a bookkeeping machine. It can print on an itemized credit sales check, and it can also be used to post to an accounts receivable ledger. The sales check provides control over all charge sales, deposit sales, c.o.d. sales, employee sales, exchange sales and deliveries. The customer's name and address would have to be imprinted on the sales check by the salesperson.

In the NCR sales register, a visible journal tape is produced which provides an historical record of every sale in the order of its incurrence. Daily register totals are also printed on the journal tape. This tape is optically scannable, by specialized equipment (to be discussed later), as input to a computer where the data will be processed and totals determined. These totals must check with the totals previously determined by the different registers of the sales register. Once again, another form of control is provided over input being fed into a data processing system.

Accounting and Bookkeeping Machines

A very common piece of equipment found in both large and small firms for use in processing business data is some type of bookkeeping machine. Essentially, the bookkeeping machine combines the functional capabilities of the two most common office machines, the adding machine and the typewriter. The adding machine prints amounts vertically on a paper tape in a single column, totals these internally, and when a particular key is depressed, prints a total or subtotal. The typewriter performs no arithmetic function but has the ability to print characters horizontally across a wide page, or on multiple forms through the use of carbon paper. A bookkeeping machine combines the listing and totaling capabilities of the adding machine with the horizontal printing feature of the typewriter.

A simple bookkeeping machine can do the following things:

1. Write and complete one or more records at one time.
2. Compute balances and accumulate totals.
3. Control accuracy as a by-product of recording transactions.
4. Process transactions at machine speed.
5. Produce a uniform and legible record.

For our purposes, bookkeeping machines may be classified into four different types. The first two types are basically numerical or nondescriptive adding machines, while the last two more truly fit the function more commonly required of accounting machines:

1. *Rear-feed carriage.* This is basically an adding machine with a rear-feed-type carriage. Such machines may or may not have a tabulating carriage and are used primarily by smaller business firms or by branch offices of larger firms where activity is relatively light. Usually only one, or rarely more than two, totals are provided.
2. *Front-feed carriage.* This type of machine is basically an adding machine with a tabulating-type front-feed carriage which permits faster posting and providing one or two totals. This class of machine and along with class 1, above, should be considered as being in a low price range.
3. *Automatic bookkeeping machines, nondescriptive.* While the automatic bookkeeping machine is still basically an adding machine, it incorporates many automatic features which eliminate operator decisions and manual operations.

    Usually incorporated in this machine are automatic tabulation and return of the carriage, automatic opening and closing of the carriage, automatic totaling and subtotaling, automatic punctuation, and automatic ribbon color control (credits in red).

    These features naturally make the posting operation simpler, faster, and less susceptible to operator error.

Automatic bookkeeping machines are available with two or more accumulators.

4. *Bookkeeping machines—descriptive.* This is similar to the machines in the previous class but also incorporates typewriter capabilities.

The typewriter allows for complete description of all entries—names on vouchers, payroll checks, reports, etc.—and is usually recommended where multiple applications may be performed on one machine.

The price of machines found in classes 3 and 4 are in the medium to high price range category. Prices will, of course, depend on the optional features desired by the individual selecting the equipment to be used. When selecting a bookkeeping machine, it is important to balance the additional cost of a larger or more elaborate machine against the anticipated clerical savings.

As one studies these various classes of machines available, he should not lose sight of the fact that they are all being manufactured and all are being used to process data in different types of situations where varying degrees of complexity are involved.

It should be particularly noted, in the discussion of these four classes of bookkeeping machines, that they are arranged from the simple to the complex, from the machines which can do only a few things to those which are extremely versatile. The prices of the machines vary much in the same manner.

The most simple bookkeeping machine is a rear-feed machine. It is electrically operated and accumulates one total. New balances are printed after each posting with the depression of a single key.

This equipment has a numeric keyboard, which means that it can only print numeric information. Any system in which the machine is used, therefore, must be capable of using numerically coded data.

This machine is capable of accomplishing all of the things which it has been previously stated a bookkeeping machine was capable of accomplishing, but in the context of a simple data processing system.

Front-feed bookkeeping machines have several distinct advantages: (1) They simplify and speed up form handling. (2) They guide forms into exact columnar position. (3) They provide a chute to hold forms firmly in place. And (4) they provide an easier visual means to align the form for the next entry. All of these features are made to facilitate the processing of data, and as such, they are important.

The 4000, 5000, and 6000 series of the Burroughs Corporation are numeric machines and, consequently, cannot describe items of information in letters or words. Data are entered through the numeric keyboard, and computations can be performed either by automatic or manual keyboard control.

The Sensimatic F 1000 is the descriptive model. The Sensimatic series (Figure 6–21) can be expanded to include punched paper tape or

Courtesy of Burroughs Corp.

FIG. 6–21. Bookkeeping Machine.

direct punched card output with the addition of available data recording devices. If this is done, it makes it possible for this by-product of the Sensimatic operation to be used as input in a computer system.

The statement was made earlier that a bookkeeping machine could write and complete two or more records at the same time. This is made possible by using transactions forms, journals, and ledgers which have been especially designed. The columns on these documents have been so planned that by the use of carbon paper all of the records can be made at the same time by imprinting them simultaneously or by repeat printing. The operation of the machine using carbons was illustrated in Chapter 4. An example of repeat printing is shown in Figure 6–22.

Courtesy of Burroughs Corp.

FIG. 6–22. Repeat Printing Bookkeeping Machine.

It should be noted from this example that the importance of recording the correct data in the proper column cannot be overemphasized. In the earlier bookkeeping machines, program control bars were built into the equipment which would cause the bookkeeping machine to position itself in the right column following a prescribed sequence by depressing the proper key. The analogy might be drawn between this program control bar and the tabular stops on a typewriter with the control bar representing a particular set of tabular stops for a given application.

Later, as the machines became more automatic, the control bars also served as a means of triggering certain automatic functions. These same control bars have now been built in such a way that four different program schedules can be contained on what is called a program control

Courtesy National Cash. Register Co.

FIG. 6–23.   Large-Scale Bookkeeping Machine.

center (formerly the control bar). All that is required in the selection of one of the four programs is to turn a convenient knob. This feature has given machines of this type greater versatility without having to take time to change the control bars.

Now, also in larger machines (Figure 6–23), the programming or directing may be performed internally in the machine thereby eliminating the necessity to even change program bars or panels. These machines can be instructed or programmed to accumulate, print, and control punching (where punched tape is a feature) of a line total, a zero line proof or balancing procedure to prove the accuracy of distribution, and automatic totals for all memory units at the completion of a posting run.

The F 5000 series of the Sensimatic has the added feature that it has two printing heads. This dual printing head arrangement allows the simultaneous printing of two forms separately. The advantage of this arrangement is that one would have two original copies rather than having to deal with carbon copies, which can become difficult to read if the copies are not carefully handled. For example, it would be particularly desirable in an accounts receivable application where an original printing of both the statement and ledger are desired.

One of the advantages of a data processing system such as this is that in addition to the original hard copies which are created, either punched cards or punched paper tape may be created which can serve as direct input to almost any computer system.

DESK-SIZE COMPUTERS

Most of the manufacturers of business machines are now making desk-size computers. These machines are designed to retain the best features of bookkeeping machines along with the speed, memory, and computing capabilities of computers. In terms of data processing, these several makes of machines have both the capacity and the speed to handle relatively large volumes of paper work.

All of the makes of these machines presently on the market emphasize simplicity of operation and programming and reasonable rental cost per month.

All of the systems will accommodate a variety of inputs—punched paper tape, edge-punched cards, tabulating cards, and the keyboard. The feeling is, quite naturally, that business data will be in one of these forms in the medium-sized businesses for which these computing systems are designed.

Programming assistance is supplied readily to the user of the equipment. One manufacturer offers to do all of the necessary programming, at no cost, for the applications which a prospective user of the equipment envisions when he installs the equipment. Any future alterations to existing programs or writing of new programs will be done by the manufacturer for a small fee. The programs are punched into paper tape and are used either in loops or in strips. When they are not in use they can be easily stored away.

Another make of computer has a programming language all its own called SWIFT. It is composed of 38 simple English command statements: Add, Subtract, Multiply, Divide, etc. The programmer writes the program in SWIFT language on a work sheet. A typist types it on the input-output station (a console typewriter) and produces a reference document which provides documentation for the program. The electronic processor simultaneously translates the English program into machine language and

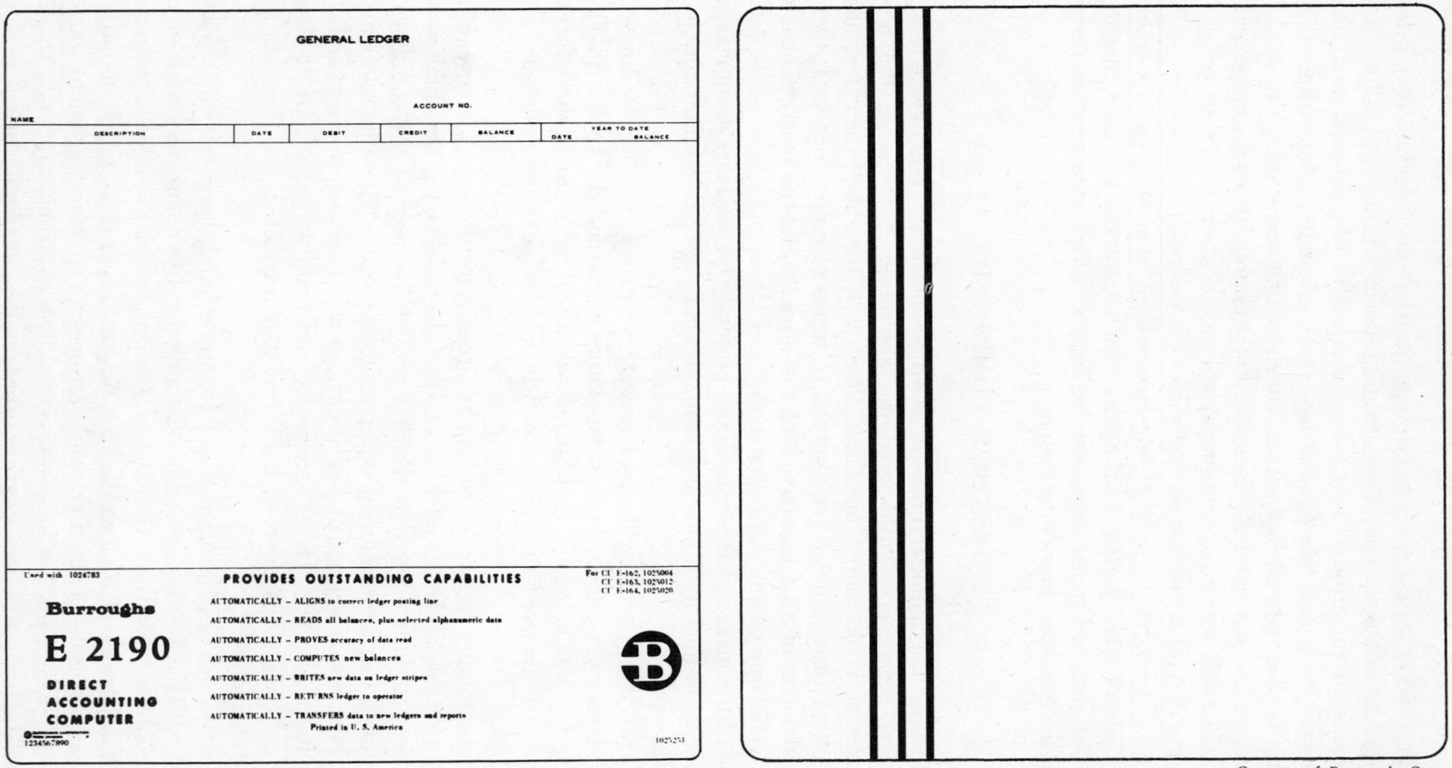

Courtesy of Burroughs Corp.

Front of Magnetic Striped Ledger Card. ***FIG. 6–24.*** **Back of Magnetic Striped Ledger Card.**

punches it into a paper tape which then becomes the program input to the system and instructs the equipment in its operation.

Storage in the different systems is accomplished in different ways. One system has two separate memories. For data storage, it has 60 registers (plus additional capability with auxiliary units which may be purchased or rented). The second memory contains 1,118 alphanumeric characters exclusively for internal program storage.

Another system utilizes core storage as well as magnetic striped ledger cards (Figure 6–24) to store current working data. The stripes on the ledger cards store, in magnetic pulse form, pertinent alpha and numeric account data such as customer name and address, accounts receivable balances, part numbers, item descriptions, inventory balances, and minimum levels. Upon insertation of the ledger cards into the Auto Reader for invoicing purposes, the detailed headings and item descriptions are automatically typed on the invoice. When the operator lists the quantity to be shipped and other nonstandard data, the information from the magnetic stripes is able to fully complete the invoice and post the accounts receivable ledger and at the same time update the active inventory ledger accounts.

All of the systems utilize a modified electric typewriter both as a means of manually inserting data into the system and as a means for printed output. In addition to having printed outputs, the outputs can also be in the form of punched paper tape, punched cards, or edge-notched cards.

One new computer, the Typetronic 7816, is interesting in its simplicity, and a description of it is as follows:

Courtesy of SCM Corp.

FIG. 6–25. Desk-Size Computer.

The basic system consists of three desk-top components and the control console (Figure 6–25). An input-output printer resembling the conventional office typewriter, a code reader, and a code punch sit on the console and associated computing processor. Add-on components, such as a second reader and a punch and/or auxiliary printer, simply plug in to extend the range and versatility of the system.

The typing function is automated by simply "feeding" repetitive data (customers' name and address cards, product cards, pricing cards, and so

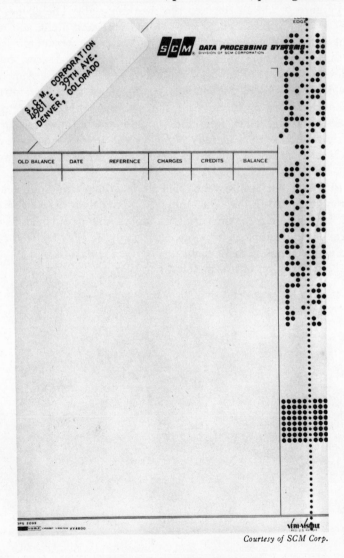

Courtesy of SCM Corp.

FIG. 6–26.   Ledger Card.

these cards are automatically typed at high speeds. The typewriter is automatically programmed to stop at predetermined locations for manual entry of variable information (quantity, shipping date, and so on). Manual entry of variable alphabetic or numeric data is possible at any time on the conventional typewriter keyboard.

The computing function is automated by performing important computations (for example, price times quantity, invoice summarizations, and so on) while the typist is performing other functions. These computations are made at electronic speeds and results can be printed, punched, or stored.

Output is in the form of typewritten documents along with a simultaneously punched paper tape.

ANNOTATED BIBLIOGRAPHY

BLUMBERG, DONALD F. "New Developments in the Small Computer Field," *Data Processing Yearbook, 1965* (ed. EDITH HARWITH GOODMAN), pp. 53–57. Detroit: American Data Processing, Inc., 1964.

The small-scale computer systems which were brought out during 1964 are discussed. Their physical characteristics and potential applications are described. Tables are given covering all the small, solid-state computers available which show their typical monthly rental, or purchase, price, processor speed, internal and external storage, special features, typical applications, and computers available.

"By the Numbers," *Administrative Management,* July, 1962, pp. 36–44.

This article is devoted to explaining the use of the hardest workers in the office—the adding machine and the desk-top calculator. The practical application of the two machines and also some of the technical aspects of the machines are explained.

GILLESPIE, CECIL. *Accounting Systems—Procedures and Methods,* chaps. vi and x. Englewood Cliffs, N.J.: Prentice-Hall, Inc., 1961.

Chapter 6 of this book explains the many types of multiple-copy forms. and automatic writing and reproducing equipment. Chapter 10 explains the use of autographic registers, writing boards, and cash registers as they apply particularly to the internal checks in a small business.

———. *Accounting Systems—Procedures and Methods,* chap. vii. Englewood Cliffs, N.J.: Prentice-Hall, Inc., 1961.

The first part of this chapter explains the different methods of posting accounts by machine. There is also a section on the methods of controlling machine errors.

JOHNSON, E. A. *Manual Methods of Data Processing Accounting Systems in Modern Business,* chaps. ix and xi. New York: McGraw-Hill Book Co., 1959.

Chapter 9 makes a summary of the principal types of equipment by which the transaction is only written once, i.e., pegboard, strip accounting, various duplicating processes. Chapter 11 explains the use of keysort cards in sorting data.

————. *Accounting Systems in Modern Business,* chap. x. New York: McGraw-Hill Book Co., 1959.

This chapter discusses the many electromechanical accounting machines, such as the adding machine, multiple-register machines, semiautomatic machines, and automatic machines. The chapter also gives a brief description of the application of accounting machines to certain accounting procedures.

LEVINE, HERMAN M. "How to Use Peg Strip Accounting Forms," *The Office,* Vol. 52 (September, 1960).

This article explains the advantages of using peg strip accounting and how it works. Many new applications of this method are brought out and explained by the writer.

MOORE, FRANCIS E., and STETTLER, HOWARD F. *Accounting Systems for Management Control,* chap. ix. Homewood, Ill.: Richard D. Irwin, Inc., 1963.

Chapter 9 of this book gives a description of the basic data processing equipment which is operated by a keyboard input method. The advantages of the bookkeeping machine and the many special devices used on that machine are clearly explained.

NELSON, O. S., and WOODS, R. S. *Accounting Systems and Data Processing,* chaps. iv and v. Cincinnati: South-Western Publishing Co., 1961.

Chapter 4 explains the many different types of manual accounting methods and devices, i.e., cash register, document control register, writing board, peg strip accounting and keysort cards. Chapter 5 goes into the concept of distribution and analysis of data by the use of electromechanical devices. It gives particular emphasis on the methods of detection of errors in machine accounting.

STEINBERG, HAROLD J. "Exploring Pegboard Accounting," *Journal of Accountancy,* Vol. 120 (November, 1965), pp. 83–84.

A form of automatic data processing available to small companies which are unable to afford the cost of electronic equipment is explored. Pegboard (one-write) accounting is a simple and low-cost system for eliminating time-consuming and repetitive office procedures. It is felt that the lack of this system's use by small business is because of a lack of understanding of how the system works. Discussed are the overall concept and its application to payroll, sales and accounts receivable, and purchases and accounts payable.

QUESTIONS

1. Why should the writing board bring about an improvement in the accuracy of data fed into a data processing system?
2. List three distinctly different situations in which you feel that peg strip accounting might be profitably used. Explain in sufficient detail so that it is easily apparent how each situation would utilize this method of recording data.

3. A keysort card is primarily used in what type of situation and for what purpose? Explain.

4. Explain how a keysort card can be used as a sorting device.

5. Under what circumstances would you recommend to a business that it employ a document control register?

6. Describe how a tab punch/reader could be used to facilitate the work of a data processing system.

7. Assuming you are an IBM sales representative, list three different applications for which you feel that it would be appropriate to recommend the use of mark-sense equipment. Support your recommendations with statements explaining why.

8. Would you recommend the purchase of a full-keyboard adding machine or a 10-key adding machine to a business client? Support your answer with statements of the reasons why.

9. How do calculators and adding machines differ?

10. It has been said that a cash register can be used as the hub of a data processing system in many retail stores. Do you agree or disagree? Explain why.

11. Enumerate five controls which cash registers provide. Explain how each one works.

12. Describe the basic features of a bookkeeping machine.

13. Under what circumstances would it be advisable for a business to obtain a bookkeeping machine? Explain.

14. What function does the program control bar perform? Explain.

15. Enumerate several uses for the magnetic ledger card. How does it work, and what advantages does it have?

16. Under what conditions might you recommend a desk-size computer to a business client? Explain in reasonable detail.

17. Describe the advantages as well as the disadvantages of the new electronic calculator.

CHAPTER 7

The Punched Card

PUNCHED CARDS have long been used as a medium of control. It is known that as early as 1725 some use was being made of the punched card to control equipment in weaving patterns in cloth. This technique was perfected as early as 1804 in equipment which utilized an endless belt of punched cards for its weaving pattern control.

Punched cards continued to be used for control purposes throughout the early 19th century, but it wasn't until the pressure of the statistical work required by the 1880 U.S. census that punched cards were considered as data mediums for calculating and tabulating devices. The U.S. Census Bureau engaged Dr. Herman Hollerith, a noted statistician, as a special agent to aid it in solving its problem of handling the masses of statistical data which increased as the population increased. Dr. Hollerith felt that some utilization of mechanical techniques would be required, and by 1887 developed a system of recording data employing punched holes in paper strips which could be "read" automatically by a magnetic principle and used to actuate statistical equipment. The pattern of punched holes used in this system became known as the Hollerith Code and is the punched card code most widely used today.

Somewhat paralleling Dr. Hollerith's work was that of James Powers, an engineer, who was hired by the U.S. Census Bureau to develop mechanical equipment to aid in tabulating the 1910 census.

It was through the efforts of these two men, Hollerith and Powers, and others who became associated with them that the use of the punched card as a business data medium grew in acceptance and developed into the punched card information processing systems we know today.

THE PUNCHED CARD AS A UNIT RECORD

The original documents used to record the daily transactions of the normal business vary widely in size, content, and the arrangement of records. Some of these documents may be in loose-leaf form either to facilitate individual page removal and replacement, when the documents are filed as a unit, or to permit them to be filed under many differing classifications where a distribution of the data is desired. Others may be the varied individual forms representing invoices, sales tickets, freight bills, memos, etc., which originate outside the specific business firm and are really the by-products of other firms doing business with it.

It would be ideal if these varied documents could merely be gathered up, thrown into a hopper, and fed into a machine which would then choose the information necessary to produce whatever report management desired at that particular time. Obviously, however, such a procedure is impossible; the original documents must be converted into some uniform type of record before they can be used in data processing equipment. The punched card serves as such a record and, as each card is designed to contain certain facts concerning a business transaction, is sometimes called a *unit record*. After the unit record data are punched in the card and the data verified (checked), they are now coded in machine language form and are ready to be processed automatically through the various punched card machines or be used as input to a computer system to produce the desired finished reports.

One way to visualize a typical unit record would be to think of the individual debits and credits to ledger accounts. Thus each of the individual sales cards "debiting" a given customer's account as well as the returns and payments "crediting" this account are unit records. A file containing these unit record debit and credit cards would be the equivalent of the hand postings made to a traditional accounts receivable subsidiary ledger account.

WHAT CAN THE PUNCHED HOLE IN THE CARD DO?

Depending upon the information punched into the card and the capability of the machine through which the card is being processed, the hole punched in the punched card can be used for many purposes. Some of the many practical results which can be expected from the punched hole are as follows:

It will add itself to something else.
It will subtract itself from something else.
It will multiply itself by something else.
It will divide itself into something else.
It will list itself.
It will reproduce itself.
It will classify itself.
It will select itself.
It will print itself on the card.
It will produce an automatic balance forward.

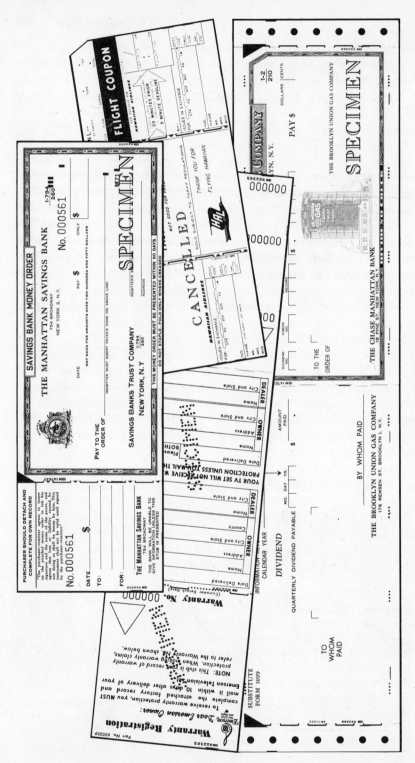

FIG. 7-1. Special Length Cards.

It will file itself.

It will post itself.

It will reproduce and print itself on the end of a card.

It will be punched from a pencil mark on the card.

It will cause a total to be printed.

It will compare itself to something else.

It will cause a form to feed to a predetermined position, or to be ejected automatically, or to space from one position to another.

The punched card, as we shall investigate it, is a thin piece of cardboard 7⅜ by 3¼ inches in size. These particular dimensions were those of our paper currency in the period of development of the punched card and were arbitrarily chosen to also be the standard size for the punched card. This type of card has become accepted as the standard card for use with all data processing equipment utilizing the punched card for either the input or output of information.

SPECIAL FEATURES AVAILABLE WITH THE CARDS

Though the standard card is the most common card size used, it is far from being the only size that can be used in standard punched card equipment. Special cards are all the same height as the standard card, but they may vary in length from one third the size of the standard card to a document 16 inches in length (Figure 7–1). These are "special" in that they are used for special or particular purposes in certain machine installations where there is a need for a card shorter or longer than the size that has become the standard.

A recent innovation in card form has been rounded corners on standard cards (Figure 7–2). This feature is particularly advantageous in

Courtesy of IBM.

FIG. 7–2.   **Rounded-Corner Card.**

types of applications that involve the repetitive use of the cards. The rounded corner cuts down on damage to the card from "dog-earing" through constant handling. It also permits the card to be inserted more smoothly into envelopes and equipment feeders, trays, files, and racks.

The basic or standard color for cards is off-white, but many other colors and color combinations are available where there is a need for color identification for the various types of information punched in cards or for special preference requirements. These colors may be in the form of stripes or bands across the card, solid-color cards, partial or overall tinted cards, or even combinations of colors, stripes, and tints to provide an almost infinite variety of combinations that can be secured by special order.

Other special features available on cards include:

1. Prenumbering and prepunching of repetitive or consecutive series of numbers for tallying and control purposes.
2. Special scoring and creasing of cards to facilitate tearing or folding.
3. Corner cuts, notches, holes, and perforations for identification purposes.
4. Tabs or stubs that extend beyond the general area of the given sized card which may serve as receipt stubs or evidence of some action taken.
5. Special printing on the face of the card so that it may be used as an invoice, check, etc.
6. Cards attached in the form of books or continuously folded cards.

Many other types of special features are also available as required for special purposes but are not used in sufficient quantity to deserve mentioning here.

BASIC TYPES OF CARDS

With the expansion of the use of punched cards into many different types of business, variations developed in the format of the card itself. These variations came about as a result of the particular uses the card was called upon to serve and the punching techniques utilized in the preparation of the card.

These variations have resulted in the cards being classified into four general types: transcript cards, dual cards, mark-sensed cards, and summary cards. Special design layout forms have also been developed to aid in a more efficient arrangement of the data to be placed on each of these types of cards.

Each of these types of punched cards has certain design limitations and special requirements in their use. Special design layout forms are available for each of the basic types of cards. These facilitate the design of a given card by providing spacings, lines, and check features which are available to that type of card. The layout form for the transcript card is shown in Figure 7–3.

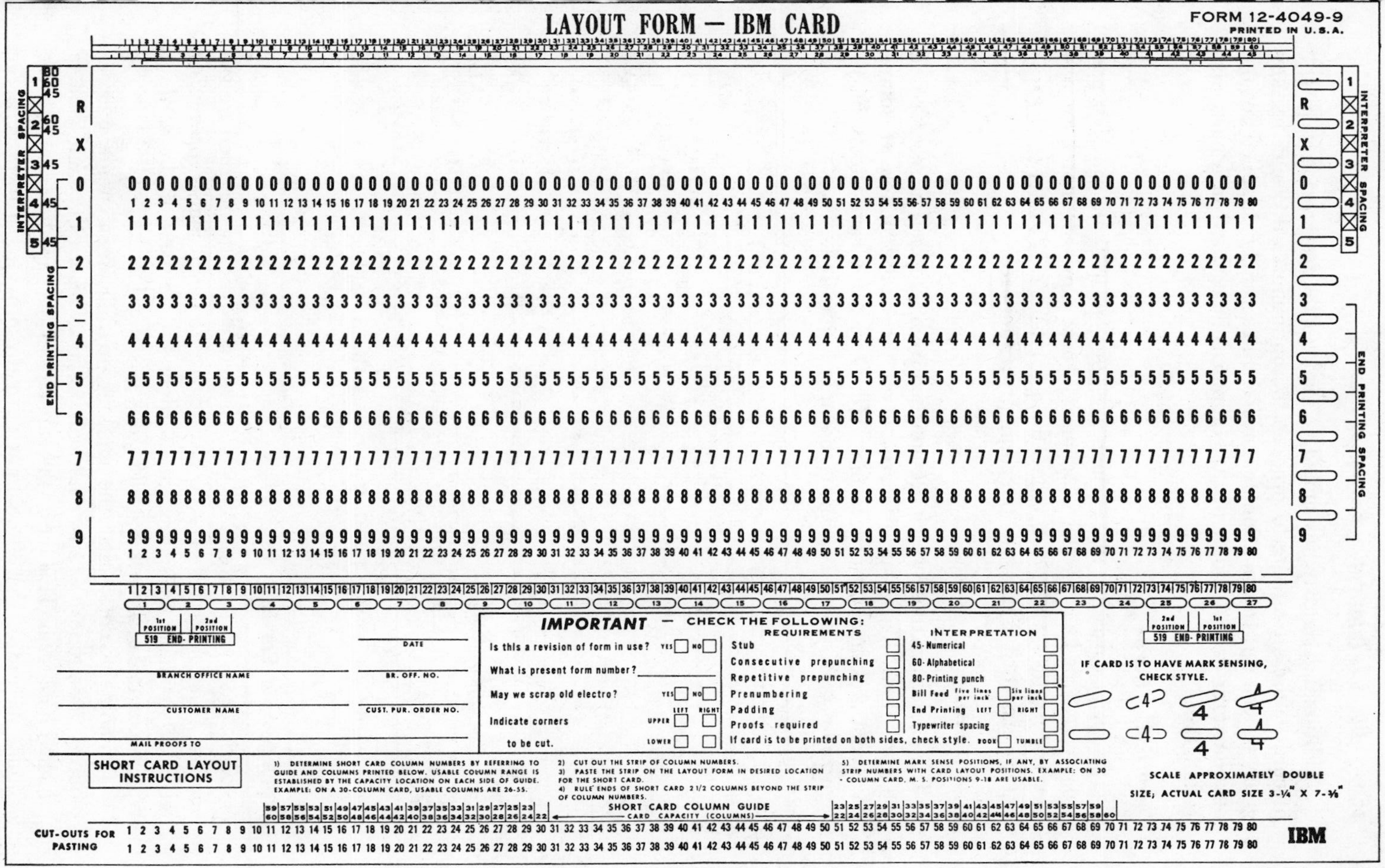

FIG. 7-3. Transcript Card Layout Form.

Courtesy of IBM.

Additional design studies should be made of the features of each type of card before attempting to produce the optimum card design for any given procedure. Information for such studies can be supplied by the manufacturer or distributor of the equipment being used in a particular installation.

Transcript Cards

Transcript cards are those which are punched from information previously recorded on another document. These cards do not have any physical features which distinguish them from some other types of cards but are classified only by the punching procedure used.

Dual Cards

Dual cards are those which are punched from information recorded on the card itself. This type of card serves the dual function of source document and machine-processable card. Dual cards vary widely in design and use. A typical example is shown in Figure 7–4.

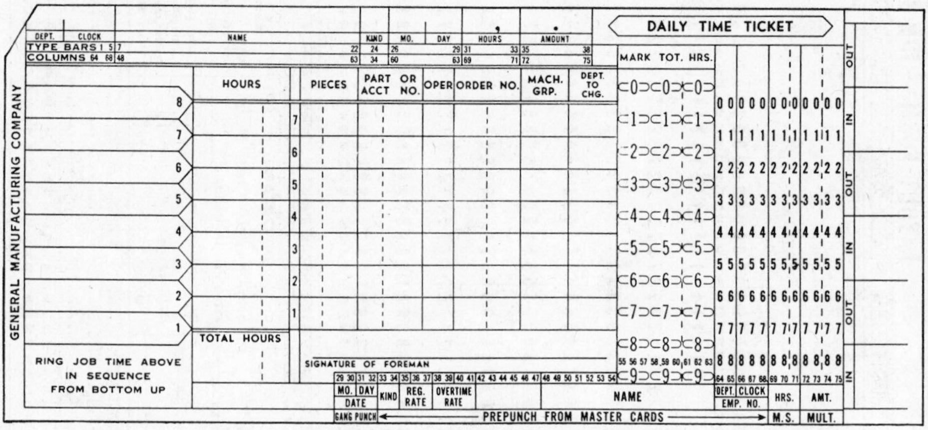

FIG. 7–4. Dual Card.

Mark-Sensed Cards

Mark-sensed cards are those which are automatically punched by the machine from electrically sensed electrographic pencil marks, previously recorded manually in significant positions on the face of the card. A typical example of a mark-sensed card is shown in Figure 7–5.

It should be noted that the marking to indicate a single number requires three times the space normally used to record the same data in punched hole form. This limits the capacity of the card to 27 mark-sense columns instead of the 80 columns normally provided. However, if the

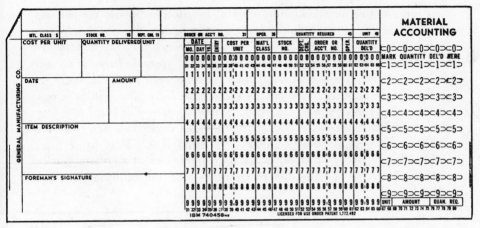

FIG. 7–5.   Mark-Sensed Card.

marked data are not to be recorded in the card containing the markings, but are to be read and punched into another or other cards, then both sides of the card may be used to provide a maximum of 54 mark-sense columns. This would, of course, require that the card be processed at two different times to permit both sides of the card to be read.

Summary Cards

Summary cards are those which are punched automatically with totals which have been accumulated from data being processed in the accounting machine or calculating punch. These cards, like the transcript cards, do not have any distinguishable physical features. A layout form used for transcript cards (Figure 7–3) can also be used in the design of summary cards.

PUNCHED CARD CODING

The standard IBM card is commonly called an 80-column card as there are 80 vertical columns available for punched holes. These vertical columns are numbered from left to right on the card from number 1 through 80.[1] Any one, several, or all of the punched columns can be selected and read or interpreted as individual alphabetical letters, numbers, or charac-

---

[1] Some Remington Rand Univac punched card equipment utilizes the same standard-sized card, but the punching is in a 90-column arrangement made up of columns 1 through 45 in the upper half of the card, and columns 46 through 90 in the lower half of the card. Round holes are punched in the six punching positions of a single column in both the upper and lower halves of the card for data representation. Numbers are represented by a single hole or a combination of two holes punched in a single column. Alphabetic characters are represented by a differing series of combinations of two or three holes punched in a single column.

ters representing pertinent information. In addition to the vertical columns there are also 12 horizontal rows in which the position of the punched hole or holes indicates to the machines whether the information in a given column is a letter, a number, or some special character such as &, $, #, %, etc. These horizontal rows are numbered from the top to the bottom of the card by zones and digits (Figure 7–6). The first three rows are the 12, 11 (sometimes called "X"), and 0 zones. The third row from the top down through the bottom row are the digit rows and are numbered for the digits they represent: 0 through 9.[2] Thus by a given punched hole, or set of holes, in the horizontal rows of a certain vertical column, it is possible for the machine to read the information represented.

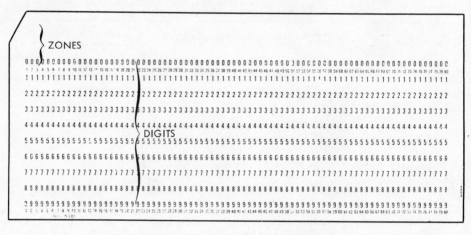

FIG. 7–6. Zone and Digit Rows.

Data to be processed in accounting machine or computer systems must be punched in the card according to a predetermined standard arrangement. This arrangement, or card design as it is usually called, is generally preselected for each individual business unit, as almost every firm has its own peculiarities as to the information pertinent to its general type of business, the arrangement in the original document of the information to be recorded in the cards for that firm, and other design features that will be touched upon later in this chapter.

This standard arrangement or grouping of information in the design of a card is made possible through the use of *fields* of information. A field of information is the designation given to any single unit, or group of information, punched into a column, or succeeding columns, in a card.

---

[2] It should be noted that while we have specified rows representing 3 zones and 10 digits, there are only 12 rows in the card. This results from using the third row as both the "0" zone and the digit zero.

Typically, this would be the data needed to represent the recording of each fact concerning a business transaction and would include such items as an address, name, invoice number, amount of a sale, etc. After the card has been punched and checked (verified), it is a permanent *unit record* which can be used to provide the information required in the many phases of data processing.

If a field consists of a single zero or number, it is punched into the card by a single rectangular punch in a predetermined column of the card (column 11, Figure 7–7). However, a field consisting of a single letter of

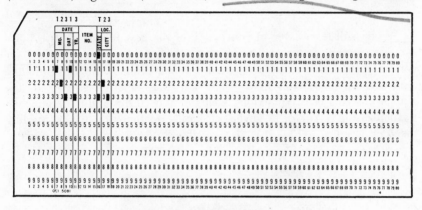

FIG. 7–7.   Field Punching.

the alphabet requires two holes to be punched in a given column of the card (column 16, Figure 7–7). Two holes are required as there are 26 letters in the alphabet, but only 12 possible positions in the card to record a letter. The combination of a high or zone punch (12, 11, or 0) with a low or digit punch (0 through 9) is used to provide the coded language of punched cards that represents the letters of the alphabet (Figure 7–8) and other special characters (Figure 7–9).

Letter	Combination Punch	Letter	Combination Punch	Letter	Combination Punch
A	12,1	J	11,1		
B	12,2	K	11,2	S	0,2
C	12,3	L	11,3	T	0,3
D	12,4	M	11,4	U	0,4
E	12,5	N	11,5	V	0,5
F	12,6	O	11,6	W	0,6
G	12,7	P	11,7	X	0,7
H	12,8	Q	11,8	Y	0,8
I	12,9	R	11,9	Z	0,9

FIG. 7–8.   Punching Procedure for the Letters of the Alphabet.

Special Character	Combination Punch	Special Character	Combination Punch
#	3,8	@	4,8
,	0,3,8	%	0,4,8
$	11,3,8	*	11,4,8
.	12,3,8	⌷	12,4,8
&	12	/	0,1

FIG. 7–9. Punching Procedure for the Special Characters.

As you will learn later in your study of the key punch, the two holes required for any letter of the alphabet and the three holes required for certain special characters are actually punched simultaneously into the card by the depression of a single key that is quite similar to the comparable key on a typewriter. A single digit (0 through 9) is punched by depressing a key on a keyboard similar to that of a 10-key adding machine (Figure 7–10). It is also possible to use a combination numeri-

Courtesy of IBM.

FIG. 7–10. Numerical Keyboard.

cal and alphabetical keyboard (Figure 7–11) with the key punch in which one keyboard is superimposed upon the other. By using a shift key, similar to the shift key used on the typewriter, a section of the keyboard serves the dual purpose of punching both alphabetical and numerical information in the card. The complete card code alphabet, punched with 26 key strokes, along with the coding for numbers and the most commonly used special characters, is shown in Figure 7–12.

If the field consists of a series of information, say three columns wide, it will be necessary to predetermine which columns are to contain this field of information. After the selection of the specific columns to be used,

charter is the small
thing information
agreed to when you sign
or stop a number for
one thing
she be a 80 field

Courtesy of IBM.

FIG. 7–11.   Combination Alphabetical and Numerical Keyboard.

the information would be punched as it is normally read, from left to right. Thus, numerical information, such as an invoice number 574, would be punched just as it is written, the five first, then the seven, and last the four. This would be read or interpreted as five hundred seventy-four.

In many instances the series of numbers to be inserted in a given designated field fails to fill completely the columns set aside for that entry. Consider an example in which the invoice number 574 is only three digits wide, but the punching instructions require this information to be punched in a five-column field. It should be evident that if the machine is to list, add, subtract, etc., such a series of numbers, the significant digits must be aligned to provide a meaningful report or answer. In punched card accounting the digits are aligned in exactly the same manner as they would be if we were writing them down by hand preparatory to adding up a series of numbers. The "unit" digits would all be in the same column,

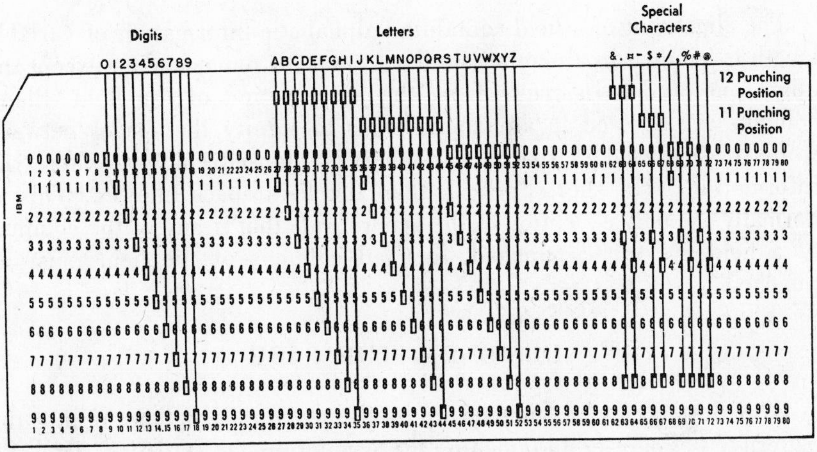

FIG. 7–12.   Card Code Punches.

the "tens" digits would be in another column, the "hundreds" digits in still another, and so on through all the significant digits.

In punching numerical information into a card, we follow this same procedure of aligning the units, tens, hundreds, etc., columns except we require all the columns in the entire field, designated for a group of information, to be punched with either a digit or a zero. If, as in the problem above where we have three columns of information to be punched in a five-column field, the series of numbers for this given card is not of sufficient length to fill the entire field, then zeros must be punched in the two columns to the left of the number and the actual field will be punched as 00574 (Figure 7–13). This procedure serves to keep the significant digits 5, 7, and 4 in their proper relation to the significant digits of invoice numbers punched in other cards.

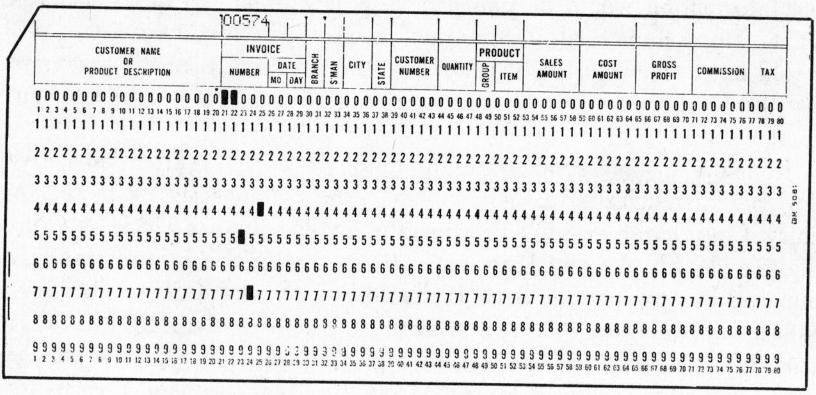

FIG. 7–13.   Field Punching.

The alignment of a field containing alphabetic information of variable length is handled in a manner similar to that for numeric data except the alignment of data is made from the left position of the field. Blank columns are allowed in alphabetic fields to signify the spaces between words or are used to space over otherwise unused columns where the information is of shorter length than the field space allowed. This is normally the only exception to the general rule that if any of the columns of a field are to be punched, then all columns of the field must be punched.

DESIGNING THE CARD

Card design can be summed up as the technique of determining the pattern to be followed in punching the accounting and statistical data of a given business firm into the cards to be processed in the accounting machine system used by that firm. At first glance, it might seem reasonable that so long as the data are put into the cards in the same columns every time, you should be able to process the cards and arrive at the reports required by the management of that firm. It is true that this procedure could possibly serve the purpose in a somewhat limited manner, but it certainly would not be a reasonable or economical method of doing so. The actual design of the card or cards to be used in a specific business is quite important. This normally requires either detailed knowledge of the entire accounting and machine system of the firm, or a study to obtain this information, to produce the optimum design for that firm.

To produce an optimum design for a particular procedure, it is essential to have a complete knowledge and understanding of the statistical, accounting, and managerial reports to be prepared from the cards, and the purposes each of these reports is expected to serve. The punched card is only a tool in the hands of the operators and clerks to be utilized in producing the desired reports. To design such a tool properly, it is also essential that you have a thorough knowledge of the machines available and the procedures to be followed in processing the data through the machines to be used.

Determination of Card Data

One of the first steps in card design is to determine the actual data that will be required in the card to meet the total needs of the business firm under consideration. To accomplish this, the following factors must be considered in the order of their presentation.

REPORT REQUIREMENTS. The most important factor affecting card design is the requirements of the finished reports to be prepared. These reports must be kept in mind constantly so that all the necessary information can be included in the card and properly arranged to facilitate the report preparation. Consideration of this factor alone could provide an ideal card design; however, these requirements may have to be subjected to some modification, as you proceed with the design of the card, to conform with some of the limiting conditions to be discussed later.

AVAILABILITY OF DATA. The next most important factor is the determination of the availability of the desired data as to whether the information to be used in the punching procedure is available in the original documents. If not, or if too much expense is involved in getting this information included in the documents, it may be necessary to revise the list of information desired, or to substitute other data which will accomplish similar purposes.

The coding procedures followed in the originating documents must be considered at this point, as the punched card is limited in the number of columns of data available. If coding has been properly considered in the design of the original business forms (Chapter 3) and if the amount of data to be recorded is not too large for the card, there is no problem. However, if either of these conditions exist, additional code consolidating techniques, to be described later, must be applied.

At this step in the study it should also be determined: if dual cards (cards which serve both as originating documents and as processing mediums) can be used advantageously to replace some of the original records; if available information can be used in ways not originally planned, or if it will be needed in the foreseeable future; and if it is desirable or necessary that the card be identified with the original record

Information Available and Required for Reports	Columns in other Cards	Sequence on Source Documents	Method of Punching	R-Reference C-Classification Q-Quantitative	Card Field Size		Final Design		Interpretation		
					Trial	Final	Field	Sequence	Field	Size	Sequence
				TOTALS →							

CARD DESIGN AID — TYPE OF CARD: CARD NAME: SOURCE DOCUMENT: Form 22-6214-1 Printed in U.S.A.

Courtesy of IBM.

FIG. 7–14.   A Work Sheet for Card Design.

from which it was punched and, if so, what method of reference punching should be used in this identification.

SUMMARIZATION OF DATA.   The final results of the above studies should then be prepared in list form on a work sheet (Figure 7–14) to aid in the assignment of the proper number of columns to each of the necessary fields. The actual sequence of the information listed is not too important at this point, but it is quite important that the list be as complete as possible before proceeding with the preliminary work necessary to develop a properly designed card.

Preliminary Work for Card Design

When we have completed the determination of the card data necessary to provide the report requirements of management, when we know that the data are available from the source documents, and when we have prepared our list of the data on the work sheet, we are ready to begin an analysis of the work sheet data in the preliminary work of actually designing the card or cards necessary in the procedures desired by this firm.

COLUMNS IN OTHER CARDS. If the company has other cards already designed for other procedures, or if several cards are being designed or redesigned simultaneously, the *alignment principle* is one of the most important factors to be considered in assigning the information available to specific card fields. A given item or field of information in the new card should always be placed in the same columns previously assigned to it in other cards.

A card designed for use in various accounting machine operations with other types of cards (such as a customer name card used with accounts receivable cards to list a statement of account, a daily time ticket card used with labor distribution cards to obtain a zero balance, or a labor distribution card with material distribution cards for cost analysis) must be aligned with these cards in the control fields that are common to both, and it is preferable that any other type of information common to the several cards should also be placed in corresponding columns. This alignment assures that the fields necessary for sorting and controlling procedures will be available in the same columns in all cards to be used together. Control-panel wiring is also facilitated when quantitative fields are placed in the same columns on all cards to be used together. A convenient layout form developed to assist the card designer in following the alignment principle, where several cards are to be used in the same processing operation, is shown in Figure 7–15.

A typical example showing the design considerations necessary in applying the alignment principle to a multiple-layout form is shown in Figure 7–16. This example involves the design of cards to be used in a rather common payroll application. The upper card in the illustration is a card 1, the middle card contains columnar headings common to both cards 3 and 4 as well as those specifically applicable to each of these cards, and the lower card contains the headings for cards 2, 5, and 9.

Card 1, the employee name and statistical data card (sometimes called personnel data card), is used as a master card in the check-writing procedure and in providing the information needed in calculating the tax deductions to be made from the employee's salary each pay period. This would normally be prepared from personnel records at the time the employee is added to the work force.

Card 2, representing current earnings for the period, is prepared from current payroll data and is taken from either a foreman's "time-worked" sheet or the time clock card itself.

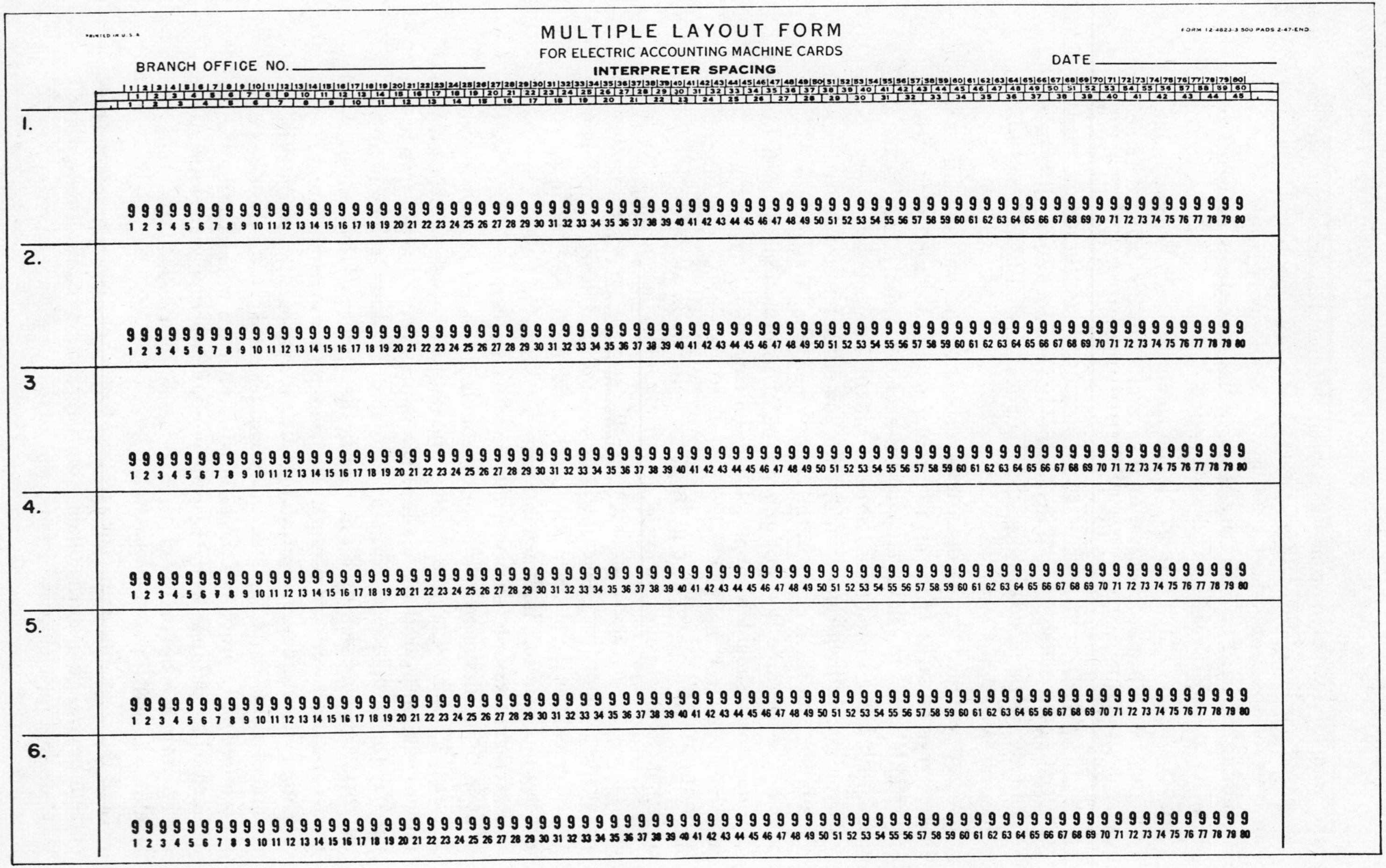

FIG. 7-15. Multiple-Card Layout Form.

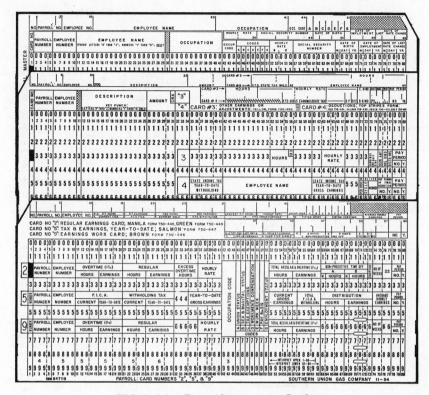

FIG. 7–16.   Data Alignment in Cards.

Card 3 is used to report other earnings such as commissions, bonus, and earnings which are not associated with the employee's regular hourly, weekly, or monthly earnings.

Card 4 shows the typical information needed for the required or authorized deductions which are customarily withheld from an individual's pay check. Such a deduction card may be prepared from a deduction authorization memo signed by the employee or it may be a dual card which will serve as both the authorization by the employee and as the machine-processable document. It would, of course, be necessary to furnish a card for each applicable deduction as required in our previous description of a unit record.

Card 5, the earnings-to-date card, shows the accumulative status of the salary payments made to the employee over a period of time. This card would provide the year-to-date information that would be used in determining if the accumulated maximum salary limits had been reached in considering the employee's deduction for the social security tax and the employer's liability for unemployment insurance. The new updated card prepared with each payroll payment would normally be prepared in a summary punch operation at the time the current paycheck is written on an accounting machine.

Card 9, the earnings work card or check card, contains pertinent information needed in the check-writing procedure and is used, along with the other cards above, to prepare the actual check itself.

Data common to all six cards includes column 1 (card number), columns 2 through 5 (payroll number), columns 6 through 10 (employee number). Occupation and other codes in columns 42 through 51 are common in cards 1, 2, 5, and 9. Pay period (columns 78, 79, and 80) is common data in all cards except the statistical data card (card 1). Earnings information in cards 2 and 9 is common in providing hourly rate data and detail information on overtime, regular, total hours, and total earnings (columns 11 through 31, 37 through 41, and 52 through 62). The deduction cards (3 and 4) have description and amount (columns 12 through 31) in common.

There are, of course, other items common to two or more of these cards, but the data listed above are typical of an application of the *alignment principle* in cards that may be used together in one or more processing applications.

Once we have completed the proper coordination of the various cards of the firm, in aligning the information common to cards that may be used together in the accounting procedures to be applied, it is necessary to consider further the design of each of these various cards on an individual basis. A separate form should be used for the detail necessary for each card to be designed. Typical layout forms for the different types of cards were previously illustrated under "Basic Types of Cards."

SEQUENCE ON SOURCE DOCUMENTS. In Chapter 4 the layout of the business document was stressed. The layout becomes much more important when the ultimate use and disposition of the data are considered. This is particularly true when one considers the design and layout of data on a punched card.

In card punching, it is desirable that the key punch operator be able to read the information needed from the originating document by letting the eye read from left to right and from the top to the bottom of the page as we are accustomed to do in any normal reading function. If this pattern is not followed, it not only makes it difficult for the operator to be accurate in randomly selecting data from the document, but it is very tiring to the operator as well.

If the document layout is properly planned, the key punch operator's task will be greatly simplified and will result in both improved accuracy and increased output.

As previously stated, it is important that the ultimate use of the data be considered in the design of any business document. However, this becomes imperative in documents to be used in key punch operations as the disadvantages are so great that the card data design may be forced to conform to the arrangement of the data on the originating document. The many limitations and restrictions which poor card design places upon any automated card system may be so severe that the economic feasibility of the system itself may be questioned.

METHOD OF PUNCHING. Assign to each field the method by which it will be punched, i.e., keypunched, duplicated, summary punched, gang punched, or calculator punched. All similar punching operations should be grouped together to simplify wiring, and to eliminate interspersed skipping on the key punch.

TYPES OF INFORMATION. All information available for punching in the card should be classified as one of the three following basic types:

1. *Reference data,* which is used to identify the original source of data (date, invoice number, batch number, etc.).
2. *Classification data,* by which the transaction is cross-indexed and classified to produce the desired summaries (state, department, customer number, part number).
3. *Quantitative data,* which may be subjected to addition, subtraction, multiplication, or division (quantity on hand, unit price, sales amount).

After each item or field of information is so classified, consideration should be given to arranging the data in the following manner: reference information should be placed to the left of the card; classification information should be placed in the center of the card; and quantitative information should be placed to the right of the card.

The four important considerations above (columns in other cards, sequence on source documents, methods of punching, and types of information) have been discussed in the order of their importance in determining the position of information on cards. It is evident, however, that there will be frequent conflicts among these requirements, and when such conflicts arise, it will be necessary to use the good judgment that should come to you as you gain experience in resolving these conflicts on some sort of priority basis.

SIZE OF FIELDS. Our next step is to determine the number of columns required to record each type of information to be punched in the card. For reference and controlling fields the columns required will be determined by the largest single number to be recorded, as indicated by the codes which have been devised for the machine application. Thus, 2 columns might be left for the month (12 being the largest number), 2 for the day, 4 for invoice numbers if the number series is repeated after 9,999 is reached, and 2 for branch if there are 99 branches or less.

With the quantitative fields, the problem becomes more difficult. In the first place, the space needed to record the largest amount may not be known, and in the second place, this amount may be very unusual. It is a good plan to provide enough columns to take care of all except the unusual cases, which may be handled by punching extra cards or by using the class selection device. For example, in most typical retail stores, sales to individuals would rarely exceed a total amount of $999.99 for any single purchase. A five-column field in the card would be adequate for any sale up to this amount. However, if there were a sale in the amount of $4,684.40 to one individual, under some special circumstance, this might be recorded in a five-column field by punching four cards of $999.99 and one card for $684.44 (or you could use any combination of five-digit numbers totaling the $4,684.40).

The possibility of consolidating certain fields on the card should be considered at this time. Several types of information can be carried in a single field if they do not occur simultaneously, and the original list should be checked for this possibility. Particularly in the case of quantity and amount fields, it may be preferable to use successive cards, with different quantities and amounts in a specific quantity and amount field in each card, rather than have the data fields spread over a wide area of one card.

The total of the number of columns assigned to all fields will indicate if the data you desire to punch in the card is within the capacity of the card, or if it will exceed it. When the columns total less than about 100, the decision must be made whether to use two cards or to reduce the number of columns to 80. If the total number of columns reaches 100 or more, it is generally evident that more than one card is needed. If more than one card is indicated as being needed, it will require separating or classifying the desired information into blocks or groupings to determine what information is to be placed in each card. Your decision to make such a division may be based upon any one of several schemes:

1. Place repetitive or recurring information in one card and temporary or nonrepeating information in a second card. This might be typical of instances involving detail and master cards.

2. Use different cards for different source documents where more than one source document is used in recording the data used in a single procedure.

3. Make one of the new cards a dual card or mark-sensed card which may be used as both a source document and as a machine-processable document.

4. Use different cards for different degrees of detail or as "double-entry" cards, each of which affects two different accounts. Examples are accounts payable and payables distribution cards, accounts receivable and sales cards, and payroll and labor distribution cards.

5. Use separate cards to produce the desired form of report. As an example, customer invoice procedures may contain heading cards, miscellaneous data cards, and detail commodity cards. Such an arrangement may actually result in a better-designed form of invoice and permit the use of very simple procedures in its preparation.

Where the total number of columns is only slightly above the maximum of 80 columns available in the card, it may be possible to use some of the following expedients to bring the actual requirements within the capacity of the card without omitting any of the fields desired:

1. You may reduce the size of the controlling or reference fields by using these fields as subclassifications of other fields. Invoice numbers may be reassigned each month, salesmen's numbers may be for each branch rather than one series for all branches, or store numbers for each branch or state instead of one series of numbers for all the stores owned by the firm.

2. Attempt to reduce the size of the controlling or reference fields to eliminate one or more digits through some recoding procedure. As an example, a series of numbers from 1 to 26 would require two columns, but the 26 letters of the alphabet would only require one column.

3. It may be possible that all of the digits in a reference or control field are not absolutely essential to preserve positive identification. Only four digits of a six-digit invoice or part number might be all that is necessary for its identification.

4. To repeat an already-mentioned technique, reduce the size of quantitative fields where amounts rarely exceed the capacity of the reduced field and use several cards whose totals will add up to the amount required.

5. Multiple punching can be used in some fields where the data are not to be listed or added. This could even be desirable at times in fields used solely for sorting purposes.

6. The group-sorting device may also be used to eliminate certain common information from detail cards.

INTERPRETATION. Data fields which are to be interpreted should be arranged according to the method of filing used. The more important information should be put in a prominent location to aid in its visual selection and reference.

At the present time the most commonly used interpreters will only interpret and print 60 characters of information on any single line. (The IBM 548 prints on either the space above the 12-zone punch position or between the 12- and 11-zone punch positions. The IBM 557 will print on any one of 25 different lines on the card.) Consideration should be given, if the total number of columns to be interpreted exceeds 60, to the placement of the most important data on the first line and data of lesser importance on the second, or other lines. If only slightly more than one line of data is scheduled for interpretation, it would, of course, be preferable to recheck the data to determine if any columns of interpreted data can be eliminated so that the interpretation may be limited to one line.

Changes in setups on the interpreter can be simplified by preprinting the type bar numbers to be used in each different setup in the printing spaces between the punching rows (Figure 7–17). This is particularly

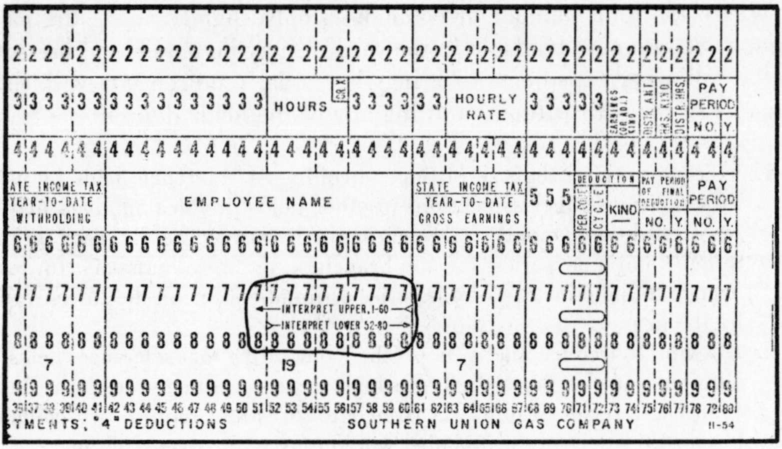

FIG. 7–17.   Interpreter Setup Instructions.

useful when there are several changes of machine setups in the interpretation of 80 column cards.

Machine Considerations in Card Design

To design uniform machines to do the various tasks of automatic accounting required in the many types of business, it is necessary to accept some construction specifications and typical methods to be used in the performance of the machines as standards. Whenever a standard is accepted, it puts some basic restrictions on any procedure or application that varies from this standard. In machine accounting these restrictions are such that they do not necessarily limit the overall accounting routine itself, but they are factors that must be considered in applying the requirements of a given business to specific procedures.

Each type of machine to be used in a given installation must be investigated to determine the specific limitations applicable to its use.

ANNOTATED BIBLIOGRAPHY

DeParis, Joseph R.   "Card Punching Still Prime as Computer Input," *Data Processing Magazine,* Vol. 7 (May, 1965), pp. 40–84.

Despite the sophisticated advances in data processing hardware and techniques, keypunching and verifying cards continue as the major medium for creating machine-sensible computer input. Now this system is being improved upon. At present the procedure is to punch cards from source documents and then to do a card-to-tape operation. A device will soon be marketed which will change this basic cycle to one in which, for many,

Some just have only one field
is a records
Several relative record is called filed

7—The Punched Card   173

application cards will be eliminated and keying will be done directly to magnetic tape from source document data. The essential features of this device are described.

INTERNATIONAL BUSINESS MACHINES CORPORATION. *An Introduction to IBM Punched Card Data Processing. A General Information Manual.* White Plains, N.Y., n.d.

The IBM punched card is explained and illustrated in the first section of this manual. Methods of using this card are explained, and the types of coding used are also considered.

———. *Punched Card Data Processing Principles,* "Section 1: The IBM Card and Its Preparation." White Plains, N.Y., 1961.

A complete and thorough discussion of the characteristics and uses of the IBM card is given in this booklet. The machines used in punching and verifying the punches are also explained and illustrated.

MESTEMACHER, ROY. "Basic Automatic Data Processing," *Hospital Accounting,* May, 1964, pp. 6–9.

The history and development of the punched card approach to automatic data processing are traced, beginning with Babbage's "analytic engine." Also described is a basic unit record installation. Each ADP system has three main stages: input, processing, and output. The items which constitute a punched card system are as follows: the language converter, the data classifier, the data manipulators, and the report producer. Each such item may contain one or more pieces of equipment.

NELSON, O. S., and WOODS, R. S. *Accounting Systems and Data Processing,* chap. xviii. Cincinnati: South-Western Publishing Co., 1961.

The first part of this chapter explains the punched card and its characteristics. The chapter also discusses quite a few different ways in which the card can be used in an accounting system.

RANDALL, C. B.; WEIMER, S. W.; and GREENFIELD, M. S. *Systems and Procedures for Automated Accounting.* Cincinnati: South-Western Publishing Co., 1962.

Chapter 6 in this book explains the characteristics and uses of both the IBM and Remington Rand punched cards. Special types of cards, such as mark-sense cards, are also discussed.

STAININGER, GEORGE E. "The Punched Card: A Unit Memory Device." Paper in the *Proceedings of the Fourth Annual Accounting Systems Conference, 1960.* Reprinted in *Management Services Handbook* (ed. HENRY DE VOS), chap. v, pp. 245–54. New York: American Institute of Certified Public Accountants, 1964.

Staininger describes at first the characteristics of the punched card and then—in detail—its applications.

WANOUS, S. J., and WANOUS, E. E. *Automation Office Practice.* Cincinnati: South-Western Publishing Co., 1964.

The second section of this book is devoted to describing the standard punched card. The methods of using this card and the advantages of recording numerical information on cards are also discussed.

QUESTIONS

1. Why is a punched card often called a unit record?
2. Why would anyone be interested in using punched cards of different colors?
3. Carefully describe the function of each of the four general types of punched card. Be certain to differentiate between each type.
4. What is the difference between the Hollerith or IBM card and the Remington Rand Univac card?
5. How would you describe a field of information?
6. What is the function of zone punches?
7. How many holes must be punched in a card column to represent numerical data? Alphabetic? Special Characters?
8. Briefly sketch the basic layout of a punched card and indicate how you would punch your name and today's date in the card.
9. Why must "zeros" be punched in all the columns to the left of the largest significant digit in a field when the data are not large enough to utilize all the columns of the field?
10. What basic data must be determined before the preliminary card design work can be started? Why?
11. What is the correlation between the design of the punched card and the business document from which the data are to be transcribed?
12. Discuss the *alignment principle* as it applies in the field of card design.
13. What is the significance of classifying data as reference data, classification data, and quantitative data?
14. What alternatives exist when there are more data than can be accommodated on one punched card? What factors or conditions might lead you to choose one alternative over another?
15. Under what conditions might it be necessary or desirable to have a punched card interpreted?
16. (*a*) Using the information found on the Time Card in Figure 1–2, page 12, design the layout of a punched card assuming that you were intending to transcribe the data from the timecard and punch it into the punched card. In doing this, be certain to follow the recommendations of this chapter. (*b*) Explain how you have designed each field of information as well as the reason for placing each field of information where you have it.

CHAPTER 8

Punched Card Machines

IN CHAPTER 4 the basic data processing functions of originating, classifying, sorting, calculating, summarizing, recording, and communicating were shown to be fundamental to the processing of business information. The capabilities of manual and mechanical processing methods were then applied to these same functions in chapters which followed.

In this chapter the capabilities of electromechanical or, as they are more commonly known, punched card machines, will be related to these same basic functions. By now, it should be apparent that these functions apply to the processing of all data regardless of the methods or equipment used in accomplishing the actual processing procedures.

In manual data processing, utilizing the pen or pencil, all of the basic functions were performed by hand or manually. It was discovered, however, that part of the repetition and transcription could be facilitated through the use of specialized forms, carbons, mark sensing, and other techniques.

In mechanical data processing the same required data processing functions were performed, but mechanical devices were used to increase the speed and accuracy of some of the processing procedures.

Now, with punched card equipment, the same basic processing functions are performed even faster and more accurately. In a punched card data processing system, once the data are coded and punched into the card or other machine-acceptable form, all the processing functions can be completed on this equipment. However, given punched card machines can only perform a specific function or functions, and the procedures necessary are completed in their proper sequence by transporting the data, in its punched card form, from machine to machine.

It will be discovered later, when the computer is studied, that these same procedures, based on the fundamental concepts in Chapter 4, must be followed step-by-step in electronic data processing. In EDP the data are originated in one of many machine-acceptable forms. The computer is instructed in the processing steps it is to follow by instructions stored in the available "memory." The data are fed into the computer, and all the processing functions necessary to the procedures required are completed automatically, with the individual processing steps being performed in millionths or even billionths of a second.

Note particularly that the procedures to be followed in the processing of business information are exactly the same—regardless of the methods used: manual, mechanical, punched card, or electronic data processing. It is only the equipment and the functions performed by given equipment that are new as one progresses in the techniques which permit business information to be processed at faster and faster speeds.

PUNCHED CARD MACHINE CAPABILITIES

The processing capabilities available through the use of punched card equipment include all the basic data processing functions. These functions are provided through the techniques of punching, verification, classifying, reporting, arithmetic calculations, and communication.

The International Business Machines Corporation and the Univac Division of the Sperry Rand Corporation are the two major manufacturers of punched card equipment in the United States. The National Cash Register Company and others, however, manufacture specific types of punched card equipment.

The equipment available in punched card systems is both flexible and variable. It is flexible in that some given machines are capable of performing more than one function in meeting the demands of the procedures required. It is variable in that many combinations of equipment are available to perform most given procedures, some of which will provide more efficient results as well as much greater speed in completing the function(s) necessary.

Punching

Card punching is a primary activity in a punched card system, as it provides the data input medium required by the system. Card punching can be performed under a variety of circumstances. Some punched cards may be provided as simply as those punched by a hand-operated device, others as complexly as those punched as the by-product of an accumulation or calculating procedure in accounting machines or calculating punches.

CARD PUNCHING. The basic method of converting source information into the punched card, in automatic machine-acceptable form, is through the use of card punch equipment (Figure 8–1). This function is performed by an operator who reads the source information and depresses keys on the keyboard of the equipment (Figure 8–2) which cause coded holes to be punched into selected vertical columns of the card. Depending

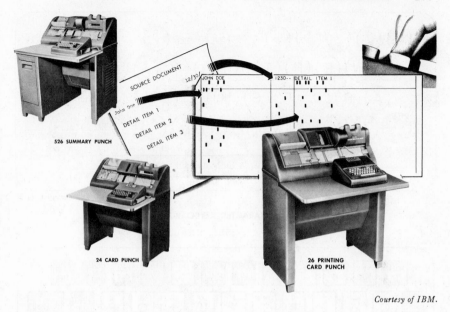

Courtesy of IBM.

FIG. 8–1. Card Punch.

on the model of the equipment, numeric, alphabetic, or a combination of numeric or alphabetic information may be punched. If a printing card punch is used, the data punched may also be printed, column by column, at the top of the card directly above the coded punch in the card. If a card proof punch is used, an adding machine tape may be produced, as a by-product of punching, where a printed record of the data and a total of one of the punched fields is also desired.

There are five basic card positions on the card punch (Figure 8–3). First, the *card hopper* where the input cards are stored until they are fed downward to the punch bed in feed position where they are held under the *card lever pressure finger.* Cards are advanced from the feed position under the *punching station* where they advance column by column as data are punched or the column skipped because no data are required. Once the card is punched or fed through the punching station, it moves to the read bed and is positioned under the *reading station* as a second card is positioned under the punching station. This card advances synchronously with the card in the punching position and may, if so instructed, be "read" by the brushes at this station so the data may be transferred (duplicated) into the card under the punch to perform the duplication function below. As cards advance through the reading station

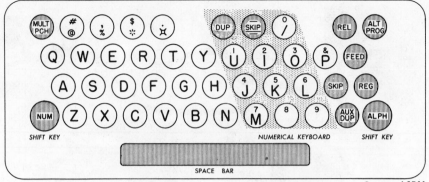

Courtesy of IBM.

46-CHARACTER KEYBOARD

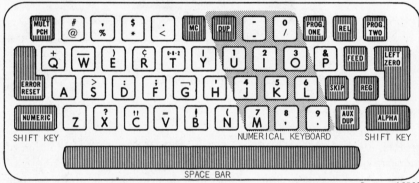

Courtesy of IBM.

64-CHARACTER KEYBOARD

FIG. 8–2.   Card Punch Keyboards.

they are eventually "stacked" in the *stacker position* until either the punching operation is completed or the stacker position acquires sufficient cards to push the toggle type *main line switch* to "off" position which cuts the electrical power to the equipment.

The *program unit* at the top center of Figure 8–3 is controlled by a program card wrapped around the program drum (Figure 8–4). This program card has coded holes punched in it which are read by the program unit and instruct the machine in such automatic operations as the automatic skipping or duplication of certain columns or fields in the data card. These columns or fields in the program card are also defined by coded punches. Inasmuch as the operating mode of the equipment is always numerical when it is under program control (alphabetic when under manual control), there is a provision for an automatic shift to the

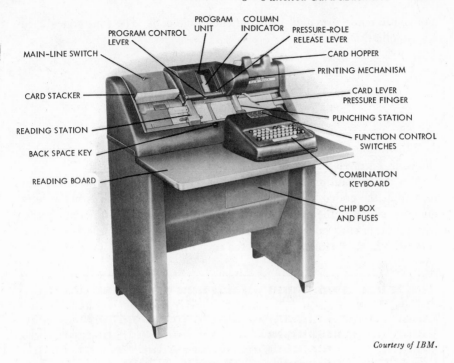

Courtesy of IBM.

FIG. 8–3.   IBM 26 Printing Card Punch.

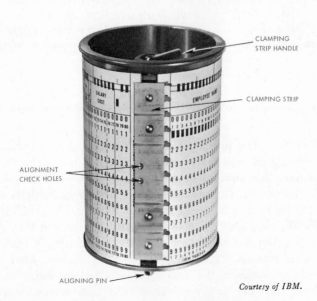

Courtesy of IBM.

FIG. 8–4.   Program Drum.

alphabetic mode provided by a punched hole code. The four codes used are as follows:

Code	Function
12	Field definition
11	Start automatic skip
0	Start automatic duplication
1	Alphabetic shift

An illustration of a typical program card and the operation controlled is shown in Figure 8–5.

A word of caution to the student is always necessary at this point regarding the coded holes in the program card. This code is not in any manner related to the coded information to be punched in the data cards. The program card code is only used to control certain automatic operations which may be performed on the card punch.

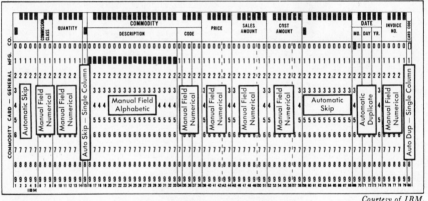

Courtesy of IBM.

FIG. 8–5.   Program Card.

DUPLICATING.   The primary function performed by card punches is that of recording or even originating, in punched hole form, the needed data. However, this equipment may also duplicate all or part of the information in one card into another card. This permits data, such as a date, in a master card to be duplicated into all the cards to follow (Figure 8–6). Thus the data only have to be punched once and they are accurately and quickly punched into other cards. Duplicating is performed by the equipment through "reading," at the read station, what is in the master card and punching the same data into the card being punched in the punch station. The newly punched card then moves into the read position, as the master card is fed into the stacker position, where it

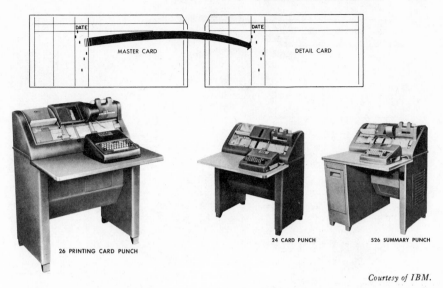

FIG. 8–6. Duplicating.

becomes, in effect, a new master card to provide the data to be placed in the new card now in the punch position. This read-punch combination operation is performed one column at a time as the two cards move to the left, under their respective positions, from column to column.

The function of duplicating reduces the work to be performed on each card and, while assuring accuracy in the transferral of data, increases the productivity of the equipment operator.

REPRODUCING. The card punching function, like that of duplicating, causes data to be transferred from one card to another. However, where duplicating on the card punch transfers data from one card to another, which passes the data to the third and is performed one punch at a time, reproducing is performed in various reproducing machines by transferring data from one deck (group) of cards to another, card by card (Figure 8–7). This transferral can be the complete copying of one card into another, or only selected data may be transferred. Also, if desired, the data in one card may be moved, as to its columnar placement as it is transferred, through the use of wired control panels (Figure 8–8) which serve to tell the machine what is desired.

The major features of the 514 Reproducing Punch, which is typical of reproducing equipment, include:

1. Two feed hoppers, primary and secondary, and their respective card stackers. The feed hoppers accept data and/or blank cards, depending

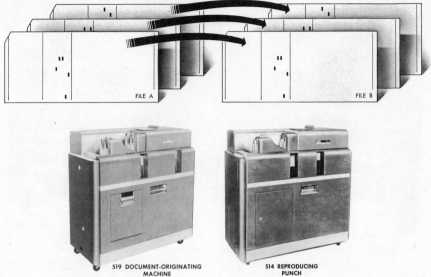

FILE A   FILE B

519 DOCUMENT-ORIGINATING   514 REPRODUCING
        MACHINE   PUNCH

Courtesy of IBM.

FIG. 8–7.   Reproducing.

on the function desired, and after the function is completed feeds the cards into the card stackers.

2. A comparing indicator unit which indicates if there is any variance in the data in each of the original, or master, deck of cards and the cards which have been reproduced. If a variance is discovered, the comparing indicator will show not only that an error exists but the columns in the card which are in error.

3. A summary punch cable which is used to connect the reproducing punch to an accounting machine to permit the summary punching of data read and gathered by the accounting machine.

4. A switch board which provides switches which alter the function to be performed by the equipment. These alternatives include some variations in the functions of reproduction and verifying, gang punching, a combination of reproduction and gang punching, mark-sense reading and punching, as well as blank-column and double-punch detection.

5. A wired control panel which permits the operator to predetermine the columns to be read, or selected, from input data and columns to be punched in output cards.

GANG PUNCHING.   Another function, somewhat similar to that of duplicating and reproducing, is that of gang punching. This is performed on basically the same equipment as used in reproducing (Figure 8–7) and is like both duplicating and reproducing in that data is punched from one card to another. However, gang punching is punching all or part of the data in a master card into succeeding cards (Figure 8–9). It is similar to duplicating in that a master card is used for all cards to be gang punched. It is also similar to reproducing in that all or part of the data from a single card can be punched into other cards, but gang punching is the production of one or many cards from a single card rather than a one-for-one reproduction.

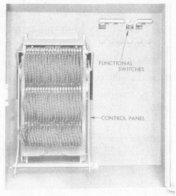

Courtesy of IBM.

FIG. 8–8. 514 Control Panel and Switches.

There are two basic types of gang punching. *Single master card gang punching* uses one master card placed in front of a deck of blank or detail cards to produce all the other cards desired. Where groups of data decks are desired from a number of master cards containing different data, the function performed is called *interspersed gang punching*. In this last form of gang punching, the master cards are interspersed into a deck of blank or detail data cards. As a master card is read, its data will be placed in all the cards which follow until another master card is read. This new master data is then placed in the cards following this second master card.

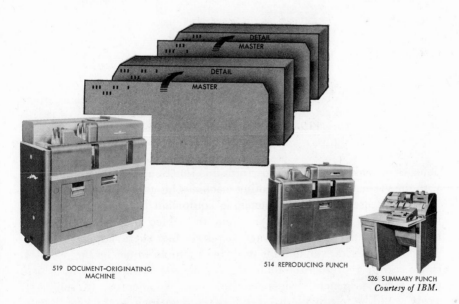

519 DOCUMENT–ORIGINATING MACHINE

514 REPRODUCING PUNCH

526 SUMMARY PUNCH
Courtesy of IBM.

FIG. 8–9. Gang Punching.

Gang punching may be performed separately or in combination with reproduction and summary punching for both alphabetical and numerical information.

SUMMARY PUNCHING. This function is that of automatically converting data, read into or developed by one of the various accounting machines, into coded punched holes in a card. Several types of summary

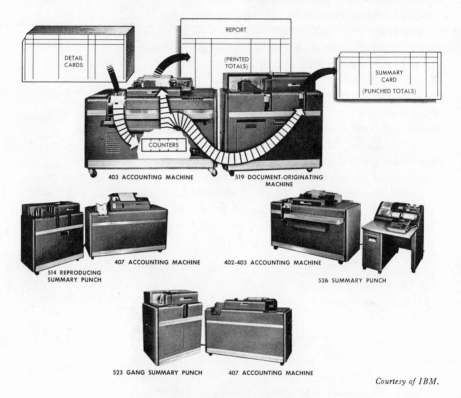

Courtesy of IBM.

FIG. 8–10.   Summary Punching.

punches, or equipment which perform this function, are available for use with the various types of accounting machines (Figure 8–10).

A major use of summary punching equipment is to provide summarized totals of large volumes of data to reduce the volume of card handling and the ensuing storage requirements where large masses of data must be held available for use. One example would be the use of a single card to represent the total sales for the day, week, or month which could serve as general ledger account data. Another use of summary cards would be to provide balance forward data such as the year-to-date information needed in a payroll procedure to determine if the payee is subject to a F.I.C.A. tax deduction or if deductions have previously been made on the maximum requirement.

MARK SENSING.   The mark-sense technique of automatically punching cards from especially marked areas on a card (Figure 8–11) has been discussed at length as to design, production, and use in both Chapters 4 and 7 and is mentioned here only as another method of performing the punching function on punched card equipment.

CONVERSION.   Punched paper tape may be produced as a by-product of the operation of a cash register, adding machine, or typewriter. This is

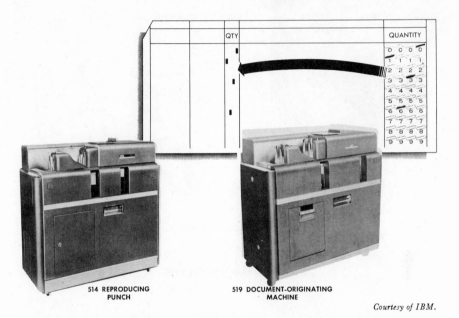

514 REPRODUCING
PUNCH

519 DOCUMENT-ORIGINATING
MACHINE

Courtesy of IBM.

FIG. 8–11.   Mark-Sensed Punching.

a form of data origination at the point of the transaction. It has many valuable uses which will be developed in depth in later chapters.

If the processing system in use is a punched card system, the punched paper tape will not be an acceptable processable data medium. This is the function of paper tape conversion to transfer the coded data on the punched paper tape to coded data in punched card form. Once the reel of tape is fed into the tape-to-card punch, the data in it are automatically converted to punched cards (Figure 8–12).

Other conversion devices convert punched cards into punched paper tape code and create punched cards as a by-product of typewriting.

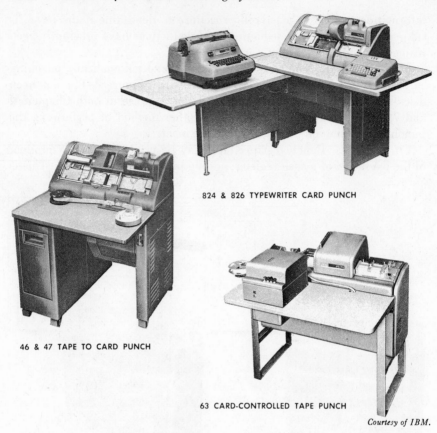

824 & 826 TYPEWRITER CARD PUNCH

46 & 47 TAPE TO CARD PUNCH

63 CARD-CONTROLLED TAPE PUNCH

Courtesy of IBM.

FIG. 8–12.   Conversion.

Verification

Recording the data in the form of punched cards is, of course, necessary to provide input data for punched card and many computer information processing systems. Inasmuch as the data recorded on punched cards are used as input to these systems, it is essential that they be correct both as to the data and their placement in the card. Inaccurate data can only result in inaccurate and unusable reports. In computer room jargon, this is sometimes expressed, "garbage in—garbage out" (GIGO).

CARD VERIFYING.   One of the most common pieces of equipment used to check the accuracy of the data in the card is the card verifier (Figure 8–13). In appearance the card verifier is quite similar to the card punch. However, where the depression of a key on the keyboard of the punch causes one or more holes to be punched in a given column of the card, the

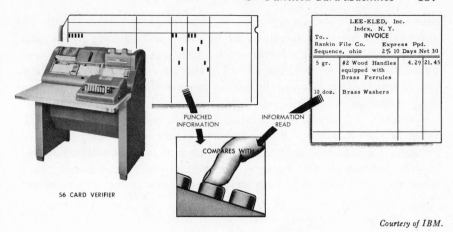

Courtesy of IBM.

FIG. 8–13.   Verifying.

depression of the same key position on the verifier will merely result in a check of the holes in the card to determine if those holes agree with the ones which should be there for that given number, letter, or character. If the coded holes are satisfactory, the card moves to the next column, where the operation is repeated and continues until the data check of the entire card is completed. As the card is checked and is moved into the next operating position, a notch is cut in the upper right edge of the card to indicate that verification is completed (Figure 8–14).

When the data in the card do not agree with the key depressed, the error light comes on and the keyboard locks. An error key is depressed and a second attempt at verification is made. If the data and the de-

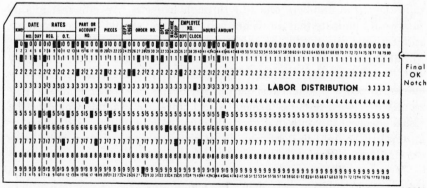

Courtesy of IBM.

FIG. 8–14.   Verified Card.

pressed key still do not agree, a third attempt is made. If still no agreement is found on the third try, the card will advance to the next column in the card, but an error notch will be cut in the top of the card above the column error (Figure 8–15). This provides a ready identification of cards with errors and the column in error after the verification of a deck of cards is completed.

EDITING.   While still a verification function, editing differs from verifying in that a hole, or holes, punched in a given column or set of columns in a card may represent a valid code as far as a verification test may be concerned—for instance, the number six (6). However, in a given statistical data field, only certain particular codes may represent

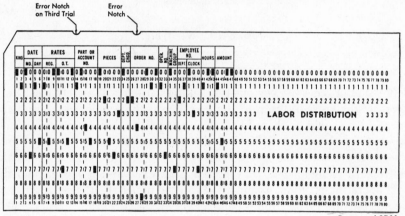

Courtesy of IBM.

FIG. 8–15.   Error Card.

valid data: the numbers one (1) through five (5). An edit test of this data would indicate that a 6 is not valid data and should not be accepted, and it will be rejected by the editing equipment.

CHECKING.   The word "check" is frequently used interchangeably with "verifying" and "editing." More commonly, checking should only be considered a physical test performed by people rather than the previously described tests performed by machines. An example would be the visual check of the data in a given column by holding two cards together up toward the light to determine if, in given columns, the punched holes are similar or different.

PROVING.   The function of proving is generally used in conjunction with the calculation of data in which the results obtained are "proved"—usually by some technique of reverse arithmetic. This proof may be performed either by people or machines.

CROSSFOOTING. To crossfoot is to add up a group of totals to determine if the answer agrees with the total obtained from the associated mass of data. Usually, it involves a test of the total of horizontal versus a total of vertical totals of the same set of arrayed data.

COMPARING. The function of comparing is normally performed by looking or testing for similarities in given data. However, it may also be used in testing for differences in the data.

DOUBLE-PUNCH DETECTION. The phrase "double-punch detection" is almost self-explanatory. In punched card systems it involves a test of data, in a given column, to determine if more than one punched hole is present in a column which should only contain a single punch. An example would be a test to determine if a character or an alphabetic letter is present in a numerical field of information. If a double punch is found in such a field, an error condition exists.

BLANK-COLUMN DETECTION. The function of blank-column detection involves a specific test for columns which should contain data, but in which none is present. This is usually an error condition which should be brought to the attention of the equipment operator.

Classifying

A number of techniques either perform, or aid in, the function of classifying data into groups or patterns of data in punched card information processing systems. These techniques include those of sorting, selecting, sequence checking, merging, matching, and programming.

SORTING. The procedure of arranging a deck of cards into groups, which are in turn arranged in either a numerical or alphabetical sequence, according to any particular classification punched in them is that of sorting (Figure 8–16). It was the need for a fast and efficient method of sorting data, to facilitate the reporting function, that prompted Dr. Hollerith to develop the sorter as one of his first pieces of punched card equipment.

Sorting is perhaps the classification function most frequently required in punched card work, and a set of specialized equipment has been developed for just this purpose.

NUMERICAL SORTING. In a numerical sort the selection switches on the sorter must first be set for numerical sorting, then the data must be sorted on each column of the field to be arranged. If there is only a single column in the field, a single pass through the sorter will put the data in the desired order, if it is removed from the sorter's stacking pockets properly. However, if there are more than one column in the field of data, the procedure is usually to sort first on the units position of the data, then the tens, hundreds, etc., until all the columns have been sorted.

BLOCK SORTING. A procedure used where large volumes of data are to be arranged, or where more than one sorter is available for use, is that of block sorting. This usually involves breaking the card deck down into blocks of data by sorting on the largest significant digit first. Then other sorters may be used to continue the sorting process. Even if only a single sorter is available, block sorting may be advisable as the first block may be sorted and processing started on other equipment while the sort of the second and following blocks of data is completed. The value of block sorting depends entirely on the need or ability to utilize other equipment to speed up the information processing.

ALPHABETIC SORTING.   In an alphabetic sort, where it is necessary that there be two coded holes in each column to represent a letter (see

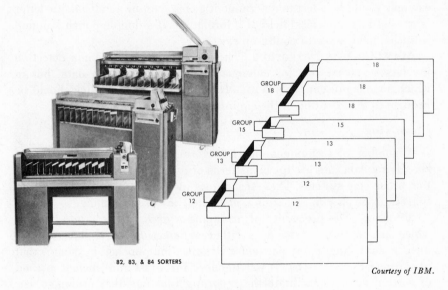

82, 83, & 84 SORTERS

Courtesy of IBM.

FIG. 8–16.   Sorting.

Figure 7–8), two sorts must be performed on each column in the field before progressing to the next. The first sort, in each column of data, would be a numerical sort as described above. The second sort, in each column, would be a zone position sort with the selection switches on the sorter set for this type of sort. When the two sorting runs are completed on the units position of the left-most or first column of the field, you progress to the second and following positions until sorting is completed for the field.

MULTIPLE-FIELD SORTING.   When the data are to be classified, in sequence, by several fields of information for a given procedural run, the importance relationship of the fields must first be determined. The sorting procedure starts with the least important or minor field and proceeds through the increasingly important intermediate and major fields of data.

SELECTING. Punched cards containing coded data representing certain particular qualities or other characteristics may be selected (Figure 8–17) from data decks on sorters and collators, of which the IBM 88 Collator is representative.

The collators aid in the major data processing problem of filing and file maintenance where the records must be kept accurate, up to date, and accessible. The principal use of these machines is in feeding and compar-

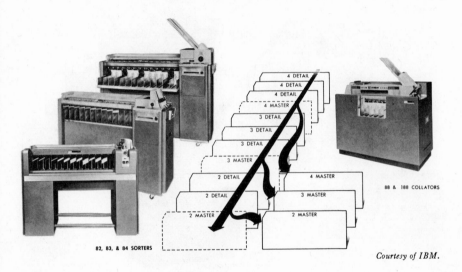

82, 83, & 84 SORTERS

88 & 188 COLLATORS

Courtesy of IBM.

FIG. 8–17. Selecting.

ing two decks of cards simultaneously and either matching them against each other or merging them together in some order. The functions performed include those of selection, sequence checking, merging, merging with selection, matching, and limited editing in the form of either, or both, blank-column or double-punch detection.

Typical selection procedures would include:

Cards punched with specific digits.
Certain types of cards for a specific date.
All cards containing a specific number.
All cards higher than a specific number.
All cards lower than a specific number.
Cards between two specific numbers.
First card of each group.
Last card of each group.

Unmatched cards.
Cards out of sequence.

SEQUENCE CHECKING. A test to determine if cards are arranged in either an ascending or descending order is that of sequence checking. This procedure is performed on any of the collators by comparing each card fed into the machine with the previous card. As long as the proper sequence is maintained, normally an ascending order, the operation continues through the deck of cards. If a card is discovered out of order, an error condition exists, the error light comes on, and card feeding is

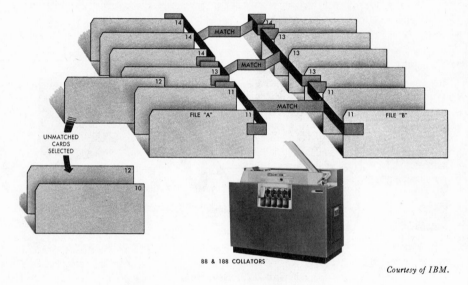

88 & 188 COLLATORS

Courtesy of IBM.

FIG. 8–18.   Matching.

automatically stopped. Sequence checking may be performed independently or in conjunction with a matching, merging, or selecting procedure.

MATCHING. The procedure to determine if the cards in two files are exactly the same, regarding specific data, is termed "matching" (Figure 8–18). This involves a series of checks on pairs of cards previously arranged in a given sequence. After the check is completed, the two matched decks of cards are stacked separately. If desired this procedure may be combined with a selecting procedure in which the unmatched cards in each deck are pulled from their respective decks and filed separately in two additional stacker pockets of the machine.

MERGING. When two decks of cards, already arranged in sequence, are to be combined to produce one deck of cards, then they are merged. Merging is performed on any of the collators by placing one of the two sequenced decks in each of the primary and secondary feed hoppers on the equipment. As the procedure is started, the card in the first file of cards is compared with that in the second file. If the first deck's card is the lower in sequence, it is fed into the stacker where the two decks will be merged (Figure 8–19, *A* and *C*). If the card in the second file is the lower (*B*), it will be placed in the stacker hopper first. If the cards are both of equal value (*D*), the card from the primary file will be fed to the stacker first. From this last it will be seen that it may, in some procedures, be quite important as to which deck of cards is placed in the primary feed file of the equipment.

PROGRAMMING. The use of the term "programming" in conjunction with punched card accounting machines is quite different from its use in conjunction with electronic computers. In punched card procedures, programming refers to the function, performed by the accounting machine, by which the machine can distinguish cards of one grouping from those of another and thereby permit individual totals of these groups to be printed. There are three classifications of totals available under programmed control. These are major, intermediate, and minor totals whose classification is determined by a previous analysis of the relative importance of the data in the groups as described above under sorting procedures.

Reporting

The end result of most information processing procedures is usually some form of statement, report, or analysis. These may be prepared for external use (customer statements, shipping notices, or purchase orders) or they may be strictly limited to internal usage (ledgers for record keeping or the many types of analyses which serve as management aids). In the punched card information system, the accounting machine performs, by far, the majority of the reporting functions required of the system.

There are several different accounting machines available, but in general they differ only in their input/output speeds and in their accumulating capacity. All the accounting machines operate automatically in both the feeding of cards and the printing of results. However, some of the machines differ in the number of lines that can be printed from one card. Some are limited to printing only one line from a card. Others can print three lines from a single card and, for this reason, are called multiple-line-print (MLP) machines. Information previously punched in cards can be read into these machines, and the functions of accumulating data by addition and subtraction, comparison, selection, programming, and detail data and group data printing can all be performed. The function of summary punching may also be performed if a summary punch is cable-connected.

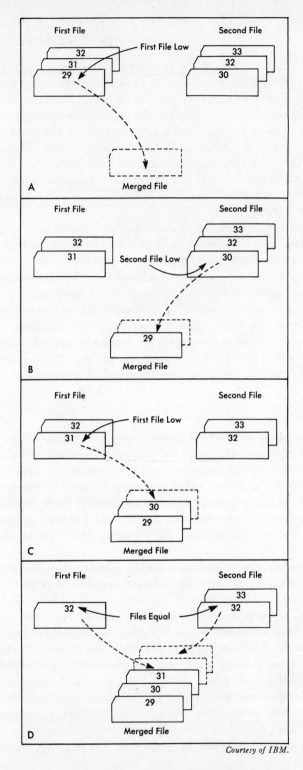

Courtesy of IBM.

FIG. 8–19. Merging Operation.

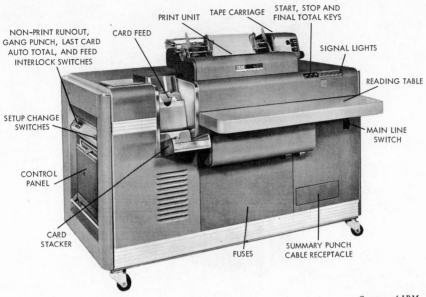

NON-PRINT RUNOUT, GANG PUNCH, LAST CARD AUTO TOTAL, AND FEED INTERLOCK SWITCHES

CARD FEED

PRINT UNIT

TAPE CARRIAGE

START, STOP AND FINAL TOTAL KEYS

SIGNAL LIGHTS

READING TABLE

SETUP CHANGE SWITCHES

MAIN LINE SWITCH

CONTROL PANEL

CARD STACKER

FUSES

SUMMARY PUNCH CABLE RECEPTACLE

Courtesy of IBM.

FIG. 8–20.   IBM 402 Accounting Machine.

The automatic control of the functions performed by the accounting machine (Figure 8–20) is based on instructions given in the form of "point-to-point" wiring on a prewired control panel (Figure 8–21) inserted into the machine. The originating electrical impulse is usually obtained through the reading brushes (one for each card column) as the card is read into the machine and passes over the two or three (depending on the equipment model) reading positions (Figure 8–22). The impulse is picked up on the control board through contact with the terminal end of a wire leading from the reading brush. It is then transferred to the control hubs (positions) on the control panel through short wires provided for this purpose. It is the placement of these wires that is referred to in "wiring" a control panel. The electrical input to the control hubs, on the panel, serve to activate the control desired—printing, comparing, selection, adding, group indication, totals, and many others.

The pattern of wiring required to produce a given report is usually first performed, in pen or pencil, on a "layout" sheet (Figure 8–23) which serves as a permanent record of the wiring necessary to do a given procedure. Whenever a procedure is used repetitively, as most business procedures are, the wired control panel is usually sealed with a cover and filed in a rack from which it may be "pulled" whenever that procedure is to be run.

Courtesy of IBM.

FIG. 8–21.   Control Panel Inserted in the Machine.

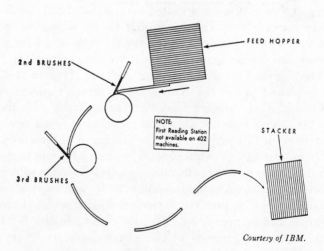

Courtesy of IBM.

FIG. 8–22.   Path of Card through the Type 402 Accounting Machine.

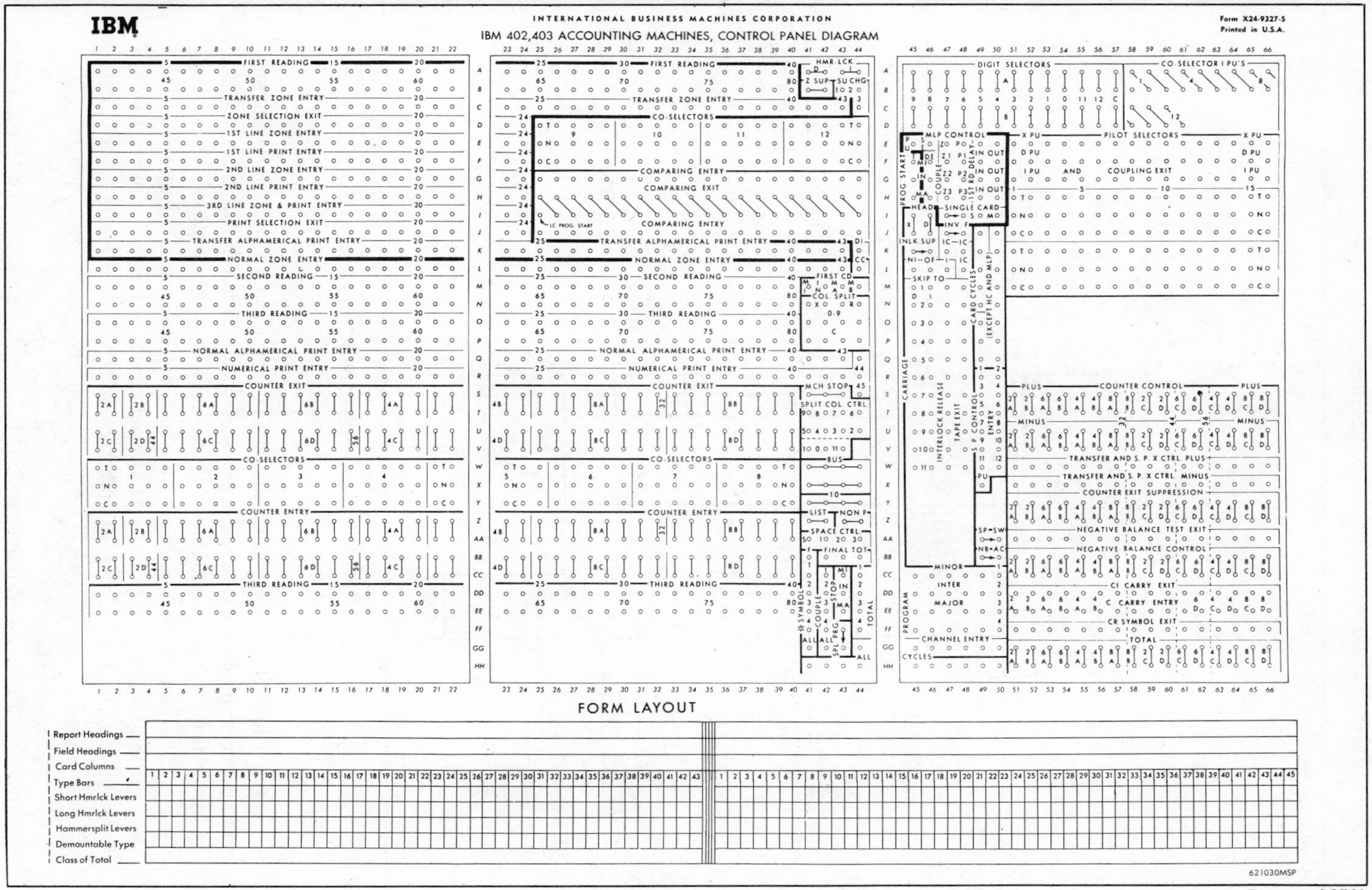

FIG. 8–23. Wiring Layout Sheet.

Courtesy of IBM.

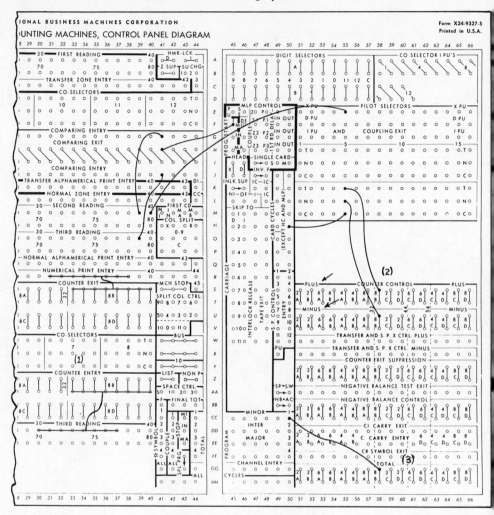

FIG. 8–24.   Counter Control.

The arithmetical function of accumulating, by addition and subtraction, is accomplished by sets or groups of counters much like those found in the ordinary adding machine. These counters are, however, activated by electrical impulses obtained from the control panel (Figure 8–24) through the counter entry hubs (1) which are told by the counter control hubs (2) to add (PLUS) or subtract (MINUS). Printing the totals accumulated in the counters is accomplished by some given control wire wired to the total hubs (3).

Form Feeding.   The movement of the form, on which printing takes place, is controlled from two sources as it feeds over the platten roller.

Single, double, and triple spacing is normally controlled by impulses provided from the wired control panel (Figure 8–25) which cause spacing on command after various patterns of listings and totals are performed in the printing operations.

Skipping spaces on the form, to position given information as desired, is accomplished through the form control tape carriage (see Figure 8–20) located on the top right side of the machine. Form-feeding carriages are available for many types of output forms (Figure 8–26) which vary widely in shape, style, and even in the number of copies to be produced simultaneously.

A prepunched narrow paper tape, with its ends glued together to form

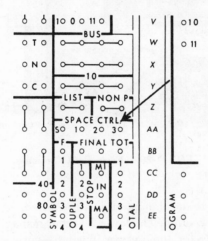

FIG. **8–25.   Space Control.**

a loop, is placed in position in the carriage control unit (Figure 8–27). This loop rotates as the form feeds over the platten and is "read" as it moves past a set of brushes. When a brush drops through one of the holes punched in the tape, it makes an electrical contact which instructs the carriage in the form movement desired. The holes required in guiding a typical form to position itself properly for data is shown in Figure 8–28.

PRINTING.   The function of printing is performed on accounting machines by type bars or type wheels which contain, on their face, the numbers, letters, and characters provided on the given machine. These type bars position themselves as they are "instructed" by the electrical impulses obtained through the control panel. On command, a hammer-like device behind each type bar strikes the bar and causes the character, which has been positioned to print, to strike against an inked ribbon held in front of the paper to reproduce the printed character on the report form.

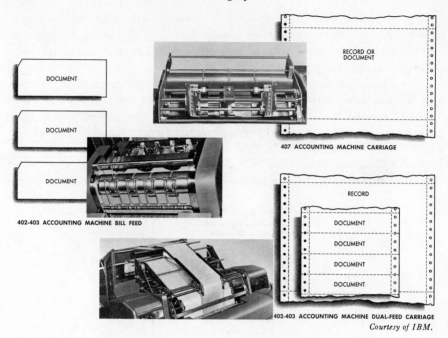

407 ACCOUNTING MACHINE CARRIAGE

402-403 ACCOUNTING MACHINE BILL FEED

402-403 ACCOUNTING MACHINE DUAL-FEED CARRIAGE

Courtesy of IBM.

FIG. 8–26.   Form Feed Carriages.

Reports vary as to the amount of detail required, on the basis of who is to receive the information. The lower levels of management are normally directly responsible for some given function—such as those of sales or purchasing. Using the sales manager of a branch store as an example, his report needs would require such detailed information as sales by salesman, type of product sold by each salesman, and the number of calls made by the salesman in obtaining his orders. The general sales manager of the firm would not need this detail but would want sales by each branch and products sold by each branch. In turn, those on an even higher level of management would probably be concerned with a wider scope of operations. They would need only a total of sales by products along with other summarized reports from the other phases of operations for which they are responsible.

DETAIL PRINTING.   The accounting machines (Figure 8–29) have the capability of giving any level of detailed information needed. In fact, this detail may be in such depth as to contain part or all of the data in each single card of the large deck of cards required in a given procedure. It is through this detail printing function that reports are prepared which show the complete detail concerning each transaction. Typical would be the report mentioned above of the store's sales by product and by salesman. During such a listing operation the accounting machine adds,

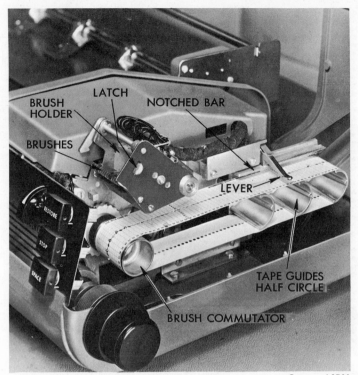

Courtesy of IBM.

FIG. 8–27.   Tape Inserted in Carriage.

subtracts, crossadds or cross-subtracts, and prints many combinations of totals.

GROUP PRINTING. In group printing, or tabulating, the data are read from each card, as above, but are held in the counter control units of the equipment rather than being listed as read. When all of the data required for a given group or class of information are complete, the machine is notified that it is time to print out the data gathered onto the report form. Any descriptive information required to identify the totals printed would also be added to the report at this time. Group printing is used in preparing all types of reports where summarized totals are desired.

CARD PRINTING. Closely associated to the reporting function is the interpreting, on the card, of the data contained in the coded holes punched in the card (Figure 8–30). Depending on the model of interpreter used, the data in the card may be printed on either of two lines near the top of the card or on various lines throughout the body of the card.

Printing data contained in the card on the card may also, as previously

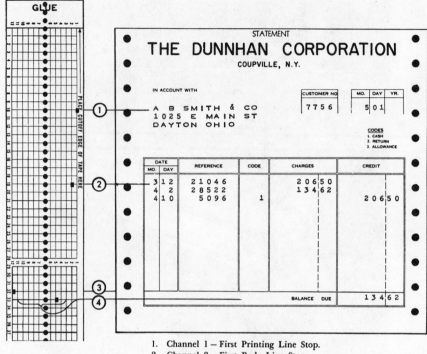

1. Channel 1 – First Printing Line Stop.
2. Channel 2 – First Body Line Stop.
3. Channel 12 – Overflow Start and Page Total Control.
4. Channels 3 to 11 – Normal Stops.

22″ Maximum
Length of Form

Courtesy of IBM.

FIG. 8–28.   Control Tape and Statement Form.

mentioned, be performed by the printing card punch as a by-product of the punching operation. Unlike the printing performed on the card punch, which may be 80 columns long with each character printed just above the related punched character, the 60 columns of printed characters on the interpreted card (Figure 8–31) have no relationship whatsoever with the data punched directly underneath those printed characters. In fact, a careful study of the interpreter's printing will show each character to be slightly wider than a single card column.

Interpreting is necessary to aid in distinguishing the various groups of cards from one another and in permitting any manual filing, sorting, or selection of cards that might be required in the processing procedure.

END PRINTING.   In end printing, up to eight digits of information may be printed in bold print on each of one or two lines near the end of the card (Figure 8–32). The data printed in these positions may be supplied by the card on which the printing is made, a card under the comparing brushes in the read unit, or from an emitter inside the machine. This

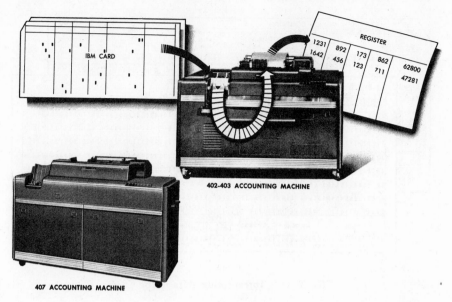

Courtesy of IBM.

FIG. 8–29.   Detail Printing.

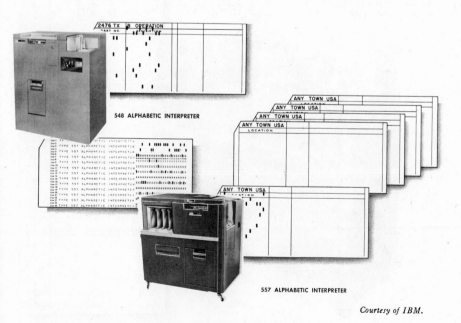

Courtesy of IBM.

FIG. 8–30.   Interpreting.

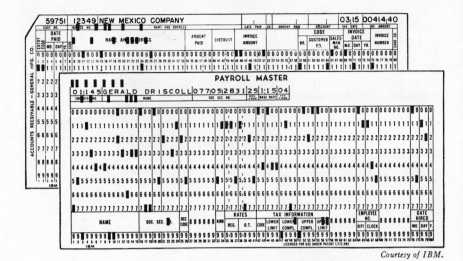

Courtesy of IBM.

FIG. 8-31.   Interpreting Data in the Card.

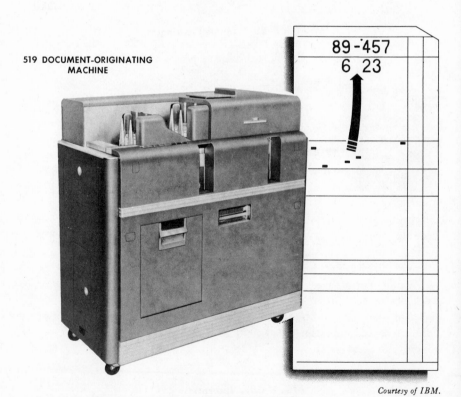

Courtesy of IBM.

FIG. 8-32.   End Printing.

end-printing operation is performed on the document originating machine and may be done simultaneously with gang punching, summary punching, reproducing, and mark-sensed punching procedures.

End printing is particularly useful in procedures in which prepunched cards are stored in racks or bins for convenient reference and selection. Personnel attendance cards, stored for insertion in a time clock, and inventory cards, stored for selection (picking) at the time of the sale of the items represented, are typical examples of the use of end printing.

Arithmetic Capabilities

The computation of a result, through the use of one or more of the arithmetic techniques of multiplication, division, addition, or subtraction can be performed by a number of different punched card machines.

COUNTING. The accounting machines, calculators, electronic statistical machines, and sorters equipped with special devices are particularly adapted to keeping a count of the number of cards, or particular items punched in them, as they are fed through the equipment.

ACCUMULATING. This function is that of gathering data, usually through addition and subtraction, pertaining to a common classification to provide a total of that class of data. This function is also performed by a number of punched card machines of which the accounting machines, summary punches, accumulating reproducers, and the calculators are typical.

CALCULATION. The techniques of multiplication and division are usually performed in punched card machines (as they are in adding machines, calculators, and even most electronic computers) through a process of multiple addition and reverse addition (subtraction) steps. Thus multiplication of five times twenty (5 × 20) would involve the addition of the number twenty (20) for five (5) times, or the reverse, to provide the answer one hundred (100). The division of the number one hundred (100) by five (5) would involve the number of times the number five (5) could be subtracted from one hundred (100) and would provide the answer, twenty (20).

Calculation, as illustrated above, is performed in punched card systems on calculators and calculating punches (Figure 8–33). The factors used in the calculations may be read from one or a series of cards, be emitted by a device within the machine, or may be developed as a result of a series of other calculations. The results obtained may be punched into the data cards fed into the equipment or into a blank trailer card which follows the data cards.

The function of calculation, where volumes of this type of work are required, has been taken over by the electronic computers. Formerly, more extensive and faster calculating punches were marketed than those available at present. The cost of this equipment was considerable, and the

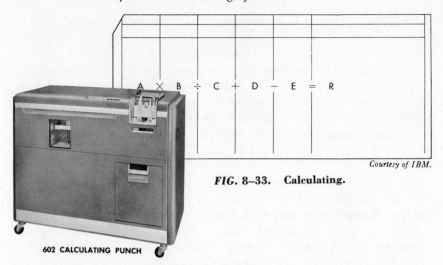

A × B ÷ C + D − E = R

Courtesy of IBM.

FIG. 8–33.   Calculating.

602 CALCULATING PUNCH

functions performed were limited to just those of calculating and punching. The newer and smaller electronic computers handle these functions at very high speeds and perform many other duties as well—in fact, replace the entire punched card system at times—at not too much additional cost. So, it has only been the smaller, less costly, calculating punches which have survived this competition.

Communication

The communication activity of punched card equipment is based on the ability to transport the data punched in the card from one point to another rather than the physical movement of the card itself. Though there are more sophisticated and faster methods of data communication involving punched cards, the most familiar type of punched card communication equipment is the IBM Data Transceiver (Figure 8–34). Two models of Data Transceivers (one of which prints on the card being punched) have been available for many years. These are, basically, modified card punches which are cable connected to a separate Signal Unit which converts the data read in the card to impulses which are transmitted over telephone or telegraph lines. Similar equipment at the receiving point reverses this procedure to produce punched cards from the impulses received (Figure 8–35). Either set of equipment may be switched to receive or transmit data. Transmission speeds vary from 3 to 30 cards per minute depending on the number of columns of data in the cards and the type of Signal Unit available.

Other methods of communication utilizing punched cards are discussed in Chapters 12 and 18.

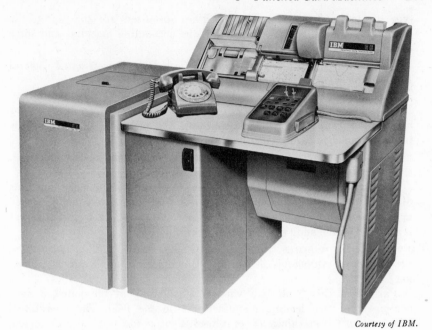

Courtesy of IBM.

FIG. 8–34.   IBM 66 Data Transceiver.

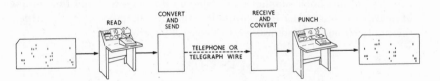

FIG. 8–35.   Communication via Punched Card.

ANNOTATED BIBLIOGRAPHY

FRIEDMAN, BURTON DEAN. *Punched Card Primer.* New York: American Book-Stratford Press, Inc., 1955.

This simple and brief book gives a general introduction into the uses and limitations of punched card equipment. All of the major machines using the punched card are explained, and then a brief introduction to punched card equipment application and installation is given.

INTERNATIONAL BUSINESS MACHINES CORPORATION. *Punched Card Data Processing Principles,* Sections 2 through 7. White Plains, N.Y., 1961.

This IBM Personal Study Program gives a complete discussion of the important machines which process a punched card in order to prepare some type of data information. The machines discussed are the sorter, the reproducer, the collator, the calculator, the accounting machine, and some of the less commonly used machines.

————. *An Introduction to IBM Punched Card Data Processing. A General Information Manual.* White Plains, N.Y., n.d.

This manual explains the basic principle of punched card accounting. Information is recorded only once on a card. The card is then available for many other uses. The manual also shows the many applications of the principal punched card related machines.

NELSON, O. S., and WOODS, R. S. *Accounting Systems and Data Processing,* chap. xix. Cincinnati: South-Western Publishing Co., 1961.

The first part of this chapter is devoted to explaining the basic functions of punching, sorting, and tabulating with particular stress being placed upon automated aspects of card processing. The second part of the chapter is centered on the additional function of calculating.

RANDALL, C. B.; WEIMER, S. W.; and GREENFIELD, M. S. *Systems and Procedures for Automated Accounting.* Cincinnati: South-Western Publishing Co., 1962.

Part II of this book is a very detailed study of the punched card equipment of two leading manufacturers in the field. The operational principles of the machines are examined, their production rates discussed, and their functions in a punched card accounting system analyzed.

SALMON, LAWRENCE J. *IBM Machine Operation and Wiring.* Belmont, Calif.: Wadsworth Publishing Co., Inc., 1962.

Part I of this book supplies knowledge on the operation and functioning of nearly all punched card machines in common use today. Part II furthers this study by building a knowledge of control-panel wiring.

QUESTIONS

1. In what way does punched card data processing differ from mechanical and manual data processing? Are there any special similarities? How will these differences and similarities change when an electronic computer system is utilized?

2. Which of the basic data processing concepts are being performed by the card punch? Explain.

3. Trace the movement of the card through the card positions found on the card punch and explain the functions of these positions.

4. What is the function of a program unit in a card punch? Explain.

5. What basic functions can be performed by a card punch? Explain fully.

6. Explain the differences between duplicating, reproducing, and gang punching.

7. What is the purpose of summary punching?

8. How does the card verifier work? What is its function?

9. In what way do the verification functions, card verifying and editing, differ?

10. Discuss the various types of sorting which are possible, indicating their various areas of usefulness.

11. Discuss the functions of a collator and discuss the importance of these functions in a punched card data processing system.

12. How does the printing on the card of data from the card differ when it is performed by the Card Punch and the Interpreter?

13. What functions can accounting machines perform? Discuss fully.

14. How does the use of the term *programming* differ in punched card and in electronic computer systems?

15. What makes it possible for an accounting machine to skip spaces on a form?

16. What type of calculations can an accounting machine perform? By what means can the remaining arithmetic operations be performed?

CHAPTER 9

Punched Card

Application—CASE STUDY

THE PAYROLL procedure case study which follows is that of a small assembly-type manufacturing firm employing a few hundred people. The equipment utilized is minimum capacity IBM Series 50 punched card machines. These include a 402 Accounting Machine, 514 Reproducing Summary Punch, 602A Calculator, 77 Collator, 82 Sorter, 56 Verifier, and a 26 Printing Card Punch. The personnel in the data processing department consists of a supervisor and two operators.

The procedures to be described are subdivided into five major procedures. The procedures were so subdivided because of the limited capability of the equipment used and also as an aid in controlling the flow of data and to permit better internal control over the data processed.

1. Earnings Cards. This procedure produces the earnings cards for each of the individual workers and a tabulated listing and total of these earnings for the period.
2. Payroll Deduction Register. This procedure assembles all the deductions, other than the income tax and social security taxes required by law, and lists these for a deduction register.
3. Year-to-Date Register. This procedure produces a tabulated report of the year-to-date earnings and new year-to-date cards for each employee while assembling cards to be used in later procedures.
4. Current Earnings Register. This procedure is to prepare an earnings register for the current period to be used in internal control procedures.
5. Payroll Checks. The production of the individual payroll checks, and their associated statements of earnings and deductions, is, of course, the end result desired of any payroll procedure.

Earnings Cards

Step (1) in the development of earnings cards (Figure 9–1), for each employee working during the current week, is the completion of the

210

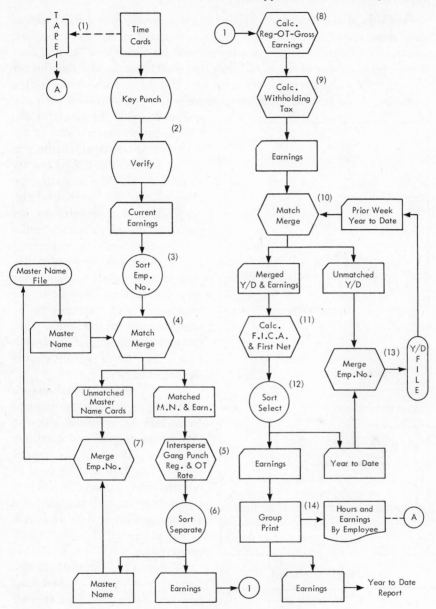

FIG. 9–1. **Earnings Card.**

timecard. Each week, in this firm, a new group of timecards is prepared manually, but the cards could be produced automatically as a by-product of some machine procedure if faster equipment and more time for processing were available.

One side of the timecard (Figure 9–2) shows the pay period ending data, department number the employee is assigned to, his clock number, and the date he was hired. Space is provided for time clock "in and out" stamps for each day of the week, daily and weekly totals, and the number of regular time and overtime hours worked. Provision is also made for the signature of the payroll clerk who compares the hours worked each day and week with the totals of the time spent on various jobs or account numbers to which the employee was assigned. This last information is provided by the other side of the timecard (Figure 9–3) and is detailed by department, by job or account number, by work order number, and by batch or release number for regular and overtime hours for each day worked. These hours are crossfooted and balanced to be sure the totals of the hours, regular and overtime, for each job equals the totals of the hours worked each day.

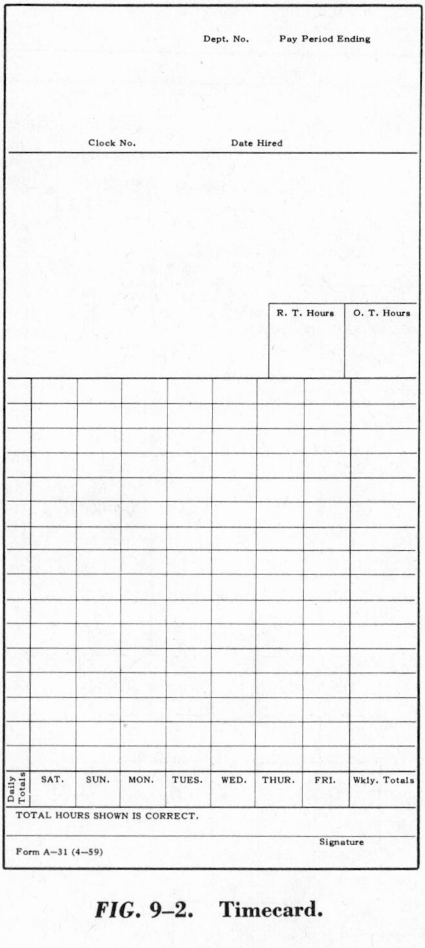

Once the above calculations are made and verified, an adding machine tape is prepared showing total hours, regular and overtime, for all employees for the payroll period. This tape will be used in internal control procedures to prevent errors in data transcription and changes in the data while it is being processed for the check preparation.

In step (2), the data in the timecards is first punched into punched cards and then verified back against the source data in the timecards to produce a current earnings card for each employee. These are then sorted (3) by employee number on the sorter to put them in sequence by employee number. Master name cards are then pulled from their file and match merged (4) in the collator with the current earnings cards. The unmatched master name cards, which represent employees who did not work this current week are held intact for the moment. Though the diagram does

FIG. 9–2.   Timecard.

LABOR DISTRIBUTION

CLOCK NO.	NAME				DEPT.NO.	WEEK ENDING		APPROVED:						Do Not Fill In TOTAL	

DEPT. NO.	Job No. or Acct. No.	WORK ORDER NUMBER	REL. NO.	Saturday Hours		Sunday Hours		Monday Hours		Tuesday Hours		Wednesday Hours		Thursday Hours		Friday Hours		Total Hours	Premium Hours
				Reg.	O.T.	Reg.	O.T.	Reg.	O.T.	Reg.	O.T.	Reg.	O.T.	Reg.	O.T.	Reg.	O.T.		
Form A—30 (4—59)			TOTAL																

FIG. 9–3.   Timecard.

not show any unmatched current earnings cards, it is possible for such to exist if a master name card is not made and placed in the master name file whenever a new employee is added to the work force. These cards would have to be checked to determine if they represent valid employees. If so, then a master name card would be prepared and the sets of master name and earnings cards would be manually placed, in proper sequence, into the matched file resulting from procedure (4).

Data pertaining to each individual's regular and overtime hourly rate and number of dependents claimed would be interspersed gang punched (5), in the reproducing punch, into his earnings card from his master name card. These two sets of cards would then be separated in the sorter through a sort separate procedure (6). The master name cards would be merged (7) back with the unmatched master name cards, previously obtained (4), into sequence by employee number and filed in the master name file. The earnings cards separated in step (6) are taken to the calculator where the regular and overtime rates are multiplied times the respective hours worked to obtain regular, overtime, and total gross earnings, which are then punched into the earnings cards (8). On a second pass through the calculator (9), the deduction necessary for withholding tax is calculated and punched into the card.

Cards representing each individual's total earnings for the year, through last week, are pulled from the year-to-date file and are match merged (10) in the collator with the earnings cards. The unmatched cards again represent employees who do not have earnings this week and are held for filing with the updated year-to-date earnings cards of this week's employees. Social security taxes are based on the first $6,600 of earnings each year, and earnings for the previous weeks of the year must be considered in determining if additional F.I.C.A. taxes are applicable to this week's earnings.

The matched earnings and year-to-date cards are then fed into the calculator (11) where the applicable F.I.C.A. tax and a first net pay amount are calculated and punched into the earnings cards. *First net pay* is a term commonly used in tabulator departments to represent gross pay less the deductions for income and social security taxes. This amount, less the other deductions, will eventually provide the net pay amount of the check to be written.

A sort select procedure in the sorter (12) separates the earnings cards from the year-to-date cards. These year-to-date cards are merged, or sorted, by employee number (13) with the unmatched year-to-date cards from step (10) and filed in the year-to-date file.

The earnings cards, now containing hours and amounts of earnings, both regular and overtime; deductions for withholding and social security taxes; and the first net pay amount are group printed (14) on the accounting machine to show hours and earnings for each employee. The total hours shown by this report are then checked against the total hours shown on the adding machine tape prepared in step (1), of this procedure, to be sure that all the timecards were properly keypunched and that no cards have been lost or misplaced in the ensuing processing procedure. The earnings cards are held for the payroll deduction register procedure.

Payroll Deduction Register

A payroll clerk prepares a list (1) of any new deductions authorized by employees since the last payroll was prepared (Figure 9–4). These are keypunched and verified (2) to prepare the new deduction cards, which are added to the regular deduction cards. These are then sorted (3) by employee number to arrange them in employee number sequence. The current earnings cards, produced in the previous procedure, are matched against the current deduction deck of cards in a match select procedure (4) in the collator. This procedure produces three separate stacks of cards. First, the unmatched deduction cards representing deductions for employees who have no earnings this particular week. These are returned (5) to the payroll clerk who will file these for next week's payroll procedure. Second, the current earnings deck of cards which will be held for the preparation of the year-to-date register. And third, the current deductions which are applicable to those who have earnings this payroll period.

The current deduction deck is then fed into the accounting machine where the deductions applicable to each employee are group printed (6) for the deduction register. The crossfooted totals from this register are sent to the payroll clerk (7) who will hold these for checking purposes against other reports to be prepared.

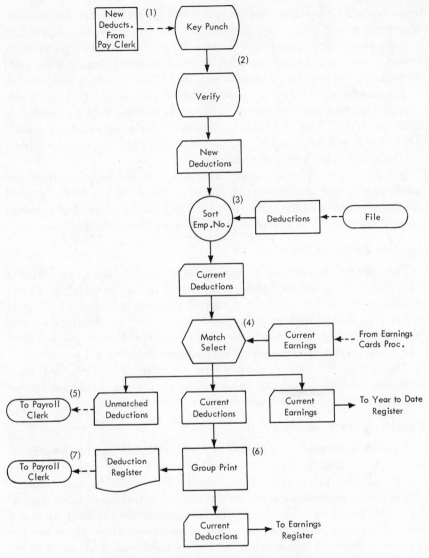

FIG. 9–4.   Payroll Deduction Register.

Year-to-Date Register

In the first step of this procedure, (Figure 9–5), the year-to-date earnings cards, representing earnings up through last payroll period, and the master name deck of cards are pulled from their respective files and are merged (1) together in the collator. This merged deck is then merged (2) with the current earnings cards for this payroll. This new deck, containing previous and current earnings, are fed into the accounting machine and are group printed (3), by employee, to prepare the current year-to-date register. This report is balanced (4) against data from the previous year-to-date register and the current earnings register, prepared in the next procedure, to be sure of data accuracy and control.

Simultaneously with the preparation of the year-to-date register, a new year-to-date earnings card, whch includes the current week's earnings, is summary punched on the cable-connected reproducing summary punch. These cards will be filed (5) in the year-to-date file for use in conjunction with next week's payroll procedure.

The prior period year-to-date cards are sort selected (6) from the master name and earnings cards. These are filed for use in the payroll check preparation procedure. The remaining master name and earnings merged deck will be held for the preparation of the earnings register.

Current Earnings Register

The merged master name and earnings cards, above, are merged (1) with the current deduction cards used in the preparation of the deduction register to produce a current earnings register file (Figure 9–6). This deck is then group printed (2) to prepare the current earnings register. The totals from this register are crossfooted and balanced (3) back against the earnings report prepared in the procedure above.

The earnings register file deck is then sort selected (4) into deduction card and earnings card decks which will be used in the check preparation and the master name deck which will be returned to its file.

Payroll Check Procedure

The first step in the preparation of the payroll check and its associated statement of earnings (Figure 9–7) is to merge (1) the current earnings cards and the prior year-to-date cards. This deck is then merged (2) with the deduction cards and the deck obtained is, in turn, merged (3) with the name and address file to produce the properly arranged deck of cards to be used in the check preparation. These cards are fed into the accounting machine and through a combination of group printing and listing (4) prepare the payroll checks and employee earnings statements. These will be delivered to the payroll clerk after they are scanned and sight checked for any obvious errors.

The payroll clerk, as a part of a separate manual procedure, will probably run an adding machine tape on the net amounts of these checks and compare it with previously prepared report totals to be sure the total amount paid is correct. This total amount may also be used to determine the necessary funds to be transferred, from the regular bank account, to the special payroll bank account.

The check file deck of cards will be sort selected (5) into each

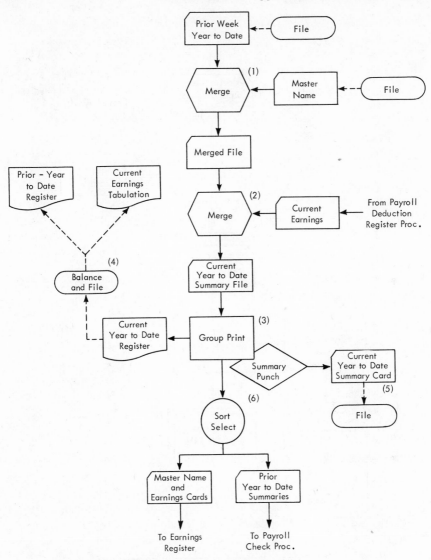

FIG. 9–5. Year-to-Date Register.

classification of card present in the deck. The name and address, earnings, and year-to-date cards will be returned (6) to their respective files for future use. The deduction cards will be put through the reproducing punch and reproduced (7). The original deduction cards will be returned (8) to the payroll clerk who will file them for future payroll deductions.

The reproduced deduction cards will be sort selected (9) by type of deductions, which may be individually tabulated to prepare various de-

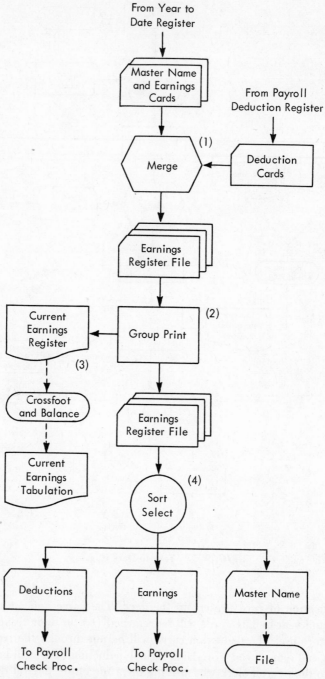

FIG. 9–6.   Current Earnings Register.

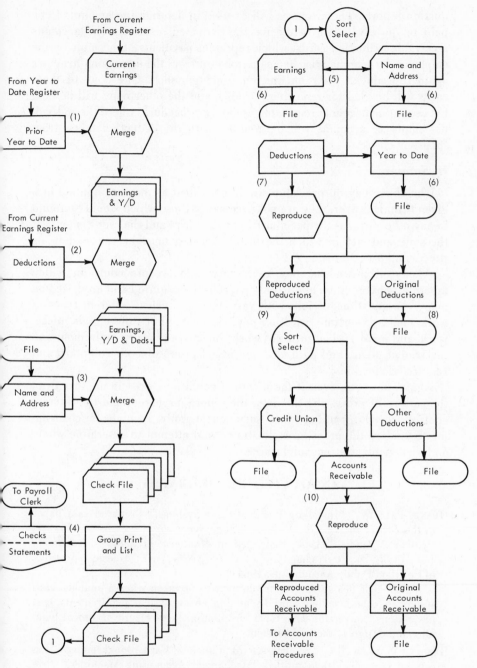

FIG. 9-7. Payroll Check Procedure.

duction reports. These reports will be used in determining amounts to be paid to those who are to receive the deducted amounts. The accounts receivable deduction cards, which represent payments on account by the employee for merchandise he has purchased from the employing firm, are again reproduced (10) on the reproducing punch. One copy of these cards will be filed for reporting purposes and the other copy will be held for use in the accounts receivable updating procedure, where the individual employee accounts will be credited with the deduction taken from their pay check.

In Summary

The above payroll procedures were described as they are applied in a given firm. However, they are not necessarily those which would be found in any other firm, as the peculiarities of each firm and the requirements of the state and city in which the firm is located must be reflected in its processing procedures.

A payroll procedure may be a very complex procedure in which monthly, semimonthly, and weekly payrolls are required and are based on many classifications of jobs with varying wage scales; different types of work such as overtime, vacation pay, sick pay, shift differentials, piece-work, and many special forms of work; incentive rewards; retirement and investment plans; and an almost unlimited group of both voluntary and required deductions.

Again, however, even if the identical conditions exist in another firm, the pattern of processing the data, the reports prepared, and the internal control procedures utilized may vary considerably. It might be challenging to analyze the procedures illustrated and attempt to determine where and why such variations might occur.

ANNOTATED BIBLIOGRAPHY

HUSKE, PAUL W. "Installing Punched Card Systems." Prepared as a paper in the *Proceedings of the Fourth Annual Accounting Systems Conference*, October 27 and 28, 1960. Reprinted in *Management Services Handbook* (ed. HENRY DE VOS), chap. v, pp. 254–65. (New York: American Institute of Certified Public Accountants, 1964).

This article deals with the simple steps to be taken when a punched card system is to be installed: initial planning (basic system requirements, cost projections, conversion time table, installation factors) and technical planning and design of the basic system.

HYMAN, WALKER R. "Weaknesses of Punched Card Bookkeeping." Excerpted from an article entitled "Mechanical Accounting Machines," *Proceedings of the Fourth Annual Accounting Systems Conference*, October 27 and 28, 1960. Reprinted in *Management Services Handbook* (ed. HENRY

DE VOS), chap. v, pp. 267–70. (New York: American Institute of Certified Public Accountants, 1964).

The value of the statistics in relation to the cost and difficulties of punched card accounting must be considered. A thorough and exhaustive review by management of the necessity for various data is of prime importance before considering any mechanization, particularly punched card. Management must be thoroughly warned of the shortcomings and high costs of punched card accounting before making any decision.

SWYLER, JAMES K. "Case # 1—Punched Card System," *Proceedings, National Automation Conference,* pp. 68–72. New York, 1964.

The punched card data processing system used by a small-town bank to process checking accounts, savings accounts and Christmas Club accounts is described. Specific topics examined include the selection of the equipment, the numbering system used, the education of employees and customers, the results obtained from the system, and the employee and customer acceptance of the system.

QUESTIONS

1. What are some of the internal control techniques present in the described procedures? Explain the function of each.
2. Why does the pattern of data processing in a given procedure vary from firm to firm, even though the same fundamental input data is used to produce basically similar reports?
3. Could any of the individual tabulated reports and registers used in the described procedure be eliminated? If so, what is their value to this firm? If not, why?

CHAPTER **10**

Electronic Computer

Development

AN AUTOMATIC computer was first conceived in 1786 by J. H. Muller, a German engineer. He proposed a device to generate data for functions from algebraic formulas involving their differences. Though Muller developed his ideas on paper in great detail, he did not attempt to produce the machine due to the tremendous engineering and technical difficulties that would have been impossible to surmount at that time.

Charles Babbage (1792–1871) was born the son of a banker at Totnes in Devonshire, England. He taught himself mathematics, and when he entered Cambridge in 1810 found he knew more in this field than his teachers. In working with the logarithm tables available then to perform calculations related to his statistical work, he discovered a number of errors and became intrigued with the idea of developing the series of numbers in these tables by some mechanical method. This, he felt, would eliminate the human errors seemingly always present in the calculations required in the development of such a complex series of numbers.

So, in 1812, at the age of 20, Babbage conceived the idea of what he called his Difference Engine, which he presented in detail to the societies of his day. He was granted financial help from both the Royal Society of London and the English government to aid him in the development of the equipment.

The Difference Engine was basically a specially designed adding machine for the computation of polynomials (such as $x^2 - 2xy + y^2$) with an accuracy up to six decimal places. A working model of the Difference Engine was completed in about 1822. It used the concept of "state" (either the presence or absence of holes) in a type of punched card that had been used in controlling the Jacquard Frame Loom. The basic operational idea involved the constancy of the difference in the third power of a sequential series of numbers (Figure 10–1).

Babbage later proposed and tried to build a similar machine with accuracy up to 20 decimal places. This work was sponsored by the government, but engineering and other technical problems prevented it from being completed on schedule, and financial support was withdrawn in 1833.

A larger model of the Difference Engine was eventually completed in 1859 and was put to use in calculating life tables for insurance ratings in

X	X^3	1st Difference	2nd Difference	3rd Difference
1	1			
		7		
2	8		12	
		19		6
3	27		18	
		37		6
4	64		24	
		61		
5	125			
20	8,000			
		1,261		
21	9,261		126	
		1,387		6
22	10,648		132	
		1,519		6
23	12,167		138	
		1,657		
24	13,824			

FIG. 10–1.

1863. George Scheutz and his son, from Sweden, and an Englishman, each constructed Difference Engines several years after Babbage's death. Both of these gave good, reliable service for many years.

Babbage conceived the idea for an Analytical Engine to perform digital computations in 1833, about the time his finances were cut off on building the Difference Engine. This idea has since proven to be the fundamental basis for the development of modern computers, and the Analytical Engine is considered the ancestor of today's general-purpose electronic computers. Babbage is often spoken of as "the father of computers."

In his proposals for the Analytical Engine, Babbage utilized an input of data in the form of punched cards or handset dials. He described the use of punched cards in his equipment as being somewhat similar to those used by the French inventor Jacquard. The holes in his cards, however, represented mathematic symbols rather than machine controls. He is quoted as saying it "weaves algebraic patterns" just as the Jacquard Loom weaves flowers and leaves.

The input data was processed by using flexible arithmetic controls which performed the calculations required in what Babbage called a "mill." Internal storage, which he termed a "store," was designed in the form of counters which provided 50,000 units of available information (1,000 numbers of 50 digits each). Output was also flexible, as it could be in the form of punched cards or a printed page (actually a mold from which type could be set). The development of the Analytical Engine soon ran into almost insurmountable engineering problems and financial difficulties. A model of the Analytical Engine was never completed, due to the mechanical production difficulties and the resulting costs, and the idea of automatic computing machines was to be forgotten for over four decades.

Dr. Vannevar Bush and some associates at Massachusetts Institute of Technology constructed a large-scale analog calculator in 1925. It was basically a mechanically operated computer, though some electric motors were utilized in its construction. In 1935 Dr. Bush and associates started to construct an improved model of their 1925 analog computer. This equipment had considerably greater capabilities. It was completed in 1942, but the project was kept secret and was not announced until after World War II had ended.

Dr. George R. Stibitz started to work on the Bell Model 1 in 1937 at Bell Telephone Laboratories under the supervision of Samuel B. Williams. The Bell Model 1 was a semiautomatic computer which used telephone relays to perform its computations. It was completed in 1939 and was used in computing complex numbers used in the design of telephone transmission networks and transformers. Though in the true sense this was not an electronic computer, as it utilized electrical relays rather than electronic circuits, this equipment was used in the first public demonstration of an automatic computer. This demonstration was in conjunction with the September, 1940, meeting of the American Mathematical Society in Hanover, New Hampshire.

Stibitz later, in 1942, developed under a government contract a "relay interpolator" at Bell Telephone Laboratories under the direction of E. G. Andrews. This equipment performed arithmetic operations under the control of a program recorded on paper tape.

A revised model was constructed in 1943, during the war, to be used as a "ballistic computer," which could be termed a general-purpose computer. In this same period, Stibitz also built an "error computer" to search files of paper tape for selected data. These models were also based on government contracts and were completed at Bell Telephone Laboratories.

Other early relay-type computers included the IBM Pluggable Sequence Relay Calculator, B.A.R.K. (Sweden), Zuse, the Imperial College Computing Engine, and the A.R.C. (Automatic Relay Computer).

In 1935 Dr. Howard Aiken, then a graduate student at Harvard University, studied Babbage's plans and ideas and decided that modern engineering capability would permit the development of equipment such as Babbage had envisioned. In 1937, after performing some initial work on his project, Dr. Aiken went to the International Business Machines Corporation for both financial and technical help on his proposal. Both were forthcoming from IBM, and in 1939 IBM started to work on this project with Aiken serving as consultant to J. W. Bryce, C. D. Lake, B. M. Durfee, and F. E. Hamilton, all IBM engineers.

The Automatic Sequence Controlled Calculator (ASCC), also known as Mark 1, was the product of this combined effort and proved to be the largest of the relay calculating devices ever to be constructed. Its computational capability was close to that of the early electronic computing devices which followed.

The ASCC was completed in 1943—but not publicly announced until 1944 due to wartime security regulations—to become the first of a series of equipment that was to develop into the electronic computer as we know it today.

A second model of the ASCC, the Mark 2, was started immediately after Mark 1 and was completed in 1947. Both were basically electromechanical in nature. Later, models 3 and 4 were built, each an improvement on the others and, consequently, considerably faster in their calculating ability. In all models, instructions were fed into the machines by punched cards as they were needed, and the calculations necessary were automatically performed. These equipments were all designed for scientific work and were used by engineers, physicists, and mathematicians to compute long series of complex arithmetical problems.

The first truly electronic computer was developed as a result of needs made apparent by World War II. Dr. John W. Mauchly had proposed the development of a computer for statistical work in weather data calculations as early as 1940. During the war, the Army needed help in developing firing tables for use in ballistics research and turned to the University of Pennsylvania (which had and was using an analog computer in its research work) for help. Dr. Mauchly teamed up with J. Presper Eckert and developed plans for the construction of an electronic computer. After the initial submission of these plans to the Army, a government contract was signed with the Moore School of Electrical Engineering in 1943, and Dr. Leland Cunningham, who had been using punched cards for ballistic calculations, became a consultant on the project.

After a period of two years (1945) the first completely electronic, high-speed, computer was produced as the Electronic Numerical Integrator and Calculator (ENIAC). Over 18,000 vacuum tubes were used in its construction. The ENIAC could perform 5,000, 10-decimal-digit, calculations a second and multiply at a speed up to 300 calculations a second (compared to a maximum of 1 per second on the fastest relay-type calculator), but it occupied a room over 100 feet in length (1,500 square feet) and used up to 100 kw. of electrical power.

One of the first problems assigned to ENIAC was one in nuclear physics which was solved in about two hours of computation over a two-week period of time. It has been estimated it would have taken about 100 man-years to have solved this problem using conventional techniques.

ENIAC was installed in the Ballistic Research Laboratory, at the Aberdeen Proving Grounds, Aberdeen, Maryland, in 1946. It was used in Ballistic research until October, 1955 when it was retired.

The EDVAC (Electronic Discrete Variable Automatic Computer), was the second computer designed by Mauchly and Eckert and built at the University of Pennsylvania. It was started about 1946 but was not finally completed until 1952. It was smaller in size (only 3,500 vacuum tubes required) but larger in capability than the earlier ENIAC. It utilized the binary system of number notation and was completely internally programmed (rather than using externally wired boards and other external input). Though other computers utilizing similar characteristics became operational before EDVAC, they were all based on ideas proposed for this equipment. Thus, the EDVAC is considered to be the prototype of serial-type computers which utilize internally stored, serially ordered, instructions.

Dr. John von Neumann of atomic energy fame had joined Mauchly and Eckert at the Moore School of Electrical Engineering in 1945 to learn more of their project and to determine if it might be applicable to the type of research he was involved in at that time. During his stay at Moore, Von Neumann attended a series of conferences held by Mauchly and Eckert on computers and discussed many ideas with them. The result was that Von Neumann published a paper on computers and described them in great detail. This paper was published soon after this period and sometime before Mauchly and Eckert developed their EDVAC. There has been considerable speculation as to whether Von Neumann obtained his information from Mauchly and Eckert or vice versa or if the ideas were a product of joint stimulation by discussions between them. However, there has been sufficient fame and other rewards resulting from the paper, the Institute of Advanced Study Computer (produced later), and EDVAC to satisfy all concerned.

As an outgrowth of Von Neumann's work with Mauchly and Eckert at Moore, the Institute of Advanced Study of Princeton University and the

Moore School of Electrical Engineering proposed a study to produce, as a joint project, the IAS Computer for the U.S. Ordnance Department. This was completed by Princeton in 1952. It used a punched paper tape input/output system, the binary number system, one-address instruction commands, asynchronous timing, and a cathode-ray-type storage tube in its design. Addition and subtraction were performed in 10 microseconds and multiplication in 300 microseconds. The basic design of the IAS has been copied and improved upon many times in the production of a number of the single model and a few of the commercial-type computers produced since its development.

The EDSAC (Electronic Delayed Storage Automatic Computer) was completed in May, 1949 as the first serially operating computer. This equipment used many of the ideas proposed for EDVAC and was constructed under the direction of M. V. Wilkes at the Mathematical Laboratory of the University of Cambridge in 1949. Mercury delay lines were used for storage, and depending on the size of the digit involved in the computation, it only took 34 to 70 microseconds (millionths of a second) to perform the addition and subtraction function. Input was in the form of five channel punched paper tape and output was to a tape punch or teleprinter.

A second English computer the ACE (Automatic Computing Engine), using EDVAC and Von Neumann ideas, was started in 1945 by Turing, Womersley, and Colebrook at the National Physical Laboratory, London, and was completed in 1950. The ACE used punched cards for its input and output, delay-line-type storage and less than 1,000 vacuum tubes in its operation. It was faster than EDSAC and more reliable. The ACE was the first computer to use the "two-address code" for instructions, with each instruction containing both the location of the number (address) to be operated upon and the location of the next instruction.

The Whirlwind 1 computer was produced at M.I.T. in 1950 under the direction of J. Forrester. It was the first to use the electrostatic cathode-ray tube, devised by Forrester, for storage. One of the first attempts to use magnetic tapes for external storage was on the Whirlwind. Input and output were both normally performed by punched paper tape and teletype. However, output could be displayed on the face of a large cathode-ray tube for visual inspection or photographing. Addition or subtraction required 5, and multiplication 40, microseconds in the Whirlwind.

PRODUCTION MODEL COMPUTERS

Mauchly and Eckert resigned their positions at the University of Pennsylvania in 1946 and organized their own computer company, the Electronic Control Company. Shortly thereafter, they procured a contract from the National Bureau of Standards and proceeded to develop what became the UNIVAC 1 (Universal Automatic Computer) in 1951. This was the *first* truly *commercial computer* to be produced on the assembly line.

The Electronic Control Company was later purchased by the Remington Rand Corporation which was quite active in the production of punched card and other electromechanical equipment. This firm, in turn, became the Univac Division of Sperry Rand Corporation, which today is one of the leading producers of computers and associated equipment.

The second production model computer, the CRC 102 (NCR 102) computer, was produced in 1952 by the Computer Research Corporation. This company was soon absorbed by the Electronics Division of the National Cash Register Company. The third piece of equipment to be produced for commercial distribution was the IBM 701 which was developed in 1952 by IBM. This was a successful computer but, as with most computers of its day, was strictly limited to scientific applications.

Business Applications

With the increasing use of computers in the scientific and engineering areas, considerable interest developed among businessmen as to how the computer could aid them in combating the expanding load of paper work in record keeping and in solving problems of data manipulation for managerial use. *The first use of computers for processing business data* was in a Bureau of the Census application on the UNIVAC 1 in October, 1954.

Though IBM had aided Dr. Aiken in the development of the Automatic Sequence Controlled Calculator (ASCC) at Harvard University in the period 1937 to 1943 and had developed punched card calculators in the 1940's, it did not enter the computer field until 1952 when it produced the IBM 701. The IBM 701 was a scientific application computer, but it served to develop a staff which produced the IBM 702, a small commercially oriented computer, and the IBM 650, a general-purpose computer with special business capabilities, in 1953, and many others which followed. The IBM 650 was first used in Boston, Massachusetts, on a business application in December, 1954, and later became the most popular of all the first-generation grouping of computers.

The IBM 650 was one of the first all-purpose computers (served the requirements of both scientific and business applications). It utilized vacuum tubes in its electrical circuits, magnetic-drum-type storage, and punched cards for both input and output of information. The IBM 650 has been termed, by many, the "model T" of computers because of its comparatively low price, broad usage application, general reliability, and wide acceptance. With the development of the IBM 650 and its ability to adapt itself to applications of both scientific and business problems, IBM assumed the position of leading producer of computers by 1955—a position it has continued to consolidate as time has passed until it is now the "giant" in the field.

MODERN COMPUTER CAPABILITIES

Many different models of computers were constructed during this early period of development. In nearly every instance each progressive development added new features to the design of even newer computers.

Storage

By the early 1960's, only a comparatively few years after the first business application of computers, data storage devices of computers had passed through various stages utilizing relays, vacuum tubes, and mercury delay lines, into the era of magnetic drums, cores, disks, tapes, cards, and films.

Storage capacities have advanced from a few hundred or thousand items stored internally in the computer to many thousands of items stored internally in conjunction with literally millions (in some instances even billions) of items stored in external devices that are immediately available to the computer on its demand. Internal access speeds have advanced from thousandths of a second (milliseconds) to millionths of a second (microseconds), and in some of the newer equipment to billionths of a second (nanoseconds).

Input/Output Devices

Input and output devices have changed from handset dials, paper tape, and paper cards to include cathode-ray tubes, magnetic tape, console typewriters, on-line analog computers, magnetic ink characters, and optical scanning devices. Some success has even been achieved in control by human voice commands and in output in the form of machine "spoken" words.

Input/output capability has changed from setting or reading a few dials on the face of the equipment to the computer's automatic acceptance of over two thirds of a million bits of numerical data per second from magnetic tape units.

Some of the more powerful units, by using buffering devices which operate on assigned priorities, have a number of completely different input and output units from which they will accept input data and to which they may feed output data. These larger computer systems have increased computational capabilities to permit the computers to be working on two, three, four, or more problems simultaneously. These utilize differing series or sets of internally stored instructions, external storage devices, and input/output units—all under priorities which may be assigned by the operator.

Paper tape can now be read at speeds up to 1,800 and punched at

1,000 characters per second. Punched cards can be read as fast as 2,500 and punched at 800 cards per minute. In addition to devices that serve as both input and output, optical character reading can be performed at up to 2,000 characters per second and magnetic ink characters may be read at 1,200 characters per second. Also, the demand for business reports has led to the development of on-line printers which will print up to as many as 2,000 lines of data per minute.

Internal Circuitry

Internal circuitry has changed from electromagnetic relays to vacuum tubes and on to transistors, diodes, and other solid-state devices such as the solid logic technology (SLT) of today. The speed of operation has advanced from a few hundred closings of a relay per minute to speeds which are measured in terms of milliseconds, microseconds, and a few hundred nanoseconds.

Experimental circuitry is being developed that operates in billionths of a second (nanoseconds) and even in trillionths of a second (picoseconds).

To give some concept of how fast these speeds are, a space ship traveling at a speed of 100,000 miles per hour would only move 1¾ inches in one microsecond. Another comparison, in terms of time rather than speed, is that there are as many nanoseconds in one second as there are seconds in 30 years. Any illustration—either in terms of speed or time—of an operation involving picoseconds is almost beyond imagination and everyday comparisons.

Internal computer speeds now permit addition to be performed as fast as 6 million numbers per second, multiplication at 2 million numbers per second and access to fast memory at 13.3 million numbers per second.

Space and Other Requirements

The first computers, which utilized vacuum tubes in their operation, were massive in size and often required the space of a number of average-sized rooms just to house the components.

The operation of the large number of vacuum tubes necessary for a typical computer brought a demand for not only considerable power requirements but also many differing levels of voltage. These electrical demands were supplied by separately housed power supply units. These power units, as well as the tubes themselves, generated a vast amount of heat. Enough, in fact, to melt the components in some of the various units. This heat had to be offset by blower fans inside the units and by large-capacity air-conditioning equipment to keep the rooms and equipment at operatable temperatures.

The computer, the associated power supplies, and the air-conditioning equipment all made heavy demands on the electrical service required. It was quite common to see heavy cables two or three inches in diameter laced across the floor from unit to unit. It naturally follows that this demand for large amounts of electrical power made the operation of the equipment quite expensive.

In the late 1950's, computers were developed to utilize the then newly developed solid state electronic devices, such as transistors and diodes, to replace the vacuum tubes previously used. These computers have become known as the second generation of computers. The solid-state devices were quite small in size, relative to vacuum tubes, had low power requirements, generated only a small amount of heat in their operation, and proved themselves to be much more reliable than the tubes they replaced.

As the operational speed of the internal circuits of the computer increased, the distance along the wires and between the components became a critical factor in their performance. Electricity travels at the speed of light, which is about 186,300 miles per second. However, when you consider a circuit operating in billionths and even trillionths of a second, a length of wire a relatively few inches in length can slow up the time it takes the current to flow from one device to another. Thus, smaller and more compact components became a necessity for performance as well as for the size and weight requirements of the space program, where most of these developments evolved.

In conjunction with these solid-state devices, etched-circuit boards and the solid logic techniques of the 1960's involving monolithic circuits came into use and eliminated much of the conventional wiring previously used in electronic circuits. These further cut down on the space requirements. Now, even the larger business computers only require a good-sized room for their installation, and the smaller ones are installed in a desk-style cabinet.

The techniques available in the production of these devices and circuit boards also permitted mass production and assembly lines to be utilized instead of previous manual and hand-writing assembly techniques. This resulted in increased efficiencies, which reduced cost while at the same time providing a more reliable and standardized product.

Computer Operating Costs

With the advent of these second-generation computers, their cost began to decrease. Now, relatively powerful systems are available for the smaller or the medium-sized firms at a price previously paid for punched card calculators and accounting machines.

Where the early computers were individually designed and hand-assembled, the new equipment now flows from the assembly line, where most of the components used are produced and assembled through automated techniques.

The performance capabilities and operating reliability of the solid-state components and etched-circuit boards are such that costs, in terms of both component replacement and the resulting nonoperating down-time, are now at a near minimum. Preventive maintenance checks, automatic within some equipment, have also been developed that test the operating level of the components to allow replacement of items that appear to be failing before there is any loss of operating efficiency.

Power demands of solid-state circuitry are quite low, relative to that of vacuum tubes, and the costs associated with this lower demand for electrical power have decreased. These lower power demands have also cut down on the need for special air-conditioning provisions until the normal air conditioning provided in most modern offices is adequate to dissipate the small amount of heat generated by the computer system.

TYPES OF COMPUTERS

There are two distinct families of computers. These are the analog and the digital computers, each of which has its individual place in the field of computation.

Analog Computers

The analog computer is used to solve problems of the type that normally originates as physical realities. These problems are solved by substituting an equivalent or analogous relationship, generally in the form of electronic voltages, which may be manipulated, higher or lower, to correspond to the larger or smaller size of the variables in the physical problem. A much simplified example of this technique would be to let a volt of electricity be the equivalent of a degree of temperature (a pound of pressure or vacuum, a unit of volume, or some other measurement). As the temperature increased or decreased this would be sensed by the equivalent of a thermometer which would, in turn, increase or decrease the voltage fed into the computer. As the voltage (temperature) reached predetermined levels, which had previously been stored in the memory system of the computer, the computer would activate a valve to either increase or decrease (as needed) the flow of fuel feeding the furnace serving as the heat source.

Data represented by the voltages can be assigned, by its very nature, any value between the maximum and minimum voltages permissible. The accuracy of the analog computer is, therefore, limited by the precision with which these voltages can be controlled.

The most common method of describing physical problems is in the mathematical form of either linear or nonlinear differential equations and associated algebraic, transcendental, and perhaps arbitrary relationships.

Combinations of analog computing units may be needed in solving more complex problems by having each unit provide the equivalent of one of the various equations that may arise where a number of variables are present. In a typical problem these variables need to be assigned various values to provide alternatives for some type of optimum operation.

In analog computers the representative quantities are always *continuously variable* and normally require interpretation in some form of measurement process.

Typical output of the analog computer may be in the form of a graphical presentation of the relationship of one variable as a function of another variable, either in the form of plotted data or pictorial drawings prepared by printers or recorder traces, or electronically plotted by utilizing oscilloscopes or cathode-ray tubes.

Other outputs may be in the form of voltages or pulses which may be used to control temperatures, pressures, and flows by actuating the many differing types of control devices available. These electronic outputs may also be used as inputs to digital computers, where their storage and computational capabilities provide additional information that may, in turn, be used as input back into the analog unit originally providing the information or to another analog computer.

The more common usage of the analog computer is in areas where control, in some form, is the end result. Typical of these is its wide use in industry to actuate various controls in many types of automatic processes such as those used for machine tools and in the flow of materials (both liquids and solids). Many uses have also been discovered for the analog computer in radar work, guided missiles, and the space program in general.

By referring back to the temperature-voltage example, previously used in describing the manner in which the analog computer operates, and adding similar analogies of pressure, volume, and physical properties of the input material, it is not hard to envision, in a very simplified manner, how these computers can be used in the automated control of an oil refinery. Here, the specific gravity and other physical properties of the crude oil being fed into the refinery system would be tested and checked at regular intervals. As the oil flows through the system, various stages of differing pressures, vacuums, and temperatures are required to break it down into the refined products required. By varying these factors, larger or smaller quantities of a given product, or combinations of products, may be produced as the demand for products change.

For each set of products to be produced from a given column of crude oil, with its specific physical properties, there is a series of required temperatures, pressures, and other factors to produce the optimum level of production of each of the end products desired. It would require many employees to perform all the functions needed and to adjust all the valves and controls necessary to do this refining process, and even then many of the tests and readings required could only be made periodically. Consequently, manually operated refineries do well to achieve more than 75 percent efficiency in attempting to reach optimum production levels. Through the use of computers, which can be continually "on line" checking all the factors, it has been possible to achieve 95 percent or better efficiency in automated plants.

As a word of caution, the automated refinery does not rely completely on analog computers for its operation. Many computers of the analog type serve to provide the input required for one or more digital computers where the larger memory capability allows all the inputs to be weighed against previously stored instructions and formulas. Computations are made to determine the optimum function controls required, and this information is then sent back to the various analog computers which, in turn, make any necessary adjustments required of the control devices.

Digital Computers

Data are represented in the circuitry of a digital computer by a pattern of coded electrical pulses, or "spurts" of electrical energy. In the memory of the computer these pulses may magnetize certain patterned spots on component parts of the computer (magnetic drums, disks, and films) or magnetize the component part itself (magnetic cores).[1] These data cannot be of a continuous nature as in the analog computer, but must represent discrete numbers such as quantities and amounts. It is this ability to accept and manipulate discrete data that makes the digital computer so adaptable to business data and problems.

Both the analog and digital computers can be used in making mathematical calculations, but as previously mentioned, the accuracy (in terms of data lost through rounding techniques) of the analog unit depends upon the precision control of voltages. In the digital unit, accuracy depends on the number of value positions available for the manipulation of data. Just as in the case of hand calculators the more place values available—the less rounding needed—the more accurate the answer to the computation. Thus you only need to add the electronic equivalent of additional place or value positions to increase the accuracy of the digital computer.

SCIENTIFIC COMPUTERS. It was mentioned in the discussion of the development of computers that there are two different types of *digital computers*. These are those that are particularly adapted to the calculations needed in *scientific* work and those that have not only calculational ability but also can store the tremendous mass of data typical of the records necessary in a *business* firm of any size at all and print out the many types of reports needed by management.

---

[1] See Chapter 12 for detailed information on these devices and the techniques used.

The need for accurate calculations in the development of atomic energy, guided missiles, and other war-related projects put increased emphasis on the development of digital computers suitable for engineering and mathematical research problems. Funds were made available by the federal government, and a number of universities and equipment manufacturers started to work and, as time passed, brought out continuously improved equipment models.

These earlier pieces of equipment were all specifically designed for their computational ability, and emphasis was placed on the computational speed and accuracy of their circuitry. Provision for the storage of data was not a great problem in scientific work. All that was needed was sufficient storage facilities to store the coded set of instructions necessary to tell the computer the logical steps it was to follow in solving a given problem, an area for the data that was to be manipulated and the data to be used in the manipulation, and a place to store the resulting answer. As an example: instructions for the machine to accept input of one number (say a 4) and a second (say a 2), an instruction for the second to be added to the first, and an instruction either to hold the resulting answer (now a 6) for further manipulation or display the answer, in one of many forms, to the operator.

BUSINESS COMPUTERS.   Computers used in business have requirements that are distinctly different from those used in the scientific areas.

Speed Requirements.   Computational ability is not nearly the problem in business data processing it is in scientific data processing. Much of the total computer time spent in business processing procedures is spent in reading in data, in searching through masses of information in internal or external memory storage for the associated data to be processed, and in preparing detailed reports for managerial use.

Most of the computational need in processing business data involves very simple addition, subtraction, and only occasionally the techniques used in multiplication and division. The period required in searching out the associated data in the processing of a typical business transaction is usually of a long enough duration that any arithmetical application can normally be completed long before the next bit of data is found and prepared for processing.

Storage Requirements.   Where the scientific computer only needed modest amounts of storage for the computational work performed, the business computer has large storage requirements.

In a typical business firm, daily transactions will involve many areas of associated records. The sale of merchandise will touch upon records pertaining to sales, personnel (salesmen), payroll (commissions or salaries), cash or accounts receivable (customers), inventory (items in stock), and any number of other records in some individual firms. The purchase of merchandise affects purchases (requisitions or purchase orders), accounts payable (creditors) or cash, inventory (items in stock), and other associated accounts. Other transactions all have their impact on their associated records.

It should be obvious that any one of these typical business records may actually require the storage of hundreds or even many thousands of individual records for the processing of just a single day's transactions. Accounts receivable, accounts payable, and inventories are particularly demanding in terms of storage requirements. In fact, the demands are normally so great that it is not economically feasible for most firms to purchase a computer that has sufficient storage capacity to meet all their storage requirements simultaneously.

BASIC PROCESSING METHODS.   There are two basic methods of processing data on digital computers: batch or sequential processing and in-line or random access processing. At present the batch or sequential method is the most widely used method of business data processing. Lack of economical mass storage devices has limited the use of random access methods. There is, however, an ever increasing trend toward the random access method as research progresses in providing internal storage devices which have improved access speed in the selection of data from these storage units.

Batch or Sequential Processing.   To limit the total storage required for the complete processing of a given transaction, the data to be processed in a given transaction may be divided, in terms of the accounts it affects. Each division, or batch, is then processed against the storage provided for only one (or more) of the affected accounts.

Typically, the files of status information will be stored in external storage files such as punched cards or on magnetic tape. Here the data would normally be arranged in an alphabetic or numeric sequential order. The transaction data would also have to be sorted into sequence before the processing could proceed at a reasonable operating speed. It is because of this sequential ordering that this process method is sometimes called the *sequential method*.

In the sales example cited above, the daily sales could be accumulated in groups, or *batches* as they are more commonly called in data processing procedures, for a day or other time period until a sufficient quantity of this type of transaction is collected to make it feasible, in terms of the "setup" preparation required, for a given computer processing run.

These *batches* of sales transactions would then be processed (Figure 10–2) in conjunction with, say, the account records of all the customers of the firm. One transaction item, or a small group of these records, would be read into the computer's internal storage, the related accounts receivable status record would then be read in, and the processing performed to update the status records to include the current information on the customer account record. Where desired, the information could be

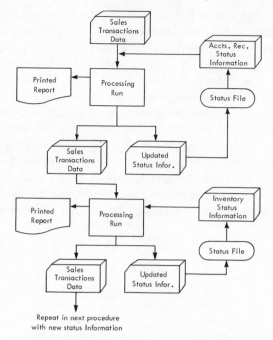

FIG. 10–2.   Batch Processing.

printed in the form of a report, as in a listing of accounts receivables. Additional transactions and related status records would then be read in and the process repeated until this *batch* of transactions is completely processed. These same sales would then be processed, in turn, with the inventory records which contain data on all the items in stock. Here the items sold would be deducted from the balances on hand to provide new balances, which reflect the actual number of these items on hand out in the warehouse or in the salesroom. Other individual transaction runs would update each of the other accounts that the sales, for the day or period, affected.

In-Line or Random Access Processing.   This method of processing follows much more closely the typical production of data and the pattern of processing that would be preferred in most business firms. In the course of a period of time we may make sales, order merchandise, pay accounts due, buy or sell assets, or do any of the many other procedural operations resulting from day-to-day business transactions. It is obvious these transactions will not occur in a patterned order but will be random in the nature of their occurrence.

In *batch* processing, we have to wait for a sufficient number of each type of transaction to occur before we can economically process the data. In *random access* processing, the transactions are prepared for input to the data processing system in the random order in which they occur. This means that within a short span of time every account is updated to reflect the transactions which have occurred rather than being forced to wait while batches of each given type of transaction have accumulated.

The requirements of a computer system capable of processing random data are considerably different from those used in batch processing. The major requirement is that the system have available a relatively vast memory storage capability.

Just as would be the case in any type of record-keeping system, any given transaction has to be processed with its respective status records. Consequently, if we are to be able to process (Figure 10–3) all transactions as they occur, we must have available, in storage, the status information pertaining to all aspects of the business. When you stop to

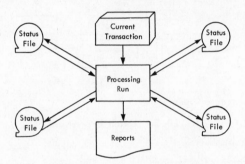

FIG. 10–3.   In-line Processing.

consider the scope of information required to store all the data pertinent to employees, customers, creditors, merchandise inventory, and the many facets of business records, it becomes apparent that vast storage provisions must be made. In even a fairly small firm the storage need for this status information may run into many millions of units of data.

In addition to the status information requirement, we would have to provide the instructions needed to tell the computer what to do with each unit of transaction data as it is fed into the computer system. These instructions would have to be made in such depth of detail that each logical procedure used in the processing of the transaction would need to be spelled out in individual steps. It is not at all unusual for a set of instructions, for a given processing procedure, to involve several hundred up to several thousand individual steps. When these steps in a single procedure are multiplied by the many procedural applications necessary in processing any random transaction that may occur, we have to have many additional million bits of storage available.

In conjunction with the need for tremendous storage files, the equipment must have the facility to select, at high speeds (normally thought of as *access time*) any single unit of status information needed. The techniques involved in providing this ability in equipment will be discussed in the following chapter, but in general, the cost of high-access-speed equipment with very large internal storage capabilities has been economically prohibitive. Most equipment with vast storage facilities is currently in the form of *disk files*. Here the data is stored on stacks of disks, each of which resembles a phonograph record.

The design of disk-type storage is such that it requires some mechanical method of moving a read and/or write head from position to position and record to record. As a result the access time to reach a given bit of information has been much slower than desired, and the cost of manufacture has been fairly high.

The demand for *in-line* processing equipment is such that it has promoted a considerable amount of research effort in this area. We will undoubtedly see some of the results of these large expenditures of funds in the relatively near future.

IN SUMMARY

To summarize the development of business computers, they may be classified into rough groupings by their generation or period of development. The first- and second-generation computers have been pretty well established, and today we are in what appears to be, and is becoming known as, the third generation of development. Figure 10–4, showing pictorially the development of IBM computers, is typical of the developments in the different generations of computers.

First-Generation Computers

Many of the forerunners of present-day computer manufacturing firms found their beginning in the development of one or more pieces of equipment in the late 1940's and early 1950's. Most of these were single units of a semi-special nature but later were improved and modified to become the ancestors of more general-purpose equipment. The know-how and staffs developed in this period provided the technical background and the leaders of many of the firms existing today.

The sequential development of computers in the initial development stage which produced the first-generation computer was, first, in the adoption of electromagnetic relays, which were then used in punched card equipment to provide control over the calculations performed. The sequential input of both instructions to the equipment and the data to be acted upon was generally through the use of punched paper tape or manually set dials or switches. In equipment produced in the intermediate stage, sequential contact was performed by externally wired plug-

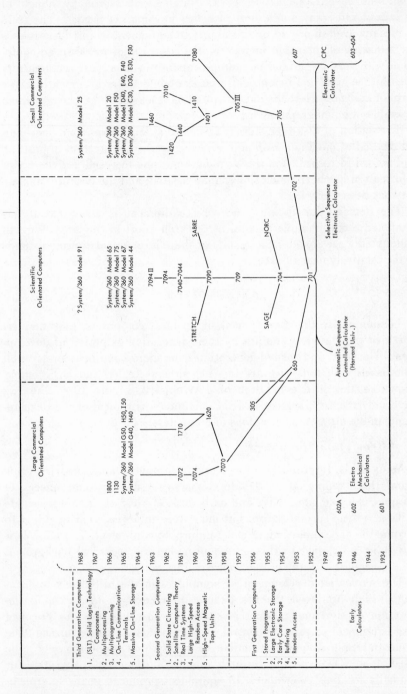

FIG. 10-4. **IBM Computer Development.**

boards similar to those used on punched card equipment. Later, the input of both instructions and data utilized punched cards as the input medium.

Storage of data was minimal at first, but as needs arose and techniques became available, storage capability increased. At first, the relays themselves "held" or indicated the data, but as time passed, mercury delay-line storage, massive banks of vacuum tubes, and electrostatic memory using a cathode-ray tube (simliar to the TV tube of today) were used. Finally, in the later part of this initial development stage, magnetic cores (discussed in detail in Chapter 12) were almost universally used to provide internal-type memory or storage.

One of the more important development concepts of the first-generation period was that of the internally stored program. This utilized internal memory banks to store either part or, later, all the instructions to the equipment to perform the solution of the problem under consideration. The data on which the calculations were to be performed were also stored in memory and called for by the equipment as it was needed in the calculations. Intermediate results would be held in storage as needed, and final answers were either placed in storage or outputed in the form of punched paper tape, punched cards, dial settings, or light indicators to the operator of the equipment.

Another development concept of this period was that of buffering, which ordered the input, output, or movement of data and instructions through a type of priority system so that data, instructions, and calculations would not be commingled and become meaningless.

Buffers serve as temporary storage devices in that as data is fed to the computer it is held until the proper time (in terms of priority or nonuse of a given part of the system) and is then fed into the operating system. In the case of outputs from the computer, the reverse procedure takes place in temporarily storing output information until the proper output device is available. An example of this last would be where a printer is currently busy on one set of output data but another set has also been prepared and is held in the buffer until the first job is completed.

Another important development of this first-generation period was that of random access to data. Most equipment of this period could only process data in some form of serial or sequential order. This was usually satisfactory in the processing of mathematical or engineering data of that period but was very inefficient in the processing of business data.

As an example, customer data in the form of accounts receivable would probably be stored in alphabetical order, but sales are never made on this basis. To process sales on account, they must be accumulated for some period of time and then put in order and processed. This lag between time of sale and final processing meant that some accounts were not up to date. If each sale (and even more important when applied to all the transactions of a typical business) could be processed as it was completed by selecting the balance stored in memory directly—rather than serially searching down through the file until that customer is found—not only sales but all types of transactions could be processed as they occurred.

Second-Generation Computers

With the development of the transistor and other solid-state components (Figure 10–5), along with techniques to produce circuit-board-type wiring, the stage was set for the second generation of computers. This period is generally conceded to have started about 1958 with the introduction of the IBM 1620 and IBM 1401. Of course, computers produced

Courtesy of IBM.

FIG. 10–5.   Second and Third Generation Components.

by other manufacturers and additional IBM equipment were quick to follow the initial introduction of solid-state computers.

Some of the major advantages of the use of solid-state circuitry included those of size, reliability, and lower heat dissipation and power requirements. These advantages permitted an increase in efficiency and greater operating power and capability at a lower cost per unit of work performed.

Equipment which had previously required several rooms full of components could now be housed in a single room of average size, and in smaller models, desk-size computers became available for smaller business firm needs.

The previously used vacuum tubes (and thousands were used in early computers) were now replaced by transistors and diodes, which were much more reliable over long periods of time than were the vacuum tubes. These could be tested periodically to determine their operating level and could be replaced before this level fell to a point that would affect efficient operation. When computer users adopted testing schedules utilizing regular preventive maintenance techniques, they solved many of their problems relating to the upkeep and avoidance of downtime on their computer systems.

Solid-state circuitry required a comparatively low power requirement with a resulting decrease in heat dissipation. In the first-generation equipment, special large-volume air-conditioning units were required to keep the operating environment—both for the equipment and the operators—at a level that could be tolerated. Now, in most instances, the regular air-conditioning system provided adequate cooling.

In every way—including the original cost of the equipment, operating cost, reliability, maintenance, and physical facility needs—the use of solid-state circuitry resulted in a lower cost per unit of output produced. This lower cost, in turn, made the equipment available to many other users and the "computer age" truly came into being.

The concept of random access data processing was further developed by most computer manufacturers, and removable disk packs (see Chapter 12 for details) were developed which permitted machine-readable files to be stored nearby for quick insertion into disk drives when a given file of data (such as accounts receivable, inventory, or accounts payable) was needed to process current transactions. Magnetic drums, cores, and film were also made available for use in random access data processing. Through an extension of these techniques the concept of "on-line real-time" data processing (see Chapter 13) began to be more than just a possibility.

Another major development in this second-generation period was that of high-speed magnetic tape units which made available reels of magnetic tape. These provided relatively cheap data storage which could be placed on tape drives as needed and utilized directly by the computer at high speeds. Even though this data had to be processed sequentially (serially), these magnetic tape units provided usable massive data storage at an economical cost.

Data transmission and communication devices were developed in this period to provide the capabilities necessary to develop fundamental techniques necessary to sending and receiving data from both local and remote data processing centers.

Manufacturers began to develop computer systems which could be expanded from a small or medium-sized system to a large system. These computers were expanded by compatible equipment units utilizing what is often termed the "building block principle." Thus a system could expand with the growth and need of the firm rather than being completely replaced by a new system.

The developments of this period resulted in a realization that the computer was not only here to stay but—to business in particular—it was to become more than just a device to replace the calculators and punched card machines. Its capabilities provided management with the means, for the first time, of having a true management information system capable of meeting most of their needs (through historical records, statistical data, forecasts, and other management science techniques).

Third-Generation Computers

Today, we are still in the early stages of the third generation of equipment. In the 1960's, we began to see the development of miniaturized components for use in the space programs. By the mid-1960's, these became microminiaturized and utilized what is now termed solid logic technology (SLT) to incorporate the components required in many circuits into small solid blocks (Figure 10–6). These SLT components require low voltages, produce very little heat, are far more reliable than comparable components of the past, and are ultrasmall in size.

Massive data storage capabilities are now available to provide reliable high-speed access to literally millions to billions of units of stored data.

There is almost an endless expansion and implementation of new techniques in data collection, data transmission, and data communication which permits the utilization of remote terminal and display unit facilities to be on-line with centralized computer installations.

Courtesy of IBM.

FIG. 10–6. Solid Logic Technology (SLT) Component.

On-line real-time systems' capabilities are becoming a reality through the use of these remote facilities and newly developed multiprogramming and multiprocessing techniques. Executive control programs (see Chapter 15) have been developed which permit many individual operating programs to be processed in what, to the uninitiated, appears to be a simultaneous operation through multiprogramming. Not only can many operators using remote facilities communicate with the computer at one time, but it is now possible for computers to communicate with other computers through multiprocessing. This permits local computers, of a given firm, to communicate with the large centralized computers of that firm to provide and receive data and to utilize the additional processing capabilities of the large computer as they are needed locally.

With the "hardware" developments of the third-generation computers, the capabilities of these machines have now become so extensive and complex that the only limitation—now and in the foreseeable future—seems to be in the imaginative and creative ability of the humans who devise new usage techniques and develop the "software" to implement them.

Truly, at this stage, man's abilities to fully utilize the equipment available are lagging far behind the capabilities of this equipment. This in itself is one of the greatest challenges ever presented to a single generation in the development of man.

ANNOTATED BIBLIOGRAPHY

Burck, Gilbert. "The Boundless Age of the Computer," *Fortune*, March, 1964.

This article tells the story of the impact of the computer on the past and forecasts future impact. The great changes in the computer and its importance in business are summarized. The warning is extended that tomorrow's executives must make use of the computer or they will not succeed.

Chapin, Ned. *An Introduction to Automatic Computers*, 2d ed. Princeton, N.J.: D. Van Nostrand Co., Inc., 1963.

Chapter 9 of this book gives a fairly complete history of not only computers, but also of all types of data handling equipment. It gives the history of both hardware and software. Chronological tables of the developments in data handling and the development of automatic computers are also illustrated.

"The Cranky Grandfather of the Computer," *Fortune*, March, 1964.

This article is about Charles Babbage, a man who was 120 years before his time. Babbage produced the first practical mechanical computer, the "Analytical Engine," in 1822.

Desmonde, William H. *Computers and Their Uses*. Englewood Cliffs, N.J.: Prentice-Hall, Inc., 1964.

The essential characteristics of digital data processing machines and their uses are presented. Specialized instruction in design, programming, and applications are not provided, but concepts basic to all of these areas are explained by examples. Punched card machines, organization and functions of a computer, information representation, machine logic, elements of programming and algebra, magnetic-tape operations, and programming techniques are discussed.

HANDEL, PAUL VON. *Electronic Computers.* Englewood Cliffs, N.J.: Prentice-Hall, Inc., 1961.

An introduction to both analog and digital computers. It explains the basic structure of computers, number systems utilized, and programming and control considerations necessary for a satisfactory computer installation.

QUESTIONS

1. Why is Babbage often spoken of as the father of computers?
2. When was the first modern-day computer developed, where, and by whom?
3. Describe the characteristics of ENIAC, the first completely electronic, high-speed computer.
4. Which well-known computer manufacturers of today are pioneers in this field of endeavor?
5. Has the development of computer capabilities been rapid? Explain. Give some examples.
6. For what were the early computers used? Explain.
7. In general, what were the physical characteristics of the first computers?
8. Have the physical characteristics of computers changed through time? Explain.
9. It seems, at times, that we have heard of computers most of our lives, but just how long ago was it that computers were first used in business data processing?
10. What are the two major families of computers? Describe the features of each and how they differ in functions performed.
11. What are some of the distinguishing features of computers designed for scientific work? Of those designed for business processing systems?
12. How did the concept of programming these machines change through time?
13. What operating problems were experienced with the first-generation machines?
14. Were these problems in question No. 13 in any way alleviated by the second generation of machines?
15. Which of the two basic methods utilized in processing business data on digital computers is most widely used today? Why?
16. Of the two basic processing methods, which is the most desirable in

terms of following the pattern of transactions found in a typical business firm?

17. What are some of the advantages of solid-state circuitry?
18. Describe several characteristics which differentiate third-generation computers from second-generation computers.

CHAPTER 11

Computer Organization

and Codes

IN EVERY business information processing system, whether it is a manual, mechanical, punched card, or electronic computer system, certain basic elements must be present. These elements must provide the means to achieve the required basic data processing concepts of origination, classification, sorting, calculating, summarizing, recording, and communicating.

Input must be provided, as data and information must have some way of getting into the system. Once the data are in the system, there must be some provision for the *storage* of the information so that it can be utilized at a later date. It may be reclassified, manipulated arithmetically, or recalled for presentation in its original form. There must also be some provision for the *control* of the input of data into the system, the *storage* of that data, the *processing* of the data to meet the requirements of given procedures, and an *output* in the form of reports or analyses.

In the electronic computer processing system the *input* of data is performed by various types of input devices which also frequently serve as output devices as well. Typical input devices include those accepting punched cards, magnetic tape, punched paper tape, magnetic ink, films, analog computer output, optically scanned data, and typewritten material, and there is always the provision for data to be entered into the system through the switches and buttons on the console of the computer itself.

The *central processing unit* of the computer system is made up of three distinct sections which perform different functions. First, the unit provides a control section for the *control* of all the operations performed by the computer through predetermined instructions (programs) stored internally in the machine. This control section directs and coordinates the entire computer system as a single multipurpose machine.

Second, this unit provides an *arithmetic-logical* section. The arithmetic part of this section performs the operations of addition, subtraction, multiplication, division, shifting, transferring, comparing, and storing. The logical part of this section provides the machine's ability to test various conditions found during processing procedures and to take any action required as the result of the test. Such a test might be one to determine if one number is larger than, equal to, or less than another number. The next procedure to be performed would then vary depending on the condition found in the test.

The third and last section provides the memory or *storage* facilities required for the retention of the input information, the program which directs the processing, and the files of data needed for reference or additional processing. This storage consists of two distinct types: *internal storage*, which is contained in the central processing unit itself; and *external storage*, which is contained in separate storage devices external to the central processing unit but which is available, on demand, to the computer when it is requested by the control section. A third type of storage is that of *off-line storage*, which provides data storage in some form that is not interconnected to, or directly usable by, the computer. An example of this last is that of punched cards filed in a storage cabinet. Data stored in both the internal and external storage devices accessible to the computer on demand must, of course, be filed in some machine-acceptable form which is understood by the particular computer in use. Off-line storage data may or may not be in a machine-acceptable form, depending upon the need of the system.

Output devices in a computer system record or write information as directed by the computer. This output may be presented in some coded form (such as punched cards, punched paper tape, magnetic tape, magnetic disks, or console lights), it may be printed out on paper (by typewriters or various types of printers), displayed on some form of display tube (similar to television), or even presented in the form of electrical impulses used to direct other computers (particularly to analog computers which direct various physical control devices).

STORED PROGRAMS

It has long been the desire of man to have machines lighten his load. As mechanical devices were developed, they did this to some extent, but such devices still required the personal attention of man in the performance of each function, such as in turning wheels, twisting knobs, pulling handles, and depressing keys. With the invention and development of the computer, however, much of the old dream began to be realized. For the first time, man could "write out" a set of instructions which could be used to direct the computer in an extensive procedural operation, store these instructions in memory, and provide the data necessary to the procedure. All he had to do was punch a button telling the machine to "get started" and literally wait while the work was completed at a fantastic speed.

This self-directing ability of the computer is centered in the control section of the central processing unit. This unit acts upon a series of prepared coded instructions which have been fed into the memory section of the computer—usually in internal storage—to direct the computer in performing its data processing task.

The series of coded instructions used in directing the computer in performing a given procedure is known as a *program*. The fundamental ideas necessary to the preparation of such a program (programming) are presented in Chapter 15. The individual steps of the program are those logical steps necessary to complete the processing procedure. These will, of course, vary with the computer in use and the procedure under consideration but would normally direct the various devices under the control of the computer in the manipulation of the data. Data would be read into the computer, stored in storage, processed as directed, and the results indicated in some output form. The possible variations of such a stored program provides the data processing system with almost unlimited flexibility.

COMPUTER DATA CODES

Just as data must be communicated between people in the form of spoken words or written words or symbols, so must data be communicated from humans to computers. Though experimental efforts are being made in directing the computer in its work by voice communication, the many complexities of human languages have, to date, restricted this means of instruction to a limited number of commands. Consequently, almost all computer instructions have been in some form of writing. As you will learn in Chapter 15, the more modern program languages can be written in the English language, and these are acceptable to the machine. However, the English language is a very inefficient language for internal computer usage, and a provision has been made for the computer to convert the English language instructions to some form acceptable to the computer. The codes and symbols acceptable vary with the computer and the associated input, output, and storage devices in use, and the conversion to these language forms is an almost automatic operation. Consequently, there may be some question as to the necessity of man being able to "speak" the language of the computer. However, in the course of writing, testing, and correcting a program, it is sometimes necessary to determine what—and where—data are contained in storage and what are the individual operations as they are performed on the data. This, plus the fact that most input forms of data are also in some form of code, makes it necessary for those associated with computer systems to get acquainted with some of the various forms of data representation used.

Binary Codes

Nearly every code form utilized in computer communication is based on some adaption of the binary number system, as this has proven to be the most efficient system for use in computers. This system differs from the decimal number system, which is based upon tenths and the digits 0

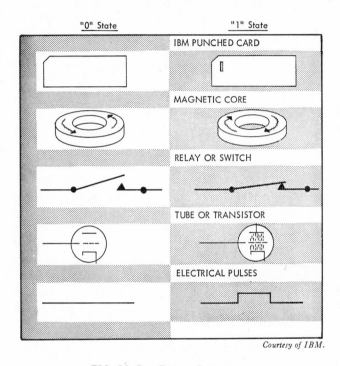

Courtesy of IBM.

FIG. 11–1.   Binary Indicators.

through 9, in that data can only be represented by two digits in the binary system; 0 and 1. These binary notations are also called *bits* with the 0 condition described as *no bit* and the 1 state described as a *bit*.

The representation of two possible conditions or states, termed a binary mode, can be expressed in many ways, and many different forms of binary modes are found in computer coding (Figure 11–1). In the punched card the 0 state is expressed by the absence of a hole in the card and the 1 state is the presence of such a hole and indicates the presence of data. In the magnetic core, a small unit of storage used in computers, current flows either in one direction or the other. In the case of relays or switches, the circuit is either open or closed. In electronic tubes or transistors, current either doesn't flow or it flows. And, for continuous electrical currents, there is either no pulse, or surge of current, present or there is such a pulse. These are only typical binary mode representations and certainly do not exhaust the many conditions which might also indicate a 0 or 1 state.

Once the 0 and 1 state is understood, we need to progress to an explanation of how the presence of such a bit or no bit can be utilized in the representation of data to the computer. If we had a series of such states (Figure 11–2) and assigned each bit position a progressive value of

etc. ←	2^6	2^5	2^4	2^3	2^2	2^1	2^0	Power of 2
etc. ←	7	6	5	4	3	2	1	Place position
etc. ←	64	32	16	8	4	2	1	Place (bit) value

FIG. 11–2.   **Place Value of Binary Numbers.**

powers of the number 2, the first place position would represent 2^0 (two to the zero power) and have the place value of 1, the second would represent 2^1 or a place value of 2, the third 2^2 or a place value of 4, the fourth 2^3 or 8, and so on until our series of place positions are all assigned a place value. It is also interesting to note that as you progress in the series from right to left, each place position is double the value of the previous. Thus with the first position assigned a place value of 1, you double this and arrive at the place value of 2 for the second position, double this for a value of 4 for the third position, again for an 8 in the fourth, and so on for the series.

64	32	16	8	4	2	1	Bit Values
0 +	0 +	0 +	0 +	0 +	0 +	0	= 0
0 +	0 +	0 +	1 +	0 +	0 +	1	= 9
1 +	0 +	1 +	1 +	0 +	0 +	1	= 89

FIG. 11–3.   **Binary Place Value Addition.**

These place-positioned values (Figure 11–3) indicate that if there is a 0 or no bit condition in each of the place positions in a series, there is no data representation. If there are 1's or bits in the first and fourth place positions (with no bits in the other positions), there is a binary coded representation of the decimal number 9. $(1 \times 2^0) + (1 \times 2^3) = (2 \times 1) + (1 \times 8)$ which, in turn, equals the decimal number 9. If there are bits in place positions one, four, five, and seven there is the binary representation of $(1 \times 2^0) + (1 \times 2^3) + (1 \times 2^4) + (1 \times 2^6)$ or $(1 \times 1) + (1 \times 8) + (1 \times 16) + (1 \times 64)$ which equals the decimal number 89.

To obtain the binary equivalent of a decimal number, select the largest binary place position (highest power of 2) whose value does not exceed the decimal number. Deduct its decimal value from the decimal number and repeat until there is no remainder left. For example, to obtain the binary equivalent of the decimal number 86, the largest power of 2 which does not exceed 86 is 2^6 whose decimal value is 64. Deducting 64 from 86 leaves 22. Next would be 2^4 or 16 which deducted leaves the decimal 6. Then deducting the decimal value of 2^2 or 4 we obtain a 2 whose binary equivalent is 2^1. Thus, $2^6 + 2^4 + 2^2 + 2^1 = 86$. However, to write these in binary form we must assign binary values "0" or "1" to each of the series of place positions affected, or $(1 \times 2^6) + (0 \times 2^5) + (1 \times 2^4) + (0 \times 2^3) + (1 \times 2^2) + (1 \times 2^1) + (0 \times 2^0)$, which binary values, in turn, becomes the binary number 1010110.

The above method is not difficult when you are accustomed to working with binary numbers or the binary number is not too large a value. Where this is not the case, however, another method is available to aid in conversion. This method is to make a continued division of the decimal number by 2 and record any remainder not divisible by 2. Reading the remainders from bottom to top and placing them in order from left to right the binary equivalent desired is obtained. Using the same example above:

		Remainder
2	86	0
2	43	1
2	21	1
2	10	0
2	5	1
2	2	0
2	1	1
	0	

Reading upward we obtain 1010110 or 86.

Now that we have seen how the equivalents of decimal numbers are represented in the binary number system, we need to consider how the arithmetical operations of addition, subtraction, multiplication, and division are accomplished using binary numbers. First, let us recall one of the things which must be remembered in the decimal number system. If one is adding a column of decimal numbers, there is no problem if the total of the units position does not exceed the number 9. However, if the total is 10, 11, or more you have to put down the unit number of the answer and "carry" the 10's, or larger, portion of the answer over to the next, or 10's, column of the numbers you are adding and continue until all columns are added.

In binary addition the same general rule of "carry" holds except that now there are only two possible numbers (0 and 1) to add. Thus a set of rules can be developed which may be followed in the addition of binary numbers by using a matrix of numbers to array our data as illustrated in Figure 11–4.

	0	1
0	0	1
1	1	0

0 + 0 (column 1, row 1) = 0
0 + 1 (column 1, row 2) = 1
1 + 0 (column 2, row 1) = 1
1 + 1 (column 2, row 2) = 0, carry 1*

* If a series of 1's are to be added, each time a 1 is added to a 1 a carry results. Thus you may have several "carrys" to start with when adding the next column.

FIG. 11–4.   Binary Addition Matrix Array.

To follow a practical example of binary addition, take the numbers 0011 + 0100 + 0101 as shown in Figure 11–5. In the first, or units, column add the 1 in row one to the 0 in row two, and following the rules above obtain an answer of 1. Then adding this 1 to the 1 in row three we obtain an answer of 0 with 1 to carry. In the second column, add the carried 1 to the 1 of the first row to obtain a 0 with a carry of 1. This 0 when added successively to the 0's in the second and third rows provides an answer of 0 for this column. In the third column, add the carried 1 to the 0, the answer 1, this added to 1 provides an answer of 0 with one to

	8	4	2	1	*Bit Values*		
	1	1	1		"Carry" values		
	0	0	1	1	= Digit	3	
+	0	1	0	0	= Digit	4	to be added
+	0	1	0	1	= Digit	5	to be added
	1	1	0	0	= Answer	12	

FIG. 11–5.   Binary Addition.

carry. This 0 is added to 1 for a column total of 1. In the fourth column, the carried 1 is added to the successive 0's for a column total of 1. Thus, the complete total is 1100 which is equivalent to the decimal number 12. This also "just happens" to be the total of the decimal equivalents of the three binary numbers $(3 + 4 + 5)$.

In decimal arithmetic, if a larger number is subtracted from a smaller number, a unit digit must be "borrowed" from the first column to the left which contains a decimal digit. This rule also carries over into binary arithmetic and follows in the rules for subtraction developed from the binary subtraction matrix array in Figure 11–6.

	0	1
0	0	1
1	1	0

$0 - 0$ (column 1, row 1) = 0
$0 - 1$ (column 1, row 2) = -1, or 1 with 1 borrowed
$1 - 0$ (column 2, row 1) = 1
$1 - 1$ (column 2, row 2) = 0

FIG. 11–6. Binary Subtraction Matrix Array.

An example of binary subtraction is shown in Figure 11–7 where the number 00101 is subtracted from 11001. In the first column, 1 is subtracted from 1 leaving 0. In the second, $0 - 0 = 0$. In the third, $0 - 1$ (following the rule above) $= 1$. (In effect, what has happened is that an eight is borrowed as two 4's and when one 4 is subtracted there is a balance of 4 left.) In the fourth column, $0 - 0$ (the 1 was borrowed for the previous column) $= 0$. And in the last column, $1 - 0 = 1$ for a complete total of 10100. Converted to decimal equivalents, $25 - 5 = 20$.

If the subtraction problem above was reversed, i.e., 11001 from 00101, where a larger number would be subtracted from a smaller, the numbers would be arrayed just as they are above (with signs reversed) and the resulting answer would be a negative number.

	16	8	4	2	1	Bit Values
			1			'Borrowed' values
		0	1			(2–4's for the 1–8)
+	1	⟋	0	0	1	= +25
−	0	0	1	0	1	= − 5
	1	0	1	0	0	= 20 Answer

FIG. 11–7. Binary Subtraction.

	0	1
0	0	0
1	0	1

0×0 (column 1, row 1) = 0
0×1 (column 1, row 2) = 0
1×0 (column 2, row 1) = 0
1×1 (column 2, row 2) = 1

FIG. 11–8.   Binary Multiplication Matrix Array.

Rules for multiplication can be developed from the binary multiplication matrix array as shown in Figure 11–8.

To multiply in the binary system, you follow the same procedure as in the decimal system. First you multiply the multiplicand by the multiplier.

128	64	32	16	8	4	2	1	*Bit Value*
				1	1	0	1	= 13 Multiplicand
				1	0	1	1	$\times$ 11 Multiplier
				1	1	0	1	= 13 First operation
	1	1	1					"Carry" values
			1	1	0	1		+ 26 Second operation
	1	1	0	1				+ 104 Third operation
1	0	0	0	1	1	1	1	= 143 Answer

FIG. 11–9.   Binary Multiplication.

If these numbers each contain two or more digits, there will as a result be two or more rows of numbers forthcoming which need to be totaled before the answer is obtained. Thus, both the rules of multiplication and addition must be applied. Multiplying 1101 (13) by 1011 (11) thus produces the answer 10001111 (143) as shown in Figure 11–9.

	8	4	2	1	128	64	32	16	8	4	2	1	*Bit Values*
								1	1	0	1		= 13 Answer
Divisor 11 =	1	0	1	1	1	0	0	0	1	1	1	1	= 143 Dividend
					1	0	1	1					− 88 First Operation
					0	1	1	0	1	(1	1)		= 55 Result Balance
						1	0	1	1				− 44 Second Operation
						0	0	1	0	1	1		= 11 Result Balance
							1	0	1	1			− 11 Third Operation
										0			= 0 Remainder

FIG. 11–10.   Binary Division.

The rules for division in binary numbers follows exactly the same rules for long division in decimal numbers. When determining how many times the divisor will go into the dividend, the rules of multiplication are needed, and when you are determining if there is a remainder, the rules of subtraction are required. As an example, follow the division of 10001111 (143) by 1011 (11) to obtain the resulting answer 1101 (13) in Figure 11–10.

It must also be remembered that subtraction can be performed by using the complement of the number to be subtracted and adding to produce the proper answer.

$$\begin{array}{ll} 25 & 25 \\ -13 \text{ or} & +99987 \text{ Complement of 13} \\ \hline 12 & 100012 \text{ (Always ignore the last carry)} \end{array}$$

Multiplication may be performed by the repeated addition of the multiplicand the number of times indicated by the multiplier.

$$\begin{array}{rr} 10 & 10 \\ \times\ 5 & +10 \\ \hline 50 & +10 \\ & +10 \\ & +10 \\ \hline & 50 \end{array}$$

Division can be accomplished by determining how many times the divisor can be subtracted from the dividend.

$$10 \div 5 = 2 \quad 10 - 5 = 5 - 5 = 0 \text{ (Answer 2)}$$

These last methods of subtraction, multiplication, and division are all used in some different makes and models of computers, and the use of binary arithmetic is equally applicable to these methods. This presentation of how arithmetical calculations are performed in computers is to develop "just a glimmer" of the technical aspects involved and to allow the reader to have some understanding of how these "electronic brains" perform.

BINARY CODED DECIMAL SYSTEM. Once the binary number system is grasped, it is easy to understand the binary coded decimal system of numbers. If you use only four positions of place values—8, 4, 2, and 1—it will be seen that these four positions can provide the binary equivalent of the decimal digits 0 through 9 (Figure 11–11). Then, if these groups of four bit values are assigned the units, tens, hundreds, thousands, etc., designation (as is done in a series of digits in a number in the decimal system), one is then able to express the decimal number 6,452 in binary coded decimals (BCD) as

Thousands	*Hundreds*	*Tens*	*Units*	
6	4	5	2	Decimals
0110	0100	0101	0010	Binary coded decimals

instead of 1100100110100 as in binary code.

8	4	2	1	Bit Value	
0	0	0	0	=	0
0	0	0	1	=	1
0	0	1	0	=	2
0	0	1	1	=	3
0	1	0	0	=	4
0	1	0	1	=	5
0	1	1	0	=	6
0	1	1	1	=	7
1	0	0	0	=	8
1	0	0	1	=	9

FIG. 11–11.   Binary Representation of Decimal Digits 0–9.

The BCD system is subject to the same procedures used in performing arithmetical calculations as was the binary system of numbers. In addition it is possible to adapt the binary coded decimal system to provide, in addition to numbers, the alphabetic letters and characters needed in processing business data.

To momentarily recall the Hollerith punched card code, numbers were expressed by a single punched hole in the digit punch area. Letters and characters were provided by the addition of a zone punch(s) in combination with a digit punch. Now to return to the binary coded decimal system. If four binary bit positions provide the numeric digit needed, we can add two additional binary bits to the bit array and assign them A and B zone designations to provide the zone bit(s) required in combination with a digit bit in the designation of letters and characters (Figure 11–12). Where three zones—12, 11 and 0—were provided in punched card code the B bit can be the equivalent of the 11 zone, the A bit can be the equivalent of the 0 zone, and a combination of both the A and B bits can be the equivalent of the 12 zone. Usually a seventh bit position is added to provide what is called a "check" bit, which permits computers to check automatically the data as entered into the machine for valid data codes. This procedure is termed a *parity check*, which in some equipment is an even number of bits (even parity) and in others an odd number of bits (odd parity). As data are transmitted, each character is automatically checked to determine if the correct parity condition exists (Figure

Check Bit	Zone Bits		Numeric Bits			
C	B	A	8	4	2	1

FIG. 11–12.   Bit Positions, Seven-Bit Alphameric Code.

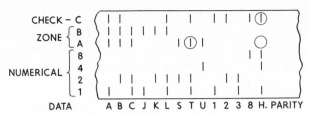

FIG. 11–13.   Even Parity, Horizontal Check.

11–13). In the illustration, check bits are added for the letters A, B, L, T, and the numbers 1, 2, 8.

In some equipment there is also a horizontal parity check performed on each channel at the end of a given unit of data where bits are added for the parity condition found in each channel. If a bit had not been recorded, such as the circled item above the letter T, there would have been a horizontal parity bit necessary, see blank circle, and the horizontal parity bit for the A channel would not have been required. However, the parity needs for the C channel would not be in agreement with the parity needs for the horizontal parity column. This would be sensed automatically and a check made as to where the error might be by a reread procedure.

Some equipment recently developed is so sophisticated that once it has determined where an error, such as the above, exists, it can automatically make a decision to correct the error and insert the missing bit or bits required. Not all bit errors are this simple, so only certain types of errors are automatically corrected.

SIX-BIT NUMERIC CODE.   Another binary code that should be mentioned is the *Six-Bit Numeric Code* which is utilized in the popular IBM 1620 computer. As indicated in the name assigned, six positions of binary notation are used in the representation of numbers.

These positions are divided into three groupings (Figure 11–14). First is a C or parity check bit which is utilized in checking the accuracy of the recording of the data in the other groups. This code is normally odd parity, so the C bit is only used when the net effect of the other bit positions is an even number of binary bits.

Check Bit	*Flag Bit*	*Numeric Bit Positions*			
C	F	8	4	2	1

FIG. 11–14.   Bit Positions, Six-Bit Numeric Code.

The *F* or flag bit position is a special-purpose binary bit which is used to indicate a negative number in a numeric field (F–4–1 represents a –5); the leftmost (highest-order) digit in a field of consecutive digits in arithmetic operations and the internal transmission of this field;

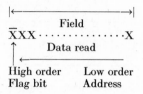

and a few other specialized uses.

The numeric bit positions are assigned 8, 4, 2, 1 place values (Figure 11–15) as are the first four place positions in other binary codes.

Decimal Digit	Place Value					
	C	F	8	4	2	1
0	1	0	0	0	0	0
1	0	0	0	0	0	1
2	0	0	0	0	1	0
3	1	0	0	0	1	1
4	0	0	0	1	0	0
5	1	0	0	1	0	1
6	1	0	0	1	1	0
7	0	0	0	1	1	1
8	0	0	1	0	0	0
9	1	0	1	0	0	1

FIG. 11–15.   Six-Bit Numeric Code.

In representing alphabetic or special characters in the Six-Bit Numeric Code, two numeric value groupings are used (Figure 11–16) with the first

	One Digit						One Digit				
C	F	8	4	2	1	C	F	8	4	2	1
0	0	0	1	0	0	0	0	0	0	0	1

FIG. 11–16.   Letter *A* in Six-Bit Numeric Code.

group indicating the equivalent of zones as used in punched card coding. However, if you will note the zone digit columns of Figure 11–17, there are 8 zones (0 through 7) used in this code. The letter A is thus coded as a combination of a "4" zone digit and a "1" numeric digit.

HEXADECIMAL CODE. To offset the disadvantages of the long strings of zeros and ones in the binary code representation of large numbers, a base 16, rather than a base 2, number system is utilized in several computer systems, which includes the widely used family of computers in the IBM System/360.

In the hexadecimal number system each hexadecimal digit represents

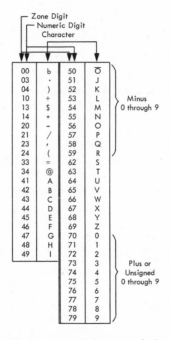

FIG. 11–17. Alphameric Codes.

four binary digits (Figure 11–18). Just as in base 10 number systems, 10 numerical symbols are required, and in base 2, or binary, 2 symbols are necessary, the base 16 hexadecimal system utilizes 16 symbols. These symbols include the familiar 0 through 9 numbers and in addition use the letters A through F to provide a total of 16 symbols, whose place values 1 through 16 are assigned in ascending order, first to the 0 through 9 and then to A through F symbols.

In the illustration above, the hexadecimal representation of the decimal numbers 16 through 31 is provided by a 1 in the "carry" position. Other decimal numbers are provided by using larger hexadecimal values in carry positions.

Decimal	Hexadecimal	Binary	Decimal	Hexadecimal	Binary
0	0	0000	16	10	10000
1	1	0001	17	11	10001
2	2	0010	18	12	10010
3	3	0011	19	13	10011
4	4	0100	20	14	10100
5	5	0101	21	15	10101
6	6	0110	22	16	10110
7	7	0111	23	17	10111
8	8	1000	24	18	11000
9	9	1001	25	19	11001
10	A	1010	26	1A	11010
11	B	1011	27	1B	11011
12	C	1100	28	1C	11100
13	D	1101	29	1D	11101
14	E	1110	30	1E	11110
15	F	1111	31	1F	11111

FIG. 11–18.   **Decimal, Hexadecimal, and Binary Notation.**

To convert binary numbers to hexadecimal notation, simply divide the number into groups of four binary digits, starting from the right, and replace each group by the corresponding hexadecimal symbol. If the left-hand group is incomplete, fill in zeros as required. For example, the binary number

$$111110011011010011 = 0011/1110/0110/1101/0011$$
$$= \quad 3 \quad\quad E \quad\quad 6 \quad\quad D \quad\quad 3$$
$$= (3E6D3)_{16}$$

If the binary number is a fraction or a mixed number, care must be taken to mark off groups of four bits from each side of the binary position. Thus the binary number

$$1011001010.1011011 = 0010/1100/1010.1011/0110$$
$$= \quad 2 \quad\quad C \quad\quad A \quad\quad B \quad\quad 6$$
$$= (2CA.B6)_{16}$$

Similarly, to convert hexadecimal numbers into binary, substitute the corresponding group of four binary digits for each hexadecimal symbol and drop off any unnecessary zeros. For instance, the hexadecimal number

$$(6C4F2E.7B8)_{16} = \quad 6 \quad\quad C \quad\quad 4 \quad\quad F \quad\quad 2 \quad\quad E \quad\quad 7 \quad\quad B \quad\quad 8$$
$$= 0110/1100/0100/1111/0010/1110.0111/1011/1000$$
$$= (11011000100111100101110.011110111)_2$$

The meaning of hexadecimal numbers is made clear by expansion in powers of 16. For example, the hexadecimal number 2CA.B6, above, means (when decimals are substituted for hexadecimal symbols)

$$(2 \times 16^2) + (12 \times 16^1) + (10 \times 16^0) + (11 \times 16^{-1}) + (6 \times 16^{-2})$$
$$= (2 \times 256) + (12 \times 16) + (10 \times 1) + (11 \div 16) + (6 \div 256)$$
$$= 512 + 192 + 10 + 0.6875 + 0.0234375$$
$$= 714 + 0.7109375 = (714.7109375)_{10}$$

In working out an example of this type, it is best to arrange the products in a vertical column for convenient addition.[1]

EXTENDED BINARY CODED DECIMAL INTERCHANGE CODE. Other terminology, closely associated with computer coding, which will be used in conjunction with various equipment in data to follow is "words" and "bytes." A "word" is a varying group of binary bits (depending on the computer system involved) which is acceptable to the equipment as a unit of input. In some equipment, a "word" may be subdivided into several "bytes." In the IBM System/360 a word is 32 binary bits long, but may be subdivided into four bytes of 8 binary bits each. Each byte

Bit Positions → 01

4567	00				01				10				11			
23	00	01	10	11	00	01	10	11	00	01	10	11	00	01	10	11
0000	NUL				BLANK	&	–						>	<	‡	0
0001							/		a	j			A	J		1
0010									b	k	s		B	K	S	2
0011									c	l	t		C	L	T	3
0100	PF	RES	BYP	PN					d	m	u		D	M	U	4
0101	HT	NL	LF	RS					e	n	v		E	N	V	5
0110	LC	BS	EOB	UC					f	o	w		F	O	W	6
0111	DEL	IDL	PRE	EOT					g	p	x		G	P	X	7
1000									h	q	y		H	Q	Y	8
1001					·		,	"	i	r	z		I	R	Z	9
1010					?			:								
1011					·	$	,	#								
1100					←	*	%	@								
1101					(	)	~	'								
1110					+	;	_	=								
1111					‡	¢	±	✓								

Courtesy of IBM.

FIG. 11–19.   Extended Binary Coded Decimal Interchange Code.

may be used to represent two four-bit binary digits (place values of 8, 4, 2, and 1), an eight-bit binary digit (place values of 128, 64, 32, 16, 8, 4, 2, and 1), or a single eight-bit BCD character (four zone bits and four digit bits with place values of 8, 4, 2, and 1). Such a byte provides a possible 250 six-bit combinations for letters, digits, and symbols, for greater versatility in both binary and decimal operations, in what is called an Extended Binary Coded Decimal Interchange Code (EBCDIC), which is illustrated in Figure 11–19.

A fairly recent attempt to develop an acceptable standard code for all

[1] International Business Machines Corporation, *A Programmer's Introduction to the IBM System/360 Architecture, Instructions, and Assembler Language*, (White Plains, N.Y., 1966), p. 28.

uses has resulted in the American Standard Code for Information Interchange (ASCII—pronounced "askey") shown in Figure 11–20). This code utilizes the eight-bit byte, described above, or two sets of binary coded decimal codes to convey a single number, letter, or character.

Bit Positions ——— **76**

4321	00	01	10	11	00	01	10	11	00	01	10	11	00	01	10	11
	\<— X5															
	00				**01**				**10**				**11**			
0000	NULL	DC_0			₺ blank	0					@	P				P
0001	SOM	DC_1			!	1					A	Q			a	q
0010	EOA	DC_2			"	2					B	R			b	r
0011	EOM	DC_3			#	3					C	S			c	s
0100	EOT	DC_4 STOP			⌐ $	4					D	T			d	t
0101	WRU	ERR			%	5					E	U			e	u
0110	RU	SYNC			&	6					F	V			f	v
0111	BELL	LEM			'	7					G	W			g	w
1000	BKSP	S_0			(	8					H	X			h	x
1001	HT	S_1			)	9					I	Y			i	y
1010	LF	S_2			*	:					J	Z			j	z
1011	VT	S_3			+	;					K	[			k	
1100	FF	S_4			,	<					L	\			l	
1101	CR	S_5			-	=					M	]			m	
1110	SO	S_6			.	>					N	↑			n	ESC
1111	SI	S_7			/	?					O	←			o	DEL

Identification of Control Symbols and Some Graphics

NULL	Null/Idle	V TAB	Vertical tabulation	$S_0 - S_7$	Separator (information)
SOM	Start of message	FF	Form feed	₺	Word separator (space,
EOA	End of address	CR	Carriage return		normally non-printing)
EOM	End of message	SO	Shift out	<	Less than
EOT	End of transmission	SI	Shift in	>	Greater than
WRU	"Who are you?"	DC_0	Device control ① Reserved	↑	Up arrow (exponentiation)
RU	"Are you . . .?"		for data link escape	←	Left arrow (implies/
BELL	Audible signal	DC_1 –			replaced by)
FEo	Format effector	DC_3	Device control	\	Reverse slant
HT	Horizontal tabulation	DC_4 (stop)	Device control (stop)	ACK	Acknowledge
SK	Skip (punched card)	ERR	Error	②	Unassigned control
LF	Line feed	SYNC	Synchronous idle	ESC	Escape
		LEM	Logical end of media	DEL	Delete/Idle

Courtesy of IBM.

FIG. 11–20.   **American Standard Code for Information Interchange.**

Though all the possible combinations provided by this code are unassigned as yet, it is possible to eventually provide for 256 combinations of numbers, letters, and characters.

Punched Cards. The code used to represent data in punched cards was discussed at length in Chapter 7 and will not be reviewed here. However, it is important to realize that today the punched card is still the most common form of input data medium used in all but the larger computer systems.

PAPER TAPE CODES. The use of paper tape as input and, to a lesser extent, as output data mediums in computer systems has been slowly increasing. Many small mechanical devices such as the typewriter, adding machine, and cash register have been adapted to produce, as a by-product of recording a business transaction, punched paper tape which may be used as direct input to the computer processing system. More will be said about this use in Chapter 13 "Integrated Systems Techniques."

Paper tape codes are often referred to as 5-, 6-, 7-, and 8-channel codes. The term "channel" stems from the fact that the impressions or holes representing data are made in imaginary channels which run the length of the tape. The numbers referring to the channel codes refer to the actual number of channels used in recording the data, sometimes called channel widths.

The 5-channel tape utilizes the Telegraph Code developed by Jean Maurice Emile Baudot, of the French Ministry of Posts and Telegraph, in 1870 (Figure 11–21). This code has been used so extensively in Teletype

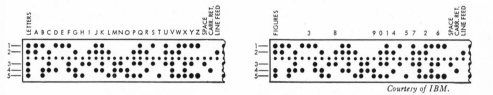

Courtesy of IBM.

FIG. 11–21.   Baudot Paper Tape Code—5 Channel.

transmissions that you will often hear it referred to as the Teletype Code. A close analysis fails to reveal any apparent relationship between the pattern of punched holes and the number, character, or letter presented. However, the code was developed on the basis of using fewer holes for the letters and numbers most frequently used at the time. When you recall the frequency of use of the letters was based on the French language, it is easy to understand why the code has no apparent relationship to our English letters.

The number of pulse and no-pulse code combinations in a 5-channel paper tape code provides a maximum number of 2^5 or 32 available combinations. Six of these are set aside as signals to the equipment to execute basic machine functions such as space and carriage return. The teletype keyboard is similar to that of the typewriter and has the ability to "shift," with a given key depression, to produce either of two type characters. This feature is utilized in the basic machine function to pro-

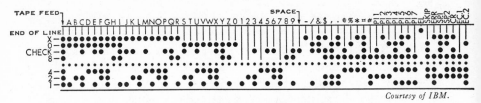

Courtesy of IBM.

FIG. 11–22.   Punched Paper Tape—8-Channel Code.

vide signals to instruct the machine to either print letters or figures. This permits the remaining 26 basic code combinations to be extended to 52 positions and provide a total of 58 positions.

The 6-channel code is often termed the Press Code as it is used almost exclusively in newspaper press data transmission. It differs from the 5-channel code only in that the additional channel permits the transmission of both upper and lower case letters.

The 7-channel code, a binary coded decimal code, is used mainly in electronic computer systems and utilizes the four bottom channels for 8, 4, 2, and 1 valued binary bits to represent a digit. These are used in combination with two zone bits to represent letters and characters. The remaining channel serves as a check or parity bit.

The 8-channel code (Figure 11–22) is similar to the 7-channel code in regard to data representation. The additional eighth channel provides additional code combinations, which are used for machine functions. This channel code was originally used in the operation of electric type-

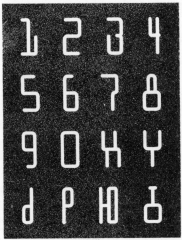

Courtesy of National Cash Register Co.

FIG. 11–23.   NOF Optical Type Font.

writers but it has since been adapted for use in wire transmission.

The parity check available in both the 7- and 8-channel codes is particularly important in data transmission as it permits an automatic check, by the receiving station, on the parity of each character received to determine if the bit combinations represent valid data.

NOF OPTICAL FONT. The National Cash Register Company has adapted a particular-shaped type font (Figure 11–23) for its use as an input to its optical reader. This type font may be attached to NCR adding machines, cash registers, and accounting machines so that, as a by-product of the operation of the machine, a printed paper tape is produced by the equipment which may be read as a human-language record or fed directly into the optical reader. This reader scans the printed paper tape at speeds of up to 31,200 characters per minute and the data read are used to either produce punched paper tape or serve as direct input into a computer system.

Optical scanning is achieved, using this font, by assigning five vertical channels (Figure 11–24) which are "read" by the two horizontal heads

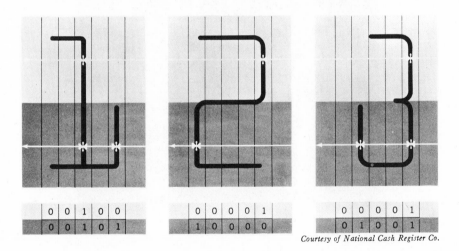

Courtesy of National Cash Register Co.

FIG. 11–24. Scanning the NOR Optical Type Font.

(represented by arrows in the illustration). As these heads sweep across the character, the type print lines encountered are recorded. This recording is in binary form and is shown below the figure in the illustration. The top binary line represents the findings of the top scanning head and the bottom binary line that of the lower head. The binary combinations found as the character is read are then interpreted into a computer system code if it is to be used as on-line input to a computer system or into a paper tape code if punched paper tape is to be produced.

Magnetic Ink Characters. The use of special type font characters printed on checks, deposit slips, and other documents by using an ink which has special magnetic qualities was developed through the joint efforts of the banking profession and computer manufacturers (Figure 11–25). The shape of the characters permits easy visual interpretation, and the special magnetic ink permits reading or interpretation by machines.

The standardized set of adopted characters includes the 10 digits (0 through 9) and four special symbols. These symbols include one to

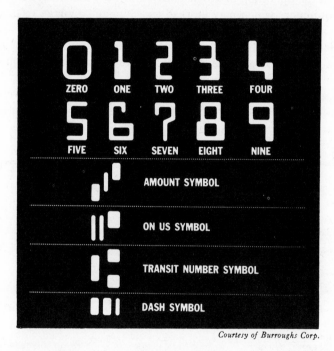

Courtesy of Burroughs Corp.

FIG. 11–25.   E13B Type Font Characters.

indicate that the digits following represent an "amount"; and an "on us" symbol which indicates the next data are applicable to the local bank on which the check is drawn and includes two sets of digits—first the type of transaction (deposit, withdrawal, etc.) and then the customer account number—separated by a symbol representing the equivalent of a "dash"; and a "transit number" symbol which indicates the data following are codes representing the local bank's assigned American Bankers Association number and the routing necessary to clear the check through the Federal Reserve Bank check clearing system.

Magnetic ink character recognition (MICR) has been adapted to some

special purpose uses, but is almost exclusively used in the banking industry.

The characters are printed at the bottom of the document in three
carefully defined and prescribed areas (Figure 11–26). The *amount field*,
to the right of the document, contains the dollar amount of the check (or
other document) and contains space for ten digits and two amount-field
symbols.

The *on-us field* is located in the central area of the document. This area
contains 20 spaces for characters, but only 18 are normally usable due to
differences in preprinted and postprinted (printing inscribed at the bank
after document is used in a transaction) tolerances. The on-us field is
usually divided into two areas, one for the transaction code, to the right,
and the other for the customer account number.

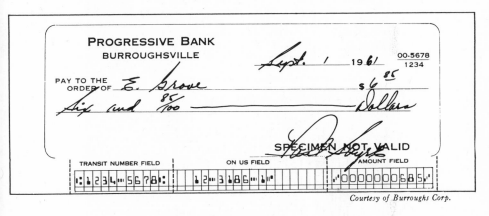

Courtesy of Burroughs Corp.

FIG. 11–26. MICR Bank Check Encoding.

The *transit number field* is positioned near the left edge of the document. Space is provided for 11 characters; four digits for the transit
number, four digits for the American Bankers Association number, a
separating dash symbol, and a beginning and ending transit number
symbol.

A special *auxiliary on-us field* may be used on extra-wide documents
and is found at the extreme left edge of the document. As many as 16
characters plus an ending symbol can be placed in this special field.

MAGNETIC TAPE. Magnetic tape is the most widely used form of data
medium input in the larger computer systems in which their computational capabilities are so great that the computer would be actually
standing idle in between the time it takes to feed in one punched card and
another.

Physically, magnetic tape comes on reels, which may contain up to

2,400 feet of the ½-inch-wide tape. It looks like the tape seen on home tape recorders. Data are recorded as magnetized spots or bits in the metallic oxide found on one side of the tape. Once recorded, information on tape is permanent unless new data are written over the old (the old is removed as the new is added) or a special effort is made to erase the data. This ability to write new information over old means that tape can be used over and over again with significant savings in recording costs.

Data are recorded on the tape in the form of small magnetized spots (Figure 11–27) in either 7- or 9-channel form. Both utilize the binary

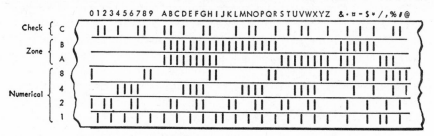

Seven-Track Tape

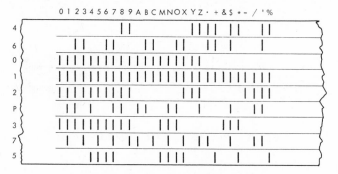

Nine-Track Tape (EBCDIC Code)

FIG. **11–27.   Magnetic Tape Data Formats.**

coded decimal system in recording digits, letters, and characters in conjunction with a check bit. However, the 7-channel code is a modification of the 7-channel paper tape code, and the 9-channel code is either in the form of the Extended Binary Coded Decimal Interchange Code or the newer American Standard Code for Information Interchange. The number of channels used, however, may vary with the computer manufacturer and the computer system with which the tape is to be used. Magnetic tape is always an even parity device. Data are read from the tape as it is moved past the read gap of the two-gap head (Figure 11–28) or the read-write gap of a one-gap head (Figure 11–29). As the magnetized spots

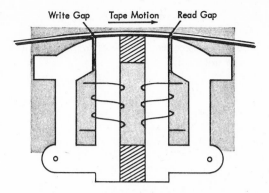

FIG. 11–28.   Two-Gap Read-Write Head.

on the tape move past the gap, small currents are generated in the read coil of the head. The presence and absence of these induced pulses of current is interpreted into data by the computer circuitry. Writing data is accomplished by small pulses of electrical current furnished by the computer circuitry, flowing in the write coil of the head which, in turn through induction causes data previously written on the tape to be removed and the new data recorded.

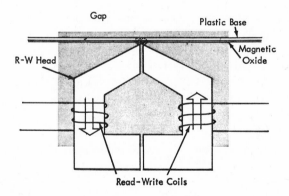

FIG. 11–29.   One-Gap Read-Write Head.

ANNOTATED BIBLIOGRAPHY

IRWIN, WAYNE C. *Digital Computer Principles*. Princeton, N.J.: D. Van Nostrand Co., Inc., 1960.

Developed as a training course at National Cash Register Co., the approach is in number systems and the methods of computation available, the need for and use of symbolic logic, and the controls which may be utilized in the reduction or elimination or errors.

SCHMIDT, RICHARD N., and MEYERS, WILLIAM E. *Electronic Business Data Processing.* New York: Holt, Rinehart & Winston, Inc., 1963.
Chapter 6 presents an excellent review of some of the uses of "arithmetic operations and data notation."

SUTHERLAND, IVAN E. "Computer Inputs and Outputs," *Scientific American,* September 1966, p. 86.

SYSTEMS AND PROCEDURES ASSOCIATION. *Business Systems,* Vol. 11, chap. xix. Cleveland, Ohio, 1963.
An excellent discussion of counting systems, internal accuracy checking and computer languages.

QUESTIONS

1. Describe the functional purpose of each segment of an electronic data processing system.
2. Describe fully how it is possible for a computer to direct itself through a series of steps.
3. Why is the binary numbering system so peculiarly well fitted for use by a modern-day electronic computer?
4. Express the number 67 in the binary number system. Explain on a step-by-step basis how you arrived at your result.
5. Take the numbers 75, 31, and 96, express their binary equivalents and add them, reflecting the answer in binary form.
6. Carefully explain how addition takes place in the binary numbering system. In short, how did you apply the rules for addition to the problem which was posed in question 5?
7. Express the number 3,768 in binary coded decimal form.
8. How are letters formed in the binary coded decimal system?
9. Explain the function of a parity check in the transmission of data.
10. Differentiate between a hexidecimal code and a binary code. Would there be any advantage to the hexidecimal coding system?
11. What is a "word" in so far as an electronic data processing system is concerned?
12. Differentiate between a "word" and a "byte."
13. What is the importance or significance of trying to develop a standard code? In this regard, what situation exists today between the various manufacturers of computers.
14. Differentiate between the NOF Optical Font and Magnetic Ink Characters. In which ways are they the same and in which ways are they different?

CHAPTER 12

Computer Equipment

THE particular equipment utilized in a given computer system is dependent upon a number of factors, which are considered in detail in Chapters 19 through 21. However, to perform a given set of applications, there may be a wide variety of equipment available—each grouping of which has its own desirable characteristics.

For instance, in the case of speed requirements, it is certain in nearly every installation that at some point in acquiring fast access and computational capability, the costs associated with speed must be reconciled against this need for speed.

In other instances where there are many I/O devices available, they must all be carefully analyzed to determine which will best serve the purposes desired. Factors weighed in this consideration must not only include the processing system itself but also the place where the data originate. For example, is the place near or far from the central processing unit? The type of business, the originating sources of the data, the transmission distances to be involved, and the type of output data to be provided are other factors to be considered.

The above discussion only scratches the surface of the many decisions which must be made in selecting specific equipment for a given system. However, it should indicate some need to be familiar with the many types of equipment available and the capabilities of each.

Almost any classification of computer equipment requires some arbitrary decision as to the placement of a given device. An example of this is the magnetic tape unit which serves both as an I/O device and as an on-line memory device. To alleviate this problem the discussion to follow will classify these devices as those which are: (1) sequential in nature, which includes most of the more common I/O devices; (2) direct access storage devices, which serve either as an extension of internal memory or as an on-line storage device; (3) internal memory devices, whose components are more commonly found as a part of the central processing unit; and (4) the teleprocessing devices, which are on-line units which may be isolated from the computer area and operated from another area many miles distant.

SEQUENTIAL DEVICES

The class of device which either inputs or outputs data in sequential units of data assumes many and quite differing forms. Some of these have been in use since the development of the first computers, while others have only recently been perfected to the point where they now have practical and accepted usage.

Punched Cards

Punched cards are used both as input and output to computers, and many different models of card readers, punches, and reader-punches are available for use with the different computer systems (Figure 12–1). Reading speeds of commercially available equipment vary from as low as 100 cards per minute up to 2,000 cards per minute. Card punching is a

Courtesy of General Electric Co.

FIG. 12–1.   GE 1,000-per-minute Card Reader.

slower operation because of the techniques required, but punching speeds may be as fast as 500 cards per minute.

Punched Paper Tape

Paper tape readers (Figure 12–2) serving as input to computer systems operate at speeds up to 1,800 characters per second. Paper tape

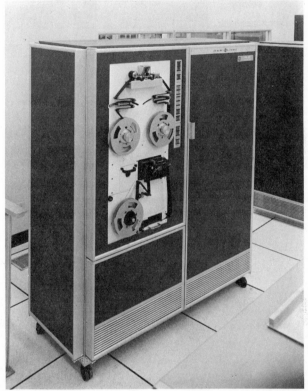

Courtesy of General Electric. Co.

FIG. 12–2. General Electric PTS–200 Perforated Tape Reader/Punch.

punches, as with card punches, are slower than their readers. However, commercial punches operate at speeds up to 300 characters per second.

Magnetic Ledger Cards

Ledger cards with magnetic stripe(s) either across the front or back of the card are utilized in many of the smaller types of computers. Most computers of this type are normally classified as electronic bookkeeping or accounting machines, such as those described in Chapter 6. Though the

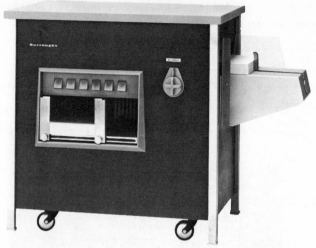

Courtesy of Burroughs Corp.

FIG. 12–3.   Burroughs A 4003 Automatic Ledger Reader.

Type	Number of Tracks	Inches per Second	Characters or Bytes per Inch	Characters or Bytes per Second
729 II................	7	75	200 or 556	15,000 or 41,667
729 IV................	7	112.5	200 or 556	22,500 or 62,500
729 V.................	7	75	200, 556, or 800	15,000, 41,667, or 60,000
729 VI...............	7	112.5	200, 556, or 800	22,500, 62,500, or 90,000
7330.................	7	36	200 or 556	7,200 or 20,016
7340 Model 1..........	10	112.5	1,511	170,000
7340 Model 2..........	8	22.5	1,511	34,000
7340 Model 3..........	10	112.5	1,511* or 3,022*	170,000* or 340,000*
2400 Series Model 1......	7	37.5	200, 556, or 800	7,500, 20,850, or 30,000
	9	37.5	800*	30,000*
2400 Series Model 2......	7	75	200, 556, or 800	15,000, 41,700, or 60,000
	9	75	800*	60,000*
2400 Series Model 3......	7	112.5	200, 556, or 800	22,500, 62,500, or 90,000
	9	112.5	800*	90,000*
2400 Series Model 4......	7	37.5	200, 556, or 800	7,500, 20,850, or 30,000
	9	37.5	800* or 1,600*	30,000* or 60,000*
2400 Series Model 5......	7	75	200, 556, or 800	15,000, 41,700, or 60,000
	9	75	800* or 1,600*	60,000* or 120,000*
2400 Series Model 6......	7	112.5	200, 556, or 800	22,500, 62,500, or 90,000
	9	112.5	800* or 1,600*	90,000* or 180,000*
2415 Model 1, 2, 3.......	7	18.75	200, 556, or 800	3,750, 10,425, or 15,000
	9	18.75	800*	15,000*
2415 Model 4, 5, 6.......	7	18.75	200, 556, or 800	3,750, 10,425, or 15,000
	9	18.75	800* or 1,600*	15,000* or 30,000*

* Asterisk indicates bytes.

FIG. 12–4.   Characteristics of IBM Magnetic Tape Units.

magnetic striped ledger card (Figure 6–24) is usually hand inserted for reading or data entry, readers (Figure 12–3) are now available that automatically feed and read data on the card at approximately 50 cards per minute.

Magnetic Tape

Nearly all the computer manufacturers have a series of magnetic tape units compatible with their computers. These differ basically in two ways: one is in the density in which the data is packed on the tape (characters per inch) and the other is in the speed with which the mechanism can read and write data on the tape. A typical series of tape units and their specifications are those manufactured by IBM (see Figure 12–4).

The magnetic tape unit (Figure 12–5) serves both as an on-line input

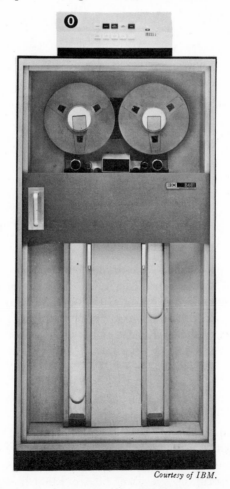

Courtesy of IBM.

FIG. 12–5. The IBM 2401 Magnetic Tape Unit.

and output device. It performs the function of transferring the tape on one reel to another, past a read, write, or read-write head where data is read from the tape to the computer system or written on the tape from the computer system. Speeds vary with the tape unit used, but data may be read or written on some of the faster units at the rate of ⅓ million alphanumeric or ⅔ million numeric characters per second.

Typewriter Consoles

Almost every computer system has a device which permits some form of manual entry into, and control over, the central processing unit. This usually takes the form of a typewriter (Figure 12–6) whose keyboard allows the operator to instruct the computer in its action and to report,

Courtesy of IBM.

FIG. 12–6.   Typewriter Input Unit of the IBM 2030 Processing Unit.

in printed form, specific data from the computer as requested by the operating program of instructions. The input speed of these devices is, of course, dependent upon the ability of the operator to use the typewriter keys. Output is usually at some optimum operating speed limited by the mechanical design of the equipment and is usually around 10 characters per second.

On-Line Printers

One of the major characteristics of a business information processing system is that it provides large masses of "human readable" output. This is normally provided by printing devices (Figure 12–7). The characteristics of such printers vary considerably from manufacturer to manufacturer and even in the different computer systems furnished by a given manufacturer. However, typical printing speeds of 600 to 1,000 lines, of 100 or 132 characters per line, per minute are not at all uncommon and highly

Courtesy of RCA.

FIG. 12–7.   RCA 70/243 Hi-Speed Printer.

specialized printers[1] have been developed which will print up to 31,250 lines per minute.

In printing typical business statements and reports, spacing on the form is almost as big a problem as printing. Some of the printers now in use will skip spaces on the report at a rate up to 75 inches per second to eliminate any waiting time on the part of the printing mechanism for form movement to take place.

Optical Scanners

There has been a steady improvement in the capability and reliability of optical scanning devices (Figure 12–8) over the past few years. These devices provide a sophisticated input technique that can serve many types of business problems in converting source data from originating documents directly into a machine-recognizable form.

There are two basic types of readers: (1) those that handle individual documents in the form of paper sheets or cards and (2) those that accept continuous rolls of paper such as cash register or adding machine tape.

---

[1] Series 690 Printer by Radiation, Inc.

Courtesy of Farrington Electronics.

FIG. 12–8.   Farrington Model 3010 Document Reader.

These types can both be subdivided into those that read a single print font style and those that are multifont readers which can read from a few up to hundreds of printing styles, including hand-printed characters. The capability of these machines can also be described as those which can only read a single line for each insertion of a document, those which can read an entire document at a single insertion, and those which read lines progressively as the roll of paper feeds past reading heads. Some readers also provide a sorting capability in outputting the scanned document into a few or as many as 12 different stacker bins.

Magnetic Ink Character Recognition

The use of MICR, previously described in Chapter 11, has grown rapidly since its development only a few years ago. Its general usage is in banking and related fields in reading the data on checks and other banking documents directly into summarizing devices or computers for calculations, processing, and sorting the read documents into stacker bins for classification and storage.

MICR devices (Figure 12–9) all have similar reading characteristics, as the first models were designed around a single set of specifications. These were produced, however, by a number of manufacturers, and each

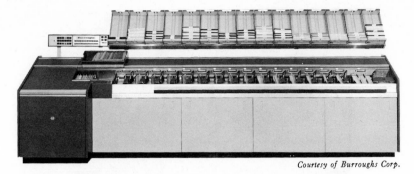

Courtesy of Burroughs Corp.

FIG. 12–9. Burroughs MICR Sorter-Reader.

firm built in their own unique ideas in fulfilling the requirements of the specifications.

DIRECT ACCESS STORAGE DEVICES

The need for fast access storage devices to serve as an extension of the internal memory of the central processing unit brought about the development of several forms of mass data files. The design of these is such that under certain circumstances they may be directly accessed by the computer and become an integral part of memory, though their general usage is to provide large files of on-line storage of data.

Magnetic Drum

Drum storage is normally an internal type of memory which provides stored data. The data may be entered or recalled at a very fast access rate compared with other mechanical types of memory. Drums are also used as external on-line storage devices (Figure 12–10) where fast access memory is required. The physical size of the drum limits it as to the quantity of information available relative to the cost of such a unit, but some external storage units provide up to 4.1 million characters or 8.2 million digits of data.

Data are normally represented in binary coded decimal form on magnetic drums with four bits for digits, two for zone bits, and a check bit. The drum is a round cylinder, which rotates at very fast speeds. Its surface is plated with a material which will become magnetized when exposed to a magnetic field. Data storage is in the form of invisible rings or tracks around the cylinder which have been divided up into sections; these sections are, in turn, subdivided into character locations (Figure 12–11). The number of these tracks, sections, and characters will vary with the make and model of equipment but, in general, has a direct dependence on the physical size of the particular drum considered.

Courtesy of UNIVAC.

FIG. 12–10.   UNIVAC FASTRAND II Mass Storage System.

Reading and writing data on the magnetic drum is accomplished by one or more read, write, or read-write heads, as shown in Figure 12–12. In some instances, where very fast speeds are desired, a separate head is used for each track. These operations are performed in essentially the same manner as those described for magnetic tape. Once placed on the drum, data are permanent until written over, as the magnetism is retained indefinitely. A few milliseconds are normally required for access to data on magnetic drums, but in some drums this access time may be lowered to approximately ½ millisecond (500 microseconds). However, as soon as the data are located, the act of reading and writing data records can be performed at rates up to 1,200,000 characters or 2,400,000 digits per second.

Card Random Access Memory (CRAM)

CRAM is an on-line storage device which reads and records data on a mylar magnetic card, 14 inches long and 3¼ inches wide (Figure 12–13). Each card has seven invisible data recording tracks which can be individually addressed for reading or writing data. Each track has a storage capacity of 3,100 alphanumeric characters, so each card has a maximum storage capacity of 21,700 characters.

Two hundred and fifty-six (256) cards are stored in a cartridge (the equivalent of 69,000 punched cards) which may be inserted in or removed from the CRAM unit (Figure 12–14) in approximately 30 seconds. Any

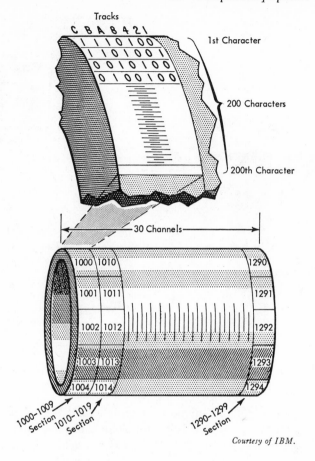

Courtesy of IBM.

FIG. 12–11. Typical Drum Storage Schematic.

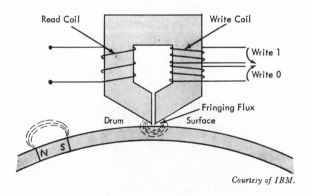

Courtesy of IBM.

FIG. 12–12. Recording Data on the Drum.

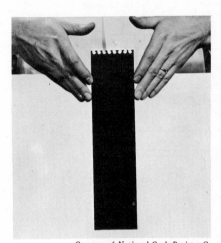

Courtesy of National Cash Register Co.

FIG. 12–13.   **CRAM Card.**

Courtesy of National Cash Register Co.

FIG. 12–14.   **NCR 353 CRAM Unit.**

one of the 256 cards and any position of data on that card may be selected independently at a speed which allows the transfer of data at a rate of 100,000 characters per second. The cards are held suspended from rods inside the cartridge which move, on orders from the computer system, to allow the card to fall into a vacuum, which pulls it in position to be wrapped around a rotating drum turning at a speed of 400 inches a second (Figure 12–15). Read and write heads (Figure 12–16) are positioned so that data may be read in a similar manner to that of reading magnetic tape.

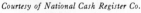

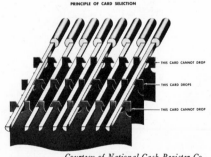

Courtesy of National Cash Register Co.

FIG. 12–15.   **Principle of Card Selection.**

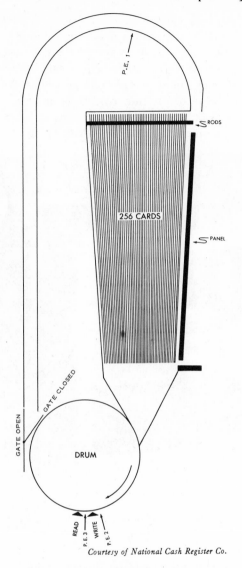

Courtesy of National Cash Register Co.

FIG. 12–16. **CRAM Feed Diagram.**

The data code used on CRAM cards is the six-bit alphanumeric binary coded decimal code with a check bit and an eighth channel, termed a clock channel, which is used for internal circuitry timing purposes and has no relation to the data represented.

Magnetic Disks

Magnetic disks are very similar in appearance to the phonograph records used in the popular juke box. These "records" are metallic disks which are coated on both sides with a ferrous oxide recording material. They are permanently mounted, one above the other, on a shaft which rotates at high speeds to spin the disks and permit mounted read and write heads to obtain or record data. In some equipment a single pair of read and write heads move in and out between the records and up and down on a shaft from record to record as they read from or write on the disks. In other equipment, two or more heads or a series of heads, one for each record, are used to perform the read and write functions. Of course, the

Courtesy of General Electric. Co.

FIG. 12–17.   General Electric DS–20 Disc Storage Unit.

greater the number of heads, the faster the data may be read or written but, as might be expected, the more expensive the unit.

Though quite similar in the function performed, disk memory files have developed in two distinct types. At first all disk files were permanently mounted in a case, with usually 25 or 50 disks in a module and one or two modules to a file (Figure 12–17). More recently, disk files have been made more compact and mobile. They are mounted, in a covered carrying case, in units of six disks, which provide ten recording surfaces, as the top and bottom of the file are not usable (Figure 12–18). These disk packs may be quickly mounted in a disk storage drive unit (Figure 12–19) for process-

Courtesy of IBM.

Courtesy of IBM.

FIG. 12–18. **IBM Disk Pack.**

FIG. 12–19. **IBM 2311 Disk Storage Drive.**

ing purposes or replaced with another disk pack and placed in a file cabinet for storage until the recorded data are needed again.

Data are addressed, or located, on the disks by the disk number, the sector on the disk, and the track number (Figure 12–20). The disks are numbered consecutively from bottom to top of the file with the bottom number being 00, the next 01, and so on. There are five assigned sectors on each side of each disk. These are assigned sector addresses 0 through 4 for the top of the disk and 5 through 9 for the bottom of the disk. There are usually 200 tracks of recorded data on each side of the disk which have addresses 000 through 199. The number of characters available, per sector per track, varies with the density of the data stored.

Some disk files are limited by the manner in which data are stored, as some equipment specifies the number of characters available in a given record length; if more space is needed for a given data record, personnel data on an employee for an example, then two or more record lengths would be required (Figure 12–21). If the recorded data required just one additional character to be stored in a second record length, then the balance of that particular record length would be unusable for other data. In some disk files, record lengths may be flexible to permit the recording of variable lengths of data records. This variable record length capability results in the more efficient use of the storage space.

Data are usually recorded in BCD form in disk files; however, some

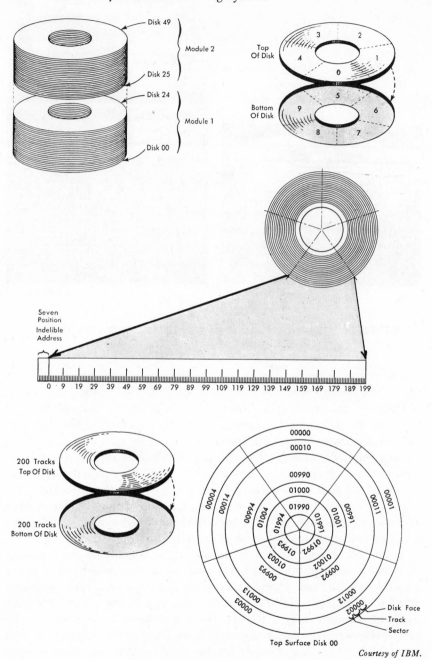

Courtesy of IBM.

**FIG. 12–20.   Information Arrangement and Addressing in IBM
Disk Storage Units.**

computer systems are found which use some other form of binary representation. The speed with which data may be read or recorded is directly dependent upon the speed of rotation of the disk, the density with which the data are packed on the disk, and the number of read and write heads available for the transfer of data. Most common makes of equipment have one or two read and write heads. The Burroughs machine, however, has a read and write head for each track on the disk. Typical transfer speeds would be a transfer rate of 156,000 characters or 312,000 digits per second for disk memory files.

The volume of storage provided by disk files is usually dependent on the number of disks available in the file and the density of the data packing, and on whether the record lengths are fixed or variable. Disk packs are small and portable and provide a maximum of 7.25 million characters or 14.5 million digits per pack. Disk files provide up to approximately 0.25 billion characters or 0.5 billion digits per file unit.

Magnetic disk memory has two major features which makes it such a desirable form of data storage. First, it provides for a tremendous volume

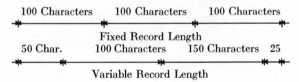

FIG. 12–21.   Fixed and Variable Record Lengths.

of data to be stored in its disks. The need for this large volume of data in business information processing systems was previously described in contrasting the requirements of such a system with those of a scientific data processing system. The second major feature is its ability to search the mass of stored data and retrieve any given bit of this data at random and to make it immediately available for processing. This ability to select any given bit of data from the mass during the processing procedure is known as *random access data processing.* This random access to data in magnetic disk memory files contrasts with the necessity of selecting data in sequence from magnetic tape files (where any selection of random data requires the serial reading of all data stored on the tape in between the desired units of data).

Until recently, with the announcement of the IBM 2321 Data Cell Drive, disk memory had been the only form of random access storage device available at a cost which could normally be justified.

Data Cell

The IBM 2321 Data Cell Drive (Figure 12–22), which is an on-line direct-access storage for the IBM System/360, offers an economical solution to the storage of large, sequentially organized data records requiring random reference. The Data Cell Drive houses ten removable and interchangeable data cells (Figure 12–23) each of which contains 200 strips of magnetic tape 2¼ inches wide and 13 inches long. Each of these strips provides 100 tracks for data, and each track provides 2,000 eight-bit bytes (previously described under magnetic cores) of data. The total storage capacity of the 10 removable cells in a Data Cell Drive is 400 million characters or 800 million digits of data. The transfer rate of this data is 55,000 characters or 110,000 digits per second.

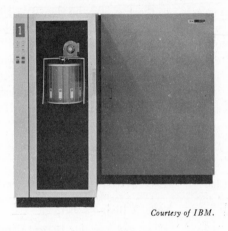

Courtesy of IBM.

FIG. 12–22.   IBM 2321 Data Cell Drive.

INTERNAL MEMORY DEVICES

The memory devices used as internal storage for data in conjunction with the central processing unit of the computer generally utilize the fastest and most capable type of such device available at the given stage of development. Thus many of the devices previously used as internal memory have been replaced by faster and more efficient devices. Also, some of the previously discussed direct access storage devices may be found to have been used for internal storage at times in the past and may even still be utilized, in a few instances, in computers for this purpose today. The particular devices most commonly used for internal memory today, however, are the items which follow.

Magnetic Core

Magnetic core memory is composed of a large number of tiny rings or cores of ferromagnetic material, each threaded at the intersection of a fine lattice of wires. Each core is only a small fraction of an inch in diameter,

Courtesy of IBM.

FIG. 12–23.   IBM 2321 Data Cell.

and because of this size, core memory is very compact. Inasmuch as its operation is based on the flow of electricity, it is very fast, stable, and re- liable.

The binary states of "on" and "off" are determined by the direction of the polarity or magnetic state of the core. If a wire is threaded through the center of the core rings, and a current of electricity sent through the wire, the core will become magnetized. The polarity of the magnetism is deter- mined by the direction of the flow of this electricity (Figure 12–24). If the direction of the current flow is reversed, the polarity of the core will be reversed. In any instance, once the core is magnetized it will retain that polarity indefinitely or until reversed.

Inasmuch as it takes a specific amount of current flow through the wire

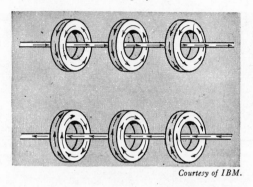

Courtesy of IBM.

FIG. 12–24.   Polarity of Magnetic Cores.

to magnetize the core, all of a series of cores strung on the wire will have the same polarity. To permit the selective magnetism of a given core, two wires, each with their own string of cores but having a single core in common (Figure 12–25), are placed at right angles to one another. If only half the current needed to magnetize a core is sent through each wire, only the core at the intersection of the wires will be magnetized. To permit all cores to be selectively magnetized, the cores are placed on a screen or lattice of wires to form a magnetic core plane (Figure 12–26).

If several planes of cores are placed one above another and the same position in each of these planes is designated as part of a binary coded decimal character location, the cores in this position may be selectively magnetized to form the binary configuration for the letter A, 1 11 0001

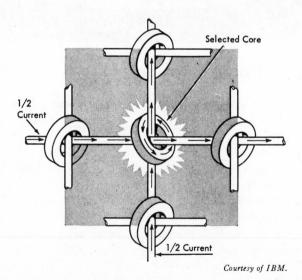

Courtesy of IBM.

FIG. 12–25.   Selecting a Core.

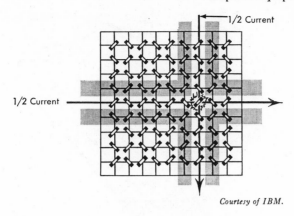

1/2 Current

1/2 Current

Courtesy of IBM.

FIG. 12–26.   Magnetic Core Plane.

(Figure 12–27). All the other core positions also serve to represent individual BCD character locations. The number of cores in a plane vary with the equipment make and model, and many use several stacks of such planes to provide a magnetic core storage unit. A given core position, in the stack of planes, provides a computer "word."

A third wire, termed a "sense" wire, is run diagonally through each core in a given plane (Figure 12–28). When a given position is to be tested, or read, for its magnetic state, current flows through the two wires previously described, and if the data stored is a 1 and is changed to a 0 by the test, this will be sensed by the sense wire (Figure 12–29), and the computer will "know" what was in this core position.

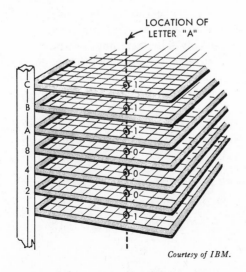

LOCATION OF
LETTER "A"

Courtesy of IBM.

FIG. 12–27.   BCD Character Locations.

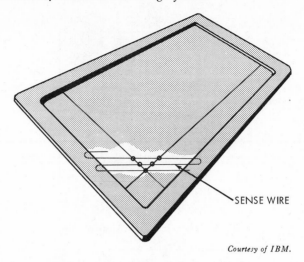

Courtesy of IBM.

FIG. 12–28.   Sense Wire in Core Plane.

It should be noted that in the test the core tested was changed from a 1 to a 0. This, of course, changes the data stored in this core and this is not desired in a read operation, as it may be necessary to read this same data many times before the data are written over in the recording of different data. To prevent the destruction of data in a read operation, the computer automatically reproduces, or regenerates, the same binary state condition present in the core before the test. This is accomplished by sending an "inhibit" pulse, which is reverse to the current flow of the "read" pulse, through the third wire to regenerate the data which was "read out."

Until recently, core storage has been quite expensive and limited in its use to internal storage only. There are now, however, some external on-line directly addressable storage devices which utilize magnetic core memory (Figure 12–30), some of which provide over 2 million bytes of storage. Access time is always very fast for magnetic core memory and may be so

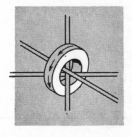
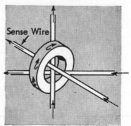

Courtesy of IBM.

FIG. 12–29.   Core Sense Wires.

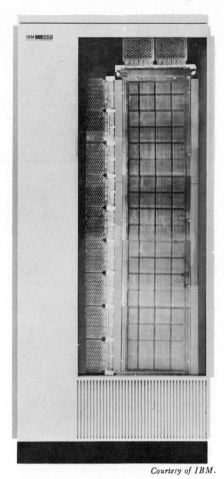

Courtesy of IBM.

FIG. 12–30. IBM 2361 Core Storage.

fast as to provide an effective cycle time of 125 nanoseconds per character.

Thin Film Memory

Thin film memory may vary in form somewhat from manufacturer to manufacturer, but basically such an element consists of a deposit on an extremely thin film of some base material which contains a uniform deposit of magnetic storage materials having high packing density.

National Cash Register Company is utilizing a unique cylindrical thin film memory in its NCR 315 Rod Memory Computer (Figure 12–31). The basic memory storage element is a "rod" (Figure 12–32) which is a beryllium-copper wire electroplated with a thin film of nickel-iron material and

Courtesy of National Cash Register Co.

FIG. 12–31.   NCR 315 RMC Rod Memory Computer.

wrapped with a ribbon of copper. Each rod is only 0.015 inch thick and 6 inches long but is capable of storing 40 binary digits which serve in random, sequential, real-time, and remote inquiry processing. A group of these rods is inserted through a stack of solenoid planes to make up a memory module (Figure 12–33). Central processing units utilizing these modules are available with 40,000, 80,000, 120,000, or 160,000 characters of this new thin film memory. Basic read-write transfer time of data in the 315 Rod Memory Computer is 800 nanoseconds (0.8 microseconds) for a 12-bit word. A four-bit group of characters can be transferred in 200 nanoseconds.

The Radio Corporation of America has developed a "scratch-pad" memory for use in the larger models of the Spectra 70 Series computer system. This memory consists of 128 four-byte words whose access time is 300 nanoseconds per word. This very fast, though limited, memory utilizes a micromagnetic thin film technique and is used in conjunction with a main magnetic core memory which varies in size from approximately 16K (16,000) to 524K bytes in various models.

Univac Division of Sperry Rand Corporation is also utilizing a limited

Courtesy of National Cash Register Co.

FIG. 12–32.   NCR Cylindrical Thin Film Memory Rod.

Courtesy of National Cash Register Co.

FIG. 12–33. NCR Rod Memory.

amount (128 36–bit words) of thin film plated wire memory in the control unit of the UNIVAC 9300 computer system. The access time of this memory is 667 nanoseconds. The core memory varies from 16K to 65K 36–bit words depending on the needs of the user of the system.

TELEPROCESSING DEVICES

Developments in equipment and techniques which permit the timely flow of data over distance has now provided management with the ability to utilize the question-answer-decision-reaction cycle in gathering and responding to data throughout the firm irregardless of whether the firm is a local organization or one spread over large segments of the world.

The devices to provide this capability have evolved over a relatively short span of time. They are, however, rapidly assuming a position of great importance in the gathering, transmission, and communication of data within the plant, from store to store, and division to headquarters.

Pushbutton Telephone

One of the more recent innovations to provide input to, and output from, a computer system is the pushbutton telephone (Figure 12–34). The first of these was the Touch-Tone telephone developed by the Bell System. This provides either a set of buttons for manual entry or an automatic entry using a Touch-Tone Card Dialer which reads a prepunched plastic card (Figure 12–35) to enter the calling information. The General Telephone and Electronics System plan to introduce their competitive Touch-Calling telephone when they complete the necessary central exchange installations.

It has been predicted that when the pushbutton telephone is connected

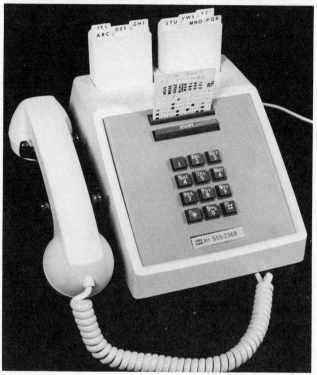

Courtesy of Bell System.

FIG. 12–34.   Touch-Tone Telephone.

to a central utility type computer system it will eventually serve the house-wife in her record keeping, grocery ordering, and other shopping; the student in solving his homework problems; and the husband in his busi-ness applications.

Audio Response Units

Both RCA and IBM have developed devices whose output is in the form of spoken words. Inquiry for this information is usually made by pushbutton-type telephone. This serves as input to the audio response system by asking for such information as the status of a given stock on the New York Stock Exchange, the number of pieces of a given inventory item, or the balance due from a particular customer of the firm. The inquiry is forwarded—usually over some type of communication device—to the central processing unit of a computer system. Once this information is interpreted and the files have been contacted for the answer to the query, the data are put in the form of a coded message and returned to the response unit. This message consists of a series of addresses which correspond to vocal words which are stored in analog form as audio signals on the magnetic drum of the response unit.

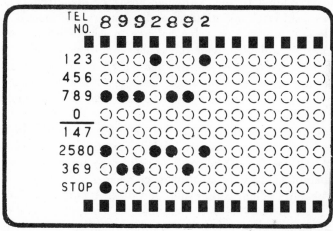

Courtesy of Bell System.

FIG. 12–35.   Touch-Tone Telephone card.

The IBM 7770 Audio Response Unit has been in operation since February, 1965, and the more recent 7772 Audio Response Unit since July, 1966. The RCA 70/510 Voice Response Unit was first installed in October, 1966. Both systems are relatively easy to use and lower in cost than other communication devices. The general availability of pushbutton telephone permits wide use of this type of equipment.

Other Teleprocessing Devices

The chapter on Integrated Systems Techniques, which follows, utilizes many of the teleprocessing and associated devices in the explanation and application of the techniques necessary to provide such integrated systems. The discussion of these additional teleprocessing devices will be deferred until that chapter.

SUMMARY

Memory Storage

The memory system used in storing data internally in a given computer system depends on the processing requirements of the firm and the equipment makes and models available which will provide those needs. Each type of memory system has its limitations—particularly in physical size, speed, and volume of storage possible. These limitations, when added to the purchase or rental costs of the various types of memory, must be carefully weighed in determining whether the capabilities of the system are those best fitted to the particular needs of the given firm. Some procedures need fast computational ability, others vast amounts of storage, while still others need some balance in computational speed and storage capacity to best provide the system requirements. Those systems requiring large volumes of storage may need it directly available in random access form (core or drum), on-line to be called in as needed (tape or disk files), or off-line for data only needed occasionally (disk packs or punched cards).

New equipment announcements have altered the picture in terms of both speed and memory capacity, and it is certainly expected that this trend will continue. Today, however, *in delivered equipment,* a ranking in speed capabilities of the internal memory devices most commonly found would probably be film, core, drum, and disk. A ranking in storage capacity of these memory devices would be disk, core, drum, and film. The ranking in terms of cost per unit of storage would possibly be film, core, drum, and disk.

Input/Output

The type of input and output available and desired will also be an important consideration in the choice of a computer system. In the smaller systems of today, the punched card is, by far, the most popular type of input, probably because of the many conversions of unit record (punched card) equipment to computers. In the larger systems, an input of punched cards is too slow to be economically feasible when considered in relation to the processing capabilities of such a system, and magnetic tape is the most popular input to these large systems. However, in the large systems, smaller computers (termed "slaves") or conversion equipment are used to convert the originating data, usually punched cards or punched paper tape, into the magnetic tape input form.

Output may be thought of in two ways—as processing output to be used in other processing procedures, which will probably be in some binary code form of machine language, and as English language output to be used as historical records or in the business decision-making process. Volume-wise, processing procedure output will, today, generally be in the form of magnetic tapes while some printing device will produce the required reports and analyses. However, printing will probably be an off-line operation in large computer systems, as these systems most economically produce magnetic tape as their output. This tape is then processed on smaller computer systems to produce the printed data.

ANNOTATED BIBLIOGRAPHY

BELL, W. *A Management Guide to Electronic Computers.* New York: McGraw-Hill Book Co., 1957.

This book, written to help the businessmen understand electronic computers, gives a simple, nontechnical explanation of what an electronic computer is and what it will do. Factual information about the present state of electronic business systems is also presented.

CHAPIN, NED. *An Introduction to Automatic Computers.* Princeton, N.J.: D. Van Nostrand Co., Inc., 1963.

This book gives some generally useful information, concepts, considerations, precepts, and methods of approach with respect to the automatic computer. A more complete and technical description of how the computer works is given in this book than in most other books of this nature.

EVANS, DAVID C. "Computer Logic and Memory," *Scientific American,* September, 1966, p. 74.

LAURIE, EDWARD J. *Computers and How They Work.* Cincinnati: South-Western Publishing Co., 1963.

This book introduces the reader to the functions of the middle-sized computers. It presents information in the simplest terms and confines consideration to those elements basic to the operation of computers.

MARTIN, E. WAINRIGHT. *Electronic Data Processing: An Introduction.* Rev. ed. Homewood, Ill.: Richard D. Irwin, Inc., 1965.

This book provides the general manager with an understanding of the capabilities and limitations of the electronic computer, gives him some idea of the impact of the computer upon the management profession, and describes the management considerations involved in its use. The purpose of the book is to introduce the subject to those who aspire to specialize in the area of *information technology.* The impact of the computer on modern society, the basic objectives of data processing, the concepts of systems, the elementary components of data processing, and the functions of and principles underlying punched card machines are examined. Characteristics of stored programs, basic programming techniques, software, and procedure-oriented languages are explained. Particular types of equipment such as magnetic tape, random access files, and magnetic tape files are described. Also discussed are systems analysis and design; conversion processes; organizing and staffing a centralized data processing facility; human relations; administrative and economic problems involved in installing an EDP system; and the impact of information technology upon management.

NELSON, O. S., and WOODS, R. W. *Accounting Systems and Data Processing,* chap. xxi, Cincinnati: South-Western Publishing Co., 1961.

Chapter 21 is a good introduction to the characteristics of an automatic digital computer and its particular application to accounting needs. The four common units in a computer are explained, and some of the basic methods of storing data are stated.

QUESTIONS

1. From a systems analyst's point of view, what are the factors which must be harmonized and resolved before any type of computer installation can be made?

2. Describe four different forms of input to a computer in reasonable detail.

3. Try to imagine separate situations where each of these forms of input might conceivably be used. Describe each of the situations as clearly as possible.

4. Is it mandatory to have an on-line printer in every EDP installation? Explain. Under what circumstances would an on-line printer probably be advisable?

5. What are some of the practical problems involved in using optical scanners? Explain.

6. Describe the relative merits and shortcomings of the following three forms of storage: (1) magnetic drum, (2) data cell, and (3) magnetic disks.

7. For what use is the magnetic core form of storage frequently used? Why?

8. Enumerate some frequently used types of output devices. Discuss the likely uses for each device.

CHAPTER 13

Integrated Systems

Techniques

THE TERM Integrated Data Processing (IDP) was first coined by the American Management Association and United States Steel in 1954.[1] However, it was never clearly defined and, over the years, came to have a meaning entirely different from the earlier one.

CONCEPTS

Originally, IDP referred to the use of paper tape producing and paper tape actuated equipment for data handling. It soon found common usage, however, in referring to any system which recorded data in a common language form at the point of origin, or as close to it as possible, and carried out all further manipulations automatically without additional manual copying. Typical examples would be the use of computers by the accounting department to prepare payrolls and determine tax liability; use by the purchasing department to keep track of inventory levels and determine when reorder points are reached; and use by the production department to control production machinery automatically. Here, each of the steps and procedures associated with a particular job are integrated in the sense that the entire operation is done by the machine without further instruction or manipulation by the human worker.

As time passed, a new concept evolved: that operations of such departments should be integrated or unified on a departmental level rather than on a particular problem level. In this way, unnecessary duplication would be eliminated and the results of each application could automatically be applied to the next successive problem area.

---

[1] Alan O. Mann, "A Publically Regulated System of Management Control Services," in *Management Control Systems*, edited by Donald G. Malcolm and Alan J. Rowe (New York: John Wiley & Sons, Inc., 1960), p. 246.

There can be no doubt that management in the past has placed far more importance upon the installation of automatic machines to improve production efficiency than to bring improvements in other areas. One of the basic reasons for the tremendous increase in office paper work and consequent increase in clerical costs has been the failure to attack the problem from an overall viewpoint. Instead, most attempts directed toward work simplification and the use of mechanical applications have been made on a limited basis. Individual problem areas in a particular business may have been automated in certain instances, but collectively they were not able to produce the desired information quickly.

Norman E. Sklar defines Integrated Data Processing as:

. . . A network of related subsystems developed according to an integrated scheme for performing the activities of a business. It is a means of uniting men, materials and machines to accomplish the objectives of the business. It specifies the content and format, the preparation and integration of information for all functions within a business that will best satisfy the planning, organizing, directing and controlling needs of the various levels of management.[2]

This concept unites data accumulation, communication, computation, processing, and control. The product of such a system is information in a form that can be used by all levels of management in the performance of their duties.

Another, more current point of view, regards an integrated system as one which is largely computerized. It is a system designed to provide timely collection, processing, and reporting of all necessary management information. It will supply on-line data in real-time so that management can exercise control instantly.

In reality, the three points of view mentioned reflect the maturing and development of the entire field of data processing. As computers become more widely accepted and used, it is quite natural that the concepts in the field of data processing will revolve more completely around the computer.

Mr. William J. Crowley states, however, that "there does not exist today a single system which is completely intregrated for complete management control."[3] The system may be completely integrated when it refers to internally generated facts, but it cannot, as yet, synthesize for management decision purposes all the political, economic, fiscal, facts etc., which management would like to have at its fingertips in order to remove all hazards from business projections and decisions.

Mr. Crowley goes on to point out, "the 'total integrated' system as

---

[2] Norman E. Sklar, "Integrated Information Systems," in *Business Systems* (Systems and Procedures Association, 1963), Vol. II, pp. 21–24.

[3] William J. Crowley, "Can We Integrate Systems Without Integrating Management," *Journal of Data Management*, August, 1966, p. 16.

generally expected to develop is, even in its most modern concept, a limited system. It gives the top executive a clearer, more timely picture of what he already knows, better than anything else in the world, but it does nothing at all with respect to unsolved, unanswered problems that hang eternally over his head like a dense smog."[4]

The concept of electronic data processing is often confused with IDP. The relationship between them is that of a part and the whole. The conception of integration, today, includes electronic elements, and a system cannot be truly integrated unless it does include such elements. This does not mean that in the future, electronics will be the method used in data processing. If electronics can be replaced by better methods of handling and processing, those methods will be used in the process of integration. At the present time, however, electronics is the most efficient method available.

PLANNING FOR IDP

Analysis of Information Requirements

Before making any concrete plans to integrate more fully any existing data processing system, the individual doing the planning should stand back and take note of the objectives of the business. This done, the next task is to determine the information which will be necessary to assist management to achieve these objectives more fully.

Management will not be the only group in need of information, however. The stockholders have an important stake in the business and are entitled to be told how well the enterprise is doing; they have a right to be informed about the status of their equity in the business as of a given point in time. The public at large, as well as outside creditors, are entitled to much of the same information. Information which the U.S. Department of Internal Revenue requires may be of a somewhat different nature. The requirements of local taxing authorities also differ widely. There are many governmental regulatory agencies which also demand information from many different types of business. For publicly owned corporations, the SEC requires precise information on a regular basis. This, in addition to what the trade associations seek, makes the information required from any accounting system voluminous and varied.

MANAGEMENT. The information required by management is extremely varied. Certain types of information are required for planning, while other types are required for control. When information is needed for either of these purposes, it must generally be specific and detailed. The level of management to which the information is sent will determine, in part, the quantity of detail submitted. The timing of the submission of

----

[4] *Ibid.*, p. 17.

information will be apt to vary in accordance with the level of management to which the information is given.

STOCKHOLDERS.   Information is generally submitted to stockholders only at periodic intervals and in a summarized form, in quarterly or semiannual and annual reports. The information is designed to provide information on, and to explain, the results of current operations, usually in comparison to previous results.

CREDITORS.   Information is seldom prepared especially for creditors. The information in which they are interested is that which will indicate the general ability of the enterprise to repay money owed, as well as that which will help evaluate the skill of management in operating the firm on a continuing profitable basis.

U.S. INTERNAL REVENUE SERVICE.   The information which is required is prescribed by law to fulfill the tax obligations of a particular business.

GOVERNMENTAL REGULATORY AGENCIES AND LOCAL TAXING AUTHORITIES.   These agencies, particularly as they affect certain types of business, are becoming more numerous all the time. Supplying the variety of the information which they require is also becoming more burdensome.

Securities and Exchange Commission.   Many publicly owned corporations are required to file annually statements with the SEC, and the form and content of these statements is clearly prescribed.

The problem of how to meet all of these varied demands for information made upon a particular business is a difficult one at best. If the handling of the problem has not been carefully worked out previously by the person concerned with the data processing system, the task becomes even more formidable. A basic principle of IDP is to utilize one piece of data for as many different purposes as possible, depending upon the information required. To do this requires a great deal of thought and planning.

To apply the Integrated Information System concept to a total business system is a tremendous undertaking. A large company's operations are very complex and do not remain static long enough to permit the simultaneous gathering and evaluation of information about all the company's operations. It is also difficult to have a sufficient quantity of qualified staff personnel who have the necessary imagination to visualize the total operations at one time.

As one means of coping with these problems, the analyst could use a "subsystems" approach. The total business system may then be conceived as a number of major subsystems, which are interdependent, yet, for purposes of analysis, may be considered as entities in themselves.

Major Subsystems Selection

The selection of the major subsystems is dependent on the organizational structure, the products of the organization, and customer and management requirements. Each subsystem selected must take into consideration the varying information needs for all levels of management.

Defining the major subsystems and their interrelationships is the most important part of the application of the Integrated Information Systems concept. For example, in a business organized according to product line, the accounting for inventory within that product line would undoubtedly constitute a major subsystem.

ANALYSIS. When analyzing each major subsystem, the following questions should be considered:

1. *What* should be done and its purpose?
2. *Who* should do the work organizationally?
3. *Where* should the work be done physically?
4. *When* is the work to be done? Time and sequence.
5. *How* is it to be done?[5]

DESIGN. The system should be designed so that it can be changed with reasonable ease. It is important to make sure that when changes in the system become necessary it will not be necessary to alter the entire system. Changes will undoubtedly become necessary, due to the inability of anyone to specify the ultimate information requirements the first time. Changes are also inevitable because of the dynamic character of business. Also, regulatory bodies continue to impose changing requirements on many forms of business enterprise.

Data should be captured in a machine-processable language as close to the source as is feasible and economically possible as a by-product of another operation. This simply means that the areas where data originate must be automated—data must be captured in a "common language" form as the automatic by-product of the initial operation. This "common language" may be punched paper tape, punched cards, or even magnetic tape. The data then may be used throughout a self-perpetuating machine system to process and communicate information without further manual operations.

One company which has been in the forefront in developing a totally integrated data processing system is the Mead Corporation of Dayton, Ohio. It is one of the largest manufacturers of paper in the United States.

When this company approves a project for studying and designing a particular subsystem, the systems project group is generally composed of representatives from many fields of specialized technical knowledge. In addition to the leader, there are representatives from cost accounting, systems analysis, manufacturing, industrial engineering, and operations research. The management of this corporation is convinced that developing a smooth-working integrated subsystem requires the combined abili-

---

[5] Sklar, *op. cit.*, chap. xxi, p. 13.

ties of such a group of people. The abilities of this group are much more technically oriented than many people might assume necessary.

IMPORTANCE OF A COMMON LANGUAGE

It has already been stated that one of the basic principles of IDP is to capture data automatically as a by-product of the initial recording in a "machine common language." This means that the data captured must be in a form in which it can be processed—free of human intervention—by other machines in the accounting process. In order for this to be possible, all of the machines utilized must be capable of being activated by the data in the form in which it is initially captured. It is because of this that the term "common language" has been coined. This common language concept becomes extremely important when one thinks of handling large volumes of data both quickly and accurately. Card code and channel code are the two "common language" codes used.

Card Code

It has been emphasized in previous chapters that the hole in the card was used as a means of activating any of the basic pieces of punched card equipment. In other words, the hole—or holes—located in a particular position on the card constitute a code whereby either alphabetic or numeric data can be expressed. Today, card code is capable of communicating with practically any business machine, either directly or by going through a converter. This is one means of processing data automatically when it is initially captured in code form.

Channel Code

Channel code is used with both punched tape and magnetic tape. The idea of transmitting data by means of paper tape is not new. We have been using the idea ever since the invention of the teletype, which utilizes a five-channel tape. Channel code gets its name from the fact that either the impressions or holes are made in imaginary channels which run the length of the tape.

COMMON LANGUAGE EQUIPMENT

Data-Originating Media for Integrated Data Processing

Typewriters, adding machines, calculators, bookkeeping machines, and cash registers are probably the most frequently used in making a record of data soon after it has been captured at its source. Several business machine manufacturers have produced equipment which can be used as attachments to these basic recording devices. Generally, these attachments produce the punched paper tape or punched cards as a by-product of the operation of the recording device. The tape-producing machines are also capable of being activated at a later time by their own or other coded paper tape data.

The Bell Telephone System produces the teletypewriter (Figure 13–1), which is capable of producing hard copy as well as five-channel tape in the same operation. Also note the Flexowriter (Figure 13–2), which is a typewriter with the capability of producing punched paper tape as a by-product of any typing operation. This tape can be used to activate any punched paper tape oriented input equipment. Figure 13–3 illustrates a tape punch adding machine, which communicates its answers electrically for direct punching into tape or tabulating cards.

Courtesy of Teletype Corp.

FIG. **13–1.   Teletypewriter.**

As indicated in Chapter 7, the fastest and probably most extensively used method of originating data on cards is by means of the key punch. The operator depresses keys on a keyboard similar to that of the standard typewriter, and the data are punched, one character at a time, into the cards. Punched cards can also be prepared by hand punching or by mark sensing—whereby electrographic pencil marks are placed in a designated position on the card.

A Magnetic Tape Keyed Data-Recorder (Figure 13–4) is also available whereby information from business documents can be directly transcribed into magnetic tape. All data transcribed are verified at that time.

The common language medium used in any particular case will be determined by the remainder of the data processing equipment which is to be used. A consideration of primary importance is the choosing of a

Courtesy of Friden, Inc.

FIG. 13–2.   Model 2303 FLEXOWRITER* Automatic Writing Machine.

common language medium which is compatible with either the existing or projected data processing equipment.

The machines which have just been described are typical examples of ways business data can be converted into the desired common language medium.

Courtesy of National Cash Register Co.

FIG. 13–3.   NCR Tape Punching Adding Machine.

*A Trademark of Friden, Inc.

Looking at an example of a paper tape application, let us say a salesman sends in a handwritten order. From it, a typist, using a tape-punching typewriter, prepares a production order. Upon removing from a customer master file a strip of punched paper tape or an edge-punched card on which have been recorded in five-channel code the customer's name and address, shipping instructions, and other standard data, she feeds the common language medium into the reader unit of the typewriter. From this tape, all the prerecorded information desired is automatically typed on the order.

As the first tape is refiled, a second tape containing an organized

Courtesy of Mohawk Data Sciences Corporation.

FIG. 13–4.   MDS 1101 Keyed Data-Recorder.

description of the standard product ordered is pulled from a product master file. The information coded thereon is then also automatically reproduced on the order by the same reader unit. All the typist has to add is the variable information (some 5 to 15 percent of the total) such as the current date and number of the order, quantity of material ordered, color, sizes or weights, and so on. When the typing of the order has been completed, it can, if desired, be automatically verified by the same tapereading device.

A second complete by-product tape, containing all the data from the standard tapes used, along with the variable information added, is automatically produced by the machine. By means of a tape-to-card converter, this tape can be used at the tabulating center to produce a punched card for various bookkeeping and statistical purposes. Since this eliminates manual keypunching and subsequent verification, there is a considerable saving in time and effort.

From the same automatic typing, an invoice, a packing slip, and even a shipping label can be produced without further human intervention. The use of this tape to produce statistical data automatically makes it possible to produce accurate and timely reports, rather than just historical records, for the use of management.

PRECODED DATA. Various methods have been devised to more carefully assure the accuracy of data at the time it is captured at its source. Where humans record the data in the first instance, there is a real likelihood of error. Efforts have been made, therefore, to devise ways of verifying the majority of data surrounding a transaction before the transaction occurs. This is done by recording in advance all of the fixed data concerning a transaction on some form of document. In this way, the accuracy of this much of the data can be predetermined. There is also the desire, as well as the necessity if the principles of IDP are to be followed, that the fixed data recorded be machine processable from this point on. There has been a variety of innovations in this area.

Machine-Recognizable Printed Characters. Although one of the newest mediums, machine-recognizable printed characters present one of the most interesting potentials for reducing data processing costs.

There are two types of character recognition equipment: optical and magnetic ink. The optical equipment scans the character, determines the presence or absence of ink in certain positions, and from this information, establishes the character. Because of this recognition technique, the type font used is somewhat stylized. A typical optical font which is used by NCR equipment was illustrated in Figure 11–23.

Magnetic ink character recognition (MICR) or the reading of magnetic ink type characters involves the recognition of differences in intensities of magnetism present in the ink used in the printing of the data. For this reason, portions of some characters are exaggerated to provide greater intensity and permit differentiation.

In using magnetic ink characters, much greater care is required in imprinting than is the case with optically recognizable characters. This factor tends to limit the use of magnetic ink character recognition equipment to banks and similar organizations which can enforce rigid imprinting requirements.

Symbols printed in magnetic ink on checks can be run through magnetic character recognition machines, read by the equipment, and recorded directly on magnetic tape for filing and processing in the regular computer system.

Machine-Recognizable Printed Codes.   The printed code is another medium involving optical scanning. Various codes have been devised for this purpose. The gasoline credit card is probably the best known example of this method. It is embossed with the customer's account number and with a code interpreting the customer's account number in machine language. An example of this code is shown in Figure 13–5.

When the customer makes a purchase, his credit card is placed in an imprinting machine where his account number as well as the code identifying the account number is imprinted on a sales invoice. The printed

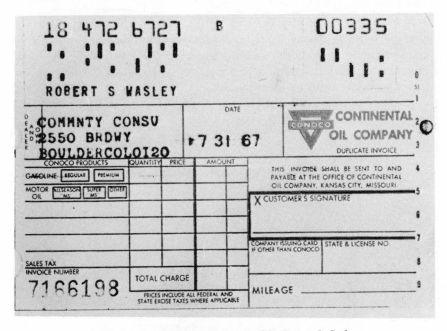

FIG. 13–5.   Machine-Recognizable Printed Code.

code on the invoice identifying the customer, as well as the code identifying the amount of the sale, will then be optically interpreted so that it can be prepared for computer input on punched cards or magnetic tape. Millions of gasoline credit cards users are billed in this way on a monthly basis.

Machine-Recognizable Perforated Codes.   This idea is a recent innovation of the National Cash Register Company. It is their answer to the problem of automatically collecting data in a credit sale type of transaction.

Every customer is provided with a credit card containing his name, address, and account number, all in embossed letters. The card also contains certain oblong shaped holes which are the customer's account number in "automation" code.

The salesperson cannot forget to record an account number because the cash register, built to go with this system, will not operate unless the credit card is placed into the credit card reader. The only exception is when a special button is used to release the register mechanism for a customer who does not have a credit card. In this event, the customer's account number can be entered through the register keyboard.

The information on the credit card is imprinted on the sales ticket. This information also serves as a direct input to the computer.

Machine-Recognizable Perforated Tags. The perforated tag is a medium designed primarily for the retail industry. Varying amounts of data can be punched into the tags, depending upon the needs of the user. For example, the manufacturer, department, style, size, class, color, season, fabric, and price can be recorded automatically. The data punched into these tags can be read instantly by a reader. An example of a perforated tag is shown in Figure 13–6.

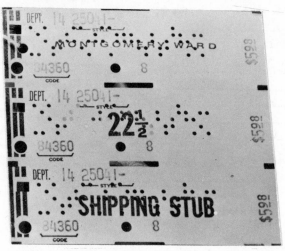

FIG. 13–6.   Perforated Garment Tag.

Optical Scanning Punch.   Both the IBM and Remington Rand Corporation have developed punches which will read normal pencil marks. The punch translates the pencil marks into punched holes. No special symbols need to be used. The numeral to be duplicated may be entered on the card, or it may be circled or have an "X" marked through it. The value of any mark is determined by its position on the card, rather than by the mark itself. An example of a punched card designed for this purpose is shown in Figure 13–7.

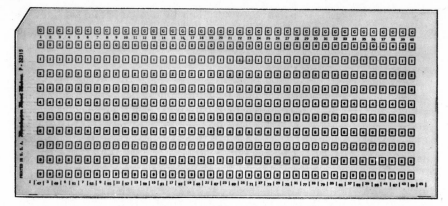

FIG. 13–7. Optically Scannable Card.

There are also optical mark page readers which will provide direct entry to a computer of information recorded in lead pencil form.

COMMUNICATIONS EQUIPMENT

Integration means the linking together of the data producing operations which go on at separate, and often geographically scattered, locations in such a way that the data produced at the various sources are expressed in a common language form so that they can be read by other machines in the system.

In an IDP program, communication is the bridge connecting the points where data originate and the points where the data are to be used or processed. Computer technology has taken tremendous strides in the past few years by greatly increasing the operational speed and storage capacity of computers while, at the same time, reducing their cost. This greatly increased capacity has thrown a tremendous strain on communication facilities, however, because if the necessary quantities of data are not transported to the computer at a speed sufficient to keep the computer fully utilized, the technological gains which have been made cannot be utilized adequately. Communication equipment, therefore, is now the most important link of all in this chain of operation for processing data.

Data can be transported manually or transmitted by means of electrical circuits. If a business has come to the conclusion that it can afford and can adequately use a computer, it is quite unlikely that it will consider transporting data manually from the location where it arises to the central location of the computer. There was a time when the invoices might have been sent by airmail or when the punched cards were sent by special delivery, but this time is rapidly passing. With computer costs as high as they are, it is imperative that adequate data be available and on hand at all times to be processed by the computer. The speed and capacity of the means of data transmission, thus, have become all important.

Data Transmission Services

The quality and speed of data transmission varies with the type of carriers and the equipment over which it travels. The type of communication channel used has a direct bearing on the directional (one-way or two-way) capability of the service. In addition, the channels are divided into grades or bands of service. The significance of the widths of the bands is that as the bands become wider, the greater is the frequency range. As the frequency range becomes greater, the clarity and speed of transmission will increase.

TYPES OF COMMUNICATION CHANNELS. There are three basic types of communication channels or circuits available in terms of directional capability. These are the *simplex*, *half-duplex*, and *duplex* channels. The *simplex* type of channel provides for one-way transmission of data, and its ability to carry information would be comparable to the ability of a doorbell or one-way street. The *half-duplex* channel can carry information in both directions but in only a single direction at a time. The *duplex* channel, sometimes called a full-duplex circuit, is the most versatile of all in its ability to transmit information in both directions simultaneously.

GRADES OF CIRCUITS. In addition to types of circuits, there are also bands or grades of circuits whose capacity is in terms of basic line speed expressed in characters per second, bits per second, or words per minute. Telegraph grade channels have transmission speeds in the 45 to 75 bits per second range. This grade is utilized in data transmission by the various types of teletype equipment and data transceivers, along with other equipment.

Industry has used the teletypewriter for data transmission for many years. It not only can produce hard copy at the time the transaction is recorded but also it can produce and can be activated by five- or eight-channel paper tape. Since it utilizes paper tape, it is readily integrated into a data processing system.

The *narrow-band* grade, like the telegraph grade, has a slower speed than those needed for voice transmission and is also called a *subvoice* grade channel. Generally, the transmission rate for this grade is within the range of 150 to 600 bits per second. The TWX or Teletypewriter Exchange Service utilizes this band and has over 60,000 subscribers in the United States who transmit data via five-channel paper tape at the rate of 60 words per minute. Many of the newer data collection (Figure 13–8) and data communication systems also utilize this grade channel as it is relatively inexpensive.

The *voice-band* grade channels carry information over a range or band

Courtesy of IBM.

FIG. 13–8.   IBM 1030 Data Collection System.

width of approximately 3,000 cycles per second. This channel may be subdivided for certain usage into subvoice channels composed of bands of 150 to 200 cycles. The 100-Speed TWX Service uses the voice-band grade for reading, transmitting, and punching eight-channel paper tape at

Courtesy of IBM.

FIG. 13–9.   IBM 1009 Data Transmission System.

the rate of 100 words per minute. The Bell Telephone System's DATA-PHONE equipment and many other data transmission systems, for example (Figure 13–9), use this grade of channel to transmit data encoded on punched cards, punched paper tape, and magnetic tape. The cost for the use of this grade channel is similar to the cost of a voice long-distance call.

The DATA-PHONE, manufactured by the Bell Telephone System, has been developed with a capability of changing voice capability to a data transmission capability and vice versa. A picture of a DATA-PHONE is shown in Figure 13–10. It will be noted that it looks like a large standard

Courtesy of the Bell Telephone System.

FIG. 13–10.   DATA-PHONE.

telephone set. Commonly, it utilizes the more consistently dependable voice-grade telephone circuits and converts all channel codes—including those which provide check bit channels for automatic checking purposes. By this means, data is transmitted by the use of electrical signals or impulses. For example, a DATA-PHONE converts electrical signals picked up from punched cards one at a time by means of an IBM 056 transceiver, a 1001 Data Transmission System, or from punched paper tape by means of Dataspeed Tape Sender (Figure 13–11), and converts them to tones suitable for telephonic transmission. Dataspeed Tape Senders can transmit data at the rate of 1,050 words per minute. Connections are made by dialing a distant location for the purpose of obtaining a clear line. At the other end, DATA-PHONES convert the incoming tones back to electrical pulses which feed into teletypewriters, Dataspeed Tape Receivers (Figure 13–11), or other business machines, producing an exact duplicate of material transmitted. Punched card, paper and magnetic

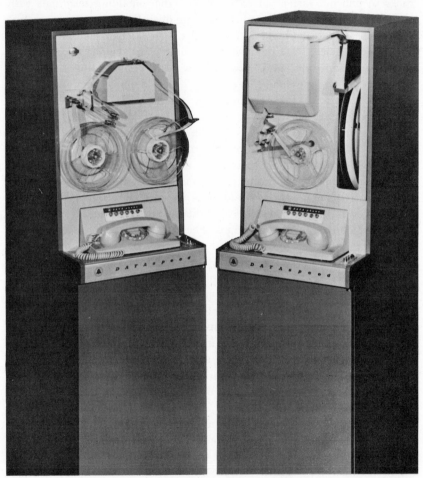

Courtesy of the Bell Telephone System.

FIG. 13–11.   Dataspeed Sender and Receiver.

tape, facsimile, "live" handwriting, and medical telemetric data can now be sent via DATA-PHONES.

An interesting example of how this equipment has been put to work is in the trucking industry. This industry has found that improved data communication has not only facilitated the processing of data but has also improved shipping service. Trucks are loaded and sent on their way without waiting for the time-consuming preparation of bills of lading. These bills are recorded on paper tape and transmitted to the distant terminals concerned while the truck is en route. This not only permits the trucks to pull out faster but also provides the unloading terminals with advance information to be used in planning operations.

Another service available over voice-band grade channels is Wide Area Telephone Service (WATS), which is similar to regular long-distance telephone service in that it provides two-way conversation between a large number of telephones. However, it has a more economical rate treatment than long distance for larger volumes. Wide Area Telephone Service permits a customer to contact a large number of telephones within a specified area at a fixed monthly rate and is basically designed for the customer who has widespread large volume of outgoing traffic.

The *broad-band* grade of circuit, sometimes called the wide band, involves a microwave or radio relay communication system operating at superhigh frequencies above 4 million kilocycles per second. Data transmitted over this band must be continually amplified and repeated by stations which use dishlike antennas. These stations can be seen on many high buildings and on towers spaced at intervals of 20 to 35 miles along highways. American Telephone and Telegraph's Telpak is a private line service carrying 12, 24, 60, or 240 voice channels connecting two or more points. It can accommodate the transmission of data, telemetering of information, and facsimile as well as telephone conversations.

Telpak is a typical leased wide-band program and costs a minimum of $15 per mile of leased circuit per month on an unlimited usage basis. However, when you consider that a system such as the IBM 7710 Data Communication Unit would transmit up to 5,100 characters per second over such a band, the cost per unit of data sent can be quite low where the volume to be sent is high.

Radio frequencies are very efficient carriers of data. They are also the fastest and the most expensive. Recently, on a test basis, 20 million bits (3.3 million characters) per second were transmitted over a TV circuit.

There are several radio frequency carriers, including radio bands themselves. Another is microwave. Generally, microwave signals have a short range and must be amplified and retransmitted on the average of every 50 to 90 miles, depending on the terrain. Line-of-sight transmission, such as microwave, is affected by weather disturbances, birds flying through the signal path, low cloud formations, etc.

One of the newer means of transmitting messages is tropospheric forward scatter propagation. This technique sends out multiple signals, as from the large end of a funnel. These signals scatter and bounce off the troposphere, which ranges from 5 to 8 miles above the earth's surface. One or more of these signals are picked up by a distant terminal.

Irrespective of the type of transmission facilities, or the rate of speed at which it is accomplished, the transmission of data is accomplished through the use of signals or impulses. Combinations of signals or the absence of signals are used to form codes which represent the letters of the alphabet, numbers, and special characters. These impulses are called "bits." A character of information is comprised of five to eight bits. In data communication terminology, a "word" is defined as five characters plus a space.

In order to transmit these bits and characters over any carrier, a modulation-demodulation unit must be placed at the terminal ends of the circuit. These units (modulation) pick up electrical signals from a punched card or paper tape reader, and convert the signals to a frequency that is acceptable to the carrier. After this conversion, the pulses are sent along the circuit. At the other end, a demodulation unit performs the conversion function. These units may be built into the terminal equipment or may be separate.[6]

According to David Sarnoff, it is technically feasible to establish, over the next few decades, a communication system by which governments, businesses, or individuals may establish contact with anyone, at any place, by voice, sight, or document.

The principal catalyst responsible for these capabilities will be the ocean-spanning satellite. Its impact will occur in three distinct phases:

1. A global system of synchronous satellites, already nearly at hand, that would be within direct line-of-sight range of up to one-third of the inhabited globe providing capabilities for communications to develop to the point of fixed telephone dialing between users anywhere in the world.
2. The next decade may mark the beginning of international satellite communications between any two cities rather than through national terminals. This would become economically feasible through the use of nuclear-power synchronous satellites. Person-to-person voice communications could be provided through fixed or mobile telephone and even pocket-radio links between individuals and earth terminals.
3. This last phase would follow the establishment of services contemplated under Phase 2 resulting in a new dimension in individual communications that might lead to the incorporation of television as well as sound in a two-way pocket-size device equipped with a decoding circuit responsive to one code out of several million possible arrangements of pulses transmitted from similar units elsewhere in the world.[7]

HANDWRITING TRANSMISSION TERMINALS. Handwriting transmission terminals are utilized to transmit written messages or sketches over communication lines (Figure 13–12).

---

[6] Leighton F. Smith, "Data Communication—Next Big Step in Data Processing." Reprinted from the June 1963 issue of *Journal of Data Management* and copyrighted by the Data Processing Management Association.

[7] "Tomorrow's Communicating World," *Florist and Nursery Exchange*, May 17, 1967.

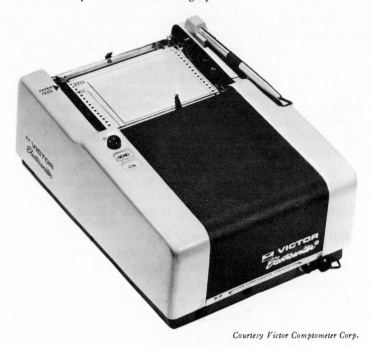

Courtesy Victor Comptometer Corp.

FIG. 13–12.   Electrowriter.

The message originating at the transmitter is written with a ballpoint pen on regular paper. As the pen moves on the paper, varying tones are generated and transmitted by means of the data set over a communication line to the receiving data set and its associated receiving business machine. There the tones are interpreted and the receiving pen reproduces the handwritten copy.[8]

FASCIMILE TERMINALS.   Fascimile terminals are basically duplicating devices. One of the large builders of duplicating equipment in this country is installing a fascimile transmission network to span one third of the continent. It will be possible to transmit anything written, typed, or hand drawn, over phone wires between the 10 different offices of this company. At the originating station, the document to be transmitted is fed into the scanner, which converts the image into electrical signals for transmission. At the receiving station, the electrical signals are reconverted into images, and a duplicate of the original document is reproduced by conventional xerography.

VISUAL DISPLAY TERMINALS.   Visual display terminals are used to provide visual presentation of information stored within a computer

---

[8] Edward C. Gentle, Jr., *Data Communications in Business—An Introduction* (New York: American Telephone and Telegraph Co., 1965), p. 129.

Courtesy Bunker Ramo Corp.

FIG. 13–13. Teleregister Visual Display Unit.

system. These terminals are connected to the computer by data communication channels and are used for inquiry to the memory of a computer system.

The terminal consists of a keyboard, a signal generator-interpreter, a buffer, and a visual display screen similar to a television screen [Figure 13–13].

An operator queries the computer system for desired information by pressing the keys. Coded signals are generated and transmitted by means of the data sets over the communication channel to the data set. The computer interprets the signals and searches memory for the desired information. The information is transmitted, again using the data sets, back over the communication channel to the visual display terminal in the form of coded signals. The signals are interpreted and visually displayed on the screen.[9]

DATA COLLECTION SYSTEMS

Automatic data collection implies the recording of the pertinent data about a transaction, in machine-readable form, at the time the transaction

[9] *Ibid.*, p. 131–32.

occurs. Some data collection systems collect and record the transaction data in batches in machine-readable form for later processing. Others feed the data directly into real-time computer systems to provide up-to-the-minute information for operational decisions.

Data collection systems consist of various types of input devices, a central receiving and processing device, and the necessary interconnecting communication links.

The input devices accept and transmit data from prepunched cards, badges, dials, or levers. Communication facilities transmit the data from the input units to the output units or computer system. Output units generally record the transmitted data on punched cards, punched paper tape, or magnetic tape.

Transmitting data collection systems are now being widely used in production control, inventory control, and employee attendance applications, to name a few. Their installation, however, should only be accomplished after a detailed systems study. An automatic data transmission system in and of itself will not solve problems. It will only create more of them if not properly implemented.

IBM 1030 Data Collection System

The IBM 1030 system is an example of a data collection system (Figure 13–8, p. 317). It accepts data from the standard 80-column IBM card, from plastic identification badges prepunched with the Hollerith code, from a data cartridge which can be preset with up to 12 digits of variable numeric information, and from a manual entry unit which will accept variable numeric information. Up to 24 input units can be accommodated in one system. A digital time unit is available which automatically records the time each entry is transmitted via the system.

The system may be operated on-line where the information is fed directly into the processing unit, or it may be operated off-line where the data are recorded at the central station in punched cards. A maximum of 24 printers can be associated with any one system.

Communications between the central control unit and the various satellite stations is by multiwire cable; however, communications between the central control unit and the central processor (computer) can be by means of a standard telephone circuit.

ON-LINE REAL-TIME SYSTEMS

The term "on-line real-time" is of comparatively recent origin in the computer field. It implies that everyone using the system has a point-of-origin device which provides a direct keyed entry to the system via teleprocessing. Each such device permits a two-directional information flow such that the person using it receives responses to his request in sufficient time that the information received can be useful in making decisions. In many such systems there is direct visual output via cathode-ray tube devices or it may be in typewritten message form.

In the earlier years of computer usage, data was processed in batches. Like data, as evidenced by business documents, was gathered together and made into a batch. The batch was converted into machine-processable form, and then processed by the computer. As soon as this batch of data was fully processed, another batch of different type would be processed.

A real-time system is quite different in that in order for a response to be received in real-time, all transactions must be processed in random order. This involves the updating of the master file or description of the current situation with every transaction, regardless of the type of transaction or how frequent the transactions occur.

"Response time is the time the system takes to react to a given input. If a message is keyed into a terminal by an operator and the reply from the computer is typed at the same terminal, 'response time' may be defined as the time interval between the operator pressing the last key and the terminal typing the first letter of the reply."[10]

The speed of the response time differs from system to system depending upon the actual needs. The more rapid the response time, the more sophisticated must be the equipment and the programming, and all of this makes for greater cost. For example, the speed of response varies from the airline reservation systems which give a maximum response time of about three seconds to the system used for controlling production in a paper mill where a five-minute response time is adequate.

There have had to be a number of technological advances to make such a system workable:

1. The storage capacity of computers has been increased manyfold without a commensurate increase in cost.
2. The speed of access to stored data has also been increased manyfold without a corresponding increase in cost.
3. The operating speed of computers has increased from millionths to billionths of a second for one calculation with an actual decrease in cost of the equipment.
4. Terminals have been developed to directly link the computer with a telecommunication network.
5. Completely new programming techniques have been developed to cope with the problems created by this type of data processing whereby it is possible for many remote terminals to make inquiries of the computer at the same time.

Remote terminal devices are usually attached to the central processing unit of the computer via input/output synchronizers. The synchronizer may contain several core buffers which form an interface between the

[10] James Martin, *Programming Real-Time Computer Systems* (Englewood Cliffs, N.J.: Prentice Hall, Inc., 1965), p. 4.

input/output (I/O) devices and the computer. Input data is generally transferred to the buffer. When a buffer is full, the central processing unit will be interrupted. Information can be read from, or placed into, buffers by ordinary read and write commands.

In such a system, there are going to be many programs involved. Because of this, a special control program remains in storage at all times. Two of its main purposes are to handle I/O requests as well as the programs needed to process the data. The control program, sometimes termed an executive program, is supervisory in nature as compared with operational programs which actually process data. Other important functions of the control program are storage allocation and the reading in of operational programs as needed.

Whenever an I/O operation is complete, the running operational program is interrupted, and control goes to the control program.

As an example of what has been discussed in this section:

. . . the housewife of 1970 may replace the check writing process with her kitchen telephone if some tests now being conducted by the Bank of Delaware in Wilmington are successful. By utilizing a standard Touch-Tone Card Dialer telephone and a set of plastic cards (one for each store, utility, mortgage company, or other organization to which she sends a monthly payment), she will be able to contact the bank computer, access her cash transfer account, and instruct the computer to transfer funds from her account to the account of the organization to which she owes money.[11]

TIME-SHARING

One application of real-time systems is in the area of time-sharing. The concept of time-sharing is typified by having a large, general-purpose computer facility available to many users who are in themselves remote from each other. The service which the users receive is instantaneous (it seems to the user), although the users and the system are independent of each other.

These benefits are made possible because of the system of executive programming (to be discussed in Chapter 15). Through this system, the central processor devotes only a short period of time to each user's program before going on to the next, but the delay is not apparent to the user. Assuming 20 users of the system made inquiries, almost simultaneously, the computer would process a small segment of the program of each user going from one to the other in rapid succession. It can act with such speed that each user will commence receiving a response to his inquiry almost as soon as he completes the inquiry.

---

[11] Dale L. Reistad, "What Telecommunications Will Do for Banking," *Banking*, December, 1965, p. 108.

The individual user of the computer time-shared system has a console or teletypewriter in his office. He is connected by telephone line to the central computer. When he wants some current information about his business he will dial his identification number or password, and then dial the inquiry. The computer takes over at this point and prints out the result of the inquiry on the user's teletypewriter.

It is possible through time-sharing to present a continuous video presentation that keeps up with changing environmental factors. For example, engineering drawings can be examined and modified at will on this video display screen.

As an example of what is being done in the area of setting up time-sharing computer utilities, Com-Share, Inc. of Ann Arbor, Michigan, was recently opened. It is estimated that it has the potential of serving 1,000–1,200 customers out of four computer centers at rates of $40 per month for a one-hour minimum to $10 per hour for 2,000 hours of computer time monthly.

For example, one of the most ambitious time-sharing plans yet developed is one for hospitals, with the goal of offering wide-range computer services to 180 hospitals in Minnesota. Participating hospitals are linked directly to the computer center, which houses two Honeywell H-200 communications computers, by private lines provided by Northwestern Bell Telephone.

This particular system is unique in that it is one of the first systems in the country to make use of the new Model 35 Automatic Send-Receive Set (Teletype Corporation) on other than a trial basis. The Model 35 is a teletypewriter that can be partially controlled by program tapes to speed and simplify the preparation on material for transmission.

This system initially provides hospitals with accounting services, but later will add inventory control, personnel and payroll accounting, a dietary control system, and a laboratory test report system. The group has identified 150 distinct administrative and clinical areas where EDP can help hospitals, and it plans to develop programs to cover these areas.

Once the possibilities of such a system are realized, it begins to stimulate everyone's imagination. There are those who are talking of having "information utilities" where groups of business firms could store their basic data which could be obtained at a moment's notice through the use of a communication device. To date, the teletypewriter is the most frequently used, although it is a relatively slow means of communication.

There are four potential problem areas in ambitious programs such as this—cost, speed, security, and the data base.

Cost: Although the performance per dollar of a large computer system (within a given family) is better than a small one, a system that is large because it integrates several small computers may not show a cost advantage, since it requires a supervisory program that can be very complex and requires more machine memory space and operation time than all the working programs put together.

Speed: In addition to the adverse effect of the supervisor, if the terminal devices of the system have different codes from the central computer, speed is decreased because of the translation time needed. Also, machine time must be used to control data transmission between the computer and remote devices.

Security: It is felt that the important part of this question is that it has been raised. Service centers, by their highly respected operations, have shown the problem can be solved by using special file controls which require coded keys to access these files.

Data Base: The data base for such a system may be more complicated than most, since it must isolate and control interaction between the various subscribers.

The most promising use of a time-sharing system will be for systems which: (1) avoid the complexity of using several programming languages; (2) avoid the inefficiency of swapping a multitude of different programs in and out of computer memory; and (3) avoid the burden of maintaining and protecting a multitude of unrelated files.

CASE STUDY 13–1[12]

Barclays Bank Ltd., Great Britain, the largest bank in the world outside the United States, has purchased a $32 million Burroughs B8500 electronic information processing system for what will be one of the largest on-line realtime banking systems in use anywhere.

Special TC-500 terminal computers, located at most of Barclays' 2,500 branches throughout the United Kingdom, will be connected by telephone lines to the B8500 central system at the bank's headquarters in London.

The system will process all aspects of the bank's operations, including instantaneous inquiry and immediate updating of customer files. Burroughs President Ray W. Macdonald is quoted as saying that "it will also operate as a service center to handle the accounting needs of Barclays' commercial customers."

An operator querying the central computer from any of the bank's branches in the United Kingdom will have a response within two and one half seconds maximum, regardless of how far the branch is from London. The system is capable of handling up to one million transactions per hour.

An important feature of the computer is that it will be able to compensate for any possible component failures within the system by immediately identifying a malfunction and re-arranging the work flow to maintain its processing operations.

---

[12] "Barclays Bank Ltd. Purchase Giant Burroughs Computer Complex," *Management Services*, May–June, 1967, p. 8.

The system will include data display units and a high-speed, random access disk file with four billion characters of memory and an average access time of 30 milli-seconds.

The central B8500 will be installed at Barclays early in 1969 and the complete on-line real-time system will be operational in 1970, prior to decimalization of the currency in Britain.

CASE STUDY 13–2[13]

One of the first companies to move toward implementation of a totally integrated, all-embracing information handling network utilizing electronic data processing is The Mead Corp., fifth ranked manufacturer of paper in the United States, with annual sales exceeding $500 million.

Real-Time Control

The ultimate system will include continuously updated central files, which will contain and make instantly available to management all information needed for the most advantageous day-to-day control of the business. Files will be fed by two-way data transmission units, capable of inputting information from the mills and field sales offices directly into on-line, real-time computer systems which will evaluate the incoming data, flash instructions back to the originating source, and update the master files.

Mathematical models will be used to forecast future sales, to determine production equipment required to satisfy the need, and to schedule when and how often grades of paper should be produced.

In accounting, the system will pinpoint profit contribution by item, by sales area, by customer, by producing mill, even by individual production machines.

And in the plants, papermaking machines and other production processes will be under on-line, closed-loop computer control.

The administrative vice president said: "We expect to have a totally integrated, computer-based information system whereby corporate management (which determines the direction of the company and sets overall goals) will receive performance reports, to guide the business on the most profitable course, and reliable information for planning and forecasting.

"Operating management, responsible for establishing objectives needed to carry out the corporate aims and for setting up schedules to accomplish those objectives, will get the performance reports it needs on a real-time basis. That is, the information will be available in time to influence the course of events—to capitalize on opportunity or avoid trouble buildups before they become serious. What we're after is dynamic information we can use right now, not an accumulation of historical facts.

"Progress, or the lack of it, will be continually measured against objectives, and primarily on an exception basis."

---

[13] "Total System in the Mill," *Business Automation*, July, 1965, pp. 23–29.

Production Lines On-Line

The large scale computer system at Dayton will maintain the master data files, process transactions and inquiries and produce both the operating responses and management reports required. Fully equipped data centers are to be set up at mill locations for controlled data input. Sales offices (and, for order entry only, customer offices) will be equipped with terminals capable of transmitting or receiving data in computer compatible form.

Direct input of orders into the computer will let sales people know immediately whether or not the order can be filled from inventory, whether it will have to be entered into production, or if part of it will be available soon from in-process inventories. Later on, if the situation changes or the customer is pressing for shipment details, the salesman will have the ability to inquire into the particular status of the order and find out exactly where it is in production or inventory.

The salesman will be able to make his inquiry, via telephone, directly into the computer's memory. Probably, he will get his answer from a computer-controlled audio response unit.

Marketing management will have random access to the computer's master sales analysis and forecasting files, and will receive, in addition, regular reports measuring market performance and potential by sales area, pinpointing the most profitable lines and grade structures and analyzing profitability by geographic location, by customer, by salesman and by item. Fast, reliable data will make for better long and short range forecasts and for more efficient advertising and promotion campaigns.

Mead's 250 merchant-customers will benefit from the system's capabilities—especially its ability to provide tight control of their own stock inventories. It will also contribute to maintenance of a high service level for their customers, which is an increasingly complex problem in view of the proliferation of paper lines and grades.

The company's own product line is vast and varied, comprising more than 100 separate items ranging from beer case carton stock to saturable transparentizable white overlay paper. Products are grouped into six areas—pulp, boards, containers, papers (for office use, printing, labels, etc.), industrial papers, and packaging. Mills and plants that produce these products, many of which are available in varying grade, size, weight and form, are located throughout the United States, in Canada, Holland, and Switzerland.

Sales offices and mills in this country are currently linked to the computer center in Dayton via leased telephone lines. Future plans to improve data transmission capability will include an increase in line requirements to accommodate direct order entry devices at each sales office, and data collection equipment at all mill locations. Microwave facilities may be required for the interface of process control and production scheduling between the larger mills and the computer center.

The trigger for the company's highly sophisticated computer processing cycle will be customer activity. Orders, order changes, or inquiries will put the entire system in motion. In a computer run requiring a few seconds at most, the incoming order will be checked for credit against master accounts receivable files, and, if OK and available from stock, immediately scheduled for shipment through the related computer shipping sub-system.

If the order calls for a "make" item, it will be entered into the scheduling sub-system which will scan current production schedules and in-process inventory tabulations, assign a manufacturing date and then immediately record this date in the shipping sub-system. At this point, the order entry sub-system will be flagged to print an order acknowledgement which will be sent to the customer.

Meanwhile, the scheduling sub-system will be constantly monitoring production, in order to update performance at the various manufacturing units, keeping track of schedule lags, breakdowns in equipment, repair and maintenance plans, so that an up-to-the-minute production schedule is always available. In addition, the sub-system will maintain surveillance over set order production dates and, when "make" time arrives, will automatically issue instructions to the mill, including operating and raw material specifications.

Progress Reports

As the required mill operations are performed, data collection devices at the various equipment stations will inform the master computer center of the progress of the order (for order status inquiry response) and of the completed production date. The mill will record this production performance data through data centers for transmission to the central computer at Dayton for redistribution to the appropriate sub-systems. Daily shipping schedules will be supplied to the warehouse and completed shipping data will be flashed back to the central computer to trigger the printing of bills of lading.

The master computer will transmit other information to the billing sub-system, where the invoice will be printed, to the accounts receivable system, for updating the A/R file, and to various data storage files, for statistical and analysis purposes.

Item withdrawal from stock inventory and material withdrawals from stores inventory will be continually adjusted to reflect current status. These files, in turn, will activate the purchasing sub-system which monitors all requisitioning and purchase order writing operations. Accounts payable receives its data from the purchasing sub-system.

While all this is going on, sub-systems for sales analysis, forecasting, and economic data will be updated, along with a cost analysis system, incorporating work standards, payroll data, stores usage, and production run costs.

All along the line, the system will flag the attention of both operating and corporate management to the exception situations. And, of course, the system will provide all needed performance and control reports on a periodic basis. The idea, however, is to hold report production to the minimum because of the opportunity management has to inquire directly into the random access, continuously updated master information files for current data on any given situation.

Integrated Process Control

One of the most sophisticated of Mead's present computer operations is in the area of manufacturing process control. A computer control system is functioning on one of the paper machines at the Chillicothe Paper Company Division and it is said to be the first such system planned from the start for eventual integration into a total computerized management information program.

The system encompasses virtually every important control problem on the paper machine, which includes some 200 variable influencing factors. Approximately 20 of the most important measurements are flashed to the computer where computations are performed, and from which instructions are directed back to the paper machine operators so they can make any necessary changes required to maintain standard operation.

A number of factors, such as stock flows, machine speeds, temperatures, and pressures are under closed loop control. This is particularly helpful in making grade changes.

The computerized control system is credited with an integral part of the program which has achieved a 20 percent decrease in grade change time, 15 percent increased speed, 19 percent increase in production, and a 2 percent increase in machine efficiency. In addition, machine operators are now able to hold closer quality tolerances in producing better, more uniform grades of paper.

The paper machines are the key production facilities and represent a large capital investment. Their time is rated in terms of hundreds of dollars per hour, so the payout for even a fractional increase in yield can be measured in tens, or even hundreds, of thousands of dollars a year. The company makes and sells some 600 different grades and basis weight papers, which underscores the importance of faster grade change time.

The corporation as a whole operates some 40 paper machines, and has already made plans to install process control computers on additional lines, including a new multimillion dollar machine at its Kingsport, Tenn. mill. Each of the new computers will have the capacity to handle control chores for several machines.

ANNOTATED BIBLIOGRAPHY

American Management Association. *Establishing an Integrated Data Processing System.* Special Report No. 11. New York, 1956.

This report explains the many benefits and pitfalls in establishing an IDP system. It goes through, in considerable detail, the whole process of establishing the IDP system, from the preliminary study to the problems after installation and use. Reports of actual company experiences show how the complete process was done and how accurate information was obtained.

Barry W. J. "Systems Integration: The Big Plan," *Administrative Management,* Vol. 23 (November, 1962), pp. 30–32, 36.

This article outlines the steps that should be taken in installing an integrated information system. It shows how the data output of the corporate activity as a whole is used as source information for the individual functions.

CANADIAN INSTITUTE OF CHARTERED ACCOUNTANTS. *Integrated and Electronic Data Processing in Canada.* Toronto, Ont., 1957.

This is a collection of eight articles by chartered accountants on integrated data processing and its many phases. They include a definition of integrated data processing, the types of equipment used, and the role of communication in integrated data processing.

CREON, MARTIN J. "The Total Integrated Approach in Business Systems for R&D," *Control through Information—A Report on Management Information Systems.* Management Bulletin No. 24. New York: American Management Association, 1963.

This article explains a new data processing system called "Product Administration and Contract Control" (PACC) developed by Sperry, which has created a method of control and planning in the important field of research and development.

Dun's Review & Modern Industry. "Information Storage and Retrieval," Special Supplement, September, 1965, pp. 162–63.

The large increase in the volume of records that must be maintained has created an information storage and retrieval problem. Various developments to aid in combating this problem are discussed including: no-drawer lateral suspended filing equipment; new microfilm system such as Video document filing and retrieval; and reference-document retrieval system called inverted indexing. It is concluded that the development of a system of retrieval should precede the change to automation.

GRUBINGER, ERIC N. "A Practical Look At On-Line Time Sharing," *Business Automation,* February, 1967, p. 46.

HUNSBURGER, HAROLD G. "What Integrated Data Processing Aims At," *NAA Bulletin,* Vol. 38 (February, 1957), pp. 733–39.

This article defines and attempts to relate all sizes of business to the concept of integrated data processing. The distinction between integration of data processing as a concept and of electronic equipment as an advanced method of application is also emphasized.

IFFT, L. G., JR. "Integration of Data Processing and Its Impact on Accounting," *NAA Bulletin,* September, 1962, p. 17.

The impact of integrated data processing on the business world and some reflections of current trends in this field are discussed. The article also points out some possible problem areas and shows some of the organizational effects of IDP on the accounting function within that organization.

JONES, JACK DWAINE. "Electronic Data Communications," *Data Processing Yearbook, 1965* (ed. EDITH HARWITH GOODMAN), pp. 63–66. Detroit: American Data Processing, Inc., 1964.

The types and purposes of electronic data communication equipment, the teletype, voice, and broadcast services available from the common carriers are discussed. The roles of the systems designer, the user, the equipment supplier, and the common carrier in establishing a suitable system are analyzed. Figures are included showing typical data processing system designs.

MEERS, R. EUGENE. "Real-Time Data Accumulation," *Data Processing Year-book, 1963–1964,* pp. 65–70. Detroit: American Data Processing, Inc., 1963.

Four questions that a businessman might have about real-time data accumulation and data communication systems are discussed. These are: How can this equipment be best used to the advantage of the business? What type of system or equipment is best suited to the business? What features must the system have? Can the cost of the system and equipment be justified economically by savings? The types, functions, features, and accessories of various data accumulation and data communication equipment are also briefly explained.

MEERS, RICHARD E. "Data Collection and Accumulation Closes the Information Processing Loop," *Automation,* January, 1963, pp. 70–74.

This article goes into the importance of having accurate and timely source information for any effective data collection and accumulation system. An explanation of the difference between nonmonitored and monitored types of systems is also explained. The economic justification considerations are also considered at the conclusion of the article.

MORKS, MARTIN R. "Integrating the Systems, Programming and Data Processing Functions," *NAA Bulletin,* Vol. 43 (April, 1962), pp. 61–67.

This article shows the importance of cooperation between the systems, programming, and data processing groups. The author reflects that the development of electronic data processing is best served when one organizational unit is responsible for these three functions.

NELSON, O. S., and WOODS, R. S. *Accounting Systems and Data Processing,* chap. vi. Cincinnati: South-Western Publishing Co., 1961.

This chapter clarifies some conflicting concepts of IDP and explains the common characteristics of IDP. The importance of common language machine systems and the different types of common language equipment are explained in the latter part of the chapter.

SPRAGUE, RICHARD E. *Electronic Business Systems.* New York: Ronald Press Co., 1962.

OLRT systems (on-line, real-time) are discussed and the potential uses of this new concept are forecast for the future. OLRT types of EDP equipment are intended for use in the actual operation of the organization and will record or transmit data when the pertinent event occurs. To provide assistance in this new concept, the text contains information on the design of OLRT systems and describes the expected impact on the management of organizations moving into this area of EDP.

QUESTIONS

1. What are the essential characteristics of an integrated system in your own mind? Explain.
2. What are some of the problems involved in providing management with a completely integrated system? Explain.

3. Why does the text recommend a subsystem approach to the development of an integrated data processing system? Do you think that other problems might also be involved?

4. What are some of the major factors to be considered when planning and developing an integrated data processing system?

5. What is the significance of a "common language form" in an integrated data processing system? What are its forms?

6. Describe four types of data originating equipment which are capable of capturing data in a common language form.

7. Referring to question No. 6, are the data which are captured only captured in common language form? Explain. What is the importance of this?

8. Describe three examples of precoded data. What is the advantage in trying to incorporate this idea in an IDP system? Explain.

9. What is the significance to a prospective user of the types of communication channels and grades of circuits which are available to be used? Explain.

10. Why are the communications media considered to be of such vital importance to the development of the IDP systems of the future?

11. What are two methods of transmitting data via communication lines which do not utilize either card code or channel code?

12. What do you believe the areas of applicability might be for the methods of transmitting data which you described in question No. 11?

13. Describe several means of data communication.

14. What is it which makes an on-line, real-time data processing system unique?

15. Describe some of the technological advances which have taken place which make on-line real-time data processing possible.

CHAPTER 14

Electronic Computer

Systems Controls

As BUSINESS organizations become larger, management becomes less able to exercise personel control over the daily affairs of the business. Greatly increased physical size, geographical dispersion, and increasing numbers of employees make the job of overseeing and directing extremely complex. Management, to fulfill its responsibility, has to depend more and more upon systemization. This involves building a system to process the data, seeing that checks and controls are built into it, making sure that everyone understands the system, and then endeavoring, through both the internal and the external auditing functions, to see that the system is followed. This is done until the system is proven to be deficient or inadequate in some way, and then the system has to be altered to conform to changed conditions.

As clerical procedures have become more and more automated, fewer workers have generally been needed. It has become more difficult for one group to check upon the work of another. With the growth in size of the average business unit has come the mechanization, and later the computerization, of many of the clerical data processing activities. The net effect of all of this is that management has come to rely more on machines and less on people to see that procedures are being properly followed.

What assurance can management have that prescribed procedures are being followed and that the output of the machine is accurate? This problem is of particular relevance to the systems analyst who is called upon to remodel an existing data processing system or to design a completely new one. It is also important to the external auditor, the certified public accountant, who is called upon to certify as to the adequacy of the system of internal control, which in turn will determine the extent of the audit checking which he must accomplish before he can certify as to the validity of the audited financial data.

It is therefore essential that anyone interested in the field of data processing to realize how important controls are to the ultimate users of the data, whether they be management, creditors, stockholders, or the government. A thorough understanding of internal control is particularly important.

Many of the intermediate steps in traditional business information processing procedures (i.e., maintenance of journals and ledgers) are either consolidated or nonexistent in an EDP system. This has resulted in the loss of an "audit trail," which has long been considered essential in tracing—backwards—from a record or statement to determine the individual originating documents and the basic transaction which led to the recorded end results. Chronological journals, classified postings to one or more classes of ledgers, listings, proofs, trial balances, etc., could be produced in the computer system. However, this would be requiring paper work to be prepared just for testing or checking purposes. This would not only be expensive but would also offset many of the advantages offered by an EDP system. Consequently, without visible evidence to support records, transactions, and other financial and nonfinancial data, the auditor must devise and adopt new procedures to verify the reliability of the information.

The audit of computerized accounting systems, as with manual and mechanical systems, must be planned to fit each individual situation. The planning and approach to such an audit engagement is, of course, left to the judgment of the auditor, but regardless of the approach used, the audit of any EDP system must be based on the sound verification of reliable source data. Equally important is the proving of the accuracy of the output of the system.

There are two distinctly different approaches to testing and verifying that the source data used in an EDP system are accurately developed and properly utilized in producing the end products of that system. One involves a direct verification of the output from the source data without really considering the method of source data conversion to its computer input form or the actual method of processing the data. This approach is usually referred to as the *"around-the-machines"* audit approach. The logic of this concept is that if input can be proven correct and was processed to produce the output, then it is assumed that the output must be equally correct. The manner in which the system operates in proceeding from the creation of the source data to the production of its output is of secondary importance.

Simplicity, logic, and familiarity are some of the advantages gained by the use of this approach. In addition, this method minimizes the need for specialized knowledge concerning EDP equipment, and there is little interference with processing operations during the conduct of the audit. There are, however, three main problems associated with the around-the-machines approach. First, the apparent or actual disappearance of the audit trail may make it difficult, if not impossible, to trace other than very large groups of data from its output form back to its source. Second, changes in operating instructions might make the sampled items used in the test applicable to only a limited number of transactions. And third, a large variety of transactions coupled with a large volume can make the testing of samples of data impractical from the standpoint of cost in comparison with the results obtained.

A second approach which does not require the tracing of input to output is referred to as the *"through-the-machines"* approach. This method involves a detailed examination of EDP operations and an evaluation of the accuracy and propriety of these procedures. The logic behind this method is that if correct source data are used and the processing procedures are accurate, then there is no need to trace input to output because the output of the system must be accurate. This approach is entirely dependent on the consistency of processing operations, which is generally quite satisfactory in most electronic business information systems.

The application of through-the-machines auditing requires a fairly comprehensive knowledge of machine operations and a good understanding of the techniques of systems design and of audit procedures which have been developed in conjunction with the growth of EDP.

Experience has shown that a combination of the applicable features of each method is perhaps the best approach to auditing an EDP system. The around-the-machines approach to auditing is familiar to all auditors, as it is the technique most often used in the audit of manual systems. The new control procedures used in the through-the-machines approach are not nearly so well known. Yet, a technical knowledge of the through-the-machines approach is extremely important in auditing EDP systems and should be familiar to all accountants, managers, and others concerned with the reliability to be placed on data produced in an electronic business information system.

INTERNAL CONTROL

The adequacy of the network of internal controls present in a system is generally recognized as the key element to be depended upon in determining the reliance to be placed upon the accuracy of the data processing system. Internal control has been defined as "the plan of organization and all of the coordinate methods and measures adopted within a business to safeguard its assets, check the accuracy and reliability of its accounting data, promote operational efficiency, and encourage adherence to prescribed managerial policies."[1] Because this is a very broad definition, a

---

[1] Committee on Auditing Procedure, *Auditing Standards and Procedures* (Statements on Auditing Procedure No. 33 [New York: American Institute of Certified Public Accountants, 1963]), p. 27.

distinction needs to be made between types of control available and particularly between the administrative controls and internal accounting controls.

The Committee on Auditing Procedure of the American Institute of Certified Public Accountants made the distinction in this way:

   a) Accounting controls comprise the plan of organization and all methods and procedures that are concerned mainly with, and relative directly to, safeguarding of assets and the reliability of the financial records. They generally include such controls as the systems of authorization and approval, separation of duties concerned with record keeping and accounting reports from those concerned with operations or asset custody, physical controls over assets, and internal auditing.

   b) Administrative controls comprise the plan of organization and all methods and procedures that are concerned mainly with operational efficiency and adherence to managerial policies and usually relate only indirectly to the financial records. They generally include such controls as statistical analyses, time and motion studies, performance reports, employee training programs, and quality controls.[2]

It should appear from this distinction that the systems analyst and designer, as well as the independent auditor, is primarily concerned with "accounting controls." Professors Bower and Schlosser point out that "the basic purposes of internal control are to bring reliability into the financial information system and to safeguard assets."[3]

There are certain characteristics of elements of a satisfactory system of internal control which must be recognized. They are as follows:

A plan of organization which provides appropriate segregation of functional responsibilities,

Personnel of a quality commensurate with responsibilities,

A system of authorization and record procedures adequate to provide reasonable accounting control over assets, liabilities, revenues and expenses, and

Sound practices to be followed in performance of duties and functions of each of the organizational departments. . . .[4]

The responsibility for their existence as well as their success rests solely with management.

Organization and Personnel

When one is considering the segregation of functional responsibilities, the first point which is generally mentioned is the separation of the operating, custodial, and accounting functions among individuals and

---

[2] *Ibid.*, p. 28.

[3] James B. Bower and Robert E. Schlosser, "Internal Control—Its True Nature," *Accounting Review*, Vol. 40 (April, 1965), p. 339.

[4] Committee on Auditing Procedure, *op. cit.*, pp. 28–29.

	Yes	No	Not App.	Comments

GENERAL CONTROLS:

1. Are all new systems and programs (including major revisions) authorized by management and approved by users prior to use? ____ ____ ____

2. Are general systems developed independent of EDP department? ____ ____ ____

3. Are personnel of computer department denied access to company assets (cash, securities, inventories, etc.)? ____ ____ ____

4. Is there a separation of duties between programmers and computer operators? ____ ____ ____

5. Is there a physical separation of work areas in EDP department?
   a) Computer room ____ ____ ____
   b) Control and audit section ____ ____ ____
   c) Program and tape library ____ ____ ____
   d) Programming ____ ____ ____

6. Is access restricted to the EDP work areas?
   a) Computer room ____ ____ ____
   b) Control and audit section ____ ____ ____
   c) Program and tape library ____ ____ ____
   d) Programming ____ ____ ____

7. Is there up-to-date documentation of computer programs and does the documentation show?
   a) Program name ____ ____ ____
   b) Date completed and name of person preparing ____ ____ ____
   c) Date effective ____ ____ ____
   d) Purpose of program ____ ____ ____
   e) Narrative description of program ____ ____ ____
   f) General block diagram (flow chart) ____ ____ ____
   g) Detailed block diagram (flow chart) ____ ____ ____
   h) Record layout (card, disk, tape, etc.) ____ ____ ____
   i) Input (form and source) ____ ____ ____
   j) Output (form and distribution) ____ ____ ____
   k) Program edits and halts ____ ____ ____
   l) Complete operating instructions ____ ____ ____
   m) Are program changes approved and the revision number and effective date shown ____ ____ ____

8. Are computer operators denied access to program documentation? ____ ____ ____

Courtesy of A. M. Pullen & Company, Greensboro N.C.

FIG. 14–1. Section of Internal Control Questionnaire.

departments in order to serve as a check upon unauthorized activity.

An EDP system tends to eliminate much of the separation of duties and cross-checking formerly done. This is in part due to the decreasing number of workers involved. In assigning responsibilities for the control of EDP systems, many managements have sought to retain a basic division of duties by:

1. Making certain that the programming and systems development activity are kept organizationally separate from the operation of the equipment itself.
2. Holding the operating departments which supply the input data responsible for its authenticity, accuracy, and completeness.
3. Establishing the data processing center as a separate unit organizationally independent from the operating units, restricted from any direct control over the assets, and without authority to disburse funds, issue inventory, etc., in order to reduce pressures that may develop to process the data improperly either to manipulate the results or to cover fraudulent activity.
4. Requiring the recipient and user of the processed data to perform checking procedures to verify that the data which have been received as accurate. For example, comparing accumulated batch totals with the current output totals.

To emphasize the importance of control and the separation of functions, one public accounting firm uses a checklist questionnaire to ascertain the existence of these controls in a client's EDP installation. (One section of this questionnaire is shown in Figure 14–1.)

The qualifications of the personnel involved in an EDP system are considerably higher than was formerly the case when clerical personnel were solely involved. On the whole, they need to have a broader background with greater appreciation of what is taking place both from an accounting point of view and from the point of view of the more technical aspects of computer operation.

System of Authorizations and Record Procedures

Under a manual system, any program of authorizations and record procedures tends to be detailed and involved. With a computerized system, documentation takes the place of this part of the control system.

Adequate program documentation, which is important for reviewing the proposed program, is close to essential for operating and modifying programs and reconstructing lost data. It is also necessary to enable other interested parties (management, auditors, system analysts, and outside agencies) to understand the operations of the system.

The basic test in judging the adequacy of documentation is to ask whether a typical programmer can fairly readily read his way to an understanding of the system without supplementary information and discussions. For a system of average complexity, this could require:

1. A general, written description of the overall system (including a statement of its objectives), a description of the basic flow of information through the system, and a broad description of the separate processing steps and interrelationships between computer runs.
2. A general system diagram to accompany and illustrate the description.
3. For each computer program, a description of the functions performed by the program and a general description of how the program accomplishes them, with particular attention to features of the program or logic that would otherwise tend to be obscure.
4. Block diagrams showing the sequence of operations performed by the programs, with one or two levels of detail, as required, for clarity. The most detailed level, however, should be less detailed than the source language listings.
5. Record descriptions showing the form and content of all inputs and outputs and memory locations.
6. Program listing in source language and in object code.
7. Program operating instructions for loading control cards, switch setting, halt procedures, sources of input, and disposition of output.[5]

These forms of system and program documentation would convey a detailed understanding of what the system does and how it does it.

Control Practices and Methods

Control practices in a manual system usually involve checks made in a variety of ways throughout the data processing activity. An automated or computerized system is no exception to this, although the checks and controls are of quite a different nature. There are controls that can be built into the data processing system itself (input-processing-output). Of equal importance are the controls which must be developed to protect the data and the equipment from accidental or intentional harm. There are also controls, whose usefulness must not be overlooked, which are built into the hardware by the equipment manufacturers.

All of these controls must be considered by the person designing a computerized data processing system. The controls utilized in a given system should be adequate to protect the owner of the system commensurate with the risk involved and the cost which he is willing to assume. The problem is not solely one of there being adequate ways to control the processing of data in a computerized system. Instead, it is a problem of anticipating and building into the system sufficient controls to be adequate to cope with the risks which will be encountered.

---

[5] International Business Machines Corporation, *Management Control of Electronic Data Processing*, #F20–0006. 1965, p. 11.

SYSTEM CONTROLS

Input Controls

The input of data into a computer system involves the most probable source of error in such a system. Obviously, machines will operate just as well with incorrect data as with correct data. A computer is accurate in its operation, but the results obtained can only be as accurate as the data fed into the system. Therefore, if an error is introduced anywhere between the origin of the transaction and its input into the computer, the error will be carried forward.

There are three distinct problem areas associated with error elimination in the input function. These problems are: to assure that raw data are properly transcribed into machine-acceptable language, that the data to be processed include all of the transactions that took place, and that the transactions are processed only once. Specific input controls may be classified as transcription controls, control totals, and labels.

TRANSCRIPTION CONTROLS. Transcription controls check the accuracy of the conversion of raw data into machine-acceptable language. If cards are keypunched from the source documents, independent verification of the accuracy of the data punched in the cards is necessary after they have been punched. While duplication of time and effort is necessary in this procedure, the verification of input data has, in many instances, proven to be an economical operation in the long run. If the data are produced in machine-processable form as a by-product of the transcription of the data on typewriters, adding machines, or cash registers (see Chapter 6), both the coded data and a copy readable by humans are also produced in the process. This permits the data to be checked visually and verified as to its accuracy either as, or after, it is prepared.

CONTROL TOTALS. Control totals also aid in establishing the accuracy of input data. Control totals are always taken on batches, or groups, of source documents. These are usually batches of preselected and sequenced logical transaction groups, as most EDP systems presently in use are serial-type processing systems. However, in a random access system, these batches may be composed of completely random and unrelated transactions, and the ability to process random data is one of the major advantages of such a system. Control totals for input data are usually obtained from adding machine tapes or from totals previously prepared by originating departments; they normally do not require any extensive additional work in their preparation. Careful planning and coordination in the use of control totals can help to provide a reasonably high degree of internal control with very little effort and consequently very little expense.

Batch totals are a form of control totals where input data are grouped into an economic processing unit. Totals of the batch may even be accumulated before source data are converted to input form. After data conversion is made to a machine-readable language, the batch totals previously taken may be compared to the totals on the input data. Thus, this is a good check to assure that all the source documents are being processed. As will be mentioned later under Output Controls, batch totals may also be used as a check on the processing unit through a comparison of output totals and the totals taken prior to the input of the data into the system.

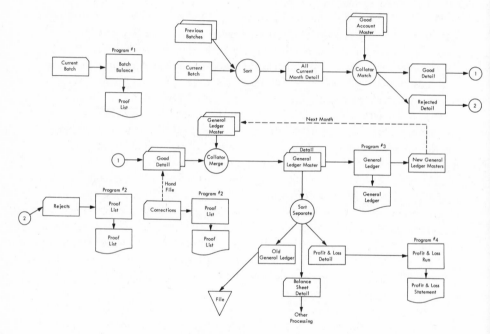

FIG. 14–2.   Flowchart.

An illustration of several programs where batch totals are used as control devices follows. This is a common routine where cards are used as input to a computer system. The flowchart and work sheet, Figures 14–2 and 14–3, represents in diagramatic form the way it is intented that the controls should work.

Program No. 1 in the flowchart represents a current batch of documents being read into the computer so that the balances can be listed and totaled. For example, the current batch might represent 100 journal vouchers which represent one week's business, and for which a prelist has been prepared. When the debit and credit parts of the journal vouchers are listed, the net debits and credits should balance to zero, and the total should be compared with the prelist total to be certain that it agrees. All of these totals would be recorded on the work sheet.

The control procedures, which it is intended that the employees should follow, should be clearly spelled out in the Manual of Procedures.

Continuing on the flowchart, the apparently correct batch of 100 journal vouchers would be sorted or merged with the previous batches of journal vouchers for the month which have been verified. This will produce a file containing all the journal voucher detail for the month. This current month journal voucher detail file should then be run through the collator to be matched with a Good Account Number Master File. This is done so as to verify that there are valid account numbers for all of the accounts indicated on the punched card journal voucher file. Any

Program #1—Balance	*Card Count*	*Total*	*Total Debits*	*Total P & L*
Batch #1................	100	–0–	490	370
Batch #2................	200	–0–	670	550
Batch #6................	100	–0–	350	275
Month to date totals....3000		–0–	22,000	18,000
Program #2—Proof List				
Month to date totals......3000		–0–	22,000	18,000
Less: Rejects...........	20	100	70	50
Plus: Corrections.......	20	100	70	50
Month to date..........3000		–0–	22,000	18,000
Program #3—General Ledger		*Total*	*Total Debits*	*Total P & L*
Previous months general ledger.........–0–			——	30,000 Next
This month's detail...................–0–			22,000	18,000 Month
Current month general ledger..........–0–			——	48,000
Program #4—P & L			*Total P & L*	
Total P & L—Current month...............18,000				

FIG. 14–3.   Control Work Sheet.

cards which do not match will be treated as rejects. This procedure could be followed at the time each batch is processed, or several batches could be processed together at the end of the month, depending upon the quantity of error which is anticipated. The reason that the coding is checked on each card is to verify that all entries will be properly charged to an existing account. The charge may not be to the right account, however.

All of the rejected cards must be kept track of because they are part of the system. In Program No. 2, therefore, a listing is made of the rejects so that a *track* will be retained of the data which temporarily left the system. Corrections are made for the rejects, and the corrected cards, which are going back into the system, are again listed to provide a *track*. The total of the data which went back into the system at this point must be equal to the data which previously left the system. These totals are again recorded on the work sheet.

The corrections are now hand filed into the file of correct journal vouchers previously accumulated, and this detail is then merged into the General Ledger Master File. The net effect of this is to add the current detail into the file of data accumulated during the remainder of the accounting period to date.

Program No. 3 updates the General Ledger Master File by punching cards which contain the summarized year-to-date totals. These cards will then be used as the general ledger file when additional details are accumulated and summarized next month. A general ledger may also be printed out at this time.

In Program No. 4 the General Ledger Master File and the monthly detail cards may be sorted so as to separate the old general ledger cards from the Profit and Loss and Balance Sheet detail cards. From this sort, a monthly profit and loss statement might be prepared.

It should be specified in the Manual of Procedures that the control work sheet be maintained by a control group or by someone not directly involved in the processing of the data. The instructions to the operator, which indicate how the program should be run, must also be included in the Manual of Procedures.

The control work sheet is preprinted and should be designed so as to contain the proof figures which have already been mentioned. In Program No. 1, each batch of data processed, as well as the number of cards in each batch, is recorded on the control work sheet. The detail totals for each batch are also recorded. In Figure 14–3, other detail columns, which are for simplification not included in the illustration would probably be necessary or desirable. In Program No. 2, the month-to-date totals minus the rejections plus the corrections should balance to the month-to-date totals. Program No. 3 in effect reflects the updating of the general ledger balances which apply to the types of data being processed. All of such balances should agree with the monthly printed general ledger balances. The Profit and Loss details, as reflects in Program No. 2 and No. 3, should agree with the printed profit and loss statement as provided through Program No. 4.

Hash totals are a form of batch total in which the totals of grouped data are not in dollar amounts. Hash totals, for example, are totals of data which would not normally be added, such as stock numbers, unit prices, and so forth. These totals are meaningless in themselves but are very useful for control purposes.

Record count controls can be found in many forms and vary considerably depending upon the particular data processing system in use. Some of the more typical types of record count controls follow.

Prenumbered documents are one form of record count control when appropriate accounting is made for all numbers to see that each number is present or accounted for. When data are recorded in punched cards, a simple *card count* is a good control technique. The best technique would involve a card count that is independent of the computer operating group. This independent count may then be compared with the number of cards the operator processed to assure that all cards were subsequently processed. When paper or magnetic tape is being used, controls should also be established to assure that the number of records read on the tape agrees with the number of source documents.

Record counts are usually carried at the end of the deck of cards being processed or the reel of tape, as the case may be, and compared each time the deck or reel is processed. As with batch and hash totals, record counts may also be used to check on the accuracy of the central processing unit. Although record counts may be a useful proof of processing, they will not indicate the occurrence of specific errors when the controls are out of balance. *Duplicate records* may be used in some cases to determine where the errors exist. In other situations, a *rerun of the routine* may help to eliminate the difficulty. This last is especially applicable in the processing of magnetic tape where machine errors may occasionally occur in reading the data from the tape.

LABELS. Labels are another form of control over input. These are especially useful in regards to the control of magnetic tape reels. Tape labels may be classified as either external or internal labels. *External labels* are visible labels which are attached to the reel of tape. These labels usually contain such information as serial number, length of tape, name, date of run, date of the last work processed, output tape address, the numbers of the runs it is used in conjunction with, and the tape address for each of these runs. This label should also contain the date on which it can again be written on. Thus, external tape labels make certain that the correct tape will be processed and that data will not be destroyed until no longer of any value.

Processing Controls

Some of the more challenging and versatile controls available in a computer system are those which are written into the computer program by the coders. Many such controls are available, all designed to test the validity of the data as well as the accuracy of the processing equipment. Some controls of this type are also provided in library routines available from the computer manufacturers.

The extent to which these programmed controls are utilized depends upon the ingenuity of the programming staff, the demands of the supervisory and maintenance personnel of the data processing center, the type and capabilities of the equipment, and the need for certain controls in a given processing run, weighed against the costs to be incurred because of the additional processing time required.

Sequence checks may be incorporated into programs to ensure that the desired order of records is maintained. This not only applies to data comprising a group of similar transactions which have been sequenced for entry into the system, but to groups of data made up of presequenced sets of data groups where one or more items from each of the respective groups are required in the processing procedure. "By comparing sequential control numbers, such as voucher numbers, check numbers, stock numbers, and employee numbers from one record to the next, records which are out of sequence, gaps in the sequence, and duplicate numbers can be quickly and efficiently located and emitted for further attention."[6]

Internal labels are usually assigned to a group of data associated with given processing procedures or "runs." These are used extensively in magnetic tape records and are checked prior to processing in what is sometimes called *identification comparison checks*. These labels provide checks on the tape librarian and computer operator and on the equipment to assure that the proper tape and tape drive have been selected before the data are entered into the system.

A number of *internal label* routines are available for use today. The checking of an internal label is similar to checking the external label except that the actual check is usually performed through some combination of programming and checking by inquiry through the console typewriter. Information desired from internal labels is particularly concerned with data to determine if this is the proper tape to be used and if this is the only tape of its type necessary for this run or if a series of tapes is required.

Identification comparison is also used in avoiding the use of incorrect disk memory files. A comparison may be made of some common items appearing in the file and in the data to be processed. Such a comparison may be related to a memory address, stock number, or unit of issue.

Check points are sometimes used to facilitate the recording of data before the processing run is completed. This technique avoids the necessity of reprocessing an entire procedure should an error or machine failure result before processing is completed. Check points also provide an intermediate starting point for any necessary rerun.

Balancing controls are very similar to those used in controlling manual processing procedures. Typical would be an accounts receivable posting procedure where, as the transactions are posted to the individual ledger accounts, beginning balances are added to transaction amounts to obtain

---

[6] U.S. Department of the Air Force, Auditor General, Comptroller, *Guide for Auditing Automatic Data Processing Systems* (Washington, D.C.: U.S. Government Printing Office, November 1, 1961), pp. 6–8.

a net balance of each account. The total of all the net balances of the individual accounts must then agree with the control balance in the "general" ledger account. *Zero balancing* may be used if the two totals are subtracted from each other to provide a zero answer if correct.

Crossfooting balance checks are used to determine if the sum of the horizontal totals of arrayed data agree with the sum of the vertical totals.

Limit checks, sometimes called *tolerance checks,* are programmed into the system to call attention to any data exceeding or less than certain predesignated limits. Typical limits would be a maximum dollar amount for payroll checks, a maximum number of inventory items to be issued at one time, percentage variations, minimum stock item levels, and maximum credit to be extended to a given individual. Any abnormal items would be printed out, noted on reports, or otherwise called to the attention of management for any action required.

Limit checks may also be provided to check the results of any arithmetic procedure and determine if the capacity of equipment accumulators or registers has been exceeded and if there is a danger of significant data being lost because of the overflow condition.

Some fields of data require the presence of blanks in their format. Where such fields are present, they must be checked in the processing procedure by *blank transmission tests.* Similarly, nonsignificant zeros should be removed before transactions are posted to data records, as these could replace significant data in the storage file.

Where a series of multiplications is to be performed, the final results may be checked through the use of *proof figures.* In such a procedure an arbitrary figure, larger than any of the data multipliers, maybe selected as such a proof figure. Each multiplicand is multiplied twice, once by the data multiplier and then by the difference between the multiplier and the proof figure. The totals, of both multiplications, for the series of items are then compared with the product of the multiplication of the total obtained by the multiplication of all multiplicands and the proof figure.

Validity checks are comparisons of the account or file number recorded in the input data with lists of existing accounts or file numbers stored in internal memory to detect erroneous entries which might otherwise be made to existent accounts. For example, if a portion of a salesman's payroll were coded for posting to a production expense account, it would be rejected as invalid, although the designated account exists.

Self-checking numbers. Incorrect identification numbers (accounts, files, products, employees, etc.) can be detected with over 95 percent reliability by making certain mathematical calculations with the digits in the basic number and comparing a digit in the result with a check digit included as a suffix in the identification number. This technique is used most frequently when the code number is originally recorded by hand and subsequently keypunched. In such cases, the check is performed either by a device connected to the keypunch or by the computer in an input editing or checking run.[7]

There are many types of *error routines*. These serve to pinpoint error conditions, permit corrections to be made more easily, and give some assurance that correction has been taken before the data are reentered into the system.

Some error routines are termed *diagnostic*, as they are used to determine what caused the error condition found to exist. These are usually printed out to aid in their correction. If desired, the processing run may either be halted for correction or continued after a proper "note" of the error has been made by the computer. Other error routines are used after processing instructions, such as COMPARE, to analyze the results if an impossible or error condition is found in the comparison.

Failure to post to a disk memory file may be detected in an *alteration test* by comparing the contents of the file before and after each posting procedure to determine if the contents of the file have been altered.

If the total of a field of input or output has been prenumbered, the system can perform a *check of totals* by accumulating a corresponding total and comparing it with the predetermined total.

Output Controls

Control totals, previously mentioned under input controls, such as hash totals, dollar amounts, and record counts, are basic in the control of the output of data. As the batches of data are processed, the computer can be programmed to develop its own batch totals. These totals are then checked by an independent department—usually the internal auditors—to be sure that they agree with the previously prepared control totals. If these independently derived batch totals are in agreement, the data processed must be the data delivered to the EDP department for processing.

A periodic read-out or print-out of totals and account balances is sometimes used for an audit trail after a certain number of transactions are processed at specified time intervals. Magnetic disk, tape, and internal storage files may occasionally be "dumped" (printed-out) for similar usage. The extent to which such print-outs are performed is a decision which must be made by management after consideration is given to the usefulness and the cost of such a procedure. After such a print-out, an occasional hand check of data samples from source document through to a report, or from the report back to the source document, may be justified as a basis for a continuing assurance of the normal level of accuracy expected in output data produced by computer systems. The selection of the above data samples may be made through the utilization of some of the

---

[7] International Business Machines Corporation, *op. cit.*, p. 9.

systematic sampling techniques available through the use of the computer.

Reports and analyses may occasionally be prepared for submission to the groups where transaction data originated for their approval. Typical of these groups would be credit departments, labor and personnel departments, and inventory control and purchasing departments.

Another problem of control over the program and data files is closely associated with the familiar saying, "Don't put all your eggs in one basket." This suggests, in connection with data files, that perhaps a set of duplicate tapes should be stored in another geographical area to protect the data from a specific disaster which might occur in the computer area. If such a set of "backup" tapes were available, loss of the original tapes would not paralyze the firm. Certainly, every precaution must be taken to make certain that at least key elements of the business accounts are safe.

On a smaller scale, protection of data tapes from the possibility of accidental loss in the form of a mutilated tape or a tape written over in error is usually provided in the retention of tapes prepared in the immediately previous procedures. The tapes retained are usually termed three-generation tapes and are often called "son," "father," and "grandfather" tapes. Some form of retention schedule must be adhered to.

Control by exception is another form of output control. If management can assume that the daily routine and nonexceptional items are satisfactory, then it may concentrate on the exceptional or special items in its decision-making function. These could involve a check of any error or unusual conditions found as a result of the programmed controls previously described. More probably, however, exception items of most concern to management would be those related to limit, tolerance, or reasonableness checks. Typical items might be sales which exceeded credit limits; proposed sales to customers who do not have approved credit; notice of a deviation from fixed sales prices previously established; differences discovered between priced items on purchase orders and prices on related invoices; notification of any unusual stock withdrawals, sales, or percentage changes; and exceeding of minimum, maximum, or other set limits. Control by exception is a widely used and most effective control technique.

The use of prenumbered standardized forms is another form of output control. Nonstandard or modified data forms will not be compatible with standard forms. If numerical accountability is required, then each form must be accounted for and the possibility of ficticious or fraudulent statements, invoices, or checks will all but be eliminated.

SECURITY CONTROLS

Input controls and the various tests and checks built in and made on the equipment and its operation are very important. However, if there is no control over the program itself which instructs the computer in its operations, there can be no assurance that the output developed will be satisfactory.

Accuracy and control over instructional programs are very much related to program controls. If a program is incorrect, all transactions processed by the program will be incorrect. The possibility of accidental or deliberate alteration of a program exists both while a program is being used and when it is being stored in the internal memory of the equipment. However, programs which are properly stored and controlled outside the operating computer system are not altered so easily.

Once the programs have been developed, tested, and put in operation, they should be kept, along with the data files resulting from procedural operations, under the control of someone responsible for their safekeeping. This individual, or librarian, should be responsible for these files, usually in the form of reels of magnetic tape or disk packs. He should see that they are properly stored and cared for and that they are only issued to authorized personnel. A record, or log, should be kept of any withdrawals of these items indicating to whom they were issued, when they were issued, and when they were returned.

A log, or record, should also be kept in the computer operating room indicating the exact time the program was put in operation and when the procedure was completed. This record has been facilitated by some of the computer manufacturers installing a timing device on the computer which records the use time of the computer. Such a record, when tied to the librarian's record, will alert auditors to any extended use of a program which, conceivably, could indicate that changes or alterations might have been made in the program steps through console intervention. Most individual processing runs are of relatively short duration—in processing time required—and any unusual time usage should be investigated for a satisfactory explanation.

In connection with possible console intervention in the programmed procedures, a copy of the console typewriter output should be delivered daily to the auditors. Instructions to the computer from the console, print-outs from the computer in the form of error, halt, and exception notices, and a record of any console input into the system will all be recorded on the console output form. Any unusual items found on this form should be completely explained to the satisfaction of the auditors.

In the early period of a computer installation, many changes are necessary in correcting and improving the procedural programs. However, once this initial stage is past, a controlled copy of each program should be kept by the auditors, and any subsequent changes to the program must be properly authorized and recorded. On a surprise basis, these programs should either be checked against the regular procedural programs or used to process procedural data as a check to determine if any changes have been made without notification. Of course, tests may also be devised using test decks of input data, whose results have been predetermined by the auditors, to check on the reliability of the program to do the required job and to test the program to be sure limits, controls, and exceptions are being recognized as it processes data.

Tape rings (Figure 14–4) are usually provided with reels of magnetic tape. These small plastic rings fit into the side of the reel holding the tape and must be inserted before data can be written on the tape. The presence of the ring does not hinder reading the tape. The ring is removed when the tape is just to be read to avoid any possibility of accidentally writing over data that are to be retained for future use.

Preventive maintenance, though not "built-in" as such, is one of the more important techniques used today in the avoidance of component

Courtesy of IBM.

FIG. 14–4. Tape File Protection Device.

and subsequent equipment failures. The components and circuitry of the computer of today are quite stable in their performance and are designed to operate over a reasonably wide range or level of operation with accurate results. Most component failures are preceded by a decline in efficiency and operation under reduced voltage conditions. If these components are tested periodically under such conditions, it is possible to determine their threshold, or lowest level, of proper operation. The items which are weakening and failing will normally be detected long before there is any loss of operating performance. The replacement of these failing components before they fail is certainly a positive approach in avoiding errors before they occur.

BUILT-IN CONTROLS

The use of *parity bits* is probably the most widely used control built in by manufacturers. The parity bit, described in more detail in Chapter 11, is a binary digit (bit) which may be added in the parity bit channel when required to provide the proper number of bits to make the coded data either an all odd or all even number of bits. Whether this number is even or odd depends on the requirements of the system in use. These bits are counted every time the tape is processed to be sure that the correct number of bits are present. This is a very important control technique, as magnetic bits may be covered by particles of dust, not be readable because of tape flaws, or even become "lost" if a reel of tape is dropped.

Duplicate circuitry is occasionally provided for particularly critical circuits in some equipment to assure a high degree of machine accuracy. The space requirements and cost of this duplication prohibits its general use.

Used rather widely in early computers, but to a lesser extent today, is the utilization of double or reverse arithmetic. As implied, double arithmetic consists of performing the same operation twice and comparing results. An example would be in the multiplication of $A \times B$ to obtain C. B would then be multiplied by A, subtracting C to arrive at zero. These operations would be performed simultaneously, utilizing different circuits to obtain the results.

Echo checks are sometimes used at points in the procedure where data are transferred in the system. As this transfer is made, an echo is sent back to the original source of the data. If there is any variation between the transferred data and the original data, a machine failure is indicated.

In Chapter 11, in the discussion of magnetic recording devices, it was mentioned that some equipment had combination read-write or dual reading heads provided. These *dual heads* serve as control devices in that data written may be read and checked for agreement with the original data, or the data may be read by two heads and checked for comparison.

CASE STUDY
A Small Inventory, Billing, and Accounts Receivable System[8]

This case study describes how a relatively small EDP user effectively organized the responsibilities and used programmed control and external control techniques to achieve a high degree of reliability in an EDP system for inventory, billing, and accounts receivable. It also illustrates some effective control techniques applied in connection with the use of disk memory units.

The EDP user is a wholesaler maintaining a warehouse which fulfills orders received either through salesmen or directly from customers. The EDP system maintains both the inventory records and the customer account bal-

---

[8] *Ibid.*, pp. 28–30.

ances on disk files which are updated as each transaction is processed. The details of the customer account balances are maintained in separate punched card files.

Division of Duties

The company's operations are divided into the following six groups, all of which report directly to a general manager: sales, warehouse operations, data processing, credit, cashier, and accounting. These organizational distinctions provide for a clear separation of duties between the sales personnel who contact the customers, the warehouse employees controlling the physical inventory, the data processing group which prepares the invoices and maintains the inventory and customer records, the credit manager who authorizes lines of credit and undertakes collection activity, and the cashier who handles the payments received from customers. In addition, the accounting department and its control records are segregated from the foregoing groups, and this department has no access to the company's assets or authority over its operations.

The common division of responsibilities between development of the EDP system and its operation was not carried out in this company because of its size. The systems development and programming was performed by the two employees who, together with three keypunch operators, currently operate the system. In the absence of this division of responsibilities, the general manager closely supervised the systems development and testing and continues to closely review its operations.

Source Data Control

The data processing cycle begins with the receipt of a customer order. Such orders are received by telephone calls either from salesmen or directly from customers. The telephone operator prepares an order form which includes the customer's name, account number, and quantities ordered. In addition, the operator notes the number of different products ordered. No additional control procedures are exercised at this time as procedures have been incorporated in an editing run to ascertain the validity of the customer and reasonableness of the order. Since all sales are made at listed prices, there is no need to obtain approval for the prices of the items ordered.

Control of Input

The sales orders are forwarded by the telephone operator to the data processing unit, where the keypunch operators prepare punched cards recording customer's number, date, product code and quantity for each item ordered, and the total number of items ordered. Both the customer number and the item codes are self-checking numbers which are checked by the keypunch machine. Because of this control, plus the other control procedures in the editing performed by the computer, the company does not consider it necessary to verify the keypunching.

The customer orders are accumulated and three or four times a day are processed by the computer. In the first processing operation, the data from the card is stored in work space on a disk file, and several editing routines are performed to detect errors in the input and to identify orders requiring the specific approval of an operating department:

The input is reviewed for completeness of data in all appropriate fields (for example, presence of a quantity when a product code appears).

The number of product items is counted by the computer and compared with the total-items-ordered field in the input to check against the omission of any items ordered.

The product code number in the input is traced to the inventory file to check its validity (both the inventory and customer account disk files are online during the editing run).

The customer account number in the input is traced to the customer account file to ensure its validity.

Approximate sales values are calculated when the inventory files are checked and are accumulated with the customer's account receivable balance to determine whether the customer's credit limit will be exceeded by the new order.

The customer's account file is searched for the presence of a "do not bill" code which indicates that for credit or other purposes, no further sales may be made to this customer without prior approval.

All quantities expressed in individual units are reviewed to ensure that they are less than a case quantity as a check on the order quantity recorded (if they exceed a case quantity, there is a probability that the quantity amount is incorrect).

In addition to the editing procedures at this time the computer establishes a hash total control over the customer numbers and counts the number of individual orders included in the batch.

Errors and other unusual items disclosed by the editing routines are printed on exception listings and forwarded to the appropriate operating department for its review or authorization. For example, orders from customers for which no master file has been established are reported to the sales department for their investigation and authorization of a new customer file. The sales department will also be advised of orders with improper product codes or other missing input data, and individual item quantities in excessive case units, for checking to the order form or clarifying with the customer. Orders which would exceed the authorized credit limits and orders received from customers subject to a "do not bill" code are reported to the credit department for disposition.

By these editing procedures and referral of errors and orders requiring specific authorization back to an operating department, the company has clearly asserted the responsibility of the source operating departments for the accuracy and authorization of the input data. The completeness of the input data is not assured by these procedures, but the company believes that, because its orders are for current delivery, the loss of an order would result in its not being shipped and would be promptly reported by a customer. Alternatively it would appear that the orders written by the telephone operators could be numbered and noted in a simple register which could be proved daily against the total orders processed or referred to the sales and credit departments. This could also control the orders being held by the latter two departments.

Billing and Recording Controls

The customer orders passing the editing test and stored in the work area of the disk file are processed in a second operation to prepare the sales invoice and update the customers' accounts and the inventory records. Invoices with preprinted numbers are used, and the number of the first invoice is inserted at the beginning of the processing in order that the customers' records will contain the invoice number for reference. During the processing customer account numbers are totaled and orders counted for comparison at the completion with the totals accumulated during the editing process to ensure against loss of data. The sales prices stored in the inventory master files are used to calculate the invoices. No checking of this calculation is performed by the computer. However, it is considered that the credit limit check, which is performed a second time when a customer account file is updated, serves as a limit control against any possible large overbillings.

The customer account numbers and the product numbers are also used as the address of the file locations in the disk files. Such numbers are also stored in each file record. As a check that the proper file location has been addressed by the computer, the customer and product numbers in the input data are compared with the numbers stored in the master files before processing such files. The possibility of writing over and destroying an active account when opening a master file account for a new customer or product is controlled in two ways. A punched card file is maintained for all unused addresses of customer accounts and product files. When new accounts are to be opened, the addresses are selected from the card file and the address selected is withdrawn from the file. As a second check against writing over an active file, before a new address is used it is searched for the presence of a code symbol which should have been recorded when the address location was previously erased at the time of closing the prior account at that address.

Interesting control procedures are followed in posting inventory master files during the billing process: The balance at the beginning of the day is not altered for each transaction, but instead, each sales (or receipt) and the new balance resulting are posted in separate fields. This provides a restart point in the event of error or computer malfunction during the day's operation. It also permits the computer to check its own processing the following morning when each inventory file is checked to ensure that the prior balance, plus the receipts and less the sales, equals the recorded closing balance, and only then is the prior balance adjusted to the new balance. During this daily balancing routine, the inventory master files are reproduced on a separate disk file which is retained until the following day's master files are reproduced. The customer account master files are similarly copied each morning. The input for the transactions processed each day is filed together and, with the copied master files, provides a means of reconstructing current master files if such becomes necessary.

Sales are posted to the customer account master files during the billing run and are also accumulated in a separate record for the day. A daily report is prepared by the EDP system, showing the sales for the day and the invoice numbers used. A copy of this report and a punched card record for each customer invoice is forwarded to the accounting department, where a control total of the accounts receivable is maintained together with a punched card file of the details of each customer's balance.

Use and Review of Processed Data

Copies of all sales invoices are forwarded to the warehouse supervision to serve as shipping instructions. The preparation of the invoice in advance of the shipping is possible in this company as it very seldom encounters an out-of-stock condition. The warehouse supervision is also furnished by data processing with a unique aggregate shipping manifest. The manifest is prepared from the inventory master files and reports the total of each product item to be shipped each day. On the basis of this manifest the products are withdrawn from their storage locations and brought to the shipping department, where they are then broken down by invoice quantity. Separate performance of these two functions assures that the quantities being billed agree with the quantities by which the inventory records have been reduced. It also helps the warehouse management to separate the shipping function from the storage operations of the warehouse and thereby adds to the physical control it can exercise over its products which are very subject to pilferage.

Comprehensive sales reports are prepared daily by the EDP system. These reports to the sales department and general manager indicate sales by product, product group, salesmen, district, and type of customer, and show both daily sales and cumulative sales for the month. These reports, designed principally for operating purposes, provide a sensitive analysis of the operations as recorded by the EDP system. Management believes that its daily review of these sales reports and the attention given to them in the sales department would disclose any significant error in the recorded data. It is also believed that the monthly commission statement prepared for each salesman also would be a likely source of notice of any error not otherwise detected.

The accounting department also checks the reliability of the EDP system. It reviews the sales register and accounts for all of the preprinted invoice forms used during a month. By comparing the total sales reported in the sales register for the month with similar totals on the various sales analyses, it checks that the data reviewed by management is the same as entered in the accounts. The total sales are posted to a manually maintained summary account used to control the total accounts receivable. The credits to this control account for cash received are derived from two sources: (1) the cashier, who reports directly to the accounting department the cash received and deposited, and (2) the EDP system, which reports the net cash received, the commission allowed, and the total credit to the customer accounts. The accounting department ensures that both of the cash amounts agree, reviews the reasonableness of the total discount allowed, and then posts the total cash credit to its accounts receivable control account.

At the end of each month, the punched card file containing the detail of the customers accounts receivable (which is culled daily for items paid) is processed with the customer accounts master files to prepare statements for the customers of their balances. In this processing the computer checks the balance it has recorded in each customer master file with the balance indicated by the punched cards. The grand total of all the customer statements is checked by the accounting department to its control total of accounts receivable.

Two external control methods are used by the company to ensure the reliability of inventory records maintained by the data processing system: First, each week the system produces a list of the balances on hand for each product. This listing is checked by warehouse personnel by physically counting the inventory present in the warehouse. The second control over the inventory records is exercised by the accounting department. Each month it reviews the sales and cost-of-sales report produced by the data processing system from the data recorded in the inventory mastery files. With the statistical data accumulated from the purchases and sales prices, the accounting department is able to closely forecast the gross profit relationship for each product group; it uses this information to check the cost-of-sale amounts received from the inventory.

ANNOTATED BIBLIOGRAPHY

BONI, GREGORY M. "Impact of Electronic Data Processing on Auditing," *Journal of Accountancy*, September, 1963, pp. 39–44.

"The computer should not be allowed to impede the auditor. Ways must be found to utlize for positive good the tool which is available." The auditor must become conversant with test decks, he must learn not to rely on print-outs, and he must become intimately involved in the system with which he is concerned.

CADEMATORI, KENNETH G. "The Experience of Auditors with EDP," *Price Waterhouse Review*, Vol. 4, No. 2 (Summer, 1959).

A very clear explanation of the problems involved in auditing an EDP installation are given. The author then points out the steps he feels that the auditor should take in coping with the problem. An excellent job is done in pointing out the many forms of control which exist in an EDP system.

FITZPATRICK, ROBERT J. "The Influence of EDP on Internal Control," *The Controller*, March, 1961, p. 123.

The author discusses the various types of controls which exist in a computer system. These involved (1) program controls, (2) operation or machine controls, and (3) controls over peripheral equipment.

HASKINS AND SELLS. *Internal Control in Electronic Accounting Systems.* New York, 1965.

This book brings the reader up-to-date in this involved area quickly and in a readily understandable way. The explanations are complete but not wordy.

INTERNATIONAL BUSINESS MACHINES CORPORATION. *Management Control of Electronic Data Processing.* #F20–0006–0. 1965.

This manual describes current methods for controlling data processing procedures. Detailed discussions of controlling input, processing, and output are included.

IRWIN, WAYNE C. *Digital Computer Principles.* Princeton, N.J.: D. Van Nostrand Co., Inc., 1960.

Developed as a training course at National Cash Register Company, the approach is in number systems and the methods of computation available, the need for and use of symbolic logic, and the controls which may be utilized in the reduction or elimination of errors.

KELLY, THOMAS J. "Impact of Electronic Data Processing Upon Auditing Procedures," *Internal Auditor,* Vol. 19 (Winter, 1962), pp. 18–23.

The author points out that the greatest loss to the auditor in an EDP system is the loss of the information trail. He then points out some of the techniques which have been developed to counter this problem. Some of the techniques are auditing records produced by the system and the use of test decks to verify the accuracy of the operation of the system.

McDERMOTT, GEORGE J. *"Controlling and Evaluating Data Processing Operations,"* *Systems and Procedures Journal,* July–August, 1965, pp. 24–27. Also printed in *Journal of Data Management,* July, 1965, pp. 26–29.

Described is a method for scheduling and controlling data processing operation which involves seven steps: classifying the type of job to be processed; classifying the operations required for each job; assigning operating code numbers to each programmer, machine operator, and keypuncher; designing the source documents to incorporate all the salient information related to data processing activities; developing a key punch format; designing a system of data input sequencing and processing; and designing a computer program which will accumulate computer usage time by program job number and department. Some of the advantages of this new method are outlined including the fact that this system provides records of computer usage for previous jobs which can be compared to current job performance.

PORTER, W. THOMAS. "Evaluating Internal Controls in EDP Systems," *Journal of Accountancy,* August, 1964, pp. 34–40.

The author first discusses auditing procedures and methods still used in non-EDP installations, the "around-the-computer" approach. He compares this with the new test-deck or "through-the-computer" approach. The advantages of the test-deck approach are emphasized.

WOOLMAN, K. D. "The Impact of Electronic Data Processing on the Chartered Accountant," Data Processing and Management Services, 36th Chartered Accountant in Australia, August, 1965, pp. 109–25.

Presented is a discussion of computer systems which relate to the design of audit procedures. Among the topics explored are: the nature of a computer; developing an installation; the controls built into a system; storage, input and output devices; various communication methods; and integration and real-time computing. Also examined is the impact of the auditor on electronic data processing. It is concluded that improved communication between the installation manager and the auditor can be very desirable.

QUESTIONS

1. When an auditor speaks of an "audit trail," what is he speaking about? Why does he consider it to be of importance?
2. Why does the auditor consider that there is an "audit trail" problem when he comes to a computer installation?
3. Differentiate between "around-the-machines" audits and "through-the-machines" audits.
4. When is internal control of concern to business management, and why should we, who are interested in the design of data processing systems, also find it of vital concern?
5. Discuss your concept of what is meant by "a system of authorization and record procedures" when one is discussing internal control in data processing.
6. Discuss your concept of what is meant by "appropriate segregation of functional responsibilities" when one is discussing internal control in data processing.
7. Why is the documentation of a system considered to be so important to the solution of the problem of how to maintain adequate internal control?
8. How is the principle on internal control "segration of functional responsibilities" ideally carried out in EDP installation?
9. Discuss three forms of input control, making certain to point out the significance of each method.
10. Differentiate between machine controls and built-in controls.
11. Explain the concept of parity bits and describe how they are used.
12. Discuss sequence checks and limit checks, describing what they are and pointing out some of their areas of applicability.
13. Why is the function of a tape librarian considered to be an important one?
14. What are some forms of output control? Discuss their usefulness.
15. How has the function of the auditor changed with the advent of electronic data processing systems?

CHAPTER **15**

Software Development

Up to this point, our discussion of computers has emphasized the development and capabilities of the equipment, or *hardware* as it is often termed.

Equally important is the development and availability of *software*—usually in the form of programs—to assist in directing the computer in its processing of data through the equipment.

The computer is capable of solving problems of tremendous complexity, with unbelievable speed and extreme accuracy. One of its most significant features is in its ability to solve problems from start to finish without human intervention in the intermediate steps of computation.

At first, the program of instructions to the computer had to be written in great detail. However, as will be seen, the depth of detail required in the program of instructions has been considerably reduced through the development of software.

STORED PROGRAM CONCEPT

Since a computer must be directed as to the procedures to be followed, a program is basic to its operation. The program provides a complete set of coded detailed steps and procedures directing the computer to perform a data processing task. It will be stored in memory and interpreted by the control unit of the machine, making it possible for the computer's performance to be self-controlled. Any such self-controlled performance includes a series of actions or movements, each depending on another and requiring no operator intervention in the completion of the series. The series can be very short or very long; it can be completely sequential or the next action to be taken can be chosen by the last action completed.

The operation of an automatic record player is a good example of a series of actions, each depending on the one immediately preceding it. When records are loaded on the spindle of a record player and the player

362

is turned on, a record drops, the playing arm moves into position, and the record plays; upon completion, the playing arm returns to a neutral position and the next record in sequence drops into place; the playing arm returns to the starting position on the new record; this record plays, and the cycle continues, without need for intervention or assistance by anyone, until all of the records have been played. This series of actions is called a program, and it is stored in the record player (Figure 15–1).

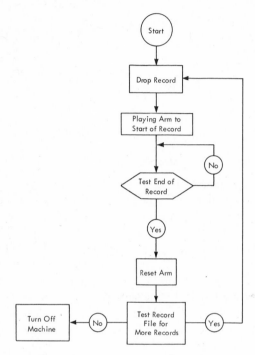

FIG. **15–1.   Block Diagram of a Program.**

Any person planning to code a program should have the following knowledge and background: (1) He should know precisely the information which is desired out of the system; (2) he should also be fully acquainted with all of the types of data which will be fed into the system; (3) he should know the characteristics of the files which will be used to store partially processed data; (4) he must understand the instructions which will be used to guide the computer in its operation; and, (5) he must be aware of the characteristics of the equipment available to carry out the procedures.

In data processing systems, the program controls the entire flow of data in and out of various processing units. If, for instance, original data are punched into cards, the program controls the reading of this data and its transport to various processing areas for addition, subtraction, multiplication, division, modification, classification, recording, and any other kind of action to which data can be subjected.

In stored-program systems all of the instructions needed to complete a procedure are written in the form of program steps. These program steps are made available to the machine by various methods, the most common of which is punched cards. (However, most of the larger computer systems normally use magnetic tape.) The data processing system stores these program steps in some type of storage medium (see Chapter 12). Thus, when a procedure is to begin, the stored program is loaded into the system, and the entire procedure can be performed from beginning to end without further intervention. The program calls in the input data as needed, enabling the computer to perform in sequence the stages required in the processing of the data.

PROGRAMMING CONCEPTS

Machine Language Instructions

When the first computer programs were written, they had to be written in a language acceptable to the computer. Since each make of computer had its own language, the programmer had to be trained in the techniques of coding for a particular computer system. This involved the writing of instructions in the form of long lists of numbers or number codes. Such a system, because of the detail and complexity involved, was prone to numerous errors. The possibility of transfer of knowledge between the coding required for two different computers was slight, and this created many difficult situations. For example, if a firm desired to change its computer, it also had to change all of its programs. Creating an equally difficult problem was the fact that the programs had to be prepared or coded in *machine language*. Obviously, coding in machine language made it necessary for the programmer either to memorize or to have readily available the many instruction codes which a particular computer used.

An even greater problem in machine language coding, however, was keeping track of the data and instruction locations. Learning the instruction codes was not too difficult, but the instruction and data addresses were different for every instruction and for every program written. Thus when the command ADD was given in a machine language program, not only did the proper instruction code have to be indicated but also the specific memory address of the quantity had to be added. Since all but the simplest programs contain several hundred coded instructions, and programs of thousands of instructions are not at all uncommon, keeping track of what is stored in various memory locations and determining which locations remain unused was quite an involved task. Furthermore, when changes had to be made or when errors were discovered in the program, all the address locations which followed usually had to be changed, necessitating an almost complete rewrite of that portion of the program.

An example of a program coded in machine language is illustrated in its application to the IBM 1401 system. This system does not require this level of coding to be used as it also utilizes some of the more sophisticated programming techniques to be described later in this chapter. Because the 1401 system uses a variable word length concept, the length of an instruction can vary from one to eight characters depending on the operation to be performed.

The format of such an instruction might look as follows:

OP Code	*A- or I- address*	*B-Address*	*d- Character*
A̲	072	423	

This form of machine language instruction consists of an operation code followed by two three-character addresses. The two-address instruction is required to move data from one location to another, to perform arithmetic operations of addition or subtraction, to compare two fields, or to edit.

The OP code is always a single character that defines the basic operation to be performed. In this case, the letter A̲ indicates an add instruction.

The underlining of the operation code designation is called a "word mark" and in its use here indicates to the computer both the beginning of an instruction (the next to be processed) and the end of the execution of an instruction (the current item being processed).

The A-address always consists of three characters. It can identify the units position of the A-field, or it can be used to select a special unit or feature such as a tape unit.

Instructions that can cause programs to branch out of a normal sequence use the I-address to specify the location of the next instruction to be executed if a branch occurs.

The B-address is a three-character storage address that identifies the B-field. It usually addresses the units position of the B-field, but in some operations it specifies the high order position of a record storage area. The d-character is used to modify an operation code.

Referring now to the preceding illustration of a 1401 system instruction, the add instruction A̲ causes the field whose units position is in storage location 072 to be added to the field whose units position is in location 423. This operation continues until a word mark for the high order position of the information stored in B-field is sensed. The word mark stops the operation being performed and causes the program to advance to the next instruction.

Some examples of instructions of varying lengths follow:

Operation	Instruction Format			
Read a card	OP Code I			
Select stacker	OP Code K	d-character 2		
Branch	OP Code B	I-address 400		
Branch if indicator on	OP Code B	I-address 625	d-character 1	
Add	OP Code A	A-address 072	B-address 423	
Branch if character equal	OP Code B	I-address 650	B-address 0680	d-character 4

Processors

Many of the difficulties and inconveniences of coding programs directly in machine coding can be simplified or eliminated through more advanced systems of program writing.

Experience has shown that computers can be programmed to recognize instructions expressed or written in other languages and to translate those instructions into their own language (Processor Programs).

For example, the first simplification of the programming process came with the use of letters and Arabic numbers in place of basic number codes. The programmer blocks out his problem and then uses a series of symbols to represent each step in the process. Thus, for an instruction such as "load address," instead of writing 01000001, the programmer need only remember "LA." These symbols, or mnemonics, are punched into cards and run through the computer where an "assembly program" or "processor" translates them into a machine language program.

This machine-produced program, known as an object program, is then used to direct the actions of the computer in its processing of business data. The object program is usually punched into cards and an object program card deck is thus produced. As soon as this program is considered to be satisfactory, the execution run may be started. Figure 15–2 diagrams the sequence of operations.

This technique simplified programming, but it still required one instruction for every step performed by the machine.

It soon became obvious that the processor could take on the additional task of assigning storage addresses to data. These data, then, could also be referred to mnemonically—further simplifying the programmer's job.

In the early processors, the programmer first assigned a symbolic name and an actual address to an item of data; thereafter he referred to that item by its name. He also indicated where in storage the first instruction was to be placed; other instructions were assigned addresses in sequential locations by the computer, under control of the processor program.

The next step in expanding the power of programming systems was to eliminate the need for the programmer to specify any of the addresses. He simply indicated how much storage would be required, and the

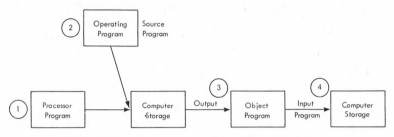

FIG. 15–2. **Preparation of an Object Program.**

processor took over the entire task of allocating storage to data and instructions.

As a result, computers became a lot easier to program. Further evolution of programming expanded on the basic theme of using a prewritten program, or processor, to perform many of the functions formerly requiring manual translation.

Interpreter

"An interpreter is a processor which translates a program into machine language and executes the instructions at the same time. When an interpreter is used, no object program is created since the source program is also the object program. Because of this characteristic, interpreters are often called "load and go" processors."[1]

Macro Instructions

In programming, certain types of instructions are repeated frequently. Over and over, almost any program uses commands to read a card, update a disk file, move a record, and so on. Each time they appeared, the programmer had to write and rewrite the series of detailed instructions which told the machine exactly how to go about this particular task.

This was a clerical job the computer could do:

It led to the development of *macro instructions*—macro, in this case, implying a long sequence of steps. With macro instructions, the programmer could

---

[1] Systems and Procedures Association, *Business Systems*, Vol. II., chap. xix, p. 45.

write one instruction to, say, "read a tape" and the processor could then automatically insert the corresponding detailed series of machine commands. In this way, the programmer could avoid, for the first time, the task of writing one instruction for every machine step.

To handle the more complex problems of simultaneous operation of the computer and input/output equipment, programmers developed special routines called input/output control systems. Basically, an input/output control system makes it possible for the programmer to write a problem as if it were a simple sequential operation; get a record, process it, and put the result into an output format. The input/output control system program makes it possible to provide the machine language coding necessary to schedule operations, to identify errors, and to provide efficient routines for reading and writing tape, card, and disk records.[2]

In addition to input/output control systems, programmers developed other standard programs to take over other repetitive tasks. Programs to sort and merge records, report generators to simplify specification of formats, and utility programs all take clerical burdens off the programmers and put them on the machine.

Compilers

The distinguishing feature of a compiler program is that one instruction in the source program can lead to the creation of many machine instructions in the object program. For example, a programmer can bring a complete subroutine into an object program simply by writing its name once.

The user of the computer language COBOL, which is a widely accepted language for handling business data processing problems (see Chapter 17), must have a COBOL compiler for his computer in order that it may process the programs written in COBOL and translate them into numeric codes which are understandable to the computer. The same would be necessary for a computer to accept any of the other computer languages commonly in use today.

SYSTEMS PROGRAMMING

There are several levels of systems programming which have evolved over time, some of which are fairly new in their actual application of multiprogramming. Each of these is designed to assist in some degree of automatic and simultaneous machine action in processing one or more programs.

1. Simultaneity of input/output permits the computer system to read one instruction while processing a second and outputting the results from another.
2. Interleaved programming permits the alternate processing of two or more programs.

---

[2] *Data Processor*, Vol. 8, No. 4 (October, 1965), p. 6.

3. Priority multiprogramming permits two or more programs to be processed in an order based on a priority structure.
4. A blend of interleaved and priority multiprocessing is sometimes desirable where one program is, in terms of time, either input or output bound. When this occurs, the priority program takes precedence, but the other is processed on the basis of available time.
5. Multi-user-operator programming involves a time-sharing capability where many users—normally at remote terminal I/O stations—have access to a single computer on a shared basis.

Executive Programs or Multiprogramming

In reading this far the reader would undoubtedly imagine that separate programs would be utilized to accomplish all of the many and varied business data processing chores. It would seem reasonable that as a data processing chore had to be accomplished that the necessary program would first be placed in the memory of the computer and then it would be utilized to direct the activities of the computer in the accomplishment of a particular task. As soon as the checks were written, the reports printed, etc., the program would be processed in small batches.

Due to the recent improvements in computer hardware the speed of the machines has been increased manyfold. At the same time, memory capacity and the access time to memory have also been increased tremendously without a relative increase in cost. With these improvements the computer has become too fast to depend upon human intervention to switch it from job to job, so programmers created executive programs to help to increase the throughput of the machines. Such programs enable the machine, for example, to (1) write a tape record, (2) process a second record, and (3) read a third one.

Executive programs increase the efficiency of the computer system by holding several operating programs in storage at the same time, making them immediately accessible upon demand.

With the increasing speed, capacity, and use of the computer, the concept of utilizing the computer to service remote locations evolved. The function of the executive program broadened to serve as the bridge between batch processing and service to remote locations. The resulting executive program could be used to control a system which processes batch programs only, or a system dedicated to the control of telecommunication devices, or any combination of these two.

To efficiently handle on-line inquiries or data entering the data processing center from remote locations, the needs of the remote devices must be satisfied quickly. This means that the computer's batch processing must be suspended when the interruption from the remote device occurs. To gain efficient system operation the control program must provide this service automatically.[3]

[3] Robert S. Dines, "Telecommunications and Supervisory Control Programs," *Computers and Automation*, May, 1966, p. 22.

In addition to controlling the input from remote terminals, the responsibilities of the executive program can be divided into the following classifications:

Scheduling the allocation of computing time to the tasks at hand.
Allocation of memory and storage involving the assignment and utilization of hardware.
Control of input and output for operating user programs.
Control over service operations.

All of these areas are closely interrelated and frequently depend on each other.

TIME-SHARING.   Executive programs can be utilized to enable the computer to perform many different tasks almost simultaneously. With the present state of development of computer hardware and software, the men who have studied and developed computers envisioned their use by many different users of data on a shared basis, thereby making the capabilities of the computer available to many more people. Time-sharing thus evolved and can be defined as "the simultaneous access to the computer by many users who are in effect sharing its use or times."[4]

This idea has considerable appeal because many firms and organizations could utilize the capabilities of computers even though they could not justify having one themselves.

DATA BASE.   As computers have been made larger, with greater storage capacities, and as the concepts of on-line, real-time, and time-sharing have become reality, the problems of collecting and converting data and organizing these into data files for maximum utility have become significant.

The problems are those of trying to balance the amount of on-line storage available with the data that it is felt should be kept in storage (the data base) as well as organizing it for efficient utilization. This information would normally be subdivided into the necessary information groups to run a business: (1) customer file, (2) vendor file, (3) personnel file, (4) product information file, (5) inventory file, (6) general ledger accounting file. The key idea in the data base concept is that the data base serve the information needs of every department, thereby eliminating the need for duplicate files.

Since internal, on-line storage is expensive, the quantity of data as well as space considered necessary for the data base becomes significant.

DATA CHANNELS.   The concept of time-sharing is predicated on the ability of numerous data users at remote locations having access to the

---

[4] Systems Development Corporation, *Software Trends—Hardware Characteristics* (Computer Research Series No. 5, [New York: American Institute of Certified Public Accountants, 1966]), p. 17.

data at will. This means that inquiries from various locations can be made almost simultaneously.

During the earlier stages of the development of the computer, the channel along which the data flowed to the computer could only accommodate data flowing in a continuous stream, and the speed of the channel constituted the speed by which data could be directed to the computer.

With the advent of the IBM System/360 a completely new concept in data channels was developed. Two different channels were developed, and they are of two general types: multiplexor channels and selector channels.

The multiplexor channel separates the operations of high-speed devices from those of lower speed devices. Operations on the channel are in two modes: a "multiplex" mode for lower data rates and a "burst" mode for the higher.

In the multiplex mode, the single data path of the channel can be time-shared by a large number of low-speed input/output devices operating simultaneously; the channel receives and sends data to them on demand. When operating in the burst mode, however, a single input/output device captures the multiplexor channel and does not relinquish it from the time it is selected until the last bit of data is serviced.

Examples of low-speed devices that can operate simultaneously on the multiplexor channel are: printers, card punches, card readers, and terminals.

Examples of input/output devices that operate in the burst mode are: magnetic tape units and disk, drum, or data cell storage.

PROGRAMMING CLASSIFICATIONS

While the first computer programmers were, of necessity, jacks-of-all-trades, programming soon generated its own subspecialties. The first logical division of programming came with the distinction between *applications programming* and *systems programming*.

Applications Programming

The people who write applications programs are the ones who write the programs which cause the computers to accomplish certain data processing tasks, such as billing, payroll, etc. They are very often individuals who have been trained or hired by a specific company and are usually highly knowledgeable of the problems for which they are programming.

Many application programs are developed by computer users in this way. They may also acquire examples of these same types of programs for computer user groups or from the program libraries maintained by some of the computer manufacturers.

Systems Programming

The systems programmers write the programs that run the computing equipment and generally are employed by the computer manufacturers. There are many computer routines which are common to many different data processing tasks, and it is these routines which are generally developed by these individuals. These programs are often referred to as program packages, and they can include such types as: control programs which operate the input and output equipment; testing programs which are designed to detect electrical and mechanical malfunctions; and utility programs which control output formats.

When a programmer who is writing an applications program comes to a point in his program where one of these program packages (macro instructions) would fit, he can utilize the program package which is obtainable from the computer manufacturer, rather than working out this part of the program independently. He knows that this package has already been tested and proven. Through the use of such program packages, the writing of applications programs can be speeded up immeasurably, and the task of the applications programmer can be made a whole lot easier.

An important subdivision of system programming is programming language development—producing the assemblers, FORTRAN, COBOL, and other translation programs. With programming languages, applications programmers can instruct a computer in a language closer to English and normal mathematical notation rather than use the ones and zeros of machine language. Programming language development, then, is the creation of programs which permit the computer to translate a natural language statement into the numerical, machine language instructions, or object programs, that actually operate the computer.

PROGRAMMING LANGUAGES

FORTRAN—*Fo*rmula *Tra*nslation—is a language system written in the period 1954–1956 by IBM personnel under the general direction of John W. Backus. It is a mathematical language and has its greatest use in scientific applications. Problems are coded for the computer in a style which closely resembles ordinary mathematical notation, and which requires virtually no knowledge of the computer on the part of the coder.

A typical FORTRAN statement might be as follows:

ROOT = (−B + SQRT[B**2 − 4.*A*C])/(2.*A)

to symbolize the mathematical formula:

$$ROOT = \frac{-B + \sqrt{B^2 - 4AC}}{2A}$$

With such a statement the computer would search out the data enclosed in the innermost set of brackets and perform the calculations required, then progress to the larger set of brackets, and finally divide by the sum of 2 multiplied times A. The double asterisk indicates exponentation; a single asterisk indicates multiplication; the minus sign, subtraction; the plus sign, addition; and the slash symbol, division.

FORTRAN has been adapted to both small- and large-scale computers and has been used extensively with IBM equipment. The ideas utilized in the design of FORTRAN have been adapted to other manufacturers' computers under many different program names.

The United States government is the largest single purchaser of computers for use in its many diversified applications. Purchases have been made from most, if not all, of the firms producing computers. It was this government ownership of many brands and types of computers that began to create major problems. If one agency outgrew a given computer, or if there was a need for one agency to share time on its computer with another agency, it was impossible to shift the programs created for one piece of equipment to another.

Finally, in 1958, the Department of Defense initiated the idea of having a joint committee formed which would be composed of representatives of the government, large private users, and the major computer manufacturers. These individuals were brought together to develop a language code which would enable one program to be translated into the machine languages required by other computers.

Due to the different coding techniques needed in mathematical and business coding it was decided that two standard program languages were needed rather than one. The outcome was the development of ALGOL and COBOL.

ALGOL, an *Al*gebraic *O*riented *L*anguage is an automatic coding language designed for wide usage in coding computational applications. It had been started in 1958 but was extensively implemented in the early 1960's.

COBOL, the *Co*mmon *B*usiness *O*riented *L*anguage, like ALGOL is not designed to be oriented to any particular computer in its utilization of a vocabulary of machine functions. When using COBOL, the coder is concerned with writing the functions he wants performed and not with exactly what machine instructions will ultimately be supplied by the COBOL compiler.

Each of the computer manufacturers who anticipates selling equipment to the government—and most of them do, of course—is writing a COBOL compiler which will translate the basic COBOL language into the machine language for his particular computer. In this way a program written in COBOL could be compiled by an IBM 1410 using its COBOL translator to produce a program for the IBM 1410 or if compiled by an NCR

315 COBOL translator, a program would be produced for the NCR 315. Similarly, COBOL programs can be translated into machine language for any computer for which a COBOL translator has been written.

OTHER TYPES OF
COMPUTER SOFTWARE

In addition to the compilers and other processors already discussed, there are software techniques available from computer manufacturers and user groups which should be considered.

Debugging Aids

Certain debugging aids are essential in installing a computer. One of these debugging aids is a *memory print (dump) program* which will cause the contents of memory to be printed out in some form to permit it to be analyzed and edited by the programmer. Memory print programs can vary in their sophistication from a very simple program to one which will actually interpret the contents of each area of memory to determine whether the information in that area consists of data or machine instructions. In the case of instructions, the instructions can be edited from machine language into a mnemonic form, which is easier for the programmer to read. This is particularly important in computers where addresses or operations in the machine language would appear in binary or octal rather than decimal digits. In such cases, it is particularly important that the memory print program edit these binary or octal configurations into a number system form the programmer can easily read.

The tape print program is another important debugging aid. A tape print program in its simplest form reads the contents of a tape and prints it out. This enables the programmer to check the data written on the tape to see if the data are correct. The tape print program in a simple form would just print the data from the tape in a consecutive manner, item by item, for the entire length of the print line used by the particular computer in use. In more complex tape print programs, each tape record would be printed out on a separate line. Some tape print programs enable the programmer to type in the account number of the desired record. The program then searches the tape to find the indicated account number and prints the appropriate record for that account. These are some examples of the options that can be built into debugging aids to make them more effective. Programs such as the memory and tape print programs are often called *utility routines*.

Operating Systems

An *operating system* is a group of programs designed to increase the efficiency and effectiveness of the computer in its day-to-day operations by reducing setup time through automatic program sequencing and selection. The program tape which contains all of the installation's program is the heart of the operating system. The program tape is created by converting the programs from punched cards to magnetic tape or by using magnetic tape as the output from the assembler or compiler.

One way in which an operating system might function would be the following: The first program on a program tape would be a program locator routine which is followed successively by a production program, a locator, then another production program, etc. This tape, when mounted on a tape unit, permits the operator to call in the first program from the tape (the locator) and specify the particular program he desires to run. The operating system automatically searches the program tape to find the program the operator has specified. The operating system would verify the tape labels for each input file and write tape labels on the output files. Control is then transferred to the production program, which performs its own processing. At the conclusion of the production program, the locator is read into memory to search the program tape for the next production program scheduled to be run. The automatic setup procedures are again performed without operator intervention or manipulation of card decks.

Another function of an operating system is to provide a method of dating reports, payrolls, etc., and inserting variable constants (such as factors, rates, and dates) into the programs where they are needed. The dating systems provided by the manufacturers today vary from no dating system at all to rather complex dating systems which include calendars and tables of special dates used to vary processing requirements. Operating systems eliminate production program decks and their inherent disadvantages (such as getting cards out of sequence, dropping a deck, losing cards, and card reader jams, which may occur as frequently used program decks become worn). This eliminates the necessity of periodically reproducing the decks to keep them in good condition. Also, by automatically sequencing and selecting the production programs, these operating systems reduce operator intervention to a minimum. This tends to limit the opportunities for operator errors. Operating systems and instruction tapes are not new, as they were first developed for some of the earlier types of computers. It is just recently, however, that computer manufacturers have been including operating systems in their software packages.

Application Packages

Another type of software is the *application program package*. Though such programs have been available in limited numbers for some time, only recently have manufacturers devoted considerable time to the development of program packages for certain rather specialized applications such as demand deposit accounting for banks and customer billing for utilities. These programs have been standardized, tested, and debugged for use in these specialized applications. The appeal of such an application package is quite clear. If a customer acquiring a computer can be provided fully tested and debugged programs needed for his application, then all that remains to be done is to convert the present data to punched cards, or magnetic tape, or other suitable input to his computer. This brings about a substantial reduction in planning, programming, and conversion costs.

Of course, such application programs must be broad enough in their application to cover nearly every condition peculiar to this industry application. Consequently, these programs may be relatively inefficient in that the needs of the particular firm may not be as extensive as those of the industry as a whole and it may take additional time to process his data. However, these application programs do permit quick conversion to, and utilization of, a computer, and they can always be modified for efficiency as time permits. Where a firm has unique problems, these application programs may have to be modified to the extent that it may be more economical to prepare their own individualized programs.

In addition, some of the original program packages have been found to be deficient in control features as a result of an attempt to perform maximum processing on minimum computer systems.

Sources of Software

The manufacturer is, of course, the primary source of these software programs. There have been some other very interesting developments in the field, however.

In August, 1955, representatives of several aviation companies met in Los Angeles to talk about their mutual computing problems. It was their feeling that with the difficulties involved in this area, they ought to get together and exchange programs and experience.

Out of that meeting came a remarkable idea for a new kind of organization: the computer user group. Since then, the growth of computer user groups has been phenomenal. They are primarily composed of IBM computer users, and the major groups are as follows:

SHARE: Formed in 1955. It is open to users with an IBM 700 or 7000 series computer, or a System/360 Model 50 or higher (but also including the model 44) installed or on order.

GUIDE: Formed in 1956. It is open to commercial users with an IBM "large scale" computer installed or on order—defined as a 705, 1410, or 7000 series computer with a minimum of 20,000 positions of high-speed memory and six magnetic tape drives on line, or equivalent; or a System/360 Model 40 or higher, with a minimum of 64,000 bytes of high-speed memory.

COMMON: Formed in 1961. It is open to scientific or commercial users with an installed—or on order—1130, 1620, 1800 or a smaller System/360.

User group rules are simple. A computer installed or on order, attendance at one of the biannual meetings, a willingness to contribute worthwhile programs (conforming to certain standards of documentation), and discussion of information and ideas are all the credentials a prospective member needs. No dues are required, but a cooperative spirit and participation in project work are expected.

As a group member, the computer user can draw what he needs from a reservoir of superior computing thought distilled from a continual, critical interchange of ideas among the entire membership. More specifically, he can expect to do considerably less programming and checkout on everything from utility routines to complete systems.

As computer users have become more sophisticated, they have paid more attention to specialized problem solving.

Application-oriented groups have been formed to help satisfy complex programming needs. These organizations include CEPA (Civil Engineering Program Applications); HEEP (Highway Engineers Exchange Programs); ACUTE (Accountants Computer Users for Technical Exchange) open to public accounting firms only; and ECHO (Electronic Computing—Hospital Oriented).

Out of the cooperative spirit of the users groups, IBM has established a program library in Hawthorne, New York, composed of 2,000 active computer programs. Members of the user groups are expected to contribute programs to this library on a nonproprietary basis. The programs, however, are available to all IBM users.

CASETTE A

GENERAL ELECTRIC ANNOUNCES THE 645 LARGE-SCALE TIME-SHARING COMPUTER[5]

General Electric has announced its largest and latest computer system, the 645, designed specifically for large-scale, time-sharing operations. Time-sharing, which allows multiple simultaneous use of a computer's full power, promises to radically reduce costs of computing while boosting the computer's usefulness. Most computers process information one batch at a time. Although its cost is high, more than $150,000 monthly rental in some versions, it replaces so many individual computers and allows so many more problems to be solved by computer that the cost of computing can be cut drastically. Time-sharing has for the most part been confined to experimental and educational projects but the 645 brings instant computing within the reach of most businessmen and researchers. Early prototypes of the 645 were ordered by MIT's Project MAC and by Bell Telephone Laboratories. Project MAC (Machine Aided Cognition) is a research program sponsored by the Advanced Research

---

[5] Commerce Clearing House, *Automation Reports*, July, 1965.

Projects Agency under an Office of Naval Research contract. Ohio State University's computation center has also ordered the 655 computer for educational time-sharing work.

GE News Release (52,011)

CASETTE B[6]

The world's first "live" computer service for savings banks and loan associations is now in operation in New York City. About one and a half million savings accounts in the New York metropolitan area will be handled by the on-line center. Ten metropolitan savings banks are charter subscribers to the New York center.

The new on-line service makes available to banks instantaneous computer service on a public utility basis with the subscriber buying only as much service as he needs. The service is designed to be utilized economically by any size banking institution and has the advantage of providing small and medium-size banks with the same advanced data processing system used by some of the largest savings banks.

The new service offers processing of both savings and mortgage accounts by directly connecting tellers' machines at subscribing banks via telephone lines with an NCR 315 CRAM computer located at the data processing center. Although the 315 computer is handling all banks simultaneously, none has access to any of the other banks' records. Each receives individual reports.

The center is capable of handling bank subscribers as much as three hundred miles away. A center in Pittsburgh opening later this year has contracts with eighteen savings and loan associations in the area. NCR is planning similar on-line computer processing centers in the next eighteen months in Chicago, Los Angeles, San Francisco and Boston.

NCR News Release (51,650)

CASETTE C[7]

Time-Sharing

Several other developments also reflect the growing interest in computer time-sharing:

C-E-I-R, Inc., goes "on the air" this fall with a time-sharing service for scientists and engineers in the Washington, D.C., area. Subscribers are paying $250 a month for 50 hours' use of the system, plus $25 for telephone lines in the District of Columbia (slightly more in Maryland and Virginia) and $35 to $125 rental of a Teletype console. Software for the system, including a mathematical programming language called BASIC, was developed at Dartmouth University in a project aided by funds from the National Science Foundation.

---

[6] *Ibid.*

[7] "Time-Sharing Grows," *Management Services*, September–October, 1965, p. 8.

Computer Sciences Corporation's Service Bureau Division plans to offer time-sharing service to small and medium-sized organizations in Southern California, starting with San Diego. However, instead of simply charging for the service on an as-used basis, CSC will cooperate with the customer in marketing computer time to potential users in the immediate area and will share in the profits. CSC will install UNIVAC 1004 or IBM 1400-series processors in facilities provided by the local organizations for direct access to CSC's UNIVAC 1107 computer.

ANNOTATED BIBLIOGRAPHY

COLEMAN, DAVID, AND COHN, THEODORE. "Some Specialized Uses of Data Processing Centers," *Management Services*, September–October, 1965 pp. 40–46.

Data processing centers are a growing industry, which is evident by the growing number of businesses utilizing them. To aid businesses in deciding whether or not to use such a service, various criteria that should be considered are discussed, including: computer application offered by the centers; jobs which are suitable for the center; and procedures to follow in selecting the center. It is concluded that with the equipment and technical skills available at data processing centers, there is no limit to their usefulness.

CUTLER, DONALD L. *Introduction to Computer Programming.* Englewood Cliffs, N.J.: Prentice-Hall, Inc., 1964.

Digital computers and the programming languages used with them are described. Data representation and organization, flow diagramming, impact-output, and advanced fixed-point techniques are among the problems analyzed. To illustrate the discussion, a hypothetical computer is used as a model.

Data Processor, "Words That Move Machines," Vol. 8, No. 4 (October, 1965), p. 4.

This article emphasizes and explains the importance of different types of programs in order that a computer can do the job intended for it.

DINES, ROBERT S. "Telecommunications and Supervisory Control Programs," *Computers and Automation,* May 1966, p. 22.

This article describes how a supervisory control program integrates computer equipment, programming, remote stations, and operations so that these elements are one.

FLORES, IVAN. "Multiplicity in Computer Systems," *Computers and Automation,* July, 1966, p. 19.

Multiprocessing, multiprogramming, and multicomputing are carefully differentiated and explained in this article.

INTERNATIONAL BUSINESS MACHINES CORPORATION. *IBM 1401 System Summary,* #A24–1401–01. Reprinted April, 1966.

This publication describes the programming systems of this machine as well as the equipment which goes with it.

McRae, T. W. *Introduction to Business Computer Programming.* London: Gee & Co., Ltd., 1963.

Although there is no doubt that mathematicians make good programmers, an extensive knowledge of mathematics is not required for programming. In fact, no preliminary qualifications other than basic common sense are required for programming. It is suggested that each profession do its own programming. Therefore, this book is designed for accountants, bankers, managers, and others who may wish to gain a general knowledge of programming. The various aspects of computer programming examined include: preparing a program, debugging, making flow diagrams, control, and timing. The background of business computers, EDP organization, and computer systems is also discussed.

System Development Corporation. *Technical Memorandum,* "A Description of the Data Base System," December, 1962.

Included in this document is a synopsis of the data base function, as well as a description of each component part of the system.

QUESTIONS

1. What is meant by a stored program concept?
2. Describe the function which a program performs in a data processing system.
3. What were some of the problems encountered when programs had to be written in machine language?
4. How has the nature of programming changed through the years?
5. What is a processor program?
6. Describe how an object program is produced.
7. Differentiate between assemblers and compilers.
8. What part does "macro instruction" play in facilitating the work of the programmer?
9. Describe how the art of programming has become more sophisticated and increased in its ability to get work accomplished over the last 15 years.
10. What are the functions of an executive program, and what has occurred in the development of hardware in recent years, which has made the development of programs of this type imperative? Explain this in *your own words* as you understand it.
11. Using your own judgment, knowledge, experience, and imagination, describe several areas of business where you feel that time-sharing a computer facility might be successfully worked out. Be certain to explain *why* you think this could be done.
12. How does the work of applications and systems programmers differ? In which ways is it the same?
13. What differentiates COBOL from other programming languages?
14. Describe as completely as you are able two sources of software available to a user of computers.

CHAPTER 16

FORTRAN Programming

Language

THE MOST commonly used computer language for the manipulation of numerical data in solving arithmetical problems is the FORTRAN (*Formula Trans*lation) language. A number of variations of FORTRAN have been developed, with FORTRAN II being the most widely used. One of the more recent versions, FORTRAN IV, is also being used quite widely, as it is more advanced in its application and permits the use of techniques which simplify certain complex problems.

Though the use of FORTRAN is quite prevalent in major computer systems, each such system must be investigated to determine thé particular version of FORTRAN that is acceptable. In addition, a given version of FORTRAN will have been modified (sometimes extensively) for its adaptation to a given computer. Considering the many different FORTRAN languages, as well as their numerous modifications, the approach we shall follow will be a limited rather than an extensive one, and will be based on FORTRAN II, as it is more universally applicable. In addition, FORTRAN II is upward compatible in that it may be utilized in FORTRAN IV, while the reverse is not true. For those desiring a more in-depth description of the use and particular characteristics of FORTRAN IV, it is suggested they refer to one of the many excellent books available.

With such a cursory approach, and in consideration of the many modifications of the several FORTRAN languages, the student should not expect that this material will develop him into a programmer for any specific computer system. The aim of the programming section of this text is, rather, to acquaint the student with the characteristics of programming in general and with the terminology associated with two of the major languages (FORTRAN and COBOL), and to give him a broad grasp of the nature of programming along with an understanding of the duties and problems of programmers. Specifically, a student completing this material should be able to communicate with programmers, should have developed some empathy in connection with the art of programming, and to some extent be able to follow the logical steps of a given business application programmed in these major languages.

FORTRAN

As in the case of all symbolic computer languages, FORTRAN requires the use of a compiler. The FORTRAN compiler is part of the software provided by the manufacturer. It permits the computer to accept a program written in FORTRAN as input and to produce as output a program written in the computer's own machine language. The compiler as well as the program it produces will be different for each make and, usually, for each model of computer. In some organizations with sophisticated programming talent available, the compiler furnished by the manufacturer may be further modified to extend its capabilities or to just do a specific job more easily. In fact, most of the different FORTRAN languages have had as a basis of their development either the design and production of a more powerful and versatile computer system or the incorporation of improvements made on the language, by programmers working on government projects or for business firms.

The FORTRAN compiler program is fed into the computer and is followed by a source program—which is the set of instructions necessary to solve a given application problem—written in a symbolic format. (This symbolic format or language will be explained in the following material.) The result, in the form of computer output produced by the reading and processing of the compiler and source decks, is a third program, known as an object program. It is this compiled object program, which is processed in turn with data (pertinent information related to the given problem in the form of constants), that executes or produces the solution to the problem in the form of the answer(s) specified by the original symbolic language program.

FORTRAN Alphabet

The basic FORTRAN alphabet is composed of the following alphanumeric characters.

1. The 10 numerical digits 0, 1, 2, 3, 4, 5, 6, 7, 8, and 9.
2. The alphabet A, B, C, . . . X, Y, and Z, utilizing only capital letters.
3. Eleven special characters, five of which are punctuation characters ., ( ) \$, a small b to indicate spacing, and five algebraic symbols + − * / =

ELEMENTS OF FORTRAN

There are two major kinds of numbers used in the FORTRAN language. These are known as fixed-point or integer and floating-point or real numbers and refer to the mode of operation in a given FORTRAN program. Fixed-point or integer mode indicates that the numbers used will always be whole numbers (integers) and *must not* be written with a decimal point. Floating-point or real mode indicates that the numbers used may be either whole numbers or decimal fractions and must be written with a decimal point.

In conjunction with the mode of operation, the user must remember that (1) it is not permissible to use mixed modes in any given expression and (2) the results of any calculations made with fixed-point values will always be expressed in whole numbers—thus $15 \div 4 = 3$ and not 3.75 (the values are truncated, not rounded).

In addition to the two kinds of numbers used, there are major classifications of FORTRAN elements which are termed constants, variables, expressions, statements, and subprograms.

Constants

Numbers which are used in computations that do not change from one execution of the program to another are called constants. The form of the constants are always numerical, but they may be either whole or fractional numbers. Examples of both fixed-point and floating-point constants are:

Fixed Point	*Floating Point*
12	12.
−1	−1.
2012	20.12
−256	$6.95E + 5 \quad [6.95 \times 10^5]$
674	$6.9E - 5 \quad [6.9 \times 10^{-5}]$

Variables

Symbolic representations which will be used to assume a value in a program are called variables. As a variable these are assigned some type of name, as the value is expected to change for either different executions of the given program or at various points within the program. In the example, $I = 4 * J$, both I and J are variables inasmuch as J may assume different values and, in turn, cause I to change in value.

Variable names always start with a letter: This initial letter may be the entire variable name, or it may be followed by a series of characters (excepting the special characters). Variable names usually cannot exceed six characters for most processing equipment, and the equipment capabilities should be checked if more than six character variable names are desired. Variables may utilize either whole or fractional numbers depending on the mode of operation.

In the fixed-point or integer mode, an expression which is to represent an item which is variable in the proposed program *must always* begin with either I, J, K, L, M, or N. In floating-point mode of operation, the expression representing a variable name *must always* begin with the letters A through H or O through Z. Examples of fixed-point and floating-point variables are:

Fixed Point	*Floating Point*
K9	HOUR
MANNO	RATE
I	TIME
JOB	SALARY
NUMBER	B4

Variables may also be subscripted in the common notation form A_i to provide a sub-index to a series of variables named A. In FORTRAN language this simple form of single subscripting is expressed as $A(I)$. For example, if an array is a list of numbers 3, 5, 9, 7, 6 and the name assigned to this array is LIST, then the third item of the array would be LIST(3), which would have a value of 9.

Variable names may also assume a subscripted form when they are used in the representation of arrays of either 1, 2, or 3 dimensions. If a two-dimensional matrix or table MTBL was in the form:

	Col. 1	*Col. 2*	*Col. 3*
Row 1	3	5	9
Row 2	7	6	4
Row 3	10	2	7

then the item in row 2, column 1 would be MTBL(2,1) and its value would be 7. Similarly, a given position in a three-dimensional array N, a given position might be subscripted N(1,3,1) and represent some given value assigned to this position of the array.

Expressions

Any valid series of constants, variables, and mathematical functions which are connected by operational symbols form an expression. Arithmetic expressions, of which there are two basic types, are frequently found in FORTRAN. Both types involve the usage of arithmetic symbols; however, one is usually called an arithmetic statement and the other an arithmetic or operational expression.

ARITHMETIC STATEMENTS. This type of statement involves the use of the arithmetic symbol = as in

$$A = B + C$$

In all FORTRAN statements involving the use of the equal sign the symbol is used in the sense of "being replaced by" rather than "being equivalent to." In the statement $A = B + C$ it indicates that what was previously stored in A is now replaced by what is stored in both locations B and C after they have been added together. B and C memory locations will remain intact after this statement is processed but A has been replaced by the total, $B + C$.

ARITHMETIC OR OPERATIONAL EXPRESSIONS. This type of expression involves the use of FORTRAN arithmetic symbols which are:

+ addition
− subtraction
* multiplication (x)
/ division (÷)
** exponentiation (x^y)

The use of these symbols individually is in the traditional arithmetic sense (same as noted in parenthesis), and typical examples include:

X+Y	A/B+C
A−B	X**Y
K*J	C*B**A/D

There is, however, a specific hierarchical relationship assigned to these symbols in the pattern of the processing to take place, when several of these symbols are used in a given algebraic formula, that must be remembered.

The first operation performed in the compilation of an algebraic formula in the FORTRAN language is to analyze the statement for parentheses. Then the processing sequence is performed as follows:

1. Operations inside parentheses.
2. Exponentiation (as it occurs left to right).
3. Multiplication and division (as it occurs left to right).
4. Addition and subtraction (as it occurs left to right).

The use of parentheses is most important in writing FORTRAN programs. Without the parentheses the statement

$$A/B+C$$

would result in A being divided by B and then the results added to C. This may not be what is desired at all, and the parentheses provides the technique that will permit A to be divided by the sum of B+C as in

$$A/(B+C)$$

An extended example of how the computer would process a complex mathematical statement would be as follows:

$$A = B - (C+D)**E*F + G/(H+I) + J$$

The first step, as noted above, would be to analyze the statement for parentheses; then $(C+D)$ would be processed to produce a sum X (called X, etc., for convenience in explanation) and $(H + I)$ to produce a second sum Y, X would be exponentiated to the power E and the product would be multiplied by F to produce Z. G would be divided by Y to produce W. Now that all operations excepting addition and subtraction are performed, they will be processed in the order in which they occur, and Z would be subtracted from B, with the remainder added to W and J in turn. The net result of this calculation would then replace the value previously assigned to A.

Statements

Along with the arithmetic expressions, statements form the basis of a FORTRAN program. Each statement performs a single aspect of the given problem and serves to direct the manipulation of data by various equipment to produce the desired result(s) of the application program. These statements are classified in several different ways in various FORTRAN texts and manuals; however, our grouping will be format and specification, input/output, dimension, and control statements.

FORMAT AND SPECIFICATION STATEMENTS. The data to be read into the computer from its input form must have some orderly arrangement. In the case of punched cards, these data would have been assigned to predetermined columnar fields in the input. To be sure that the particular data needed in the given application are read from the card, there is a FORMAT statement that specifies how data are to be read.

Inasmuch as in some instances all the data in a card are needed, while in others only certain data are needed (and the balance not used), and that the data characters themselves may be in differing forms such as numbers, letters, etc., different types of FORMAT specifications are provided to permit the flexibility required.

FORMAT statements by themselves do not cause anything to "happen" in the FORTRAN language in the compilation of instructions in the object program and thus are termed nonexecutable. It is when they are used in conjunction with executable statements that they serve to specify "how" the data are to be transmitted, either to or from the computer. It is in this "how" function that they prescribe the pattern (format) of the data to be read, printed, or punched when used with executable statements such as READ, PRINT, or PUNCH. The function of the FORMAT statement will be made clear as the various forms of such statements are described.

The *F specification* indicates that the data to be selected is a floating point number which contains a decimal point. A format statement such as

FØRMAT (F8.2, F5.1, F5.0)

would indicate that the data are to be found in the card (Figure 16–1) in three successive fields. The first field of eight card columns would contain numerical data or blanks with two decimal places (such as 46824.83, 00462.12, or bb001.20). The second field of five card columns would contain numerical data or blanks with a single decimal place (b23.4 or 024.0). The third set of data would follow in card columns 14 through 18 and would contain numerical data or blanks in five columns with no

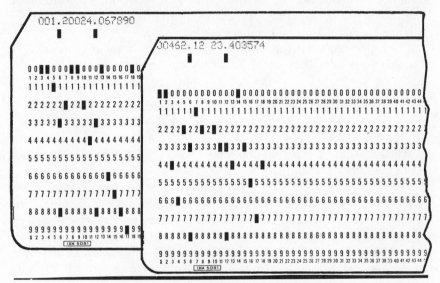

FIG. 16–1. FORTRAN Data Cards.

decimal place (03574 or 67890). It also should be noted that if the data examples above had not been punched with the decimal point, the computer would still have read the data as if the decimal was present. Frequently, on input, an expressed decimal point will override the specification.

In output form the F specification causes numeric internal data to be printed out in floating-point form, but without exponent. Typical output might be 107., −786., 0.007, and 12.4.

The *E specification* is designed to handle real numbers in floating-point mode, utilizing the E exponent to provide input and output of large numbers (usually in scientific and mathematical applications). The scientific notation 3×10^4 ($= 30,000$) is written in FORTRAN as 3.0Eb04. Thus, the E literally means "times 10 to the."

Typical card input under the E specification might be provided by a statement

FØRMAT (E9.2,E12.3)

which would read data into memory from a card—starting with card column 1—such as −4.57E−07 and b3456.296Eb08. The E refers to the format in E notation form, the 9 and 12 in the two statements refers to the number of card columns to be read for each input data, the − or (blank) indicating in the first case that the exponential is negative and positive in the second, and the 07 and 08 to provide the power of the exponential.

In output form the E specification converts internal numerical data from floating-point form to floating point with exponent. Typical output for 123.4, .002, and 16.3 may show them printed as 0.1234Eb03, 0.02E−01, and 0.163Eb02 respectively.

The *I specification* is used to read data in integer form and later output it in this same form. A typical FORTRAN statement such as

FØRMAT (I3, I10, I6)

would read data into memory as from card columns 1 through 19 of a given card containing data such as 321−456734896748315 as 321, −456734896, and 748315.

When this data was output under the I specification it would be printed out in the same exact form.

The *X specification* is used when specific columns of the input card are to be ignored rather than accepting all the consecutive data from card column 1 to some other card column. For instance, data in a card such as 13.4465329674.8 may all be valid data. However, a given application may only be concerned with the first four and last five columns, and it is the X specification which permits the data in columns 5 through 10 to be ignored in a given reading of this card. The format statements to permit this selective reading of data would be

FØRMAT (F4.1,6X, F5.1)

and the data read would be 13.4 and 674.8 with the six columns of data in between ignored.

Data output under the X specification would print this same data out with six print positions open between the two units of data.

The specifications up to this point have all been used in reading and printing numeric data. The *H specification* performs these same functions for alphameric data. This specification was named for Dr. Hollerith, who invented the punched card code, as it can utilize any of the valid Hollerith code characters (numbers, letters, and special characters).

When the H specification is used with a read statement as in

READ 1
1 FØRMAT (20Hbbbbbbbbbbbbbbbbbbbb)

the 20 characters read on the card (columns 1–20) will be placed in memory. If these FORTRAN statements were followed by a statement

PRINT 1

the data read in from the card would be printed out in its exact form. This series of statements might be applicable to reading a heading for a report such as BALANCE SHEET from a card and printing it out on the report.

If an additional statement

READ 1

followed the above, then a series of cards could be read and the data in them listed on a report. This type of application might involve a listing of the names of the employees in a given department.

The H specification may also be used for labeling. As an example

2 FØRMAT (59X,7HJØURNAL)
PRINT 2

will cause the word JOURNAL to be printed after skipping 59 spaces on the form.

Other specifications, including A, D, O, and L specifications, are available in more sophisticated and advanced FORTRAN language developments. Each of these specifications has its own unique advantages. Some increase the capability of the language, while others increase the power by making it easier to perform more complex techniques. It is suggested that if additional information is desired on these that an in-depth FORTRAN text or manual be consulted.

INPUT/OUTPUT STATEMENTS. As might easily be surmised, statements which instruct the equipment in where to get data for the given application and what to do with the data after it has been manipulated in accordance with the instructions provided by the program are termed input and output statements.

There is quite a variety of I/O statements available in the many versions of FORTRAN, depending on the input equipment available and the form in which the data must be provided to be acceptable to each type of equipment. Punched card readers would require data to be punched in card code form; paper tape readers would only read certain paper tape codes (5, 6, 7 or 8 channel); magnetic tape units would only accept a specific size of magnetic tape (7, 8, 9, or 10 track) and given tape codes (binary, binary coded decimal, EBCDIC, or ASCII), etc. Output equipment will also vary with the given installation and might include line printers, punched cards or tape, magnetic disk, drums, tapes, etc.

In this survey of the FORTRAN language only the more commonly used I/O statements, READ, PUNCH, and PRINT will be illustrated. In each case, however, remember that under the section discussing FOR-MAT statements it was explained that the format of the data to be read into or output from the application *must* be specified by some specific FORMAT statement, whose specifications would depend on the type of data provided.

A FORMAT statement with a label (name or location in the program by which this specific statement is known) 10 such as

10 FØRMAT (F3.1, 6XF4.2)

might be either followed or preceded by an I/O statement such as

READ 10, HØURS, RATE

and would indicate to the equipment that a punched card was to be read for hours, and rate in which the hours and tenths of hours worked would be found in the first three columns of the card, and the rate in dollars and cents in card columns 10, 11, 12, and 13.

Similarly, if the statement was

PRINT 10 HØURS, RATE

the data would be printed out on the line printer with hours in the first three print positions and rate in print positions 10, 11, 12, and 13 with six blank print spaces in between the two sets of data.

A statement

PUNCH 10, HØURS, RATE

would cause the data representing hours and rate to be punched in card columns 1, 2, 3 and 10, 11, and 12 of a card by the card punch equipment.

Other specifications in format would, of course, cause the data to be read, printed, or punched in different form and/or in other positions in the respective operation specified.

DIMENSION STATEMENTS.   Just as in the case of FORMAT statements, the DIMENSION statement is a nonexecutable type of statement. The function performed by the DIMENSION statement is to provide the FORTRAN processor program with the information to permit it to allocate locations or positions in the computer's memory for data to be stored.

If only a single subscripted variable is to be stored in memory then a statement

DIMENSIØN RATE (3)

would serve to set aside three positions in memory for a variable named RATE, which might provide the rate per hour data to be used in computing payroll.

In the case of a two-dimensional array or table to store data, the statement

DIMENSIØN TABLE (5,6)

would provide memory storage for five rows of data six columns wide. An example might be a table listing the number of stores in a region or state.

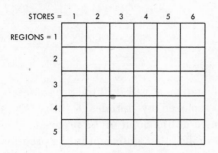

Similarly, variables which have triple subscripts, as in the case of three-dimensional arrays of data, would be described by a statement such as

DIMENSIØN ØPR (5,4,3)

Thus, "operations" for a given firm might be a group of stores located in several states which in turn were classified into regions each encompassing several states.

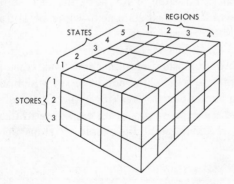

CONTROL STATEMENTS. Most FORTRAN statements are performed sequentially in the order they are found in the program. However, in many programs it is necessary to alter this sequence to achieve the desired results. Statements which have this ability to alter the execution sequence of a program are termed control statements.

Unconditional GO TO Statement. When it is necessary to shift from the normal sequential execution of the program and it is desired to shift to a specific statement number in the program, the unconditional GO TO statement is used as in

$$\cdots$$
$$\cdots$$
$$X = 2$$
$$Y = 4$$
$$\text{GØ TØ 5}$$
$$10 \ X = 3. * Y$$
$$5 \ Y = 4. * X$$
$$\cdots$$
$$\cdots$$

where the GØ TØ 5 statement will shift the program to statement 5, which says Y should be replaced by 4 times X $(4 \times 2 = 8)$. Statement 10 would not be executed at this point in the program. However, it may be a point of entry from some other statement in the program.

Computed GO TO Statement. When it is desired to shift to another point in the program but you don't want to go to a specific statement number, as it depends on the value of some variable as to the exact point to switch to, another form of the GO TO statement is available. This is termed the computed GO TO, as the statement to be switched to depends on the "computed" value of the variable.

In this form of statement

$$\text{GØ TØ (5, 10, 2), K}$$

would indicate that if the value of K was 1, the next statement executed would be 5; if K was 2, the next statement would be 10; and if K was 3, statement 2 would be executed next.

IF Statement. At times it is necessary to change the processing sequence of the program when certain conditions exist. In such an instance, it is necessary to test for the condition(s) which may exist. Thus, the IF statement makes a decision-making type of control available, as in a test to determine if the gross pay of an employee to date has exceeded the $7,800 level, at which point the employer stops deducting for the social security tax.

$$\text{IF (GRØSS} - 7800.) \ 10, 20, 30$$

If the gross pay minus $7,800 is negative (less than zero), statement 10 would be the next statement executed, and social security taxes would be calculated on the current pay amount. If the answer is exactly zero, then statement 20 would be executed next, and only the amount of current pay necessary to bring the gross up to $7,800 would be used in the social security tax calculation. If the answer to GROSS − $7,800 was positive, then statement 30 would be executed next, and no deduction would be made for the social security tax.

Another form of the IF statement is available, called the Logical IF, that has more power and greater capability than the above, but it is not available unless FORTRAN IV is used.

DO STATEMENT. One of the most powerful statements available in the FORTRAN language is the DO statement. In many programs it is necessary that a series of instructions be repeated for a given number of times with some variable being modified each time the instruction is performed. A form of repeating instructions is possible using the IF statement in conjunction with other statements as in

```
      . . .
      . . .
      . . .
   10 J = 0
   20 J = J + 1
   25 ACR (J) = ACR (J) − PMT (J)
   30 IF (200 − J) 40, 40, 20
   40 . . .
      . . .
      . . .
```

in which a list of 200 accounts receivables is updated by deducting payments made on account. In the looping procedure to be followed, it is desired that each account (1 through 200) be updated for any payments to that account. J is first assigned account number 1 in statement 20, and statement 25 proceeds to update account 1. Statement 30 says $200 − J$ is greater than zero, so return to 20 where J becomes 2, and this account is updated. This looping continues until $200 − J = 0$, at which time the program moves on to statement 40.

The looping procedure above required a minimum of three statements (10, 20, and 30) using the IF statement. This same procedure can be performed in a single statement using a DO statement as in

```
      . . .
      . . .
      . . .
   30 DØ 40 J = 1, 200
   40 ACR (J) = ACR (J) − PMT (J)
   50 . . .
      . . .
      . . .
```

in which case statement 40 would be performed for all accounts numbered 1 through 200, after which statement 50 would be performed.

If the increment steps in the numbers above had been desired to be 2, statement 30 would have been written

$$30 \text{ DØ } 40 \text{ J} = 1, 200, 2$$

which would have updated only accounts 1, 3, 5, etc. Some of the specific rules governing the use of DO statements are as follows:

1. In some instances multiple looping is desired, and DO statements may be placed within other DO statements. However, each inner DO loop must be within the range of the outer loop.

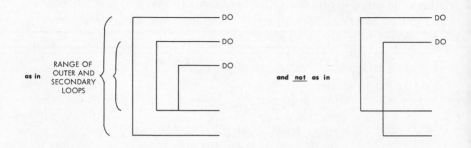

2. Transfers to statements out of the range of a DO loop are permitted, but it is never possible to return to the loop from outside that specified range.

3. When a DO statement is completed and passes control in a normal manner to the next statement, the index, the variable—J in the above illustration—may not necessarily continue to contain the last value assigned to it, and to reuse J it must be reassigned a value. If transfer is out of the range, the value then assigned to J remains. The value of J also remains in the case of an inner loop procedure which is still within the range of a larger loop.

4. No statement within a loop may redefine the value assigned to the index of that loop. In the illustration the J of DØ 40 J = 1, 200 may not be changed until after the loop is completed and the instructions which follow move beyond its range: statement 40.

5. The last statement in the range of a DO statement must be an executable statement. Statements such as DIMENSION and FORMAT and other information statements could not be used as a last statement.

CONTINUE Statement. The CONTINUE statement is not a control statement and causes no action when the object program is executed. It is included at this point, however, as it ratifies one of the rules of the DO statement that the last statement in the range of a DO must not be one that causes a transfer of control. A return to the DO is not possible, except to start at the beginning, when such a transfer is made. The CONTINUE statement may also be used to provide a transfer statement for an IF statement following the completion of a DO loop. An example of a CONTINUE statement would be

```
              . . .
              . . .
              . . .
30  DØ 60 J = 1,200
40  ACR(J) = ACR(J) − PMT(J)
50  IF (ACR(J)) 80,60,60
60  CØNTINUE
70  GØ TØ 100
80  . . .
              . . .
              . . .
```

PAUSE Statement. When it is desired to temporarily halt the computer during an object program execution the statement

PAUSE

is used. After the reason for the halt has been corrected, the depression of the START key on the computer will cause the program to pick back up at the point it left off.

STOP Statement. When it is desired that the program come to a final halt in its execution, a

STØP

statement is used. After a STOP is used, that run of the program is complete, and any continuation of the program is not possible.

END Statement. The END statement is one of the previously discussed nonexecutable statements. However, it provides a signal to the FORTRAN processor that all the statements for a given program have been translated. Such a statement *is required* to be the last card of a FORTRAN program deck.

COMMENT CARD. Usually, it is desired to describe the program, give it a name, note who prepared the program, or make some other comment. This capability is provided by punching a C in column 1 of a card in the program deck and punching the information desired in columns 2 through 72 of that card. The C identifies the card as a comment card, and the data contained is ignored in the translation of the program into machine language. If the program deck of cards is listed out, however, as on an accounting machine or printer, the comment cards will be listed along with the other cards.

Subprogram

In instances where it is necessary to perform a given set of calculations a number of times in a program or to perform some standard calculations involving arithmetic functions, FORTRAN permits the use of two subprogram techniques.

THE FUNCTION. First a given set of mathematical functions is available as an integral part of the FORTRAN compiler. These vary somewhat with the compiler but usually include the following:

Type of Function	FORTRAN Name
Natural logarithm	LØGF
Trigonometric sine	SINF
Trigonometric cosine	CØSF
Exponential	EXPF
Square root	SQRTF
Arctangent	ATANF
Absolute value	ABSF

Note that function names are always six or less alphabetical or numerical characters in length (no special characters), always start with a letter which must be an X if the value of the function is an integer. (These restrictions apply specifically to FORTRAN II.) In many instances, programmers with ingenuity have developed additional functions which would follow the basic idea and patterns of those "built-in" functions listed above.

The function subprogram is used when a particular mathematical function cannot be defined as a single arithmetic statement. When such a calculation is performed, only a single value is provided to the main program.

An example of the use of these functions would be in solving an equation such as

$$X = Y + \sqrt{C + D}$$

which would be written in FORTRAN as

$$X = Y + SQRTF (C + D)$$

with

$$FUNCTIØN \; SQRTF \; (C + D)$$

being used to perform the calculation after both C and D had been defined.

THE SUBROUTINE. Subroutine subprograms are usually used where one or more programs are part of a single, more comprehensive program or where more than one value has to be provided to the main program. These programs would usually be prewritten and found in a program library and would be predefined as to limits, variables, etc., applicable to each subroutine program, or they can be (and commonly are) written by the individual programmer.

To cause an exit from the main program to the given subroutine, the FORTRAN statement CALL would be used as in

CALL MEAN

which would cause the program to switch to the subroutine program named MEAN. This program would then be executed until it reached a statement at the end of the subroutine where the FORTRAN statement

RETURN

would then cause the main program to be continued at the point where it had transferred to the subroutine MEAN.

Various levels of subroutines may CALL in other subroutines which, in turn, may CALL in other subroutines before returning to the main program.

FORTRAN PROGRAM TO PREPARE A DAILY CASH REPORT [1]

The following data relate to the daily transactions of the Medina Federal Savings and Loan Association:

RMORT = Receipts on mortgage loans.
RSAV   = Receipts on savings accounts.
COUT   = Cash paid out.
CHAND = Cash on hand at end of day.
CHECK = Checks on hand at end of day.
FUND   = A permanent cash fund amount which is required to begin each day's operation. If this amount is not in the fund, a check must be drawn and cashed to provide this amount.
RECON = A reconciliation to check for cash overage or shortage for the day.
RTOT   = Total of fund and receipts.
OTOT   = Total of on hand and cash paid out.
REIMB = Reimbursement of fund from cashing check.
DEPOS = Deposit.

Required

FORTRAN program to provide: (1) a reconciliation to determine cash overage or shortage; (2) a breakdown of the amount of cash and checks on hand at the end of the day; (3) a calculation to show any amount needed to reimburse the fund if fund is lower than requirements; and (4) the total amount of cash and checks available for deposit.

Flowchart

The logical flowchart of a procedure which will process the data given in this problem to produce the output required is illustrated in Figure 16–2.

---

[1] Adapted from *A FORTRAN Primer with Business Administration Exercises* (C20–1605 [White Plains, N.Y.: International Business Machines Corporation: 1964]), pp. 40, 41, 110.

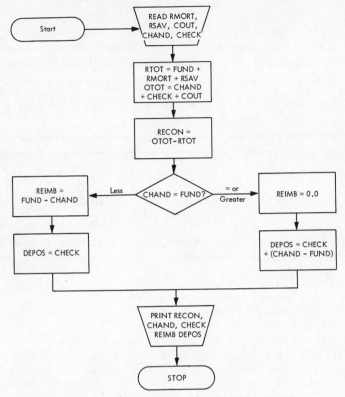

FIG. 16–2.   **Flowchart for Daily Cash Report.**

The FORTRAN Program

Line[2]

```
 1     C     DAILY CASH REPORT
 2     C     C SPROWLS
 3     C     FORTRAN II (1620)
 4    10     FORMAT(5F8.2)
 5           FUND = 40000.00
 6           READ 10,RMORT,RSAV,COUT,CHAND,CHECK
 7           RTOT = FUND + RMORT + RSAV
 8           OTOT = CHAND + CHECK + COUT
 9           RECON = OTOT − RTOT
10           IF(CHAND − FUND) 11,12,12
11    11     REIMB = FUND − CHAND
12           DEPOS = CHECK
13           GO TO 13
14    12     REIMB = 0.0
15           DEPOS = CHECK + (CHAND − FUND)
16    13     PRINT 14,RECON
17    14     FORMAT(F10.2,26H OVERAGE(+) OR SHORTAGE(−))
18           PRINT 15,CHAND,CHECK
19    15     FORMAT(F10.2,13H CASH ON HAND,F10.2,15H CHECKS ON HAND)
20           PRINT 16,REIMB,DEPOS
21    16     FORMAT(F10.2,19H TO REIMBURSE FUND,F10.2,12H FOR DEPOSIT)
22           STOP
23           END
```

[2] The line numbers do not appear in the program or on the cards but are used here for ease of reference in the description which follows.

Description of the Program.

Line 1. A comment card for the name of the procedure.

Line 2. A comment card showing the person preparing the program.

Line 3. A comment card indicating the language and computer used.

Line 4. Statement numbered 10 indicates that the format of the input card is 5 floating-point numbers, each of which takes up 8 columns on the card. Each of these numbers consists of 5 digits to the left of the decimal point, the decimal point, and 2 digits to the right of the decimal point (5 dollar and 2 cents positions maximum). The first number will be in card columns 1 through 8, the second in columns 9 through 16, and so on through column 40.

Line 5. FUND is defined as $40,000.

Line 6. A READ statement indicating that cards will be provided in the FORMAT of statement 10 (line 4) with data for receipts on mortgage loans, receipts on savings accounts, cash paid out, and cash on hand at the end of the day.

Line 7. RTOT is defined as the sum of the fund, the receipts on mortgage loans, and the receipts on savings accounts.

Line 8. OTOT is defined as the sum of cash on hand and cash paid out.

Line 9. RECON is defined as OTOT (Line 8) less RTOT (Line 7).

Line 10. An IF statement which says that if the cash on hand at the end of the day minus the $40,000 required in the FUND is: (1) less than zero—a negative amount—then the next statement is line 11 or (2) exactly zero or (3) greater than zero then the next statement is line 12.

Line 11. If line 10 was negative, this statement (11) calculates the amount required to reimburse the FUND.

Line 12. The amount to be deposited can only be the checks received if the FUND needs reimbursement in line 11.

Line 13. This is a GO TO statement which says the next program step is to be found in statement 13 which is found later in the program.

Line 14. Statement 12 was to be the next step if the FUND did not need reimbursement, so REIMB is set to 0.0.

Line 15. The amount to be deposited if the FUND is satisfactory is the sum of the checks on hand and the cash on hand above the FUND amount.

Line 16. Statement 13 is a PRINT command to show amount of cash overage or shortage determined by the reconciliation. The format of the printed data is to follow that required by statement 14.

Line 17. Statement 14 indicates the format of some operation (PRINT in line 16) to be a floating-point amount of 10 columns with 2 decimal places followed by 26 positions of alphameric data containing OVERAGE (+) or SHORTAGE (−).

Line 18. A PRINT command which says use format statement 15 to print cash and checks on hand at the end of the day.

Line 19. The format specified by this statement 15 is to be a floating-point number of 10 columns, 2 of which are decimal places, 13 positions of alphameric data containing the words CASH ON HAND, another 10-column (2 decimal places) floating-point number, and 15 positions of alphameric data containing the words CHECKS ON HAND.

Line 20. Another PRINT command which will utilize statement 16 for a format to print data regarding amounts to reimburse the fund and to be deposited in the bank.

Line 21. This format statement is a 10-column floating-point number (2 decimal places) followed by 19 positions of alphameric data, TO RE-IMBURSE, and a second 10-column floating-point number (2 decimal places) followed by 12 positions of alphamerica data, FOR DEPOSIT.

Line 22. STOP indicates a permanent halt.

Line 23. END indicates to the FORTRAN processor that this completes the translation to machine language of the FORTRAN statements in this program.

Typical Output

A set of data which would represent typical output (based on specific given data) of the FORTRAN program illustrated is shown in Figure 16–3.

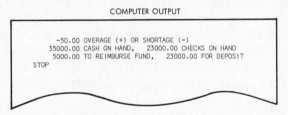

COMPUTER OUTPUT

```
     -50.00 OVERAGE (+) OR SHORTAGE (-)
  35000.00 CASH ON HAND,    23000.00 CHECKS ON HAND
   5000.00 TO REIMBURSE FUND,    23000.00 FOR DEPOSIT
STOP
```

FIG. 16–3.   Daily Cash Report.

ANNOTATED BIBLIOGRAPHY

ANDERSON, DECIMA M. *Basic Computer Programming*. New York: Appleton-Century-Crofts, 1964.

A basic approach to programming using FORTRAN and the IBM 1620 Computer.

———. *Computer Programming FORTRAN IV*. New York: Appleton-Century-Crofts, 1964.

A text for beginning programmers learning the FORTRAN IV language.

COLMAN, HARRY L., and SMALLWOOD, CLARENCE. *Computer Language.* New York: McGraw-Hill Book Co., 1962.

An autoinstructional introduction to FORTRAN.

DIMITRY, DONALD, and MOTT, THOMAS, JR. *Introduction to FORTRAN IV Programming.* New York: Holt, Rinehart & Winston, Inc., 1966.

An elementary, though detailed, approach to learning the FORTRAN IV language.

HARRIS, L. DALE. *FORTRAN Programming (II and IV).* Columbus, Ohio: Charles E. Merrill Books, Inc., 1964.

Though primary attention is given to FORTRAN II programming, the added features and capabilities of FORTRAN IV are also presented for those who desire to use it.

HARTKEMEIER, HARRY P. *FORTRAN Programming of Electronic Computer.* Columbus, Ohio: Charles E. Merrill Books, Inc., 1966.

An introduction to FORTRAN programming and the processing of such programs on the IBM 1620 Computer.

INTERNATIONAL BUSINESS MACHINES CORPORATION. *FORTRAN.* A General Information Manual, F28–8053. White Plains, N.Y., 1961.

A discussion of FORTRAN, the language format, its use, and FORTRAN processor requirements.

LEDLEY, ROBERT STEVEN. *FORTRAN IV Programming.* New York: McGraw-Hill Book Co., 1966.

Though this book is designed to serve as an elementary text for beginners, it is a rather complete and exhaustive treatment of the language.

McCRACKEN, DANIEL D. *A Guide to FORTRAN Programming.* New York: John Wiley & Sons, Inc., 1961.

A concise presentation of the essentials of FORTRAN programming.

———. *A Guide to FORTRAN IV Programming.* New York: John Wiley & Sons, Inc., 1965.

Fundamentals of FORTRAN IV with 15 case illustrations of its application.

OSWALD, HENRY. "FORTRAN—Towards a 'Universal' Language," *Data Processing Yearbook 1965* (ed. EDITH HARWITH GOODMAN), pp. 89–98. Detroit: American Data Processing, Inc., 1964.

The adaptability of the programming language, FORTRAN, to the solving of business problems is discussed. An examination is made of the nature of both its language and its processor. The evolution of FORTRAN is described, its present applications noted, and its future potential explored.

QUESTIONS

1. Explain the function performed by a FORTRAN compiler. What are the steps that take place in the compilation and processing procedure for a given problem?
2. Briefly describe the composition of the basic FORTRAN alphabet.

3. What are the two major kinds of numbers used in the FORTRAN language? Describe or define these.

4. Name and describe the major elements of the FORTRAN language.

5. List examples of five of each of the following:
    a) Fixed-point constants.
    b) Fixed-point variables.
    c) Floating-point constants.
    d) Floating-point variables.

6. Describe what is meant by arrays of 1, 2, or 3 dimensions.

7. What is an arithmetic statement? Describe its use.

8. List the arithmetic or operational expressions used in FORTRAN. Describe their function.

9. Describe the hierarchical assignment of processing steps involving an arithmetic expression containing several or all of the operational expressions.

10. Name and briefly describe the four groups of statements as they are classified in this text.

11. Name and describe the two types of subprograms.

CHAPTER 17

COBOL Programming

Language

THE United States government has always been the largest user of computers and computer technology. There are numerous different manufacturers of computers, and each manufacturer produces different sizes and models with different characteristics and capacities. The government uses a wide variety of this equipment.

The need to develop program languages which would be equally applicable to the equipment produced by both a given manufacturer and that produced by all manufacturers became acute as time went on. This resulted in a proposal by the Department of Defense in 1958 that a committee of manufacturer and user representatives be organized to see what could be done to develop a language which would be acceptable to most equipment. The language produced by this committee was to be used in the processing of business data. This language became known as COBOL, an acronym for *Common Business Orientated Language*.

COBOL

Like the English language, COBOL is built up from its smallest possible units, a set of characters (letters, numbers, punctuation marks, etc.). These characters are used to form meaningful words by following certain rules, just as in English we find different types of words, such as nouns, verbs, conjunctions, etc. These types of words are combined, following the rules of grammar, to form expressions, statements, sentences, and paragraphs. Also, as in the English language, the different types of words in the COBOL language are combined, using COBOL's rules of grammar, into statements, sentences, etc.

All computers are constructed so that certain sets of characters are meaningful to their operation. A set of such characters is referred to as a "computer character set." Because of the physical characteristics of each type of computer, the character sets for different types of computers may not be identical. Of course, all programs written in COBOL for a given computer must contain only characters from that machine's character set.

Names

Any language must contain words which stand as symbols for things. In English they are known as "names" or "nouns." COBOL also employs names which the coder uses to refer to things he is handling in his program. In ordinary language we do not usually have to distinguish consciously between the name of an object and the object itself, but this is very important in COBOL. A coder must always keep in mind that when he gives an item of data a name and then refers to that item by writing the equivalent of its name in the program, he is referring to the data, not to the name. Thus a name can be said to represent the value of the associated data item.

The portion of this chapter which follows will introduce the reader to COBOL. There are many more intricacies to writing a successful COBOL program than are explained here. The object here is only to give the reader a feeling for what the COBOL programming language is about.

There are four general categories of names in COBOL. They are data-names, procedure-names, condition-names, and special-names.

Data-Names

Data-names are names given to the data used in a program. As the reader will see, data-names usually will represent a number of values during the course of a program. For example, if a program is written to compute the payroll for a business firm, the coder might name one item of data MAN-NUMBER. Then, as the payroll is processed, the data-name MAN-NUMBER refers to the man number of the man whose pay is currently being computed.

Procedure-Names

Procedure-names are names assigned to individual portions of a program so that one procedure statement can refer to another by its individual procedure-name.

Condition-Names

A condition-name is a name which is assigned to denote one of a number of values which may be assumed by an item of data. For example, suppose a dealer in tires identified each of his tire sizes in inventory by number. The number of tires on hand for any item of inventory will vary. Therefore, the tire size 850 × 14 will constitute a condition-name whose value will change from time to time.

Special-Names

Special-names are names which may be assigned by the coder to various physical parts of a computer. For example, one card punch unit might be named MASTER, while another punch unit might be named DETAIL. Then at any time the programmer refers to either device he uses the special names.

Rules for Forming Names

In COBOL, names may be formed by combining any of the following characters: the letters A through Z, the numerals 0 through 9, and the hyphen. In addition the following rules must be followed.

1. Names must not contain blanks.
2. They may contain from 1 to 30 characters.
3. They may neither begin nor end with a hyphen. However, hyphens may be used freely elsewhere in the name.
4. Data-names, condition-names, and special-names must contain at least one alphabetic character. Procedure-names may consist exclusively of numerals if the coder so desires.

CONSTANTS. The occasion often arises for data to have a fixed value never to be modified in a given program. Such a fixed value which never changes during the execution of a program is called a constant. For example, suppose a program were written to handle the sales of a wholesale house. Assume that for certain types of items, a 10 percent tax must always be added. Since this value of 10 percent never varies, it would be convenient to be able to write it directly at the time the program is written, rather than having to enter it as data every time a sale of this type of item is made.

Program Divisions

A COBOL program is made up of four divisions, the Identification Division, the Environment Division, the Data Division, and the Procedure Division.

IDENTIFICATION DIVISION. This division is used to identify or label the program and to provide any other such pertinent information required. This division may run from one to seven paragraphs long. Each paragraph can be identified in the following manner:

Program-ID.—Program-Name.
Author.—Author-Name.
Installation.—Any sentence or group of sentences.
Data-Written.—Any sentence or group of sentences.
Data-Compiled.—Any sentence or group of sentences.
Security.—Any sentence or group of sentences.
Remarks.—Any sentence or group of sentences.

Only the Program-ID paragraph is required, and it must appear in the first paragraph of the program. The use of the other identification paragraphs is optional. The program-name should be used in referring to the source program, the object program, and all associated documentation.

ENVIRONMENT DIVISION. This division is organized into two main sections—the CONFIGURATION SECTION and the INPUT-OUTPUT SECTION. The names of each of these main sections are fixed and must always be given at the beginning of their respective sections. The names of the paragraphs following each section are also fixed, and their names must also be given at the beginning of any paragraph used.

The overall structure of the ENVIRONMENT DIVISION of the source program is shown below. Note the periods at the end of the division statement, the section statements, and the paragraph headings. It is important that these always be there.

```
ENVIRONMENT DIVISION.
   CONFIGURATION SECTION.
      SOURCE-COMPUTER. computer-name.
      OBJECT-COMPUTER. computer-name.
      SPECIAL NAMES. device-name . . . switch-name.
   INPUT-OUTPUT SECTION.
      FILE CONTROL. SELECT. . . .
      I/O-CONTROL. APPLY. . . . .
```

In the CONFIGURATION SECTION, the coder writes the overall specifications for a particular computer. This section is composed of three paragraphs: the SOURCE-COMPUTER paragraph, which contains a description of the computer for which the program was written; the OBJECT-COMPUTER paragraph which describes the computer which will actually execute the object program (compiled program); and the SPECIAL-NAMES paragraph, which equates the hardware names that are recognizable by the compiler to the names the coder wishes to use in writing the source program.

The INPUT-OUTPUT SECTION consists of two paragraphs. The FILE CONTROL paragraph usually identifies and describes at least two files: the input file and the output file. It is not feasible to read data from a COBOL file, process it, and return it to its source. Instead, most procedures call for reading data from one or several files, processing it, and writing in one or more new files.

For example: "SELECT TIME-TICKET FILE, ASSIGN TO GO." This informs the computer that a file named TIME-TICKET FILE, is to be processed through a data input unit, probably a card reader, called GO.

The command "SELECT TIME EXTENDED-PAYROLL-FILE, AS-SIGN TO SO" informs the computer than the processed payroll data should be assigned to the computer unit named SO, which in this case may be assumed to be a magnetic tape unit.

The I/O CONTROL paragraph allows the coder to specify what input-output techniques will be established.

The ENVIRONMENT DIVISION is the portion of a COBOL program that would necessarily be changed when moving the program from one computer to another.

DATA DIVISION. To quote from Donald L. Roun:

The purpose of the DATA DIVISION is to clearly and meticulously define the input and output as well as any information that is to be stored within the computer for future use.

Through the DATA DIVISION we communicate with the computer in regard to the following:

1. The output, or outputs, of the computer program.
2. The input, or inputs, to the computer program.
3. The items of information to be stored within the computer for later use.

To communicate with the computer we must first very carefully identify each input and output record with a specific name. Secondly, we must specifically designate the number of characters that represent each input and output record. Finally, we must identify each item of information in a record by the precise name and again indicate the number of characters which represent it.[1]

The DATA DIVISION is composed of three sections. These are:

FILE SECTION.
WORKING-STORAGE SECTION.
CONSTANT SECTION.

If any of the sections are not required in the particular program being written, they may be omitted.

File Section. A file can be thought of as the total input or output of a computer of a particular type. In the illustration used in the ENVIRONMENT DIVISION, the time tickets constituted one file, while the updated payroll information constituted another file. Each file must have a name, and these two files were called TIME-TICKET FILE and EXTENDED-PAYROLL FILE. Any names are suitable as long as they conform to the COBOL rules for writing names.

Descriptions of the files to be used will follow the FILE SECTION heading and will be indented four spaces on the program worksheet and will be preceded by FD (File Description). The File Description will

---

[1] From Donald L. Roun, *An Introduction to COBOL Computer Programming for Accounting and Business Analysis* (Belmont, Calif.: Dickinson Publishing Co., Inc., 1966). Reprinted by permission of the publisher.

generally include a name for the file, such as described above; a description of the input to the file, such as CARD-IN; a description of the size of each individual record in the file, i.e. if a standard punched card was being used it would be RECORD CONTAINS 80 CHARACTERS; and, if the input or output to the computer is on magnetic tape, it is desirable to place a name on the tape for control purposes. If the file record is a punched card or paper tape, the statement should be made LABEL RECORDS ARE OMITTED. On a program work sheet, the description of the TIME-TICKET FILE would be as follows:

```
FD  TIME-TICKET,
    DATA RECORD IS CARD-IN,
    RECORD CONTAINS 80 CHARACTERS,
    LABEL RECORDS ARE OMITTED.
```

The nature of the data on each record, described as CARD-IN in the previous example, must all be carefully described. The computer needs to know the name of the items; whether the item will consist of numbers, letters, or a combination of numbers and letters; and the number of characters represented by the item.

Since a description of the CARD-IN record would be a subsection of the description of the TIME-TICKET FILE, the identification of the CARD-IN file is preceded by 01, while its description is preceded by 02.

```
01  CARD-IN.
    02 THIS-WEEKS-PAY PICTURE 9999.
    02 FILLER PICTURE X.
    02 WITHHOLDING PICTURE 999.
    02 FILLER PICTURE (76).
```

Note the position of the periods, once again, at the end of each sequence of information. They are essential to communicate with the computer.

The word FILLER is used only to identify a space or a group of spaces. Donald Roun says:

The output of the computer program in the DATA DIVISION is described in identically the same fashion as the input files and records that we have just discussed. *In each case the file, record, and each item of information within the record must be given a distinct name so that it may be specifically identified.* As you will note, each of the output files has a specific purpose and is designed to satisfy that need; yet basically, the form is the same as our description of the input files.[2]

---

[2] *Ibid.*, p. 3-1.

In the process of describing files and records, it often becomes necessary to also describe their format. Referring to the previous illustrations of the CARD-IN record you will note the presence of picture clauses.

A *picture* clause is used to indicate the size of an item, its *class*, the presence or absence of an operational sign and/or an assumed decimal point. It also provides additional information which would otherwise have to be specified in other Record Description clauses. The word *picture* with the identifying numbers and symbols will follow each file description entry.

The following characters are typical of those which may appear in a *picture* clause:

Character	Meaning and Use
9	A 9 indicates that the character position will always contain a numeric character.
V	A *V* indicates the position of an assumed decimal point. Since a numeric item cannot contain any character other than numerals and an operational sign, the actual decimal point cannot appear. Therefore, an assumed decimal point is used to provide the processor with the information concerning the alignment of items involved in computation.
S	The character *S* is equivalent in meaning and use to the sign clause, it indicates the presence of an operational sign. If used, it must always be written as the leftmost character of the *picture*.
A	The character *A*, when used in a picture, indicates that the character position will always contain either a letter or a space.
X	The character *X*, when appearing in a *picture*, indicates that the character position may contain any character in the computer's character set.
Z	The character *Z* specifies zero suppression of the indicated characters. Zero suppression is the process of replacing unwanted zeros, to the left of significant digits, by blanks so they will not be printed.
$	The single dollar sign, like the *S* character above, is placed in the leftmost position of a *picture*, and specifies that a dollar sign character is to be placed in that position in the data. The use of several $ signs at the left of a *picture* provides a floating $ symbol which will appear to the left of the first significant digit.
	This character represents an actual decimal point. When used to describe a character position:
	1. The data being edited is aligned by decimal point.
	2. An actual decimal point will appear in the indicated character position.

Following is an example of how different pictures might look utilizing the symbols just given:

If Picture Is:	And the Charac- ters in the Item Are:	Then the Item Will be Used in Procedures as:	And its Class Will Be:
99999	12345	12345	NUMERIC
999V99	12345	123.45	NUMERIC
S999V99	−12345	−123.45	NUMERIC
XXXXX	123AB	123AB	ALPHANUMERIC
AAAAA	ABCDE	ABCDE	ALPHABETIC
999X99	123.45	123.45	ALPHANUMERIC
999XX	123AB	123AB	ALPHANUMERIC

Working–Storage Section. The WORKING–STORAGE SECTION is used to describe areas of storage where intermediate results and other items are stored temporarily. If it is desired to have the computer print out information from what has been in storage, the format for the print-out must be indicated in the same way the CARD-IN record was described. The records which are to be retained in storage must also be described in the same way. Each Record Description entry begins with the special level number 77.

Constant Section. This section is used to describe constants which will be used in the PROCEDURE DIVISION. It always begins with a CONSTANT SECTION heading.

In a payroll situation, following the examples which have been previously used, the CONSTANT SECTION would probably contain the following tax withholding information because the associated constant rates would apply to all employees.

77 FED-HOLDING, PICTURE V999, VALUE IS .044.
77 STATE-WITHHOLD, PICTURE V99, VALUE IS .01.

PROCEDURE DIVISION. The first three sections of a COBOL program, the IDENTIFICATION DIVISION, the ENVIRONMENT DIVISION, and the DATA DIVISION are all describing the program, the equipment or the data, and procedures which are going to be used in a particular program. It is not until one gets to the PROCEDURE DIVISION that one is actually developing coded steps. The output of this division is what creates a program which will direct the activities of a computer.

In this division the coder specifies what he wants to do with the data described in the DATA DIVISION. His ideas are expressed in terms of meaningful English words, sentences, and paragraphs. Every COBOL sentence must end with a period. The coder will naturally require the use of some action verbs. The COBOL verbs form the basis of the PROCEDURE DIVISION of a source program. These verbs fall into two main categories, program verbs and processor verbs. The former denotes the data processing steps the object program is to perform while the latter directs the processor.

The COBOL verbs are listed below:

PROGRAM VERBS

Input/Output	OPEN
	READ
	WRITE
	CLOSE
	ACCEPT
	DISPLAY
Data Manipulation	MOVE
	EXAMINE
Arithmetic	ADD
	SUBTRACT
	MULTIPLY
	DIVIDE
	COMPUTE
Sequence Control	GO TO
	ALTER
	PERFORM
	STOP

PROCESSOR VERBS

ENTER
EXIT
NOTE

Input-Output Verbs. The open verb is used to initiate the processing of one or more input and/or output files. At least one of the two optional clauses (*input or output*) must be written. An *open* statement can name just one file or it can name all of the files to be processed by the program. In other words, the coder can open all the files at one time, if desired, or he can open one or more at a time according to the requirements of the program. In any case, an *open* statement must be executed for a given file before a *read* or *write* statement pertaining to that file can be executed. Some examples of the use of the *open* verb are:

OPEN INPUT BACK-ORDERS
OPEN OUTPUT STATISTICS

The function of the *read* verb is to get the next record from an input file and make it available for processing.

The *write* verb is used to release a record for its insertion into an output file. Examples follow:

WRITE INVOICE
WRITE MASTER-OUT FROM WORK-AREA
WRITE VOLUME FROM TABLE

Data Manipulation Verbs. The movement of data from one place to another within the computer and the inspection of data are implicit in the functioning of several of the COBOL verbs. The two main data manipulation verbs are *move* and *examine*. The *move* verb has as its primary function the transmission of data from one area to another. *Examine* involves the inspection of data within the computer, with or without movement.

However, other verbs may perform the manipulation function incidental to their main purpose. For example, execution of the *compute* verb can involve editing of, as well as movement of, the result.

The Arithmetic Verbs. COBOL also provides a verb corresponding to each of the four basic arithmetic operations: *add, subtract, multiply* and *divide*. A fifth arithmetic verb, *compute*, is provided to permit the coder to include arithmetic expressions in his source program. Arithmetic operations may also be performed by the use of $+$, $-$, $*$, and/for addition, subtraction, multiplication, and division respectively.

The Sequence Control Verbs. Four of the verbs in COBOL are designed to specify the sequence in which the various source program procedures are to be executed. These verbs are referred to as the sequence *control verbs:* they are *go to, alter, perform,* and *stop.* Unless one of these verbs is encountered, the statements, sentences, and paragraphs of the PROCEDURE DIVISION of a source program are executed one after another in the order of their appearance. The verbs *go to* and *perform* are used to interrupt the normal execution sequence and to transfer control to some other point in the program. The other two verbs are supplementary—*alter* provides a means of modifying *go to* statements and *stop* is used to halt execution of the program.

Processor Verbs. Processor verbs are those verbs which only serve to direct the processor in its work. The verb *enter* makes it possible to utilize existing routines written in a language other than COBOL. An example would be ENTER AUTOCODER, which would then be followed by a program written in Autocoder language. To return to the COBOL program the same verb would be used in ENTER COBOL. The verb *exit* is required following a *perform* which has conditional action in its statement and *note* is used, as it connotes, to make a note or record for information only.

The independence of the procedure and data divisions leads to a major advantage of COBOL. With rather minor changes a COBOL source program can be compiled for running on any computer for which a COBOL processor exists. The data division does depend somewhat on the object machine to take account of such machine characteristics as variable versus fixed word length format, the handling of signs, and tape formats. It usually turns out, however, that changing the data division is far less work than rewriting the whole program, and the relative machine independence is in fact achieved.

COBOL PROGRAMMING ILLUSTRATED

In order for COBOL to be compatible with all makes and models of computers, it is necessary that separate compiler programs be written for each make and model of machine. The significance of these compiler programs was explained in Chapter 15. It should be remembered, however, that every computer has its own unique physical characteristics. The function of these compiler programs is to take a common programming language and cause it to be translated by a particular machine in such a way that the output of this machine will be consistent with the output of all other makes and models of computers.

The writing of a program in COBOL is not as simple as the above statement might make it appear, because all COBOL compilers are not written under the assumption that all COBOL programs are going to be written in the same way. Carl H. Reynolds says:

The professional designers and implementors of systems software are notoriously loath to standardize. For one thing, they believe that standards limit the degree to which they can exercise their creative skills. Also, the technology of programming is changing so rapidly that professionals are always finding a better way to do things.[3]

In short, *there is no absolutely correct way to write a program in COBOL.* In a general way, however, one can say that the programs are written in the same way, but when it comes to specifics—these are going to be determined by the way in which the compiler is written.

Payroll Program

This first example of a COBOL program is a complete but simple program which will be illustrative of most of the many of the points made in the first part of this Chapter.

THE PROBLEM. Phillip Thompson, certified public accountant, has three employees. The weekly payroll is $850. Assumptions: (1) the employer is responsible for remitting 8.8 percent quarterly to the federal government for federal insurance contributions, 4.4 percent being deducted from employees' salaries and 4.4 percent representing the employer's contribution; (2) the employer is responsible for remitting a total of 2.7 percent quarterly to the state for unemployment and disability insurance, and .4 percent to the federal government; and (3) income tax withholdings amount to $210.

---

[3] Carl H. Reynolds, "Software Standards," *Data Processing Magazine*, March, 1967, p. 26.

REQUIRED. Prepare a program to compute the amount of money Mr. Thompson must pay his employees this week.

It should be noted that the program is written on work-sheet paper expressly designed for the purpose (See Figure 17–1). The two control cards at the beginning are necessary parts of the program at this installation. The first card, which contains $IBJOB, instructs the computer that that which follows is a new job, and the second card, containing $IBCBC, is saying that the new job is in COBOL language.

A series of numbers is used to identify each of the steps on the program sheet. The first three numbers of the series, at the top of the first page, indicates the page number, and the second set of three numbers indicates the line number on that page. Thus the first 010010 represents page 10, line 10. As you will note, both the page and line numbers progress in stages of 10. This is to permit the insertion of other program steps when additions and other changes are required. The four principal divisions of the program are the IDENTIFICATION DIVISION (010010), the ENVIRONMENT DIVISION (010080), the DATA DIVISION (010160), and the PROCEDURE DIVISION (020170).

The IDENTIFICATION DIVISION is used to identify the program and what is being done. In this case, the program is identified in line (010020) as a PAYROLL PROBLEM. It is further identified in the following lines by author, installation, date written, date compiled, security, and remarks. The PROGRAM-ID (010020) is the only entry which is essential, however.

The ENVIRONMENT DIVISION (010080) is used to identify the specific characteristics of the computer which is being used. The two sections in this division which must always be specifically identified in the program are the CONFIGURATION SECTION (010090) and the INPUT-OUTPUT SECTION (010120). The CONFIGURATION SECTION identifies the SOURCE-COMPUTER as well as the OBJECT-COMPUTER. The SOURCE-COMPUTER (010100), compiles the source program into machine language, while the OBJECT-COMPUTER (010110) is the computer upon which the object program (or machine language program), will be run. Each computer in this case is an IBM 7044. The INPUT-OUTPUT SECTION (010120) consists of a single paragraph, the FILE CONTROL (010130). In this problem the two files described in the FILE CONTROL paragraph are the input and output files (010140) and (010150). These describe where the data to be processed are going to come from, and where the data are to be placed after being processed. IN applies to the name which has been given to the input device, i.e., card reader, and OU identifies the output device. The ENVIRONMENT DIVISION of the COBOL program is the portion which will normally be changed when the program is adapted from one computer to another.

The DATA DIVISION (010160) is composed of three sections, any of which may be omitted if the program has no need of them. The three sections consist entirely of entries and are the FILE SECTION (010170), the WORKING-STORAGE SECTION (020020), and the CONSTANT SECTION (020130).

The FILE SECTION describes the files which are mentioned in the FILE-CONTROL section. A file description entry is always preceded by FD. This can be noted on lines (010180) and (010270). It is essential to identify each input and output record or file by a specific name, i.e., PAYROLL-FILE (010180) and OUT-FILE (010270), and indicate the number of characters which represent it. Each item of information within a file, i.e., CARD-IN (010220), must also be given a name and the number of digits which it will take to represent it. In this case, a description of the PAYROLL-FILE is contained on cards, and they are named CARD-IN. The way in which the data are contained on the cards is described on lines (010230) to (010260). Total pay is indicated in the first three columns on the card, there is a space, and then the amounts withheld are contained in the next three columns. The rest of the card is blank. When an IBM 7044 is used, it is assumed that a punched card has 84 columns because the logical records in the 7044 are grouped in six-bit blocks.

Where either the input or the output files are not on magnetic tape the statement LABEL RECORDS ARE OMITTED, line (010190) is included.

The WORKING-STORAGE SECTION (020020) is used to describe areas of storage where intermediate results are temporarily stored. In this example, lines (020030 to 020060) describe the size of the FICA payments, and the size of the contributions payable to the state, as well as the net amount of the payroll and the total amount of income tax withholdings. If there is to be a print-out from WORKING-STORAGE, it must be remembered, in this particular installation the print-out will be 132 characters wide. What is to be done with each of the 132 characters must be described here. The width of the print-out is determined by the type of printing equipment available.

The CONSTANT SECTION (020130) describes constants which will be used in the PROCEDURE DIVISION. In this case, the FICA contributions as well as the employer's contributions for Unemployment Insurance would be regarded as constants. The rate of tax in both instances would remain the same.

The PROCEDURE DIVISION (020170) develops the coded procedural steps in the program. It specifies what is necessary to be done with the data in the DATA DIVISION. Note the important position of the action verbs in each of the statements. They are START, OPEN, READ, COMPUTE, MOVE, WRITE, CLOSE, and STOP. The statements in this

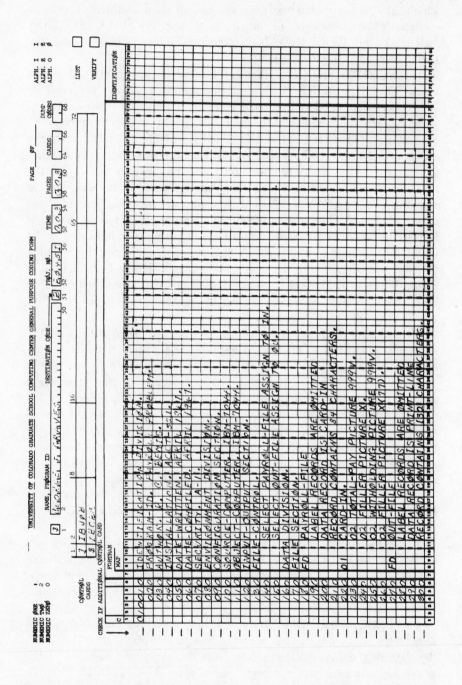

NUMERIC ONE 1
NUMERIC TWO 2
NUMERIC ZERO 0

ALPH. I I
ALPH. Z Z
ALPH. O O

NAME, PROGRAM ID: R. C. Leemig

CONTROL CARDS
1 2 IBJOB
8 IECC

CHECK IF ADDITIONAL CONTROL CARD

DESTINATION CODE

PROJ. NO. 62451   TIME 203   PAGES 303   CARDS   DUMP CODES

LIST   VERIFY

IDENTIFICATION

```
010  IDENTIFICATION DIVISION.
020  PROGRAM-ID. PAYROLL PROBLEM.
030  AUTHOR. R. C. LEEMIG.
040  INSTALLATION. ACCT-501.
050  DATE-WRITTEN. APRIL 1947.
060  DATE-COMPILED. APRIL 1947.
070  SECURITY. A-11.
080  ENVIRONMENT DIVISION.
090  CONFIGURATION SECTION.
100  SOURCE-COMPUTER. IBM-7044.
110  OBJECT-COMPUTER. IBM-7044.
120  INPUT-OUTPUT SECTION.
130  FILE-CONTROL.
140    SELECT PAYROLL-FILE ASSIGN TO IN.
150    SELECT OUT-FILE ASSIGN TO OU.
160  DATA DIVISION.
170  FILE SECTION.
180  FD  PAYROLL-FILE
190      LABEL RECORDS ARE OMITTED
200      DATA RECORD IS CARD-IN
210      RECORD CONTAINS 84 CHARACTERS.
220  01  CARD-IN.
230      02  TOTAL-PAY PICTURE 999V.
240      02  FILLER PICTURE X.
250      02  WITHHOLDING PICTURE 999V.
260      02  FILLER PICTURE X(77).
270  FD  OUT-FILE
280      LABEL RECORDS ARE OMITTED
290      DATA RECORD IS PRINT-LINE
300      RECORD CONTAINS 132 CHARACTERS.
```

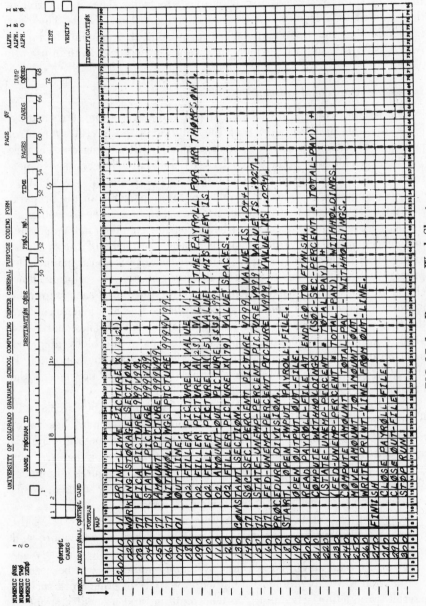

FIG. 17-1. Program Work Sheet.

division are expressed in readily understandable terms. The PAYROLL-FILE and the OUT-FILE, both of which were previously described in the FILE SECTION, are opened. The data from the PAYROLL-FILE is read into storage. Necessary calculations are made. The net payroll is then moved to a location in storage called AMOUNT-OUT. The next instruction is for the computer to print out the amount found in AMOUNT-OUT, following which the two files which have been in use are closed.

Inventory Control Application

The second example of a COBOL program illustration starts with a block diagram (Figure 17–2) of the solution to an inventory control application. This will follow with a partial COBOL program (Figure 17–3) which illustrates the PROCEDURE DIVISION necessary to perform the necessary steps indicated by the block diagram.

This example is designed to emphasize the importance of the preparation necessary before the computer program can be written as well as of the actual program itself. As described in earlier chapters, it is important that an intensive study and analysis of each problem of the business information processing system be completed and procedural manuals be prepared. These manuals may be in the form of essay description, flowcharts, or block diagrams, but regardless of the form used each step to be performed must be indicated. In the computer coding of a given problem, the analysis of the specific application usually results in flowcharts and block diagrams. The individual procedural steps of the block diagrams must be coded into a program language acceptable to the computer. It should be particularly noted in the example to be followed how closely the program steps follow the steps in the block diagram.

THE PROBLEM.   A certain company employs about 1,000 workers in building small- to medium-sized electric motors. The company has a normal inventory of 20,000 stock items. Four hundred of these are motors and related items which are built for stock; the remainder are raw materials and subassemblies. The company also manufactures equipment on special order, but this type of finished product is never stocked, nor is it included in the inventory control system.

Inventory records in the past have been kept on ledger cards. As the company's business has expanded, this method has become more and more cumbersome, expensive, and time-consuming, and the company has decided to obtain an IBM 1401 tape system computer. It will be used in conjunction with this problem, along with a variety of other work such as payroll, production scheduling, cost accounting, and a small amount of engineering calculation. The company anticipates that keeping inventory control records with the computer will only reduce costs slightly, but that it should provide more accurate inventory control information, reduce clerical delay, and eventually provide the basis for a more thorough management control of the company's inventory position.

The master file is to be on magnetic tape and will contain the following information:

Part number
Abbreviated Alphabetic Description
Quantity on Hand
Quantity on Order
Reorder Point (the point at which more stock is ordered)
Reorder Quantity (the size of the order that is placed)
Code Character (indicating whether this is a finished item for sale, a raw material, or a subassembly)
Unit Price for Finished Goods
Year-to-Date Sales for Finished Goods

In this case study, there are four types of transactions to be processed against this master file:

1. Adjustments in the quantity on hand. These are a result of such things as recounts, loss, and spoilage.
2. Receipts. These refer to inventory items received in the stockroom.
3. Orders. These are orders placed through purchases or production control for materials, subassemblies, or finished stock.
4. Issues. These refer to stock which has been issued by the stockroom either to purchasers or to the manufacturing operation.

THE PROGRAM REQUIRED. The PROCEDURE DIVISION of a coded COBOL program (Figure 17–3) to perform the procedural steps illustrated in the block diagram of Figure 17–2, follows the steps of the application in a logical progression.

The processing required may be summarized as follows: The inventory tape is to be updated daily by the transaction cards being processed against the old master file. Adjustments (1) replace the quantity on hand in the master file record with the transaction quantity (Trans. Qty.). Receipts (2) are added to the master file quantity on hand (QOH). Since the system is being set up so that nothing is ever received in the stockroom that was not ordered, either by purchasing or production control, receipts also represent a fulfillment of an order that was placed previously. Therefore, receipt quantities (TQ) are subtracted from quantity on order (QOO). Order (3) are added to the quantity on order (QOO) in the master file.

Issues (4) are subtracted from the master file quantity on hand. However, before an issue quantity (TQ) is subtracted from the quantity on hand (QOH), a test is made to determine whether there is enough stock on hand to supply the amount specified. If there is not, an out-of-stock or shortage message is printed out and the quantity on hand is

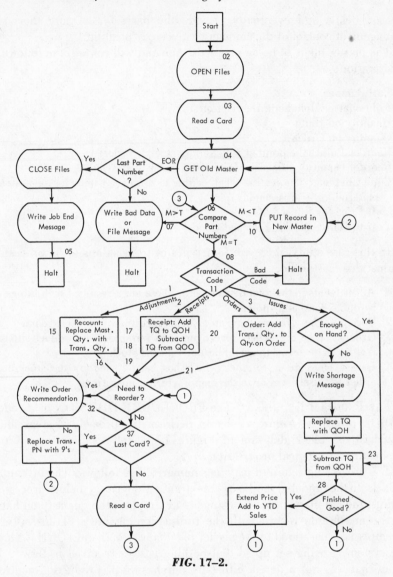

FIG. 17–2.

reduced to zero by replacing the transaction quantity (TQ) with the amount of stock on hand (QOH) and deducting it from itself. If the quantity on hand plus the quantity on order falls below the reorder point, a recommendation to purchasing or production control is printed indicating that more of this item should be ordered. This quantity is not added to the quantity on order until it is subsequently received through an order transaction—that is, until purchasing or production control responds to the order recommendation.

```
01  PROCEDURE DIVISION.
02    OPEN INPUT OLD-MASTER-FILE OUTPUT NEW-MASTER-FILE.
03    ACCEPT TRANSACTION-CARD FROM CARD-READER.
04  MASTER-READING. READ OLD-MASTER-FILE RECORD AT END GO TO
05    WRAPUP-TEST.
06  COMPARISON. IF PART-NUMBER OF OLD-MASTER IS GREATER THAN
07    PART-NUMBER OF TRANSACTION-CARD GO TO WRAPUP-TEST.
08    IF PART-NUMBER OF OLD-MASTER IS EQUAL TO PART-NUMBER OF
09    TRANSACTION-CARD GO TO CODE-TESTING-ROUTINE OTHERWISE
10    GO TO MASTER-WRITING.
11  CODE-TESTING-ROUTINE. GO TO RECOUNT, RECEIPT, ORDER, ISSUE
12    DEPENDING ON TRANSACTION-CODE. MOVE 'BAD CLASS
13    CODE JOB HALTED' TO MESSAGE.
14    DISPLAY MESSAGE ON PRINTER. STOP 1.
15  RECOUNT. MOVE TRANSACTION-QUANTITY TO QUANTITY-ON-HAND.
16    GO TO REORDER-ROUTINE.
17  RECEIPT. ADD TRANSACTION-QUANTITY, QUANTITY-ON-HAND.
18    SUBTRACT TRANSACTION-QUANTITY, QUANTITY-ON-ORDER.
19    GO TO REORDER-ROUTINE.
20  ORDER. ADD TRANSACTION-QUANTITY, QUANTITY-ON-ORDER.
21    GO TO REORDER-ROUTINE.
22  ISSUE. IF QUANTITY-ON-HAND IS NOT LESS THAN TRANSACTION-
23    QUANTITY GO TO SUBTRACTION-ROUTINE. MOVE
24    QUANTITY-ON-HAND TO MESSAGE-A. MOVE PART-NUMBER OF
25    TRANSACTION-CARD TO MESSAGE-B. MOVE TRANSACTION-QUANTITY
26    TO MESSAGE-C. DISPLAY MESSAGE ON PRINTER. MOVE
27    TRANSACTION-QUANTITY TO QUANTITY-ON-HAND.
28  SUBTRACTION-ROUTINE. SUBTRACT TRANSACTION-QUANTITY,
29    QUANTITY-ON-HAND. MULTIPLY UNIT-PRICE BY TRANSACTION-
30    QUANTITY GIVING TOTAL-PRICE. ADD TOTAL-PRICE,
31    YEAR-TO-DATE-SALES.
32  REORDER-ROUTINE. IF QUANTITY-ON-HAND + QUANTITY-ON-ORDER
33    IS GREATER THAN REORDER-POINT GO TO LAST-CARD-ROUTINE.
34    MOVE PART-NUMBER OF TRANSACTION-CARD TO CARD-1. MOVE
35    MASTER-CODE TO CARD-2. MOVE REORDER-QUANTITY TO CARD-3.
36    DISPLAY CARD ON CARD-PUNCH.
37  LAST-CARD-ROUTINE. IF LAST-CARD GO TO REPLACEMENT-ROUTINE.
38    ACCEPT TRANSACTION-CARD FROM CARD-READER. GO TO
39    COMPARISON.
40  REPLACEMENT-ROUTINE. MOVE HIGH-VALUE TO PART-NUMBER OF
41    TRANSACTION-CARD.
42  MASTER-WRITING. WRITE NEW-MASTER FROM OLD-MASTER. GO TO
43    MASTER-READING.
44  WRAPUP-TEST. IF LAST-CARD GO TO CLOSEOUT. MOVE
45    'FILE OR DATA ERROR JOB HALTED' TO MESSAGE.
46    DISPLAY MESSAGE ON PRINTER. STOP 2.
47  CLOSEOUT. CLOSE OLD-MASTER-FILE, NEW-MASTER-FILE. MOVE 'JOB
48    FINISHED' TO MESSAGE. DISPLAY
49    MESSAGE ON PRINTER. STOP 3.
```

FIG. 17–3. **COBOL Program for Inventory Control Case Study.**

If the issue is for finished goods, the transaction quantity is multiplied by the unit price to determine the amount of the sale, which is then added to the year-to-date sales.

When the last transaction card is read by the computer, it will be sensed. When this last card is completely processed, the equipment will halt, and the processing procedure will be completed.

To summarize how this application relates to the work of other departments within the company: The sales department sends, to the data processing center, notices of sales of standard items. These become the issue transactions. Sales and engineering together determine the raw materials and subassemblies required to manufacture special orders and these, in turn, become issue transactions when these items are removed from stock and are delivered to the manufacturing floor.

When production control receives a notice that the level of stock of a standard item produced by the firm has fallen below the reorder point, it is production control's responsibility to schedule the production of more of this item. In doing so, the need will be created for raw materials from the stock room, which once again become issue transactions. When items go into the stock room after being completed in manufacturing, they become receipt transactions.

When an order recommendation for raw materials goes to purchasing, a purchase order is normally immediately placed with a vendor—taking into account any special consideration such as the combination of orders, quantity discounts, etc. As soon as purchasing places the order, an order transaction goes to data processing, where it is added to the quantity on order.

ANNOTATED BIBLIOGRAPHY

CHAPIN, NED. *Programming Computers for Business Applications.* New York: McGraw-Hill Book Co., 1961.

    This book gives an introduction to programming, using more modern techniques applicable to the more common programming languages. It stresses COBOL but is not limited to it. It is designed to help one learn how to program or code computers but not to teach the computer itself.

INTERNATIONAL BUSINESS MACHINES CORPORATION. *COBOL. A General Information Manual.* White Plains, N.Y., 1961.

    A thorough approach to the background, basic concepts, and the language of COBOL.

JUNKER, J. P., and BOWARD, G. R. "COBOL v. FORTRAN: A Sequel," *Datamation,* April, 1965, pp. 65–67.

    A series of tests made by the United States Air Force Data Service Center indicates that COBOL is superior to other higher languages for data processing applications. The tests were run in order to answer several questions concerning language selection in the programming of data processing applications. The testers wanted to discover if FORTRAN was better than COBOL, as some had maintained. The tests made, and their results, are described.

McCAMERON, FRITZ A., *COBOL Logic and Programming*. Homewood, Ill.: Richard D. Irwin, Inc., 1966.

This is a COBOL manual for beginning programmers. Its object is to present the basic nature of COBOL in such a way that the reader may gain an understanding of the language's use. It is written in textbook style.

McCRACKEN, DANIEL D. *A Guide to COBOL Programming*. New York: John Wiley & Sons, Inc., 1963.

This book gives an easy-to-understand discussion of the application of computers to the problems of business. While explaining the particular characteristics of the COBOL method, it also presents good background information on data processing needs and methods.

RAUN, DONALD L. *COBOL Computer Programming for Accounting and Business Analysis*. Belmont, Calif.: Dickinson Publishing Co., Inc., 1966.

A book designed to assist the business student to understand COBOL programming, and, in the author's opinion, accomplishes its task admirably.

SAMMETT, JEAN E. "COBOL—Past, Present, Future," *Data Processing Yearbook, 1962–63*, pp. 76–82.

This article, as the title implies, attempts to describe the various phases in the COBOL activity. The article includes a look at the future possibilities of COBOL and at how it is related to other activities now underway.

SAXON, JAMES A. *COBOL, A Self-Instructional Manual*. Englewood Cliffs, N.J.: Prentice-Hall, Inc., 1963.

A programmed-learning approach to COBOL.

U.S. DEPARTMENT OF DEFENSE. *COBOL Specifications*, 1960, 1961, 1962, and 1965.

These specifications explain the development of the COBOL language (history of COBOL), and serve as manuals for those who want to learn COBOL.

QUESTIONS

1. Differentiate between data-names, procedure-names, condition-names, and special-names. What is the significance of each of them?
2. What are the basic divisions of a COBOL program?
3. Briefly describe the function of each division of a COBOL program.
4. What is the purpose of the File Section in the Data Division?
5. What types of information would be included in the description of a file?
6. What is the function of a picture clause? Illustrate and describe.
7. How does the procedure division of a COBOL program differ primarily from the other three divisions of such a program?

8. What functions are performed by program verbs? Describe and identify precisely.

9. Why is it possible to learn a certain programming language but yet be unable to write a program which will run correctly the first time it is tried?

CHAPTER 18

Use of Computers

by Management

EARLY digital computers were bulky, heavy, generated an excessive amount of heat, and were relatively expensive per digit of data processed. Programming was a difficult and time-consuming task, and there was little assistance available from the manufacturers in the form of software. In short, the early users of digital computers were hardy souls who had to have a great need for the processing capability and comparatively greater speed the computer had to offer to cause them to venture into the maze of problems involved in converting their mechanical or punched card accounting systems to one of the early computerized systems.

All of the initial problems surrounding the use of computers made a conversion to a computerized system a very expensive undertaking. In the beginning it was quite natural to consider a conversion, for example, because a clerical bottleneck existed or there was a need to provide better service to customers. The computer could also usually handle the clerical work more quickly with fewer personnel, and many of the earlier computerized systems were justified solely on the basis of cost saving in the performance of clerical tasks. Those firms, however, who have allowed their computers to remain in their office strictly as a bigger, better calculating machine have not realized the full potentialities of the equipment and, in most instances, have soon become disenchanted and dissatisfied with their installation.

The greatly increased I/O speeds, memory capacity, access time, and diminishing costs per unit of data processed, as well as the availability of greater software assistance, has made it possible for the computer to be used in a much wider variety of ways to perform a greater scope of services for management.

Information accumulated and summarized by computers is being used, for example, to measure performance, evaluate progress, assist in decision making (by simulating assumed conditions), forecast business conditions, set company objectives, set standards, and allocate resources.

Applications for digital computers are being found not only in business and industry but in engineering, science, medicine, and law, to name a few of the areas.

Many of the earlier business users of computers have gone through an evolutionary process in the development of their computerized systems. The computer has made it possible for them to go from the relatively simple automation of clerical tasks to complex applications and improvements in existing procedures which assist management in top-level decision making in controlling and coordinating widely scattered business units.

AUTOMATION OF CLERICAL TASKS

When businessmen first started to look at computers as a means of assisting them in some of their data processing tasks, the tasks which they first considered were those which had large volume, where the clerical operations were largely repetitive, and where there were peaks in the periods during which the data had to be processed. The computer, with its speed, seemed to be ideally suited for this type of operation. Payroll and billing applications were usually among the first to be converted to computers. Sales analyses and the updating of inventory records followed as a logical outgrowth of the billing operation. Public accountants who were doing write-up work for their clients quickly saw the applicability of these techniques to their work, and some installed small systems of their own. Also, within the last 8 to 10 years, computer service bureaus have grown up in many communities with the purpose, in part at least, of providing the smaller businessman with computerized service for his routine data processing tasks.

Payroll Procedures

Often, a payroll procedure is thought of as being rather simple, as nearly everyone has had some association with the basic items necessary for payroll computation. However, more typically, such a procedure turns out to be fairly complicated, and can be very complex under some circumstances.

The payroll procedure, used in the following discussion, as well as other procedures, are just typical examples of "a" business and not necessarily those which would be followed by any given firm. Some of the processing runs, which are arbitrarily numbered in a consecutive order, would not be desired by some firms, and others, which are not included, would be required by other firms.

The form of the machine-processable document used as input to the data processing system would, by necessity, vary with the type of processing equipment, and the following procedures could utilize almost any of the various types of processors available. Punched cards are used in the illustrations which follow as the input media, but punched paper tape, magnetic tape, information taken from the various types of internal and external storage units of the computer, and even optically scanned data, would serve equally well. Regardless of the type of input used, however, the end result in the form of reports, statements, and analyses would all be comparable.

ABSENTEE REPORTS. In any payroll procedure the initial procedure would be to obtain the daily hours worked by each employee from time

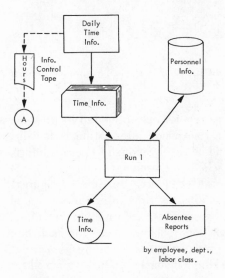

FIG. 18–1.   Absentee Reports.

sheets or timecards and convert this information into some type of machine-processable document. The first typical process run (Figure 18–1) would utilize timecards and the current employee magnetic disc file to determine if any of the employees in the current file had not reported for work in the current work period. The end result of this procedure would be to produce absentee reports which would list the absentee by employee, department, etc. These reports would be invaluable to the department head or to the foreman in determining the amount of reliance to be placed on a given employee to produce a given amount of work, or in recommending this employee for advancements in job classification and raises in pay. It could also be of use to the personnel department, which could follow up on absences and determine whether the employee is ill, has some other justified excuse, or has resigned without notice.

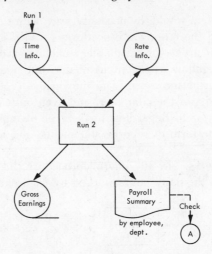

FIG. 18–2.   Payroll Summary Report.

If these absentee reports were prepared by an integrated data processing system, where time clock information is fed directly into the computer, reports could be timely enough to permit information to be used in machine and job scheduling each day.

PAYROLL SUMMARY REPORT.   In Run 2 (Figure 18–2) the magnetic tape file which contains the time information is used as input, but this time in conjunction with rate information including assigned rates for each type of operation (such as those for each hour, week, or month worked, or piece produced), to calculate gross earnings for each of these employees and to simultaneously produce a payroll summary report. This

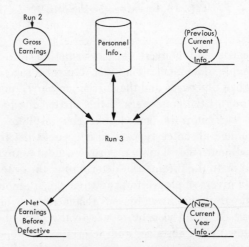

FIG. 18–3.   Net Earnings before Deductions.

report can be by employee, department, or any other breakdown desired. It can be used as control data against which later reports can be checked for assurance that no data have been added or removed and, perhaps, also provide an audit trail (or track) for verification procedures. At this point the time information file will have served its purpose and will be filed and held for future use on another run.

PAYROLL REGISTER. The illustrations used (Figures 18–3 and 18–4) show that it takes two processing runs to produce the payroll register. This would, however, vary with the capability of the equipment used; the register might possibly be completed in only one run or it might require several processing runs, as certain procedural steps are required which must be followed in a patterned order.

The gross earnings information tape produced in Run 2 will be one of

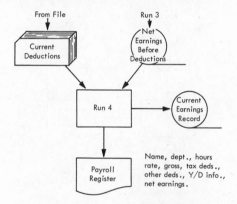

FIG. 18–4.   **Payroll Register.**

three inputs used in Run 3 (Figure 18–3). The other two types of input include the necessary data pertaining to the employees who have worked this particular period. The first of these is the personnel records disk file, which contains tax information, such as number of dependents, needed in the calculation of taxes to be withheld. The second is the current year-to-date information tape file which contains, along with other information, earnings to date and taxes withheld up through the last pay period. The output possible from this information input can vary somewhat, but the illustration shows the production of a net pay before deductions tape. The personnel disk file would be returned to the personnel record file if it is in disk pack form. The current information file would be updated into a new tape with income tax deduction information which has been calculated in this run and will be held for next week's processing run. The gross earnings file may be used in later procedures. A new tape file for net earnings before deductions will be produced in this run.

The payroll deduction cards applicable to the current payroll are now pulled from our deduction card file (Figure 18–4). These, along with the net earnings before deductions tape, serve as inputs for Run 4.

One of the outputs of this particular process is a current earnings record which brings the information from the net earnings before deduction tape and the current deduction into a single record.

The second output of this process run is the payroll register. This register serves as a detailed listing of the payroll as it is to be made and also contains a total which would represent the funds to be provided at the bank to cover the payroll checks.

Where manual journals and ledgers are used, data from the register may serve as the entries required to record the payroll information. Typical of these data would be the debit(s) to labor expense(s) and the

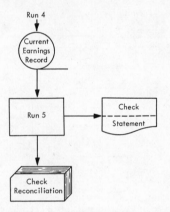

FIG. 18–5.   Payroll Check Preparation.

credits to wages payable, the deductions taken for the required taxes payable, and the many other authorized deduction items.

To aid in internal control procedures, the total hours worked may be checked back for agreement with a calculator run ticket of total hours worked made from the original timecards (Figure 18–1), and the gross earnings can be checked back against our payroll summary report produced in process Run 2 (Figure 18–2). This register may also serve as an invaluable report in furnishing an audit trail which both the internal and external auditors may follow when it is necessary to reconstruct the procedures used in processing these data.

CHECK AND STATEMENT PREPARATION.   Run 5 (Figure 18–5) utilizes the current earnings record produced in Run 4 to produce the payroll check and its attached statement of deductions which goes to the employee. The preparation of the payroll check is, of course, the fundamental purpose of any payroll procedure. However, with the complexity of modern payrolls (involving many different pay bases, such as regular, overtime, holiday, and vacation, and the many deductions), the statement of earnings has also become quite important to employees.

This run also produces a check reconciliation net paid card for each employee which contains the amount paid, the employee number, and the check number, as well as other possible information, which will be used in bank reconciliation procedures when the bank statement is received. These cards will be filed with other outstanding check cards in the payroll account file.

DEDUCTION REGISTER AND ASSOCIATED REPORTS. In Run 6 (Figure 18–6) the deductions information (either the current deductions cards or the current earnings tape record) is used to prepare a deduction register. Also, any number of deduction reports can be prepared such as: bonds, union dues, United Fund, insurance, etc. Each of these deduction reports represents funds withheld from the employees' pay which are being held

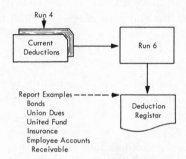

FIG. 18–6. Deduction Register.

until it is time to pay them out to someone else. The various totals provided by this deduction register would serve as the journal entry amount to be credited to the respective ledger accounts.

INDIVIDUAL EMPLOYEE EARNINGS RECORDS. In Run 7 (Figure 18–7) the updated current earnings tape along with the previous current year information and personnel information disk are used to prepare the individual employee earnings records. These records contain the detail of each employee's earnings over a period of time (usually a year) along with basic statistical information pertaining to him. Typical information found in such a record would be the employee's name, address, social security number, date employed, date of birth, sex, marital status, number of exemptions, rate of pay, and occupation classification.

The earnings information would be nearly identical with that provided in the payroll register previously described, except that it would contain the detail by employee for each payroll over a period of time instead of detail for all employees for a single payroll. The information is necessary

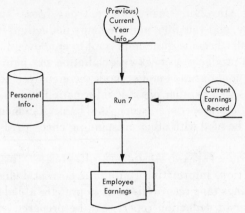

FIG. 18–7.   Employee Earnings Records.

in determining the cutoff point for social security and income taxes withheld and both federal and state unemployment taxes payable by the employer.

Billing Procedures

The types of companies which have probably had the greatest billing problems are those with large numbers of customers, such as the public utilities, the insurance companies, and the oil companies with their credit card business. Even staggering the billing periods by using "cycle billing" could not alleviate the tremendous clerical work load involved.

As a result, when many public utilities converted their data processing systems to computers, they designed their meter reading documents in the form of mark-sensed punch cards, with one card for each customer. All that the meter reader was required to do was to blacken certain squares on the card indicating the quantities of gas, water, or electricity which had been consumed. He read the meters in a given neighborhood on a cycled basis and turned his mark-sensed cards in at the end of each day. The data marked on the cards were then reproduced, in coded punched hole form in cards, on a mark-sensing reproducer. These cards were then in a suitable form to be used as input to a computer.

Constant data concerning rates would be retained in computer storage. When the quantities of electricity and gas which had been consumed by each customer were read into the computer, it was an extremely rapid operation to have the quantities multiplied by the rate and to produce a printed statement as an output of the operation.

Sales Analyses and Inventory Records

Organizations making sales to many customers were not far behind in computerizing their operations. They saw in the computer, however, the capacity not only to speed up the billing operation but to utilize the same data to make detailed sales analyses and to keep inventory records on a perpetual basis. With the computer's capacity for the storage of data and with the tremendous speeds of the processing unit, analyses of sales of almost any complexity could be easily and quickly accomplished.

For example, assume that a man walked into a department store to buy a suit of clothes or a woman to buy a dress. Information on the resulting sales slip which would be of particular interest to the sales management in the future included:

1. The name of the person to whom the merchandise was sold.
2. What was sold.
3. The size of the garment.
4. The make of the garment.
5. The color of the garment.
6. The cost of the garment.
7. The selling price of the garment.

With a computerized accounting system, not only could the person who purchased the merchandise be billed for it at the appropriate time but also the information could be readily stored in memory, summarized, and printed out to produce analyses and reports for management.

Insofar as inventory records are concerned, they could be stored in memory and recorded by make, size, color, and cost. When the information concerning the sale was read into the computer, inventory records would be updated as the data describing the item sold was stored in memory.

Use by Certified Public Accountants

The average CPA has been somewhat slow in grasping the benefits to be derived from EDP. The American Institute of Certified Public Accountants has been concerned with this, and as a result, in 1966 published the third in their Computer Research Series entitled *Computer Applications to Accounting Operations* in an endeavor to show their members how computers could be and were being used by members of the profession. This study indicated that, in most instances, the CPA's are using the computer to handle write-up work applications which involve keeping books and making statements for clients of their firms.

The observations of a certified public accountant in a rural area of Colorado are of interest:

Write-up work can overwhelm the creativity in Certified Public Accounting firms which specialize in servicing the small businessman. In recent years, this trend has been growing. Our firm, for instance, which handles primarily small businessmen, ranchers and farmers, recently found itself backed into a situation in which we were spending more time fighting the battle of paper work than doing the professional work of auditing, tax practice and management services.

In our association with the small businessman, we were always concerned about the lack of efficiency in bookkeeping practices, and we were always expounding the need for controls, checks and balances, and pointing out the need for meaningful management reports. But there were too many times when we were not able to carry out our desires because of the same problems—lack of time on our part and the expense to the client. Our review of electronic data processing convinced us that a computer application could be directed toward a combination of paper work reduction and improved managerial control. In addition, we were positive the results of making such a change would result in simpler accounting procedures and business systems for our clients.[1]

Computer Service Bureaus

Computer service bureaus are usually individually organized business firms and are found in most of the larger population centers. They provide a wide range of services to customers. They process customers' routine accounts on a regular basis, provide scientific or numerical analysis, and serve as an overload standby facility when large corporations have peak needs or emergency volumes of data. Finally, the bureau may be used to process a high volume of data on an irregular basis. Service bureaus usually sell time at a given rate per hour based on volume needs. Most customers are companies that cannot, because of size, justify their own computer installation.

The principal application use of service bureaus is to process routine accounting data, serving the primary need of most smaller companies. This enables the smaller company to have the facilities and advantages of a computer at a reasonable cost while at the same time avoiding long-term capital equipment expenditures or contracts for equipment and staff services. The bureau provides highly qualified programmers and systems analysts. This avoids the problem of training staff for these purposes, and means that the firm will only pay for this staff when there is a need for this work. The use of a bureau insures that accurate and timely reports will be available to bureau users, and delivery schedules are often guaranteed as a part of the service contract.

IBM's Service Bureau Corporation has recently announced that more than 70 of its local service bureaus will be tied into a national network linked by 12 central processing stations by 1969.

Each of the local bureaus will be equipped with a System/360 data processor, ranging in size from the basic Model 30 up to the Model 75. Local customers requiring the use of even larger 360's will have them

---

[1] Charles A. Taylor, "Using the Computer for the Small Business Client," *Colorado CPA Report*, Vol. XXX (April, 1966), p. 11.

available through data communications links between the local bureau and the Central Processing Bureau.

IMPROVEMENTS IN PREVIOUS DATA PROCESSING SYSTEMS

It was pointed out earlier in this chapter that there has been a clearly perceptible evolution in the way computers are being utilized throughout American industry and commerce. In many cases, a new computer user first considers automating existing clerical routines. As soon as these operations are mastered, and the user begins to realize more fully the capabilities of the computer, he generally endeavors to improve upon his existing data processing system. For example, in using the computer the user is quickly impressed by the ease and speed with which data can be accumulated and summarized, as well as the many different ways whereby accounting functions can be integrated because of their use of identical data. With greater amounts of current information available, the planning function (standards, budgets, forecasts) can be carried out in a much more complete and adequate manner.

In 1965 the American Management Association questioned 288 companies as to the extent to which computer information was being used by their business managers. In this group there were 90 manufacturers of nondurable goods, 103 durable-goods manufacturers, and 82 service firms. One should note in Figure 18–8 the many uses which this study found for computer information. However, it is also interesting to note the variance in given applications in providing information for various purposes among the different types of business enterprise.

In manufacturing planning and control procedures, there are many areas in which the results of computer operation can provide information timely enough to allow management to make the decision necessary in not only day-to-day operations but in forecasts and budgets for both capital and operational expenditures. Typical information needed for these purposes includes the following:

1. Work priorities—used to assign critical work loads to specific machine stations and to expedite particular orders.
2. Machine loading or utilization—valuable in production scheduling. These inform management which machines are idle or down for maintenance and also serve as a measure of machine efficiency.
3. Machine downtime—measures machine efficiency and helps pinpoint downtime as a result of worn-out, poorly designed, carelessly used, or improperly maintained equipment.
4. Employee attendance; unproductive time and cause—provides information relating to absent employees as well as inefficiently operated equipment.

Planning		Sales and Customers (Percent)	Goods Produced (Percent)	Finances (Percent)	Materials Purchased (Percent)	Manpower (Percent)
Forecasting	Nondurable goods	74	60	46	33	18
	Durable goods	68	55	42	35	36
	Services	41	15	37	17†	23
Evaluating progress	Nondurable goods	68	52	54	21	19
	Durable goods	62	51	61	32	34
	Services	52	23	39	32	20*
Setting objectives	Nondurable goods	62	50	40	31	22
	Durable goods	55	40	42	32	28
	Services	38	15	32	17*	24
Allocating resources	Nondurable goods	31	46	37	21	26
	Durable goods	26	35	32	23	28
	Services	22	15†	22	17*	16†
Seeking new products, companies, markets	Nondurable goods	38	18	14	12	7
	Durable goods	47	16	14	10	8
	Services	37	13	12	4†	2†
Controlling						
Measuring performance	Nondurable goods	72	58	59	30	36
	Durable goods	62	63	64	40	60
	Services	40	18	35	23	43
Setting standards	Nondurable goods	48	48	42	24	29
	Durable goods	36	46	42	30	38
	Services	24	10	21	17	26
Administering						
Decision making	Nondurable goods	68	61	51	41	24
	Durable goods	54	58	54	46	39
	Services	40	16	40	27*	27
Coordinating	Nondurable goods	43	44	33	27	17
	Durable goods	32	33	31	22	26
	Services	27	13	20	18*	16
Directing	Nondurable goods	51	44	43	26	17
	Durable goods	42	43	39	23	33
	Services	28	9†	32	18*	22
Communicating	Nondurable goods	44	30	29	18	13
	Durable goods	42	35	37	25	25
	Services	30	15†	23	16*	20
Delegating	Nondurable goods	27	18	17	9	9
	Durable goods	14	14	16	12	12
	Services	11	4†	10	9†	10

* No banks or insurance companies are in this group.

† No banks, insurance companies, or department stores are in this group.

Source: M. Valliant Higginson, *Managing with EDP—A Look at the State of the Art* (Research Study No. 71 [New York: American Management Association, Inc., 1965]), p. 55.

FIG. 18–8. Uses for Computer Information.

5. Labor efficiency; scrap materials: rework necessary to bring work up to standard; quality control; job status and work location—provide the foreman and supervisors with information needed to determine performance by each work station and its operator.
6. Stores receipts and issues; tool requisition and return; work in process; material shortage; inventory; shipping notices—aid in controlling material through the production process and to out shipment.
7. Cost of production—includes analyses of labor costs, cost of materials, and factory overhead. Other reports may include actual costs, variances from standard or average costs, unit or job costs, and others.

M. Valliant Higginson says:

The adoption of computers for controlling companies has created more impact than their adoption for planning or decision making. The reason is twofold: (1) computers are more easily applied to control activities; (2) the need for control in companies has been more acute. Many of the changes that are now occurring, bringing a breakthrough in management techniques, have resulted from the use of EDP for control purposes.[2]

One should also realize that all of the purposes (planning, control, administration) for which computerized information is being used are all part of the management function. In other words, the computer has progressed from merely being a clerical tool to one which management looks upon as being capable of providing meaningful assistance in the management function.

An interesting illustration of the use of the computer for control purposes is now utilized by a Caterpillar Tractor Company franchise dealership. The dealer headquarters maintained 13 widely dispersed warehouses and commercial outlets for the parts inventory for their line of products. This necessitated the maintenance of approximately 40,000 different types of spare parts at each of the 13 warehouses. The management of this franchise was highly conscious of service to their customers and as a result felt that it was imperative that adequate stock of parts be maintained at each warehouse and commercial outlet.

Maintaining such a sizable parts inventory necessitated a tremendous investment as well as the storage, protection, and maintenance of this stock. It was a continuous problem, therefore, to attempt to provide the service which management felt was paramount, try to minimize the investment in inventory, and at the same time have the parts available at all of the warehouses when they would be asked for.

Initially, the company attempted to keep its inventory records with cardex cards and then switched to bookkeeping machines. From this they went to punched card equipment. In all three instances, however, they were highly dissatisfied with the inaccuracy of the information they

---

[2] M. Valliant Higginson, *Managing with EDP—A Look at the State of the Art* (Research Study No. 71 [New York: American Management Association, Inc., 1965]), p. 86.

received as well as with its slowness. They felt that the inaccuracy was due to the poor quality of clerical employees they were able to hire but that the equipment was responsible for the lack of speed. Both of these factors materially reduced the service the company could render to their customers.

As a means of solving the problem, top management installed an IBM System/360 Model 40 computer system and completely standardized the clerical procedures surrounding the preparation of input data for the computer. All of the 13 warehouses were then connected by teletype, so that all of the input data could be fed continuously to the computer which was centrally located.

By having accurate inventory information more quickly, they have been able to reduce their investment in inventory by approximately 20 percent, in addition to being able to render much better service to their customers, which in turn has enabled them to increase their sale of parts. They are obtaining a great deal of information about their sales which was not available on a timely basis before, as well as being able to determine the quantities to be ordered for replacements by means of an economic order quantity formula.

To this point, the computer is still being utilized primarily by operating management.

CONTROL AND COORDINATION OF WIDELY DISPERSED ACTIVITIES

There are coming to be more and more large business concerns in the United States. This is being brought about by growth in population as well as by corporate combinations and mergers. An important problem today in financial accounting circles developing out of this trend is the question of how these conglomerate corporations report the results of their various activities in their financial statements. As corporations have grown in size, it has frequently meant that they have increased the number of places from which they do business both within the continental United States and around the world. The more widely dispersed business activity has become, the greater has been the problem of coordination for management. Also, where management is not able to personally supervise what is taking place, it must depend upon procedures, built-in controls, and a flow of data concerning current operations, in order to see that present activity is conforming to plans (budgets) set previously. The computer and telecommunication equipment (even using satelites to relay data) has done a great deal to bridge this gap.

Using computers for this purpose has meant that more complicated and sophisticated information systems have had to be developed. One aspect of this problem is that in order for a computer to be utilized to its fullest in the coordination of physically diverse activities, there must be standardization of the chart of accounts between the different business units, as well as in the procedures followed in the accumulation of data and the reports prepared from the accumulated data.

In many instances, in order that companies might bring this about, it has meant a much more complete and searching revamping of their existing system than had previously been necessary when clerical procedures were automated or when management extended the use of the computer to the planning and control areas.

The Westinghouse Electric Corporation in Pittsburgh has one of the best known examples of the type of computer system being described. It ties together about 300 plants, field offices, warehouses, distributors, and appliance repair centers.

Martin Greenberger says:

One interesting application of their system is a "Cash-management information program" that keeps a running account of the cash flow. All receipts and disbursements of the various Westinghouse divisions are immediately transmitted by teletype to the telecomputer center and recorded in the appropriate accounts. When the balance in any of the corporation's 250 regional bank accounts falls below a preset level, the computer automatically orders a transfer of cash from the central bank account. When the balance in the central account is higher than necessary, the treasury office invests the excess in marketable securities, notifying the computer as it does so. The net result is that the company's management knows the company's cash position at all times and is able to put formerly idle funds to work earning interest.[3]

More and more business concerns operating in any and all parts of the world are finding that it is only through computer systems, such as the one described at Westinghouse Electric, that they can adequately cope with the problems with which they are confronted.

TOP-LEVEL ADMINISTRATION WITH EDP

Different levels of management have quite differing responsibilities. Most of the heirarchies of management, below the top level, are primarily concerned with current operating problems. How to keep the various segments of the firm operating efficiently and effectively conforming to budget standards is a never ending source of concern to all operating management.

The prime responsibility of top management, on the other hand, is to be concerned with the future. They should be frequently asking themselves "what if" types of questions. What would be the position of the company if this or that happened in the future? Operations research

---

[3] Martin Greenberger, "The Uses of Computers in Organizations," *Scientific American*, September, 1966, p. 200.

techniques can often be of assistance with problems of this type. Operations research has been described as:

. . . an approach to problem solving for executive management characterized by:

The use of mathematical, economic, and statistical descriptions of models of business problems. The development of methods or rules to yield measures of the relative profitability of alternative courses in action.

Application to decision-oriented problems in situations of conflict, complexity, uncertainty.

Analyses of relationships which determine the probable future effects of decision choices.[4]

In considering the use of computers in management decision making, be assured that no complicated "human type" decisions have yet been made by a computer as such. It is possible, however, for a computer to utilize programmed instructions, which must be written by humans, to make such decisions as to whether one amount is larger or smaller or equal to another amount, or, if certain conditions are present, to decide whether the conditions fulfill the answer to a yes or no question. These programmed instructions can be quite complicated in nature at times, and it is very important to realize that the use of the computer in solving this type of problem is limited only by the ingenuity of the programmer.

Only in the sense that the human decision process is based on the recall of information stored in the mind—and is influenced by the experiences the individual has had—can there be any parallels in the thinking processes of humans and machines. However, as computers grow in complexity and storage capacities to the point where they more closely follow the patterns of the human mind, and as these computers reach *maturity* in terms of experiences—it is not too far in the realm of fantasy for them to more nearly equal their glamorous billing as Giant Electronic Brains.

To answer "what if" types of questions often involves the use of simulation techniques. Simulation is the designing of models of real-life situations in numeric form and then utilizing a computer to determine the outcome of a wide variety of assumed circumstance by varying different factors in the model. An interesting problem in simulation involving linear programming which came to the authors' attention is that of a large pulp and paper manufacturer. This problem involves the question of how much money should be spent on the propagation of a forest and at what point in time the timber should be harvested. The trees which the company is planting come to maturity within approximately 30 years. They can be harvested sooner or later than this as the occasion may dictate.

---

[4] Harvey M. Wagner, "Practical Slants on Operations Research," *Harvard Business Review*, Vol. XLI, No. 3 (May–June 1963), p. 62.

In the initial stages, one of the big costs is the planting of the forests. Following this, the trees must be pruned. The pruning of the lower branches is done to provide a greater amount of air circulation among the trees, which in turn provides for healthier trees. It also serves to reduce the danger of fire.

There is also the matter of "high thinning." This involves the trimming of the trees much further off the ground as the trees grow older, and this has to be done by hand with long ladders and saws. When there are millions of trees involved, this can involve a lot of human labor. The thinning of the trees when they come to a certain size is also a considerable cost item.

These are the major cost factors involved. The other side of the coin is, of course, the amount of lumber and, eventually, the amount of revenue which will be derived from the forest if it is harvested within a varying amount of time, probably a six- or eight-year period. One of the factors which can be varied is the second trimming. This is the "high trimming." However, if the trees are not high trimmed, there is going to be more trimming in terms of hand labor when the trees are felled.

The company has put in a great deal of time, money, and effort in developing models which are as nearly typical of the situation as possible so that top management can have better information on which to make future policy decisions when and as these mathematical models have some relevance to the decision being made.

This is only one of many types of questions which top management has turned over to operations research technicians and computer specialists.

The top management of the Frisco Railroad is utilizing simulation to assist them in finding solutions to some of their most prevalent problems. They have scheduled for completion by June 1, 1968, test runs on their network model for computer simulation of operations on that part of the railroad system which handles about 90 percent of the traffic and includes five major terminals. Through the computer simulation, Frisco plans to test new blocking policies and patterns and to try out varying concepts of short-train versus long-train operation.

It was emphasized that the network model and the computer will be acting in an advisory capacity. Simulation runs can provide indicators and show trends, and it is anticipated that with proper inputs and programming, the model will be able to predict the consequences of alternative decisions for such operational questions as:

1. How should schedules be arranged between given sets of points?
2. How do advantages and disadvantages stack up as between short trains run frequently and longer trains run less frequently?
3. How much preblocking should be done? And where should it be done?

4. What are the best blocking policies for each yard on the system?
5. How should car-classification activity be distributed among Frisco's various yards?
6. What cars should be classified into what trains at each yard?
7. What changes in yard layouts are advisable? And is there a need for new facilities, say a new hump yard?[5]

The reader should note in the previous example that the management intended to use the results of the computer simulation as an adviser in the solution of the problems enumerated. As effective as the new mathematical techniques may be, they still do not necessarily give the answers to the problems which have been posed. They are not a substitute for management experience and judgment.

ANNOTATED BIBLIOGRAPHY

AMERICAN MANAGEMENT ASSOCIATION (FINANCE DIVISION). *Data Processing Today: A Progress Report.* New York, 1960.

An analysis of new concepts in management information systems. Specific computer applications are presented to illustrate how these new concepts are being implemented.

BOEHM, GEORGE A. W. "The Decision-Making Potential of Computers," *Computer-Based Management for Information and Control.* American Management Association Management Bulletin No. 30. New York: American Management Association, Inc., 1963.

This article explains how the computer helps improve the operation and profitability of a business by: (1) Demanding and providing great understanding of the business; (2) permitting better analysis and information for all levels of planning, decision, and control; (3) reducing the cost and improving the quality of the information processing operations which it automates.

BURTON, A. J., and MILLS, R. G. *Electronic Computers and Their Business Application.* London: Ernest Benn, Ltd., 1960.

This book is intended to help businessmen to understand what is involved in the use of large-scale electronic digital computers in business applications. The book is divided into three sections—equipment, techniques, and applications—with particular emphasis on the last section.

CAMERON, B. B., and MIDDLETON, D. M. "Production Control Through EDP," *The Chartered Accountant in Australia,* March, 1966, pp. 681–88.

A discussion of broad techniques for production control through the use of a computer, with specific reference to a manufacturer who makes assemblies requiring a number of levels of subassembly, is presented. Examined are selective inventory policies, production planning based on sales forecasts, projection of manpower and equipment requirements and manage-

---

[5] Abstracted from "Why Computers Mean Better Railroading," *Railway Age,* April 17, 1967.

ment reports. Though a computer is not an essential tool of production control, it is contended that its speed has opened the way for better control of inventory and production by manufacturing organizations.

ENRICK, NORBERT LLOYD. *Management Operations Research.* New York: Holt, Rinehart & Winston, Inc., 1965.

A simplified, relatively nonmathematical in form, operations research book geared for immediate application to typical business problems of today.

HUMFREY, R. D. "Process Control on the Computer—A General Review. Office Equipment Review," *Canadian Chartered Accountant,* February, 1965, pp. 141–43.

Out of the development of the scientific and business computer has emerged the computer for process control. Process control is different from just automated procedures. Computer control of processes provides the means to constantly measure performance against established parameters and to initiate corrective action when necessary. Automated operations do not have this capability. The process control computer, the functions of the process control computer, process control applications, and the acceptance and application of process control in industry are examined.

LLOYD, B. H. "Statistical Quality Control as a Management Tool," *Canadian Chartered Accountant,* January, 1966, pp. 30–34.

Even though precise measures of quality are unavailable or are subject to varying interpretations, the control of quality is shown to be possible through the use of the management tool known as statistical quality control. Among the topics discussed are statistical sampling, risks of sampling, control charts, inspection departments, cost of defective conditions, quality summary reports, and interpretation of controllable costs. It is suggested that management develop an acceptance toward this technique because the quality of a product will continue to be an influencing factor for its marketability.

MARTIN, E. WAINRIGHT, JR. *Electronic Data Processing: An Introduction.* Rev. ed. Homewood, Ill.: Richard D. Irwin, Inc., 1965.

This book is aimed at providing the general manager, who does not expect to specialize in computer technology, with an understanding of the capabilities and limitations of the electronic computer and of the management considerations involved in its use.

MOELLER, EDWARD F. "Case Study No. 2—P a p e r T a p e (ODT) System," *Proceedings, National Automation Conference 1963,* pp. 73–77. New York, N.Y.: American Bankers Association, 1964.

Described is the way in which a bank with 10,500 checking accounts and 11,000 savings accounts converted from three semiautomated posting machines to fully automated paper tape processing system. The new system was the Cummins Original Document Processing System (ODP). It utilizes the identification technique of stamping a small perforated code in the upper left-hand corner of the document and provides complete comparability with the magnetic ink character recognition check-handling system.

MOORE, FRANCIS E., and STETTLER, HOWARD F. *Accounting Systems for Management Control.* Homewood, Ill.: Richard D. Irwin, Inc., 1963.

A systems approach to the considerations required of management in typical business applications. These are not specific EDP applications, but the problems and solutions used would be equally appropriate in a computer system.

MYERS, CHARLES A. *The Impact of Computers on Management.* Cambridge, Mass.: MIT Press, 1967.

The book is made up of a group of papers presented by a gathering of well-known scholars at a conference held at MIT in 1966 on a variety of subjects, all of which bear on the title of the book.

PRICHARD, JAMES W., and EAGLE, ROBERT H. *Modern Inventory Management.* New York: John Wiley & Sons. Inc., 1965.

In order to compete successfully in the business world or to work efficiently in the public sector, the contemporary inventory manager must utilize the scientific advances that have been made in his field. The problems treated include the replenishment process, economic order quantity, reorder point and safety stock objectives, system consequences, and demand forecasting. Tables, formulas, and a case study are incorporated into the discussion.

SHUCHMAN, ABE. *Scientific Decision Making in Business.* New York: Holt, Rinehart & Winston, Inc., 1963.

The background and growth of operations research, how to develop and evaluate models necessary in this type of research, what tools and techniques are available to solve problems having given characteristics, and some examples of operations research applications.

SIMON, HERBERT A. *The New Science of Management Decision.* New York: Harper & Bros., 1960.

A review of some of the changes that have occurred as a result of the new decision-making techniques the computer has made available to management.

SWYERS, WILLIAM E. "A Computerized Approach to Timekeeping," *Management Accounting,* October, 1965, pp. 25–31.

A computerized timekeeping system is described, where the reporting of employee time and payroll distribution for accounting purposes has been integrated into one reporting system which supplies vital source data for the centralized timekeeping operation performed in the home office. Areas of the operation that are examined include the accumulation of time, calculation of gross pay, the preparation of input data, and the preparation of the forecast. Diagrams showing the layout of the installation are also presented. The basic objectives of the system are outlined as a conclusion.

ZELNICK, JOEL. "Credit Analysis by Computer," *Financial Executive,* June, 1966, p. 26.

How an economic simulator in a computer program reduces cost of evaluating and developing credit policies.

QUESTIONS

1. In what ways has American business enterprise predominantly used the capabilities of the computer to date? Why has this pattern of use developed as it has? Explain.

2. If all potential business users of computers could benefit from the experience of those who have already installed computers, what do you see wrong in a business deciding to utilize a computer based upon the saving of certain clerical costs?

3. Do you feel that the payroll application illustrations in this chapter describe a traditional payroll system, or do they describe the applications of an enlightened computer user? *Clearly explain your opinion.*

4. Carefully explain the basic characteristics of cycle billing.

5. Looking at it from the point of view of a public utility, what do you see as the advantages of using marked-sensed punched cards as a means of recording the readings performed by the meter readers? Explain.

6. What other types of sales analyses might businesses making sales to many customers want to make other than the ones enumerated in this chapter? List as many possibilities as you can, carefully explaining why each possibility has been included.

7. Under what circumstances would you recommend that a business client of yours use the services of a local computer service bureau? Explain each point which you make.

8. Explain several means whereby a businessman can gain better control over his operations by computerizing the procedures in certain operations of the business.

9. As companies grow larger and larger in size and become more diverse in their activities, how are computers helping management to maintain control over what is going on? *Think your answer through carefully.*

10. What is simulation and how is it used in business management? In what ways might a computer facilitate its use?

11. This chapter outlines various business applications in which a computer can be utilized. It would appear that the computer is capable of doing a wide variety of things. Do you, therefore, feel that every business should have a computer? Discuss in reasonable detail.

12. Are the decisions made by the computer similar to those made by management? In what way?

13. Is there any possibility in the foreseeable future that the computer will replace some or all of the functions performed by management?

CHAPTER 19

The EDP

Justification Study

In THE complex industrial firm of today, management is continually faced with decisions which will have a major impact on the operation of the firm. Some of the more publicized decisions are those dealing with plant expansion, acquisition of other firms, and movement into different types of product lines. Other decisions which may also have a tremendous impact on the future of the firm include such internal decisions as production levels, product mix, marketing policies, and changes in accounting systems and procedures.

It is this last type of decision with which we will be concerned in this chapter. The impact of such decisions, however, is not limited to just the accounting records and the procedures to be followed in providing the data required for these records. Typically, when a firm enters into a consideration which involves a system change to a computer system—and this applies equally to changes from manual, punched card, and even other computer equipment—the decision will not only have its impact on top management and those who are assigned to the study team to investigate the feasibility of the change, but it may, in addition, have an even greater impact on the other personnel of the firm. Also, such a study will have its effect on the financial structure of the firm, as it may involve either a large expenditure or a long-term fund commitment, depending on a decision to purchase or rent the equipment and the required related items.

It is possible that the acquisition of a computer will require a centralization of the data processing procedures in place of the decentralized system currently employed. Such a change may result in the complete disruption of presently established lines of communications or work patterns which may have evolved over years of operations and are now firmly established in the firm's corporate structure. On the other hand, even though there may not be a relatively complete change in operations, there will probably be many major changes required in almost any firm involved in such a systems-change decision. New managerial policies will undoubtably have to be implemented, and different methods of providing and capturing the originating data may have to be devised. Not only will there be probable changes in the data itself which may be required for newly proposed reports and analyses, but many of the conventional reports of the past, which have become a tradition in the minds of those relying on them, may be completely eliminated.

In some instances new and unfamiliar job titles will replace the old ones which disappear. Normally, however, most of the current job classifications will remain, even though many of these will be completely changed as to the routines and procedures to be followed. This will undoubtably bring about many changes in personnel requirements. Existing employees may have to be shifted into other positions, the duties of which are new and different, and this will probably involve the development of training programs to aid these employees in learning their new jobs. Additional personnel may be required for some of the more technical and highly skilled positions which will be developing.

The work area required in the processing of data will also probably be changed or altered in terms of the actual amount as well as type of space required.

Thus it must be realized that any organization considering the adoption of electronic data processing must consider a multitude of problems which will be precipitated by a change to EDP. Such a decision is of significant importance, both to present and future operations, in the development of the firm. The monetary outlays required are certainly of major importance, but they may be relatively insignificant in relation to the effects the change to EDP may have upon the organizational structure, the physical facilities, and, perhaps most important of all, the personnel of the firm.

THE APPROACH TO THE INVESTIGATION

Traditionally, the management personnel of most business enterprises have not given their personal attention to data processing methods and procedures. These routine duties have in many instances in the past been supervised by those of the junior executive level. Even the controller has not always been greatly concerned with procedures and methods, except when questions of internal control or the possibility of improved reporting, clerical accuracy, or cost reduction have been raised. Even then, it is not unusual for the active work and review to be delegated to a subordinate with instructions to investigate the problem, initiate appropriate changes, and prepare a memo reporting on the action taken.

This situation has been changing rapidly in recent years. In companies which have considered EDP installations, department heads, controllers, treasurers, presidents, and even boards of directors have found they must take an interest and participate actively in this new development in data processing. Such management support is not only desirable, but it is an absolute necessity if the study is going to be successful in establishing a basis for an objective expression of opinion in regards to the feasibility of the firm changing its data processing system.

One of the primary reasons for this recent interest of management in data processing is that the investment in an "in depth" systems study and evaluation will involve a substantial expenditure, regardless of whether the results support recommendation of the conversion of the present system to electronic data processing or not. The cost of the study alone is often large enough to require the president's approval. If conversion is recommended by the study, the necessary expenditures which will be required will almost certainly necessitate approval of the board of directors. All levels of management must be willing to cooperate so that the study can be completed as economically as possible and so that the results can accurately reflect the true situation in the company.

A systems study will necessarily cut across established organizational lines. The study teams will, at least, be considering the possibility of consolidating the data processing activities of a number of different departments into an integrated system. Again, the active participation and support of all levels of management is a necessary prerequisite to a successful systems study.

Integration of a system often results in the activities of some departments being altered or even eliminated. Changes of this type usually meet considerable resistance, and the support of top management may be required to make the desired changes.

Another important consideration which may have to be faced, is that some basic, traditional, time-honored company policies may need to be altered. The effective use of an EDP system calls for centralization of many management functions which may have formerly been decentralized. Procedures may be changed from being performed by autonomous departments to being a responsibility of the centralized data processing department. This certainly will have a disrupting effect on "chains of command" and may eliminate some "little empires" which have been built up over time in various sections and departments. It is possible that the basic functions performed by some groups will be completely changed.

Methods used by management in its control of operations may be affected. More data will probably be available, which will permit the use of analytical tools not previously possible. Management must be made to realize that its customary routines will be upset, in case of a systems change, and prepare to face it. In some instances it may be highly recommended that the data processing department, in conjunction with equipment manufacturers, initiate a management training program in which management will be shown the significance and interpretation of the new information to be developed from the new system and taught how to appraise intelligently and control the results in its direction of operations. Management is often surprised to learn there is a real need for an occasional reappraisal of the data really needed to operate the business properly.

Management will be wise to issue a statement of the objectives of the study and to outline the broad general methods by which they are to be attained. Such a statement is needed to ensure the cooperation needed by the study team in its survey of overall company policies and objectives—a survey which is to serve as a framework on which the decision will eventually be based. The release of a similar announcement to all employees, if carefully and tactfully composed, can also be of immeasurable value in the conduct of the study. In addition to the information above, this statement should include an enumeration of the need for a systems study and, perhaps, should also include a statement of management's policies regarding the displacement of personnel, changes in job classifications, etc., which may result from the systems change. It is well to remember, change of any type is usually viewed with suspicion and distrust, and is aggravated severely if an employee suspects that his own job may be at stake. Management's assurance of the employees' future can result in the study team receiving increased cooperation from those on whom they will be dependent for information regarding the existing operational system.

The consequences of any systems study are far-reaching. The procedures required in the operation of a typical EDP system and the results of the study itself often bring about changes in the basic organization of the firm. All levels of management must realize this and be willing to support any well-based decisions of the study group if the study is to be fruitful.

To sum up this area of discussion, there are several aspects to be considered by management in its approach to an EDP feasibility investigation. Areas which must be specifically delineated include: the definition of the problem; the scope of the study to be made; the ultimate objectives which management hopes to achieve; the organization, selection, and training of the study team; and the authority to be delegated to the team in carrying out its mission. A timetable must be developed, at least in skeleton form, to indicate to the study team members and management in general the time to be allotted to the study.

Problem Definition

The problem itself and the scope of the study should be so stated that there will be little doubt in the minds of the study group as to the extent of the investigation and the areas to be covered within the firm. The problem may be as limited as one involving a determination of the feasibility of acquiring a computer to do the current record-keeping procedures.[1] It may also be so broad in scope as to include the possibility of a completely integrated data control system involving operations research techniques and other tools of scientific management.

The investment required in a modern computer is always significant. It is not unusual for an electronic computer system to have a value in excess of several hundred thousands or even millions of dollars. To this cost must be added the expense of installation, personnel training, programing, and planning. In many instances these additional expenses have equaled the cost of the equipment. As a result of this large investment, the decision as to whether a computer should be installed is a major one required of top management. In order for them to be able to make a truly intelligent decision they must have information prepared in depth which will give them a sound basis for making the decision. Appraising the economics of a computer installation is not significantly different from the techniques used in the appraisal of any other large capital investment. However, the problems involved are different from those normally faced by managers and businesses in the selection of office equipment in general in that they are much more complex.

Objectives Desired

The formulation of objectives to be derived from an EDP feasibility study is quite important. First, a formal set of objectives forces management to give the whole subject matter serious thought. In the process of arriving at a set of objectives, the problems involved, in attaining these objectives, will come to be more clearly defined. Second, a framework will be developed within which the study team can operate, so it will know exactly what is expected of it, the limitations under which it must work, and the time allowed to reach a conclusion.

Objectives desired are often taken for granted, and many considerations which should have been investigated may have been overlooked. In

---

[1] Such a limited consideration has, at times, been suggested by some business firms, but anyone with experience in installing business computer systems would never consider such a limited approach in justifying the system.

retrospect, top managers of companies which have made major changes in its systems have indicated that their work would have gone much more smoothly if they had adopted a formal slate of objectives. In a systems study, unlike some other areas requiring management consideration, the definition of the problem and statement of objectives is not a purely academic task. However, it cannot be emphasized too strongly that management will find it profitable to consider their objectives in an unbiased, common-sense manner before embarking on a systems study.

The desired objectives should indicate the various approaches to be followed and even, perhaps, the emphasis necessary to achieve the end results desired. Normally, the objectives will be centered around one or more basic types of economic advantage. There have, however, been instances where the glamour of being one of the first to install a computer has outweighed the importance of other possible considerations and has sometimes led to regret later for the actions taken.

Typical objectives that may encourage a firm to automate its office may include one or more of the following items, which are only representative of the many conceivable reasons which may be proposed by any specific firm:

1. An attempt to reduce clerical costs through a reduction in the required clerical force. (Part of the gains here may be offset by a general upgrading of the positions retained.) If there is a reduction in clerical help, some savings in the office space requirements may result.
2. Eliminate conflicting and overlapping services by combining some of the many functions and activities now performed by separate departments and branches in the preparation and processing of data and in duplication in file maintenance.
3. Improve employee relations by providing them with additional information in such reporting areas as those of payroll, pensions, taxes, insurance, etc.
4. Increase the productivity of clerical operations through greatly improved processing techniques which are not only faster but which also become more accurate with the elimination of human intervention in the processing and preparation of reports.
5. Obtain greater operating efficiency in data processing through increased speed, improved accuracy, and decreased equipment idleness due to infrequent "downtime" and reliability of the computer system.
6. Reduce expenses through faster billing procedures. This may be realized in the reduction of interest charges on borrowed capital previously necessary because of the longer carrying time on customer accounts.
7. Provide more flexibility for the expansion of the firm's data processing capabilities as growth occurs.
8. Improve customer relations and competitive position through accuracy and timeliness in reporting, billing, and in the notification of scheduling or shipping changes or delays.
9. Permit more timely decisions by management. This is made possible through the current reports and data provided by the speed of the computer and

more complete reporting in the form of information which would not have been economically feasible or available using conventional methods.

10. Gain greater control of information and a consequent strengthening of the organizational structure through improved system and accounting controls which minimize human intervention by incorporating checks and balances which are automatically performed as the data is processed.

11. Permit the use of operations research and other management science techniques which could bring such typical future benefits as the reduction of inventory investments and other working capital requirements; reductions in production costs through more efficient scheduling, parts control, and costing techniques; and reductions in selling costs through improved market and sales analyses.

As a summary, the basic objectives of any EDP study must be to enable the firm to earn a larger net profit than is possible under its present system of operation. The larger net profit must accrue through improvement in many specific areas of operation such as: savings in clerical work, improved overall clerical performance and greater operating efficiency in the processing of data, speedier collections on accounts outstanding, improved customer relations and services, and better and more timely reports for use in management decisions.

Authority Delegation

The authority delegated to the group should be clearly outlined. This is necessary as not only those conducting the study but those with whom they will have contact must fully understand the powers and responsibilities which have been assigned to the group. This is particularly essential where functional procedures tend to cut across departmental lines as departmental jealousy or fear of loss of departmental controls may lead to non-cooperation or even downright hostility to any proposed change.

It is not unusual for some segment of top management, as well as many of those in the various levels of middle management to be outright dubious of the necessity of even considering an electronic computer. The assignment of authority from top management may have to be used at times to override, and we hope overcome, any resentment to the study being made, the interruption of work that will occur as the study progresses, and to lessen the general resistance that is always present in any change. Support of top management throughout the assignment is an absolute requirement for the success for any systems-change decision.

Committee Considerations

The decision as to the composition of the study committee is, of course, vital. There are several alternatives available, and all have been used with varying degrees of success by different firms. Such a committee may involve only company personnel, be completely contracted out to a consulting firm, or may represent some degree of combination of consultants and company employees.

The amount of training required to qualify the members of the study team for the work expected of them will depend on the knowledgeability of the individual members in the general area of systems analysis and electronic data processing.

A tentative time schedule will have to be developed to guide the committee in the progression of their assignment.

ORGANIZATION OF THE STUDY GROUP. One of the first considerations in the organization of such a study group is to select the individual who will be in charge of its direction. His duties will include the review of the work of the members of the study team, make policy decisions within the framework management provides, see that the work is proceeding according to schedule, and generally direct the systems study activities.

If possible, this data processing coordinator should hold a rank comparable to that of a vice president. Experience has shown that there is a positive relationship between the extent of the success of the study and its resulting system implementation and the level of management to which the study group is responsible. It is advisable that the head of the EDP study rank high in the executive hierarchy and that there be a minimum number of levels between himself and top management.

The actual committee should be held to about six or no more than eight members to avoid inflexibility in making the decisions necessary as they proceed at each stage of the undertaking. This does not mean that there will never be more than these six or eight people working on the study at one time as key individuals will be called upon to aid at various times, especially during the systems study, and clerks will be called upon to do much of the "leg work" involved. Neither does this indicate that this many people will be "permanently" employed in these duties as much of the time only key committee members will be at work in specific areas of study.

SELECTION OF THE STUDY GROUP. When the firm has no qualified individuals, or cannot spare them for the period required for the study, it may be necessary to turn the complete responsibility over to professional consultants. This is normally not recommended, however, for several reasons. First, the consultants, except perhaps in the case of the external auditors, will rarely have any knowledge of the firm's detailed procedures and requirements. Next, company personnel will not receive training in the systems work, programming, and operational techniques required of them at a later date in the installation and operational stages—if a decision is made to install a computer. The consultant will have little or no responsibility for the continuing operations of the computer system. And, finally, most of the "know-how" developed in the study will belong to the consultant and will be lost, as far as the firm is concerned, when the study is completed.

For the reasons outlined above it is preferable that the study be made by company personnel if at all possible. It may be desirable to use an experienced consultant to direct and guide the committee in the procedures which need to be followed if an overall successful feasibility study is to result, but again the actual work should be performed by company personnel.

If the company has employees who have previously been associated with such a study in another firm or have special training and/or background in computers and electronic data processing, there is little doubt that these people should be included on the investigation committee and should be given particular consideration. If administratively qualified, it may be that one of these individuals should be placed in charge of the direction of the study group.

Also, inasmuch as one of the most vital areas of the study is that of systems analysis, at least one of the committee members should be from the accounting or systems departments. This may, in some instances, be the controller himself or someone high on his staff.

Where the organizational structure of the firm is based on departmental assignments, representatives from the major departments who are familiar with the respective functions of the departments should be included. This serves at least two purposes: (1) these representatives bring authoritative know-how in their respective areas to the committee and (2) generally, their departments will tend to be more cooperative if the personnel of the departments feel they have been represented in the decision-making process. Others on the committee might include some individuals from top management, production control, personnel, and marketing.

All members of the study committee should be highly qualified individuals who have a genuine interest in the future of the firm. In addition, some of the qualities which members of the study group should possess are as follows:

1. They should be familiar with company philosophies, systems, and objectives. In other words, they should know what makes the company "tick."
2. A knowledge of accounting is essential, in that the members should be skilled in systems analysis, know legal and audit requirements, and know what is expected of the system in general.
3. Since they will be making many recommendations to management, they should have sound judgment and objectivity in that they can draw logical conclusions from a set of given information.
4. Since the members of the team will be working together for an extended period of time, they must have demonstrated a spirit of cooperation in previous assignments.

5. The group should be composed of a panel of very thorough people as many small details must be satisfactorily dealt with.
6. They should be imaginative people who will avoid falling into "ruts" left by someone else, for the synthesis stage of the analysis requires creative thinking—the art of generating new ideas. The success of any new system largely depends on the judgment-seasoned creativity of the systems committee.
7. If at all possible, the team should be chosen from a group who have demonstrated some research capability, as the major tasks will be concerned with fact-finding. For this ability to do effective research, people holding graduate degrees are often chosen to be members of the survey team.
8. Since the members will be dealing with company employees who may resent the innovation which the group represents, they must be capable of exerting the utmost in tact and diplomacy.
9. Above all, the group must have the confidence of management.

It is obvious that it would be almost impossible to find all, or even most, of these qualities in one person, let alone in each of the several people comprising the group. Consequently, these requirements must necessarily apply to the group as a whole, and not to each individual member of the group.

TRAINING THE STUDY GROUP. Since most of the members of the survey team probably won't possess the specialized knowledge required of them as the study progresses, they should undergo a period of training. This training normally includes visiting installations which are in operation in other firms, talking with the personnel of these firms, taking notes, and generally finding out what goes on and is required. Most computer manufacturers offer intensive courses of instructions which range from a week to three weeks in length. Becoming familiar with books and periodicals related to the study area can also be invaluable during this period of training. Nearly all business trade associations have information available concerning computers in their various phases with particular emphasis on the industry represented by the trade association. Some universities are beginning to offer courses in data processing with emphasis on EDP and computers. Incidentally, the growth of collegiate courses in this area may tend to alleviate some of this general background problem in the future and permit the members of such a team to spend more training time in studying specific equipment and its related procedures. For the present, however, with a lack of computer-trained personnel in most businesses, training the study group remains a very important aspect of the considerations necessary in conducting a systems-change feasibility study.

Scheduling a Timetable for the Study

The time required for a typical systems-change decision study will, of course, vary considerably with the definition of the problem and the extent of the objectives desired. Such a study may involve only a few months or (and this is not at all unusual) continue for as long as a year or more. It is very important, though, that the outlined scope of the study be investigated as thoroughly as possible and in sufficient depth of detail to allow management to make the major decision involved.

There should be, if possible, some provision for scheduling the time required for the study. It is important that the information needed be obtained and developed properly and that some deadlines be set for the completion of the various segments of the study and the study as a whole. If the individuals involved in the study have not had previous experience or are not guided by an experienced consultant, these deadlines will have to be set by some estimation technique and it should be understood that some flexibility will have to be provided.

GENERAL CONSIDERATIONS. The committee's basic obligation involves the major question whether electronic data processing equipment will increase overall company efficiency in terms of financial savings, customer relations, and operating efficiencies. To accomplish these ends the committee will have to determine the company's requirements for data processing and place particular emphasis on the areas in which the greatest improvements can be made. These requirements should not only include those of the record-keeping system but, perhaps of even greater importance, those involving new managerial techniques which are so broad as to include such areas, among others, as purchasing and/or production, marketing, and inventory control.

If the answer to the above question is in the affirmative, then the committee will attempt to recommend the system which will best fit the requirements determined. This will be accomplished by evaluating applicable available equipment, both as to cost and ability to perform the work required, and by developing detailed data which will permit the committee to compare the costs of the proposed system with the costs of the present system.

To accomplish these goals, the committee will need a broad view of the organization when charting the flow of information throughout the firm.

Once the questions of should the firm install a computer and, if so, what computer should it acquire are answered, the committee has fulfilled the obligation for which it was appointed. However, in many instances this does not complete the assignment for all of the members of the committee, as these individuals now have the background necessary to make them the logical ones to supervise training programs and systems applications, as well as the installation and operation of the computer.

QUESTIONS

1. Why is the statement made in the chapter that it is most important for top management to be intimately involved in determining whether a company

should convert its data processing system to an electronic data processing system?

2. What are some of the areas of problem which may arise when the decision has been made to convert to EDP?

3. List and explain some of the many reasons why management should advise employees that a computer is under consideration and continue to keep them advised as time passes.

4. What are some of the possible impacts that the acquisition of a computer may have upon individual employees of the firm?

5. Which of the objectives mentioned in the chapter as typical of those of companies who want to automate their data processing systems do you consider to be the most valid or important? Be certain to explain why you have made the choices you have made.

6. Why is it necessary to have a justification study made prior to the acquisition of a computer? Wouldn't it be easier and quicker for top management to make the decision, and then go out and procure one?

7. What would be the composition of an ideal study group to make a computer justification study? Explain your answer fully.

8. What would be some desirable personal characteristics for members of an ideal study group?

9. What are some of the essential things which a study group must do in preparing itself for its task?

10. How may the members of the study group become familiar with the specialized knowledge which will be required for them to reach their decision?

CHAPTER **20**

The EDP

Justification Study

(CONTINUED)

ONCE THE approach to the justification study has progressed to the stage where management has outlined the problems confronting the firm in this area and the study team has been selected and organized, the survey of the existing systems is the next procedure to be considered.

To review and add additional depth to the initial discussion of systems analysis in Chapter 5, the systems survey should investigate the following basic areas:

1. Scheduling requirements.
2. Review of current operations.
3. Analysis of forms and reports.
4. Work volume estimates.
5. Cost of present operations.
6. Personnel requirements and considerations.

Scheduling Requirements

As mentioned in the previous chapter, one of the early duties of the study committee is to determine a timetable for the study. This timetable must, of course, be extended through the conversion and implementation of the computer if a decision is reached to automate. It is with such a decision in mind that the following scheduling requirements are proposed.

Scheduling requirements must be planned as far in advance as possible to anticipate the problems which will arise in any change from one system to another.

Experience has shown that there is a distinct tendency to underestimate the time required—not only for the survey as a whole but for many of the phases which the study will have to encompass. Areas which must be considered in scheduling are those involving: personnel, work volume estimates, programming and its related aspects, new forms and supplies, files, physical space requirements, installation considerations, conversion plans and peripheral equipment.

Most firms will have some realization of the time it will take to organize the study, to select and train the committee, and to gather the data needed for a decision on the feasibility of office automation. Few, however, come close to estimating correctly the time and effort which will be required to implement the decision.

A typical breakdown of the relative percentage of time involved in the various phases of a systems investigation and implementation is as follows:

Organizing for the investigation	15%
Investigating and designing the system	15
Training programmers and systems people	7
Flowcharting and block diagramming	14
Programming	10
Program assembly, testing, and debugging	21
Planning and preparing for the conversion	5
Parallel operation and system checking	7
Miscellaneous	6
	100%

PERSONNEL. One of the personnel problems mentioned earlier, but so important that it warrants repetition, is to prepare the workers for the change. Scheduling the conversion may require the issuance of bulletins, group meetings, and other continuing notification of the progress of the study. This may even involve some general educational sessions involving lectures and/or films on related subject areas. To promote proper cooperation, maintain good morale, and a high peak of efficiency, the worker should be informed as to why the change is needed.

The number and types of personnel required after the change-over should be ascertained so that staff can be provided to facilitate adequately the promotion of a smooth, efficient transition. Any personnel needed to fill the newly developing technical positions must have time and the opportunity to receive the necessary training required of the new positions. This then, brings up a consideration of any needed educational training which may have to be provided either by the firm itself or by computer manufacturers.

WORK VOLUME ESTIMATES. A schedule must be completed for work volume estimates for the new operations. These will not only help to determine the forms and supplies needed and manpower requirements, but are necessary determinations before programming routines can be started.

PROGRAMMING AND RELATED ASPECTS.   Much preinstallation systems work must be planned in advance. Procedures such as flowcharting, block diagramming, programming, testing the individual program runs for accuracy, and testing all the runs for consistency and compatibility must be provided for. It is essential that programs be set up and debugged before the equipment is delivered and installed, as monthly payments will be starting (or amortization of the cost, if outright purchase is made) and management will expect operational returns on these costs. Time must be scheduled for each of these work areas.

In reference to the previous listing giving the relative percentage of time involved in the various phases of a system investigation and implementation, only 7 percent of the time shown is spent in training programmers and systems people. This percentage is relatively small because only a comparatively few people are involved in this phase of the work. However, the time required to train such individuals properly and allow them to develop and become proficient in their work will probably be from four to nine months. This depends, of course, on the individuals involved, the complexity and extent of the new system, and the characteristics of the equipment selected. This means that training cannot be started until a decision is made that automation is feasible and the equipment is selected to meet the requirements of the particular system. Consequently, considerable time must elapse before actual programming can begin.

Then, the period required for the almost integral effort of flowcharting and block diagramming, programming, and program assembly, testing, and debugging will represent nearly 50 percent of the total effort required. A small advantage is gained, however, in that the planning and preparing for the conversion phase may be progressing simultaneously during this same period.

Once a decision is made to automate, nearly every firm so far involved wants to get the computer installed and complete the change-over as rapidly as possible. It is very hard for management to realize that, even though the feasibility study committee has taken perhaps a number of months to reach its decision, only approximately one third of the effort required for computer implementation has actually been expended. This often explains the rush to get the computer installed and the pressure, put on the systems people and the programmers, to start using the computer as early as possible. Only incomplete, improperly controlled, and inefficient programs can result, and then management will be dissatisfied with either, or both, the computer or the results to be forthcoming.

NEW FORMS AND SUPPLIES. The design of new forms must be undertaken as early as possible as not only the data to be shown on each form, but its format as well, must be set before programming can proceed.

Timing must be given careful attention when ordering the new forms to assure delivery in advance of the date the forms will be needed. Timing must also be considered regarding any supplies required by the new system, as these must also be on hand before they are required.

FILES. Decisions must be made regarding any files to be converted in the new procedures. First, consider what files are to be converted. Then, give thought to what will be the form of these new files (punched card, magnetic tape, or magnetic disk); what are the best procedures to be followed in their conversion; what files, if any, will be consolidated or merged with others; what will be the new filing patterns and sequences; and finally, if not stored in some type of machine memory, what will be the physical location of those files.

These problems involving file design and arrangement can be exceedingly complex and time-consuming; therefore, schedules should provide for the procedures necessary.

PHYSICAL SPACE REQUIREMENTS. General floor space requirements should be ascertained, along with lighting, power, heat, and ventilation needs. The possibility of remodeling and face lifting should be considered and generally planned so the work can be completed far enough in advance to allow the installation of the equipment.

INSTALLATION CONSIDERATIONS. Planning the actual installation takes much thought and consideration. The actual time for the installation must be set. Conditions should be examined to determine the most suitable time.

CONVERSION PLANS. Decisions must be made concerning whether the system should be installed at one time or in parts. A time should be set when existing procedures will be discontinued and when the new procedures will take effect.

EQUIPMENT. Once the timing schedule is completed, the requirements determined may indicate, or play some part in, the consideration of additional peripheral equipment or even perhaps, a larger, smaller, or otherwise different type of computer than originally anticipated. Therefore, scheduling should not be put off until the equipment is chosen.

SUMMARY. Schedules should be as realistic as possible. They should not only provide a timetable for the progression of the work, but should also be used as a basis for reporting achievement of the various phases as completed. There should be regular formalized reports prepared to keep management (all levels concerned with the project) properly informed. These reports not only serve as historical records, but should also indicate delays and problems which have come up and aid any department or functional area affected in replanning its timetable.

Review of Current Operations

In reviewing the present operations, care must be taken to obtain clear and concise information. The information should include the organizational structure and the chain of command within the firm. The review should spell out the procedures currently in use and indicate the function every person concerned with each given procedure performs. The existence, maintenance, and proper use of policy and procedural manuals, if any, should be documentated.

Flowcharting should play an important role in the review of the organization's current operations. These flowcharts should include each department's procedures, and there should be an overall chart which shows the main lines of movement of the data required. These charts should indicate the origination of data into the system, the files maintained, the sequence of operations, and the reports produced.

At this point, it might be a good idea for the committee or consultants to meet as a group to challenge the existing operations. Questions should be asked in respect to the purpose and results of each of the procedural operations. Some examples of typical questions include the following: Have conditions changed since the operation was established? Is the operation a result of habit? Is the operation created by an incomplete previous or subsequent operation? How necessary is the result obtained in each operation? Is there any possibility the end result could be changed and the procedure eliminated? Can the needed results be secured as a by-product of another operation or in some other manner?

Other information which may be required in such a review concerns equipment and office layout. Detailed diagrams could be made, disclosing the floor plan in relation to the flow of work. The present office layout should be challenged as to whether it serves a functional purpose in aiding the flow of work.

Existing equipment used in the current operations should receive much attention. Consideration should be given to its operating condition as well as to the possibility of its obsolescence in a systems change. The use of the equipment should also be investigated. Just how much is the equipment used? Are existing machines operating close to capacity? Is proper control exercised over equipment to prevent unauthorized functions from being performed?

Though personnel is discussed in more detail later, part of the review should include a listing of job classifications and the number of employees.

Notes should be made on employee turnover, morale, training, supervision, and how each would be effected by a change to an EDP system.

In summary, the survey of existing procedures and operations should reveal relationships of personnel, equipment, and documents in the origination of documents, processing procedures, resulting records, and final reports.

Analysis of Forms and Reports

The forms and reports used in the current operations will be noted on the flowcharts previously prepared in the review of present operations. Detailed analysis of these should be made questioning each item as follows:

.01 Is the form being made out in proper place and by the proper person?
.02 Is all the information really needed? Is all the necessary information included?
.03 Do we get the correct number of copies? Are the proper persons receiving them? Is the line of transportation the best?
.04 Is the form designed for the best use, for both maker and reader?
.05 Could the form be eliminated through substitution as a by-product of another form?[1]

Additional questions should be those concerning the descriptive headings used, the sequence of the data, the reason for this sequence, how often the form is referred to in its normal usage, and what are its file retention requirements.[2]

As the data on each of the different forms are assembled, the committee or consultant will have to study each form in its relation to the present system. The use of each of the present forms in both the current and the proposed EDP system should be questioned. The firm should not accept the data collected or the reporting forms used in their present operations as either ideal or even usable for the new system to be developed. Every effort should be expended at this stage in the study to provide more efficient forms for use in future operations—regardless of the equipment system to be implemented.

In addition to the attempt to develop more efficient forms,[3] special attention should also be given to the possibility of a standardization of

---

[1] U.S. Treasury Department, Internal Revenue Service, Data Processing Division, Systems and Procedures, *A Notebook for the Systems Man* (Washington, D.C.: U.S. Government Printing Office, February, 1963), p. 13.

[2] Also see Chapter 5.

[3] Form design requirements are discussed in more detail in Chapter 4.

forms. This requires that care be taken to avoid duplication of data so that information provided on one form is not also being provided on other forms.

Forms which are improperly designed will lead to unnecessary and even duplicated work effort. This will quickly be reflected in a loss of efficiency in their use.

The same review procedures should be applied to report forms which are prepared for management. It is important to remember, at this point, that the data included on the present reports—as well as the reports themselves—may have little relevance to the information management actually needs.

The information determined necessary should be presented in a format that is understandable and convenient to use and that requires very little effort in its interpretation. Timing is a very important consideration which should not be overlooked when evaluating reports for management. Each report should be available by the time it is needed and when it will serve management best.

From the analysis of existing forms and reports, the committee should know the wants and needs of management. It should have, in part, revealed whether or not the currently used forms and reports are all necessary; it should have uncovered the possibility that additional reports or data forms might be necessary to facilitate managerial decisions.

The various input and output devices used by EDP systems, as well as the types of forms which various systems are able to utilize in the production of reports, should be carefully analyzed before considering new forms and reports. Different types of forms and reports recommended by equipment manufacturers should be carefully considered and studied to determine which will best provide the requirements of the firm.

When the committee has completed the analysis of existing and possible new forms and reports, it should then reach a decision regarding the reports to be recommended to be produced, the data to be included, the format in which this data is to be presented, the number of copies required, and when the reports are to be produced. This information is vital in the design of any system. The volume of data to be presented and the pattern of the format to be used can not only have considerable effect on the output equipment requirements but also on the acceptability of the document produced by those who will be using it in their daily routine.

It must be constantly kept in mind that one of the major considerations in changing to an EDP system is that of improving the quality, quantity, and timing of needed reports. In some cases, reports of given types, particularly those involving extensive mathematical computation, cannot be produced manually due to the excessive costs involved and time required for their production. These may, however, be made available through a modern computer system at a cost which can be justified, and the reports can still be timely enough to aid management in its decision-making processes.

Work Volume Determination

A careful analysis should be made regarding the work volumes required in each individual department of the firm relative to every clerical procedure with which it is concerned. This information will be required in determining present cost of operations as well as in estimating costs of proposed systems to be considered.

Some of the procedures to be followed in determining departmental work volumes are:

1. Check the procedural flowcharts previously prepared for the work to be performed in each individual department.
2. Determine the data required by every function performed by the department in each procedure which flows through this area. This not only includes the data originating in the department, but the data, probably already in some type of report form, required from others.
3. Analyze the reports prepared by each department's personnel as to what data are included, for whom the report is prepared, the number of copies required, and the use to which the data will be put.
4. Build a file of each procedural flow and attach a copy of each related report prepared by the various departments.

After this information has been recorded for each individual department, it can be combined to determine the work volume of the entire company.

This work volume data should then be analyzed, both as a whole and by the individual department, to determine if the work volume findings will be adaptable to an EDP system. Where the work volume is small and the procedures required are varied, it is quite probable that EDP would neither be practical nor economical. However, when it is found there is a large amount of work involving duties of a similar nature in several areas, an EDP system should probably be considered.

Work volumes may also be used to determine procedural areas which may be consolidated or otherwise simplified to either improve the system in general or to cut the costs involved, or both.

Work simplification and standardization should be given special consideration. This may involve only the procedural aspect or it may also include form design or redesign. A typical procedural improvement might be in the preparation of a machine-processable document at the time of the recording of the original transaction. A form improvement might be to include additional data on a standard report preparation which would serve the needs now filled by two or more reports. This might be accomplished by using partial carbons for some copies of the report, which would omit some of the data included on other copies but not needed or desired by some users of the report. This might involve cost or profit data which some users should not have access to.

Depending on the depth of the completed work volume study, the findings in procedural areas which appear to be subject to systems improvement may have to be supplemented by additional depth of detail regarding the procedural flow of the data.

The quantitative data gathered on the number of various transactions which occur throughout the firm's operation should be analyzed in terms of the work loads which may result. If the daily level of these transactions is fairly constant, then summarization of the data will be relatively simple for determining work loads for the day, week, month, or year. However, when there are definite cyclical effects present in the business cycle of the firm, additional consideration will be required to prevent "bottlenecks" developing in the system in these periods of exceptional activity. This information is necessary in the determination of the operational time required in the schedules to be developed for processing the various procedures involved.

Other quantitative data to be gathered in work volume determination is that which conerns the files required for both the originating and reporting data. Here, not only the number and types of files and records required are important, but also the information concerning *what data* are stored in these files and records and how the data are to be utilized. This knowledge is vital in determining the size and type of electronic memory storage required of an EDP system.

Cost of Present Operations

At first, many of the applicable costs related to as broad an area as the clerical systems and procedures of a given firm may appear to be rather nebulous and hard to determine. However, such an analysis is a vital and necessary requirement in a justification study, as it is impossible to ascertain if a change may be feasible until the present cost of these operations is known and is compared with the estimated costs of the new system recommended.

Some of the major areas of costs to be considered include those of personnel, forms and supplies, equipment, and the physical space required to house the staff, files, and equipment. These costs may be determined, for some time period which allows a comparison of present and future costs, either by departmental or by functional analyses, whichever method is easier in the particular firm under consideration. How this is done may, in part, be set by the manner in which the system study is performed. If the entire system is to be replaced or revised, as it would be in a completely integrated system, then costs may be "lumped" together to a much greater extent than is possible in partial automation. In such a major revision, costs of individual procedures would no longer have the comparability possible where only selected procedures are to be automated and present procedural costs can be directly weighed against the new.

PERSONNEL. Personnel costs, at first glance, may not appear to be too difficult to determine, as clerical personnel are usually separated both physically and functionally from production personnel. Where this is the case, these costs can be fairly easily determined unless the systems analysis was made by function. In this case, personnel costs would have to be allocated, on some predetermined basis, to each function performed by each individual. However, it will normally have been discovered in the systems study that, particularly in the origination of data, this clear-cut demarcation is not always present.

To mention an example of job classifications in which clerical functions may be present, in addition to the primary function, foremen may be used to prepare a roster of production workers present (or absent)—though in a firm of any size this will probably be part of the duties of timekeeping, which is a clerical function. The foremen, however, will probably either oversee or perform the duty of recording the time spent by each worker (and maybe each machine) on each job or contract—unless a data collection system is in use, and this probably would not be the case if office automation is not already a *de facto* condition.

Other mixed functions to be found in the plant, among many, would be:

1. In receiving and shipping where records may be kept on incoming and outgoing items, on the related freight charges on these goods, and on the physical condition of the merchandise received.
2. In materials inventory control and maintenance where records may be kept of such things as goods on hand, the minimum and maximum stock levels of each item recommended, order quantities and normal suppliers of each type of good, and to whom and for what purpose items are to be released into the production stream.
3. In tool and miscellaneous supply storage where the records needed would be somewhat similar to those above in material inventories along with data on frequency of use and stock item condition in the case of such items as tools which are checked out, used, and returned.
4. In equipment maintenance shops where detailed records will be kept on downtime and on the labor supplies, and parts used in maintaining each piece of equipment. Many of these records, and their associated duties, may be replaced either totally or in part in the systems change, depending on the extent of the automation deemed feasible.

FORMS AND SUPPLIES. The current cost of forms and supplies used in the present system is largely a matter of record. However, if only part of the procedures are to be automated, the affected forms and supplies for these procedures will have to be separated costwise from those which will continue to be used.

Where new forms are to be designed, there will be initial setup costs for their reproduction as well as the costs involved in the time spent on the actual design of these forms. This last cost may be more than anticipated, as form design is exacting work and requires consideration of all the related procedures and documents as well as the technical requirements of any new equipment under consideration.

EQUIPMENT. The cost of the equipment presently in use should also be easily determined by consulting the accounting records. Here, however, the net or book value of these items may have little relationship to either actual market value or their value in terms of the ability of the equipment to serve the firm over an extended time in the future. Depreciation previously recorded on this equipment may not have been properly determined in the first place, such as where an error was made in estimating the life of the equipment or where one of the accelerated methods of depreciation may have been utilized for tax purposes.

A new life estimate may have to be made if the equipment is to be considered for use in the future or a salvage or disposal value may have to be determined if it will be replaced by other equipment in the newly proposed system.

Equipment costs to be considered are those on all the items of equipment used in the clerical operation. This will not only include the bookkeeping equipment itself, but the files, desks, chairs, cabinets, typewriters, calculators, and any other related equipment. Many of these items may not be required in the new system if there is a reduction in clerical personnel.

PHYSICAL SPACE. If a detailed cost system is in use, the cost of the physical space required in clerical procedures may already be allocated to the record-keeping function. If not, some method of allocating these costs should be determined, as some of these costs may be transferred to other functions if a new electronic computer is installed.

OPERATIONAL EXPENSES. Operational and the many types of expense such as light, heat, air conditioning, and personnel related costs, such as life insurance, hospitalization, and pensions, should all be determined and detailed, in as much depth as feasible, as many of these costs will be severely altered if the system is automated.

Personnel Requirements and Considerations

It is important that the employees be advised as early as convenient in the planning stage of the fact that a possible systems change is under consideration. Experience has demonstrated, in studies made of the impact of automation on office personnel, that if management will impress upon the employees the need for a systems change and then keep them informed of progress as it is made, employee problems will normally be minimized. These studies also indicated that in instances where management deliberately avoided discussing the systems change with employees, knowledge of the study prevailed anyway, unfounded rumors quickly became rampant, and the feasibility study results proved unsatisfactory.

Resistance to change is inherent in most of us for the basic reason that we are sure of the familiar and fearful of what we do not understand. Fear and misunderstanding usually take over when management does not explain the benefits, in human terms, to be derived from new methods and equipment. This may result in the plans for the change being handicapped by the withholding or delay in providing needed information, and the possible results of the change may very probably become severely distorted by these efforts to resist change.

The more the employee knows about the changes to be implemented the more he will become aware of the fact that business automation still requires people to get the work ready for the machines, requires people to tell the machine what to do, requires people to operate them, and also requires people to interpret the results obtained.

All workers associated in any way with clerical procedures must be made to feel that they are not on the outside, but that the success of the entire project depends on each playing some part in it. They should be encouraged to submit ideas and suggestions concerning the change-over. Careful consideration and acknowledgment should be given to any constructive ideas forthcoming.

Fear of loss of jobs and of the future are natural reactions to any mention of the word automation. There is plenty of justification of these fears as far as the production line, and its associated machinery, is concerned, and there is little question that these fears have received considerable publicity in connection with our continuing national unemployment problems. However, nearly every study made of business office automation, and there has been a large number of these studies, has concluded that very few personnel have been displaced as a result of it, that most of the positions affected have been upgraded, and that often after a short period of adjustment, the total staff is as large as it was before automation.

The clerical positions which are normally affected by office automation are those which involve repetitious and routine procedures. There is generally a large turnover of the employees holding these positions because of the dullness and drudgery associated with these positions. Many of these people have relatively little training for more advanced work, and there is a tendency for them to shift positions relatively often in hopes of finding "greener pastures" and more challenging positions. Others who have training or special abilities tend to advance from these routine jobs as new positions present themselves. This turnover rate is the answer to the low displacement record in office automation. It is not unusual for the systems-change decision along with the period of preparing and waiting for the equipment to be delivered after the order is placed (usually 12 to 18 months) and the actual conversion to computer processing to require a period of not less than one year and as long as three years' time for completion. This time lapse allows the firm to consolidate its work loads, hire temporary replacements where required, and use the attrition due to retirement to its advantage in the reduction of these routine-type positions.

A number of the individuals who have training or special aptitudes and abilities will be needed in the new operations. These people will have an exceptional opportunity to advance to more challenging positions in the firm. Training programs, furnished by both the firm itself and the computer manufacturer, will be available to them and completely new vistas of job opportunity will open up for those capable and interested. These individuals will, almost without exception, be upgraded in both position and compensation.

Additional procedures involving techniques not previously available will be economically feasible with the new computer installation to guide management in the decision-making processes. These techniques may involve the addition of personnel to gather additional detailed information needed as well as technical personnel such as mathematicians, statisticians, engineers, and others.

Historically, the introduction of machines into industrial and office operations has, on the whole and in the long run, increased employment and raised the standard of living. The fact is that electronic data processing has and will replace some people, but there is little evidence to support any doubt of the increased productivity gains that will be available and the probable increase in total employment that will accrue as a result. Certainly, business office automation has resulted in a decrease in the drudgery present in the day-in–day-out functions required in work involving masses of figures and data and has freed many individuals to do analysis and more advanced work which will better serve the needs of management. It opens opportunities for more people to work at jobs involving the use of intelligence and judgment. In fact, all classes of jobs from office clerk to top-level management will be affected quantitatively and qualitatively as electronic computers are installed and properly utilized.

The fears and misconceptions the average worker has concerning electronic systems can only be overcome through education. Employees can be persuaded to accept office automation by making them feel more important as a result of using the new equipment and by encouraging them to make suggestions as to how the electronic data processing system can be adapted to the needs of the firm.

Retaining sound relationships with employees is possibly one of the hardest parts of the study, but in turn it is probably the most important aspect of all. Disorganization and dissatisfaction on the part of the employees will not only have its effect on the study itself, but may be extended into continuing and long-run personnel problems.

The time spent in evaluating human relations problems, getting essential information to the employees, and keeping open channels of communication is a vital part of the program for the introduction of an electronic data processing system or any other major change in processing business information.

ANNOTATED BIBLIOGRAPHY

CANNING, RICHARD G. *Electronic Data Processing for Business and Industry.* New York: John Wiley & Sons, Inc., 1956.

    The purpose of the book is to advocate the efficient use of EDP. It is concerned mainly with the period of time that begins with management's first interest in EDP and ends with the presentation to top management of a proposed plan of action.

————. *Installing Electronic Data Processing Systems.* New York: John Wiley & Sons, Inc., 1957.

    A thorough approach to the overall area relating to the many problems of, and possible methods to approach, an electronic computer feasibility study and the implementation of an EDP System.

DENBY, EARL W. "Five-Year Shift to EDP: The Stages and Problems," *Controller,* Vol. 28 (March, 1960), pp. 114–16, 118.

    This article explains the complete change-over of the Huron Portland Cement Company from manual to electronic data processing. This shows the step-by-step transition and explains the problems encountered and how they were overcome.

MCNERNEY, JOHN. *Installing and Using an Automatic Data Processing System.* New York: McKinsey & Co., Inc., 1961.

    This book is concerned particularly with the problems that arise in installing an automatic data processing system. It focuses on the problems of a single company and its problems of processing sales orders and control of finished goods inventory and control of sales effort.

OPTNER, STANFORD L. *Systems Analysis For Business Management.* Englewood Cliffs, N.J.: Prentice-Hall, Inc., 1960.

    An analysis of business systems in terms of a feasibility study—the study itself, selection of equipment, cost-saving analysis, and possibilities of including operations research techniques. A series of case studies is provided.

PINKERTON, PAUL W. "Helping to Put Electronic Equipment to Work in Business," *NAA Bulletin*, Vol. 44, No. 9 (May, 1963).

This article is concerned with seeing that accountants use electronic data processing equipment in any manner which would be of benefit to the company. In the latter portion of the article, data areas regarded as capable of integrated processing are charted and described.

SEALLY, W. J. "Planning for EDP," *Cost Accountant*, Vol. 37, May 1959, pp. 433–5.

This article explains what planning should be made after the decision to install a specific machine has been made. The responsiblities of the people associated with this planning are also outlined. The problems that one will meet and the many alternatives that one can choose concerning the use of the computer are also discussed.

SHEGDA, MICHAEL. "Management Action and Planning for Successful EDP Installation," *Lybrand Journal*, Vol. 40, No. 2 (1959), pp. 19–30.

The cause of the disappointment of many firms in the performance of new EDP systems can be usually traced to problems in one of five areas. They are (1) management responsibility, (2) staffing, (3) survey of present procedures, (4) system design, and (5) equipment.

VIGNALI, JOSEPH A. "Ten Consequences of Inadequate Planning of Automatic Data Processing," *NAA Bulletin*, April, 1962, pp. 55–61.

The experience of the federal government in its installation of automatic data processing is related in this article. Underestimation of costs and of work load and the ineffective use of electronic equipment were a few of the consequences of poor planning mentioned here.

VOURNAS, HARRY C. "Avoiding the Pitfalls of EDP Installations," *NAA Bulletin*, Vol. 44, No. 9 (May, 1963).

The importance of knowing what to expect from an electronic data processing system and how to make the best use of this system is highlighted in this article. Some of the pitfalls that commonly occur are stated, but to achieve a successful installation of an electronic data processing system, one must start early, plan ahead, and work hard.

QUESTIONS

1. What individual problem areas must be provided for when the study group is considering the overall scheduling problem? Briefly explain each problem area.

2. Is it the function of the study group merely to arrange for the automation of existing procedures? Explain your answer.

3. Why is it necessary for the study group to be concerned with the information which is on individual forms?

4. Why is it necessary for the study group to analyze all of the reports of the existing system? Explain.

5. What does the analysis of work volume have to do with the problem of justifying an EDP system? Explain.

6. Why is it important for the study group to ascertain the size of the files required for both the originating and reporting data?

7. Should it be possible to justify the installation of a computer on the basis of cost savings? Explain your answer.

8. If your answer to question No. 7 is yes, what are the elements of cost which should be considered?

9. Automation results in a loss of jobs and unemployment. Is this statement true in regards to the results found in surveys of business office automation?

10. Examine the statement in No. 9, above, from the outlook of a given employee, now satisfactorily employed, who may not be able to cope with the demands of the new skills required.

11. Examine the statement in No. 9, above, in terms of both short- and long-run effects on employment.

CHAPTER 21

Preparing for

and Introducing

Electronic Equipment

WITH THE completion of the justification study and its associated analysis of the business information system, a decision must be made regarding the feasibility of acquiring, or converting to, an electronic data processing system.

If a decision is made to automate, the firm must then approach the problems which will accompany such a conversion. These problems will, of course, vary to some degree with the business firm and the equipment system to be acquired. However, considerations involved in the selection of equipment, the acquisition and training of qualified personnel, the plans necessary in the conversion of present methods and procedures over to the new system, and the provision for the physical facilities needed by the computer and its associated peripheral equipment all have some common features regardless of the particular system to be installed.

SELECTING EDP EQUIPMENT

The selection of the perfect computer for a given information system is rarely, if ever, possible. If for no other reason, it may be because of rapid changes in the demands for data required in the system of any modern dynamic business firm.

There are, however, certain basic facts which must be considered in equipment selection. These include the characteristics of the computer and associated equipment, aids available through some of the computer manufacturers, and company policy which is often expressed in terms of financial, personnel or physical limitations.

Computer Characteristics

Only after all facets of the previously prepared systems study have been carefully examined and the needs of the new information system have been determined can a list of the equipment specifications required be prepared. These system requirements will then have to be matched against the functions performed by the various available computer input, storage, and output devices and other special equipment such as that required in input preparation, filing, binding, mailing, etc.

Alternative approaches to meeting the general specifications of the system must be considered, keeping in mind the importance of selecting the best equipment available—for the price. Such equipment must not only be able to do the current job required, but must be expansible to meet the future needs of the firm. This may not only be in terms of larger storage capacity and greater processing speed in accomplishing current requirements, but may include the computer system's incorporation into a full-fledged integrated data processing system involving communication and transmission systems and other on-line devices.

To obtain an initial idea of the types of equipment available which might perform the data processing work required, those in charge of planning the new system, along with officials of the firm, may follow several methods of procedure:

1. They might invite representatives of the various computer manufacturers into the firm for initial discussions of the firm's needs.
2. Visit demonstration equipment showrooms of these manufacturers.
3. Visit computer installations of other business firms, particularly those with similar systems problems, and discuss with management how it solved these problems. Ask for advice as the people involved may have made some decisions regarding their own installation that they would not care to repeat if they were starting over again.
4. Consult trade organizations for general recommendations.
5. Attend seminars, institutes, and lectures on data processing.
6. Review the various forms of literature on the subject such as texts and other books, trade magazines, and data processing periodicals in general.

A particularly effective method of determining equipment which may meet the specifications of a particular company is to request given computer manufacturers to submit bids or proposals on the basis of the specifications and procedural flow charts submitted.

The list of specifications, based on the system requirements, should include, as a minimum, the following:

1. Data Origination
   a) How data originates
   b) How data is collected
2. Data Communication
   a) Data developed in the immediate system
   b) Local data transmission
   c) Distant data transmission
3. Input Data
   a) Format
   b) Coding
   c) Volume, including cyclical peaks
   d) Hourly rates of input
4. Storage Files
   a) Volume
   b) Methods of maintaining and updating
   c) Code requirements
   d) Types of access (random or serial)
5. Data Handling
   a) Types of transactions
   b) Kinds of computations
   c) Types of decisions required
6. Output Reports
   a) Kind
   b) Distribution of data
   c) Volume of each type
   d) Formats
   e) Need for timeliness
7. Special Requirements
   a) Time cycle for unit processing (speed)
   b) Common-language compatibility
   c) Expansion possibilities
   d) Cost limitations
   e) Space limitation or requirements
   f) Maintenance requirements
   g) Date of delivery and installation
   h) Site preparation requirements
   i) Personnel training
   j) Manufacturer's assistance in programming, etc.
   k) Other special requirements

The manufacturers, in turn, will respond to the bid invitation with specific proposals for implementing the system. Through this approach, management can gather the information needed and emphasis can then be placed on the relative efficiency and cost of the various makes of equipment. Today, the competence and continued support of the equipment manufacturer can be assumed, as the computer business is a highly competitive one and any major manufacturer will do its utmost to assist its customers.

A computer characteristic which must not be overlooked in the selection of a system is that of reliability. Reliability, of course, refers to the basic stability of the internal components and the associated circuitry. This characteristic has improved considerably with the widespread use of transistors and other solid-state devices. Reliability will be even more improved as the newer microelectronic components, involving "chip" transistors and unit circuitry techniques, are incorporated in commercial computers. Many types of self-checking devices and techniques are also being incorporated in some equipment to test the operating efficiency level of the various internal components and circuits.

Reliability, in a broad sense, however, may even include reliability of handling the data itself, and not only involve data reading and writing checking techniques but also include ability to test for certain types of errors and make automatic corrections so that the data becomes acceptable to the system. The replacement of a "lost" bit in data recorded on magnetic tape would be one example of this correction procedure, as the use of both vertical and horizontal check bits would pinpoint automatically the missing bit.

Aids from Computer Manufacturer

Many benefits are to be expected from the rental or purchase of a computer from its manufacturer other than the functions performed by the equipment. These include maintenance of the equipment, training programs and educational facilities, programming assistance, and program libraries. These must all be considered and the expected benefits weighed before selecting a computer system.

MAINTENANCE. Most computer manufacturers provide the maintenance required to keep the equipment in top operating condition under rental agreements. This must, however, be a separate consideration when outright purchase of the equipment is contemplated. Then it may, depending on many factors, be better for the firm to train its own staff of maintenance personnel rather than enter into a separate maintenance contract with the equipment manufacturer.

Under rental agreements or separate maintenance contracts, the availability of the manufacturer's servicing personnel must be a consideration in selecting equipment. It is a serious problem if the equipment becomes inoperable for even a short period of time, as the volume of work performed in such a system means that, with any delay at all, a backlog of data processing information will quickly develop.

In larger electronic computer systems the manufacturer may assign maintenance personnel to a specific system or to a few similar strategically located systems. In either instance the user of the equipment will be expected to provide the office and equipment space required for this personnel.

In smaller electronic computer systems the maintenance will probably be performed from a central office of the manufacturer. Here, the factors to be considered are the distance from this office and the general reputation of the manufacturer as determined from talks with other business firms who have installations serviced in this manner.

In conjunction with maintenance, the availability of other systems compatible with the one under consideration, through which the work could be performed on an emergency basis, should be investigated. Though the probability of a major system breakdown is remote today, it is always a possibility and could be a near disaster under some circumstances.

TRAINING SCHOOLS.   Most computer manufacturers provide training programs for their customer's personnel. Though this training is "advertised" as being without cost to the customer, this is not the complete picture. The personnel sent by the customer to this school will be on his payroll, and he will also provide any transportation expense involved as well as housing, meals, and incidental expenses in some instances.

Typical areas of training will include both seminars and classroom-type courses such as those for a broad survey of office automation in general for executives, department heads, and even staff members as a group; training for operating personnel on both the computer system and the supporting peripheral equipment; detailed training in the technical performance of the equipment in developing programmers and systems analysts; and, where a firm purchases the equipment and desires to do its own maintenance, training of selected personnel in the technique and use of equipment necessary to do this type of work.

It is to be expected that a more extensive training program will be necessary as the size or type of system increases in complexity and capacity. However, the quality and depth of training programs may vary from manufacturer to manufacturer on a system of a given size, and the end result of quality personnel must be a factor to consider.

PROGRAMMING ASSISTANCE.   The amount of programming assistance to be expected can vary from a complete package of tested programs down to no assistance at all.

At first mention, the completed package of tested programs sounds too good to be true. This may not be the case, however, as these will probably be very general programs for the given procedural application. This is understandable if one stops to think that these programs must be equally applicable for all other firms with similar procedural applications. Each firm has its own unique peculiarities, and if the program is broad enough to cover most of the possible differences, then it will generally be inefficient, in terms of processing time required, for any given firm. Such a program, however, may serve as a good starting point, and with the expenditure of a great deal of thought, selecting what is appropriate and then condensing it to fit a specific need, it may become a satisfactory program.

Some manufacturers will, if requested, furnish, on a full-time basis in the preparation stage, an experienced lead programmer or systems analyst to work with and guide a company's newly trained personnel in their work. This may be good under some circumstances, but care must be taken that this individual doesn't do the majority of the work requiring real ingenuity in the techniques and decisions to be made. If this is the case, the company employees will not be developing as they should and will still be inexperienced programmers and systems people when the initial work is completed. Systems work and programming are never ending jobs, as conditions and policies change and improvements can seemingly always be made. Company personnel will have this responsibility as soon as the system is in operation.

What is appropriate for one firm in programming assistance will not necessarily be so for another, so this must be a matter of executive judgment as to the capabilities of the personnel, the time to be allotted for the completion of the work, and the expense to be involved.

PROGRAM LIBRARIES. Many of the computer manufacturers keep files of programs which have been developed for either specific problems or general applications. These may be in the form of a listing of detailed instructions, a deck of punched cards, or a reel of magnetic tape, to provide a given program. Normally, these are available without charge to customer users of a manufacturer's equipment.

Many of these represent specific "routine programs"—so called because they represent programmed procedures which will be utilized over and over. A typical example would be in the case of mathematical problems where the square root of a number or a given trigonometric function of a triangle may be needed. It would be ridiculous to write a new program to do either of these calculations every time such a procedure is called for.

Some of the library programs—often jokingly called "canned" programs—represent the development of extensive programs for specific applications. Generally these are applications with broad usage and are most commonly found in areas where the business is tightly controlled by governmental regulations. Under these circumstances the problems faced in a given procedural application are very similar, and the accounts affected will probably have to conform to a standardized coding pattern.

Program libraries are also available from various user groups. These may be groups of users who have similar problems or, more commonly, groups formed by users of specific models of a given manufacturer's computers. As the individual member of the group develops or improves upon programs which serve a common purpose for the group, these are put in the user-group file which is available to all members of the group.

Members of such user groups are usually charged a very nominal fee for membership, and each appoints one or more representatives to attend the various meetings held by the group. These groups may be limited in membership to local users or extended to a regional or even a national group organization.

Purchase-versus-Lease Considerations

A decision to purchase must, of course, reflect the availability of capital funds—or the ability to secure borrowed funds at a satisfactory interest cost. There must also be serious thought given to the "opportunity cost" of alternative uses to which those funds might be applied if a decision to lease rather than purchase is made.

Usage requirements will have a bearing on the decision to purchase or lease as overtime usage results in an additional rental charge—though at a reduced rate. Consequently, a two- or three-shift operation may be the factor that results in a buy decision.

Purchasing allows the substitution of fixed costs for the major variable costs of a computer system. Therefore, a firm must be conscious of the cost-volume-profit interrelations present. The break-even point (where the revenue from sales is just sufficient to meet the total, fixed and variable, expenses involved) will be raised with the purchase of a computer, so a serious consideration must be given to sales potential—just as it would in any other major asset investment.

Technical obsolescence is not always the problem that it appears to be. If the firm has planned properly and purchased a system which is adequate and provides for anticipated growth, there should be no consideration given to replacing it unless revolutionary changes threaten to give competition an insurmountable advantage in the market. Renting provides some protection against such a contingency, but any change will probably involve considerable expenditures and some certain resulting disorganization, which must be given proper weight in any decision to change systems. Also, the rental price itself must include some provision for the possibility of obsolescence as the supplier must protect its own investment.

Amortization of the purchased investment through depreciation tends to counter the tax advantage of expensing rental payments. In fact, some of the accelerated depreciation methods permissible may even be an advantage in that the majority of the cost of the computer may be "charged off" in the early years of its use.

Another, but lesser, tax consideration is that purchase will result in additional property taxes. However, it must be remembered these taxes will also have been included in the determination of the rental fee.

If a change in computers is dictated after a few years use, it must be remembered that a secondhand market for used computers has never fully developed. If disposal is made through a "trade-in" on a new system, this will probably "tie" the purchaser to the manufacturer who sold the previous equipment. This may prevent having the freedom desired in selecting the "best" equipment for the job. Developments, both in the purchasing firm and in the company manufacturing the equipment, may be such that a change in manufacturer is the only way to assure the achievement of the performance desired in a system. In the past, many computer firms have been absorbed by others through purchase or merger and their equipment modified or discontinued; others have stopped manufacturing computers completely, and some have not advanced technologically as fast as their competitors.

As previously mentioned, maintenance will normally be included in the rental fee quoted on the equipment, but it will be an additional expense if the computer is purchased.

Most leasing contracts allow part of the rental fee to be applied toward purchase of the computer. Such an alternative permits a "trial run" of the system before the firm must make a final decision to invest in computer hardware.

In most instances leasing is more expensive than purchasing; however, leasing can certainly be justified if the usage is to be temporary, if only a few applications are to be employed, if the firm anticipates the introduction of improved models in the relatively near future, or, of course, if capital funds are not economically available for the investment required.

The decision to lease or purchase must be based on facts applicable to the particular firm, and management must consider all these facts, in terms of the impact the alternatives will have upon the firm, before finalizing their decision to purchase or lease the equipment.

Other Considerations

Management should not build up high hopes of a new system substantially reducing the cost of the data processing operation—experience indicates that it will likely be disappointed.

The expected reduction in cost is often projected as a result of decreased labor costs through the reduction of the clerical staff. Quite often, this benefit fails to materialize. The savings from the reduction in the number of people employed is usually offset by the general upgrading of the positions retained.

To utilize the full capability of a computer system, the functions it performs must be extended beyond the conventional record system. This may involve additional managerial reports, such as detailed costing procedures would provide, or it may result in the use of some of the newer operations research or management science techniques. This utilization will, of course, increase costs but at the same time will provide better managerial control and greater anticipated returns from operations. On the other hand, as the integrated systems concept is more widely adopted, there are more and more applications which can be placed on the computer. This should have the effect of getting more mileage out of each dollar spent on data processing.

Another factor that tends to keep computer costs up is that it normally is not economically feasible to program a computer to handle all situations which may arise; therefore, it is necessary to retain a skeleton force to operate a manual system to handle exceptions and special cases.

Although the cost of operating the system may remain relatively constant or even increase, the increased managerial control that is possible through a soundly conceived system should ultimately prove to be a profitable investment. This may, however, be hard to prove in dollars and cents, as better control and an ability to make better decisions are hard to quantify.

Finally, automation should never be considered in the anticipation of short-run gains or for automation's sake itself. Instead, it should be regarded in exactly the same light as any other major capital expenditure—a carefully planned investment which is expected to produce long-run benefits over the life of the asset being acquired.

PERSONNEL REQUIREMENTS

As previously discussed, personnel throughout the organization must be aware of the capabilities and limitations of an EDP system. Cooperation can only occur if the employees are favorably convinced from the beginning that the success of any system is dependent upon them individually and as a group.

Displacement Problems

To date, most of the companies involved in changes to computerized data processing systems have taken a "social trust" viewpoint toward their personnel and have generally been able to maintain sound employee relationships throughout the course of the changes. The vast majority of the studies made on employment displacement in changes to computer systems have shown very few people to have been displaced as a result of EDP. This problem, historically, hasn't begun to approach the magnitude that is generally assigned to it. Automation of the factory, however, has been another story and normally has involved sizable personnel displacement; but automation of the office seldom has.

Since the introduction of any EDP system requires an extended time period for it to be planned, installed, and put into operation, there is usually ample time to plan for the reorganization of the staff. Jobs of routine nature may be eliminated by normal attrition. These positions are usually staffed by young women among whom, traditionally, the turnover rate is very high. However, the total work force may not be reduced because the computer system can perform so many additional activities which may require personnel in data gathering and analytical interpretation procedures.

Displacement in the managerial ranks can be a major cause of internal dissension. If a firm changes its traditions by hiring people trained outside of the firm and by altering the established avenues of promotion, the resultant lack of understanding could lead directly to failure of the EDP system. The company's normal procedures regarding security of employment and opportunities for promotion must remain intact if the installation is to be successful.

Personnel who have proven themselves satisfactory employees in the past should not be discharged but, if at all possible, should be retrained for new responsibilities within the firm. Those who are not suited for or are not interested in the new, and often technical, positions should be provided jobs elsewhere in the organization. Whenever possible, these new positions should be commensurate in salary, prestige, and all other respects to their current positions.

A technique which has sometimes proven useful regarding employees nearing retirement age, who might have a particularly hard time in adjusting to the changes necessary, is to accelerate their retirement. This should be carefully planned, however, to permit a continuing use of the employee's experience and abilities on a part-time or consulting basis and to allow the individual to retain his ties with the firm so that he will feel he is still needed and is not being thrust "out in the cold."

Employee Acquisition

The firm must, of course, know which jobs are to be filled before any action can be taken. Job analyses, based on the functional descriptions developed in the feasibility study, should have resulted in definite job classifications and procedural descriptions of the positions which will be required. This permits the recruiter as well as the applicants to know exactly what is required and expected.

Past experience has shown that it is normally easier to train a person thoroughly versed in the firm's operations to do computer work than it is to train a computer specialist to have the required in-depth insight of the firm's policies and operations. However, once it is determined that qualified personnel are not available from the internal staff to fill the new positions, then management will have to turn to the labor market for personnel. Only people with a potential for growth should be hired so that normally expected promotions and advancement may be forthcoming as time passes.

Applicants must be tested for their ability to perform a given task and for their aptitude to learn the things required in the position. These tests may be designed by the firm, standardized tests may be purchased, or a professional testing service may be used. Tests, to be fair and accurate, must be professionally administered, scored, and interpreted.

Finally, after testing has been completed, interviews will also need to be conducted to delve into the applicants' personalities. Interviews are necessary since tests cannot adequately reveal indifference, ambition, or personal difficulties. The workers must be interested in the job. They should be able to pay attention to detail and have the ability to think logically and abstractly. Not only should a person have these analytical capabilities, but he should be aggressive in his actions while retaining the ability to get along with others.

The final selection of the technical personnel required can only be made after testing and interviewing the applicants.

Training

Although most of the training required is in the area of specific skills which are to be applied in the area of EDP, it must not be forgotten that EDP presents a new challenge for management also. Management personnel at virtually every level—even though they will have no direct connection with the program—must be orientated as to the potential and limits of an EDP system through educational programs. Again, full cooperation is necessary and a broad background is desirable so that the supervision and coordination of the data processing operation will be successful.

Systems analysts, programmers, and operators must also be trained. The systems analysts should have a broad general training so that they will understand the principles involved in programming the specific computer in operation. They should have a thorough familiarity with the way the business operates and must be aware of the existing internal control system. They must have formal training in EDP, but only the background of at least two years' experience can develop a top-notch analyst.

Programmers, console operators, and maintenance personnel are usually trained in their highly specialized skills in formal schools conducted by the manufacturer of the computer to be used. Again, however, proficiency can only come through experience.

A point that is sometimes overlooked is that even after the staff is complete and the systems change is in operation, there is a continuing need for a personnel development program in the firm. There is a strong demand for employees with computer-orientated training and experience, and the turnover of personnel in this area may be somewhat higher than might normally be expected. Regardless of this demand, however, there is always a need in every firm for better-trained personnel who can assume the positions which will become available through the firm's growth and normal attrition.

DEVELOPING PROCEDURAL APPLICATIONS

The development of the various procedural applications to be processed on the new computer system is a joint responsibility of both the systems staff and line management. There must be coordination between all concerned to reach the desired result of an efficient, properly developed, properly installed, and smoothly operating business information processing system. It is hard to separate this development in terms of specific areas of endeavor, as each is a part of, and dependent on, the other associated areas. However, somewhat arbitrarily we will separate the development of procedural applications into the areas of block diagramming and flowcharting, programming, debugging, testing, and converting.

Block Diagramming and Flowcharting

Block diagramming and flowcharting, as previously discussed, form the basis for the programmed instructions which must be prepared to guide the computer in its processing procedures. These diagrams and charts will probably have been developed in basic form as part of the systems survey, but once a given computer is decided upon, these will have to be reanalyzed in terms of the fundamental requirements of the system to be used. Every major type and model of computer system has its own special requirements. Some of these are the following: only certain types of input and output devices may be acceptable, both in terms of equipment and of data presentation; each processor has its own unique combinations of instructions, data, and internal codes as well as "decision-making" circuitry; and each system is a combination of various input, output, and internal and external storage devices. The net effect of these requirements will be reflected in the detailed steps necessary for a given computer system to complete a given processing procedure.

Programming

Programming is a time-consuming and expensive job, so the initial preparation should begin as soon as an EDP system is decided upon. The programming effort should be closely supervised by someone who is thoroughly familiar with company operations and the objectives of management.

Previously prepared flow diagrams are studied by the programmers so that they will be familiar with exactly what the computer is expected to do. The basic idea of programming is to develop the most efficient way of transforming the source data into usable output. This is accomplished in EDP equipment by making use of four fundamental steps:

1. The transcription of the data into a medium acceptable by the machine through a set of coded instructions.
2. Programming (instructing) the machine in the necessary operations to be performed on the data to produce the desired results.
3. Reading (feeding) this data into the central processing unit through the various types of input devices available.
4. Writing out the processed data in the form desired.

There can be thousands of individual logical instructions involved in some of these steps.

In addition to writing his own programs, a programmer has several sources of information to turn to as he develops a program. Processors, assemblers, interpreters, program generators, and other "software" are examples of sources of information (see Chapter 15). Canned programs are also available through both the manufacturer and user groups, and consulting services may be provided by manufacturers, consulting firms, and service organizations.

Debugging the Program

Debugging is the process of detecting and correcting the errors which have been made in systems design, systems analyses, coding, and programming. This is the final check for the exceptional items for which there is no provision but which may appear from time to time.

The debugging process begins at the time the program is planned and continues as the program is written and finally implemented. In the beginning stages, programmers check on each other, but as the program enters the completion stage, tests are made with pilot runs to check the program's performance on the computer with actual data whose processing results are already known.

The two major types of errors found in computer programs are logical errors and clerical errors. Logical errors, usually extremely difficult to detect, are a result of a fundamental lack of understanding of what is desired in a given situation. Clerical errors, which might be something as simple as assigning two pieces of information to the same address in the storage area, are discovered and corrected by testing techniques developed specifically for that purpose.

Testing the Program

Testing is accomplished by applying specially designed hypothetical data, which requires only a small amount of machine time, to a program to see if the desired result is achieved. This procedure is relatively ineffective in eliminating logical errors. These may, in fact, not all be discovered until the program is actually put into use.

The two most common ways to locate errors in a program are by using *postmortems* and *traces*. A postmortem involves the selection of data after a mistake has caused the program to stop running and analyzing pertinent areas as to why the program halt occurred. This analysis could result in the use of the trace technique, which involves going through the logic of the program, instruction step by instruction step, to understand where and how the error developed.

Converting

During the preparation for conversion, a systems manual should have been prepared prescribing the details of the early operation of the system. This may need to be revised as the system matures. The study and organization required in the preparation of such a manual will prevent many problems in the early stages of conversion and operation.

The far-reaching changes introduced by an EDP system require a careful appraisal of the basic functions of the organization and of the manner in which the new procedures may assist in performing those functions. The personnel whose job it is to guide the conversion in the most efficient manner must have as their major concern the overall welfare of the firm. As management attempts to solve technical and administrative problems, it must, however, remain conscious of personnel problems and try to maintain equilibrium in the organization.

The final step in the integration of the computer into the system requires the conversion of files from written or punched card form to magnetic tape or some other medium which is acceptable as an input to the computer.

Those responsible for this conversion may find that existing files are inaccurate, incomplete, and inconsistent, and that they even deviate from the correct format.

At the beginning of the period when the computer system is first used, the old noncomputer processing system should be operated concurrently —in parallel—for a period to assure the accuracy of the new system. Cross-checking will establish confidence in the adequacy of the new system. Discrepancies, whether due to inadequacy of the old system or oversights or mistakes in the new program, will be corrected without the loss of valuable data, operating efficiency, or continuity.

It is usually best to convert one or two procedures at a time so that disruption and confusion can be kept to a minimum. This allows the people involved to adjust to the changing conditions. If various departments or divisions have previously automated independently, overall efficiency and economy may suffer as personnel try to adapt to another computer system. They must not be allowed to feel resentful and fear a loss of status.

Management can expect an EDP system to offer solutions to many problems associated with:

1. An increasing volume of paper work.
2. A short supply of suitable office personnel.
3. The ever increasing cost per unit of the performance of the information processing functions.
4. New requirements for managerial, accounting, statistical, and tax data.

To achieve these benefits, management must seek cooperation and understanding from all who are in contact with the EDP system. Management must remember that conversion, which is a trying experience for all concerned, may turn out to be a never ending task as more uses are found for the computer and as new and better equipment becomes available.

PHYSICAL FACILITIES

The physical requirements of an electronic computer system can create many problems. If some effort is not made to determine these in advance and make preparations for them, serious problems will develop.

Floor Space and Design Requirements

While the actual computer installation may not take up any more floor space than present equipment, space may be a greater problem than was anticipated. From space requirements alone, you will have to have sufficient area for the dual operation of the new and at least part of the old equipment for a period of time. You may have to provide space for repairs and perhaps extensive modifications which will probably have to be made to meet the requirements of the computer system. Also, you will probably have to reorganize completely the data collection, handling, and storage areas for their most efficient use.

An existing floor with adequate structural qualities may be available, but it must also have adequate recessed channels to carry the power lines and other interconnecting cables for the equipment. These cables are fairly massive and require considerable space. They have critical lengths to be considered, as electrical power deteriorates as it travels through the wires. Also, some interconnected units of the equipment operate at speeds of millionths or, more recently, even billionths of a second and the time it takes the signal to travel from one unit to another—even though it travels at approximately the speed of light—may be longer than can be tolerated. Normally then, these cables must be run in a direct path between these critical equipment units. Another problem is that the floor must be vibration-free for satisfactory performance of some of the units utilizing high-speed rotating mechanical devices.

If adequate cable channels are not available or if the floor structure is not satisfactory—and remember there are large concentrations of weight in small areas—then a false floor must be constructed. This permits more even loading of the existing structure, tends to cut down on vibration, and provides sufficient space underneath to permit the cables to be laid in the most efficient manner. This space may, where necessary, also be used for air-conditioning and/or heating ducts.

Other problems arising from the computer room itself include acoustical floor, walls, and ceiling to cut down on noise. The materials used for this purpose must also have qualities which make them as dust- and lint-free as possible. Special nonflaking floor wax and wall paint should be used, along with special cleaning procedures. Foreign particles can, if they reach some of the magnetic data-carrying medias or reading and writing heads, either cause data to be masked and not read or cause the foreign particles to be read as data. This, of course, cannot be tolerated.

Observation windows to the equipment should normally be planned for the use of employees and visitors so as not to disturb operations. Visiting executives, employees' families, and college students are all fascinated by such a data processing center.

Preventive and corrective maintenance requires that space be provided on all sides of the computer to facilitate the removal of panels and to swing out hinged sides or tops to permit access to the interior components. Large pieces of test and repair equipment on wheels or carts must have room to move between the equipment. Data will also move within the computer room on racks, stands, and hand trucks. To obtain efficiency, data must travel a direct and short route between points of use.

For effective supervision while operating the console, the operator must be able to see the indicator lights on all on-line input and output units and the front side of the magnetic tape units.

After the technical requirements for the computer room have been met, the remainder of the data processing center can be established. The storage vault should be near those who will use it. Spare maintenance parts can be located at a distance from the center, but maintenance technicians must be able to locate them conveniently. The floor space required by the input preparation room may make it necessary to locate it some distance from the computer. However, storage and data movement must be planned to avoid congestion in the computer room and surrounding areas.

Offices for the analysts and programmers are best located some distance away from the actual computer room to avoid the noise, distraction, and confusion that exists there.

Specific floor design and space requirements are influenced by the type and brand of equipment purchased and the size and scale of the operations planned.

Power Supply

The location of the computer will not generally affect the location of the power equipment. The major consideration when designing a power system is the continuous level of electrical power between a narrow range of tolerances. Electrically triggered circuits in a computer cannot adjust to much variance in the power level. There must be no interference from varying loads of power used by other equipment.

It may be wise to consider some means to provide for contingencies which lead to power interruptions. A substitute power device with an automatic cut-in may be an inexpensive investment in the long run if there is any previous history of power failures. First, it can be quite expensive to adjust, repair, and replace computer components after power failures or surges. Also, when your computer is down, or out of order, processing will either be at a standstill or, if another computer is available, data will have to be transported to the supporting computer system.

The actual cost of power is a minor consideration in a computer installation. The required voltage levels range from 110 to 440 volts, but the increased use of transistors have lowered the need for high amperage capacities.

Lighting

Management is faced with a difficult decision when choosing the proper level of illumination, because different chores, which may require different light levels, may be performed simultaneously. Any clerical work necessary to the operation requires a good level of illumination. Maintenance personnel need a high degree of flexibility as well as adequate illumination to enable them to distinguish colors and small component parts. On the other hand, operators can best observe indicator lights and read test equipment at a lower level of intensity. A partial solution to the problem is in the use of dimmer controls for the general lighting facilities and hoods or shields for consoles and test equipment.

Air Conditioning

The constant need for air conditioning often suggests the installation of a separate cooling system for the computer complex. However, the noise generated by air-conditioning equipment requires that it be placed at some distance from the computer facilities.

Even though the newer equipment does not generate vast quantities of heat, a fairly powerful air-conditioning system may still be required. Machines and humans are most efficient at constant temperature and humidity levels. A high percentage of humidity would damage such storage devices as paper tape, punched cards, and magnetic tape. Air must be circulated so as to be completely changed every few minutes. Air intakes and ducts, however, must be situated so that drafts and hot spots are not created. Dust must be filtered from the room, as it interferes with the efficient use of magnetic tape and disk units. The air conditioner also provides a slight increase in air pressure which inhibits the infiltration of foreign particles when doors are opened.

Planning is a very important requirement in the development of an effective air-conditioning system.

OTHER AREAS OF ENVIRONMENTAL CONTROL

The most effective use of a computer complex is derived from a controlled physical environment.

Usually, smoking will not be permitted in the computer room due to the ash problem and fire hazard. Carbon-dioxide fire extinguishers may be the solution to the fire hazard. Sprinkler systems should not be used because of possible damage to the computer and the danger of electrical shock to the operators. Insurance contracts requiring a sprinkler system may complicate this problem.

Workers should be made fully aware of the high voltage utilized in the equipment and the possibility of shock or mechanical accidents.

Intercommunication systems should be employed and external telephones should be available for the use of personnel.

SYSTEM FOLLOW-UP

As with any extensive installation, the business information processing system must be observed, checked, and rechecked to determine if it is functioning in an efficient manner. As time passes, this check should be extended to include the possibility that changes should be made to incorporate any new managerial policies and functional or procedural requirements which have developed since the system was installed.

A checklist for both a checkup and reexamination of a system would include the following:

1. Make a thorough checkup as soon as possible with these objectives:
    .01 To see that all parts of the system have been installed and are working properly.
    .02 To see that the procedures are being followed.
    .03 To make modifications which may be required by operating experience.
    .04 To measure the results achieved against the objectives and expectations originally predicted.
        a) See if the quality and quantity of work comes up to expectations.
        b) See if man-power savings are being realized or delayed.
2. Make regular post-installation audits with these objectives:
    .01 To prevent inefficient or unnecessary steps creeping into the system.
    .02 To make sure that new personnel are fully indoctrinated before they begin to operate the system.
    .03 To see if the original objectives are being accomplished.
    .04 To see if the expected benefits continue to be realized.
    .05 To look for the possibility of further improvement through the introduction of new equipment or new techniques.
    .06 To look for opportunities to apply work simplification techniques.
        a) Assuming that the procedures are now accomplishing the desired results, look for possible ways to improve the methods of doing the work. This is the essence of a work simplification program— making improvements at the work stations.
        b) The actual work simplification should be done by the worker, by the supervisor, or by the worker and the supervisor working as a team.[1]

ANNOTATED BIBLIOGRAPHY

Burns, Patrick D. "Preparing for a Computer Installation," *Cost and Management*, April, 1966.

---

[1] U.S. Treasury Department, Internal Revenue Service, Data Processing Division, Systems and Procedures, *A Notebook for the Systems Man* (Washington, D.C.: U.S. Government Printing Office, February, 1963), p. 27.

This article presents a cogent and practical discussion of one company's approach to the problems encountered in the four phases of computer installation: systems design, the writing of programs, the conversion of records, and program testing.

CANNING, RICHARD G. *Installing Electronic Data Processing Systems.* New York: John Wiley & Sons, Inc., 1957.

A thorough approach to the overall area relating to the many problems of, and possible methods to approach, an electronic computer feasibility study and the implementation of an EDP System.

CONWAY, B., GIBBONS, J., and WATTS, D. E. *Business Experience with Electronic Computers.* New York: Controllers Institute Research Foundation, 1959.

This book is aimed principally at those who have been assigned responsibility for making the initial decision and for the planning, supervision, and ultimate success of the EDP system. It covers such topics as company education and the programming group, development of the applications and conversion from prior methods, and the position of the computer in the organization structure.

GARRITY, JOHN T., and McNERNEY, JOHN P. "EDP, How to Ride the Tiger," *Financial Executive,* September, 1963, p. 19.

The author is employed by McKinsey & Co., a large management consulting firm in New York City. He points out the results of a survey his firm recently made of 27 large users of EDP equipment in which it was found that many were disenchanted with their installations. The article then proceeds to point out why many of these EDP users were unhappy, as well as what should have been done to enable each installation to make a contribution to the business enterprise.

HEILBORN, GEORGE H. "EDP Equipment: Purchase, Trade-In, or Sell?— An Analysis." *Data Processing* magazine, August, 1965, pp. 44–46.

The used computer market is providing small business with a source of obtaining modern computer systems at a low cost. It is also providing large organizations with an opportunity to expand existing systems rather than purchasing, installing, and programming a completely new system. The development and analysis of the used computer market is discussed.

INTERNATIONAL BUSINESS MACHINES CORPORATION. *General Information Manual: Planning for an IBM Data Processing System,* No. F20–6088–1. White Plains, N.Y., January, 1961.

This is an excellent reference on this topic. It covers in reasonable detail almost every topic taken up in this chapter.

McMAINS, HARVEY J. "Planning—The Role of Humans in Information Systems," *Data Processing Yearbook, 1965.* (ed. EDITH HARWITH GOODMAN), pp. 159–68. Detroit: American Data Processing, Inc., 1964.

The planning processes involved in instituting and operating a computer system are discussed. The necessary equipment, the management of the computer center, and the problems of data communications are considered within the context of the long-range objectives of management. Stress is put upon the development potential of the system and the need for flexibility to allow for new data processing techniques and for changing business conditions.

OPTNER, STANFORD L. *Systems Analysis for Business Management.* Englewood Cliffs, N.J.: Prentice-Hall, Inc., 1960.

An analysis of business systems in terms of a feasibility study—the study itself, selection of equipment, cost-saving analysis, and possibilities of including operations research techniques. A series of case studies is provided.

RAVER, ROLAND. "Computer Leasing Provides Future Flexibility," *Financial Executive*, May, 1967, p. 18.

Article compares the advantages of leasing from third parties with all of the other possible options open to a computer user.

SHEGDA, MICHAEL. "Management Action and Planning for Successful EDP Installation," *Journal of Machine Accounting*, September, 1959.

The author starts by pointing out that all EDP installations have not been successful, and then he points out why—management did not take responsibility, they had not spelled out their objectives, the EDP installation had not been adequately staffed. The latter part of the article is a description of the steps which should have been followed in making the decision and installation.

WALLACE, FRANK. *Appraising the Economics of Electronic Computers.* New York: Controllership Foundation, Inc., 1956.

This book has as its purpose the presentation in nontechnical language of what a firm needs to think about when it is considering the installation of a computer. It considers: (1) organizing the computer feasibility team, (2) selecting areas for specific study, (3) analyzing present procedures, (4) constructing projected computer systems, (5) determining equipment requirements, and (6) installing the computer.

WATTS, DUANE E. *Administration and Control of EDP Projects.* First appeared as an article in the Summer, 1961, issue of *The Virginia Accountant.* Reprinted in HENRY DE VOS (ed). *Management Services Handbook,* chap. v, pp. 279–84. New York: American Institute of Certified Public Accountants, 1964.

This article discusses problems in connection with the introduction of EDP projects and shows possibilities how these problems can be avoided.

WOFSEY, MARVIN M. *Conversion to Automatic Data Processing: A Practical Primer.* Center for Technology and Administration. Bulletin No. 3. Washington, D.C.: The American University, School of Government and Public Administration, March, 1962.

Written to serve as a practical guide for those responsible for computer conversion operations.

WOLF, EDWIN D. *Rental versus Purchase of Data Processing Equipment.* Adapted from an article by Edwin D. Wolf in the February, 1962, issue of *Management Controls.* Reprinted in HENRY DE VOS (ed). *Management*

Services Handbook, chap. 5, pp. 296–302. New York: American Institute of Certified Public Accountants, 1964.

Wolf describes the factors for comparison in a rental-versus purchase decision situation and gives an analysis example showing the application of the factors for comparison.

QUESTIONS

1. Discuss four ways whereby a company's representatives might acquaint themselves with the types of available EDP equipment. What are the relative advantages and disadvantages of each method?

2. What do you think about asking a computer manufacturer to submit bids based upon specifications drawn up by your company? Are there problems involved? If so, what are they?

3. Discuss some of the possible solutions to the maintenance problem which are open to the users of EDP equipment. Do you consider this problem to be a critical one?

4. What would you consider to be a good way for your company to get started with programming, assuming that the decision has been made to install EDP equipment?

5. In justifying a computer installation, would you consider it a good idea to propose to install EDP equipment so that existing accounting procedures can be more fully automated? If you agree, explain why. If you don't agree, explain the scope of thinking which one should use to justify a computer.

6. What are the problems connected with personnel and how might they be solved, assuming the decision has been reached to install an EDP system?

7. Briefly discuss some of the training problems which are bound to arise as soon as the decision is made to install EDP equipment.

8. What are the two types of errors which can creep into a program? How are they generally found? Explain.

9. Point out some of the physical facilities which must be provided for the installation of EDP equipment. Discuss their importance.

Equipment Characteristics

of Selected Major

Computing Systems

Burroughs B 300 System

BURROUGHS B 300 SYSTEM

The Burroughs B 300 Series of computers are transistorized magnetic core small-scale general-purpose data or item processing systems. A unique characteristic is the three-address command structure of logic which normally reduces programming steps up to 40% when compared to two-address structure programming.

SYSTEM CONFIGURATION

1. I/O Equipment.
   a) Punched Card Readers (1 or 2 units).
      B 122   200 cards per minute.
      B 123   475 cards per minute.
      B 124   800 cards per minute.
      B 129   1,400 cards per minute.
   b) Punched Card Punches (1 unit).
      B 303   100 cards per minute.
      B 304   300 cards per minute.
   c) Paper Tape Reader (1 or 2 unit).
      B 141   1,000 characters per second.
   d) Paper Tape Punch (1 unit).
      B 341   100 characters per second.
   e) MICR Sorter-Readers (1 unit).
      B 103   1,560 items per minute, 13 pockets.
      B 107   1,200 items per minute, 13 pockets.
      B 116   1,560 items per minute, 16 pockets.
   f) Line Printers (1 or 2 units).
      B 320   475 lines per minute, 120 characters per line.
      B 321   700 lines per minute, 120 characters per line.
      B 325   700 lines per minute, 132 characters per line.
      B 328   1,040 lines per minute, 120 characters per line.
      B 329   1,040 lines per minute, 132 characters per line.
   g) Six-Tape Listers (1 unit).
      B 322   1,565 lines per minute numeric.
      B 325   1,565 lines per minute alphanumeric.
      B 326   1,250 lines per minute numeric.
   h) Typewriter.
      B 495   Supervisory Printer.
2. Storage.
   a) Internal.
      4,800 to 19,200 magnetic cores.
   b) Magnetic Tape (1 to 6 units).
      B 422   200 or 556 bits per inch, 90 inches per second, 18 or 50K characters per second.
      B 423   200 bits per inch, 120 inches per sec., 24K characters per second.

B 424   800 bits per inch, 83 inches per sec., 66K characters per second.

B 425   200, 556, or 800 bits per inch, 90 inches per second, 18, 50, or 72K characters per second.

c) Disk Storage (1 to 50 units).

Auxiliary storage. Overlay of additional memory on the extremely fast (average 20 microseconds access time) disks provide unlimited available memory

Disk File and Data Communications available to provide a maximum capacity of 500 million characters.

B 475   9.6 million alpha characters—14.4 numeric

3. Communication Equipment (1 to 5 units)

Various types to provide a maximum of 985 terminals

Burroughs B 2500 and B 3500 Systems

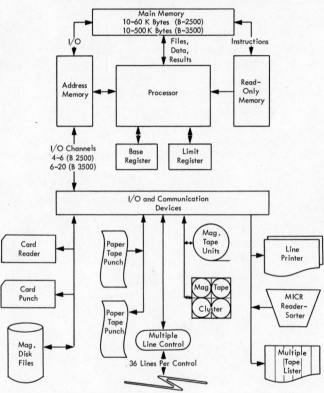

BURROUGHS B 2500 AND B 3500 SYSTEMS

The Burroughs B 2500 and B 3500 are general-purpose digital electronic computer systems suitable for a wide range of business, scientific, and data communication tasks.

SYSTEM CONFIGURATION

1. I/O Equipment.
   a) Punched Card Readers.
      9111   800 cards per minute.
      9112   1,400 cards per minute.
   b) Punched Card Punches.
      9210   100 cards per minute.
      9211   300 cards per minute.
   c) Paper Tape Reader.
      9120   Maximum 1,000 characters per second.
   d) Paper Tape Punch.
      9220   100 characters per second.
   e) MICR Document Sorter-Readers.
      13 or 16 sorter pockets, 1,565 documents per minute.
   f) Line Printers.
      9240   700 lines per minute, 120 or 132 characters per line.
      9241   1,040 lines per minute, 120 or 132 characters per line.
   g) Multiple-Line Listers.
      6, 12, or 18 individually controlled listing tapes, prints at 1,565 lines per minute.
2. Storage.
   a) Internal.
      Main Memory.
      B 2500   10 to 60K bytes magnetic core memory, 2 microseconds per 2 characters access time
      B 3500   10 to 500K bytes magnetic core memory, 1 microsecond per 2 characters access time
      Read-only Memory.   A resistive type memory containing wired interpretive routines whose access time is 100 nanoseconds
      Address Memory.   24 to 120 words, 100 nanoseconds access time.
   b) Magnetic Tape.
      Free-Standing Units.
      9391   7 channel, speed 90 inches/second, density 200, 556, or 800 frames per inch, reads 18, 50, or 72K characters per second.
      9392   9 channel, speed 90 inches/second, density 200 or 800 frames per inch, reads 18 or 72K bytes per second.
      9393   9 channel, speed 90 inches/second, density 1,600 frames per inch, reads 144K bytes per second.
      9394–1 9 channel, speed 120 inches/second, density 200 or 800

frames per inch, reads 24 or 96K characters per second.

9394–2   7 channel, speed 120 inches/second, density 200 or 556 frames per inch, reads 18 or 50K characters per second.

Cluster of 2, 3, or 4 tape stations.

9381   9 channel, speed 45 inches/second, density 200 or 800 frames per inch, reads 9 or 36K bytes per second.

9382   9 channel, speed 45 inches/second, density 1,600 frames per inch, reads 72K bytes per second.

9383   7 channel, speed 45 inches/second, density 200, 556, or 800 frames per inch, reads 9, 25, or 36K characters per second.

  c) Magnetic Disk Files.
Systems Memory, 1 to 4 million bytes, average access time 17 milliseconds.
On-Line Disk File, 10 million to 2.5 billion bytes, average access time 20 milliseconds.

3. Communication Equipment.
Remote Card Readers.
Remote Paper Tape Readers.
Teller Consoles.
Data Collection Devices.
Teletypewriters.
Satellite Computers, etc.

Burroughs B 5500 System

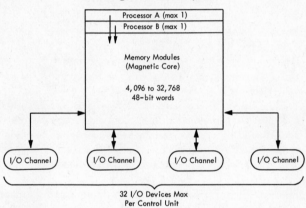

BURROUGHS B 5500 SYSTEM

The B 5500 information processing system is a large-scale, high-speed, solid-state computer which represents a departure from the conventional computer system concept. It is a problem-language-oriented system rather than the conventional hardware-oriented system with a strong interdependence between the hardware and the Master Control Program which directs the system.

SYSTEM CONFIGURATION

1. I/O Equipment
    a) Punched Card Readers (2 max.).
    B 122   200 cards per minute.
    B 123   475 cards per minute.
    B 124   800 cards per minute.
    B 129   1,400 cards per minute.
    b) Punched Card Punches (1 max.).
    B 303   100 cards per minute.
    B 304   300 cards per minute.
    c) Paper Tape Reader and Punch (3 max.).
    B 141 Reader   1,000 characters per second.
    B 341 Punch   100 characters per second.
    d) Line Printers (2 max.).
    B 320   475 lines per minute, 120 characters per line.
    B 321   700 lines per minute, 120 characters per line.
    B 325   700 lines per minute, 132 characters per line.
    B 328   1,040 lines per minute, 120 characters per line.
    B 329   1,040 lines per minute, 132 characters per line.
2. Storage
    a) Internal Memory Module (max. 8 of one model) magnetic core.
    B 460   4,096 48-bit words, 6 microseconds cycle time.
    B 461   4,096 48-bit words, 4 microseconds cycle time.
    b) Magnetic Drum (2 max.).
    B 430   32,768 48-bit words, 8.5 millisecond average access time.
    c) Magnetic Disk.
    B 452   Control (8 max.)—up to 2 Data Transmission Terminal Units.
    B 5470   Control (2 max.).
    B 451   Expanded Control (2 per B 5470—4 max.).
    B 471   Electronics Unit (10 per B 5470—20 max.).
    B 475   Storage Module (5 per B 471—100 max.).
    d) Magnetic Tape (16 max.).
    B 422   200 or 556 bits/inch, 90 inches/second, 18 or 50K characters/second.
    B 423   200 bits/inch, 120 inches/second, 24K characters/second.
    B 424   800 bits/inch, 83 inches/second, 66K characters/second.
    B 425   200, 556, or 800 bits/inch, 90 inches/second, 18, 50, or 72K characters/second.

3. Communications Equipment.

B 452	Control (8 max.).
B 487	Data Trans. Terminal Unit (2 per B 452, max. 15).
B 5480	Control (1 max.).
B 249	Control (1 max.).
B 481	Teletype Terminal Unit (15 max., all terminals).
	Teletype Units (399 max. per B 481).
B 483	Typewriter Terminal Unit (15 max., all terminals).
B 493	Typewriter Inquiry Station (8 per B 483, max. 120).
B 484	TWX Terminal Unit (15 max., all terminals).
	AT&T Data-sets (8 per B 484, max. 120).
	Various adaptors (16 max. per B 487).

Burroughs B 6500 and B 7500 Systems

Processor 1

Processor 2

Main Memory
1 to 32 Modules—Mag. Core
16,384 to 524,288
52-bit Words
(6 8-bit Bytes + 4 Control bits)

Optional

4-10 Switching Channels

Data Comm.
4 Processors

I/O
Multi-
plexor

Mag. Tape
Exchange

I/O
Multi-
plexor

Data Comm.
4 Processors

1-4 Multi-Line
Data Comm Control
Per Processor

Tape
1-16
Units

1-4 Multi-Line
Data Comm.Control
Per Processor

1-64 Line/Control

1-64 Lines/Control

Real-Time
Adapter

Disk File
Exchange
1-2 Units

Real-Time
Adapter

Real-Time
Devices

Paper
Tape
Read
&/or
Punch

Paper
Tape
Read
&/or
Punch

Real-Time
Devices

Disk
1-10
Units

Disk File
Exchange

Disk
1-10 Each
Exchange

Mag. Tape
Exchange

Tape
1-16
Units

Mag. Tape
Cluster

Printer

C.R.T.

Card
Reader &/or
Punch

Console

Other Peripheral
Controls

BURROUGHS B 6500 AND B 7500 SYSTEMS

The B 6500 and B 7500 Electronic Data Processing Systems are intermediate-scale computers whose normal mode of operation is multiprocessing and remote time-sharing under full operating system control.

SYSTEM CONFIGURATION

1. I/O Equipment.
   a) Punched Card Readers.
      9111   800 cards per minute.
      9112 1,400 cards per minute.
   b) Punched Card Punches.
      9210   100 cards per minute.
      9211   300 cards per minute.
   c) Paper Tape Reader.
      9120   Max. of 1,000 characters per second.
   d) Paper Tape Punch.
      9220   100 characters per second.
   e) Line printers.
      9240   700 lines per minute, 120 or 132 characters per line.
      9241 1,040 lines per minute, 120 or 132 characters per line.
      9242   815 lines per minute, 120 or 132 characters per line.
      9243 1,040 lines per minute, 120 or 132 characters per line.
2. Storage.
   a) Internal Memory.
      Magnetic Core.   16,384 to 524,288 words of 52 bits per word, access time for the B 6500 is 600 and the B 7500 is 300 nanoseconds per word.
   b) Magnetic Tape.
      See B 2500 and B 3500 systems for detail.
   c) Magnetic Disk.
      9372   10- or 20-million-byte capacity, 20 or 23 millisecond average access time.
      9375   100 million byte memory bank (additional 20-million-byte increments) 23, 40, or 60 millisecond average access time.
3. Communication Equipment.
   Burroughs B 300, B 2500/B 3500, and B 5500 systems.
   Burroughs Input and Display Unit.
   TWX/Remote typewriters.
   Univac DCT 2000.
   IBM 1050.
   Honeywell 120.
   Model 35 or 8A1 Selective Calling Service.
   Automatic Dial Out.
   Typewriter Inquiry Station, etc.

Burroughs B 8500 System

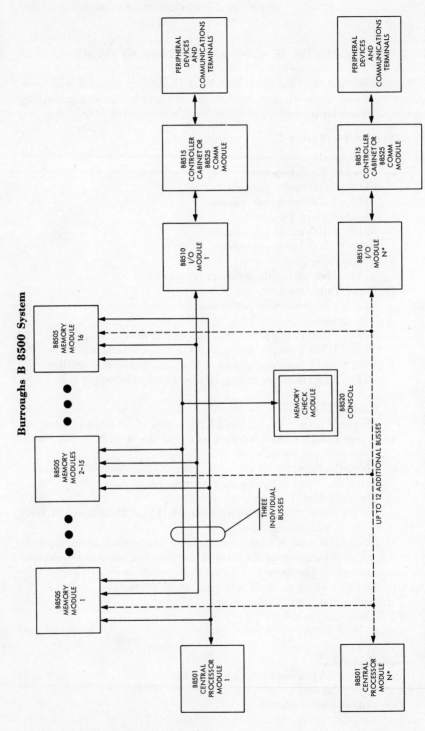

* Total combination of central processor and I/O modules can be extended to 14.

BURROUGHS B 8500 SYSTEM

The Burroughs B 8500 Information Processing System is a large information processor that controls and executes many different kinds of business and scientific data processing tasks simultaneously through the use of multiprogramming and multiprocessing techniques.

The modular organization of both equipment and programming is built upon advanced state-of-the-art features, such as monolithic integrated circuits, magnetic thin-film memory, multiprogramming and multiprocessing, and automatic job control.

SYSTEM CONFIGURATION

1. I/O Equipment.
    a) Punched Card Readers.
        9211   800 cards per minute.
        9212 1,400 cards per minute.
    b) Punched Card Punches.
        9210   100 cards per minute.
        9211   300 cards per minute.
    c) Paper Tape Reader.
        9120   500 or 1,000 characters per second, 5-, 6-, 7-, or 8-channel
                tape.
    d) Paper Tape Punch.
        9220   100 characters per second, 5-, 6-, 7-, or 8-channel tape.
    e) Line Printer.
        9241 1,040 lines per minute, 120 or 132 characters per line.
    f) Operators Console.
        8520–2 Typewriter module—Information Display System optional.
2. Storage.
    a) Internal.
        8505 Memory Module.   Thin-film memory of 16,384, 52-bit word
        capacity, 500 nanosecond cycle time (16 modules per processor
        max.).
        8510 I/O Module.   Thin-film memory of 1,024, 100-bit word
        capacity, 500 nanosecond cycle time (1 I/O Module per Memory
        Module).
    b) Magnetic Tape.
        9391   7 channel, speed 90 inches/second, density 200, 556, or 800
                frames per inch, reads 18, 50, or 72K characters per
                second.
        9392   9 channel, speed 90 inches/second, density 800 frames per
                inch, reads 72K bytes per second.
        9393   9 channel, speed 90 inches/second, density 1,600 frames
                per inch, reads 144K bytes per second.
    c) Magnetic Disk File System.
        470   200 million 48-bit word capacity, average access 30 milli-
               seconds, storage modules in 2 million bit increments.
3. Communications Equipment.
    Each I/O Controller provides up to 512 simplex channels, each of these
    may serve 1 or more adapters which, in turn, may serve 1 to many
    various types of terminals.

Control Data 3000 Series

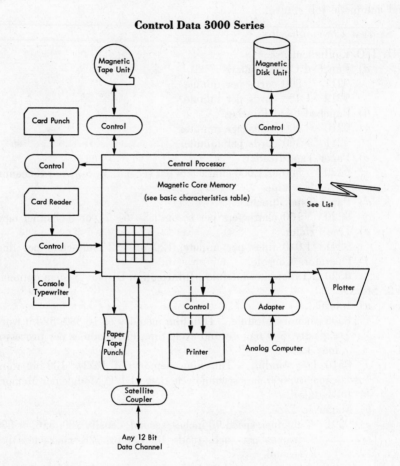

CONTROL DATA 3000 SERIES

The Control Data 3000 series is composed of two basic groups of compatible equipment.

The 3100, 3200, 3300, and 3500 computers are essentially medium-scale systems. The 3200 has four processors available—basic, scientific, data, or general. The 3100 has only the basic processor and its associated characteristics. The 3300 has the general processor with expanded speed and storage capabilities. The 3500 utilizes "intebrid" (*inte*grated hy*brid*) circuitry for faster operating capability.

The 3400, 3600, and 3800 systems are large-scale systems. The 3600 is extremely modular in design to permit high versatility in adapting it to many varied applications. The 3400 is slightly slower with limited expandability. The 3800 is faster, but otherwise similar to the 3600.

SYSTEM CONFIGURATION

1. I/O Equipment.
   a) Punched Card Reader.
      405 Reads 1,200 or 1,600 cards per minute for 80- and 51-column cards.
   b) Punched Card Punch.
      415 Punches 250 cards per minute.
   c) Paper Tape Reader/Punches.
      3691 Reads 350 and punches 120 characters per second.
      3694 Reads 1,000 and punches 120 characters per second.
   d) Line Printer.
      512 1,200 lines per minute interchangeable 48 character cartridges, 136 print positions.
      501 1,000 lines per minute, 64 characters, 136 print positions.
      505 500 lines per minute, 64 characters, 136 print positions.
   e) Optical Scanning.
      915 Page Reader. Scans ASA Standard Font at 370 characters/second (8½″ × 11″ page in 14 seconds), accepts single documents 4″ to 12″ wide and 2½″ to 14″ long.
2. Storage.
   a) Internal Memory.

Magnetic Core Memory—Basic Characteristics							
Model	Cycle Time (μs)	Add Time (μs)	Word Size (Byte)	Memory Size (Words)	Number Data Chans.	Floating Point	Number Index Registers
3100........1.75		3.50	28	4–32K	4	Opt.	3
3200........1.25		2.50	28	8–32K	8	Opt.	3
3300........1.25		2.75	28	8–262K	8	Opt.	3
3500........0.90			28	32–262K	8	Yes	3
3400........1.50		3.00	48	16–32K	4	Yes	6
3600........1.50		2.00	48	32–262K	32	Yes	6
3800........0.80		1.80	48	32–262K	32	Yes	6

b) Magnetic Tape.

			Magnetic Tape Units		
Model	*Number Tracks*	*Speed (In./Sec.)*	*Density (Bits/In.)*	*Transfer Rate (KCS)*	
601...........7		37.5	200/556	7.5/20.8	
604...........7		75.0	200/556/800	15/41.7/60	
607...........7		150.0	200/556/800	30/83.4/120	
608...........7		37.5	200/556/800	7.5/20.8/30	
609...........9		37.5	800	30	

c) Magnetic Disk.

			Magnetic Disk Units			
Disk Packs	*Max. Capacity Million Char.*	*Bits/Char.*	*Access Time Milli- seconds*	*Transfer Rate Ch./ Seconds*	*No. Disks*	*No. Heads*
852...........	2.0	7 (BCD)	145	77,730	6	10
853...........	4.096	6	145	208,333	6	10
854...........	8.192	6	145	208,333	6	10
Disk Files						
813...........100.663		6	34–110	196,000	36	32
814...........201.327		6	34–110	196,000	72	32

d) Magnetic Drum.
863   Capacity 4.1 million, 6 bit/character, transfer rate 62.5Kch. to 2Mch./second, average access time 17 milliseconds.
865   Capacity 8.3 million, 6 bit/character, transfer rate 1 million characters, average access time 17 milliseconds.
4. Communication Equipment.
Diagraphics Consoles.
273 Vector-oriented 22-inch flat-face CRT console with light pen.
274 Vector-oriented 22-inch flat-face CRT console with light pen and controller.
200 USER Terminals.   100 c/m reader, 300 l/m printer, & CRT/Keyboard Console.
210 Entry/Display System.   Displays 1,000 characters in 20 lines 50 characters each on 6″ × 8″ display on 14″ CRT.
3692 Typewriter Console.   Prints 15 characters per second from channel I/O.
6020 Conversational Terminal System.   Typewriter and visual display.

6030 Remote Terminal System.   100 c/m reader, 300 l/m printer, and 8092 Teleprogrammer.

6040 Remote Computer Station.   1,200 c/m reader, 1,000 l/m printer, 250 c/m punch, I/O Typewriter, and 8090 Computer.

Any 3000 or 6000 Series computer.

Analog Computers.

Control Data 6000 Series

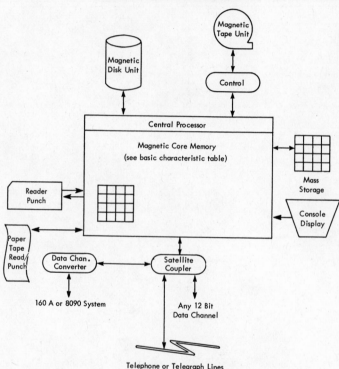

Telephone or Telegraph Lines
IBM 1009 Data Transmission Unit
IBM 7701 Magnetic Tape Terminals
IBM 7702 Magnetic Tape Terminals

CONTROL DATA 6000 SERIES

The Control Data 6000 Series are very large-scale, general-purpose computers comprised of the 6400, 6500, and 6600 compatible computer systems. Each is similar in general characteristics with memory speed being the distinctive difference. Each system is comprised of 11 independent computers —the 6400 and 6600 have 1 central processor each while the 6500 has dual central processors (131,000 maximum words of common memory) and 10 peripheral processors (each with 4,096 words of memory).

SYSTEM CONFIGURATION

1. Any of the 3000 series peripheral equipment may be attached to the 6000 computer systems via a 6681 Data Channel Converter. The 6681 permits 4 controllers to be attached.
   a) Console Display
   6612 Display. Dual 10-inch scope, 3 character sizes: 64, 32, and 16 characters per line.
2. Storage
   a) Internal Memory
   Magnetic Core Memory. See table below.

		Basic Core Memory Characteristics					
Model	*Cycle Time* *(μs)*	*Minor Cycle Time* *(μs)*	*Word Size* *(Byte)*	*Memory Size* *(Words)*	*Number Data Channels*	*Floating Point*	*Index Registers*
6400......1.0	0.1	60	32–131K	12	Yes	12
6500......1.0	0.1	60	65–131K	12	Yes	12
6600......1.0	0.1	60	65–131K	12	Yes	12

   b) Magnetic Tape
   626 Tape Unit. 150 inches per second, 800 bits per inch density, and 240,000 characters per second transfer rate. Uses one inch tape.
   c) Disk Storage
   6603 Disk Unit. 75 million 6 bit character capacity, average transfer rate of 1.11 to 1.25 million characters per second. Average access time of 201 to 268 milliseconds.
   6638 Disk Unit. 131 to 167 million 6 bit character capacity, average transfer rate 1.68 million characters per second. Average access time of 25 to 110 milliseconds.
   d) Mass Storage
   6633 to 6636 Extended Core Storage. 125 to 1,000K 60 bit word

capacity. Transfer rate 2.5 to 10 million words per second. First word access time 3 microseconds.

3. Communication Equipment

6683 Satellite Coupler. Permits direct connection to any two 12-bit data channels.

Analog Computers

GE–115 System

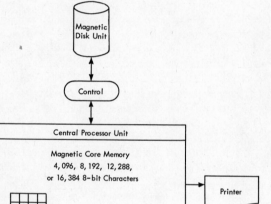

GE–115 SYSTEM

The GE–115 System is a low-cost computer system designed to replace tabulating card equipment and to serve as a remote on-line input/output terminal connected by communications lines to a central computer system.

SYSTEM CONFIGURATION

1. I/O Equipment.
   a) Punched Card Readers and Punches
      CRZ–100 Card Reader. Reads 300 cards per minute.
      CRZ–120 Card Reader. Reads 600 cards per minute. Has larger hopper capacity.
      CRP–100 Card Reader/Punch. Processes 300 cards per minute reading, punching, or mixed reading and punching.
      CPZ–101 Card Punch. Punches 60 to 200 cards per minute.
      CPZ–103 Card Punch. Punches 300 cards per minute.
   b) Paper Tape Reader.
      PTR–100 Paper Tape Reader. Reads 500 characters per second.
   c) Line Printers.
      PRT–100 Line Printer. 300 lines per minute. 104, 120, or 136 print positions using a 64 character set.
      PRT–110 Line Printer. Same as PRT–100 except printing is at 600 lines per minute.
      PRT–120 Line Printer. 780 lines per minute buffered printer. 120 or 136 print positions using a 64 character set.
2. Storage.
   a) Internal Memory.
      Magnetic core memory with 4,096, 8,192, 12,388, or 16,384 8-bit characters. Access time is 6.5 microseconds per character.
   b) Magnetic Tape.
      MTH–103 Magnetic Tape Handler. Reads/writes 200, 556, or 800 bits per inch, either 7- or 9-track, at 37.5 inches per second. Transfer rate is 7,500, 21,000, or 30,000 characters per second. One to six handlers per subsystem and one to four subsystems per GE–115 system.
      MTH–106 Magnetic Tape Handler. Same as MTH–103 except tape speed is 75 inches per second and transfer rate is 15,000, 42,000, or 60,000 characters per second.
   c) Magnetic Disc.
      DSU–130 Removable Disc Storage Unit. Capacity is 2.98 million 8-bit words per disc cartridge. Transfer rate is 77,500 characters per second. One to five drives per subsystem and one to four subsystems per GE–115 System. Average access time is 115 milliseconds.
3. Communication Equipment.
   Datanet–10. Synchronous single-line data communication controller permitting the GE–115 to serve as a remote input/output terminal for a large central computing system.

GE–400 Series
405, 415, 420, 425, and 435 Computer Systems

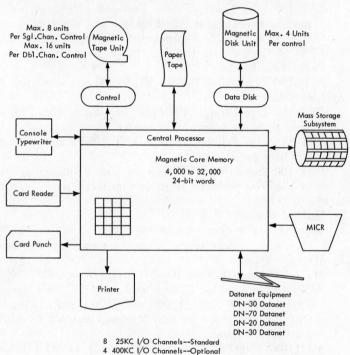

Max. 8 units
Per Sgl.Chan. Control
Max. 16 units
Per Dbl.Chan. Control

Magnetic Tape Unit

Paper Tape

Magnetic Disk Unit   Max. 4 Units Per control

Control

Data Disk

Console Typewriter

Central Processor

Magnetic Core Memory
4,000 to 32,000
24-bit words

Mass Storage Subsystem

Card Reader

Card Punch

MICR

Printer

Datanet Equipment
DN–30 Datanet
DN–70 Datanet
DN–20 Datanet
DN–30 Datanet

8   25KC I/O Channels--Standard
4   400KC I/O Channels--Optional

GE–400 SERIES

The GE–400 Series of computers are compatible business-oriented information processing systems. Their internal organization, decimal arithmetic capability, instruction repertoire, address modification capabilities, and highly efficient simultaneous read-write-compute operations provide optimum performance in a wide range of applications.

SYSTEM CONFIGURATION

1. I/O Equipment.
    a) Punched Card Readers and Punches.
        CRZ–201 Card Reader. Reads BCD/Binary/Mixed data at the rate of 900 cards per minute.
        CPZ–100 Card Punch. Punches at 100 cards per minute.
        CPZ–201 Card Punch. Punches at 300 cards per minute.
    b) Paper Tape Reader and Punch.
        PTR–200 Paper Tape Reader. Reads 500 characters per second in 5-, 6-, 7-, or 8-level codes.
        PTP–200 Paper Tape Punch. Punches 150 characters per second in 5-, 6-, 7-, or 8-level codes.
    c) Line Printer.
        PRT–201 Printer. Prints all ASCII characters on a 136-character print line at the rate of 1,200 lines per minute.
    d) MICR.
        MRS–Magnetic Reader/Sorter. Reads and sorts up to 1,200 MICR documents per minute in either on-line or off-line operations.
    e) Optical Scanning.
        COC–5 Bar Font Reader. Optically reads and sorts 1,200 COC–5 or E–13B font documents per minute. Also reads MICR characters magnetically.
2. Storage.
    a) Internal Memory.
        Magnetic Core Memory. Standard memory sizes are 8,192, 16,384, or 32,768 24-bit words. Extended memory is available up to 131,072 words. Access per word is 8.0 microseconds on the 405, 5.8 microseconds on the 415, 3.9 microseconds on the 425, and 2.7 microseconds on the 435.
    b) Magnetic Tape.

Magnetic Tape Units			
Model	*Speed* (*in/sec.*)	*Density* (*bits/in*)	*Transfer Rate* (*KCS*)
MTH–200...............	37.5	200/556	7.5/21
MTH–300...............	37.5	200/556/800	7.5/21/30
MTH–201...............	75.0	200/556	15/41.7
MTH–301...............	75.0	200/556/800	15/41.7/60
MTH–211...............150.0		200/556	30/83
MTH–311...............150.0		200/556/800	30/83/120

c) Magnetic Disc.

DSU–160 Removable Disc Storage Unit. Capacity is 7.68 million 6-bit characters per disc cartridge. Transfer rate is 208,000 characters per second. Up to eight disc drives per subsystem or 61.4 million characters on line. Average access time is 97.5 milliseconds.

DSU–204 Disc Storage Unit. Capacity is 23.5 million 6-bit characters per file with up to four files per subsystem or 94 million characters on line. Transfer rate is 41,700 characters per second for the inner tracks and 83,400 characters per second for the outer tracks. Average access time is 199 milliseconds.

DSU–270 Disc Storage Unit. Capacity is 200 million characters per file and transfer rate is from 261,000 to 333,000 characters per second. Average access time is 25 milliseconds.

d) Mass Storage.

MDS–201 Magnetic Drum Subsystem. Capacity is 4.7 million 6-bit characters per unit with up to two units per subsystem or 9.4 million characters on line. Transfer rate is 370,000 characters per second and average access time is 17 milliseconds.

MSS–388 Mass Storage Subsystem. Capacity is 1.35 billion 6-bit characters per unit with transfer rate of 83,000 characters per second and average access time of 400 milliseconds.

3. Communication Equipment.

Console Typewriter with a printing output of either 10 or 15 characters per second.

Datanet Equipment.

DN–30 (computer with 5.7 microsecond access time and core memory of 4,096, 8,192, or 16,384 18-bit words) controls a maximum of 120 I/O lines including interchange with GE–115 Remote Processing Terminal.

DN–20. Asynchronous single-line data communication controller for interchange with remote terminals including teletypewriters.

DN–21. Same as above except synchronous. Used for interchange with the GE–115.

DN–760. Remote keyboard/display terminal with cathode ray tube display.

Time-Sharing Equipment.

GE–420. Time-Sharing version of GE–415 employing DN–30 as I/O Controller.

Honeywell 200 Series

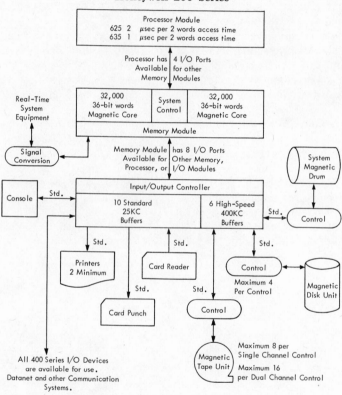

GE–600 SERIES

The GE–600 Information Processing Series provides modular, solid-state, digital computing systems for large-scale business, scientific, military command and control, and other real-time applications. Multiprogramming and multiprocessing capabilities are provided through an integrated programming and operating system.

SYSTEM CONFIGURATION

All of the input/output devices available for the GE–400 Series are equally applicable to the GE–600 Series.

Memory. Magnetic core memory is provided in Memory Modules, each of which contains 2 units of 32,000 36-bit words of memory. Normally, a maximum of 4 Memory Modules may be used with a Processing Module to provide a maximum of 262,144 words of memory. Access time (for two 36-bit words) is two microseconds for the 625 and one microsecond for the 635.

The required MDS–201 Magnetic Drum Subsystem decodes each received command and initiates the proper sequence of command operations. It also monitors entire operations, including error checking, and transmits status information to the I/O Controller.

The capacity of the MDS–201 is 9.4 million characters (in 6-bit words) per subsystem. Average access time is 17 milliseconds and the transfer rate is up to 370,000 characters per second.

The MTH–211 and MTH–311 Magnetic Tape Units are usually utilized on the 600 system due to their speed capabilities.

GE–600 Series

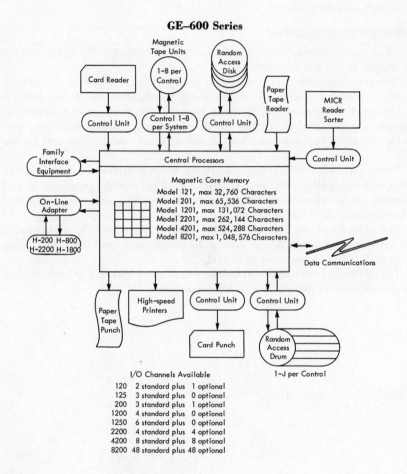

I/O Channels Available

120	2 standard plus 1 optional
125	3 standard plus 0 optional
200	3 standard plus 1 optional
1200	4 standard plus 0 optional
1250	6 standard plus 0 optional
2200	4 standard plus 4 optional
4200	8 standard plus 8 optional
8200	48 standard plus 48 optional

HONEYWELL 200 SERIES
120, 125, 200, 1200, 1250, 2200, 4200, and 8200 COMPUTERS

The Honeywell 200 Series is a transistorized, magnetic core, two-address, alphanumeric data processing series of computer systems. They are primarily adaptable to business applications in the lower ranges and both business and scientific applications in the upper ranges.

SYSTEM CONFIGURATION

1. I/O Equipment.
   a) Punched Card Readers and Punches.
   214–2 Reader, speed 400 cards per minute.
   223 Reader, speed 800 cards per minute.
   224–1 Punch, variable speeds 50 to 262 cards per minute.
   224–2 Punch, variable speeds 90 to 354 cards per minute.
   227 Reader/Punch, reads 800 and punches 250 cards per minute.
   b) Paper Tape Reader.
   209   600 characters per second.
   c) Paper Tape Punch.
   210   120 characters per second.
   d) MICR Reader/Sorter. 1,560 and 1,600 documents per minute.
   e) Line Printers.
   222–1, –2, and –3. All print at 650 lines per minute with a numeric option to print at 1,300 lines per minute. The models have 96, 108, and 130 (132 optional) respective print positions.
   222–4   Speed of 950 alphanumeric or 1,300 numeric lines per minute, 120 or 132 characters per line.
   222–5   450 lines per minute, 120 or 132 characters per line.
2. Storage.
   a) Magnetic core. Access time for 121 is 3 microseconds, 201 is 2 microseconds, 1201 is 1.5 microseconds, 2201 is 1 microsecond, 4201 is 750 microseconds (3 characters), and 8201 is 750 microseconds (8 characters).
   b) Magnetic Tape.
   204B $\frac{1}{2}$" tape, speeds 24, 36, 80, and 120 inches/second, seven models available, density 200, 556, or 800 characters/inch, transfer rate 4.8 to 96K characters per second.
   204A $\frac{3}{4}$" tape, speed of 60 or 120 inches/second, three models, density 533 or 740 characters/inch, transfer rate 32, 64, or 88.8K characters/second.
   c) Magnetic Disk.
   261   150 million character/2 stack file, transfer rate 196,666 characters/second.
   262   300 million character/4 stack file, transfer rate 196,666 characters/second.
   258   Disk Packs 4.58 million characters, transfer rate 208,333 characters/second.

259 Disk Packs 9.16 million characters, transfer rate of 147,500 or 208,333 characters per second.

d) Magnetic Drum.

270 2,621,440 characters per file, speed 1140 rpm, 512 read/ write heads, average access 31 milliseconds, transfer rate 111,000 characters per second.

3. Communication Equipment.

A very broad range of lines, speeds, and terminal devices are optional.

212–1 On-Line Adapter. High-speed memory to memory link between two or more systems.

216 series of peripheral and communication control switching allows 2 systems to share peripherals.

281, 284, and 286 Communication Controls allow the system to receive and transmit data over toll or leased communication lines.

Honeywell 800 System

ON LINE

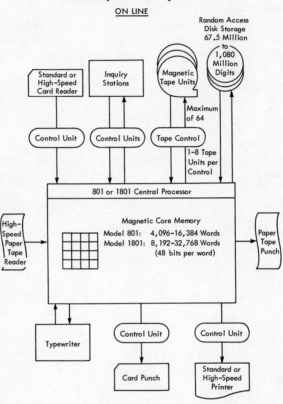

HONEYWELL 800

The Honeywell 800 is a transistorized, magnetic core, three-address, alphanumeric data processing system. It is primarily adaptable to business applications. With additional equipment it is suitable for scientific problems.

SYSTEM CONFIGURATION

1. Input Equipment—Other than magnetic tape and disc.
   a) Card to Memory.
      823–1 Standard Card Reader, 807–1, 811–1, –2, or –3 Card Reader Control. Speed of 240 cards per minute.
      823–2 High-Speed Card Reader, 807–2 or 811–1, –2, or –3 Card Reader Control. Speed of 650 cards per minute.
   b) Paper Tape to Memory.
      809 High-Speed Paper Tape Reader with speed of 1,000 char/sec.
   c) Console to Memory.
      Uses a standard electric typewriter.
2. Output Equipment—Other than magnetic tape and disc.
   a) Memory to Card.
      824–1 Standard Card Punch, 808–1, 811–1, –2, or –3 Card Punch Control. Speed of 100 cards per minute.
      824–2 High-Speed Card Punch, 808–2, 811–1, –2, or –3 Card Punch Control. Speed of 250 cards per minute.
   b) Memory to Paper Tape.
      810 Paper Tape Punch. Speed of 110 characters per second.
   c) Memory to Printer.
      822–1 and –2 Standard Printers, 806–1, 811–1 and –2 Printer Control. Printing speed 150 lines per minute.
      822–3 High-Speed Printer, 806–2, 811–3 Printer Control. Printing speed of 900 lines per minute.
      Standard electric typewriter with printing speed of 10 char/sec.
3. Storage.
   a) Internal Storage.
      Magnetic core. Access time for 801 is 6 and for 1801 is 2 microseconds.
   b) Magnetic Tape.
      808–2 Tape Units. 8 units per control and 8 controls gives a maximum of 64 units. Speed 120 inches per second.
   c) Magnetic Disc.
      Model 860–1, –2, –3, –4, –5, –6, –7, –8, or –9 disc storage and control. Average access time of 100 milliseconds.
4. Additional Input/Output Equipment.
   Honeywell 400 System for card to tape, tape to card, and tape to printer operations.
   Card to Magnetic Tape. 823–1 or –2 Card Readers, 804 Magnetic Tape Unit, 807–1, 811–1, –2, or –3 Card Reader Control. Speed of 240 or 650 cards per minute.

Magnetic Tape to Card. 824–1 or –2 Card Punch, 804 Magnetic Tape Unit, 808–1, 811–1, –2, or –3 Card Punch Control. Speed of 100 or 250 cards per minute.

Magnetic Tape to Printer. 822–1, –2, or –3 Printers, 804 Tape Unit, 806–1, –2, or –3, 811–1, –2, or –3 Printer Control. Speed of 150, 150, and 900 lines per minute respectively.

Model 20 IBM System/360 I/O Devices

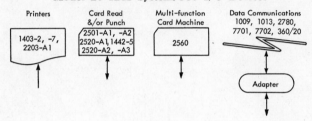

Printers   Card Read &/or Punch   Multi-function Card Machine   Data Communications 1009, 1013, 2780, 7701, 7702, 360/20

1403-2, -7, 2203-A1

2501-A1, -A2 2520-A1, 1442-5 2520-A2, -A3

2560

Adapter

Other Models IBM System/360 I/O Devices

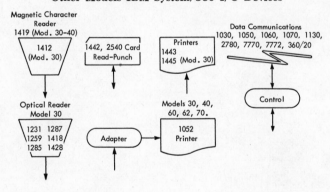

Magnetic Character Reader 1419 (Mod. 30-40)

1412 (Mod. 30)

1442, 2540 Card Read-Punch

Printers 1443 1445 (Mod. 30)

Data Communications 1030, 1050, 1060, 1070, 1130, 2780, 7770, 7772, 360/20

Optical Reader Model 30

1231 1287 1259 1418 1285 1428

Adapter

Models 30, 40, 60, 62, 70.

1052 Printer

Control

Other Models IBM System/360 I/O Devices (continued)

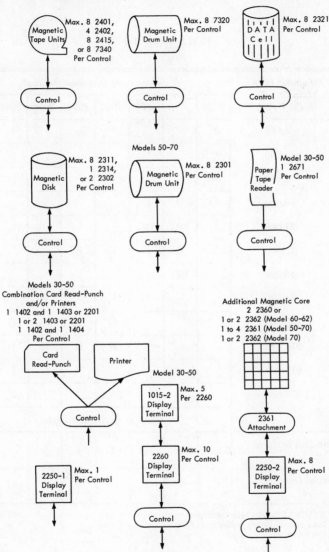

IBM System/360

Magnetic Core Main Storage (8-Bit Bytes)	System/360 Processor Options*							
	2020	2025	2030	2040	2044	2050	2065	2075
4,000	B							
8,000	C		C					
12,000	BC							
16,000	D	D	D					
24,000		DC	DC					
32,000		E	E	E	E			
48,000		ED						
64,000			F	F	F	F		
128,000				G	G	G	G	
256,000				H	H	H	H	H
512,000						I	I	I
1,050,000							J	J
Channel Outlets Available†								
Standard feature Multiplexor		1	1	1	1	1		
Special feature Selector		1	2	2	2	4	6‡	‡

* A Model 91 has also been announced.
† Each channel outlet provides up to 8 control unit connections.
‡ One required.

IBM SYSTEM/360

The IBM System/360 is a single system constructed with semicompatible components. A number of announced models encompass a wide range of application areas—commercial, scientific, communications, controls, and combinations of these. Various processors and many types of input and output devices are available to permit modifications to be made, on a building-block principle, in adapting the system to the needs of the user.

SYSTEM CONFIGURATION

1. I/O Equipment.
    a) Punched Card Reader.
        1402–N1 Card Read-Punch. Reads 800 cards per minute, and punches 250 cards per minute—both maximum (also see 1401).
        1442 Card Read-Punch (see 1440).
        2520–A1 Card Read-Punch. Reads, reads and punches, or punches 500 cards per minute.
        2501–A1, –A2 Card Reader. Reads 600 and 1,000 cards per minute depending on model.
        2560 Multifunction Card Machine. A combination 500-card-per-minute card reader, 160-column-per-minute punch, and 140-character-column-per-second printer with a selective 5-pocket stacker. Performs the traditional unit record functions of reproducing, gang punching, summary punching, collating, de-collating, and sorting.
    b) Punched Card Punch.
        1402–N1 Card Read-Punch (see 1401).
        1442 Card Read-Punch (see 1401).
        1442–5 Card Punch. Serial punching at a maximum rate of 160 columns per second.
        2520–A1 Card Read-Punch (see above).
        2520–A2, A3 Card Punch. Punches 500 and 300 cards per minute depending on model.
    c) Paper Tape Reader.
        2671 Paper Tape Reader. Reads strips or rolls of 5-, 6-, 7-, or 8-channel codes at speeds up to 1,000 characters per second.
    d) Printer.
        1052 Typewriter Keyboard (see 1401).
        1403 Printer (see 1401).
        1404 Printer (see 1401).
        1443 Printer (see 1440).
        1445 Printer (see 1440).
        2201–3 Printer. 132 print positions and 1,100 lines per minute.
        2203–A1 Printer. 120 characters per line. 300 to 750 lines per minute depending on the set of characters used.
    e) MICR Reading.
        1412 Magnetic Character Reader (see 1401).
        1419 Magnetic Character Reader (see 1401).

  f) Optical Scanning.

   1231 Optical Mark Page Reader (see 1401).

   1285 Optical Reader (see 1401).

   1287 Optical Reader. Reads single or multiple lines of hand-printed, machine-printed, or imprinted numbers; marks from cut form documents, and continuous journal tapes prepared on cash registers and adding machines.

   1418 Optical Character Reader (see 1401).

   1428 Alphameric Optical Reader (see 1401).

2. Storage.

  a) Internal Memory.

   Magnetic core memory (see Processor Options chart).

   2360–1, –2, –3 Auxiliary Bulk Storage of 65.5, 131, and 262 thousand byte capacity. Access speed of 2 microseconds.

   2361–1, –2 Core Storage of 1 and 2 million bytes capacity. Access speed of 8 microseconds.

   2362–1 Core Storage of 262 thousand bytes capacity with an access speed of 1 microsecond.

  b) Magnetic Tape.

   2401 Tape Unit (see Figure 12–4).

   2402 Tape Unit (see Figure 12–4).

   7340 Hypertape Unit (see Figure 12–4 and 1401).

  c) Magnetic Disk.

   2302 Disk Storage. 117-digit or 234-million-alphameric-character storage capacity. Maximum transfer rate 184,000 characters, 143,000 bytes, or 286,000 digits per second.

   2311 Disk Storage. 7.25 million bytes capacity per interchangeable disk pack. Average access time is 85 milliseconds and the transfer rate is 156,000 bytes per second.

  d) Magnetic Drum.

   2301 Drum Storage. 4 million bytes capacity. Average access time is 8.6 milliseconds and the transfer rate is 1.2 million bytes per second.

   7320 Drum Storage. 830,000 bytes capacity. Average access time is 8.6 milliseconds and the transfer rate is 135,000 bytes per second.

  e) Data Cell.

   2321 Data Cell Drive. 400 million byte capacity. Access time varies with position from 175 to 600 milliseconds. Data transfer is 55,000 bytes per second. The Data Cell Drive houses 10 removable and interchangeable data cells, each with a capacity of 40 million bytes.

3. Communication Equipment.

  Data Communications.

   Data Communications Adapter permits the Model 20 to function as a point-to-point data transmission terminal through the 1009 Data Transmission unit, 1013 Card Transmission terminals, and 7701 and 7702 Magnetic Tape Transmission Terminals.

1030 Data Collection System.

1050 Data Communication System.

1060 Data Collection System—for banks.

1070 Process Communication System.

1800 Data Acquisition and Control System.

1051 Attachment.

Audio Communications.

7770 Audio Response Unit. Provides magnetic drum, analog coded, recorded voice responses to inquiries made from telephone and similar terminals.

7772 Audio Response Unit. Similar to above except voice recorded in digitally coded form on an external disk file.

Display Units.

2260–1, –2 Inquiry Display Terminal which presents data from storage in either character or graphical form. Each Model 1 provides the power to support up to five Model 2 units.

2250–1, –2 Display Unit. A "TV-like" display device used to visually present, in alphameric or graphical form, computer-generated data. A hand-held light pen may be used to enter or alter data on the screen.

IBM 1130 System

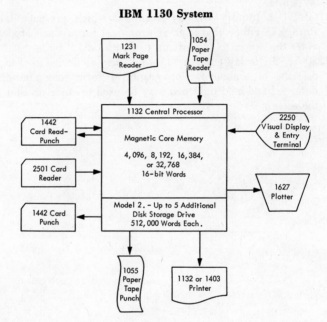

IBM 1130 SYSTEM

The IBM 1130 System is a compact, easily operated computer utilizing magnetic core memory (model 2 also has disk storage). It is a general-purpose computer designed to serve engineering and scientific applications as well as being ideally suited to small commercial applications.

SYSTEM CONFIGURATION

1. I/O Equipment.
    a) Punched Card Reader and Punch.
    1402–N1 Read-Punch (see 360).
    1442 Read-Punch (see 1440).
    b) Paper Tape Reader and Punch.
    1054 Reader (see 1401).
    1055 Punch (see 1401).
    c) Printers.
    1132 Printer. 80 Alphameric or 110 numeric lines per minute, 120 characters per line.
    1401 Printer. 465 or 600 lines per minute, 120 characters per line.
    1627 Plotter. An incremental plotter to provide the graphical presentation of digital information. Model 1 plots maximum area of 11 inches by 120 feet. Model 2 plots maximum area of 29½ inches by 120 feet. Speeds are 300 and 200 0.01-inch steps per second, respectively.

2. Storage.
    Model 1 has 4,096 to 32,768 16-bit words of magnetic core memory available with a cycle time of 2.2 or 3.6 microseconds.
    Model 2 has the above magnetic core memory plus up to 5 additional units of 512,000 16-bit words of disk storage with access rate of 28.6 microseconds per word and transfer rate of 700,000 bits per second.

IBM 1401 Sytsem

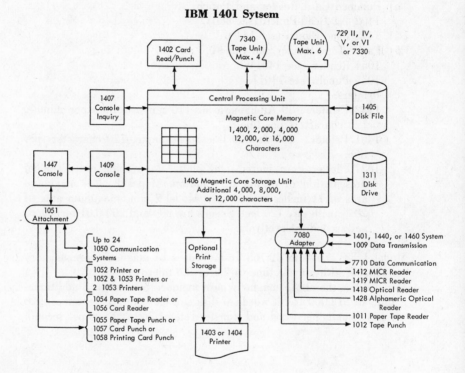

IBM 1401 SYSTEM

The IBM 1401 is a transistorized, alphanumeric, sequential magnetic core, general-purpose data processing system.

SYSTEM CONFIGURATION

1. I/O Equipment.
    a) Punched Card Reader.
        1056 Card Reader. Model 1, card pack and model 2, single card. Both read at 14.8 characters per second.
        1402 Card Read-Punch. Reads 450 or 800 cards per minute.
    b) Punched Card Punch.
        1057 Card Punch. A limited-speed card output for 1050.
        1058 Printing Card Punch. Similar to 1057 except data is printed as it is punched. It has an alphameric keyboard which can be used as an off-line keypunch.
        1402 Card Read-Punch. Punches up to 250 cards per minute.
    c) Paper Tape Reader.
        1011 Paper Tape Reader. 5- to 8-track tape at a rate of 500 characters per second.
        1054 Paper Tape Reader. Reads tape at 14.8 characters/second. Used with the 1050, 1130, and 1800 systems.
    d) Paper Tape Punch.
        1012 Tape Punch. Punches 5- to 8-track tape at speeds up to 150 characters per second.
        1055 Paper Tape Punch. Punches tape at 14.8 characters per second. Used with the 1050, 1130, and 1800 systems.
    e) Line Printer.
        1052 Printer Keyboard. A typewriter which prints 14.8 characters per second.
        1053 Printer. A typewriter similar to the above. For use with 1050, 1070, and 1800 data communications systems.
        1403 Printer. 120 or 132 characters per line depending on model. Model 2 & 7 prints 600 and model 3 prints 1,100 lines per minute.
        1404 Printer. Bill-feed printer for cards of 51 to 160 columns. Prints on continuous forms at 600 lines per minute. On cards at 400 (2 cards simultaneously at 800) cards per minute.
    f) MICR Reader.
        1412 Magnetic Character Reader. Reads and sorts documents at a maximum rate of 950 documents per minute.
        1419 Magnetic Character Reader. Reads and sorts at a maximum rate of 1,600 documents per minute.

  g) Optical Scanning.

    1231 Optical Mark Page Reader. Reads up to 1,000 marked positions on $8\frac{1}{2}'' \times 11''$ sheets at speeds up to 1,600 or 2,000 documents per hour.

    1285 Optical Reader. Reads printed paper tapes, such as those produced on cash registers or adding machines, as input.

    1418 Optical Character Reader. Reads special printer type numerical data at 300 $8\frac{3}{4}''$ or 420 $5\frac{7}{8}''$ wide documents a minute. Also provides selective stacking.

    1428 Alphameric Optical Reader. Similar to the 1418 except alphameric data is read.

2. Storage.

  a) Internal Memory.

    14,000 to 16,000 magnetic cores. Additional 4,000-core 1404 Storage Units available to provide up to 12,000 additional cores. 11.5 microsecond cycle.

  b) Magnetic Tape (see Figure 12–4 for data).

    Up to 6 model 729 II, IV, V, or VI or 7,330 Units.

    Up to 4 model 7,340 Hypertape Units with automatic cartridge loading.

  c) Magnetic Disk.

    1311 Disk Storage Drive. Utilizes interchangeable disk packs each containing 2 million characters. Average access time is 250 milliseconds.

    1405 Disk Storage. Available as a 25 or 50 disk unit (10 or 20 million character capacity). Access time: minimum 100, maximum 800 milliseconds.

3. Communication Equipment.

  1009 Data Transmission Unit. Two-way communication with Magnetic Tape or Card Transmission Terminals, or other 1401 processors.

  1050 Data Communication System which operates over leased lines through a series of input/output equipment.

  1401, 1440, or 1460 Systems for input and output.

  7710 Data Communication Unit. Similar to 1009 plus microwave and coaxial cable broad-band communication.

  7740 Communication Control Systems. A multisystem switching device. Consoles.

  1407 Console Inquiry Station. Typewriter I/O.

  1409 Console Auxiliary. Permits the addition of: Model 1—1447 Console; Model 3, or Model 2—up to 4 1026 Transmission Control Units and Terminals.

IBM 1440 System

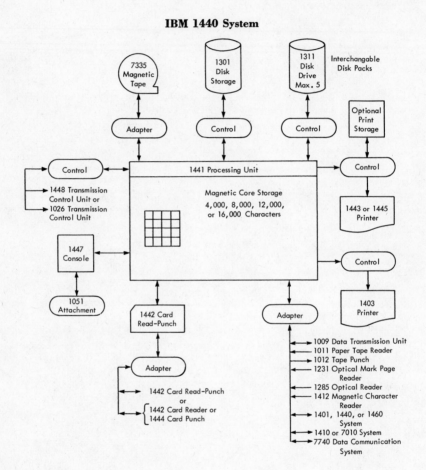

IBM 1440 SYSTEM

The IBM 1440 is a small-scale, on-line, nonbuffered, magnetic core data processing system.

SYSTEM CONFIGURATION

1. I/O Equipment.
   a) Punched Card Reader.
   1056 Card Reader (see 1401).
   1442 Card Read-Punch.   Reads 400 cards per minute and punches 160 columns per second.
   1442 Card Reader.   A "read only" model of above.
   b) Punched Card Punch.
   1057 Card Punch (see 1401).
   1058 Printing Card Punch (see 1401).
   1442 Card Read-Punch (see 1401).
   1444 Card Punch.   250 cards per minute punching.
   c) Paper Tape Reader.
   1011 Paper Tape Reader (see 1401).
   1054 Paper Tape Reader (see 1401).
   d) Paper Tape Punch.
   1012 Tape Punch (see 1401).
   1055 Paper Tape Punch (see 1401).
   e) Line Printer.
   1053 Printer (see 1401).
   1403 Printer (see 1401).
   1443 Printer.   120 characters per line. 200 to 600 lines per minute depending on the set of characters used.
   1445 Printer. 113 characters per line. 190 to 525 lines per minute depending on the set of characters used. Prints magnetic ink E-13B characters as well as standard characters.
   f) MICR Reading.
   1412 Magnetic Character Reader (see 1401).
   g) Optical Scanning.
   1231 Optical Mark Page Reader (see 1401).
   1285 Optical Reader (see 1401).
2. Storage.
   a) Internal Memory.
   Magnetic core memory.
   b) Magnetic Tape.
   7335 Tape Unit. Reads and writes tape at 20,000 characters per second. Tape density is 556 characters per inch.
   c) Magnetic Disk.
   1301 Disk Storage Unit.   28 or 56 million alphameric character storage capacity, maximum transfer rate of 90,000 characters per second.
   1311 Disk Storage Drive (see 1401).

3. Communication Equipment.
        1447 Console (see 1401).
        1009 Data Transmission Unit (see 1401).
        1026 Transmission Control Unit. Services include:
          357 Data Collection System.
          1030 Data Collection System.
          1050 Data Communication System.
          1060 Data Communication System.
          1070 Data Communication System.
        1401, 1440, or 1460 Computer Systems.
        1410 or 7010 Computer Systems.
        1448 Transmission Control Unit (see 1401).
        7740 Data Communication System (see 1401).

IBM 1460 System

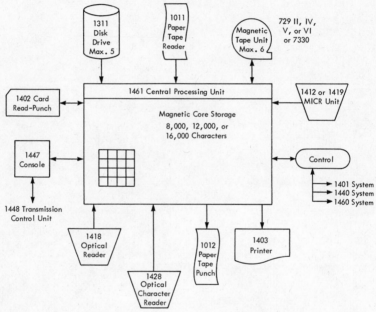

IBM 1460 SYSTEM

The IBM 1460 is a transistorized, alpha-numeric, sequential, magnetic core, general-purpose data processing system. It is designed to be compatible with the 1401 system, but to provide more power and speed as an intermediate-range system.

SYSTEM CONFIGURATION

1. I/O Equipment.
   a) Punched Card Reader.
   1402 Card Read-Punch (see 1401).
   b) Punched Card Punch.
   1402 Card Read-Punch (see 1401).
   c) Paper Tape Reader.
   1011 Paper Tape Reader (see 1401).
   d) Paper Tape Punch.
   1012 Tape Punch (see 1401).
   e) Line Printer.
   1403 Printer (see 1401).
   f) MICR Reader.
   1412 Magnetic Character Reader (see 1401).
   1419 Magnetic Character Reader (see 1401).
   g) Optical Scanning.
   1418 Optical Character Reader (see 1401).
   1428 Alphameric Optical Reader (see 1401).
2. Storage.
   a) Internal Memory.
   Magnetic core memory. Access time 6 microseconds.
   b) Magnetic Tape.
   729 II, IV, V, or VI Tape Units (see Figure 12–4).
   7330 Tape Unit (see Figure 12–4).
   c) Magnetic Disk.
   1311 Disk Storage Drive (see 1401).
3. Communication Equipment.
   Direct Data Channel provides access to and from 1401, 1440, or 1460 system. 1447 Console provides access to a 1448 Transmission Control Unit.

IBM 1620 System

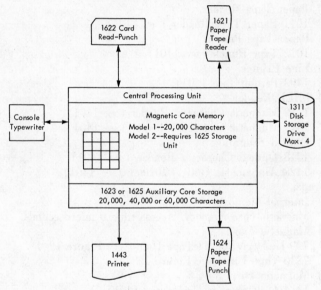

IBM 1620 SYSTEM

The IBM 1620 is a small-scale, transistorized computer designed for both commercial and scientific applications.

SYSTEM CONFIGURATION

1. I/O Equipment.
   a) Punched Card Reader.
      1622 Card Read-Punch with speed of 250 cards per minute; 236.6 of the 240 millisecond cycle are available for computing.
   b) Punched Card Punch.
      1622 Card Read-Punch with speed of 125 cards per minute; 476.6 of the 480 millisecond cycle available for computing.
   c) Paper Tape Reader.
      1621 Paper Tape Reader with speed of 150 characters per second.
   d) Paper Tape Punch.
      1624 Paper Tape Punch with speed of 15 characters per second.
   e) Printer.
      Modified IBM typewriter, same as used for input. Printing speed of Model 1 is 10 and Model 2 is 15.5 characters per second.
      1443 Printer (see 1440).
   f) Keyboard Console.
      Modified IBM typewriter with 10 numeric, 26 alphabetic, and 12 special characters printable.
2. Storage.
   a) Internal Memory.
      Magnetic core with access time for Model 1 of 20 microseconds. Model 2 speed is 10 microseconds.
   b) Auxiliary Memory.
      1623 Core Storage used to expand the main memory of the 1620 Model 1. Access time is 20 microseconds.
      1625 Core Storage is required for the 1620 Model 2. Access time is 10 microseconds.
   c) Magnetic Disk.
      1311 Disk Storage Drive (see 1401).

NCR 315 System

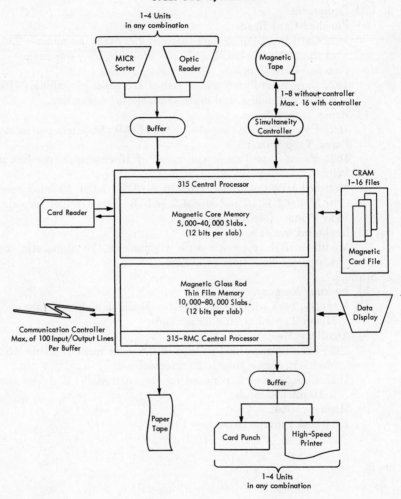

NCR 315 SYSTEM

The NCR 315 is a solid-state, transistorized, magnetic core, expandable-type computer, primarily designed for business applications.

The NCR 315 RMC (Rod Memory Computer) is a solid-state computer with thin-film memory. Designed for business, engineering, and on-line communication control. Model Mark II is a multiprogramming processor.

SYSTEM CONFIGURATION

1. I/O Equipment.
   a) Punched Card Readers and Punches.
      376–7   Read/Punch. Reads 300 and punches 60 cards per minute.
      376–8   Read/Punch. Reads 400 and punches 100 cards per minute.
      380–3   2,000 cards per minute Photoelectric Card Reader.
      383–1   400 cards per minute, 50% of cycle time is available for computing when reading 80-column cards.
      IBM 523 or 544 Card Punch. Speed 100 or 250 cards per minute with all time being computing time.
   b) Punched Paper Tape Reader.
      361–201   600 characters per second photoelectrically.
   c) Punched Paper Tape Punch.
      371–3   120 characters per second.
   d) Optical Font Reader.
      420–1   28 lines per second.
      420–2   56 lines per second.
   e) MICR Check Sorter.
      402   750 documents per minute (time sharable).
      404   600 documents per minute.
      407   1,200 documents per minute of mixed size, constant speed.
   f) Line Printers.
      340 Series of printers, 120 to 132 print positions, speeds of 680 to 1,500 lines per minute.
   g) Data Display System (CRT).
      795   256, 512, or 1,024 characters per display, 64 characters per line, and 32 lines per page.
2. Storage.
   a) NCR 315. Magnetic core using slab memory with 12-bit slab structure of 2 alphanumeric and 3 numeric. Access time 6 microseconds cycle time per slab. 5 to 40K slab capacity.
      NCR 315–RMC. Glass rods using 12-bit slab structure of 2 alphanumeric or 3 numeric. Access time 800 nanoseconds per 12-bit slab. 10 to 80K slab capacity.
   b) Magnetic Tape.
      332–204   Speed 66K characters per second, 556 bits per inch.
      333–101   Speed 120K characters per second.

333–102 Speed 83K characters per second, 556 bits per inch.

333–501 (315–RMC only) Speed 120K characters per second.

333–502 (315–RMC only) Speed 83K characters per second, 556 bits per inch.

334–101 Speed 12K characters per second, 200 bits per inch (not 315–RMC).

334–131 Speed 33K characters per second, 556 bits per inch.

c) Magnetic Disk.

365 Series. 2 million max. character capacity per unit, average access time 16.7 milliseconds with a transfer rate of 120K characters per second.

d) CRAM—Card Random Access Memory.

353–1 Access time 200 milliseconds (time sharable), transfer rate 100,000 characters per second, 5,555,200 characters per file.

353–2 Access time 200 milliseconds (time sharable), transfer rate 38,000 characters per second, 8 million characters per file.

353–3 Access time 200 milliseconds (time sharable), transfer rate 38,000 characters per second, 16,100,000 characters per file.

353–5 Access time 125 milliseconds (time sharable), transfer rate 50,000 characters per second, 82,944,000 characters per file.

3. Communication Equipment.

321 Communication Controller handles 100 input/output communication lines (any mix or speed) allowing remote input from any location directly in or out of the system. I/O devices may be any wired NCR equipment (adding machines, cash registers, accounting machines, teleprinters, or other computers).

NCR 390 System

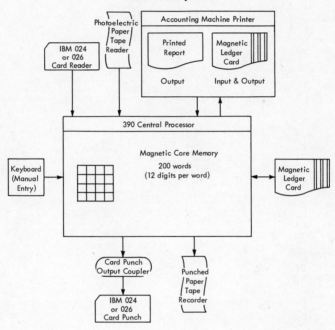

NCR 390 SYSTEM

The NCR 390 is a solid-state, fully transistorized, numeric, magnetic core data processing system primarily designed for business application.

SYSTEM CONFIGURATION

1. I/O Equipment.
   a) Punched Card Reader/Punch.
   IBM 24 or 26. Speed in or out 17 columns per second.
   Accounting Machine with speed of 2 seconds per magnetic ledger card of 216 digits and to read and position itself for the next posting line.
   386 Automatic Ledger Reader. Magnetic ledger cards at the rate of 2,400 cards per hour. Recodes at speed of 1½ seconds per card.
   582–1 Punched Card Reader. 100 cards per minute.
   b) Paper Tape Reader.
   Photoelectric Paper Tape Reader with speed of 400 characters per second.
   362 Strip Reader. Speed of 650 characters per second.
   c) Paper Tape Punch.
   462–2 Punched Paper Tape Recorder with speed of 30 characters per second.
   d) Line Printer.
   Accounting Machine Printer with speed of two 12-digit words per second. Printing positions of 260 numeric characters per line. 10 numeric characters from memory and alphabetic and other characters through the keyboard. Approximately 50% of print cycle available for computing.
   e) Console.
   Console Keyboard for manual entry, no alphabetic characters (except from direct punched card input), 10 numeric, and some special characters printable.
2. Storage.
   Magnetic core with access time of 1.2 milliseconds. Will transfer data by word, partial word, or by groups of up to 100 words.

NCR 500 SERIES

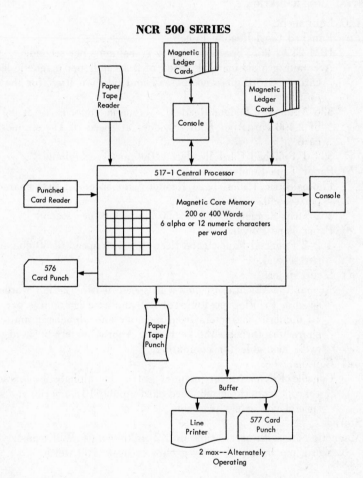

NCR 500 SERIES

The NCR 500 Series Computer is a solid-state, transistorized, magnetic core memory computer primarily designed for business applications in smaller business organizations.

SYSTEM CONFIGURATION

1. I/O Equipment.
   a) Punched Card Reader.
   582–1   100 cards per minute.
   b) Punched Card Punch.
   576–1 (Serial Printing)   25 columns per second.
   577–1   100 cards per minute.
   c) Paper Tape Readers.
   561–1   Rewind Tape Reader.   400 characters per second.
   561–2   Rewind Tape Reader.   600 characters per second.
   562–1   Strip Reader.   650 characters per second.
   563–1   Strip Reader.   50 characters per second.
   d) Paper Tape Punches.
   571–1   120 characters per second.
   572–1   30 characters per second.
   e) Line Printer.
   541–1   96 characters per line and 125 lines per minute.
   f) Optical Font Readers.
   420–1   28 lines per second.
   420–2   56 lines per second.
   g) Automatic Ledger Reader.
   586–1   Reads 2400 magnetic ledger cards per hour (320 digits at 2 seconds per card).
   h) Console.
   521–1 Control Console—keyboard entry only.
   590–1 (Magnetic Ledger).   216 digits per 2 seconds.
   590–2 (Without Magnetic Ledger).   Prints 12 characters per line at 111 lines per minute.
2. Storage.
   Magnetic core memory, 200 or 400 words, 6 alpha or 12 numeric characters per word.

NCR 615 Century Series; 615–100 and 615–200 Systems

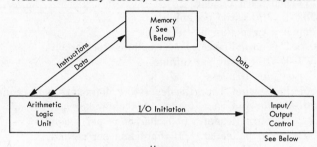

Memory
615-100 16 or 32K 8-bit bytes
615-200 32, 64, 128, 256, 384, or 512K 8-bit bytes

Input/Output

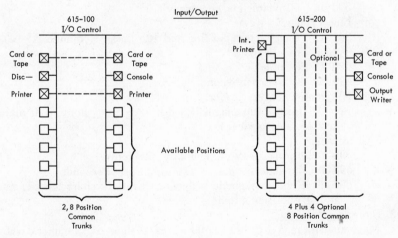

NCR 615 Century Series; 615–400 System

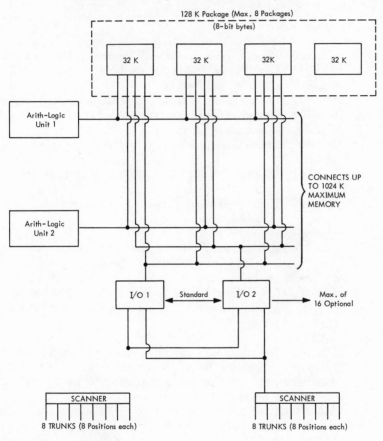

128 K Package (Max. 8 Packages)
(8-bit bytes)

32 K   32 K   32K   32 K

Arith-Logic Unit 1

CONNECTS UP TO 1024 K MAXIMUM MEMORY

Arith-Logic Unit 2

I/O 1   Standard   I/O 2   Max. of 16 Optional

SCANNER   SCANNER

8 TRUNKS (8 Positions each)   8 TRUNKS (8 Positions each)

NCR 615 CENTURY SERIES

The 615 Century Series of computers is an expandable family of computers utilizing monolithic circuitry. This family currently consists of three systems which range from the low-cost general purpose 615–100, through the medium cost and performance 615–200 with optional multiprogramming, to the 615–400—a high performance system with emphasis on multiprocessing and multiprogramming real time and time-sharing capabilities.

SYSTEM CONFIGURATION

1. I/O Equipment.
   a) Punched Card Reader and Punch.
      682–100   Photo-Electric Reader. 300 cards per minute.
      686   Card Punch. 82 to 240 cards per minute.
   b) Paper Tape Reader and Punch.
      660–101   Photo-Electric Reader. 1500 characters per second.
      662–100   Photo-Electric Reader. (Integrated into processor) 1,000 characters per second.
      665–101   Punch 200 characters per second.
   c) MICR.
      670–101   Low Cost MICR Sorter. 600 documents per minute in 11 pockets.
      671–101   High Speed MICR Sorter. 1,200 documents per minute in 18 pockets.
   d) Optical Scanning.
      420–1   O.C.R. Journal Reader 26 lines per second of journal tape imprinted with NOF Font characters of 32 characters per line.
      420–2   O.C.R. Journal Reader 52 lines per second of journal tape imprinted with NOF Font characters of 32 characters per line.
   e) Line Printers.
      640–102   450 alpha/450 numeric lines per minute, 132 print positions, 64 characters set.
      640–102 (opt)   450/900 lines per minute, 132 print positions, 52 characters set.
      640–200   1,500/3,000 lines per minute, 132 print positions, 52 or 64 characters set.
      640–210   1,500/3,000 lines per minute, 160 print positions, 52 or 64 characters set available with 6 tape 2,000 lines per minute Multi Lister Attachment.
      640–300   600/1,200 lines per minute, 132 print positions, 128 characters set.
      740–501   Remote 300 alphanumeric lines per minute available with 740–502 Card Reader Attachment (70–180 cards per minute).
2. Storage.
   a) Internal Memory.
      Thin Film-Short Rod Memory. 800 nanosecond cycle time.

b) Magnetic tape (9 track except as noted).

633–101	1,600 bits/inch, 50 inch/sec., 80 KC transfer rate.
633–121	Same as 101 except a dual unit.
633–102	1,600 bits/inch, 90 inch/sec., 144 KC transfer rate.
633–122	Same as 102 except a dual unit.
633–103	1,600 bits/inch, 150 inch/sec., 240 KC transfer rate.
633–117	200, 556, & 800 bits/inch, 50 inch/sec., 10, 28, & 40 KC transfer rate 7 track tape.
633–119	800 bits/inch, 50 inch/sec., 40 KC transfer rate.
633–201	800 bits/inch, 50 inch/sec., 40 KC transfer rate.
633–211	200, 556, & 800 bits/inch, 50 inch/sec., 10, 28, & 40 KC transfer rate, 7 track tape.
633–211	1,600 bits/inch, 90 inch/sec., 144 Kb transfer rate (9 track tape).
633–221	Same as 211 except a dual unit.
633–311	1,600 bits/inch, 150 inch/sec., 240 Kb transfer rate.

c) Magnetic Disc.

655–101/102	Integrated Disc Unit (102, a second unit optional), 4,194,304 bytes per disc pack used on 615–100 system. 2 spindles with 1 arm each, head positioning time 20–70 milliseconds, transfer rate 108 KC.
655–201	Disc Unit, 2 spindles and 1 arm each, head movement time 20–70 milliseconds, transfer rate 108 KC.
655–202	Disc Unit. Same as 201 except transfer rate of 180 KC.

d) CRAM.

353–1	See 315 System.
353–2	See 315 System.
353–3	See 315 System.
353–5	See 315 System.
653–101	Capacity 150 million bytes, 1,800 bits/inch density, 96 Kb transfer rate.

3. Communication Equipment.

621–101	Communication Multiplexer. Controller for 14 addressable lines.
621–201	Communication Multiplexer. Line concentrator, limited real-time processor or communication switcher.
622–201	Data Recorded Control Unit. Reads 1,000 CPS and writes 500 CPS.
622–401	Cal Comp Plotter Control Unit.
795	CRT Control Unit. Up to 12 CRT Units.

RCA Spectra 70

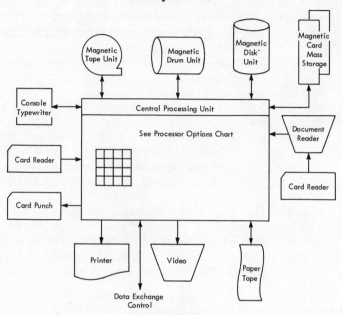

Input/Output Channels Available

70/15 1 standard channel--up to 6 trunks--each 16 devices maximum.

70/25 1 multiplexor channel--115 devices maximum.
8 selector channels maximum--each 16 devices maximum.

70/35 1 multiplexor channel--176 devices maximum.
2 selector channels--each 256 devices maximum.

70/45 1 multiplexor channel--128 devices maximum.
3 selector channels maximum--each 256 devices maximum.

70/55 1 multiplexor channel--128 devices maximum.
6 selector channels maximum--each 256 devices maximum.

RCA SPECTRA 70 SERIES

The RCA Spectra 70 Series provides an open-ended family of compatible data processing systems. These provide a wide range of system configurations designed to meet the requirements of commercial, scientific, multisystem, control, and communications applications.

SYSTEM CONFIGURATION

1. I/O Equipment.
    a) Punched Card Readers and Punches.
        70/237 Card Reader. Speed of 1,435 cards per minute by photo-electrically reading punched or marked cards. Translates the extended Hollerith code to EBCDIC for processor use.
        70/234 Card Punch. 100 cards per minute, uses extended Hollerith code.
        70/236 Card Punch. 300 cards per minute, uses extended Hollerith code.
    b) Punched Paper Tape Reader/Punch.
        70/221 Reads at 200 and punches at 100 characters per second 5-through 8-level paper tape.
        70/224 Reads (only) 5-through 8-level tape at 1,000 characters per second.
    c) Optical Scanning.
        70/251 Video Document Reader. Accepts printed documents $2\frac{1}{2}''$ x $2\frac{1}{2}''$ up to $4''$ x $8\frac{1}{2}''$. Printed characters using RCA N-2 font are read at 1,500 characters per second or from 1,300 to 1,800 documents per minute. Marked documents and punched card reading (500 CPM) is optional.
    d) Printers.
        70/242 Medium Speed Line Printer. 625 lines per minute with 132 or 160 print positions per line. Provides 64 printed characters.
        70/243 Hi-Speed Printer. 1,250 lines per minute with 132 or 160 print positions per line using a 64-character subset, 714 lpm with extended character set of 96 graphics—upper- and lowercase letters, and 833 lpm using 80 of the 96 graphics.
        70/248 Bill-Feed Printer. 600 lines per minute on continuous forms or 800 cards (2 feed channels) per minute.
    e) Video Data Terminal.
        70/752 12″ rectangular cathode-ray tube, maximum of 1,080 characters in 20 lines of 54 characters per line. Alpha-numeric keyboard. Used with the 70/35, 70/45, and 70/55 systems.
    f) MICR Reader.
        70/272 Operates several 13 to 18 sort-pocket sorter/readers at 1,600 documents per minute. Also interfaces with Burroughs 103/116, IBM 1410, and NCR 407 equipment.
    g) Audio Response.

70/510   Voice Response System. Five models, capacities of 31
or 63 words; 31 or 63 phrases, 31 or 63 words and/or phrases;
and 189 words. Used in conjunction with either private lines or
the Bell System Touch-Tone telephone.

h) Console.

70/97   Console and Typewriter. A typewriter I/O for the 70/
35, 70/45, and 70/55 Processors.

70/216   Interrogating Typewriter. A typewriter I/O for the
70/15 and 70/25 Processors.

2. Storage.

a) Internal.

Magnetic Core Memory is the basic storage for each of the series
(see processor option chart). The access time is 2 microseconds
for the 70/15, 1.5 microseconds for 4 bytes for the 70/25, 1.44
microseconds for 2 bytes in the 70/35 and 70/45, and 0.84
microseconds for 4 bytes in the 70/55.

Scratch-Pad Memory is a fast micromagnetic thin-film memory
of 128 four-byte (32-bit) words for control memory in the 70/
45 and 70/55. Access time of this memory is 300 nanoseconds.

Read-Only Control Memory of an additional 128 words (512
bytes) is provided in nonaddressable memory to contain various registers in the 70/35 and 70/45. Access time of this
memory is 480 nanoseconds.

Magnetic Core Main Storage (8-Bit Bytes)	Spectra 70 Processors				
	70/15	*70/25*	*70/35**	*70/45**	*70/55**
4,096	A				
8,192	B				
16,384		C	C	C	
32,768		D	D	D	
65,536		E	E	E	E
131,072				F	F
262,144				G	G
524,288					H

* Plus 128 (4-byte) words of micromagnetic memory.

b) Magnetic Tape.

70/432   9-channel density is 800 bits per inch, speed is 37.5
inches per second, and transfer rate is 30,000 bytes per second.
7-channel density is 200, 556, or 800 bits per inch, speed is 37.5
inches per second, and transfer rate is 7,500, 20,800, or 30,000
characters per second.

70/441   Reads 333 bits per inch (381 mode) and 500 bits per
inch (382 mode) tape at 50 inches per second for transfer rate
of 16,650 or 25,000 bits per second.

70/442   9-channel density is 800 bits per inch, speed is 75 inches per second, and transfer rate is 60,000 bytes per second. 7-channel density is 200, 556, or 800 bits per inch, speed is 75 inches per second, and transfer rate is 15,000, 41,600, and 60,000 characters per second.

70/445   9-channel density is 800 bits per inch, speed is 150 inches per second, and transfer rate is 120,000 bytes per second. 7-channel density is 200, 556, or 800 bits per inch, speed is 150 inches per second, and transfer rate is 30,000, 83,400, and 120,000 characters per second.

c) Magnetic Disk.

70/564   Capacity of 7.25 million bytes per disk pack. Data transfer rate is 156,000 bytes per second. Average access time is 75 milliseconds.

d) Magnetic Drum.

70/565   Capacity of 1 million bytes. Data transfer rate is 210,000 bytes per second. Average access time is 8.6 milliseconds.

70/567   Capacity of 4.13 or 8.26 million bytes. Data transfer rate is 333,000 bytes per second.

e) Mass Storage.

70/568   Capacity of 536,870,912 to 4,296,967,296 bytes. 1 to 8 units, 8 interchangeable magazines per unit, 256 magnetic cards per magazine. Data transfer rate 70,000 bytes per second. Average access time is 508 milliseconds (2nd half of fourth magazine).

3. Communication Equipment.

70/627   Data Exchange Control.   Permits memory to memory transfer between any two local processors and the use of shared I/O devices.

70/630   Data Gathering System.   An on-line data gathering system of varying input capabilities for use with 70/35, 70/45, and 70/55.

70/653   Communication Control.   Provides a single communication channel between RCA Spectra 70, RCA 301, or RCA 3301 System Processor telephone lines.

In addition, a wide range of special-purpose I/O devices may be utilized.

UNIVAC 418 System

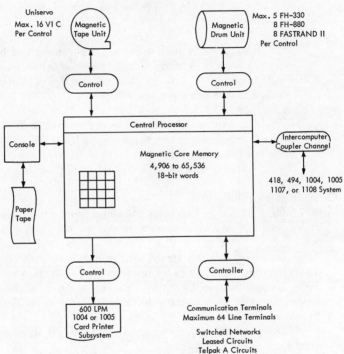

8, 12, or 16 I/O Channels Available

UNIVAC 418 SYSTEM

The UNIVAC 418 System is a large-scale, magnetic core, general-purpose computer which operates concurrently on real-time, batch processing, and communications-orientated applications.

SYSTEM CONFIGURATION

1. I/O Equipment.
   a) Paper Tape Reader and Punch.
      A Reader and Punch are available through the console operation. Speed is 200/400 characters per second reading and 110 characters per second punching.
   b) Line Printer.
      600 lines per minute Printer—1004 or 1005 Subsystem.
2. Storage.
   a) Internal.
      Magnetic core memory with a 2.0 microsecond cycle time.
   b) Magnetic Tape.
      Uniservo VI C (see 1108).
   c) Magnetic Drum.
      Flying Head 330. 262,144 18-bit word storage capacity, average access time is 8.5 microseconds.
      Flying Head 880 (see 1108).
      FASTRAND II (see 1108).
3. Communication Equipment.
   Intercomputer communication with a 418, 494, 1004, 1005, or 1108 system. Permits a dual processor configuration utilizing common I/O equipment.
   Real-Time Data Communications System.

UNIVAC 494 System

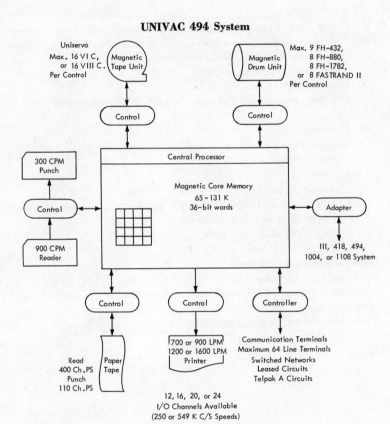

Uniservo
Max. 16 VI C,
or 16 VIII C.
Per Control

Magnetic
Tape Unit

Magnetic
Drum Unit

Max. 9 FH–432,
8 FH–880,
8 FH–1782,
or 8 FASTRAND II
Per Control

Control

Control

300 CPM
Punch

Central Processor

Magnetic Core Memory
65 – 131 K
36–bit words

Adapter

Control

III, 418, 494,
1004, or 1108 System

900 CPM
Reader

Control

Control

Controller

Read
400 Ch.PS
Punch
110 Ch.PS

Paper
Tape

700 or 900 LPM
1200 or 1600 LPM
Printer

Communication Terminals
Maximum 64 Line Terminals
Switched Networks
Leased Circuits
Telpak A Circuits

12, 16, 20, or 24
I/O Channels Available
(250 or 549 K C/S Speeds)

UNIVAC 494 REAL-TIME SYSTEM

The UNIVAC 494 Real-Time System is a large-scale, magnetic core, general-purpose digital computer designed to operate in both batch processing and real-time modes as an independent computer or as a centralized control over remote operations.

SYSTEM CONFIGURATION

1. I/O Equipment.
   a) Punched Card Reader and Punch.
      900-card-per-minute Reader.
      300-card-per-minute Punch.
   b) Paper Tape Reader and Punch.
      400-character-per-minute Reader.
      110-character-per-minute Punch.
   c) Line Printer.
      700- or 900-line-per-minute Printer.
      1,200- or 1,600-line-per-minute Printer.
2. Storage.
   a) Internal.
      Magnetic core memory with a 750 nanosecond access time (effective 375 nanoseconds possible with memory bank overlap).
   b) Magnetic Tape.
      Uniservo VI C (see 1108).
      Uniservo VIII C (see 1108).
   c) Magnetic Drum.
      Flying Head 432 (see 1108).
      Flying Head 880 (see 1108).
      Flying Head 1782 (see 1108).
      FASTRAND II (see 1108).
3. Communication Equipment.
   Intercommunication with UNIVAC III, 418, 494, and 1108 computers.
   Real-Time Data Communications System.
      Switched Networks.
      Leased Circuit.
      Telpak A Circuit.

UNIVAC 1004 and 1005 Systems

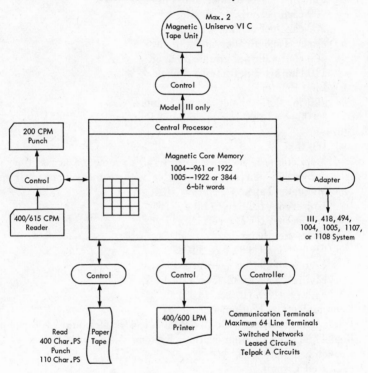

UNIVAC 1004 AND 1005 SYSTEMS

The UNIVAC 1004 is a card processor with wired programs expanded to accept tape units, auxiliary readers, read-punch units, paper tape, and communications.

The UNIVAC 1005 is similar to the 1004 except it accepts either internal stored or external wired instructions.

SYSTEM CONFIGURATION

1. I/O Equipment.
   a) Punched Card Reader and Punch.
      400/615-card-per-minute Reader.
      200-card-per-minute Punch.
   b) Punched Paper Tape Reader and Punch.
      400-character-per-second Reader.
      110-character-per-second Punch.
   c) Line Printer.
      400/600-line-per-minute Printer.
2. Storage.
   a) Internal.
      Magnetic core memory with 6.5 or 8.0 microsecond access time.
   b) Magnetic Tape.
      Uniservo VI C (see 1108). Used only on 1004 Model III.
3. Communication Equipment.
   Intercomputer communication with the UNIVAC III, 418, 494, 1004, 1005, and 1108 computer systems.
   Data Communications System.
      Switched Networks.
      Leased Circuits.
      Telpak A Circuits.

UNIVAC 1108 System

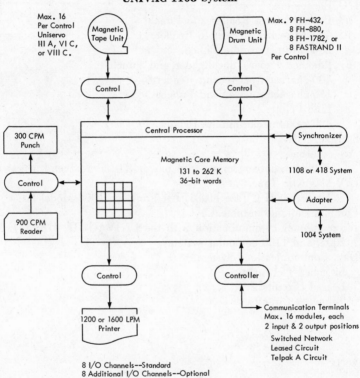

Max. 16
Per Control
Uniservo
III A, VI C,
or VIII C.

Magnetic Tape Unit

Max. 9 FH-432,
8 FH-880,
8 FH-1782, or
8 FASTRAND II
Per Control

Magnetic Drum Unit

Control

Control

300 CPM Punch

Control

900 CPM Reader

Central Processor

Magnetic Core Memory
131 to 262 K
36-bit words

Synchronizer

1108 or 418 System

Adapter

1004 System

Control

1200 or 1600 LPM Printer

Controller

Communication Terminals
Max. 16 modules, each
2 input & 2 output positions
Switched Network
Leased Circuit
Telpak A Circuit

8 I/O Channels—Standard
8 Additional I/O Channels—Optional

UNIVAC 1108 SYSTEM

The UNIVAC 1108 System operates in real-time as a solid-state, general-purpose computer which provides general-purpose utility across the entire range of data processing activity. Software in the form of program support is particularly effective and extensive. Has multiprocessing as well as multiprogramming capability. Model I is a unit processor and Model II is a multiprocessor.

SYSTEM CONFIGURATION

1. I/O Equipment.
   a) Punched Card Reader and Punch.
      900-card-per-minute Reader.
      300-card-per-minute Punch.
   b) Line Printer.
      1,200- or 1,600-line-per-minute printer.
2. Storage.
   a) Internal.
      Magnetic core memory. 750 nanosecond cycle time per 36-bit word. (375 nanosecond effective time with memory bank overlap).
   b) Magnetic Tape.
      Uniservo VI C. 200, 556, and 800 characters per inch density, 42.7 inches per second, for 8.5, 23.7, and 34.2K characters per second transfer rate.
      Uniservo VIII C. 200, 556, and 800 characters per inch density, 120 inches per second, for 24, 66.7, and 96K characters per second transfer rate.
   c) Magnetic Drum.
      Flying Head 432. 262,144 36-bit word storage capacity, 1.44 million characters per second transfer rate, 4.3 millisecond average access time.
      Flying Head 880. 786,432 36-bit word storage capacity, 360,000 characters per second transfer rate, 17 millisecond average access time.
      Flying Head 1782. 2,097,152 36-bit word storage capacity, 1.2 million characters per second transfer rate, 4.25 millisecond average access time.
      FASTRAND II. 22,020,096 36-bit word storage capacity, 150,900 characters per second transfer rate, 92 millisecond average access time.
3. Communication Equipment.
   Intercomputer communication with an 1108 or 418 system.
   UNIVAC 1004 as a multiple-function switchable satellite.
   Real-Time Data Communications System.
      Switched Network.
      Leased Circuit.
      Telpak A Circuit.

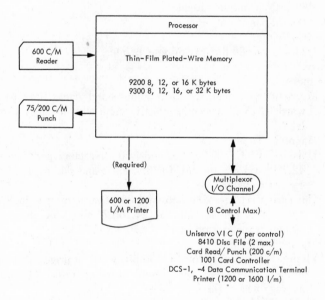

Processor

Thin-Film Plated-Wire Memory

9200 8, 12, or 16 K bytes
9300 8, 12, 16, or 32 K bytes

600 C/M
Reader

75/200 C/M
Punch

(Required)

600 or 1200
L/M Printer

Multiplexor
I/O Channel

(8 Control Max)

Uniservo VI C (7 per control)
8410 Disc File (2 max)
Card Read/ Punch (200 c/m)
1001 Card Controller
DCS-1, -4 Data Communication Terminal
Printer (1200 or 1600 l/m)

UNIVAC 9000 SERIES

The UNIVAC 9000 Series is a new computer family which embodies many bold, new design concepts in a unified and low-cost line of data processing equipment. The Series consists of small-, medium-, and large-scale data processing systems. The UNIVAC 9200 System is a small, card-oriented data processing system, but can be expanded to the higher performance card- and tape-oriented 9300 System.

SYSTEM CONFIGURATION

1. I/O Equipment—Other than through multiplexer channel.
    a) Punched Card.
        9200 400-card-per-minute Reader (serial by column).
        9300 600-card-per-minute Reader (serial by column).
              75- or 200-card-per-minute Punch (serial by column).
    b) Line Printer.
        9200 250- or 500-line-per-minute Printer (required).
        9300 600- or 1,200-line-per-minute Printer (required).
2. I/O Equipment—through multiplexer channel.
    Uniservo VI C. Magnetic Tape Unit (see 1108).
    UNIVAC 8410 Disc File. 3.2-million-byte capacity direct access storage system. Average access to single disc surface 110 milliseconds (faster with additional discs on line).
    UNIVAC 1001 Card Controller. A merging, selecting, collating machine with 2 reader stations (1,000 cards per minute each) and 7 stacker stations.
    DCS-1 Data Communication Subsystem (single line).
    DCS-4 Data Communication Subsystem (2 to 4 lines).
    Row Read/Punch. 200 cards per minute serial by row—only 9300 System.
    Printer. 1,200 or 1,600 lines per minute—only 9300 System.
    DCT-2000 Data Communication Terminal. A read/punch/printer with 256-position memory.
    UNISCOPE–300 Visual Communication Terminal. A CRT terminal with expanded keyboard.
3. Storage.
    a) Internal.
        UNIVAC 9200 8, 12, or 16K bytes, plated-wire thin-film memory with 1.2 microsecond access time.
        UNIVAC 9300 8, 12, 16, or 32K bytes, plated-wire thin-film memory with 0.6 microsecond access time.

APPENDIX **B**

Glossary of Terms

*Access time. The time it takes a computer to locate and transfer data internally, either from memory to the arithmetic unit or from the arithmetic unit to memory.

*Accounting machine. An equipment which reads information from a medium such as cards, paper tape, or magnetic tape and produces lists, tables, and/or totals on separate or continuous paper forms. Often called tabulating equipment or a tabulator.

*ALGOL. A contraction of *A*lgorithmic Language or *A*lgorithmic Oriented Language.

*Algorithmic Language. A standardized arithmetic language obtained as a result of international cooperation. Basically, a numerical language for computers, but also a means of communicating numerical procedures to individuals.

*Alphameric. A contraction of either alphanumeric or alphabetic-numeric.

*Alphanumeric. A contraction of alphabetic-numeric. To include the letters of the alphabet, numbers, and, at times, special characters such as: . , &, #, etc.

* These items are supplied by the authors. All others are excerpts from "Automatic Data Processing Glossary," Executive Office of the President, Bureau of the Budget (Washington, D.C.: U.S. Government Printing Office, December, 1962).

*Annunciator system. A signaling device, usually audible, but may include a visual indication, used for notification or calling purposes.

*Application. The system or problem to which a computer is applied.

Application study. The detailed process of determining a system or set of procedures for using a computer for definite functions or operations, and establishing specifications to be used as a base for the selection of equipment suitable to the specific needs. *Also see,* Justification study.

Arithmetic unit. The portion of the hardware of a computer in which arithmetic and logical operations are performed. The arithmetic unit generally consists of an accumulator, some special registers for the storage of operands and results, supplemented by shifting and sequencing circuitry for implementing multiplication, division, and other desired operations.

*ASCII. American Standard Code for Information Interchange.

*Audit trail. A method of providing a path or track which may be followed in tracing output data back through the processing steps used in converting input data to its final output form.

Automation. (1) The implementation of processes by automatic means; (2) the theory, art, or

Automation—*Cont.*

technique of making a process more automatic; (3) the investigation, design, development, and application of methods of rendering processes automatic, self-moving, or self-controlling.

Batch processing. A technique by which items to be processed must be coded and collected into groups prior to processing.

*__Batch total.__ The total or sum of specific data contained in a group or batch of documents containing similar characteristics. Used as control information to assure that all data of the batch have been properly processed.

*__Baud.__ (1) A unit of speed equal to the number of code elements per second. Sometimes used interchangeably with "bits per second." (2) A digital data communications term designating the smallest unit of transmission signaling speed.

*__Baudot code.__ A 5-channel paper tape code first used in telegraph communication. Developed by Jean Maurice Emile Baudot in 1870 while with the French Ministry of Posts and Telegraph.

*__Binary.__ A characteristic or condition in which there are but two possible alternatives.

Binary coded decimal. Describes a decimal notation in which the individual decimal digits are represented by a pattern of ones and zeros.

Binary coded decimal number. A number, usually consisting of successive groups of figures, in which each group of four figures is a binary number that represents but does not necessarily equal arithmetically, a particular figure in an associated decimal number, e.g., the decimal number 262 would be expressed as the binary coded decimal number 0010 0110 0010.

Binary digit. A numeral in the binary scale of notation. This digit may be zero (0), or one (1). It may be equivalent to an on or off condition, a yes or a no. Often abbreviated to (bit).

Binary notation. A number system written to the base two notation.

Bit. (1) An abbreviation of *binary digit*. (2) A single character in a binary number. (3) A single pulse in a group of pulses. (4) A unit of information capacity of a storage device. The capacity in bits is the logarithm to the base two of the number of possible states of the device.

Block diagram. (1) A graphical representation of the hardware in a computer system. The primary purpose of a block diagram is to indicate the paths along which information and/or control flows between the various parts of a computer system. It should not be confused with the term flow chart. (2) A coarser and less symbolic representation than a flow chart.

*__Bookkeeping machine.__ A combination adding machine and typewriter which has been developed to do bookkeeping work.

Branch. The selection of one of two or more possible paths in the flow of control, based on some criterion.

Buffer. (1) An internal portion of a data processing system serving as intermediary storage between two storage or data handling systems with different access times or formats; usually to connect an input or output device with the main or internal high-speed storage. (2) A logical OR circuit. (3) An isolating component designed to eliminate the reaction of a driven circuit on the circuits driving it, e.g., a buffer amplified. (4) A diode.

*__Bus.__ A pathway for the transmission of data, usually in the form of electrical impulses.

Byte. (1) A generic term to indicate a measurable portion of consecutive binary digits; e.g., an 8-bit or 6-bit byte. (2) A group of binary digits usually operated upon as a unit.

Calculator. (1) A device that performs primarily arithmetic operations based upon data and instructions inserted manually or contained on punched cards. It is sometimes used interchangeably with computer. (2) A computer.

Card column. A single digital column in a punched card normally containing a single digit, letter, or special character.

Card, edge-notched. A card of any size provided with a series of holes on one or more edges for use in coding information for a simple mechanical search technique. Each hole position may be coded to represent an item of information by notching away the edge of the card into the hole. Cards containing desired information may then be mechanically selected from a deck by inserting a long needle in a hole position and lifting the deck to allow the notched cards to fall from the needle. Unwanted cards remain in the deck.

Card, edge-punched. A card of fixed size into which information may be recorded or stored by punching holes along one edge in a pattern similar to that used for punched tape.

Card feed. A mechanism which moves cards serially into a machine.

Card punch. A machine which punches cards in designated locations to store data which can be conveyed to other machines or devices by reading or sensing the holes. Synonymous with card punch unit.

Card, punched. A heavy stiff paper of constant size and shape, suitable for punching in a pattern that

Card, punched—*Cont.***
has meaning, and for being handled mechanically. The punched holes are sensed electrically by wire brushes, mechanically by metal fingers, or photoelectrically by photocells.

Card reader. (1) A mechanism that senses information punched into cards. (2) An input device consisting of a mechanical punched card reader and related electronic circuitry, which transcribes data from punched cards to working storage or magnetic tape. Synonymous with Card reader unit.

Card reproducer. A device that reproduces a punched card by punching another similar card.

Cathode-ray tube (CRT). (1) An electronic vacuum tube containing a screen on which information may be stored by means of a multigrid modulated beam of electrons from the thermionic emitter storage effected by means of charged or uncharged spots. (2) A storage tube. (3) An oscilloscope tube. (4) A picture tube.

Central processing unit. (1) The central processor of the computer system. It contains the main storage, arithmetic unit, and special register groups. (2) All that portion of a computer exclusive of the input, output, peripheral, and in some instances, storage units.

Channel. (1) A path along which information, particularly a series of digits or characters, may flow. (2) One or more parallel tracks treated as a unit. (3) A path for electrical communication. (4) A band of frequencies used for communication.

Character. One symbol of a set of elementary symbols such as those corresponding to the keys on a typewriter. The symbols usually include the decimal digits 0 through 9, the letters A through Z, punctuation marks, operation symbols, and any other single symbols

Character—*Cont.*
which a computer may read, store, or write.

Character reader. A specialized device which can convert data represented in one of the type fonts or scripts read by human beings directly into machine language. Such a reader may operate optically; or if the characters are printed in magnetic ink, the device may operate magnetically or optically.

*Character recognition equipment. Equipment designed to be able to recognize automatically either magnetic ink characters, printed characters, printed codes, pencil characters, or perforated tags.

Character set. An agreed-upon set of representations, called characters, from which selections are made to denote and distinguish data. Each character differs from all others, and the total number of characters in a given set is fixed.

Check, automatic. A provision constructed in hardware for verifying the accuracy of information transmitted, manipulated, or stored by any unit or device in a computer.

Check bit. A binary check digit; often a parity bit.

*Check, built-in. *See* Check, automatic.

Check, duplication. A check which requires that the results of two independent performances, either concurrently on duplicate equipment or at different times on the same equipment, of the same operation, be identical.

Check, echo. A check of accuracy of transmission in which the information which was transmitted to an output device is returned to the information source and compared with the original information to insure accuracy of output.

Check indicator. A device which displays or announces that an error has been made or that a checking

Check indicator—*Cont.*
operation has determined that a failure has occurred.

Check, parity. A summation check in which the binary digits, in a character or word, are added and the sum checked against a single, previously computed parity digit, i.e., a check which tests whether the number of ones in a word is odd or even.

*Check points. These are predetermined points in a program where specific checks or tests are performed.

Check, sequence. A data processing operation designed to check the sequence of the items in a file assumed to be already in sequence.

Check, summation. A check in which groups of digits are summed and that sum checked against a previously computed sum to verify that no digits have been changed since the last summation.

Check, system. A check on the over-all performance of the system, usually not made by built-in computer check circuits, i.e., control totals, hash totals, and record counts.

Check, validity. A check based upon known limits or upon given information or computer results; e.g., a calendar month will not be numbered greater than 12, and a week does not have more than 168 hours.

Circuit. A system of conductors and related electrical elements through which electrical current flows, (2) a communications link between two or more points.

COBOL. *See* Common Business Orientated Language.

Code, alphabetic. A system of alphabetic abbreviations used in preparing information for input into a machine; e.g., Boston and New York may in alphabetical coding be reported as BS and NY. Contrasted with Code, numeric.

Code, Baudot. *See* Baudot code.

*Code, binary. A coding system in which two states or conditions are used to represent encoded data.

Code, column-binary. A code used with punched cards in which successive bits are represented by the presence or absence of punches on contiguous positions in successive columns as opposed to rows. Column-binary code is widely used in connection with 36-bit word computers where each group of 3 columns is used to represent a single word.

Code, computer. (1) A system of combinations of binary digits used by a given computer. (2) A repertoire of instructions.

Code, instruction. The list of symbols, names and definitions of the instructions which are intelligible to a given computer or computing system.

Code, machine language. Same as Code, computer (1) and contrasted with Code, symbolic.

*Code, mnemonic. A code in which the items are abbreviated and expressed mnemonically to facilitate remembering the item represented.

Code, numeric. A system of numerical abbreviations used in the preparation of information for input into a machine; i.e., all information is reduced to numerical quantities. Contrasted with Code, alphabetic.

Code, operation. The part of a computer instruction word which specifies, in coded form, the operation to be performed.

Code, symbolic. A code which expresses programs in source language, i.e., by referring to storage locations and machine operations by symbolic names and addresses which are independent of their hardware determined names and addresses. Contrasted with Code, machine language.

Coder. A person who prepares instruction sequences from detailed

Coder—*Cont.*
flowcharts and other algorithmic procedures prepared by others, as contrasted with a programmer who prepares the procedures and flowcharts.

Coding. The ordered list in computer code of the successive computer instructions representing successive computer operations for solving a specific problem.

Collate. To merge two or more ordered sets of data, or cards, in order to produce one or more ordered sets which still reflect the original ordering relations. The collation process is the merging of two sequences of cards, each ordered on some mutual key, into a single sequence ordered on the mutual key.

Collator. A device used to collate or merge sets or decks of cards or other units into a sequence. A typical example of a card collator has two input feeds, so that two ordered sets may enter into the process, and four stackers, so that four ordered sets can be generated by the process. Three comparison stations are used to route the cards to one stacker or the other on the basis of comparison of criteria as specified by plugboard wiring.

Column. A character or digit position in a physical device, such as punched card or a register, corresponding to a position in a written table or list, e.g., the rightmost place in a register or the third column in an 80-column punched card.

Common Business Oriented Language. A specific language by which business data processing procedures may be precisely described in a standard form. The language is intended not only as a means for directly presenting any business program to any suitable computer, for which a compiler exists, but also as a means of communicating such procedures

Common Business Oriented Language—*Cont.*
among individuals. Synonymous with COBOL.

Compatibility, equipment. The characteristic of computers by which one computer may accept and process data prepared by another computer without conversion or code modification.

*Compiler. A more powerful processor which can create a number of machine instructions from a single command.

*Computer, analog. A computer which represents variables by physical analogies such as: pressure, temperature, etc.

Computer, digital. A computer which processes information represented by combinations of discrete or discontinuous data as compared with an analog computer for continuous data.

Computer, general-purpose. A computer designed to solve a large variety of problems; e.g., a stored program computer which may be adapted to any of a very large class of applications.

Computer, parallel. A computer in which the digits or data lines are handled concurrently by separate units of the computer.

Computer, serial. A computer in which digits or data lines are handled sequentially by separate units of the computer.

Computer, solid-state. A computer built primarily from solid-state electronic circuit elements.

Computer, special-purpose. A computer designed to solve a specific class or narrow range of problems.

Computer, stored program. A computer capable of performing sequences of internally stored instructions and usually capable of modifying those instructions as directed by the instructions.

Configuration. A group of machines which are interconnected and are

Configuration—*Cont.*
programmed to operate as a system.

Console. A portion of the computer which may be used to control the machine manually, correct errors, determine the status of machine circuits, registers, and counters, determine the contents of storage, and manually revise the contents of storage.

Control field. A constant location where information for control purposes is placed.

Control panel. (1) An interconnection device, usually removable, which employs removable wires to control the operation of computing equipment. It is used on punched card machines, to carry out functions which are under control of the user. On computers it is used primarily to control input and output functions. (2) A device or component of some data processing machines, which permits the expression of instructions in a semifixed computer program by the insertion of pins, plugs, or wires into sockets, or hubs in the device, in a pattern to represent instructions, and thus making electrical interconnections which may be sensed by the data processing machine. Synonymous with Plugboard.

Control total. A sum of numbers in a specified record field of a batch of records, determined repetitiously during the processing operation so that any discrepancy from the control indicates an error.

Control unit. The portion of a computer which directs the coded instructions and initiates the proper commands to the computer circuits preparatory to execution.

Conversion. (1) The process of changing information from one form of representation to another: such as, from the language of one type of machine to that of another or from magnetic tape to the

Conversion—*Cont.*
printed page. (2) The process of changing from one data processing method to another, or from one type of equipment to another, e.g., conversion from punched card equipment to magnetic tape equipment.

Converter. A device which converts the representation of information, or which permits the changing of the method for data processing from one form to another, e.g., a unit which accepts information from punched cards and records the information on magnetic tape, and possibly including editing facilities.

Copy, hard. A printed copy of machine output, e.g., printed reports, listings, documents, and summaries.

*Critical path. The pathway through the network which requires the greatest amount of time in order to complete the project is called the critical path.

*Data base. The basic file(s) of data required by a firm or organization. The data in this file(s) are changed as a result of the transactions associated with the firm's operation.

Data origination. The act of creating a record in a machine-sensible form, directly or as a by-product of a human-readable document.

Data processing. (1) The preparation of source media which contain data or basic elements of information, and the handling of such data according to precise rules of procedure to accomplish such operations as classifying, sorting, calculating, summarizing, and recording. (2) The production of records and reports.

*Data punch. A portable, manual card-punching device which can punch six columns of numerical data into a standard punched card and simultaneously print the nu-

Data punch—*Cont.*
merical figures with a single machine stroke.

*Data transmission equipment. Equipment designed to transmit either card code or channel code over long distances by means of the telephone lines or by radio.

*Debugging. The process of determining the correctness of a computer routine, locating any errors in it, and correcting them. This also involves the detection and correction of malfunctions in the computer itself.

Decision. The computer operation of determining if a certain relationship exists between words in storage or registers, and taking alternative courses of action. Use of this term has given rise to the misnomer "magic brain"; actually the process consists of making comparisons by use of arithmetic to determine the relationship of two terms.

Deck. A collection of cards, commonly a complete set of cards which have been punched for a definite service or purpose.

Density, character. The number of characters that can be stored per unit of length; e.g., on some makes of magnetic tape drives, 200 or 556 bits can be stored serially, linearly, and axially to the inch.

Disk storage. The storage of data on the surface of magnetic disks.

Display tube. A cathode-ray tube used to display information.

*Document control register. A locked metal box housing a supply of continuous forms. The forms are positioned so that they can be written on and then emitted from the box with one copy remaining in the box for purposes of proof and control.

Documentation. The group of techniques necessary for the orderly presentation, organization and communication of recorded specialized knowledge, in order to

Documentation—*Cont.*
maintain a complete record of reasons for changes in variables. Documentation is necessary not so much to give maximum utility as to give an unquestionable historical reference record.

Downtime. The period during which a computer is malfunctioning or not operating correctly due to mechanical or electronic failure, as opposed to available time, idle time, or stand-by time, during which the computer is functional.

EAM. Electrical Accounting Machine, *see* Accounting machine.

*****Earliest times.** Refers to the earliest start time of an operation as well as the earliest finish time. The earliest start time is the earliest possible start time of an operation where as the earliest finish time is simply the sum of the earliest start time and its duration.

Edit. To rearrange data or information. Editing may involve the deletion of unwanted data, the selection of pertinent data, the application of format techniques, the insertion of symbols such as page numbers and typewriter characters, the application of standard processes such as zero suppression, and the testing of data for reasonableness and proper range. Editing may sometimes be distinguished between input edit (rearrangement of source data) and output edit (preparation of table formats).

EDP. Electronic Data Processing.

Encode. (1) To apply a code, frequently one consisting of binary numbers, to represent individual characters or groups of characters in a message. (2) To substitute letters, numbers, or characters for other numbers, letters, or characters, usually to intentionally hide the meaning of the message except to certain individuals who know the enciphering scheme.

*****Equipment, auxiliary.** *See* Equipment, off-line.

*****Equipment, off-line.** Equipment or devices not in direct communication with the central processing unit of the computer.

*****Equipment, on-line.** Equipment or devices which are under the control of, or in direct communication with the central processing unit of the computer.

*****Equipment, peripheral.** Devices which are necessary to a computer system. These may either be off-line or on-line devices.

Error. The general term referring to any deviation of a computed or a measured quantity from the theoretically correct or true value.

*****Error routine.** A prepared diagnostic program which searches for predetermined types of errors and advises, by computer output, of any errors and the types of error found.

Feed. (1) To supply the material to be operated upon to a machine. (2) A device capable of feeding, as in (1) above.

Field, card. A set of columns, either fixed as to number and position or, if variable, then identifiable by position relative to other fields. Corresponding fields on successive cards are normally used to store similar information.

Field length. The physical extent of a field. On a punched card it refers to the number of columns. On a tape it refers to bit positions.

File. An organized collection of information directed toward some purpose. The records in a file may or may not be sequenced according to a key contained in each record.

*****Float.** The difference between the earliest finish time and the latest finish time of any operation. It is a measure of the time leeway available for that operation.

Flowchart. A graphic representation of the major steps of work in proc-

Flowchart—*Cont.*
ess. The illustrative symbols may represent documents, machines, or actions taken during the process. The area of concentration is on where or who does what rather than how it is to be done.

File maintenance. The periodic modification of a file to incorporate changes which occurred during a given period.

Fixed length record. A record whose number of characters is fixed. The restriction may be deliberate to simplify and speed processing or may be caused by the characteristics of the equipment used.

FORTRAN. A programming language designed for problems which can be expressed in algebraic notation, allowing for exponentiation and up to three subscripts.

Game theory. A mathematical process of selecting an optimum strategy in the face of an opponent who has a strategy of his own.

Gang punch. To punch identical or constant information into all of a group of punched cards.

Gap. (1) An interval of space or time used as an automatic sentinel to indicate the end of a word, record, or file of data on a tape. (2) The absence of information for a specified length of time or space on a recording medium, as contrasted with marks and sentinels which are the presence of specific information to achieve a similar purpose. (3) The space between the reading or recording head and the recording medium, such as tape, drum, or disk.

*Generator. A program which will adopt or modify a general-purpose program to fit a specific need.

Hardware. The physical equipment or devices forming a computer and peripheral equipment. Contrasted with Software.

Hash total. A sum of numbers in a specified field of a record or of a batch of records used for checking purposes. No attention is paid to the significance of the total. Examples of such numbers are customer numbers or part numbers.

Hollerith. A widely used system of encoding alphanumeric information onto cards: hence, Hollerith cards is synonymous with punched cards. Such cards were first used in 1890 for the U.S. Census and were named after Herman Hollerith, their originator.

Hub. A socket on a control panel or plugboard into which an electrical lead or plug wire may be connected in order to carry signals, particularly to distribute the signals over many other wires.

IDP. Integrated Data Processing.

Initialize. (1) To set various counters, switches and addresses to zero or other starting values, at the beginning of, or at the prescribed points in a computer routine; (2) used as an aid to recovery and restart during a long computer run.

Input. (1) Information or data transferred or to be transferred from an external storage medium into the internal storage of the computer, (2) describing the routines which direct input as defined in (1) or the devices from which such information is available to the computer. (3) The device or collective set of devices necessary for input as defined in (1).

Input device. The mechanical unit designed to bring data to be processed into a computer, e.g., a card reader, a tape reader, or a keyboard.

Input equipment. (1) The equipment used for transferring data and instructions into an automatic data processing system. (2) The equipment by which an operator transcribes original data and instructions to a medium that may

Input equipment—*Cont.*
be used in an automatic data processing system.

Input-output.   A general term of the equipment used to communicate with a computer and the data involved in the communication. Synonymous with I/O.

Inquiry Station.   A point of entry or access to the computer system.

Integrated data processing.   (1) A system that treats as a whole, all data processing requirements to accomplish a sequence of data processing steps, or a number of related data processing sequences, and which strives to reduce or eliminate duplicating data entry or processing steps. (2) The processing of data by such a system. Synonymous with IDP. (3) The concept also applies to departments which should be unified on a departmental level to facilitate the automatic processing of data. The concept unites data accumulation, communication, computation, processing and control.

Interface.   A boundary which is common between automatic data processing systems or parts of a single system. In communication and data collection systems this may involve such items as code, format, speed, or other required changes.

Internal control.   The plan of organization and all of the coordinate methods and measures adopted within a business to safeguard its assets, check the accuracy and reliability of its accounting data, promote operational efficiency, and encourage adherence to prescribed managerial policies.

Internal label.   *See* Label, internal.

Interpret.   (1) To print on a punched card the information punched in that card. (2) To translate nonmachine language into machine language instructions.

Interpreter.   (1) A punched card machine which will take a

Interpreter—*Cont.*
punched card with no printing on it, read the information in the punched holes, and print a translation in characters in specified rows and columns on the card. (2) A processor which translates a program into machine language and executes the instructions at the same time. No object program is created.

Jam, card.   A pile-up of cards in a machine.

Justification study.   Determining for definite functions or operations a system or set of procedures for use in a computer. *Also see,* Application study.

Key.   (1) A group of characters which identifies or is part of a record or item; thus any entry in a record or item can be used as a key for collating or sorting purposes. (2) A marked lever manually operated for copying a character, e.g., a typewriter, paper tape perforator, card punch, manual keyboard, digitizer, or manual word generator. (3) A lever or switch on a computer console for the purpose of manually altering computer action.

Key punch.   (1) A special device to record information in cards or tape by punching holes in the cards or tape to represent letters, digits, and special characters; (2) to operate a device for punching holes in cards or tape.

Keysort cards.   A manual device used to speed up the sorting function. Cards are notched in the margin and are sorted away from unnotched cards by means of a sorting needle.

Key-verify.   To use the punched card machine known as a verifier, which has a keyboard, to make sure that the information supposed to be punched in a punched card has actually been properly punched. The machine signals

Monte Carlo method—*Cont.*
straightforward analytical handling.

Microsecond. One millionth of a second, 10^{-6} seconds, abbreviated microsec.

Millisecond. One thousandth of a second, 10^{-3} seconds, abbreviated msec. or ms.

Mode. (1) A computer system of data representation, e.g., the binary mode. (2) A selected mode of computer operation.

***Multiplexor channel.** A logical channel incorporated in the basic unit which permits two or more messages to be transmitted simultaneously or the use of two or more I/O devices simultaneously.

Multiprogramming. A technique for handling numerous routines or programs simultaneously by means of an interweaving process.

Nanosecond. One thousandth of a millionth of a second, 10^{-9} seconds. Synonymous with millimicrosecond.

Object language. *See* Language, object.

***Object program.** The program prepared by the computer from the processor program expressed in machine language instructions. Such a program directs the actions of the computer in processing business data. It is retained by being punched into a deck of punched cards.

Off-line. Descriptive of a system and of the peripheral equipment or devices in a system in which the operation of peripheral equipment is not under the control of the central processing unit.

On-line. Descriptive of a system and of the peripheral equipment or devices in a system in which the operation of such equipment is under control of the central processing unit, and in which information reflecting current activ-

On-line—*Cont.*
ity is introduced into the data processing system as soon as it occurs—thus, directly in line with the main flow of transaction processing.

Operations research. The use of analytical methods adopted from mathematics for solving operational problems. The objective is to provide management with a more logical basis for making sound predictions and decisions. Among the common scientific techniques used in operations research are the following: linear programming, probability theory, information theory, game theory, Monte Carlo method, and queuing theory. Synonymous with O.R.

Operator, machine. The person who manipulates the computer controls, places information media into the input devices, removes the output and performs other related functions.

Optimize. To rearrange the instructions or data in storage so that a minimum number of time-consuming jumps or transfers is required in the running of a program.

Output. (1) The information transferred from the internal storage of a computer to secondary or external storage, or to any device outside of the computer. (2) The routines which direct (1). (3) The device or collective set of devices necessary for (1). (4) To transfer from internal storage onto external media.

Output device. The part of a machine which translates the electrical impulses representing data processed by the machine into permanent results such as printed forms, punched cards, and magnetic writing on tape.

Output equipment. The equipment used for transferring information out of a computer.

Paper tape. A strip of paper capable of storing or recording information. Storage may be in the form of punched holes, partially punched holes, carbonization or chemical change of impregnated material, or by imprinting. Some paper tapes, such as punched paper tapes, are capable of being read by the input device of a computer or a transmitting device by sensing the pattern of holes which represent coded information.

Parity bit. A check bit that indicates whether the total number of binary "1" digits in a character or word (excluding the parity bit) is odd or even. If the total number of "1" bits, including the parity bit, is always even, the system is called an even-parity system. In an odd-parity system, the total number of "1" bits, including the parity bit, is always odd.

Peg-strip accounting. Composed of preprinted report forms. When forms are filled in often on a daily basis they are assembled on a peg-strip accounting board. Weekly and monthly analysis can be made when desired by adding item figures horizontally.

Picosecond. One thousandth of a nanosecond, or 10^{-12} seconds; abbreviated psec.

*Picture clause. Used in a COBOL program to indicate the size of an item, its class, the presence or absence of an operational sign and/or an assumed decimal point.

Plotter. A visual display or board in which a dependent variable is graphed by an automatically controlled pen or pencil as a function of one or more variables.

*Polling signal. A centrally controlled flexible and systematic technique used to permit stations on a multipoint circuit to transmit without competing for the line.

*Port-A-Punch. A portable key punching device developed by the IBM Corporation whereby

Port-A-Punch—*Cont.* punched cards can be punched with a hand stylis.

Primary crossbar bay. The first stage of an automatic telephone switching system using movable switches mounted on bars. The dialed information is received and stored by common circuits which select and test the switching paths and control the operation of the switching mechanisms.

*Processing, batch. Data which are similar are gathered into groups or batches and are then entered into the processing procedure.

Processor. (1) A generic term which includes assembly, compiling, and generation. (2) A shorter term for automatic data processor or arithmetic unit. (3) A computer program which translates the symbolic (mnemonic) instruction codes into machine language instructions.

Program. (1) The complete plan for the solution of a problem, more specifically the complete sequence of machine instructions and routines necessary to solve a problem. (2) To plan the procedures for solving a problem. This may involve among other things the analysis of the problem, preparation of a flow diagram, preparing details, testing, and developing subroutines, allocation of storage locations, specification of input and output formats, and the incorporation of a computer run into a complete data processing system.

Program, coded. A program which has been expressed in the code or language of a specific machine or programming system.

Program, control. A sequence of instructions which prescribe the series of steps to be taken by a system, a computer or any other device.

Punch. (1) To shear a hole by forcing a solid or hollow, sharp-edged tool through a material into

Punch—*Cont.*
a die. (2) The hole resulting from (1) above.

Punching positions. The specific areas, i.e., row-column intersects, on a punched card where holes may be punched.

Queuing theory. A form of probability theory useful in studying delays or line-ups at servicing points.

Read-in. To sense information contained in some source and transmit this information to an internal storage.

Read-out. To sense information contained in some internal storage and transmit this information to a storage external to the computer.

Read-punch unit. An input/output unit of a computing system which punches computed results into cards, reads input information into the system, and segregates output cards. The read-punch unit generally consists of a card feed, a read station, a punch station, another read station, and two output card stackers.

Read/write head. A small electromagnet used for reading, recording, or erasing polarized spots, which represent information, on magnetic tape, disk, or drum.

*Real-time. Connotes quick access to storage with an instantaneous response if desired.

Real-time processing. The processing of information or data in a sufficiently rapid manner so that the results of the processing are available in time to influence the process being monitored or controlled. Synonymous with Real-time system.

Record length. The number of characters necessary to contain all the information in a record.

Row binary. A method of representing binary numbers on a card where successive bits are repre-

Row binary—*Cont.*
sented by the presence or absence of punches in a successive position in a row as opposed to a series of columns. Row binary is especially convenient in 40-bit-word, or less, computers, wherein the card frequently is used to store 12 binary words on each half of the card.

Scanner. An instrument which automatically samples or interrogates the state of various processes, files, conditions, or physical states and initiates action in accordance with the information obtained.

Select. (1) To take the Alternative A if the report on a condition is of one state, and alternative B if the report on the condition is of another state. (2) To choose a needed subroutine from a file of subroutines.

Serial. The handling of one after the other in a single facility, such as transfer or store in a digit-by-digit time sequence, or to process a sequence of instructions one at a time, i.e., sequentially.

Simulation. (1) The representation of physical systems and phenomena by computers, models, or other equipment. (2) In computer programming, the technique of setting up a routine for one computer to make it operate as nearly as possible like some other computer.

Software. The totality of programs and routines used to extend the capabilities of computers, such as compilers, assemblers, narrators, routines, and subroutines. Contrasted with Hardware.

Solid state. The electronic components that convey or control electrons within solid materials; e.g., transistors, germanium diodes, and magnetic cores. Thus vacuum and gas tubes are not included.

Sonic delay line. A delay line using a medium providing acoustic delay, such as, mercury or quartz delay

Sonic delay line—*Cont.*
lines. Synonymous with Acoustic delay line.

Sort. To arrange items of information according to rules dependent upon a key or field contained in the items or records; e.g., to digital sort is to sort first the keys on the least significant digit, and to resort on each higher order digit until the items are sorted on the most significant digit.

Sort, block. A sort of one or more of the most significant characters of a key to serve as a means of making workable-sized groups from a large volume of records to be sorted.

Sort, merge. To produce a single sequence of items, ordered according to some rule, from two or more previously unordered sequences, without changing the items in size, structure, or total number; although more than one pass may be required for a complete sort, items are selected during each pass on the basis of the entire key.

Sorter. A machine which puts items of information into a particular order.

Source language. *See* Language, source.

Stacker, card. (1) A receptacle that accumulates cards after they have passed through a machine. (2) A hopper.

Storage. (1) The term preferred to memory. (2) Pertaining to a device in which data can be stored and from which it can be obtained at a later time. The means of storing data may be chemical, electrical, or mechanical. (3) A device consisting of electronic, electrostatic, electrical, hardware, or other elements into which data may be entered, and from which data may be obtained as desired. (4) The erasable storage in any given computer. Synonymous with Memory.

Storage, auxiliary. A storage device, such as magnetic tape, drum, or disk, which is in addition to the main storage of a computer.

Storage, auxiliary—*Cont.*
or disk, which is in addition to the main storage of a computer.

Storage capacity. The number of elementary pieces of data that can be obtained in a storage device. Frequently defined in terms of characters in a particular code or words of a fixed size that can be so contained.

Storage, external. (1) The storage of data on a device which is not an integral part of a computer. (2) A facility or device, not an integral part of a computer, on which data usable by a computer are stored, such as off-line magnetic tape units, or punched card devices.

Storage dump. A listing of the contents of a storage device, or selected parts of it. Synonymous with (memory dump), (core dump), and (memory print-out).

Storage, internal. (1) The storage of data on a device which is an integral part of a computer. (2) The storage facilities forming an integral physical part of the computer and directly controlled by the computer. In such facilities all data are automatically accessible to the computer, e.g., magnetic core, and magnetic tape on-line.

Storage, magnetic core. A storage device in which binary data is represented by the direction of magnetization in each unit of an array of magnetic material, usually in the shape of toroidal rings, but also in other forms such as wraps on bobbins. Synonymous with Core storage.

Storage, magnetic drum. The storage of data on the surface of magnetic drums.

Storage, magnetic tape. A storage device in which data are stored in the form of magnetic spots on metal or coated plastic tape. Binary data are stored as small magnetized spots arranged in column form across the width of the tape.

Storage, magnetic tape—*Cont.*
A read-write head is usually associated with each row of magnetized spots so that one column can be read or written at a time as the tape traverses the head.

Store. (1) To transfer an element of information to a device from which the unaltered information can be obtained at a later time. (2) To retain data in a device from which the data can be obtained at a later time.

*Stored Program. A complete set of detailed steps and procedures stored within the computer directing it to perform a particular data processing task.

Summary punch. A card punch operating in conjunction with another machine, commonly a tabulator, to punch into cards data which have been summarized or calculated by the other machine.

Symbol. A substitute or representation of characteristics, relationships, or transformations of ideas or things.

System. An assembly of procedures, processes, methods, routines, or techniques united by some form of regulated interaction to form an organized whole.

*System analysis. The examination of an activity, procedure, method, technique, or business to determine what is required and how the requirements may best be accomplished.

*System flowchart. A flowchart which shows the sequence of major operations which normally summarizes a complete operation.

*System, information. The network of all communication methods within an organization. Information may be derived from many sources other than a data processing unit, such as by telephone, by contact with other people, or by studying an operation.

System, information retrieval. A system for locating and selecting,

System, information retrieval—*Cont.*
on demand, certain documents, or other graphic records relevant to a given information requirement from a file of such material. Examples of information retrieval systems are classification, indexing, and machine searching systems.

System, management information. A communications process in which data are recorded and processed for operational purposes. The problems are isolated for higher level decision making and information is fed back to top management to reflect the progress or lack of progress made in achieving major objectives.

*Tabulator. *See* Accounting machine.

Tabulating equipment. The machines and equipment using punched cards. The group of equipment is called tabulating equipment because the main function of installations of punched card machines for some 20 years before the first automatic digital computer was to produce tabulations of information resulting from sorting, listing, selecting, and totaling data on punched cards.

Tape. A strip of material, which may be punched, coated, or impregnated with magnetic or optically sensitive substances, and used for data input, storage, or output. The data are stored serially in several channels across the tape traversely to the reading or writing motion.

Test data. A set of data developed specifically to test the adequacy of a computer run or system. The data may be actual data that has been taken from previous operations, or artificial data created for this purpose.

Transcribe. To copy, with or without translating, from one storage medium to another.

Transistor. An electronic device utilizing semiconductor properties to control the flow of currents.

Unit. A portion or subassembly of a computer which constitutes the means of accomplishing some inclusive operation or function.

Unit record. (1) A separate record that is similar in form and content to other records, e.g., a summary of a particular employee's earnings to date.

Update. (1) To put into a master file changes required by current information or transactions. (2) To modify an instruction so that the address numbers it contains are increased by a stated amount each time the instruction is performed.

Validity. The correctness; especially the degree of the closeness by which iterated results approach the correct result.

Verify. To check a transcribing operation, by a compare operation. It usually applies to transcriptions which can be read mechanically or electrically.

Word. An ordered set of characters which occupies one storage location and is treated by the computer circuits as a unit and transferred as such. Ordinarily a word is treated by the control unit as an instruction, and by the arithmetic unit as a quantity. Word lengths may be fixed or variable depending on the particular computer.

Word length. The number of characters in a machine word. In a given computer, the number may be constant or variable.

Word length, fixed. Having the property that a machine word always contains the same number of characters or digits.

Word length, variable. Having the property that a machine word may have a variable number of characters. It may be applied either to a single entry whose information content may be changed from time to time, or to a group of functionally similar entries whose corresponding components are of different lengths.

*Writing board. All of the basic forms surrounding a particular business transaction can be prepared at one time in writing by aligning and holding the documents in place while the transaction is recorded. The recording on all the documents is accomplished simultaneously through the use of carbon paper.

Zone. (1) A portion of internal storage allocated for a particular function or purpose. (2) The three top positions of 12, 11, and 0 on certain punched cards. In these positions, a second punch can be inserted so that with punches in the remaining positions 1 to 9, alphabetic characters may be represented.

Zone bit. (1) One of the two leftmost bits in a commonly used system in which six bits are used for each character. (2) Any bit in a group of bit positions that are used to indicate a specific class of items, e.g., numbers, letters, special signs, and commands.

Zero. A numeral normally denoting lack of magnitude. In many computers there are distinct representations for plus and minus zero.

Index

This book has been set in 11 and 10 point Bodoni Book, leaded 1 point. Chapter numbers and titles are in Bodoni Book and Bodoni #375. The size of the type page is 27 x 45½ picas.